THE HANDBOOK OF MICROFINANCE

THE HANDBOOK OF MICROFINANCE

edited by

Beatriz Armendáriz

University College London, UK & Harvard University, USA

Marc Labie

Université de Mons, Belgium

World Scientific

NEW JERSEY • LONDON • SINGAPORE • BEIJING • SHANGHAI • HONG KONG • TAIPEI • CHENNAI

Published by

World Scientific Publishing Co. Pte. Ltd.
5 Toh Tuck Link, Singapore 596224
USA office: 27 Warren Street, Suite 401-402, Hackensack, NJ 07601
UK office: 57 Shelton Street, Covent Garden, London WC2H 9HE

British Library Cataloguing-in-Publication Data
A catalogue record for this book is available from the British Library.

THE HANDBOOK OF MICROFINANCE

ISBN-13 978-981-4295-65-9
ISBN-10 981-4295-65-5

Typeset by Stallion Press
Email: enquiries@stallionpress.com

Para Georges-Antoine,
Beatriz

A mes parents,
Marc

Contents

CERMi

The Centre for European Research in Microfinance (CERMi) was created in October 2007 at the initiative of the Centre Emile Bernheim (Solvay Brussels School of Economics and Management — Université Libre de Bruxelles, Belgium) and the Warocqué Research Centre (Warocqué Business School — Université de Mons, Belgium), with the goal to become an active participant in the microfinance sector. It brings together researchers involved in microfinance and aims to study the management of a wide range of institutions, represented by NGOs, cooperatives, and commercial companies. Thanks to an interdisciplinary approach, CERMi hopes to make substantive contributions to the body of knowledge on microfinance, which may help the industry to face more effectively its future challenges. A complete description of CERMi (including an updated list of its members — permanent and associated) is available on http://www.cermi.eu.

Biographical Notes

Beatriz Armendáriz

Beatriz Armendáriz is a lecturer in economics at Harvard University, and a senior lecturer at University College, London. She is also a research affiliate at the David Rockefeller Center for Latin American Studies at Harvard University, a research associate at Centre for European Research in Microfinance (CERMi–Université Libre de Bruxelles (ULB)) in Belgium, a member of the Board of Directors of Grameen Crédit Agricole Microfinance Foundation, and a Board Member of YouthSafe. Having written numerous articles on microfinance with co-author Jonathan Morduch, Armendáriz has already written an updated second edition of *The Economics of Microfinance* for MIT Press, which appeared in April 2010. Her current research includes field work on microfinance and gender empowerment with researchers from the Innovations for Poverty Action (Yale and Harvard). She is also writing a book on "The Contemporary Latin American Economy" for MIT Press with co-author Felipe Larraín B. (Universidad Pontífica Católica de Chile). Armendáriz grew up in southern Mexico where she founded AlSol and Grameen Trust Chiapas, the first Grameen-style replications in the region.

Bernd Balkenhol

Bernd Balkenhol is Director of the Social Finance Programme at the ILO (International Labor Organization). This department works on financial sector issues relevant for decent work. For several years he has been advisor to the central bank of West African States (BCEAO) on SME finance. He is lecturer at the Faculty of Economics of the University of Geneva. He also teaches regularly at the Université Libre de Bruxelles (ULB) and the Boulder Microfinance Training Programme in Turin. His publications cover a range of issues related to access to finance. His latest book ("Microfinance and Public Policy", Palgrave Macmillan) investigates the conditions for smart subsidies to microfinance institutions. He served on the Executive Committee of CGAP, is Founding President of the Swiss Microfinance Platform and on the Executive Committee of the World Micro Finance Forum Geneva. He holds a PhD from Freiburg University in Germany and a MA from the Fletcher School of Law and Diplomacy (Medford, Mass).

Johan Bastiaensen

Johan Bastiaensen is senior lecturer at the Institute of Development Policy and Management (IOB) of the University of Antwerp and associate lecturer at the European Microfinance Programme. He teaches at the graduate level in the areas of research methods and development studies, focusing particularly on the topics of local institutions and poverty reduction, microfinance, land policies and value chains. For more than two decades, he has been cooperating with the Instituto Nitlapán of the Universidad Centroamericana, Nicaragua in teaching, research and development initiatives in the field of microfinance and rural development. In this context, he also closely followed the genesis and development of the Fondo de Desarrollo Local.

Craig Churchill

Craig Churchill is a senior technical specialist in the ILO's Social Finance Programme, where he focuses primarily on the role of financial services that the poor can use to manage risks and reduce their vulnerability, including savings, insurance and emergency loans. He chairs the Microinsurance Network, teaches at the Boulder Microfinance Training Programme in Turin, and heads the ILO's Microinsurance Innovation Facility funded by the Bill and Melinda Gates Foundation. Craig has authored and edited over 40 articles, papers, monographs and training manuals on various microfinance topics including microinsurance, customer loyalty, organizational development, governance, lending methodologies, regulation and supervision, and financial services for the poorest of the poor. His recent publication, "Protecting the Poor: A Microinsurance Compendium" (Geneva: ILO, Munich Re Foundation), which he edited, is the most authoritative book on the subject.

Robert Cull

Robert Cull is a lead economist in the Finance and Private Sector Development Team of the Development Economics Research Group of the World Bank. His most recent research is on the performance of microfinance institutions and the design and use of household surveys to measure access to financial services. He has published numerous articles in peer-reviewed academic journals including the *Economic Journal*, *Journal of Development Economics*, *Journal of Financial Economics*, *Journal of Law and Economics*, *Journal of Money, Credit, and Banking*, and *World Development*. He is also co-editor of the *Interest Bearing Notes*, a bi-monthly newsletter reporting on financial and private sector research.

Asli Demirgüç-Kunt

Asli Demirgüç-Kunt is the Chief Economist of the Financial and Private Sector (FPD) Development Network and Senior Research Manager of Finance Private Sector (DECFP), in the World Bank's Development Economics Research Group. After joining the Bank in 1989 as a Young Economist, she has been in different of the divisions, working on financial sector issues and advising on financial sector policy. She is the lead author of World Bank Policy Research Report 2007, Finance for All? Policies and Pitfall in Expanding Access. The author of over 100 publications, she has published widely in academic journals. Her research has focused on the links between financial development and firm performance and economic development. Banking crises, financial regulation, and access to financial services including SME finance are among her areas of research. Prior to coming to the Bank, she was an Economist at the Federal Reserve Bank of Cleveland. She holds a Ph.D. and M.A. in economics from the Ohio State University.

Asif Dowla

Asif Dowla is a professor of economics at St. Mary's College of Maryland. Professor Dowla is an expert on microfinance. He has published articles in reputed journals on various aspects of microfinance, for example, leasing, savings mobilization and social capital. In 1997, Prof. Dowla received a fellowship to spend a year on sabbatical at Grameen Bank. His recent book on Grameen Bank, *The Poor Always Pay Back: The Grameen II Story*, has been labeled as a must-read for anyone interested in microfinance and how it can be used to alleviate poverty. The book is in its second printing and has been translated into simplified and traditional Chinese, Bahasa Indonesia and French. Recently, Professor Dowla was awarded the Norton Dodge Award for excellence in teaching by St. Mary's College and was named Hilda C. Landers Endowed Professor in the Liberal Arts.

Greg Fischer

Greg Fischer is a lecturer (assistant professor) at the London School of Economics and Political Science. His research focuses on corporate finance and entrepreneurship in developing countries using experimental methods and applied theory. He is the co-director of the Finance Programme at the International Growth Centre, a board member and research affiliate of Innovations for Poverty Action, and a research affiliate of the MIT Jameel Poverty Action Lab Fischer holds a PhD from MIT and an AB from Princeton, both in economics.

Rients Galema

Rients Galema is currently a PhD student in the Institute of Economics, Econometrics and Finance at the University of Groningen. He is working on a PhD project titled "Commercialisation of Microfinance", which aims to investigate to what extent microfinance is interesting for commercial investors. In 2007, he completed his MPhil in international economics and business at the University of Groningen with a thesis titled "Socially Responsible Investment: Performance and Diversification". In his research he uses traditional tools from finance, like mean-variance analysis, to analyse investing in microfinance and socially responsible investment in general.

Maitreesh Ghatak

Maitreesh Ghatak is a professor of economics at the London School of Economics and Political Science. His areas of research include development economics, public economics, and the economics of organizations. His recent research topics include microfinance, property rights, occupational choice, collective action, and the economics of non-profits. He is the current Editor-in-Chief of the Journal of Development Economics, a former Managing

Editor of the Review of Economic Studies and a former co-editor of the Economics of Transition, is the director of the research group, Economic Organization and Public Policy (EOPP) at the LSE. He taught previously at the Department of Economics of the University of Chicago and holds a PhD from Harvard.

Nathanael Goldberg

Nathanael Goldberg is policy director at Innovations for Poverty Action (IPA), a non-profit organization dedicated to creating, evaluating, and replicating innovative solutions to development problems. He leads IPA's efforts to disseminate research findings and direct resources to proven development interventions. Nathanael also manages evaluations related to financial inclusion, including Targeting the Ultra Poor/Microfinance Graduation pilots designed to enable the poorest households to participate in entrepreneurship. Previously he served as chief of staff of the Microcredit Summit Campaign where he supervised industry-wide data collection and led the organization of major industry conferences including the 2002 Microcredit Summit +5 in New York. Nathanael has a Master in Public Affairs in International Development from Princeton University's Woodrow Wilson School of Public and International Affairs.

Claudio Gonzalez-Vega

Originally from Costa Rica, Claudio Gonzalez-Vega has been a professor of agricultural, environmental and development economics and professor of economics at The Ohio State University since 1982, where he is director of the Rural Finance Program, a center of excellence in finance and development recognized with the Distinguished Policy Contribution award by the American Agricultural Economics Association. He holds a Master's degree from the London School of Economics and a PhD from Stanford University. He has been a consultant for many international agencies and governments in Latin America, Africa and Asia and served on USAID's advisory committee on Microenterprise Development, chaired the technical committee of the Cooperative Research Support Program on Broadening Access and Strengthening Input Market Systems (BASIS) and is a member of the executive board of the Generation Challenge Program (CGIAR). Gonzalez-Vega has published extensively on financial policy reforms, rural financial markets, microfinance, poverty, economic development and international trade policies.

Isabelle Guérin

Isabelle Guérin is currently research fellow at the Institute of Research Development (Research Unit "Development and Societies", Paris 1–IRD). She is also research associate to the French Institute of Pondicherry and CERMi. She is coordinating the RUME Project which aims to analyse the interactions between rural finance and employment in three countries (South India, Mexico and Madagascar). Her research interests span from financial inclusion, informal finance, debt bondage and over-indebtedness to NGOs interventions, empowerment programmes and linkages with public policies. From a theoretical perspective, her work pays specific attention to the social meaning of money, debt and finance, the social fabric of markets, organizations and institutions. Her latest book, *Unfree Labour* (co-edited with Jan Breman and Aseem Prakash, Oxford University Press), examines the persistence of debt bondage in India.

Timothy W. Guinnane

Timothy W. Guinnane is the Philipp Golden Bartlett Professor of Economic History in the Department of Economics at Yale University. His research focuses on the demographic and financial history of Europe and North America in the 19th and early 20th century. Current research projects include a book on the history of Germany's credit cooperatives; collaborative research on the development of new company forms in 19th and 20th century Europe; and several research projects dealing with the demographic transition in Germany.

Begoña Gutiérrez-Nieto

Begoña Gutiérrez-Nieto is an associate professor in the Department of Accounting and Finance at the Universidad de Zaragoza (Spain). She is also an associate researcher at the Centre for European Research in Microfinance (CERMi). She has received several awards for her research in the microfinance field. She has published articles in journals such as *Annals of*

Public and Cooperative Economics, *Journal of the Operational Research Society*, *Nonprofit & Voluntary Sector Quarterly*, *Online Information Review* and *Omega*. She teaches banking and financial mathematics at the undergraduate level, and microfinance and financial management for non-profit organisations at the postgraduate level.

Valentina Hartarska

Valentina Hartarska is an associate professor at the Department of Agricultural Economics and Rural Sociology at Auburn University and an associate researcher of the Centre for European Research in Microfinance, Belgium. Her research program focuses on economic development and governance, and on financial intermediaries serving low-income populations including microfinance institutions. She has studied various issues of internal and external governance mechanisms, efficiency, outreach and impact, in cross-country, country-wide and regional contexts. She has conducted projects in several countries, mainly in Eastern Europe, Central Asia and Africa. Professor Hartarska teaches graduate and undergraduate classes in finance, management, development and econometrics at Auburn University and has taught an introduction class on agricultural development at the European Microfinance Programme, Belgium.

Niels Hermes

Niels Hermes is an associate professor of international finance at the University of Groningen, The Netherlands. He is also visiting professor at the Université Libre de Bruxelles, and an associate researcher of the Centre for European Research in Microfinance, Belgium. His research focuses on microfinance, the impact of financial liberalization, foreign banking, trade credit in emerging economies, comparative corporate governance studies and the nature and impact of corporate governance codes. He has published on these issues in journals such as *The Economic Journal*, *Journal of International Money and Finance*, *Journal of Banking and Finance*, *World Development*, *Journal of Development Studies*, and *Corporate Governance: An International Review*. His teaching focuses on international financial management, corporate governance and financial strategy, and microfinance.

Marek Hudon

Marek Hudon is currently Assistant Professor at the Solvay Brussels School of Economics and Management (ULB). He has launched the European Microfinance Programme (EMP) and is still its scientific coordinator. He is also one of the co-founders and co-directors of the Centre for European Research in Microfinance (CERMi). He has conducted research in India, Mali, Morocco and the Democratic Republic of Congo. In 2006, Prof Hudon was a visiting fellow at Harvard University where he worked on ethical issues in microfinance under the supervision of Professor Amartya Sen. Current research interests also include public policy issues in microfinance and complementary currencies. His is currently Affiliate Professor at Burgundy School of Business (ESC Dijon) where he teaches business ethics. In 2009, he has been awarded both the CEDIMES prize for Post-doctoral studies and the Merlot-Leclerq prize in public economics. He has published or forthcoming articles in journals such as *World Development*, *Journal of Business Ethics*, *Journal of International Development*, *Annals of Public and Cooperative Economics*, *International Journal of Social Economics*, and *Savings and Development*.

David Hulme

David Hulme is professor of development studies at the University of Manchester and head of the Institute for Development Management and Policy (IDPM). He is executive director of the Brooks World Poverty Institute and the Chronic Poverty Research Centre. His recent publications include *Poverty Dynamics: Inter-disciplinary Perspectives* (with T Addison and R Kanbur, 2009, Oxford University Press), *Social Protection for the Poor and Poorest: Risks, Needs and Rights* (with A Barrientos, 2008, Palgrave), *The Challenge of Global Inequality* (with A Greig and M Turner, 2006, Palgrave), a special issue of the *Journal of Development Studies* (2006) on 'Cross-disciplinary Research on Poverty and Inequality' and many articles in leading journals. His research interests include rural development, poverty analysis and poverty reduction strategies, finance for the poor and sociology of development. Dr Hulme has just completed a senior research fellowship with the Leverhulme Trust to write a book entitled "Global Poverty" (forthcoming, Routledge). This book explores the "invention" of global poverty and questions whether this has benefited poor people around the world.

Dean Karlan

Dean Karlan is a professor of economics at Yale University. Karlan is also president of Innovations for Poverty Action (IPA), co-director of the Financial Access Initiative, a consortium created with funding from the Bill and Melinda Gates Foundation, a research fellow of the MIT. Jameel Poverty Action Lab, and co-founder and president of StickK.com. In 2007, he received a Presidential Early Career Award for scientists and engineers. In 2008, he received a Alfred P. Sloan research fellowship. His research focuses on microeconomic issues of financial decision-making, specifically employing experimental methodologies to examine what works, what does not, and why in interventions in microfinance and health. Internationally, he focuses on microfinance, and domestically, he focuses on voting, charitable giving, and commitment contracts. In microfinance, he has studied interest rate policy, credit evaluation and scoring policies, entrepreneurship training, group versus individual liability, savings product design, credit with education, and impact from increased access to credit. His work on savings and health typically uses insights from psychology and behavioral economics to design and test specialized products. He has consulted for the World Bank, the Asian Development Bank, FINCA International, Oxfam, Freedom from Hunger and the Guatemalan government. Karlan received a PhD in economics from MIT, a MBA and a MPP from the University of Chicago, and a BA in international affairs from the University of Virginia.

Erna Karrer-Rüedi

Erna Karrer-Rueedi, Vice President, works at Credit Suisse in microfinance within Private Banking Investment Services and Products and has extensive experience in impact investment. Prior to her assignment with Credit Suisse in Zurich, Erna held various positions in academia and with financial services firms in the USA focusing on trends, emerging issues, and opportunities related to sustainable development and product offerings. Erna is a recently-elected board member of the European Microfinance Platform and is also an active member of several organizations that want to make an impact.

Erna Karrer was conferred a doctorate in environmental sciences from the Swiss Federal Institute of Technology, Zurich, in 1992.

Marc Labie

Marc Labie is associate professor at the Warocqué Business School of the University of Mons (UMONS) where he teaches organization studies and management. He is also visiting professor at the Solvay Brussels School of Economics and Management (ULB) and lecturing in the FIPED Executive Program at the Kennedy School of Government (Harvard University). He is one of the co-founders and co-directors of the Centre for European Research in Microfinance (CERMi) based in Mons and Brussels in Belgium. Professor Labie specializes in microfinance organizations. He has a BA in economics and social sciences and a PhD in business administration from the University of Mons. He has also studied for brief periods at the Universidad de Salamanca, at the London School of Economics and Political Science, as well as at Harvard University. He has co-authored numerous articles on microfinance. His current research focuses on corporate governance issues in microfinance.

Robert Lensink

Robert Lensink is professor of finance and financial markets at the Faculty of Economics and Business of the University of Groningen. He is also professor of development economics at Wageningen University and associate researcher of the Centre for European Research in Microfinance, Belgium. Robert Lensink's research mainly deals with finance and development, with a strong focus on microfinance. He has published many papers on microfiannce in international journals, such as *The Economic Journal, World Development and the Journal of Development Studies.*

Cecilio Mar Molinero

Cecilio Mar Molinero is professor of management science at the University of Kent, United Kingdom. His main areas of interest are data envelopment analysis (DEA), multivariate statistics, and their intersection. He has researched into the statistical properties of accounting numbers, the prediction of corporate failure, the relationship between social conditions and educational achievement, and the theory of DEA. His current research interest are, besides microcredit efficiency, the changes in the social structure of a city brought about by the right to buy protected housing, the impact on social conditions of the right to choose primary school, and various models to overcome the limitations of DEA. He has published extensively in major refereed journals, particularly in the areas of operational research, statistics, accounting, and finance.

Peter E. Marchetti

Peter E. Marchetti is currently a researcher at the Association for the Advancement of Social Sciences in Guatemala, AVANCSO, and serves as the President of the Internal Audit and Operational Committee of the FDL. He has researched and promoted agrarian reform and peasant-based development in the Dominican Republic, Chile, Peru, Cuba, Nicaragua, Honduras and Guatemala. In 1988, he began his work in developmental microfinance accompanying peasant-founded community banks. That work culminated in the establishment of two institutions designed with the needed vision of synergy between financial and non-financial development services — Nitlapán, the Institute for Research and Development at the Universidad Centroamericana and the Fondo de Desarrollo Local in Nicaragua in 1990 and 1996, respectively. In 1998 he spearheaded the creation of CREDISOL in Honduras, a microfinance initiative similar to the FDL. His broader work on emergency relief, citizen participation, land reform, and the advocacy against drug trafficking earned him the National Award for Human Rights in Honduras. He has directed university research programs since the mid-1980s and has held the post of vice-president for research and postgraduate studies at the UCA in Nicaragua and director of the same areas as the Universidad Rafael Landívar in Guatemala.

Linda Mayoux

Dr Linda Mayoux is an international consultant who has worked on gender mainstreaming and women's empowerment in microfinance since 1997 for DFID, UNIFEM, ILO, Aga Khan Foundation, Asian Development Bank, World Bank, IFAD, USAID, SDC and many NGOs in South Asia, Africa and Latin America. She is author of the Rural Finance component of the World Bank's *Gender and Livelihoods Source Book* and a *Reader on*

Gender and Rural Finance for IFAD. She is currently a global consultant for Women's Economic Empowerment Mainstreaming and Networking (WEMAN) spearheaded by Oxfam Novib. This is a global process with networks in Latin America, South Asia and Africa to remove gender discrimination in access to livelihood development services and policy-making: including financial services, technical support, value chain development and local/regional/national economic policy-making. She has set up and manages the genfinance website and Yahoo Discussion Group at http://www.genfinance.info and http://finance.groups.yahoo.com/group/genfinance/.

Aljar Meesters

Aljar Meesters is currently a lecturer and researcher at the faculty of Economics and Business of the University of Groningen. He teaches in the areas of finance and econometrics. His main research interests are applied econometrics, financial institutions in general and microfinance institutions in particular. He has published in the *Journal of Banking and Finance* and *World Development.*

Roy Mersland

Roy Mersland has extensive international management, consulting, and research experience in the field of microfinance in Latin America, Asia, Africa, and Europe. He is the founder of the Ecuadorian MFI D-MIRO where he still serves as the vice president of the board. He holds a postdoc position at the University of Agder in Norway and operates his own consultancy practice (www.microfinance.no). His academic works concern mainly the management, governance and performance of microfinance institutions but also includes works on how to bridge the gap between the disability and microfinance communities. He has published in journals like World Development, International Business Review, Journal of Banking and Finance and European Financial Management. He hosted the two first International Research Workshops on Microfinance Management and Governance in Kristiansand, Norway and has several times been the conference chair of the European Microfinance Week in Luxembourg.

Karen Moore

Karen Moore is currently a policy analyst with the Education for All Global Monitoring Report team at UNESCO. Prior to this, she worked as a research associate with the Chronic Poverty Research Centre, a UK Department for International Development-funded international partnership of universities, research institutes and NGOs. She was based first at the University of Birmingham and then at the University of Manchester. The majority of her recent research has focused on understanding the intersections between childhood, youth, intergenerational, life-course and chronic poverty, and policies to interrupt these (including social protection and microfinance), primarily in South Asia. She holds a BA (Hons) in international development from the University of Toronto, and an MSc in development studies from the University of Bath.

Jonathan Morduch

Jonathan Morduch is professor of public policy and economics at New York University and is managing director of the Financial Access Initiative (www.financialaccess.org). He is co-author of *Portfolios of the Poor: How the World's Poor Live on $2 a Day* (2009, Princeton) and, with Beatriz Armendáriz, of *The Economics of Microfinance* (2005, MIT Press; 2010, 2nd edition). Morduch has been chair of the United Nations Expert Committee on Poverty Statistics and an advisor to the United Nations, World Economic Forum, Pro Mujer, and the Grameen Foundation. He is a member of the editorial boards of the *Journal of Economic Perspectives*, and *Journal of Globalization and Development*. Morduch holds a BA from Brown and PhD from Harvard, both in economics. He was awarded an honorary doctorate from the Université Libre de Bruxelles in December 2008 in recognition of his work on microfinance.

Solène Morvant-Roux

Solène Morvant-Roux is currently a lecturer in development studies at the department of political economy, Fribourg University, Switzerland. She is also associate researcher of the Institut de Recherches pour le développement (IRD) and of the Centre for European Research in Microfinance (CERMi). Specialist in financial inclusion, she is part of the comparative project, "Rural microfinance and employment: Do processes matter?" (http://www.rume-rural-microfinance.org/) which aims to understand the interactions between access to financial services and employment dynamics implemented in three different regions and countries: India, Mexico and Madagascar and Morocco. Her research interests span from microfinance in rural areas with a focus on financing agricultural activities, debt and social institutions to migration dynamics. From a methodological perspective, her research relies on a combination of qualitative and quantitative tools.

Denis Nadolnyak

Denis Nadolnyak is currently an assistant professor at the Department of Agricultural Economics and Rural Sociology at Auburn University (USA). He is working in the areas of environmental, development, and resource economics. His current research is on the impact of climate variability on farm profitability and disaster assistance payments, the use of climate forecasts in designing crop insurance and farm programs, development finance, and economics of water use. Dr. Nadolnyak teaches at the undergraduate and graduate level in the areas of environmental and resource economics. His other research interests are international trade and the environment, industrial organization and economics of innovation, contract theory, and production economics.

William Parienté

William Parienté is assistant professor of economics at the Université Catholique de Louvain and member of the Jameel Poverty Action Lab (J–PAL). He has worked on the analysis of credit demand and the evaluation of policies improving access to credit in three countries: Serbia, Brazil and Morocco. Parienté's current research focuses on access to credit, poverty and health issues and the evaluation of public policies using experimental methods. He is involved in several field experiments in Morocco, Pakistan and France.

Jay Rosengard

Jay Rosengard is lecturer in public policy at the Kennedy School of Government, Harvard University, and has 30 years of international experience in the design, implementation, and evaluation of development policies and programs throughout Asia, Africa, and Latin America. Rosengard is currently director of the Mossavar-Rahmani Center for Business and Government's Financial Sector Program, which focuses on the development of bank and non-bank financial institutions and alternative financing instruments. In addition, Rosengard is a faculty affiliate of both the Ash Center for Democratic Governance and Innovation and the Center for International Development. He also serves as faculty chair of three executive education programs: Financial Institutions for Private Enterprise Development (FIPED), which focuses on sustainable and effective microfinance and SME (small and medium enterprise) finance; Comparative Tax Policy and Administration (COMTAX), which addresses key strategic and tactical issues in tax design and implementation; and VELP (Vietnam Executive Leadership Program), which is an innovative policy dialogue with senior Vietnamese leadership.

Stuart Rutherford

Stuart Rutherford is a researcher and writer on how the poor manage their money, and a teacher and practitioner of microfinance. His best known book is *The Poor and Their Money* (2nd edition, 2009) and is also a co-author of the recently published *Portfolios of the Poor* (2009). In 1996 he founded SafeSave (safesave.org), a microfinance provider in Bangladesh which originates and develops general money-management services that poor and very poor people value. He is a senior visiting fellow at the Brooks World Poverty Institute at the University of Manchester. He lives in Japan. More about his ideas can be found online at thepoorandtheirmoney.com.

Kazi Faisal Bin Seraj

Kazi Faisal Bin Seraj, a Senior Research Associate at BRAC, is currently working as coordinator for the Research and Evaluation Unit for BRAC West Africa Programs. His unit is responsible for carrying out research and evaluation activities for both Sierra Leone and Liberia. In Bangladesh, before being transferred to the international program, he worked as a core member for the CFPR (Ultra Poor) research team and was responsible for the publication of the baseline report for the second phase of the program. Having an academic background in economics and environmental economics, his research interests range from extreme poverty and development economics to natural resource economics, environmental policy instrument and environment and development.

Carlos Serrano-Cinca

Carlos Serrano-Cinca is a professor in accounting and finance at the University of Zaragoza (Spain). He has been visiting scholar at the Department of Accounting and Management at the University of Southampton (United Kingdom). His research interests include e-business, microfinance, multivariate mathematical models in Accounting and Finance. He was "Telefónica Professor of Quality in New Networks and Telecommunication Services" at the University of Zaragoza. He coordinates the Centre for Research in E-business at Walqa Technology Park. Dr Serrano-Cinca has published articles in journals such as *Nonprofit & Voluntary Sector Quarterly*, *The Journal of Forecasting*, *Decision Support Systems*, *Omega*, *The European Journal of Finance*, *The Journal of Intellectual Capital*, and *The Journal of the Royal Statistical Society.* His personal page is at http://ciberconta.unizar.es/charles.htm.

Jean-Michel Servet

Jean-Michel Servet is currently professor at the Graduate Institute of International and Development Studies in Geneva and research fellow in the Institut de Recherche pour le Développement (Paris), the French Institute of Pondicherry (India) and the Centre for European Research in Microfinance (Belgium). He teaches at the graduate level in Geneva and in Lima (Peru) in the areas of development studies and finance. His research deals with social finance, local exchanging trading systems, financial globalization, the history of economic thought and interdisciplinary methods. He is a member of the board of directors of Symbiotics S A and a member of the French Red Cross Comity for social credit.

A list of his publications can be found in http://www.rume-rural-microfinance.org/IMG/pdf_CV_Jean-Michel_Servet.pdf.

Guy Stuart

Guy Stuart is a Lecturer in Public Policy at the Kennedy School of Government, Harvard University. He received his PhD from the University of Chicago in 1994, and then worked for four years in Chicago in the field of community economic development. Since 1998 he has been on the faculty at the Harvard Kennedy School where he teaches courses on management and microfinance — financial services for the poor in developing countries. He uses "bottom up" methods, such as Financial Diaries and Participatory Research, to help microfinance organizations find the best way to serve their clients. He is currently conducting research on microfinance in Pakistan, Malawi and Kenya. He is the author of numerous articles and case studies on microfinance. He is also the author of a book on the U.S. mortgage lending industry, Discriminating Risk, published by Cornell University Press in 2003.

Ariane Szafarz

Ariane Szafarz is full professor of mathematics and finance at Solvay Brussels School of Economics and Management (SBS-EM), Université Libre de Bruxelles (ULB). She holds a PhD in mathematics and a MD in philosophy. Her research topics include microfinance (mission drift, governance issues), financial econometrics, international finance, epistemology of probability, and job market discrimination. Currently, she is co-director of CERMi, co-director of the SBS-EM doctoral programme in management sciences, president of the jury of the European Microfinance Programme, and president of the Marie-Christine Adam Fund. She has been visiting professor at Université de Lille II, Université Catholique de Louvain, and the Luxembourg School of Finance. She also worked a few years as an expert for the Walloon Region Statistics Department.

Marcelo Villafani-Ibarnegaray

Marcelo Villafani-Ibarnegaray is a post-doctoral researcher with the Rural Finance Program at The Ohio State University. His current work focuses on microfinance and rural finance in Bolivia and in Mexico. He has been actively involved in the sector for the past 15 years, having worked as the manager of a rural housing finance program and as a financial supervisor at the Superintendence of Banks of Bolivia. His research interests are related to finance and development, banking regulation, risk management, and microfinance.

Acknowledgments

This project was started in 2007. Little did we know then that our concerns on the future of microfinance pertaining to our mismatch idea — the enormous gap between the supply and demand for financial products, were shared. Many colleagues who had been watching carefully were aware of the fact that supply was lagging far behind. We were, however, skeptical about the effort we could extract from colleagues, as the 2008 financial crisis increased uncertainty on the extent of the damage — if at all. Writing on the future of microfinance through the lens of our "mismatch" idea seemed secondary, maybe risky and daring at this delicate financial juncture.

Our thanks go first to our colleagues who had the courage, and took the time to make insightful contributions to this handbook. We also thank our contributors for their patience. Constructive comments on each contribution were hard to collect and put together, creating unavoidable delays. These comments were ultimately taken on board by our contributors — some did this when the academic year 2009–2010 had already started. We are also grateful to all our colleagues and contributors, who were kind enough to take the time from their busy agendas to make constructive comments on other contributors' articles.

This handbook would have never been produced without Didier Toussaint, our project coordinator. His hard work from the start of the project involved making contact and following up with over 30 distant contributors, on both sides of the Atlantic. He took timely initiatives, and made wise decisions when we were on regular field trips in Africa, Asia, and Latin America. Didier also played a key role in keeping our publishers up to date. We thank him wholeheartedly.

We are most grateful to our publishers, World Scientific Publishing, for having suggested the idea of embarking on this exciting project to begin with, and for financial support. We thank Zhang Ruihe, Lim Shujuan, Shalini Raju, Grace Lu Huiru, Jhia Huei Gan, and Samantha Yong for having sequentially taken the lead in publishing this handbook. All six have delivered swift and helpful responses to our requests.

Last but not least, we wish to thank the staff of the Centre for European Research in Microfinance (CERMi) for their administrative and logistical support. Armendáriz is particularly grateful for additional support from Véronique Lahaye and Aurélie Rousseaux from the Centre Emile Bernheim (Solvay Brussels School of Economics and Management–Université Libre de Bruxelles), Kendra Gray from Harvard University, and Simon Allen from University College London. Labie thanks the Warocqué Business School (Université de Mons), the Solvay Brussels School of Economics and Management (Université Libre de Bruxelles), and the Académie Wallonie–Bruxelles for the support provided to CERMi. Without such institutional support and personalized attention, a project as ambitious as this one would not have ever come into existence.

Beatriz Armendáriz
Harvard University, University College London, and CERMi

Marc Labie
Université de Mons and CERMi

Introduction

Introduction and Overview: An Inquiry into the Mismatch in Microfinance

Beatriz Armendáriz
Harvard University,
University College London, and CERMi

Marc Labie
Warocqué Business School,
Université de Mons (UMONS), and CERMi

Microfinance — a set of financial practices designed to serve the unbanked poor — is seen by some as a magic wand against poverty that is supposed to solve it all. For others, microfinance is no more than a new wave of usurious practices reframed and glorified. These extreme views can, to a certain extent, be validated by convincing stylised facts, case studies, and, in some instances, by rigorous academic research. From our standpoint, however, the reality is to be found in nuances and perspectives. As it is often said: "The devil is in the details". Our main objective in this handbook is thus to present some of the most recent findings and research in microfinance in order to build, step by step, a nuanced perspective of microfinance where positive and negative aspects can be looked at in an attempt to deliver an objective and balanced view via a collection of articles. While these might at first glance seem scattered — reflecting polarised views and controversies at times — our stand is that the entire set of articles contained in this handbook is strongly linked to one single idea, which we have coined "mismatch". Our choice is more than pure semantics, as it will recurrently surface in the reminder of this introduction.

Most recent estimates suggest that microfinance has reached one hundred and fifty million individuals worldwide.* The number of the unbanked poor is however estimated by some authors to be around two and a half billion.[1] Put simply, microfinance could therefore be seen as currently serving a meagre percentage of those people who are excluded from access to financial services. There are, of course, debates on the relative importance of this failure to expand outreach.[2] To some, the meagre numbers alone are *prima facie* evidence of the failure of microfinance to include the poor. We disagree. From our standpoint, if well-designed, microfinance has the potential to improve the living standards of millions of unbanked poor throughout the world.

A strong criticism of microfinance, however, is that it has been around for over 30 years now, and numerous observers are rightfully beginning to wonder: "Why is it that a renowned and well-funded innovation such as microfinance is letting so many unbanked poor down?"

One answer is that the poor prefer to turn to informal sources of finance — friends, family-members and moneylenders, to mention a few. A second one is that microfinance only attracts a minority of entrepreneurial poor — savvy business individuals, for example — who are able to produce handsome returns. These returns enable such individuals to repay relatively high interest rates. A third one is that donors and socially responsible investors are obsessed with self-sustainability, forcing supply of microfinance products to be limited only to profitable and relatively safe products. Small loans to women, in particular, seem to be microfinance institutions' best bet in order to meet self-sustainability objectives.

All these answers and many more might be the right answers. We however believe that there is a mismatch between microfinance products and what the unbanked poor really need to finance their investment and consumption needs on the one hand, and to save and insure themselves against idiosyncratic (and aggregate) shocks on the other. Take the example of microloans for women. A vast majority of these borrowers are petty traders who would rather borrow and repay daily because demand is uncertain, supply from

*See, for example, S. Daley-Harris (2009), State of the Microcredit Summit Campaign Report 2007. Washington, D.C.: Microsoft Summit.

[1]See, Kendall in GGAP Report, http://microfinance.cgap.org/ or Chaia, A, A Dalal, T Goland, M J Gonzalez, J Morduch and R Schiff (2009). Half the World is Unbanked. Financial Access Initiative Framing Note.

[2]See for instance the CGAP Newsbrief, Are We Overestimating Demand for Microloans? (April 2008).

traders is often unreliable, and because the best way to preserve a good credit record is by repaying immediately after sales are completed if only because their ability to pay is often hindered by theft — in many instances from the women's own family members. Some women would also like to take their profits home to pay for food and/or unforeseen contingencies — idiosyncratic shocks such as having to spend for the illness of a family member or a friend. Others might prefer to save their savings while they are covered by health insurance. The best microfinance deal women often get, however, is a three-month loan, weekly repayments on that loan, savings facilities with limited withdrawals, and health insurance for themselves but not for their family members.

Why is there such a huge mismatch between a limited microfinance menu and the demand for financial services by a highly heterogeneous population of more than two billion unbanked poor? Imaginative minds might come up with myriad answers. We believe that this is an exceedingly complex question requiring informed responses from academics and practitioners alike. And this is precisely what our main objective in *The Handbook of Microfinance* is.

Over a 30-year period, microfinance has transformed itself drastically. Thanks to field practitioners, microfinance innovations have grown exponentially. Started initially by what is often referred to as a "civil society", microfinance was largely built upon initiatives from non-governmental organizations (NGOs), and cooperatives. BancoSol of Bolivia, for example, started as "Fundación para la Promoción y el Desarrollo de la Microempresa", a small NGO, in 1986. BancoSol is now a commercial bank serving over one hundred thousand clients in Bolivia. BancoSol exports technological know-how to a handful of Latin American countries. Another example is the well-known Grameen Bank. It started as a small pilot project with NGO-features in Chittagong, Bangladesh, in 1976. That is nearly 35 years ago! The Grameen Bank is now a well-established financial institution under the legal status of a cooperative serving over six million clients in Bangladesh, with hundreds of replications worldwide. Added to these well-documented examples from Latin America and Asia, are the often neglected but recently revived cooperative networks in Western Africa. The Réseau de Caisses Populaires de Burkina Faso (RCPB), for instance, launched in 1972, gathers over 100 financial cooperatives. The RCPB is now serving over half a million members in the entire country.

Such initiatives, alongside a thousand more, were fairly disconnected. Yearly summits, microfinance platforms, and regular practitioners' conferences worldwide have facilitated diffusion of technology and expertise across numerous microfinance initiatives. At those gatherings, strategic alliances between commercial banks and microfinance institutions, savings banks, donors, CEOs of commercial microfinance institutions, and NGOs interact. Simultaneously, think-tanks organize regular encounters with experts and academics active in the field. These world-wide gatherings in recent years point in the direction of at least five well-defined trends.

First, a change in lending methodology. At the beginning, microfinance gained popularity for having introduced solidarity groups and village banking with joint liability, mostly among women borrowers. Today, there are many more approaches. Individual lending seems to be getting most of the attention. At the same time, the excessive focus on women is being questioned.

Second, a change in the supply of financial products. Microcredit has traditionally received most of the attention, and it still does. Over the past decade, however, the almost exclusive attention on microcredit has evolved into a broader vision — as captured by the use of the word "microfinance" instead of "microcredit". The former takes into account the fact that the unbanked poor need an array of financial services other than just credit. These include savings, insurance, remittances, and many more.

Third, a larger and a more diverse pool of suppliers. In particular, microfinance clients are no longer being served exclusively by NGOs and cooperatives. Added to these traditional suppliers, the so-called downscaling banks — local commercial banks which are responding to demand for microfinance products such as consumer credit — are on the increase. Trends towards commercialization are also in crescendo. These were initially NGOs which have transformed themselves into fully regulated microfinance banks. Socially responsible investors are also contributing to an increased supply of funds available for financial intermediation via the so-called Microfinance Investment Vehicles (MIVs).

Fourth, a radical transformation in supervision and regulation. In most countries, microfinance institutions are prevented from monopolistic practices. Local authorities are no longer turning a blind eye. In particular, local governments are trying to foster competition, and stringent supervision for fully regulated suppliers is being set-up in many countries. If and when more competitive microfinance practices do take place, proactive local authorities are making it happen.

Fifth, a fundamental change in financial priorities. Focus on self-sustainability does not seem to be the greatest challenge anymore.

Microfinance has demonstrated that it can not only be self-sustainable, but also generate handsome returns. And the focus of attention is increasingly shifting towards how (if at all) those profits are being shared among different stakeholders. Questions are raised pertaining the share accruing to the operational staff, and, most importantly, to the microfinance clients themselves.

When looking at these relatively new trends, a deeper understanding is needed for the microfinance industry, which seems to be at a crossroads. Practitioners on the one hand are well aware of the need to increase outreach, but the problem is how: By re-balancing from urban to rural? From women to men household-heads? From loans for income generation to consumer loans? By the enhanced financing of agricultural activities? On the other hand, commercialization trends are posing new challenges for the microfinance industry in general, and for local authorities in particular. This is especially worrying if such trends are meeting outreach objectives, but are biased against the poorest.

Time has come to reflect upon where microfinance stands, and what its future will be 10 years down the road. Ideally, donors and socially responsible investors would like to see the industry meeting outreach objectives at a faster pace without compromising its social mission, namely, contributing to poverty alleviation. *The Handbook of Microfinance* is intended to address hundreds of questions that the industry's participants are asking themselves at this delicate juncture. And our principal objective is to shed light on what hides behind the mismatch between the demand and supply of microfinance products and thereby address critical questions.

Our inquiry begins with Part I titled "Understanding Microfinance Practices". In this section we first present context-specific survey data gathered with the main objective of measuring impact. Dean Karlan and Nathanael Goldberg provide a comprehensive review of methodologies and interventions which touch upon the mismatch problem in micro experiments carried out in Africa, Asia, and Latin America. However micro-climatic such experiments might be, the results that the authors describe deliver partial solutions, some of which can better serve the poor without compromising self-sustainability objectives. But context-specific experiments are designed through the lens of theory, a point that is nicely framed in the chapter by Greg Fischer and Maitreesh Ghatak. In their article, the group-lending methodology — the starting point of microfinance in Asia's solidarity groups and Latin America's village banking — is explained and questioned, in order to shed light on recent trends towards individual lending methodologies.

Such methodologies, in some cases, can more adequately serve a vast majority of the unbanked poor.

To better understand microfinance as it is often perceived these days, however, the historical roots of group lending methodologies are well explained in a follow-up chapter by Timothy Guinnane on the 19th century German cooperatives. This article not only delivers important insights on group lending, but also on recent trends to include existing cooperatives in the microfinance movement. Isabelle Guérin, Solène Morvant-Roux and Jean-Michel Servet in a follow-up essay remind us that in order to constructively push the limits of microfinance further, we must understand how ancient informal financial institutions operated. Their article borrows extensively from the financial diaries — a compilation of stylised facts from World Bank field researchers — a useful stepping stone for understanding the demand for financial services by the poor. This is complex indeed. But the key issue here is the swift response to the poor's demand for liquidity, which represents a gigantic challenge, if only because microfinance already faces exceedingly high transaction costs.

These costs are, however, not the only reason why microfinance institutions often charge relatively high interest rates when compared to those rates charged by commercial banks. In particular, the transformation of large microfinance institutions from non-governmental organizations into commercial banks has led to monopoly pricing of financial products. The poor are forced to endure usurious interest rates, for example, because there are few or no other alternatives out there. In a thought-provoking article, which closes this section on a silver lane, Marek Hudon severely questions microfinance institutions' malpractices — monopoly pricing — on ethical grounds. In a nutshell, Hudon's essay sends a warning remark to donors and socially responsible investors supporting microfinance outreach and innovations. Is donor's support justified in light of unethical behaviour by institutions which, at least in principle, are meant to serve the poor?

Part II, titled "Understanding Microfinance's Macro-Environment and Organizational Context" contains a series of articles on competition, regulation, management and corporate governance. These issues are country and institution-specific, but lessons can often be drawn. In reading this section, one is able to understand more clearly that outreach growth correlates with country-specific supervision and regulation on the one hand, and with institution-specific management and governance on the other.

Based on various case studies, Robert Cull, Asli Demirgüç–Kunt and Jonathan Morduch open the debate by explaining how regulation, competition, and financing interact. The researchers highlight that microfinance involves trade-offs: maximizing social objectives on the one hand, and financial performance on the other. Framing these trade-offs is clearly crucial to make critical policy choices. Jay Rosengard complements their analysis by reviewing the choices. Rosengard's focus is on regulation and supervision. He argues in favor of maintaining coherence: "to favor regulating what should be supervised while making sure to supervise what is being regulated".

The section then moves on to assess the overall impact of macro conditions on institutional performance, nicely spelt out in two complementary contributions. The first one, written by Niels Hermes and Aljar Meesters, provides an analysis of how macroeconomic, financial development, institutional and political variables may influence microfinance institutions' success. With the use of a large set of variables, the researchers provide an overall vision of macro conditions. In their view, the development of microfinance can only be understood within the context in which microfinance institutions operate. And, in particular, within context-specific financial systems as well as country-wide macroeconomic environment.

Claudio González–Vega and Marcelo Villafani Ibarnegaray follow the same path by reviewing in great detail the exceedingly interesting case of Bolivia. Their analysis clearly illustrates the need to adopt a "system's perspective" when studying institutional development. In the particular case of Bolivia — a leading innovator in the field — the approach proposed by González–Vega and Villafani Ibarnegaray sheds light on how Bolivian microfinance moved from being an alternative market to becoming the most vibrant segment of the Bolivian financial system.

The last three contributions in this section touch upon management and governance. Guy Stuart proposes a "strategic management framework", the main objective of which is to make a clear link between the constraints imposed by the government, the "public value" and the operational capacity needed for institutional success. Using a "value-creation approach" and stakeholder analysis, Stuart spells out "a triangle" with the main purpose of clarifying our understanding of the management conditions which, he argues, are needed to support sound and successful growth.

On governance, Valentina Hartarska and Denis Nadolnyak question the way external control mechanisms can actually help microfinance institutions to achieve their objectives. The researchers deliver an interesting review of various empirical studies, and show that such controls might be misleading, for it is unclear whether the mechanisms on governance that they analyze assist microfinance institutions to fulfill their missions. Marc Labie and Roy Mersland then close this section. They first deliver a literature review on corporate governance. Next, they suggest "a framework", which should be viewed as the lens for discussing corporate governance in microfinance. Their main message is that the issue of corporate governance in microfinance is under-researched and exceedingly complex, necessitating various sets of mechanisms. Their article suggests eight different venues for further research in this promising area.

In the third section of this handbook, readers will find a collection of articles related to commercial microfinance. Part III is titled "Current Trends Toward Commercialization", and begins with an article by Jean-Michel Servet. This article delivers a snapshot of corporate social responsibility which might be realistic but portrays a rather pessimistic scenario. To strike a good balance — and a less pessimistic view of corporate social responsibility — the second chapter in this section by Erna Karrer–Rüedi focuses on the experience of the Credit Suisse. It delivers a practitioners' view on how socially responsible investors view themselves. Banks in the developed world "link" a pool of socially responsible investors' savings and lend those savings to microfinance institutions of their choice. Microfinance institutions in turn lend those resources to the poor. Interestingly, spread variations across microfinance institutions are not in the picture, which in turn leaves the reader intrigued on whether the size of such spreads, which are presumably large, could be taken as a metric of corporate social responsibility.

The next chapter by Beatriz Armendáriz and Ariane Szafarz explores mission drift. Contrary to common wisdom, the researchers argue that average loan size alone does not represent a benchmark for judging whether microfinance institutions are moving away from their poverty alleviation mission. In particular, Armendáriz–Szafarz present a theoretical framework which makes an interesting point: the difference between mission drift and cross-subsidization is blurred at best, misleading at worst. If depth of outreach is region-specific, do investors have to sacrifice monetary returns in order to serve the poorest? This question is taken up by Rients Galema, and Robert Lensink in an essay where the trade-off faced by socially responsible investors between risk and return is well articulated. Specifically, the researchers show that socially responsible investors must endure lower returns or take a higher risk in order to increase portfolio outreach. This negative correlation, Galema and Lensink argue, has never been quantified.

And this first trial should be viewed as the tip of an iceberg in terms of how much social investors are willing to endure in order to offer financial services to approximately 94 percent potential clients.

But the trade-off can be somewhat mitigated if microfinance institutions become more efficient. Marek Hudon and Bernd Balkenol remind us about the importance of what they call "efficiency", namely, outreach maximization for a given set of subsidies. Suppose for a moment that a relative lower return that social investors have to endure for the sake of opening financial access to the poor is like a subsidy. Because we live in a world of limited resources, those subsidies must be selective. A straightforward way of allocating subsidies across microfinance institutions by means of social investors is to be guided by efficiency. Yet, Hudon–Balkenol would argue, this is easier said than done, for microfinance institutions differ quite widely. Not only do such institutions review different production functions, but they also offer different financial products, from microloans to savings and insurance. These differences are multidimensional, and make resource allocation of subsidies exceedingly difficult — even if productivity parameters were the only focus of scarce resource allocation.

To complete the picture, this section closes with an interesting article by Carlos Serrano-Cinca, Begoña Gutiérrez Nieto, and Cecilio Mar-Molinero, which reminds us of the so-called "double bottom line". That is, microfinance institutions are mindful not only about financial performance (or efficiency, as described in the Hudon–Balkenol essay) but also by social indicators. Econometric analysis is used to assess financial performance, and guidance is provided for extending the analysis to social performance indicators.

Finally, the fourth section aims at reviewing how unmet demand can be attended properly. It is analyzed from three different angles. The first one focuses on the challenges posed by agriculture. It starts with a contribution by Solène Morvant-Roux who clearly establishes the limits and constraints of microfinance when dealing with rural and agricultural financing. Her essay shows that even if more attention were to be devoted to agriculture lately, the market conditions experienced by a vast majority of small farmers still tend to exclude agricultural producers from financial services. The analysis is then completed with a contribution by William Parienté. Focusing on a rural area in Serbia, he shows the limitations of microcredit in order to resolve the specific needs of rural populations. Reviewing current approaches to deal with agricultural financing is portrayed as an imperative.

On an optimistic note, Johan Bastiaensen and Peter Marchetti deliver an important contribution which, albeit context-specific, shows a promising way for moving forward on the agricultural financing front. Borrowing from the experience of the Fondo de Desarrollo Local Nitlapán, and other institutions in Nicaragua, the authors show the importance of proactively promoting agricultural "value chains" in microfinance: alternative to top-down development policies, which contribute to create synergies between financial and non-financial actors in order to offer better services to small farmers. These chains, Bastiaensen and Marchetti argue, enhance efficiency, social inclusion and gender justice.

The second angle in this section concerns gender. Gender is a widely used parameter to assess social performance, that is, an indicator of social performance based on the percentage of women in microfinance. Women are not only the poorest, but also the main brokers of health and education within the household. Emphasis on women is therefore not surprisingly an important social indicator of how faithful microfinance institutions adhere to their social objectives. The numbers are striking: eight out of 10 microfinance clients are women. Somewhat paradoxically, however, women face severe saving constraints. Women's unmet demand for savings, Armendáriz argues in her essay, is due to the fact that women demand security, flexibility and commitment. None are being adequately met by microfinance institutions. Women therefore have a tendency to turn to microfinance for loans and to the informal market for savings. A follow-up paper by Stuart Rutherford focuses on the poor's savings in Bangladesh. Rutherford shows that instalment plans whereby the poor save bite-sized amounts combined with other innovative plans can boost the poor's capacity to save.

Savings are, however, only one part of the equation. The poor in agriculture, relative to their counterparts in urban areas, are more exposed to risks due to drastic changes in weather conditions, low levels of sanitation, and infectious diseases, to mention a few. Craig Churchill sheds light on this interesting topic. In his paper, he first highlights the importance of taking a broad view of microfinance with a built-in health insurance component. He illustrates nicely some latest state-of-the-art developments in microinsurance for protecting the heavily exposed poor.

In a follow-up article, David Hulme, Karen Moore, and Kazi Faizal Bin Seraj remind us that poverty is a multidimensional problem. Largely based on a Bangladeshi BRAC programme, which is specifically designed to target the ultra poor, the authors of this interesting piece document how a combination of asset delivery and skill provision can reduce poverty and vulnerability. While the authors portray BRAC's programme as exceedingly successful at reaching vast numbers of ultra poor via its carefully designed

Targeting the Ultra Poor (TUP) program, they warn us on TUC being context-specific, with limited policy implications which could easily be replicable in other regions.

The third angle in this last section is education. Not because we consider education to be unimportant. On the contrary, we think that education is in high demand by microfinance clients, particularly the poorest. But it is probably here where the mismatch is most acute. In her paper, Isabelle Guérin documents rather nicely how appalling the design of existing microfinance products is relative to what the poor actually would like to see on offer. This is a very difficult problem to tackle in the context of West Africa, she argues, because, among other problems, clients are highly heterogeneous. Gender issues are part of the equation. Linda Mayoux, in particular, delivers a "gender protocol for financial services", which touches upon normative statements for women's empowerment. The handbook closes on an appropriate note, thanks to the interesting contribution by Asif Dowla on higher education in Bangladesh. In Dowla's own words: "...there is a mismatch between what potential clients demand and what microfinance can offer in terms of financial products. Prior to the introduction of education loans by Grameen Bank, a student, specially a female student... would probably have received a general education in the local college... Now, thanks to the education loan of Grameen Bank, she is self-confident, independent, helping other people".

Microfinance success is a long and winding road. Quite a lot has already been accomplished. Much more remains to be done. Can smarter funding from donors and socially responsible investors help resolve the mismatch? Or, are stronger efforts in the field of innovation from practitioners needed? Can insights from academics help to accelerate the pace at which the mismatch gap can potentially be closed? After reading this handbook, we are left with the impression that a concerted action between the three might do the trick.

PART I
Understanding Microfinance Practices

Microfinance Evaluation Strategies: Notes on Methodology and Findings

Dean Karlan

Yale University, Innovations for Poverty Action, Financial Access Initiative, and the MIT Jameel Poverty Action Lab

Nathanael Goldberg

Innovations for Poverty Action

1 Introduction: Why Evaluate?

Impact evaluations can be used either to estimate the impact of an entire program or to evaluate the effect of a new product or policy. In either case, the fundamental evaluation question is the same: "How are the lives of the participants different relative to how they would have been had the program, product, service or policy not been implemented?" The first part of that question, how are the lives of the participants different, is the easy part. The second part, however, is not. It requires measuring the counterfactual, how their lives *would have* been had the policy *not* been implemented. This is the evaluation challenge. One critical difference between a reliable and unreliable evaluation is how well the design allows the researcher to measure this counterfactual.

Policymakers typically conduct impact evaluations of programs to decide how best to allocate scarce resources. However, since most microfinance institutions (MFIs) aim to be *for-profit* institutions that rely on private investments to finance their activities, some argue that evaluation is unwarranted, a debate discussed in Morduch (2000). At the same time, MFIs, like other businesses, have traditionally focused on quantifying program *outcomes*; in this view, as long as clients repay their loans and take new ones, the program is assumed to be meeting the clients' needs. Even if this is so, we propose four reasons to evaluate.

First, an impact evaluation is akin to good market and client research. By learning more about the impact of a product on clients, one can design better products and processes. Hence, in some cases, an impact evaluation need not even be considered an activity outside the scope of best business practices. For-profit firms can and should invest in learning how best to have a positive impact on their clients. By increasing client loyalty and wealth, the institution is likely to keep clients longer and provide them with the resources to use a wider range of financial services, thus improving profitability. Public entities may wish to subsidize the research to make sure the knowledge enters into the public domain, so that social welfare is maximized.[1] Note that this point is true both for impact evaluations of an entire program (e.g., testing the impact of expanding access to finance), and impact evaluations of program innovations (e.g., testing the impact of one loan product versus another loan product). We will discuss both types of evaluations in this paper.

Second, even financially self-sufficient financial institutions often receive indirect subsidies in the form of soft loans or free technical assistance from donor agencies. Therefore it is reasonable to ask whether these subsidies are justified relative to the next best alternative use of these public funds. Donor agencies have helped create national credit bureaus and worked with governments to adopt sound regulatory policies for microfinance. What is the return on these investments? Impact evaluations allow program managers and policymakers to compare the cost of improving families' income or health through microfinance to the cost of achieving the same impact through other interventions. The World Bank's operational policy on financial intermediary lending supports this view, stating that subsidies of poverty reduction programs may be an appropriate use of public funds, provided that they "are economically justified, or can be shown to be the least-cost way of achieving poverty reduction objectives" (World Bank, 1998).

Third, impact evaluations are not simply about measuring whether a given program is having a positive effect on participants. Impact evaluations provide important information to practitioners and policymakers about the

[1]Note that for-profit firms could have an interest in keeping evaluation results private if they provide a competitive advantage in profitability. However, for-profit firms can and have made excellent socially minded research partners. When public entities fund evaluations with private firms, they should have an explicit agreement about the disclosure of the findings.

types of products and services that work best for particular types of clients. Exploring why top-performing programs have the impact they do can then help policy-makers develop and disseminate best practice policies for MFIs to adopt. Evaluations serve as a public good and the more they are undertaken across a variety of settings and business models, the better it will be for the applicability of findings to a wide range of MFIs, not just a few top performers. Impact evaluations also allow us to benchmark the performance of different MFIs. In an ideal setting, we would complement impact evaluations with monitoring data so that we could learn which monitoring outcomes, if any, potentially proxy for true impact.

Lastly, while many microfinance programs aim to be for-profit entities, not all are. Many are non-profit organizations, and some are government-owned. We need to learn how alternative governance structures influence the impact on clients. Impact may differ because of the programs' designs and organizational efficiencies, or because of different targeting and client composition. Regarding the former, many organizations have found that they have been better able to grow and attract investment by converting to for-profits. The advantages of commercialization depend on the regulations in each country, and some critics accuse for-profit MFIs of mission drift — earning higher returns by serving better-off clients with larger loans. Some governments have run their own MFIs as social programs. Historically, government-owned programs have had difficulties with repayment (perhaps due to the political difficulty of enforcing loans in bad times), but there are cases where government-owned programs can do well (e.g., Crediamigo in Brazil and BRI in Indonesia). If, however, the main difference in impact between organizations with different governance structures is due to targeting and client composition, impact evaluation is not necessarily needed in the long-term. Impact evaluation can begin by measuring the relative impact on the different client pools. However, once the relative impact is known, simpler client profile data and targeting analysis could suffice for making comparative statements across microfinance institutions.

In this paper, we seek to provide an overview of impact evaluations of microfinance. We begin in Section II by defining microfinance. This discussion is not merely an exercise in terminology, but has immediate implications for how to compare evaluations across different programs. Section III discusses the types of microfinance impacts and policies that can be evaluated, including program evaluation and policy evaluations. Section IV reviews experimental and quasi-experimental evaluations and methodologies in urban and rural environments, and discusses some of the key results from past studies. In Section V, we review common indicators of impact and sources of data. Section VI concludes with a discussion of impact issues that have yet to be adequately addressed.

2 Definition of Microfinance

The first step in conducting an evaluation of a microfinance program is, perhaps surprisingly, to ensure that you are conducting an evaluation of a microfinance program. This seems obvious, but is not, since the definition of "microfinance" is less than clear. Broadly speaking, microfinance for loans (i.e., microcredit) is the provision of small-scale financial services to people who lack access to traditional banking services. The term microfinance usually implies very small loans to low-income clients for self-employment, often with the simultaneous collection of small amounts of savings. How we define "small" and "poor" affects what does and does not constitute microfinance. "Microfinance" as evidenced by its name clearly is about more than just credit, otherwise we should always call it microcredit. Many programs offer stand-alone savings products, and remittance services and insurance are becoming popular innovations in the suite of services offered by financial institutions for the poor. In fact, it is no longer exclusively institutions for the poor that offer microfinance services. Commercial banks and insurance companies are beginning to go downscale to reach new markets; consumer durables companies are targeting the poor with microcredit schemes, and even Wal-Mart is offering remittances services.

Hence, not all programs labeled as "microfinance" will fit everybody's perception of the term, depending on model, target group, and services offered. For example, one recent study collectively refers to programs as varied as rice lenders, buffalo lenders, savings groups, and women's groups as microfinance institutions (Kaboski and Townsend, 2005). Another study, Karlan and Zinman (2009a), examines the impact of consumer credit in South Africa that targets *employed* individuals, not microentrepreneurs. Surely these are all programs worthy of close examination, but by labeling them as microfinance programs, the researchers are making an implicit statement that they should be benchmarked against other microfinance programs with regard to outreach, impact, and financial self-sufficiency. If the programs do not offer sufficiently similar services to a sufficiently similar target group, it is difficult to infer *why* one program may work better than another. Despite their differences, these programs do typically compete for the same scarce resources from donors and/or investors. Hence, despite their differences and lack of similarities, comparisons are still fruitful since they help decide how to allocate these scarce resources. Note that this argument holds for comparing not only different financial services organizations to each other, but also interventions from different sectors, such as education and health, to microfinance. At a macro level, allocations must be made across sectors, not just within sectors. Hence, lack of comparability of two organizations' operations and governance structure is not a sufficient argument for failing to compare their relative impacts.

2.1 *Key characteristics of microfinance*

It may be helpful to enumerate some of the characteristics associated with what is perceived to be "microfinance". There are at least nine traditional features of microfinance:

(1) Small transactions and minimum balances (whether loans, savings, or insurance).
(2) Loans for entrepreneurial activity.
(3) Collateral-free loans.
(4) Group lending.
(5) Focus on poor clients.
(6) Focus on female clients.
(7) Simple application processes.
(8) Provision of services in underserved communities.
(9) Market-level interest rates.

It is debatable which of these characteristics, if any, are necessary conditions for a program to be considered microfinance. Although MFIs often target microentrepreneurs, they differ as to whether they require this as a condition for a loan. Some MFIs visit borrowers' places of business to verify that loans were used for entrepreneurial activities while other MFIs disburse loans with few questions asked, operating more like consumer credit lenders. In addition, some MFIs require collateral or "collateral substitutes" such as household assets which are valuable to the borrower but less than the value of the loan. Group lending, too, while common practice among MFIs, is certainly not the only method of providing micro-loans.[2] Many MFIs offer individual loans to their established clients and even to first-time borrowers.

[2] There is a rich theoretical literature on joint-liability lending. See for example Stiglitz (1990); Ghatak (1999); Ghatak and Guinnane (1999); Conning (2005).

Grameen Bank, one of the pioneers of the microfinance movement and of the group lending model, has since shifted to individual lending.

The focus on "poor" clients is almost universal, with varying definitions of the word "poor". This issue has been made more important recently due to legislation from the United States Congress that requires USAID to restrict funding to programs that focus on the poor. Some argue that microfinance should focus on the "economically active poor", or those just at or below the poverty level (Robinson, 2001). Others, on the other hand, suggest that microfinance institutions should try to reach the indigent (Daley-Harris, 2005).

Most, but not all, microfinance programs focus on women. It has been argued that women repay their loans more often and direct a higher share of enterprise proceeds to their families.[3] Early replicators of the Grameen Bank have spoken of their operations nearly failing until they shifted their lending practices to focus on female clients (UNDP, 2008). Today the Microcredit Summit Campaign reports that 80% of microfinance clients worldwide are female. However, the percentage of female clients varies considerably by region, with the highest percentages in Asia, followed by Africa and Latin America, and the fewest in the Middle East and North Africa. This focus on the poor, and on women, along with the simple application process and the provision of financial services in clients' own communities together form financial *access*. This is the provision of financial services to the unbanked — those who have been excluded from financial services because they are poor, illiterate, or live in rural areas.

Finally, microcredit loans are designed to be offered at market rates of interest such that the MFIs can recover their costs, but not so high that they make supernormal profits off the poor. This is an important concept because institutions that charge high interest rates can be scarcely cheaper than the moneylenders they intended to replace, and institutions that charge subsidized rates can distort markets by undercutting other lenders that are attempting to recover their costs. This has implications for impact assessments because the less clients must pay in interest, the more they could be expected to show in increased income. If we compare the impact of

[3]Higher repayment rates for females is commonly believed but not well documented. In evidence from consumer loans in South Africa (Karlan and Zinman, 2010), women are three percentage points less likely to default on their loans, from a mean of fifteen % default. Little is known, however, as to why this is so. One theory is women are simply more responsible, while some argue that women, having fewer borrowing options than men, are wary of jeopardizing their relationship with their MFI by defaulting. If this is true, we may expect to see the repayment gap diminish over time as financial access expands.

institutions that fall outside of "normal" microfinance interest rates, we could end up drawing unreasonable conclusions about the effectiveness of one program versus another, since each type of program attracts different clients and imposes different costs on its borrowers.

Note that the sustainability of an organization does not require each and every product or target market to be sustainable, but rather that the organization as a whole is sustainable. Thus organizations could charge lower interest rates for indigent or particularly poor individuals, as long as there were sufficient profits from lending to the not-so-poor to be able to cross-subsidize such a program. Such programs may, in the long run, be sustainable (if the initially subsidized program leads to client loyalty and a long-term relationship with the MFI).

2.2 *Liability structure of microfinance loans*

There are three basic models of liability employed by MFIs. Each poses the possibility of differences in potential impacts (e.g., group-liability programs may generate positive or negative impacts on risk-sharing and social capital) as well as targeting (traditionally, individual-lending programs reach a wealthier clientele).

- Solidarity Groups: The classic microfinance model, often referred to as the "Grameen model" after the pioneering Grameen Bank in Bangladesh, involves 5-person solidarity groups, in which each group member guarantees the other members' repayment. If any of the group members fail to repay their loans, the other group members must repay for them or face losing access to future credit.
- Village Banking: Village banking expands the solidarity group concept to a larger group of 15–30 women or men who are responsible for managing the loan provided by the MFI (the "external account"), as well as making and collecting loans to and from each other (the "internal account"). In India, self-help groups (SHGs) operate according to a similar format.
- Individual Lending: Individual lending is simply the provision of microfinance services to individuals instead of groups. Individual lending can be hard to distinguish from traditional banking since they have similar forms. This is especially true where MFIs require collateral (or collateral substitutes such as household items with low market value but high personal value to the borrower) from borrowers, as collateral-free lending has traditionally been one of the hallmarks of microfinance.

2.3 *"Other" microfinance services*

Many microfinance programs offer services beyond credit. The most basic such service is savings (credit unions and cooperatives, for instance, rely heavily on savings), although only a few programs focus solely on savings (on the premise that what the poor need most is a safe place to store their money). Some MFIs require mandatory savings each week from each borrower as well as each group, although, depending on the individual MFI's policies of collection of mandatory savings in case of default, this is often more appropriately called cash collateral, rather than savings. Some of these programs also collect voluntary savings, allowing clients to deposit as much as they like each week. Recently MFIs have begun to offer (either independently or bundled with credit) a wide variety of other services, including insurance (life insurance and/or health insurance), skills training, and remittances services. A popular form of training is credit with education, developed by Freedom from Hunger, which includes modules on both business and health training. While MFIs offering credit with education have demonstrated that the modules can be provided at low cost, some MFIs retain their focus on credit and savings, arguing that the poor already have all the business skills they need — what they need most is the cheapest possible source of credit.[4]

3 Types of Policies to Evaluate

We discuss three types of microfinance evaluations: program evaluations, product or process evaluations, and policy evaluations. These types encompass a wide range of activities engaged in by practitioners, donors and governments. These include: (1) microfinance services delivered to end clients; (2) loans to programs: either loans to state-owned banks which then directly

---

[4]See Karlan and Valdivia (2008) for an evaluation of the marginal benefit of business training for microcredit clients. We conduct a randomized control trial in which preexisting credit groups were randomly assigned to either credit with education (business training only) or to credit only (i.e., no change to their services). This random assignment ensures that we are measuring the impact of the business training, and not confounding our result with a selection bias that individuals who want business training are more likely to improve their businesses, regardless of the training. We find that the business training leads to improved client retention, improved client repayment, better business practices, and higher and smoother business revenues.

lend to microentrepreneurs (e.g., the Crediamigo program), or loans to second-tier lenders, who then on-lend to banks (private or public), NGOs or other financial institutions who then on-lend to the poor; (3) technical assistance to help microfinance institutions improve their operations so as to lower costs, expand outreach, and maximize impact; and (4) public policies, such as creating and strengthening credit bureaus, or establishing stronger regulatory bodies for savings and capitalization requirements.

The last of these is the most difficult to evaluate. Public policy initiatives, particularly regulation, are quite difficult to evaluate fully. We will discuss a few examples of when it is possible to learn something about the impact of the policy (such as credit bureaus), but we note that for some interventions, particularly those that are implemented at the country level, it is difficult, if not impossible, to have a full and unbiased evaluation.

We divide the types of evaluations into three, though the line between them is not always crystal clear.

First, and perhaps most importantly, "program" evaluation refers to examining whether a particular microfinance institution is effective or not in improving the welfare of its clients. Rigorous evaluation is essential to determine this because of selection bias (discussed in more detail later in the paper): maybe the people most driven or most able to improve their lives elect to participate in microfinance in the first place. So knowing that an MFI's clients are thriving is not sufficient for understanding whether an MFI caused the change.

Second, "product or process" evaluation refers to evaluating the relative effectiveness for a *particular* microfinance institution in implementing one product versus another, or one process versus another. In the case of technical assistance to microfinance institutions, then, here are examples of how evaluations can be done to evaluate not the entirety of the technical assistance, but of particular assistance given on a particular topic. Examples include credit with education versus credit without education, group versus individual liability, and incentive schemes for employees.

Third, in the case of "policy" evaluations, we refer to more macro-level policies, such as regulation of banks and introduction of credit bureaus. Often these macro-level policies do have some micro-level implementation. We put forward examples from interest rate sensitivities to credit bureaus of how to use those micro-level implementations in order to learn the impact of the policy. Some policies, implemented at the macro-level, are arguably not possible to evaluate cleanly. For example, an implementation of new hardware and software for a central bank is undoubtedly outside the scope of an impact evaluation, or changing capitalization requirements for banks may also not be possible to evaluate explicitly.

All three types of evaluations are impact evaluations. Recalling our earlier definition, each of these evaluations distinguishes the outcome from the counterfactual of what would have happened in the absence of the program, process, or policy.

3.1 *Program impact evaluations*

Historically, MFI impact evaluations have been program evaluations, i.e., they have attempted to measure the overall impact of an MFI on client or community welfare. In many cases, the full package of program services includes many components: credit, education, social capital building, insurance, etc. Thus, a program evaluation measures the impact of this full package relative to no package at all. Although useful for measuring whether the resources allocated to the program were worthwhile, such program evaluations do not clearly identify which particular aspects of successful programs produced the impact. This type of program evaluation, therefore, will not tell other programs precisely which mechanisms to mimic.

3.1.1 *Product or process impact evaluations*

Many microfinance institutions test new product designs by allowing a few volunteer clients to use a new lending product, or by offering to a small group of particularly chosen clients (often, their best) a new product. Alternatively, a microfinance institution can implement a change throughout one branch (but for all clients in that branch). We argue that such approaches are risky for lenders, and inferences about the benefits of changes evaluated in such a manner can be misleading. Such approaches do not help establish whether the innovation or change *causes* an improvement for the institution (or the client) because the group that chooses or is chosen to participate may vary substantially from those who did not choose (or were not chosen) to participate. Establishing this causal link should be important not only for the microfinance institution implementing the change, but also for policymakers and other MFIs which want to know whether they should implement similar changes. This is a situation in which impact evaluations, especially randomized controlled trials, are a win-win proposition: less risky (and hence less costly in the long run) from a business and operations perspective, and optimal from a public goods perspective, in that the lessons learned from establishing these causal links can be disseminated to other MFIs.

Examples abound of randomized controlled trials that evaluated the effectiveness for an MFI of a product or process innovation. In each of these cases, the studies measure the impact to the institution. In one study in the Philippines, a bank converted half of its group-liability Grameen-style centers to individual-liability centers. Before this test, it was unclear what the effect of such a change might be: clients may appreciate the group support of solidarity loans but dislike being on the hook for others' defaults. Moreover, there are a number of theoretical reasons why group-lending may break down under stress, e.g., a number of defaults may lead to a tipping point and "strategic default" (Besley and Coate, 1995). The bank found that under individual liability, client repayment did not change, client retention improved, and more new clients joined (Giné and Karlan, 2006). Of course, this could be driven by the selection process under group liability: all these clients agreed to borrow under group liability and therefore may be more reliable or better connected to begin with. In a further experiment, upon entry to villages for the first time, the bank randomly decided whether to offer group or individual liability. The bank found no difference in repayments regardless of the liability structure (Giné and Karlan, 2009). In ongoing work in Pakistan, a World Bank team led by Xavier Giné and Ghazala Mansuri is working with a lender to test different incentive schemes and training for credit officers.

Yet another area of evaluation focuses on repayment. Frequent payment schedules are thought to be essential to maintain low default, but all those meetings come at a cost, both for clients and MFIs (Armendariz, de Aghion and Morduch, 2005). In an experiment in India, Field and Pande (2007) examine the effect of different repayment frequencies on default. They find no difference in repayment between weekly and monthly repayment schedules, implying both banks and clients could potentially save substantial amounts of time at little cost. In follow-up work, however, they show that social capital is diminished along with reductions in meeting frequency (Feigenberg, Field and Pande, 2009). Giné, Goldberg and Yang (2009) evaluate the impact on repayment of a biometric system to identify loan applicants by their fingerprints, preventing defaulters from re-borrowing in the future under different identities. Repayment increases substantially among those predicted *ex ante* most likely to default. Moreover, this subgroup takes out smaller loans, spends more of their loans on agricultural inputs, and generates higher profits at harvest.

MFIs have typically set interest rates either ad hoc, or under the assumption that the poor will be willing to pay anything up to moneylender rates; little analysis has focused on deriving optimal interest rates based on empirical demand (Morduch, 1999). In South Africa, a consumer finance lender evaluated borrower sensitivity to interest rates (Karlan and Zinman, 2008; Karlan and Zinman, 2010), as well as the effectiveness of different marketing approaches on the likelihood that individuals borrowed. They find that some costless marketing approaches such as presenting only one rather than several loans or including a woman's photo on the mailer were as effective at increasing demand as dropping the interest rate as much as 4 percentage points per *month* from an average rate across the sample of 7.9 percent (Bertrand *et al.*, 2010). Of course, take-up can be affected by product features as well. Farmers in Malawi offered loans packaged with rainfall insurance, were 13 percentage points less likely to borrow compared to those offered credit alone. Such a difference is somewhat puzzling since the insurance was offered at actuarially fair prices. The authors hypothesize that with the limited liability implicit in the group-liability contract, the added insurance instead translates into a higher interest rate for borrowers (Giné and Yang, 2009). Alternative hypotheses from an earlier version of the paper suggested lower demand for the insured loans may be related to difficulty in understanding the new product, as take-up of the insured loans is positively correlated with education levels (Giné and Yang, 2007).

Analysis by Banerjee and Duflo (2007) of a battery of household surveys shows even the very poor have disposable income at times, and therefore the capacity to save for future needs. Psychologists have predicted that certain types of people who discount future consumption more heavily will have difficulty saving (Laibson, 1997; O'Donoghue and Rabin, 1999; Fudenberg and Levine, 2005). In the Philippines, we measured the impact of a new commitment savings product (a specialized savings account for which the client set a savings goal; her money could not be withdrawn until she reached her goal), as well as an accompanying deposit collection service, and compared the savings balances of clients who received it to clients who already had traditional savings accounts (Ashraf, Karlan and Yin, 2006a; Ashraf, Karlan and Yin, 2006b; Ashraf, Karlan and Yin, 2006c). In a study in Peru, a village banking organization measured the impact of credit with education as compared to credit without education on both the financial institution and client well-being. Repayment rates and client retention increased, as did clients' business revenue (Karlan and Valdivia, 2008).

3.1.2 *Policy evaluations*

Evaluations can also be designed to measure the impact of public policies such as financial regulation and credit bureaus. Typical regulatory policies include interest rate ceilings and regulation (or prohibition) of savings or savings protection via government deposit insurance programs. It can be difficult to design rigorous studies to measure the macro effects resulting from these types of policies. However, there are two ways in which micro-level studies can give insight into the impact of a macro-level policy. First, impacts on specific behaviors in response to policies can be estimated through micro-level interventions that inform individuals about the macro policies. Second, by measuring spillovers on non-participants in micro studies, one can calculate community-level estimates of the impacts. Typically, this does require a large sample in order to be able to generate variation on the intensity of treatment and then estimate the spillover to non-participants. Depending on the type of spillover, this may or may not be feasible.

An excellent example of the first type of study is recent work in Guatemala on credit bureaus (de Janvry, McIntosh and Sadoulet, 2007). The authors worked with an NGO, Genesis, to assign randomly some clients to receive training on the importance of credit bureaus to their credit opportunities. The clients were informed of both the stick and carrot components (i.e., paying late harms their access to credit elsewhere, yet paying on time gives them access to credit elsewhere at potentially lower rates). The authors find that the training led to higher repayment rates by their clients, but also led their clients to borrow elsewhere after establishing a good credit record. This type of study fits under both what we are calling "policy evaluations" as well as "product or process evaluation" (elaborated above). The distinction here is that this particular "process" is intended to help illuminate the effectiveness of the implementation of credit bureaus in Guatemala.

Similar approaches could be applied to a wide variety of policies such as savings regulation and interest rate policies, as well as large-scale donor agency initiatives such as financial infrastructure lending for ATMs, smart cards, and cell phone banking. Such interventions could readily be evaluated with randomized controlled trials of the end products, with treatment groups of participants compared to control groups who do not receive the services.

Regarding savings regulation, two issues in particular seem ripe for evaluation: (1) Do safer, regulated savings make a difference to individuals when choosing how or whether to save? (2) How does savings mobilization affect the larger relationship between the MFI and the client? Both of these are consequences of macro-level policies that need to be understood. Naturally, they do not encompass the entirety of the macro policy and hence should not be seen as a conclusive gross impact of a savings regulatory policy in a country. However, such evaluations can provide important information about the specific consequences that were generated, and can be expected in the future, from approving MFIs to accepting savings or regulating their management of the deposits.

Regarding interest rate policy, two areas should be of particular interest to policymakers and are ripe for carefully executed randomized controlled trials: (1) interest rate caps, and (2) consumer protection, à la "Truth in Lending" type regulation. We have little systematic evidence about sensitivity to interest rates, and not much in terms of overall demand or how different interest rates attract different clients (wealthier vs. poorer, riskier vs. safer, etc.). Three recent papers from work in South Africa and Bangladesh demonstrate more sensitivity than is commonly believed (Dehejia, Montgomery and Morduch, 2005; Karlan and Zinman, 2008; Karlan and Zinman, 2010). However, we do not have enough information, particularly across different countries and settings, to predict confidently what will happen to access to credit if interest rate caps are put in place.[5] Regarding consumer protection, many countries are putting in place laws to regulate how firms present their charges to clients, not just how much they charge. We know there can be tremendous confusion on simple matters of interest. For instance, many lenders charge interest over the declining balance (as is common in developed countries), whereas others charge interest over the initial loan size throughout the life of the loan. The latter practice offers the benefit of greatly simplified math, and could therefore be considered consumer-friendly, but the interest rate advertised will understate the APR by half. The lower interest rate advertised by an MFI competitor may come at much greater cost. Do consumers understand the difference? When given a choice in the market, do they choose the loan which best fits their cash flow needs at the lowest true cost? Depending on the term of the loan, lower payments may not mean a better deal. Studies could be conducted to understand how the different presentation of loan terms affects client behavior and outcomes (take-up, repayment, and impact) in order to then form effective public policies on consumer protection.

[5] This of course only mentions the demand side of interest rates. Supply side considerations also must be taken into account when formulating interest rate policies.

4 Methodological Approaches

4.1 *Randomized controlled trials for program evaluation*

Evaluating the impact of a microfinance program requires measuring the impact of receiving the program's services (typically credit, and sometimes savings), versus the counterfactual of not receiving the services. This can be more difficult than evaluating new products or policies (to be discussed below) because the control group must be drawn from non-clients, with whom the MFI does not have a preexisting relationship.

We discuss here three different approaches to conducting experimental evaluations of microcredit programs. In experimental evaluations, subjects are selected at the outset with potential clients randomly assigned to treatment and control groups. When evaluating the impact of an entire program, the treatment as well as the control group must be drawn from potential clients whom the program has yet to serve.

4.1.1 *Experimental credit scoring*

Credit scoring is becoming a popular tool for microfinance institutions seeking to improve the efficiency and speed with which credit is granted (Schreiner, 2002). An experimental credit scoring approach uses credit scoring to approve or reject applicants based on their likelihood of default — as with normal credit scoring — but then randomizes clients "on the bubble" (those who should neither obviously be approved nor rejected based on the bank's criteria: e.g., credit history, employment, savings balance) to either receive or not receive credit. The outcomes of those in this middle group who were randomly assigned to receive credit would be compared to those in this middle group who were randomly assigned not to receive credit. The analysis would not examine the outcomes of the clients who fell outside of this randomization "bubble" (i.e., either the extremely creditworthy or extremely un-creditworthy clients). This does have an important implication: the approach measures the impact on only the *marginal* clients with respect to creditworthiness. If access to credit is limited for other reasons (proximity to banking services), this has important implications and may cause an underestimate of the average impact of the program (if those who are most creditworthy accrue more positive benefits from participation) or an overestimate (if those who are least creditworthy accrue more positive benefits from participation). If, on the other hand, the primary contribution of the MFI is that it helps get access to those who are deemed un-creditworthy by other financial institutions such as commercial banks, then this approach hones in on the exact population of most interest. In other words, perhaps the most creditworthy have other equally good choices for borrowing, hence there is no "impact" (or minimal impact, perhaps) on them, and thus measuring the impact on those at the threshold is the exact group that benefits the most.

Note that this approach, if sample sizes permit, does not necessarily require randomization. A regression discontinuity design may also be possible if enough individuals are at or near the threshold.[6,7]

The experimental approach offers an operational advantage: it provides lenders with a less risky manner of testing the repayment rates on the marginal (or below marginal) clients. Whereas normally a lender may set a bar at a certain credit score threshold, the randomization allows the lender to lower the bar but limit the number of clients that are allowed in at that level. Furthermore, the experimentation allows the lender to adjust the credit scoring approach. A conservative credit scoring approach, which does not allow the lender to test below their normal "approve" level, will never reveal whether profit opportunities are being missed because of fear of default.

This approach was employed in a study in South Africa with a consumer lender making micro-loans, and with a microenterprise lending program in the Philippines. The lender in South Africa already had a credit scoring system, and the experimental addition focused strictly on those they normally would reject, whereas the Philippines experiment was designed as stated above, since no preexisting threshold existed. In South Africa, the lender randomly "un-rejected" some clients who had been rejected by the bank's credit scoring system and branch manager (Karlan and Zinman, 2009a).[8] Extending consumer credit to marginal customers produced noticeable benefits for clients in the form of increased employment and reduced hunger. Plus, follow-up analysis revealed the loans to these marginal clients were actually profitable for the lender. Note that these loans were made to employed borrowers; unlike traditional microfinance, the impact channel

[6]By comparing a regression discontinuity design to experimental estimates of the PROGRESA program Buddelmeyer and Skoufias (2004) provides useful insight into how far from the discontinuous point one can go without introducing bias into the impact estimate.

[7]The regression discontinuity approach may fail if some individuals near the threshold were given opportunities to improve their application and rise above the threshold.

[8]Clients with excessive debt or suspicion of fraud were removed from the sample frame, and all other rejected applicants were randomly assigned credit at a probability correlated with proximity to the approval threshold.

is not through enterprise creation or expansion. Instead the loans helped borrowers to retain employment.

A similar methodology was used by the researchers in the Philippines to evaluate the impact of loans to microentrepreneurs made by First Macro Bank, a for-profit rural bank operating in the Metro Manila region (Karlan and Zinman, 2009b). The findings are surprising. Profits increase, but mostly for men, and the effect is stronger among those with higher income. Curiously, the mechanism through which the impact takes place is not how microfinance is generally presumed to work — investment in productive activities. Here, business investment does not increase, and in fact there is evidence that businesses shrink in size and scope, including the shedding of paid employees. Together the results suggest that borrowers used credit to re-optimize business investment in a way that produced smaller, lower-cost, and more profitable businesses. The question remains as to why credit enabled this change: why did households need to borrow to reduce staff — what did they do with the money? We know they did not substitute into labor-saving devices because there was no change in business investment. One potential explanation is household risk management: individuals with access to credit substitute out of formal insurance products, while also reporting a greater ability to borrow from friends or family in an emergency. It is possible that before credit, entrepreneurs were retaining unproductive employees as a kind of informal mutual benefit scheme. Those employees, even if unprofitable, were an additional resource to turn in times of need.

4.1.2 *Randomized program placement*

We now discuss clustered randomized trials, in which the unit of randomization is not the individual but instead the market or the village. Randomizing by individual is not always feasible. For example, in implementing a group-lending program, it would be difficult to enter a rural village and randomly identify individuals to allow to join the group-lending program, while not allowing others to join.[9] Similarly, for a product innovation test, it would

[9]One could try to encourage some to join (by giving them a personal home visit to market the program) and others not, but allow everyone in the village to join. This would work if the home visit were effective in creating differential participation, but would only allow one to measure the impact on those who only joined as a result of that marketing. That does not introduce an internal validity problem, but does generate a question about external validity if those individuals are fundamentally different. In pilot experiments, we have found that such issues are moot, as home visits get swamped by the village-level marketing and we have typically not found demonstrably higher participation from those who received home visits than those who did not.

be inappropriate to assign randomly some clients from a lending group to get credit with education and others not, since the classes are given to the group as a whole.

In urban India, the Centre for Micro Finance (CMF), the M.I.T. Jameel Poverty Action Lab (JPAL) and Innovations for Poverty Action (IPA) evaluated the impact of a microfinance program in the slums of Hyderabad (Banerjee *et al.*, 2009) using a clustered randomized trial. The organization, Spandana, selected 120 slums into which it was willing to expand. The researchers, Abhijit Banerjee and Esther Duflo, randomly assigned each slum to either treatment or control. It is worth noting some differences with the FMB evaluation in the Philippines, discussed above: Spandana is a non-profit organization, where FMB is for-profit, and Spandana is a group-lending institution, where FMB lends to individuals. A baseline survey was completed in each slum, after which Spandana entered the treatment communities and offered loans to as many individuals as possible.[10] After 15–18 months, the households from the treatment slums were compared to the households in the control slums. The results show impacts on a number of dimensions, though not, critically, on average consumption. The treatment slums had greater investment in business durables, increases in the number of businesses started, and in the profitability of existing businesses. Among households that did not have existing businesses at the start of the program, those with high propensity to become entrepreneurs[11] see a decrease in consumption, while those with low propensity to become entrepreneurs increase consumption. Likely this difference is explained by investment in durable goods among those likely to become business owners. While the short-term impacts are clear, these results make it difficult to anticipate the long-term impacts. As the authors speculate, these investments may pay off in future consumption in the coming years. The increase in consumption among non-business owners has an even more ambiguous future: if these households went on a credit-fueled spending spree they will have to reduce future consumption to pay down debts. Alternatively, if they used the credit

[10]Note that for an experimental evaluation, a baseline survey is not necessary. As long as the sample size is large enough, the law of large numbers will produce statistically similar treatment and control groups. Baseline surveys do provide for further statistical precision, as well as the ability to measure heterogeneous treatment effects across more dimensions.

[11]Characteristics with explanatory power are: whether the wife of the household head is literate, whether the wife of the household head works for a wage, the number of "primeage" (18–45) women in the household, and the amount of land owned by the household.

to pay down high-cost moneylender debt, then their current consumption should remain high.

There is an important substantive advantage to randomizing at the village or market level. If there is reason to believe that a treatment has indirect effects on other individuals (spillovers), then an ideal experimental design captures such effects so that the aggregate impact of a program is measured. If spillovers are ignored in the design of an experiment, this could lead to bias in the analysis. The total program impact is the sum of the direct and indirect effects, thus it is important for policy purposes to measure both. An evaluation with such a design, conducted by Innovations for Poverty Action, is underway in Mexico. The research will measure the impact of Compartamos, a large for-profit microcredit organization operating throughout Mexico. In this study, 257 neighborhoods in northern Sonora, Mexico (65 percent urban, 26 percent peri-urban, and 9 percent rural) are randomly assigned to receive Compartamos' Crédito Mujer product, a group solidarity loan for low-income female entrepreneurs. An important contribution this study will make to the literature is the ability to measure spillovers on non-borrowers. In the three main cities in the sample, the neighborhood clusters are grouped into "superclusters" with varying intensity of treatment (penetration of financial services), creating exogenous variation in the amount of credit flowing into communities. This difference in the credit available to neighboring clusters will allow us to measure whether microfinance creates economic growth, or merely shifts resources from established entrepreneurs to new entrepreneurs. In the latter scenario, non-borrowers will be worse off from the expansion of credit even if clients prosper, while the net impact of the program can be positive or negative.[12] An alternative approach employed by Miguel and Kremer in Kenya (2004) uses variation in geographic distance from treatment to measure spillovers: comparing non-participants closer to treatment to those farther away provides an estimate of spillover effects.

[12] Alternatively, if one could collect sufficient baseline information to predict take-up within both treatment and control groups, one could do an experimental propensity score approach, and compare the predicted non-borrowers in treatment areas to the predicted non-borrowers in control areas in order to measure the impact on non-borrowers from lending in well-defined geographic areas (e.g., specific markets or rural villages). An alternative approach is to collect detailed data on channels through which impacts flow. This would be most akin to the approach employed in the adoption of agricultural technology literature (Conley and Udry, 2005). Note that this can be done in conjunction, or not, with an experimental evaluation (see Kremer and Miguel, 2007).

If randomizing by villages works, it may seem logical to ask: Why not randomize by larger units, such as branch or district/area? While such an approach might be good in theory, it greatly limits the number of effective observations in your sample if outcomes are highly correlated within geographic area. It is unusual to come across a setting with a sufficiently large sample size to make it possible in practice. Conversely, simply comparing one branch that gets the treatment to another that does not is not an acceptable strategy. It would be impossible to tell whether the *treatment* worked or whether that branch was different, for example, because it had an exogenous income shock such as a particularly good harvest or a new factory generating employment for the region, or if it had an extraordinarily good (or bad) branch manager.

4.1.3 *Encouragement designs*

In encouragement designs, the individuals in the treatment group are *encouraged* to participate in the program (e.g., the program is marketed to them), but they are not required to participate. The program is not marketed to the control group, but they are able to participate if they choose to do so. Therefore, encouragement designs may be useful in situations where it is infeasible to deny service to people who would like to participate in the program. The encouragement component, however, ensures that the treatment group contains more program participants than the control group.

In encouragement designs, it is critical that *assignment to treatment* — as opposed to *treatment* — is used to differentiate the groups when analyzing the results. In other words, members of the treatment group who do not participate are still part of the treatment group and members of the control group who do participate are still part of the control group. However, it is important to note that the more participating control group members there are, the larger the sample size necessary to detect program impacts. Dupas and Robinson (2009) is an example of this approach. Entrepreneurs in rural Kenya were provided with incentives to open a savings account with a community bank in their village. For the treatment group, the researchers paid the fee to open the account and provided the minimum balance. The control group received no incentives but were not barred from opening an account. In this case, the incentives were strong enough that 89 percent of the treatment group opened an account while only three individuals in the control group did so, but less extreme differences will work. Dupas and Robinson find remarkable impacts, despite substantial transaction fees charged by the bank ($0.50 or more) and the fact that many people in the sample never used the account after opening it. Moreover, the impacts are found only among female entrepreneurs. Four months after opening the account, women assigned to treatment show 40 percent growth in productive investment, and after six months, daily consumption is approximately 40 percent higher than in the control group.

4.1.4 *Ethical considerations of randomized evaluations*

With doubts about the reliability of quasi-experimental designs (discussed below), randomized evaluations are gaining popularity in international development (Duflo and Kremer, 2003). Particularly with poverty-alleviation programs, however, some observers and policymakers may be uncomfortable with the idea of randomizing the allocation of services to beneficiaries. In instances where the positive benefits of a program seem obvious, the need for an evaluation may come into question. However, until an idea has been properly evaluated, it is wrong to assume that you would be denying the poor a beneficial intervention. It is best to first evaluate the impact and ascertain whether the program does, in fact, have a positive impact relative to the next-best alternative, and then to determine for which types of clients the intervention works best. While microfinance might seem rather benign, there is a very real possibility that taking on debt or paying for services could leave a microfinance client worse off post-intervention. High interest rates are very common in microfinance. But not all clients have the financial sophistication to calculate their return on investment in their enterprise. Is it possible that their lack of formal recordkeeping causes some clients to continue borrowing (since cash flow increases with the credit and expanded working capital) even though they are actually generating lower profits? Such questions should be kept in mind before one assumes that a given intervention is unambiguously beneficial.

It is important to note that, as in an encouragement design, randomized evaluations do not necessarily need to deny services to anybody. Another common solution is to randomize the order in which a program expands to an area. Thus, the randomization simply makes use of the organizational constraint that existed even in the absence of the evaluation. No fewer people are served than before, but by incorporating a random component into the allocation process, one generates out of the expansion the opportunity for a clean impact evaluation. Such an approach only works on growing microfinance institutions, and ones that are able to plan far enough ahead to generate a list of target areas for a few years. Alternative approaches, such as encouragement designs, are discussed briefly above, and in more detail in Duflo, Glennerster and Kremer (2008).

4.2 *Quasi-experimental methodologies for program evaluation*

Quasi-experimental evaluations attempt to approximate experimental designs by constructing a comparison group out of similar non-participants. Quasi-experimental designs are an improvement over non-experimental evaluations such as *reflexive* (or "pre-post") designs because they can account for external changes in welfare among the study population by comparing participants to a control group. In reflexive evaluations, participants are compared only to themselves before and after the intervention. This is not a useful comparison, however, as many factors could contribute to the changes in their outcomes. For instance, participants' income could increase, but this could be due to general economic changes in the region, or simply due to participants acquiring more stable income as they age. In extreme cases, where GDP per capita in a particular country is declining, a reflexive design could show negative impact even if the program succeeded — participants may have fared less poorly than non-participants, hence the program had a positive impact even though participant income fell. We argue that such reflexive evaluations should not be referred to as *impact* evaluations, but rather client-monitoring exercises, or client-tracking exercises, since while they provide information on how clients' lives change, they in no way provide insight into the causal impact of the microfinance program on their lives.

Microfinance evaluators have used a variety of techniques to identify comparison groups. The extent to which these comparison groups adequately mimic the treatment groups is subjective. While no formal analysis of the quality of microfinance comparison groups has been conducted, evaluators would be wise to familiarize themselves with such comparisons from other settings. LaLonde (1986) finds quasi-experimental evaluations fail to match the results of randomized control trials of labor training programs. Glewwe *et al.* (2004) find that quasi-experimental evaluations overstate the impact of flip charts in Kenyan schools. With microfinance evaluations, it may be even more difficult to find a comparison group of similar non-participants, since the non-participants should have the same special (and often unobservable) determination and ability that led the clients to join the microfinance program. Evaluations that compare clients (those with this special determination) to non-clients will likely overestimate the impact of the programs (assuming this determination, or entrepreneurial spirit, leads to improved business outcomes). The extent to which this increases (or decreases) the estimate of program impact is the self-selection bias of the non-experimental approach. A related pitfall is bias from non-random program placement, in which outcomes in program villages are compared to outcomes in non-program villages. The problem with this method is that programs choose where they operate for a reason. They may target the poorest villages, for instance, or they may start cautiously with better-off clients before expanding their outreach. The bias from non-random program placement, therefore, can go either way, depending on whether the evaluation compares program villages to non-program villages that may be (even unobservably) better or worse off.

Randomized controlled trials, discussed above, solve these problems. However, as in the LaLonde and Glewwe *et al.*, studies discussed above, it would be a worthwhile exercise to conduct side by side experimental and quasi-experimental evaluations and compare the results to determine precisely how far off quasi-experimental evaluations are from experimental evaluations of microfinance programs. If quasi-experimental evaluations can be performed without substantial bias, it will allow evaluators more freedom in their choice of methodology.

Given the potential hazards, it is crucial to ensure that treatment and comparison groups are identical on as many observable dimensions as possible. Comparison group identification techniques have included:

- surveying target neighborhoods (either the same neighborhoods in which the treatment groups live or neighborhoods with similar demographics) to identify all households engaged in the informal sector, and then randomly drawing from the list;
- random walk method — starting from a particular point in a neighborhood walking X number of houses to the left, Y number of houses to the right, etc., and attempting to enroll the resulting household in the comparison group.

The quasi-experimental methodology suggested by the USAID-funded project, Assessing the Impact of Microenterprise Services (AIMS), further simplifies the survey methodology by comparing existing clients to incoming clients, suggesting that the difference in outcomes between the two groups represents the impact of the program. Karlan (2001) discusses several flaws with this methodology. The most important of these flaws is the potential bias from dropouts; if unsuccessful clients drop out, this approach is akin to ignoring one's failures and only measuring one's successes.[13] Furthermore, there may be unobservable reasons why incoming clients differ from clients who chose to enroll in the program at an earlier date. For instance, a year earlier they may have been afraid to join, they may not have had a business opportunity, they may have had a job, or they may have had child-rearing issues. Or, the delay may be due to the MFI. The MFI may not have targeted their village at the time because it was too far from infrastructure like roads and telephones, or because it was too well-off. Regardless of the reason, the AIMS-suggested approach will bias the estimate of impact. The punch line often provided to defend this methodology is that "since everyone is a client, they all have entrepreneurial spirit". This argument is flawed. It ignores the time-specific decision to join, and assumes that entrepreneurial spirit is a fixed individual characteristic. As the examples above demonstrate, it is easy to imagine that the decision to join a microfinance program is just as much about the time in one's life as it is about the personal fixed characteristics of an individual.

Alexander-Tedeschi and Karlan (2009) show this is not an idle concern. By replicating the AIMS cross-sectional methodology with longitudinal data from one of the AIMS "Core Impact Assessments" of Mibanco, an MFI in Peru, they find several significant differences between existing members and incoming clients, though the directions of the resulting biases differ. New entrants were more likely to have a formal business location, which would understate impact, but were poorer on household measures such as educational expenditures, which would overstate impact.

Coleman (1999) used a novel method to control for selection bias; he formed his comparison group out of prospective clients in northern Thailand who signed up a year in advance to participate in two village banks. This technique (later dubbed "pipeline matching") allowed him to compare his estimate of impact to the estimate he would have calculated had he naïvely compared program participants to a group of non-participants. The "naïve" estimate overstated the gains from participation because participants turned out to be wealthier than non-participants to begin with. Coleman found no evidence of impact on sales, savings, assets, or school expenditures, and he

[13]As will be discussed below, clients who exit the program can include both "dropouts" and "successful graduates". The limited evidence available to distinguish between the two types suggests those who exit microfinance programs tend to be worse off on average.

even found negative effects on medical expenditures and increased borrowing from moneylenders. His results would be more cause for concern, however, if northern Thailand were not already so saturated with credit. Sixty-three percent of the households in the villages surveyed were already members of the Bank for Agriculture and Agricultural Cooperatives (BAAC), a state bank that offered much larger loans than the village banks.

Bruhn and Love (2009) examine the effects of the simultaneous launch of 800 Banco Azteca branches in Mexico in 2002. The branches were all opened in existing consumer stores called Grupo Elektra. A difference-in-difference calculation shows a huge increase in informal businesses (7.6 percent), average income (7 percent), and even total employment (1.4 percent) in locations with an Azteca branch. However, it is not clear how reliable the results are because the communities originally targeted for the consumer stores are likely to be more economically vibrant than those without. Some of this concern is mitigated by the fact that Grupo Elektra opened banks in all of its stores, with no further targeting for bank locations (but then again they would not have chosen this strategy if they thought it unlikely to be profitable).

Before the recent randomized evaluations, the most ambitious attempt to control for selection bias and non-random program placement was Pitt and Khandker (1998). Pitt and Khandker, surveying 1,798 households who were members and non-members of three Bangladeshi MFIs (Grameen Bank, BRAC, and RD-12), used the fact that all three programs limited membership to those with landholding totaling less than one-half acre to calculate that every 100 taka lent to a female borrower increased household consumption by 18 taka. Their model ("weighted exogenous sampling maximum likelihood–limited information maximum likelihood–fixed effects") was based on the premise that while there should be no discontinuity in income between people who own just over or just under a half acre of land, participation in the MFIs would be discontinuous because those who were above the cutoff would be rejected from the programs.

The conclusions we can draw from their findings rely on specific identification assumptions, and the practical implications are also limited in that the methodology is not easily replicated in other settings (and certainly not by practitioners, as it requires involved econometrics). Morduch (1998) challenges the econometric models and identification assumptions in Pitt and Khandker. Using a difference-in-difference model, he finds little evidence for increased consumption, but does find reduction in the variance in consumption across seasons.

Khandker (2005) refined their earlier model with the benefit of panel data, finding lower impact estimates but greater total impact (from current and past borrowing in the survey rounds conducted in 1991–2 and 1998–9) and substantially lower marginal impact from new borrowing. Poorer clients were found to have larger impacts than the less poor, and money lent to men was not found to have any impact at all.

Roodman and Morduch (2009) attempt to bring closure to the issue by returning to the data and rebuilding the analysis from scratch. They are unable to replicate results from Pitt and Khandker (1998) or Khandker (2005). In fact, their estimates carry the opposite sign. Rather than concluding that microcredit harms borrowers, however, they unearth a raft of identification issues which are not solved with panel data. Their revised analysis casts doubt on *all* of the findings from the related set of papers, including Morduch's (1998) oft-cited finding of consumption smoothing. The authors conclude that the final word on the impact of microfinance will have to rest on the set of randomized evaluations of microfinance recently completed (discussed above) or underway.

4.3 *Randomized controlled trials for product and process innovations*

In a randomized controlled trial, one program design is compared to another by randomly assigning clients (or potential clients) to either the treatment or the control group. If the program design is an "add-on" or conversion, the design is often simple: The microfinance institution randomly chooses existing clients to be offered the new product. Then, one compares the outcomes of interest for those who are converted to those who remained with the original program. A similar approach is also possible with new clients, although it is slightly more difficult. In this section, we will discuss the logistics of how to change an existing product or process. The following discussion summarizes a process detailed in Giné, Harigaya, Karlan *et al.* (2006).

The flowchart (Figure 1.1) below presents three basic phases to evaluating the effectiveness of a product or process innovation on the institution and clients. Often, microfinance institutions innovate by doing a small pilot and the full launch (Phases 1 and 3), but not a full pilot (Phase 2). Furthermore, they usually forego random assignment to treatment and control, which would allow them to measure properly the causal link between the product change and institutional and client outcomes. The more common two-stage

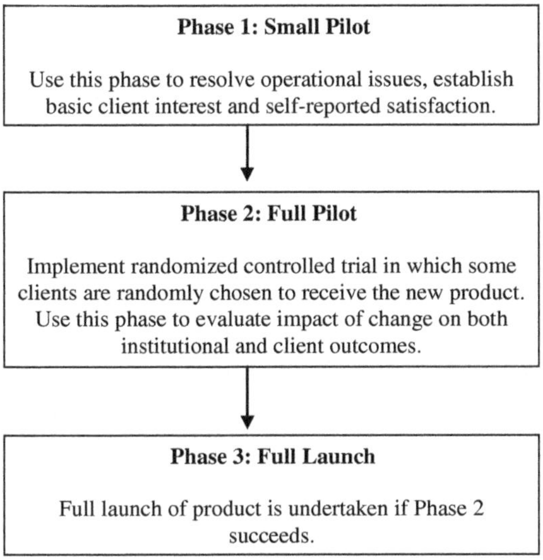

Figure 1.1: Stages of evaluating a product or process innovation.

process involves only a small pilot test to resolve operational issues and gauge interest in and satisfaction with the new product among clients who receive it (or sometimes, not even that). If the product "works", the MFI launches the product to all their clients. With the information from a full pilot in hand, the MFI can make much more informed decisions about whether to proceed to a full launch of the innovation and whether to make any changes to the product or policy.

Product innovation typically aims to solve a problem with the existing product or improve the impact and feasibility of the product. The first step is to identify the problem with the current product and potential solutions through a qualitative process. This should include examination of historical data, focus groups, and brainstorming sessions with clients and staff, and ideally discussions with other microfinance institutions that have had similar problems. Once a potential solution is identified, an operating plan and small pilot should be planned. An operating plan should include specifics on all necessary operations components to introduce the proposed change. This includes, for instance, development of training materials, processes for training staff, changes to the internal accounting software, compensation systems, and marketing materials.

In order to resolve operational issues and, depending on the complexity of the proposed change, a small pilot implementation should follow. This pre-pilot can be done on a small scale, and serves the purpose of testing the operational success of the program design change. Such an endeavor does *not,* however, answer the question of impact to the institution or the client. It instead intends to resolve operational issues so that the full pilot can reflect accurately the true impact.

After the proposed solution has been identified and a small pilot has been conducted, "testing" is not over. The impact of the product innovation on both the institution (repayment rates, client retention rates, operating costs, etc.) and the client (welfare, consumption, income, social capital, etc.) must still be determined. To measure such outcomes properly, one can not merely track the participants and report their changes. One needs a control group.

Often, a proposed solution consists of a main change but many minor issues that need to be decided. For instance, when testing credit with education in the FINCA program in Peru (Karlan and Valdivia, 2008), the type of education modules to offer had to be selected, and when testing individual liability, the optimal loan size needed to be determined. A careful experimental design can include tests of such sub-questions collapsed into the evaluation from the start. These questions often arise naturally through the brainstorming questions. Any contentious decision is perfect for such analysis, since if it is contentious, then the answer is not obvious.

4.4 *Other considerations*

4.4.1 *Determining sample size*

The minimum necessary sample size depends on the desired effect size (e.g., a 10 percent increase in income), the variance of the outcome, and the tolerance for error in assigning statistical significance to the change in outcome (and the intra-cluster correlation if using a clustered randomization, such as randomized program placement). The smaller the minimum detectable difference, the larger the variance, and the lower the tolerance for error, the larger the sample size must be. Outcomes in microfinance evaluations can be both continuous (e.g., change in income) and binary (e.g., no longer below the poverty line). Using binary outcomes can be easier since the variance is entirely determined mathematically from the mean, no data on underlying variation is needed (alternatively, if no variance data are available, one can use standardized effect sizes). Power is weakest for outcomes that have mean 0.50 (the variance is thus 0.25) when the desired effect size is a fixed percentage point increase (e.g., 10 percentage-point increase from 0.5 to 0.6 versus 0.1 to 0.2), but not a percent increase (e.g., a 20 percent increase from 0.5 to 0.6 versus 0.1 to 0.12). We recommend the free software Optimal

Design to help determine sample sizes, though most statistical packages such as Stata can provide some basic power calculations.[14]

(i) Dropouts

MFIs do not have set lengths of program participation. It is expected that clients will avail themselves of the MFIs' services and leave the programs when they have exhausted the utility of the available products. The more comprehensive the array of products offered, the longer the average client could be expected to "grow" with the program. Broadly speaking, clients who exit an MFI are of two types: those who have outgrown the need for the MFI ("graduates", who hopefully are able to access commercial banking services), and those for whom participation did not bring great benefits ("dropouts" — who were either dissatisfied with the program or were unable to pay for the MFI's services).

Without following up with clients, it is difficult to distinguish between the two types, and experienced program evaluators understand the importance of including program dropouts in their analysis. Some microfinance evaluation manuals, such as the one offered by AIMS, however, do not counsel evaluators to include dropouts. Alexander-Tedeschi and Karlan (2009) demonstrate that failing to include dropouts can bias estimates of impact. They find that after including dropouts, some of the measures of impact changed dramatically. Where the AIMS cross-sectional methodology showed an increase of US$ 1,200 in annual microenterprise profit, including dropouts caused the estimate to fall to a *decrease* of about US$ 170. It would be a worthwhile exercise to repeat this type of analysis with an MFI that carefully tracks its departing clients and records their reasons for dropping out of the program: graduation, default, or otherwise. Subgroup impact analysis among these different types (e.g., voluntary vs. involuntary dropouts) would be valuable.

In any evaluation, failure to track down a sufficiently high percentage of participants can cause attrition bias: if those who cannot be located differ from those who can (it is easy to imagine that this could be the case), the impact estimate can be affected. Those who remain with the program are almost certainly more likely to be located for the follow-up survey than dropouts, and more willing to take part in the survey. Not

[14]The software can be downloaded from http://www.ssicentral.com/otherproducts/othersoftware.html.

including dropouts at all introduces this problem to an extreme. Whether or not dropouts are less likely to experience a positive impact, if different *types* of clients are more likely to drop out (for instance, richer clients could find it more costly than poorer clients to attend weekly repayment meetings), the composition of the sample will shift and the comparison to the control group will be biased. There are econometric techniques for mitigating these issues.

(ii) Targeting

While an impact evaluation is not necessary to evaluate an MFI's outreach to poor clients,[15] when evaluating the impact of a change in program design on existing clients, it can be especially useful also to evaluate the impact on the selection process which may result from the change in design (i.e., does the change in program alter the type of client who joins?). There are a couple of ways to do this. The simpler method is to compare the demographics of the treatment and control groups, which allows one to say that the change in the program resulted in a different profile of client (e.g., poorer incoming clients) *relative* to the control group. The more powerful method is to conduct (or access) a census survey of households in the treatment and control communities and to compare the distribution of clients in the treatment and control groups to the distribution in the region as a whole. This will allow the MFI to determine the percentage of the population in a given demographic (e.g., below the poverty line) it is currently reaching, as well as the percentage of the demographic it can reach with the new design.

(iii) Intensity of Treatment

Intensity of treatment may vary both in length of treatment and quantity of services used. Studies have looked at the impact on clients after one year, two years, and even 10 years of membership. Deciding at what point to measure impact can be subjective and may depend on the intervention (credit, savings, or another product). There is no set answer but it might be debatable whether one year would be adequate to show the impact of credit, for which clients would need time to start or grow their business. Studies that fail to show impact on one-year clients should acknowledge that the

[15] This can be done with poverty measurement tools on clients and non-clients. For more information, see http://www.povertytools.org.

results do not prove that the program has no impact, merely that it has no impact after one year. The longer the time period, the more difficult it is to employ a randomized controlled trial, since one must maintain the control group throughout the study. Encouragement designs, discussed above, could be useful for longer-term studies as long as the initial "encouragement" has long lasting effects on the likelihood of being a client. However, if over time the entire control group gets treated, the encouragement design will fail to measure the long-term impacts as desired. The length of time also relates directly to the outcome measures, as we will discuss in a moment.

5 Impact Indicators

Microfinance may generate impacts on the client's business, the client's well-being, the client's family, and the community. A thorough impact evaluation will trace the impacts across all of these domains.

In entrepreneurial households, money can flow quite easily between the business and different members of the household. Credit is considered fungible, meaning it would be wrong to assume that money lent to a particular household member for a specific purpose will be used only by that person, for that purpose. It is well-known, for instance, that loans dispersed for self-employment can often be diverted to more immediate household needs such as food, medicine, and school fees, and that, even though an MFI targets a woman, the loans may often end up transferred to her husband. Thus it would be a mistake to measure only changes in the client's enterprise when evaluating a credit program.

5.1 *Enterprise income*

The most direct outcome of microfinance participation is change in household income and business profits. MFIs almost always work with clients who are engaged in the informal sector and not receiving regular wages. Therefore (as in many developing-country impact evaluations) it can be easier to measure consumption than to measure income.

Business revenue should *not* by itself be considered an impact indicator. Clients who are servicing loans will need to generate increased revenue over and above their loan repayments, or impact will be *negative*, even if business revenue has increased. Therefore, business *profit* is the preferred measure of financial impact on the business. Other business impacts include ownership of business premises and number of employees. Measuring business profits for enterprises without formal records can be difficult. Several options exist, none is perfect. When time permits, it helps to build a flexible survey which allows the surveyor to walk the entrepreneur through their cash flows, starting from their cost of goods sold (or cost of goods produced) per item to revenues per item, and then to frequency of sales. Alternatively, one could focus on funds withdrawn from the enterprise, as well as investments made into the enterprise, in order to back out the net profits. If the family consumes some of the enterprise inventory (as is often the case with buy-sell mini-grocery stores), this approach is more difficult. Similarly, measuring investment in the enterprise can be difficult when inventory levels vary considerably. Hence, this alternative approach should be used cautiously, in settings where business and household lines are kept clearly, and when inventory is not highly volatile.

Consumption or income levels (poverty)

Evaluations can attempt to determine the number of clients moving out of poverty. This of course requires measuring income (or consumption) versus a standard poverty line. Several studies have developed their own measures of poverty based on a summary statistic of indicators such as housing condition, assets, etc. (Zeller, 2005; Schreiner, 2006). The World Bank's Core Welfare Indicator Surveys (CWIQ), which use a reduced set of consumption proxies, could be used in a similar manner. While it may be easier to use such poverty correlates than to measure income, it will limit the reliability of the results and the ability to compare MFIs to other poverty-reduction programs. Depending on the resources available, however, it may be the best alternative. When resources are more plentiful, see Deaton (1997) for more detailed information on proper formulation of consumption surveys. The World Bank Living Standards Measurement Study surveys (LSMS) are also often useful as a starting point for consumption modules in countries around the world. Deaton (1997) discusses many of the advantages and pitfalls of the approaches found in the LSMS.

5.1.1 *Consumption smoothing*

In addition to changes in income, it may also be important to measure the reduction in risk. Many may use credit as an insurance device, helping to absorb negative shocks (Udry, 1994). Consumption smoothing can be difficult to measure, since it requires either frequent observations to measure the variance in overall consumption over time, or evidence of particular vulnerabilities. For example, one can measure the number of "hungry days" an individual experienced, or ask about specific negative shocks (illness, death, theft, etc.) and ask how the individual coped with each situation. Although this latter approach is easier in terms of survey complexity, it requires *a priori* knowledge of the types and sources of risk that the individuals face. If treatment group individuals are better able to cope, this indicates positive impact from access to credit.

5.1.2 *Wider impacts*

The non-monetary impacts of microfinance participation (i.e., distinct from changes in income) have been labeled "wider impacts". Important examples include children's education and nutrition, housing stock, empowerment, and social capital. While some of these outcomes (e.g., nutrition) can be related to changes in income, others (e.g., women's decision-making power) can be derived from participation in the program itself and the confidence women gain from running a business and handling money. For instance, in the Philippines, we find that offering a woman a commitment savings account in her own name leads to an increase in her household decision-making power after one year, and that this increase in power leads to more purchases of female-oriented household durables (Ashraf, Karlan and Yin, 2006b).

Potential negative impacts should not be ignored, however promising the program. Along with potential increases in children's schooling rates, many observers are concerned that increased economic opportunity may come with a dark side: increased incentives to employ children at home rather than sending them to school. Karlan and Valdivia (2008) examine this in Peru and find a decrease in child labor, though the result is statistically insignificant. Recent work has expanded outcome measures to include mental health. Fernald *et al.* (2008) finds credit access in South Africa leads to increases in perceived stress among borrowers, even when the impacts on consumption are strikingly positive (Karlan and Zinman, 2008). There are many aspects to mental health, however, and on a scale of depressive symptoms, male borrowers showed reduced symptoms. This could be because increased economic activity and responsibility can be stressful, even if leading to better economic outcomes.

The experimental design for measuring these wider impacts should be much the same as measuring changes in income or poverty, and the data for these outcomes can often be gathered in the same survey. Many of these wider impacts can be measured in a variety of ways, but there may be important differences between indicators that might not be immediately obvious. For instance, height-for-age and weight-for-age (measured in z-scores, or standard deviations) are both measures of malnutrition, but they capture different aspects of severity. Height-for-age ("stunting") is a better indicator of long-term malnutrition, while weight-for-age would better capture acute malnutrition ("wasting").

Other common indicators of nutrition and education include:

- instances per week/month of consumption of specific nutritious foods (e.g., meat, fish, dairy, vegetables) (Husain, 1998).
- percentage of children enrolled in school (Pitt and Khandker, 1998).
- percentage of possible years of education ("age grade") children have completed (Todd, 2001).
- ability to treat children's illnesses such as diarrhea (MkNelly and Dunford, 1998).
- medical expenditures (Coleman, 1999).
- value of house (Mustafa, 1996).
- access to clean water/sanitation (Copestake *et al.*, 2005).
- use of family planning methods (Steele, Amin and Naved, 1998).
- voted in local or national elections (Cortijo and Kabeer, 2004).

5.1.3 *Spillovers*

While it can be simple enough to survey participants and a comparison group of non-participants, restricting our analysis to these groups would misstate the full impact of the program, because the program can be expected to generate impact on non-participants (spillovers) as well. Spillovers can be both positive (increasing community income through increased economic activity) or negative (e.g., if the creation or expansion of participants' enterprises simply transfers sales away from competitors' businesses). This introduces a complication because we do not know every person in the community who will be affected by the program.

In the absence of this information, the cleanest method of estimating the true impact of the program is to compare the outcome of entire villages, which can be randomly assigned to treatment or control groups. However, we cannot simply compare participants in the treatment villages to non-participants in control villages because doing so would introduce selection bias — we would be comparing people who chose to join the program to others who did not. Since we do not know who in the control village would have joined the program had it been offered to them, we can compare a sample of clients and non-clients in each village to each other. This method measures the impact of *access* to microfinance (intent-to-treat effect), rather than *participation* in the MFI (treatment on the treated). From a societal perspective, one could argue this is better, as this allows us to reasonably estimate the impact microfinance could have at the macro level. The intent-to-treat effect, since it includes both participants and non-participants in the estimate, will be a lower estimate of expected impact from treating a particular individual, but it can be scaled up by dividing by the probability of participation to obtain the local average treatment effect. The estimate can also be refined with propensity score matching (PSM), if sufficient baseline data are available to predict take-up within the treatment group. This technique re-weights the treatment and control groups by the probability of participating in order to improve the power of the analysis by putting more weight on those more likely to join.

5.1.4 *Impact on the MFI*

When evaluating the effect of new products or policy changes on the MFI, the data can usually be collected directly from the MFI's administrative data. Common outcomes of interest for MFIs include the following:

- Repayment rate.
- Client retention rate.
- New client enrollment.
- Average loan size.
- Savings balances.
- Profitability.
- Composition of clients (demographics).

There are a variety of ways to measure the above outcomes. For instance, "profitability" could be financial self-sufficiency, operational self-sufficiency, return on assets, adjusted return on assets, return on equity, and so on. So long as the same definition is used to measure any of the above outcomes before and after the intervention, the chosen definition can serve as a valid indicator of impact. However, the MFI and the microfinance industry may get more value out of the evaluation if standard definitions and financial ratios are used. This way the MFI can measure its performance (and improvement) against others in its peer group. The Microfinance

Information Exchange has put forth financial ratio definitions applicable to the microfinance industry.[16]

Several of the impacts on the MFI can be considered "intermediate" indicators, implying that while they are important outputs for the MFI, they do not by themselves indicate a positive outcome for clients. New client enrollment, for example, implies more people have the opportunity to be served by the program, but this will only be a good thing for *clients* if the program improves their welfare, which would be measured through different indicators such as income (described above). Nonetheless, it should be considered a positive indicator for the program, as it has a goal of serving clients.

Evaluations often distinguish between inputs, outputs, and outcomes. Inputs and outputs are factors that contribute to achieving outcomes, i.e., impact. Inputs (e.g., funding) contribute to outputs (e.g., number of loans dispersed), and the difference between outputs and outcomes is that outputs are fully under the program's control, whereas outcomes are not. For instance, an MFI can control to whom it disperses loans, but it cannot "create" impact by running clients' businesses for them.

In some cases, the same indicators that measure program outputs can also measure client outcomes. For instance, savings balances are useful to MFIs as a source of loan capital; they are also an indicator of financial stability for clients.

While acknowledging the utility of the distinction between inputs, outputs, and outcomes, we retain the term "impact on the MFI" to indicate the *effect on the input or output* from a change in products or policies. As with impacts on clients, impacts on MFIs need to be measured against a counterfactual of no change.

5.1.5 *Timing of measurement*

One also should think practically about what types of outcomes are likely to be observed at which points in time. Perhaps the most immediate outcome one should consider is debt level. If the control group has the same quantity of debt as the treatment group, then there is direct evidence that individuals are not credit-constrained (the control group simply borrowed elsewhere). This indicates that one should examine the relative *quality* of the debt that each group acquired, since the measurable impact will be driven

[16] Available at http://www.mixmbb.org/en/mbbissues/08/mbb_8.html.

by difference across debt instruments, not from access versus no access to debt. An intermediate outcome, perhaps six months to one year, would be working capital and/or fixed assets in the business (these may be observable in a shorter time period as well). Increased profits, employment, and formalization may take longer and require one to two years, or more, in which to see the businesses grow sufficiently to observe such impacts. Furthermore, impacts on consumption may be observed immediately, if the funds are not used for the enterprise but rather for consumption. If, on the other hand, the funds are used in the enterprise and profits reinvested, it may take time before the entrepreneur is comfortable withdrawing enterprise funds and increasing consumption.

Returning to the discussion at the beginning of this paper, recall that MFIs have often focused on measuring process and institutional measures (e.g., default and client retention) to gauge their performance. However, it is important to note that these types of outcomes may not correlate with client welfare outcomes. In order for MFIs to use these measures as actual impact measures, we must first study whether or not the process and institutional outcomes correlate with client welfare. Such analysis has not been done, and would be an important contribution to our knowledge of microfinance.

6 Outstanding Issues for Evaluation

The microfinance industry needs reliable data, both to prove to donors, governments, and other stakeholders that microfinance works, and to improve its products and processes so that it can accelerate its impact on poverty. In the review of the existing impact literature, both from practitioners and academics, Goldberg (2005) finds few, if any, studies that successfully address the important selection biases relevant for an evaluation of microfinance programs. Randomized controlled trials are the most promising means to allow MFIs to assess reliably the effectiveness of their operations on poverty alleviation, and for investors and donors to learn which types of programs produce the strongest welfare improvements.

Evaluations need not be mere costs incurred by an organization in order to prove its worthiness. Quite to the contrary, a good product or process impact evaluation can help an organization improve its operations, maintain or improve its financial sustainability, and simultaneously improve client welfare. The microfinance industry has experienced tremendous experimentation, and now a plethora of approaches exist around the world. How should microfinance institutions decide which approaches to employ when? If evaluation experts worked more closely with microfinance institutions as they made these decisions, we would have better answers and, thus, prescriptions that we could provide to these institutions.

The nine hallmarks of microfinance discussed in the introduction provide a good structure for many of the open questions in microfinance product design:

(1) Small transactions and minimum balances. Certainly, microfinance is not microfinance unless loans remain under a certain manageable size, but how small is best for serving the dual needs of the client and the institution? What number of different loan products maximizes impact before becoming unmanageable for the institution and confusing for the client? What other products, such as savings and insurance, can be effective complements or substitutes for loans?
(2) Loans for entrepreneurial activity. Is a focus on lending for entrepreneurial activity essential for maintaining repayment and ensuring impact on the household? The poor face a variety of credit needs and allowing them to use credit for any type of expenditure could serve them best. Or, loosening the requirement could encourage further indebtedness without a means of escape. To what extent does business skills training help clients manage their enterprises and bolster repayment rates? Why do so many micro-entrepreneurs seem to stagnate at a certain business size, and what can be done to help them expand, employ others, and open additional locations?
(3) Collateral-free loans. To what extent do collateral requirements or collateral substitutes discourage the poor from participating in MFIs, and to what extent do they raise repayment rates? How effective are collateral substitutes compared to traditional collateral?
(4) Group lending. Recent evidence from the Philippines and the success of ASA and Grameen II have raised questions about the extent to which high repayments rest on group liability. Can individual liability work as well, or nearly as well?
(5) Focus on poor clients. What is the impact of microfinance on the poor? Does microfinance work for the very poor? What specialized services, if any, serve the "poorest of the poor"? Does one need to provide financial literacy along with the loan in order to be effective?
(6) Focus on female clients. Anecdotally, many studies report that women have higher repayment rates than men. Is this true, and if so, what program designs can work best to encourage men to repay their

loans? What products and policies can generate the greatest increase in empowerment of female clients?

(7) Simple application processes. Most MFIs have simple applications, else they would have few clients. A useful extension is to determine what types of marketing are most effective at increasing take-up of services among the poor.

(8) Provision of services in underserved communities. To what extent does offering credit and savings in poor communities deepen access and increase welfare? Do programs that conduct meetings in the field but require clients to make repayments at the bank branch have lower client retention? Can provision of services in remote areas be profitable?

(9) Market-level interest rates. To what extent do high interest rates drive out the poor? Do high rates attract riskier clients? Does subsidized credit "crowd out" market-priced services from competing MFIs?

Impact evaluation of microfinance need not be focused strictly on the impact of credit versus no credit. Instead, prospective evaluation can help MFIs and policymakers design better institutions. Good evaluation not only can deliver to donors an assessment of the benefits that accrued from their investment, but also can provide financial institutions with prescriptions for how best to run their businesses, and how best to maximize their social impacts.

References

Alexander-Tedeschi, G and D Karlan (2009). Cross Sectional Impact Analysis: Bias from Dropouts. Perspectives on Global Development and Technology.

Armendariz de Aghion, B and J Morduch (2005). *The Economics of Microfinance.* Cambridge: MIT Press.

Ashraf, N, D Karlan and W Yin (2006a). Deposit collectors. *Advances in Economic Analysis & Policy*, 6(2), Article 5.

——— (2006b). Household Decision-Making and Savings Impacts: Further Evidence from a Commitment Savings Product in the Philippines. Working Paper.

——— (2006c). Tying Odysseus to the mast: Evidence from a commitment savings product in the Philippines. *Quarterly Journal of Economics*, 121(2), 673–697.

Banerjee, A and E Duflo (2007). The economic lives of the poor. *Journal of Economic Perspectives*, 21(1), 141–167.

Banerjee, A, E Duflo, R Glennerster and C Kinnan (2009). The Miracle of Microfinance? Evidence from a Randomized Evaluation. Working Paper.

Bertrand, M, D Karlan, S Mullainathan, E Shafir and J Zinman (2010). What's advertising content worth? Evidence from a consumer credit marketing field experiment. *Quarterly Journal of Economics*, 263–305.

Besley, T and S Coate (1995). Group Lending, Repayment Incentives and Social Collateral. *Journal of Development Economics*, 46(1), 1–18.

Bruhn, M and I Love (2009). Grassroots Banking: The Effect of Opening Banco Azteca on Economic Activity in Mexico. Working Paper.

Buddelmeyer, H and E Skoufias (2004). An Evaluation of the Performance of Regression Discontinuity Design on PROGRESA. World Bank Policy Research Working Paper.

Coleman, B (1999). The Impact of Group Lending in Northeast Thailand. *Journal of Development Economics*, 60, 105–141.

Conley, T and C Udry (2005). Learning About a New Technology: Pineapple in Ghana. *American Economic Review*, 100(1), 35–69.

Conning, J (2005). Monitoring by Delegates or by Peers? Joint Liability Loans under Moral Hazard. Working Paper.

Copestake, J, P Dawson, JP Fanning, A Mckay and K Wright-Revolledo (2005). Monitoring Diversity of Poverty Outreach and Impact of Microfinance: A Comparison of Methods Using Data From Peru. *Development Policy Review*, 23(6), 703–723.

Cortijo, M and N Kabeer (2004). Direct and Wider Social Impacts of SHARE Microfin Limited: A Case Study from Andhra Pradesh. Unpublished Imp–Act report. Available at: http://www.microcreditsummit.org/pubs/reports/soc/2005/SOCRϕ5.pdf.

Daley-Harris, S (2005). State of the Microcredit Summit Campaign Report.

Deaton, A (1997). *The Analysis of Household Surveys.* World Bank.

Dehejia, R, H Montgomery and J Morduch (2005). Do Interest Rates Matter? Credit Demand in the Dhaka Slums. Working Paper.

Duflo, E, R Glennerster and M Kremer (2008). Using randomization in development economics research: A toolkit. In: *Handbook of Development Economics* 4(5), Schultz, T and JA Strauss (eds.), pp. 3895–3962.

Duflo, E and M Kremer (2003). Use of Randomization in the Evaluation of Development Effectiveness. Paper prepared for *the World Bank Operations Evaluation Department (OED) Conference on Evaluation and Development Effectiveness.*

Dupas, P and J Robinson (2009). Savings Constraints and Microenterprise Development: Evidence from a Field Experiment in Kenya. NBER Working Paper 14693.

Feigenberg, B, E Field and R Pande (2009). Do Social Interactions Facilitate Cooperative Behavior? Evidence from a Group Lending Experiment in India. Working Paper.

Fernald, L, R Hamad, D Karlan, E Ozer and J Zinman (2008). Small Individual Loans and Mental Health: Randomized Controlled Trial Among South African Adults. *BMC Public Health*, 8(409), doi: 10.1186/1471-2458-8-409.

Field, E and R Pande (2007). Repayment Frequency and Default in Micro-Finance: Evidence from India. *Journal of European Economic Association Papers and Proceedings*, 6(2–3), 501–550.

Fudenberg, D and D Levine (2005). A Dual Self Model of Impulse Control. *American Economic Review*, 96(5), 1449–1476.

Ghatak, M (1999). Group Lending, Local Information and Peer Selection. *Journal of Development Economics*, 60(1), 27–50.

Ghatak, M and T Guinnane (1999). The Economics of Lending with Joint Liability: A Review of Theory and Practice. *Journal of Development Economics*, 60, 195–228.

Giné, X, J Goldberg and D Yang (2009). Identification Strategy: A Field Experiment on Dynamic Incentives in Rural Credit Markets. Working Paper.

Giné, X, T Harigaya, D Karlan and B Nguyen (2006). Evaluating Microfinance Program Innovation with Randomized Control Trials: An Example from Group versus Individual Lending. Asian Developement Bank Economics and Research Department Technical Note Series, 16.

Giné, X and D Karlan (2006). Group versus Individual Liability: Evidence from a Field Experiment in the Philippines. Yale University Economic Growth Center Working Paper 940.

——— (2009). Group versus Individual Liability: Long Term Evidence from Philippine Microcredit Lending Groups. Working Paper.

Giné, X and D Yang (2007). Insurance, Credit, and Technology Adoption: Field Experimental Evidence from Malawi. World Bank Policy Research Working Paper.

——— (2009). Insurance, Credit, and Technology Adoption: Field Experimental Evidence from Malawi. *Journal of Development Economics*, 89(1), 1–11.

Glewwe, P, M Kremer, S Moulin and E Zitzewitz (2004). Retrospective vs. Prospective Analyses of School Inputs: The Case of Flip Charts in Kenya. *Journal of Development Economics*, 74, 251–268.

Goldberg, N (2005). *Measuring the Impact of Microfinance: Taking Stock of What We Know*. Grameen Foundation USA publication series.

Husain, AMM (1998). *Poverty Alleviation and Empowerment: The Second Impact Assessment Study of BRAC's Rural Development Programme*. BRAC publication.

de Janvry, A, C McIntosh and E Sadoulet (2007). The supply and demand side impacts of credit market information, *Journal of Development Economics*, 93(2), 173–188.

Kaboski, J and R Townsend (2005). Policies and Impact: An Analysis of Village-Level Microfinance Institutions. *Journal of the European Economic Association*, 3(1), 1–50.

Karlan, D (2001). Microfinance Impact Assessments: The Perils of Using New Members as a Control Group. *Journal of Microfinance*, 3(2), 75-85.

Karlan, D and M Valdivia (2010). *Teaching Entrepreneurship: Impact of Business Training on Microfinance Institutions and Clients*. Review of Economics and Statistics.

Karlan, D and J Zinman (2008). Credit Elasticities in Less Developed Economies: Implications for Microfinance. *American Economic Review*, 98(3), 1040–1068.

——— (2009a). Expanding Credit Access: Using Randomized Supply Decisions to Estimate the Impacts. *Review of Financial Studies*, 23(1), 433–464.

——— (2009b). Expanding Microenterprise Credit Access: Using Randomized Supply Decisions to Estimate the Impacts in Manila. Working Paper.

——— (2009). Observing Unobservables: Identifying Information Asymmetries with a Consumer Credit Field Experiment. *Econometrica*, 77(6), 1993–2008.

Khandker, SR (2005). Micro-finance and Poverty: Evidence Using Panel Data from Bangladesh. *World Bank Economic Review*, 19(2), 263–286.

Kremer, M and E Miguel (2007). The Illusion of Sustainability. *Quarterly Journal of Economics*, 122(3), 1007–1065.

Laibson, D (1997). Golden Eggs and Hyperbolic Discounting. *Quarterly Journal of Economics*, 112(2), 443–477.

LaLonde, RJ (1986). Evaluating the Econometric Evaluations of Training Programs with Experimental Data. *American Economic Review*, 76(4), 604–620.

Miguel, E and M Kremer (2004). Worms: Identifying Impacts on Education and Health in the Presence of Treatment Externalities. *Econometrica*, 72(1), 159–217.

MkNelly, B and C Dunford (1998). *Impact of Credit with Education on Mothers and Their Young Children's Nutrition: Lower Pra Rural Bank Credit with Education Program in Ghana*. Freedom from Hunger Publication.

Morduch, J (1998). Does Microfinance Really Help the Poor? New Evidence on Flagship Programs in Bangladesh. Working Paper.

——— (1999). The Microfinance Promise. *Journal of Economic Literature*, 37(4), 1569–1614.

——— (2000). The Microfinance Schism. *World Development*, 28(4), 617–629.
Mustafa, S (1996). *Beacon of Hope: An Impact Assessment Study of BRAC's Rural Development Programme.* BRAC Publication.
O'Donoghue, T and M Rabin (1999). Doing it Now or Doing it Later. *The American Economic Rcvicw*, 89(1), 103–124.
Pitt, M and S Khandker (1998). The Impact of Group-Based Credit Programs on Poor Households in Bangladesh: Does the Gender of Participants Matter? *The Journal of Political Economy*, 106(5), 958–996.
Robinson, M (2001). *The Microfinance Revolution: Sustainable Finance for the Poor.* Washington DC: IBRD/The World Bank.
Roodman, D and J Morduch (2009). The Impact of Microcredit on the Poor in Bangladesh: Revisiting the Evidence. Center for Global Development Working Paper 174.
Schreiner, M (forthcoming). Seven Extremely Simple Poverty Scorecards. *Enterprise Development and Microfinance.*
Steele, F, S Amin and RT Naved (1998). *The Impact of an Integrated Microcredit Program on Women's Empowerment and Fertility Behavior in Rural Bangladesh.* Population Council publication.
Stiglitz, J (1990). Peer Monitoring and Credit Markets. *World Bank Economic Review*, 4(3), 351–366.
Todd, H (2001). Paths out of Poverty: The Impact of SHARE Microfin Limited in Andhra Pradesh, India. Unpublished Imp–Act report.
Udry, C (1994). Risk and Insurance in a Rural Credit Market: An Empirical Investigation in Northern Nigeria. *Review of Economic Studies*, 61(3), 495–526.
UNDP (2008). *Malaysia Nurturing Women Entrepreneurs.* Malaysia: UNDP.
World Bank (1998). *World Bank Operational Manual OP 8.30 — Financial Intermediary Lending.*
Zeller, M (2005). Developing and Testing Poverty Assessment Tools: Results from Accuracy Tests in Peru. IRIS Working Paper.

Spanning the Chasm: Uniting Theory and Empirics in Microfinance Research*

Greg Fischer
London School of Economics,
Innovations for Poverty Action, Poverty Action Lab,
and BREAD

Maitreesh Ghatak
London School of Economics,
STICERD, and BREAD

1 Introduction

Microfinance continues to play an ever increasing role in approaches to poverty alleviation around the world. Yet despite the attention paid to microfinance, the design of credit contracts for small uncollateralized loans remains a bit of a mystery. From its inception, microfinance generated a great deal of interest from economic theorists. Influential papers from Besley and Coate (1995), Stiglitz (1990) and Varian (1990),[1] to name just a few, sought to explain the economic foundations of this novel lending mechanism. Yet empirical research testing these theories was for a long time largely absent. Recently, the area has seen a surge of empirical work, chiefly in the form of randomized field experiments.[2] This work has tended to focus on evaluating programs in their operational form — testing the broad impact

*We would like to thank Christian Ahlin, Jean-Marie Baland, Tim Besley, Garance Genicot, Xavier Giné, Rocco Macchiavello, Imran Rasul, Debraj Ray and Miriam Sinn, the participants at the ESF Exploratory Workshop in Microfinance and Entrepreneurship, and an anonymous referee for very helpful feedback.

[1]See Ghatak and Guinnane (1999) for a review of the theoretical literature.

[2]See, for example, Giné & Karlan (2009) and Banerjee *et al.* (2009).

of a particular microfinance institution or the effect of a specific program design feature — and has remained, by and large, distinct from the existing body of theory.

While the need to have a closer interaction between theory and empirical work seems self-evident, in the context of microfinance, the two strands of research have developed relatively independently. This paper argues that with the increasing use of randomized experiments in development research we now have a unique opportunity to bridge the gap between these two strands of research; we need to use existing theories to make sense of the experimental evidence and, in turn, to use experimental evidence to refine existing theories and suggest new ones. This discussion is essential to what we believe is the next step in the research agenda: using existing and new theory explicitly to design future experiments and using the results from these experiments to refine and extend our theoretical understanding.

Much of the early theoretical work on microfinance focused on joint liability — a small group of borrowers being held jointly liable for one another's repayments — as the key to high loan recovery rates. But while joint liability remains a feature in the majority of microfinance loan contracts, it is no longer the sole focus. Several factors have contributed to this change. A number of large micro-lenders have expanded into or converted their portfolios to individual liability loans, although the evidence on the effects of these changes remains inconclusive. There has also been a growing recognition of the potential costs of joint liability (Banerjee, Besley and Guinnane, 1994; Besley and Coate, 1995; Fischer 2009). At the same time, other features of microfinance contracts such as frequent repayment, sequential lending and dynamic incentives have risen to the fore. In this paper, we review some of the recent theoretical developments in the field focusing on these alternative features and discuss their potential interactions.

Next we turn to some of the recent empirical advances in the field. The sheer volume of empirical work necessitates that this review is incomplete and idiosyncratic, but our summary highlights a common theme. Through the creativity of empirical researchers and the willingness of microfinance practitioners to experiment and innovate, we have begun to develop a set of stylized facts that move beyond our theoretical underpinnings. Recent work on repayment frequency (Field and Pande, 2008; Fischer and Ghatak, 2010) and joint versus individual liability lending (Giné and Karlan, 2008) serve as illustrations. We also discuss issues such as group formation where important, long-standing theories still call for empirical support.

This brings us to the issue of how to bridge the chasm between theoretical and empirical research in microfinance. We argue that largely independent theoretical and empirical research in the area of microfinance has pushed our understanding to a level where the next steps require unifying these two strands and the input of practitioners. What is true throughout economics is accentuated by the pace of innovation in microfinance. We need to use theory to make sense of the experimental evidence and generalize results beyond their immediate context. In turn, we need to subject our theories to empirical testing and refine them where warranted. This discussion is essential to what we believe is the emerging research agenda: using existing or new theory explicitly to design future experiments and as the *ex ante* framework for more empirical work. We focus on the case of repayment frequency as representative of the many areas where this approach may yield great rewards.

A more effective dialogue between theoretical and field researchers can do more than just extend the frontier of academic knowledge. It can also facilitate translating research into action. Like any other field in economics, this calls for a three-way interaction between theoretical researchers, empirical researchers and practitioners. Untested theories, however insightful, are unlikely to be considered by microfinance institutions and donors, let alone influence their operations. Similarly, field experiments conducted without sound theoretical foundations have little to say about the underlying mechanisms through which a policy or program operates. Without such foundations, experiments can be limited to informing about only a particular policy in a particular location, and out-of-sample predictions can be little more than guesswork. Unifying theory and field experiments can help practitioners make sense of and utilize academic results to contribute to poverty reduction and other institutional aims.

As with most economic activity (e.g., starting a business), microfinance is a practitioner-led activity. And while a practitioner might not have a specific theoretical model or a regression result in mind when trying something new, he or she still has some implicit view of how the world works. That view can be described as a theory, however incompletely specified it might be, in the sense of having a set of causal relationships among various agents, actions and phenomena. The experience that the practitioner has in implementing his or her ideas might not constitute formal empirical research, but it generates facts that are of use to other practitioners. Academic research can find the common threads between these experiences and then try to develop a framework on which other practitioners can build. Of course, new research discoveries and experiences at the field level make this a process of continuous evolution and development.

The experience of Muhammad Yunus (Yunus, 2003) is a good case in point. He expressed frustration that what he saw during his trips to rural areas of Bangladesh to understand the causes of poverty was very different from what textbooks at the time suggested. In the accepted theory of the time, markets cleared and no one was unemployed or credit-constrained in equilibrium. His own experience and that of other practitioners suggested that this was far from true. For example, people who were willing to start a small business were not able to get a loan because formal lenders did not find them creditworthy and informal lenders charged extortionate rates. According to textbook economics, this could not happen since the forces of arbitrage and competition would equalize interest rates, which would only reflect, in equilibrium, the scarcity of capital for the economy as a whole. Yunus stepped outside the conventional mode of thinking and his innovations eventually revolutionized how we think about credit markets in relation to the poor. At the same time, Joseph Stiglitz, George Akerlof and many other academic economists were also frustrated with the standard model of the credit market and were developing tools that would eventually lead to rewriting the textbooks. They emphasized asymmetric information and transaction costs and showed that due to these problems the poor might be credit-constrained even if they have good projects. Classroom discussions of development economics now start off by talking about credit-constraints and unemployment and policies that can mitigate them.

The plan of the paper is as follows. In Section 2, we review the current state of theoretical literature in the field, capturing some of the exciting developments over the last decade. We conclude this section with a discussion of potential interactions among the various mechanisms of microfinance lending contracts. In Section 3, we review some of the recent empirical advances in the field. In Section 4, in keeping with the title of this essay, we discuss our views on how to span the chasm. In Section 5, we offer some concluding observations.

2 Theory

The first wave of theoretical work on microfinance focused exclusively on joint liability. The term joint liability can be interpreted in several ways, which can be lumped under two categories. First, under explicit joint liability, when one borrower cannot repay her loan, group members are contractually required to repay in her stead. Such repayments can be enforced through the threat of common punishment, typically the denial of future credit to all members of the defaulting group, or by drawing on a group savings fund that serves as collateral. Second, the perception of joint liability can be implicit. That is, borrowers believe that if a group member defaults, the whole group will become ineligible for future loans even if the lending contract does not specify this punishment. One form in which this can happen is if the microfinance organization itself chooses to fold its operations when faced with delinquency.

Ghatak and Guinnane (1999) review the key mechanisms proposed by various theories through which joint liability could improve repayment rates and the welfare of credit-constrained borrowers. These all have in common the idea that joint liability can help alleviate the major problems facing lenders — screening, monitoring, auditing, and enforcement — by utilizing the local information and social capital that exist among borrowers. In particular, joint liability can do better than conventional banks for two reasons. First, members of a close-knit community may have more information about one another (that is, each other's types, actions, and states) than outsiders. Second, a bank has limited scope for financial sanctions against poor people who default on a loan, since, by definition, they are poor. However, their neighbors may be able to impose powerful non-financial sanctions at low cost. An institution that gives poor people the proper incentives to utilize information about their neighbors and to apply non-financial sanctions to delinquent borrowers can do better than a conventional bank.

An exhaustive literature review is beyond the scope of this paper. However, broadly speaking, subsequent theoretical work on microfinance has gone off in four directions. The literature that we will focus on has looked at mechanisms other than joint liability, such as frequent repayment, sequential lending and dynamic incentives (e.g., Jain and Mansuri, 2003; Roy Chowdhury, 2005; Tedeschi, 2006; and Fischer and Ghatak, 2010). Another strand has focused on exploring further contractual issues that arise with respect to joint liability, such as collusion (Laffont, 2003; Rai and Sjöström, 2004) and group composition and matching (Guttman, 2008; Bond and Rai, 2008). Yet another strand has stepped out of the standard partial equilibrium contracting framework where there is a single lender and a group of borrowers and has begun to explore market and general equilibrium issues (Ahlin and Jiang, 2008; McIntosh and Wydick, 2005). The key issues are competition among MFIs and how microfinance affects the overall development process through wages and mobility. Finally, a set of papers has started exploring incentive issues that arise on the part of the lenders that are typically NGOs (e.g., Aubert, de Janvry and Sadoulet, 2009; Roy and Roy Chowdhury, 2008).

As mentioned, we will focus on the literature concerning contractual mechanisms other than joint liability. For example, microfinance organizations often use high frequency repayments. Borrowers are typically required to repay their loans in regular installments, beginning soon after the loan is given out. This aspect of the repayment schedule is usually explained as inducing 'fiscal discipline' among borrowers. Jain and Mansuri (2003) argue that an alternative rationale for this loan repayment structure lies in the difficulty of monitoring borrowers' actions. The potential for moral hazard leads MFIs to use innovative mechanisms, such as regularly scheduled repayments, which indirectly co-opt the better-informed informal lenders. Conversely, this installment repayment structure allows informal lenders to survive. Further, they show that this linkage can not only expand the volume of informal lending, but may also raise the interest rate in the informal sector.

Fischer and Ghatak (2010) propose an alternative theory based on present-biased, quasi-hyperbolic preferences in order to capture the belief of many microfinance practitioners that clients benefit from the fiscal discipline required by a frequent repayment schedule. Their work is motivated by a pervasive sense among practitioners that frequent repayment is critical to achieving high repayment rates. This belief is captured well in the following observation by Muhammad Yunus:

> "[I]t is hard to take a huge wad of bills out of one's pocket and pay the lender. There is enormous temptation from one's family to use that money to meet immediate consumption needs... Borrowers find this incremental process easier than having to accumulate money to pay a lump sum because their lives are always under strain, always difficult.[3]"

The model that captures this is stark in order to highlight one particular effect: if borrowers are present-biased, frequent repayment can increase the maximum loan size for which repayment is incentive-compatible. Intuitively, when borrowers are present-biased, the immediate gain to defaulting on any large repayment is subject to significant temptation. When these payments are spread out, the instantaneous repayment burden at any time is smaller and thus less subject to temptation. Frequent repayment also means that

[3]Yunus (2003: 114).

at the time of the first payment, the rewards (typically access to future credit) are further away from the repayment decision and thus more heavily discounted. On the other hand, so, too, is some of the repayment burden. On balance, frequent repayment relaxes the incentive compatibility constraint for present-biased borrowers. But these benefits do not come without costs. Frequent repayment imposes an opportunity cost of meeting attendance on borrowers and direct costs on the lender. It might also distort the investment incentives of borrowers toward projects that generate consistent, if meager, returns. The optimal frequency balances these costs against the positive incentive effects.

The behavioral factors motivating frequent repayment for loans can also create demand for commitment savings products, ranging from ROSCAs to formal financial products with time or amount targets. For a time, the excitement surrounding microlending seemed to crowd out interest in savings behavior, but interest has flooded back. The policy literature now broadly recognizes the importance of savings outlets for poor households (e.g., Collins *et al.*, 2009; and CGAP, 2002), and academic research has begun to unpack the many constraints households face when attempting to save. A whole body of evidence, both in developing and developed economies, documents savings anomalies that are consistent with the general insights of behavioral economics.[4] In particular, we have seen that individuals with time-inconsistent preferences and even those with conventional preferences who are subject to resource claims by others may value commitment savings products. There is a general sense that such problems are particularly salient for poor individuals; more and more, we see the tools of behavioral economics applied to specific questions concerning microfinance and informal credit markets. Basu (2008), for example, looks directly at the effect of time-inconsistent preferences on the demand for commitment savings products and their welfare implications.

Note that the quasi-hyperbolic utility functions underlying these models can come from a number of different sources, including insecure savings, demands for future consumption from other family members, or a behavioral bias towards current consumption. The theory, following standard practice, embeds them all in the parameter for present bias and represents a further step in understanding the role these collected factors may play in repayment behavior. One possible course of research would be, first, to test

[4]See Ashraf *et al.* (2006) and Thaler (1990) for a sense of this research.

the hypothesis that greater present bias, whatever its root cause, both lowers the maximum incentive-compatible loan size and improves the relative repayment performance of more frequent installments. If data supports this hypothesis, practitioners could use this knowledge to better tailor contractual terms to their customers' needs. A natural extension would be to determine the sources of present bias, as mitigating the welfare consequences of each would call for a different intervention. If insecure savings are inducing quasi-hyperbolic behavior, the optimal response would include strengthening savings mechanisms. Whereas if behavioral biases towards current consumption are inducing these preferences, such measures would have little effect. Instead, policy responses could include commitment devices if individuals were aware of their biases, or some combination of commitment devices and financial education if they were not.

An alternative view of frequent repayment focuses on the meetings rather than the act of repaying itself. Rai and Sjöström (2004) argue that frequent meetings serve as a means for the lender to extract information about borrowers' projects. By asking borrowers to report on their partner's and their own projects and punishing borrowers when reports do not match, the lender can determine if a default is strategic or if a borrower genuinely cannot repay. Under joint liability without these repayment meetings, there is no way to know if a borrower has the means to repay. It is this cross-reporting at group meetings that improves efficiency. Disentangling the effects and mechanisms behind alternative repayment structures provides an interesting opportunity for future research.

Turning back to credit mechanisms other than frequent repayment, Roy Chowdhury (2005) and Aniket (2006) highlight another mechanism often used by MFIs: sequential lending. Loans are typically not given to all borrowers simultaneously. For example, in a two-member group, one member gets a loan only after the previous member has paid a number of her installments properly. This creates an additional stake for the member who comes in later to monitor the previous one. Indeed, with simultaneous lending, borrowers will under-monitor. Sequential lending avoids the problem. In his model, Roy Chowdhury (2005) implicitly assumes that there is an escrow account such that part of the first-round borrower's revenue is taken away from her and returned to her only if the second-round borrower repays. This is a form of collateral creation, which, if practically feasible, could indeed overcome one of the key underlying problems that generate credit constraints.

Above, we discussed these alternative instruments in isolation. A potentially fascinating area of research is to look at their interactions. Some might complement each other, and some might crowd out the positive effects of one another. Consider the interaction of joint liability and frequent repayment. One potential cost of joint liability is it might sometimes lead to default by the whole group because one borrower might not be able to pay off the loans of her partners, even though she would be able to pay off her own loan (Besley and Coate, 1995). With frequent repayment and smaller repayment amounts, this constraint would be relaxed.

3 Empirics

For a long time, empirical research in microfinance long lagged behind the early wave of theoretical advances. More recently, the field has attracted a great deal of attention, inspiring randomized control trials, lab experiments and more traditional econometric work. In this section, we look at some of the areas where gaps exist between empirical evidence and our theoretical framework. In certain cases, we see what Banerjee (2005) described as the challenge to theory: observations from the "real world" that do not square with our theoretical models. In others, we see areas where long-standing theories call out for empirical tests and the iterative process of testing and reformulation that is the hallmark of scientific progress.

As discussed in the preceding section, much of the early theoretical work on microfinance focused on joint liability. Yet despite attention from theorists, empirical research lagged behind. A few academic papers exploited observational data from existing borrowing groups to test *how* joint liability worked,[5] but the question, "Does joint liability work?" was answered largely on revelation. Microfinance institutions employing joint liability were lending to poor individuals without collateral, *ipso facto* microfinance must "work". In truth, the performance of joint liability lending contracts had been mixed, and qualitative evidence documents a number of limitations. But until recently, we lacked any hard evidence on the relative performance of joint versus individual liability lending.

Motivated by this knowledge gap, Giné and Karlan (2009) analyze two randomized control trials to evaluate the efficacy of joint liability relative to

[5] Ahlin and Townsend (2007) and Wydick (1999) are exceptional examples.

individual liability on the monitoring and enforcement of loans. This paper is an interesting and important example of the experimental approach to microfinance. They find that loan repayment behavior did not differ across clients of a large Philippine bank that were randomly assigned to either joint or individual liability lending contracts. However, as they discuss in their paper, all these borrowers were already borrowing under joint liability when the experiment was carried out. As a result, it is possible that the pool of these borrowers was already safer than average (as implied by, say, Ghatak, 1999). Keeping or removing the instrument of joint liability would not make a difference if peer-screening is the most important mechanism through which joint liability works. As the authors point out, their experiment does suggest that conditional on this selection, the mechanisms of peer monitoring or peer pressure did not differ enough between contract types to affect repayment rates. However, since this sample is likely to have some selection bias, it is possible that their findings understate the extent of peer monitoring and peer pressure (the hypothesis being, the riskier the borrowers, the greater the returns from these mechanisms).

Despite this caveat, the findings of Giné and Karlan suggest an interesting way to try to test directly the effect of one mechanism (joint liability) and try to understand the channels through which it works (or does not work). In other words, it suggests how randomized control trials can be used to explicitly test out theories about specific microfinance mechanisms. The next step could be to design an experiment where the selection effect can be teased out, for example, by directly trying to measure not only variation in social connections under joint versus individual liability, but also variation in information about risk preferences, investment opportunities and other characteristics that are at the heart of our models concerning selection. As an important complement to this step, we could also design an experiment where these characteristics were randomly varied within groups governed by the same financial contracts, thus allowing us to assess causality in both directions. Finally, along the lines of the work of Karlan and Zinman (2008), a direct test of the relative importance of peer selection, peer monitoring and peer pressure would be valuable.

There are a number of ways in which the contribution of Giné and Karlan could be profitably extended. But here we would like to focus on what this tells us about the research process itself. Many of the core theories of microfinance are over a decade old and still await careful empirical testing. The scientific method is built on the iterative process of hypotheses formation and testing. Yet in the area of microfinance, as we have seen, theory and empirics have largely followed independent paths. We now turn to an area where there is an immediate opportunity for the two to evolve in tandem: repayment frequency.

As the focus of academics and, more importantly, microfinance practitioners themselves has moved away from joint liability, high-frequency repayment has attracted well-deserved attention. The typical microfinance client repays her loan in small, frequent installments beginning almost immediately after origination. Most lending contracts require weekly repayment. The intuition captured in Yunus's quote above is appealing and shared by many microfinance practitioners. Yet empirical evidence on the effect of repayment frequency is both limited and mixed. BRAC, one of the largest MFIs with nearly six million clients, abandoned a move to biweekly repayment when an experiment showed increased delinquencies (Armendariz and Morduch, 2004). In Latin America, several MFIs have migrated a portion of their clients to biweekly repayments but have been reluctant to lengthen installments further (Westley, 2004). Satin Credit Care, an urban MFI targeting trading enterprises, saw delinquencies increase from less than 1 percent to nearly 50 percent when it tested a move from daily to weekly repayment.[6] In Bolivia, BancoSol has revised its repayment policy repeatedly in response to fluctuating arrears (Gonzalez–Vega, 1997; Westley, 2004).

Recently, the importance of this issue has attracted experimental and quasi-experimental investigation. In 2000, FINCA Uganda, one of the largest and best-established microfinance institutions in Africa, introduced the "flexibility program", under which borrowing groups in selected areas could elect by a unanimous vote to change from weekly to biweekly repayment. As with many other microfinance institutions, FINCA shared the belief that frequent installments are critical for repayment performance and thus was reluctant to offer less frequent repayment despite the high costs associated with weekly meetings. One naturally worries that FINCA only offered the less frequent repayment option in areas where it felt the risks of increasing delinquency were the lowest, which would induce selection bias in estimates of the change's effects due to endogenous program placement. Using an econometric strategy designed to account for these effects, McIntosh (2008) finds that, relative to borrowing groups choosing to stay with the weekly repayment schedule, those that elected biweekly repayments have higher retention and, surprisingly, slightly better repayment performance. However,

[6]Greg Fischer's interview with H.P. Singh, November 2005.

as he notes, this tests the effects of allowing existing clients to decide from a menu of contract options and not the direct effect of changing repayment terms.

Field and Pande (2008) conduct just such a test by randomly assigning clients of a large Indian microfinance institution to either weekly or monthly repayment schedules. They find no significant effect on delinquencies, with all treatment groups reporting extremely low default and delinquency rates. As their study extends to future and larger borrowings for which the incentive compatibility constraint for repayment is more likely to bind, differences may emerge. But, for now, the evidence is silent.

Nonetheless, microfinance practitioners maintain an almost universal belief that frequent repayment schedules improve repayment rates. It is here that the experience of practitioners and the emerging empirical evidence move beyond theoretical foundations. At first glance, this belief in the importance of frequent repayment is theoretically puzzling. Classically, rational individuals should benefit from more flexible repayment schedules, and less frequent repayment should increase neither default nor delinquency. Insights from behavioral economics and psychology suggest a possible mechanism. Ariely and Wertenbroch (2002) demonstrate that externally imposed deadlines can improve task performance, and many others have described the consequences of procrastination and present bias in a range of settings.[7] Present bias has long been assumed and is now well-documented among microfinance borrowers (Bauer, Chytilová and Morduch, 2008).[8] It can also explain the importance of frequent repayment. Fischer and Ghatak (2010) show that with present-biased borrowers, more frequent repayment can support larger loan sizes. In fact, when interest rates are set competitively, more frequent repayment will relax the repayment incentive compatibility constraints for borrowers with any degree of present bias.

This does not mean that repayment frequency is unimportant for institutions, such as BRAC or ASA, that make small loans. For any given degree of present bias, the incentive compatibility constraints will only bind and repayment frequency will only affect repayment behavior for loans above a certain size. However, for sufficiently present-biased borrowers or loans where the consequences of non-payment are relatively small, this lower

---

[7]See, for example, Akerlof (1991) or O'Donoghue and Rabin (1999).

[8]More generally, Mullainathan (2005) makes a convincing argument that time-inconsistent preferences may be central to understanding many of the core issues in development economics.

bound can be quite small. Because of the heterogeneity in microfinance borrowers' utility, use of proceeds, outside financial options and susceptibility to default penalties, it is not surprising that we see a range of responses to changes in repayment frequency. Thus far, we do not know why some attempts to reduce the repayment frequency for small loans have succeeded while others have failed. A microfinance institution currently considering changing its repayment terms is left to consider the range of experimental and observational results and make a best guess as to what might happen within its own borrower pool. One aim of this theory is to underpin future experiments, thereby unpacking the mechanisms through which repayment frequency affects repayment and helping practitioners make informed decisions about their loan terms and experiment optimally.

Questions about repayment frequency are just one area where empirical evidence, intuition and experience about microfinance have extended beyond theoretical support. But there are also many areas where long-standing theories call for testing. Take, for example, the theory of group formation. Even as many microfinance institutions move beyond traditional joint liability lending, they continue to rely on groups for screening, monitoring and repayment activities. The benchmark models conclude that groups match homogenously such that similar risk types are matched together (Ghatak, 1999, 2000; Gangopadhyay *et al.*, 2005), while a competing strand suggests borrowers may match heterogeneously to maximize the potential gain from mutual insurance (Sadoulet, 1999). Ahlin (2009) makes innovative use of data from borrowing groups in Thailand to find support for homogenous matching. The continual and evolving importance of groups suggests that further work along these lines would be fruitful.

4 Spanning the Chasm

In light of the costs and consequences of frequent repayment, research could be productively directed towards understanding how to lower these costs. Some of the advances will be necessarily operational, for example, scheduling and locating meetings to reduce the direct costs to borrowers and credit officers or using innovations in communication technology, such as mobile phones, in creative ways. Others may be suggested by theory. For example, if repayment is driven by frequent payments per se rather than the social pressure or information structure of face-to-face meetings, then migration to high-frequency electronic payments would reduce costs without increasing defaults. However, if the key welfare cost of frequent repayments occurs through distorted investment decisions, such a change would have little benefit. Instead, microfinance institutions and their borrowers may be better served by loans with deferred or reduced early amortization schedules, which allow for potentially higher return investments that do not necessarily generate frequent and immediate cash flows.

Much more work is required to understand the solutions to these long-standing issues. Our movement towards these solutions will be more certain if we unite the insights of theory, field research and practitioners. Quantifying the impact of any policy changes through careful field research is essential if microfinance institutions are to assess the costs and benefits of any policy changes. A clear understanding of the mechanisms, the theory, behind any changes will facilitate translating these findings into action. And the input of practitioners will ensure that the research is grounded in reality and informed by the best thinking of all those interested in finding an answer.

Among theorists, one often hears the complaint that while randomized control trials can offer clean tests of a hypothesis, not a lot of thought goes into choosing the hypotheses to be tested. We reject this criticism. At the same time, we recognize that while the body of field experiments has generated an abundance of intriguing findings, in many cases, one genuinely does not know where to hang these results in our theoretical framework. Duflo (2005) captures this line of reasoning well when she writes, "Field experiments need theory, not only to derive testable implications, but to give general direction to what the interesting questions are". Conversely, one often encounters theory, worked out with detailed extensions and modifications of core insights, but without due attention to the facts generated by empirical research and observation.

Nearly everyone agrees, in fact it is perhaps trite to say, that closer interactions between theory and empirics would benefit the research agenda in microfinance. We would like to take this claim a step further. Yes, much can be learned from careful empirical work or randomized control trials onto which theory is fitted after the fact. So, too, is there much value in stand-alone applied theory that is tested at a later date and by a different researcher. However, we would like to suggest that there is a great opportunity within the microfinance literature to unite theory and empirics from their inception.

Consider an application to the question of repayment frequency. The interesting and important empirical results generated by McIntosh (2008) and Field and Pande (2008) have immediate policy relevance. They will likely spur other practitioners to experiment with reducing repayment frequency. But the mechanisms behind these results remain unclear. For example, the theory of Fischer and Ghatak (2010) offers several testable predictions. Repayment frequency will matter more for, (a) larger loans as the incentives for default are stronger; (b) for borrowers who are more prone to present bias; and (c) where transactions costs for organizing group meetings are lower. These predictions are testable and falsifiable. And should testing prove them false, we can refine and retest until we arrive at some generalizable understanding of how these mechanisms work.

This follows the established line of scientific inquiry and is not unique to economics or microfinance. What is unique is the situation where some methodological innovations in economics (such as randomized experiments) have made testing theories easier. With secondary (non-randomly generated data) there are always many confounding factors at work that make it hard to make inferences about even broad causal mechanisms, let alone subtle nuances of theory. Also, by their very nature, these experiments can only be carried out in close cooperation and partnership with the practitioners. These two features make the current environment somewhat unique, and, for those of us working in it, very exciting.

5 Conclusions

In this paper we have reviewed some recent theoretical and empirical work on microfinance. Our goal has been not to provide a comprehensive survey of the literature but to highlight the main themes and their interconnections. We have offered our views on how future research can bridge the chasm between theoretical and empirical work and argued that randomized experiments can play a very important role here. There is another chasm that needs to be bridged, and that is between academic research and the work carried out by practitioners. It is important to realize the two-way nature of this interaction. Practitioners are pioneers whose work — both the successes and failures — gives researchers the basic material for thinking about fundamental economic questions. Researchers use both theory and empirical work to establish some broad patterns or stylized facts that serve as a benchmark for practitioners when they think of carrying out innovations in the design of these programs, generating new puzzles and questions, and the three-way interaction continues.

References

Ahlin, C (2009). *Matching for Credit: Risk and Diversification in Thai Micro-Borrowing Groups.* BREAD Working Paper No. 251.

Ahlin, C and N Jiang (2008). Can Micro-credit bring development? *Journal of Development Economics*, 86(1), 1–21.

Ahlin, C and RM Townsend (2007). Using repayment data to test across models of joint liability lending. *Economic Journal*, 117(517), 11–51.

Alexander Tedeschi, G. (2006). Here today, gone tommorrow: Can dynamic incentives make microfinance more flexible? *Journal of Development Economics*, 80(1), 84–105.

Aniket, K (2006). *Sequential Group Lending with Moral Hazard.* Edinburgh School of Economics Discussion Paper No. 136.

Ariely, D and K Wertenbroch (2002). Procrastination, deadlines, and performance: Self-control by precommitment. *Psychological Science*, 13(3), 219–224.

Armendariz de Aghion, B and J Morduch (2005). The Economics of Microfinance. Cambridge, MA: MIT Press.

Aubert, C, A de Janvry, and E Sadoulet (2009). Designing credit agent incentives to prevent mission drift in pro-poor microfinance institutions. *Journal of Development Economics*, 90(1), 153–162.

Banerjee, A (2005). New development economics and the challenge to theory. *Economic and Political Weekly*, 40(4), 4340–4344.

Banerjee, AV, T Besley, and TW Guinnane (1994). Thy neighbor's keeper: The design of a credit cooperative with theory and a test. *Quarterly Journal of Economics*, 109(2), 491–515.

Basu, K (2008). *The Provision of Commitment in Informal Banking Markets: Implications for Takeup and Welfare.* University of Chicago mimeograph.

Bauer, M, J Chytilová, and J Morduch (2008). Behavioral foundations of microcredit: Experimental and survey evidence. Institute for Economic Studies mimeograph.

Besley, T and S Coate (1995). Group lending, repayment incentives and social collateral. *Journal of Development Economics*, 46(1), 1–18.

Bond, P and AS Rai (2009). Borrower runs. *Journal of Development Economics*, 88(2), 185–191.

Chowdhury, PR (2005). Group-lending: Sequential financing, lender monitoring and joint liability. *Journal of Development Economics*, 77(2), 415–439.

Chowdhury, PR and Ray, J (2009). Public-private partnerships in micro-finance: Should NGO involvement be restricted? *Journal of Development Economics*, 90(2), 200–208.

Collins, D, J Morduch, S Rutherford, and O Ruthven (2009). Portfolios of the poor: How the world's poor live on $2 a day. Princeton, NJ: Princeton University Press.

Consultative Group to Assit the Poorest (2002). *Microfinance Consensus Guidelines. Developing Deposit Services For The Poor.* Washington, D.C.: CGAP/The World Bank.

Duflo, E (2006). Field experiments in development economics. In: *Advances in Economics and Econometrics: Theory and Applications: Ninth World Congress.* Cambridge University Press.

Field, E and R Pande (2008). Repayment frequency and default in microfinance: Evidence from india. *Journal of the European Economic Association*, 6(2–3), 501–509.

Fischer, G (2010). Contract structure, risk sharing and investment choice. LSE mimeo.

Fischer, G and M Ghatak (2010). Repayment frequency and lending contracts with present-biased borrowers. LSE mimeo.

Gangopadhyay, S, M Ghatak, and R Lensink (2005). Joint liability lending and the peer selection effect. *Economic Journal*, 115(506), 1005–1015.

Ghatak, M (1999). Group lending, local information and peer selection. *Journal of Development Economics*, 60(1), 27–50.
Ghatak, M (2000). Screening by the company you keep: Joint liability lending and the peer selection effect. *Economic Journal*, 110(465), 601–631.
Ghatak, M and TW Guinnane (1999). The economics of lending with joint liability: Theory and practice. *Journal of Development Economics*, 60(1), 195–228.
Giné, X and DS Karlan (2009). *Group Versus Individual Liability: Long-Term Evidence from Philippine Microcredit Lending Groups.* Yale Economics Department Working Paper No. 61
Gonzalez-Vega, C, S Navajas, and M Schreiner (1995). *A Primer on Bolivian Experiences in Microfinance: An Ohio State Perspective.* Ohio State University.
Guttman, JM, (2008). Assortative matching, adverse selection, and group lending. *Journal of Development Economics*, 87(1), 51–56.
Jain, S and G Mansuri (2003). A little at a time: The use of regularly scheduled repayments in microfinance programs. *Journal of Development Economics*, 72(1), 253–279.
Karlan, D and J Zinman (2009). Observing unobervables: Identifying information asymmetries with a consumer credit field experiment. *Econometrica*, 77(6), 1993–2008.
Laffont, J-J (2003). Collusion and group lending with adverse selection. *Journal of Development Economics*, 70(2), 329–348.
McIntosh, C (2008). Estimating treatment effects from spatial policy experiments: An application to Ugandan Microfinance. *The Review of Economics and Statistics*, 90(1), 15–28.
McIntosh, C and B Wydick (2002). Competition and microfinance. University of California, Berkeley mimeo.
Rai, AS and T Sjöström (2004). Is Grameen lending efficient? Repayment incentives and insurance in village economies. *Review of Economic Studies*, 71(1), 217–234.
Sadoulet, L (1999). Equilibrium risk-matching in group lending. ECARES/Universite Libre de Bruxelles mimeo.
Stiglitz, JE (1990). Peer monitoring and credit markets. *World Bank Economic Review*, 4(3), 351–366.
Varian, HR (1990). Monitoring agents with other agents. *Journal of Institutional and Theoretical Economics*, 146(1), 153–174.
Westley, GD (2004). A tale of four village banking programs: Best practices in Latin America. Washington, D.C.: Inter-American Development Bank.
Wydick, B (1999). Can social cohesion be harnessed to repair market failures? Evidence from group lending in Guatemala. *Economic Journal*, 109(457), 463–475.
Yunus, M and A Jolis (2003). Banker to the poor: Micro-lending and the battle aganist world poverty. New York: Public Affairs.

The Early German Credit Cooperatives and Microfinance Organizations Today: Similarities and Differences

Timothy W. Guinnane*

Yale University

Microfinance institutions now occupy a central place in development policy. The economic problems that make special microfinance institutions necessary are not new, and several scholars have drawn attention to the similarities between modern microfinance institutions and older lenders. This paper uses a tight focus on one historical institution (Germany's credit cooperatives) and two of the oldest modern microfinance institutions to make a careful point-by-point comparison. Issues to consider include lending policy, typical loan sizes, sources of finance and the role of larger social and other infrastructure in shaping the institution's conduct. I conclude that despite similar goals, the historical cooperatives were different in ways that might offer lessons for microlenders today.

Microfinance institutions have become a major force in most developing countries. Many economists and development practitioners see these institutions as central to encouraging improvements in farming, the creation of small businesses, formation of human capital and the enhancement of overall welfare in poor countries. Some of the practices and questions that arise in connection with microfinance today echo questions that came up earlier of institutions formed in the 19th century. More than one recent observer has noted parallels to some historical European institutions. At some level, these comparisons are inaccurate, because the early microfinance institutions relied on a different institutional structure. On the other hand, their lending models sometimes paralleled those used today, so there is value in understanding what the historical institution can offer present practice. This paper undertakes a focused comparison of one of the strongest early

*We thank the editors and Anaïs Périlleux for comments on an earlier version of this paper.

European credit cooperative groups — microfinance institutions today with the German.

Some discussions of this sort address themselves to the question of "firsts", that is, asking whether a particular institution was the first of its type. That question quickly turns into a fruitless argument about the definition of historical microfinance. A number of important institutions made small loans long before the credit cooperatives discussed here. With care, however, we can focus on a number of lenders whose aims were most similar to those of modern microfinance institutions. Another approach is to claim that some earlier historical institution does or does not hold lessons for modern practitioners. That approach is more fruitful if treated with appropriate caution; the "best" way to undertake a certain kind of lending surely differs across time and place, but understanding the features that enhanced or impeded success in one place can only help in understanding the problem in another.

This paper has a modest but still useful goal, which is to describe the ways in which historical credit cooperatives were similar to and different from modern microfinance institutions. Other contributions to this volume offer great detail on modern microfinance institutions, and I confine my comparisons to two of the most important models operating today. One is the "group lending" model pioneered by the Grameen Bank, and the second is the "microfinance cooperative" that is especially prevalent in West Africa today.

1 Early Microfinance Institutions

Several recent papers focus on historical micro lenders and discuss their similarities to modern microfinance institutions. These discussions illustrate the need for care in understanding what an institution actually did. There is always the historical problem of separating the possibly multiple aims of a given set of people. More importantly, economists have a tendency to read into an institution a logic that might not have been there, or at least was not central to the institution's functioning. Some recent examples include Hollis and Sweetman's (1998, 2001) discussion of the Irish Loan Funds, and Phillipps and Mushinski's (2007) analysis of the Morris Plan banks in the United States. The Irish Loan Funds, which began in the 18th century, were a quasi-philanthropic local institution empowered to lend money. Hollis and Sweetman argue that they functioned much as some modern micro lenders. The Irish Loan Funds undoubtedly made relatively small loans at a time when for-profit lenders rarely did so. The question is whether we really want to think of the Loan Funds as the Hibernian equivalent of the Grameen Bank or a microfinance cooperative. Did the the loan funds employ special organizational features intended to contend with the information and enforcement problems that underlie the innovative mechanisms seen in modern micro lenders? Contemporary observers are more likely to argue that the Funds were sources of local patronage and corruption.

Something similar can be said of the Morris Plan Banks, a group of independent, for-profit lenders in the United States that started in the early 20th century. By requiring co-signers, the Plan was able to reduce the costs of screening and monitoring, just as is argued for modern joint-liability lenders. But others noted that the Plan employed a complex scheme that left many borrowers unable to understand the true cost of the loan they took. For example, the Plan required borrowers to make no-interest deposits as they paid off their loan. The Plan feature that some modern scholars have stressed, the reliance on co-signers, was standard in 19th century banking and not specific to the Morris Plan. The Plan's advertised interest rate, critics argued, badly understated the true cost of borrowing. If the critics are right, then the Morris Plan's apparent success does not reflect innovations in lending that successfully dealt with information and enforcement problems.[1]

The effort to locate the early history of microfinance in such institutions has overlooked a widespread and very old lender, the pawnshop. Brief consideration of this approach to small loans illustrates why cooperatives were seen as a dramatic improvement. Pawnshops have been a regular feature of European credit markets since the Middle Ages. Pawnshops work on a simple principle; all loans are collateralized and the lender maintains physical possession of the collateral. Thus "default" is not possible. The only way the lender can lose money is if he incorrectly values the pawned object, and the borrower does not repay. Some European historical pawnshops were for-profit firms, while others were operated by a municipal government as a service to the local population. As a lending model, pawnshops face several important drawbacks. For this model to work, customers must own mobile objects that are valuable enough to serve as collateral but easily valued and stored. An important implicit cost of a pawnshop loan is loss of the object's use. Thus pawn-based lending has little use in a society where the only

[1]See Carruthers, Guinnane and Lee (2009) for details on the Morris Plan and other small-loan lenders in the United States.

appreciable physical asset is land or tools constantly needed in production. Finally, the model itself is inherently costly: pawn objects must be valued and stored. One can see why reformers were looking for a better lending model.

2 The Formation of Germany's Credit Cooperatives

Germany's credit cooperatives themselves grew out of older local institutions. They trace their modern origins to two different strands, one associated with Hermann Schulze–Delitzch and the other with Friedrich Raiffeisen. Schulze–Delitzsch first organized credit cooperatives in the late 1840s, while Raiffeisen started later, in the late 1850s. Both of these first two strands were indirect reactions to the failed revolution of 1848. A third cooperative group associated with Wilhelm Haas started as an offshoot of Raiffeisen's group but later eclipsed the original in numbers and size. Other regional variants also emerged. The diversity in the German cooperative movement was at times a source of internecine conflict, but was also a great strength.

The cooperative movement in Germany grew rapidly throughout the century. By 1914, there were over 35,000 cooperatives in total, with a combined membership of 6.4 million people. Normally only one person per household belonged to a cooperative, so these figures imply that about 25 million Germans (well over one-third of the total population) were involved with a cooperative.[2] About 15 thousand of these institutions were the credit cooperatives that interest us. The others included cooperatives for the purchase of inputs or the marketing of output, as well as cooperative retail outlets, cooperative apartment complexes and a myriad other institutions. As we shall see, the credit cooperatives were legally distinct from other cooperatives, but often provided credit to their sister organizations. German historians stress the political role and implications of the cooperative movement. Schulze–Delitzsch, Haas and other cooperative leaders doubled as political leaders (usually Liberals), and most German governments turned from actively opposing the cooperative movement to viewing the movement as a useful bulwark against the threat of social democracy, which by the 1890s was a powerful political movement (Guinnane, 2009a).

[2]These estimates are from Fairbairn (1994: 1215–16). While he is certainly right that the cooperative movement was huge, and that German historians have not paid it sufficient attention, the figures he cites are an upper bound.

Cooperatives were free to adopt a wide variety of policies on membership and operations. Following the Prussian law of 1867 (which was preceded in some other states by similar legislation and adopted by the North German Confederation and then the Reich in 1871), cooperatives could register with a special part of the business registry (Guinnane, 2010). Registration gave cooperatives legal personality and enhanced their ability to contract in their own capacity. The 1889 Cooperatives Law, which received more attention than the ground-breaking 1867 Act, introduced two further significant changes. First, cooperatives could be formed in which owners had *limited* liability for their investments. Prior to 1889, all cooperative members had *unlimited* liability for the institution's debts in bankruptcy. Unlimited liability sounds draconian to modern observers, but was the norm for all but the very largest businesses in Germany and most other Continental countries until the early 20th century (Guinnane, Harris, Lamoreaux and Rosenthal, 2007). Liability structure mattered a great deal at the time for two reasons. Unlimited liability was thought to deter the wealthier members of a community from joining the cooperative; if the institution failed, they would be disproportionately liable for any losses. Since only members could participate in management, this feature of the liability rules would deprive the cooperative of valuable business experience as well as the capital needed to run the institution. Some spectacular failures of unlimited liability cooperatives in the 1860s had led to a small number of relatively wealthy people paying virtually all the cooperative's debts. The remaining members were either bankrupt themselves or could not be located by the bankruptcy referees. A second argument in favor of limited liability reflects the difficulty of lending to an institution whose main capital is the property of its members. This issue of course arises with any unlimited liability business organization, but was especially severe when most owners were relatively poor people with assets such as land and livestock. The Reichsbank (the central bank), for example, was, in principle, willing to lend to unlimited liability cooperatives as it would any business enterprise, but in practice could not judge the safety of such loans and generally refused to make them.

The 1889 Act also allowed a cooperative to own a share in another cooperative, thus enabling the structure of regional cooperatives that emerged in the late 19th century. This "cooperative owning a cooperative" would make no sense if both had to have unlimited liability. But additional legal impediments in the pre-1889 legislation meant that the liability changes were not enough to create the new structures on their own.

State policy toward cooperatives changed over the century. At first many governments actively harassed the new institution, viewing them as intended to assist the State's political opponents. Over time, several German governments either accommodated themselves to the movements formed by Schulze–Delitzsch, Raiffeisen and Haas, or promoted more conservative versions of the same movement. By the outbreak of World War I, cooperatives enjoyed some modest state support. Cooperatives did not pay the equivalent of corporate taxes so long as they only dealt with their own members. Some governments granted cooperative associations small amounts to offset the cost of the mandatory external audits introduced in 1889. And in 1895, the Prussian government created a special "State Cooperative Central Bank" intended to provide loans to the cooperative movement, and also to promote the cooperatives most in favor with the government. The Prussian Bank was controversial. Some accounts portray the cooperative movement as heavily dependent on state handouts, but this claim reflects a misunderstanding of what the Prussian State Central actually did. In most years, the cooperatives were collectively net lenders *to* the Prussian Bank. State policy did help the cooperatives in other less direct ways. The legal framework within which cooperatives operated was favorable, relative to that for business enterprises, especially after 1889. And the enormous protective tariffs that preserved German agriculture in the face of American and Eastern European grain imports in the late 19th century surely contributed much to the success of the rural communities in which many German cooperatives operated (Guinnane, 2009a).

While this paper focuses on the German credit cooperatives, two related sets of institutions warrant note. The German credit cooperatives were part of a much larger, interrelated set of cooperative institutions in Germany. In rural areas, these included cooperative wineries, creameries, storage and marketing enterprises, etc; in urban areas, there were cooperative grocery stores as well as enterprises that assisted craftsman with inputs and marketing. Credit cooperatives were freestanding entities, but many were allied to other cooperatives in larger regional federations. Cooperatives could also contract with one another; thus a credit cooperative might lend to a creamery cooperative, either directly or via a cooperative "Central", as discussed below. The credit cooperatives were the largest part of the German cooperative movement, measured as a proportion of institutions or total membership. The consumer cooperatives that became important in the 1880s and later had an explicitly left-wing outlook, and that political orientation has attracted the attention of historians.

The German cooperatives had numerous imitators in other countries. Most European societies experienced some version of the problems that led to the success of German cooperation, and even when local discussions did not lead to German-style cooperatives, the German experience largely framed local discussions. In some cases an effort to import the German system failed, as they did at first in Ireland (Guinnane, 1994). Sometimes the claim to have imported a "model" reflects German efforts to take unwarranted credit, or foreign effort to legitimize their efforts by pointing to the thriving German scene. But, without doubt, the cooperative movements in Italy, Austria and the Low Countries owe much to German inspiration. Other cases are less clear; the German example was much discussed in France, but only parts of the French system reflect German influence. Some countries such as Denmark and arguably the United States had for-profit credit institutions that provided many of the services due to cooperatives in Germany, so there were no serious efforts to import the German model although it was well-known (Guinnane and Henriksen, 1998). The U.S. credit union system owes its origins to Quebec's *Caisses Desjardins*, which were turn heavily influenced by the German cooperative movement. The American credit unions, however, never became the important part of the banking system that credit unions comprise in countries like Germany or the Netherlands today.

The variety of historical financial institutions that existed in historical contexts offers opportunity for confusion. Most European countries had, in addition to banks in the narrow sense, financial institutions that were formed to serve some social purpose. The most numerous and largest were savings banks (in the German example, *Sparkassen*) that were intended as safe depository institutions to encourage working-class and middle-class savings. In some countries, a Post Office savings system played this role. Most savings banks invested their portfolios in government paper and real estate, and thus did not engage in activities that would look like micro lenders today. (Some pawnshops were adjuncts of savings banks, however, and, to that extent, the savings bank was lending indirectly via the pawnshop). Often these savings banks, like the German, had explicit government guarantees for their deposits. Savings banks and credit cooperatives were distinct institutions and, in many situations, saw themselves as competitors for deposits. There were also mutual organizations that facilitated savings for the purchase or construction of a house. These building and loans (which in Germany were usually legally cooperatives) again should not be confused with a micro lender; while they existed to serve a financial need unmet by for-profit banks, they clearly were dealing with a much larger loan.

2.1 *Institutional structure*

The internal structure and governance procedures of German cooperatives were the subject of lively debate. Cooperative law required specifics, but, in most matters, cooperatives could decide for themselves. Table 3.1 lays out the general tendencies in the various strands of the German credit cooperatives. Local cooperatives consisted of a membership who elected the governing committees, in most cases a management committee (*Vorstand*) and a supervision board (*Aufsichtsrat*). Membership had to be (formally) "open" to satisfy the cooperative law, but cooperatives could and did screen members for unwanted characteristics (like alcohol abuse). The Schulze–Delitzsch cooperatives often had stiff entry fees and substantial share requirements to discourage the poor from trying to join. The rural cooperatives usually had a single, part-time staffer who kept the books and handled cash, while the larger urban cooperatives employed full-time professional staff. Most rural institutions did not have dedicated office space. The rural cooperatives were generally much smaller than their urban counterparts. The Raiffeisen group had a formal practice of encouraging credit cooperatives to restrict themselves to a single rural parish.

The relationship between local cooperatives and the regional organizations (discussed below) and the national organizations differed across groups. The Raiffeisen organization had a more rigid structure and the national federation made certain practices (such as the maintenance of unlimited liability after 1889) a condition of membership. The Haas group had independent regional organizations that came together in a national federation, but the group was usually more pragmatic than its Raiffeisen counterpart. Some Haas cooperatives adopted limited liability after 1889, although the federation recommended unlimited liability where that was practical. The Schulze–Delitzsch group stressed the independence of its member cooperatives and it exhibited the greatest heterogeneity on most organizational matters.

2.1.1 *The credit cooperative's balance sheet*

The credit cooperatives viewed themselves as small banks and their balance sheets resemble small banks in other places. Their liabilities consisted of capital, deposits and, sometimes, loans from other institutions. The rural cooperatives had very high leverage, with capital sometimes amounting to only five percent of total liabilities in their early years. Urban cooperatives tended to have larger shares and build up larger reserve funds, so they had

Table 3.1: Differences between groups of credit cooperatives in Germany.

	Raiffeisen	Haas	Schulze–Delitzsch
Location of institutions	Nearly always rural.	Nearly always rural.	Primarily urban.
Regional institutions ("Central" banks, etc)	One national central with branches.	Independent regional institutions.	No regional banks, but regional auditing associations.
Membership (size)	Usually less than 200.	Usually less than 200.	Varied widely; some cooperatives had more than 1000 members.
Membership (class)	Accepted virtually anyone in community.	Accepted virtually anyone in community.	Screened out the poorest applicants.
Management of local cooperatives	Part-time treasurer only paid employee.	Varied; usually only had part-time treasurer.	Paid professional staff.
Type of loans (duration)	Could be 10 years or more.	Could be 10 years or more.	Primarily short-term.
Type of loans (security)	Personal security, co-signers and property.	Personal security, co-signers and property.	Co-signers, inventory and raw materials.
Source of capital	Deposits.	Deposits and modest reserves.	Paid-in shares, reserves and deposits.
Legal form	Unlimited liability required.	Usually unlimited liability.	Many had limited liability after 1889; some were corporations.

lower leverage. Rural cooperatives often did not pay dividends on shares, and the Raiffeisen model stressed an indivisible reserve fund — that is, if the cooperative wound up business, it would give its remaining reserves to some local charity. The idea was to remove any incentive to make a disguised profit for members. The urban cooperatives on the other hand tended to pay attractive dividends on shares and, not incidentally, charged higher interest rates on loans. The most important category of liabilities in either case was deposits. Anyone could deposit at a cooperative. Depositors included both members and non-members. Some discussions of whether cooperatives should be taxed reflected the irritation of bankers who thought the cooperatives were unfairly competing for household deposits by the end of the 19th century. Similarly, the savings banks in some circumstances threatened cooperatives' access to deposits and vice-versa. Cooperatives could and did borrow from other financial institutions, including other cooperative institutions and sometimes commercial banks.

The credit cooperatives' assets consisted almost entirely of loans. The other only substantial asset item was investments in state bonds, or deposits at other banking institutions. Any cooperative that lent to non-members risked losing its tax-exempt status, and the practice was rare. Deposits at cooperatives shared the feature of most savings deposits at the time in that they were not demandable. Policy differed across institutions, but usually a depositor had to wait at least three months after giving notice to receive his money back. Some institutions offered higher interest rates to those who would agree to a six-month notice policy. This feature of the deposit structure helped to make cooperatives less vulnerable to the runs that plagued banks in other contexts. But they were not specific to cooperatives: the *Sparkassen* usually had similar provisions.

2.1.2 *Lending policy*

Cooperatives had a formal mechanism for deciding on credit applications. Some used their management committee for this purpose, others had a special credit committee and some delegated decisions about, at least, smaller loans to the treasurer. Cooperatives did not explicitly link credit decisions to a member's capital investment in the institution, as is sometimes claimed in the literature. In some cases, cooperatives made loans to new members on the day they joined, and after the new members invested only the minimal nominal amount needed to satisfy the law. Cooperatives could and did reject credit applications; in the manuscript records I have examined, there are denials for several reasons, including doubts about the project's advisability and worries about the security offered. In many instances, a member reapplied for a loan after remedying the worrisome feature of the original application. Many members never took a loan, even after belonging to a cooperative for years. Guinnane (2001) notes that this behavior implies that the cooperative was an important externality; it could be in a shopkeeper's interest for his customers to have low-cost credit, even if he did not need it himself.

Cooperatives relied on three types of loan products in the period prior to World War I. Most loans had a fixed duration and amortization schedule. Rural cooperatives, in particular, favored this approach. Some rural cooperative loans were of very long duration, as much as 10 years or more. Most loans made by rural cooperatives were for at least five years. Cooperative leaders thought that farmers needed long-term loans, while the cooperatives, even with a three-month recall provision, were funded from short-term deposits. Another product, most popular with small businesses, was a current account where the borrower paid interest on the debit balance and received interest on the credit balance. Instead of disbursing a specific amount to the borrower, the cooperative simply set a maximum net loan the individual could have. Urban cooperatives especially often made loans by discounting a bill of exchange. Artisans were often paid for their product with a bill of exchange (a type of promissory note). They could hold the bill until its maturity, or take it to a bank to receive cash early. This type of lending, which amounts to a loan with the bill itself as collateral, was typical of commercial banks of the day.

Security for loans was up to the local cooperative, but we see several patterns. Larger longer-term loans often had some form of property as security. Rural cooperatives made some mortgage loans, and many cooperatives secured a loan on tools or other equipment. Depending on how a promissory instrument was drafted, it might make some inventory or raw materials the property of the holder if the drawer did not make good the loan. But the most common security was personal, in the sense that the borrower would pledge to repay the loan, and one or more co-signers would guarantee the arrangement.

2.1.3 *Regional institutions for cooperatives*

The 1870s and 1880s saw the growth of two kinds of regional cooperative institution. One was simply a regional group that existed to share information, lobby governments and publish some type of newspaper or newsletter. These groups functioned as auditing societies after the introduction of mandatory audits in 1889. The other was a regional "Central", a sort of specialized bank for cooperatives. The relationship between local cooperatives and these regional organizations differed across groups. The Raiffeisen association had regional auditing associations and a single Central; the Haas group had regional auditing associations and multiple Centrals; the Schulze–Delitzsch group created regional auditing associations but never really had Centrals.

Prior to 1889, many cooperative associations had undertaken voluntary external audits of member associations. These audits were viewed as a way of encouraging good practice and uncovering fraud before the consequences became an embarrassment. Competition among the several branches of the cooperative movement sometimes took the form of damaging generalizations about the problems of a particular strand in the movement, and each cooperative group understood that it was in their interest to police their own members (Guinnane, 2003). The 1889 Cooperatives Act formalized the external audits. Under this law, every cooperative had to undergo an external audit at least every other year. The audit could be done by a cooperative auditing association, or by someone appointed by the local court. The only sanction the auditors could apply to a deficient cooperative was expulsion from the association, but knowledge of this action was like a death sentence for most cooperatives. This way of approaching external auditing was that preferred by the cooperative movement itself. Rather than a government official, who might be hostile to the movement, politically motivated, or simply ignorant of the special situation of these often very small enterprises, the 1889 law gave the several branches of the cooperative movement the chance to keep their own houses clean (Guinnane, 2003).

The auditing provisions of the 1889 law reflect a long concern about the management and control of cooperatives. The early cooperative leaders recognized that governance was going to be a major issue for them. Especially in rural areas, there was a shortage of people trained in the business methods needed to run a cooperative. And groups committed to volunteer management (such as Raiffeisen and Haas) faced the problem of motivating unpaid people. The several cooperative groups dealt with this problem in several different but related ways. First, they all commissioned and printed numerous cooperative advice manuals and printed forms that helped guide untrained treasurers and managers. Second, they all published periodicals intended for the local cooperative leadership. Much of the content of these periodicals consisted of advice about specific issues, such as how to secure a loan on land. Finally, most regional organizations set up training courses for the treasurers and managers of the local cooperatives. These courses, most of which lasted three or four days, would take the students through the basics necessary to operating their enterprise. More importantly, perhaps, it gave the regional leadership the opportunity to impress on the locals that a problem in one cooperative would quickly become a problem for all (Guinnane, 2003).

Governance and management issues differed slightly between rural and urban cooperatives, in part because the latter were larger and more willing to hire full-time staff. A second type of regional institution was almost entirely limited to rural cooperatives. The early Centrals were legally corporations whose shares were owned by local member cooperatives. After 1889, a Central could be a cooperative as well, and later institutions took that form. A Central's liabilities consisted primarily of deposits from its member cooperatives, and its liabilities were dominated by loans to member cooperatives. Centrals could also borrow from commercial and state banks, and those with excess deposits would buy state paper or deposit funds at other intermediaries.

The urban cooperatives rejected the idea of Centrals, and these regional banks became a major point of contention among the several groups. But they clearly reflect a solution to the special problems of credit cooperatives in rural areas. To take advantage of local information and social ties, the rural cooperatives had to operate in a fairly small region. But this structure made it very difficult for a single cooperative to diversify both its assets and liabilities. Seasonality was an additional problem; most members of a rural community needed credit precisely when savers might also want to use their funds for their own operations. Finally, rural credit cooperatives were highly leveraged and, as a consequence of their lending policy, illiquid. Their leaders understood this problem but viewed it as a necessary consequence of the need for long-term loans in agriculture. Making it possible for them to draw easily on outside funds was viewed as a way of allowing them to make long-term loans, to serve their clientele, without risking failure due to illiquidity.

Examination of the balance sheets and loan flows of the many Centrals within the Haas group suggests that these regional banks worked well. On the one hand, there were incidents of shocks in one part of the country (for example, to wine production, which was relatively localized) where the Centrals were able to, in effect, borrow from one group of coops to lend to another. There were also two additional practices not stressed at the time. One important function was to allow credit cooperatives (which typically had excess deposits at posted interest rates) to invest in a portfolio of other cooperatives in their region. A credit cooperative would deposit cash at its Central, which would then lend the money to another member of the group such as a creamery. This approach reduced the credit cooperative's exposure to problems in any one cooperative in the group. The system also helped to insulate, for good or ill, the cooperatives from the rest of the money market. A second practice was to allow a cooperative to start making loans before it was able to attract significant deposits. Especially in the eastern parts of Germany, which were on average poorer and had great inequalities in wealth, the first credit cooperatives found it very hard to raise funds from local depositors. Their Centrals were able to fund the first few years of lending to prove that the model was viable.

The Centrals were helpless in the face of truly aggregate shocks, such as the financial panic that spread from the United States in the period 1907. This panic illustrated a serious weakness in the entire system. Cooperatives working with a Central had to agree to use their Central exclusively; they could not lend to or borrow from anyone else. This provision was intended to keep local cooperatives out of trouble. A few cooperatives had gotten into serious trouble when they tried to invest in esoteric financial instruments they did not understand (Guinnane, 1997). The exclusivity was also intended to prevent a type of free-riding that reduced the Central's ability to work in a panic. Healthy cooperatives would withdraw their funds from the Central to invest, at higher rates, in the Berlin money market. This left the Central with the impossible task of assisting troubled cooperatives at the same time as its own balance sheet deteriorated. No serious observer thought the Centrals could function as lenders of last resort. But credit cooperatives that abused the relationship in this way make it tough for the Central to help member cooperatives that were in a weakened condition.

2.1.4 *The relationship among the several branches of the movement*

One strength of the German cooperative movement was its diversity, although many leaders in the 19th century did not see things that way. The cooperative law created a flexible enterprise that could be adapted to many different purposes and made consistent with different ideologies. By the end of the 19th century there were, in addition to the Raiffeisen, Haas, and Schulze–Delitzsch cooperatives described above, cooperatives organized by both ultra-conservative and left-wing organizations.

The relationship between the three main branches of the credit cooperatives was at times quite difficult. Raiffeisen gave lip service to Schulze–Delitzsch's role as the movement's founder, but Raiffeisen also ignored many of the precepts Schulze–Delitzsch thought central to the organization's functioning, such as building up cooperative reserves or reliance on short-term loans. Schulze–Delitzsch clearly thought the Raiffeisen variant a danger to the entire cooperative movement, and used his role in parliament to force the Prussian government to declare important Raiffeisen practices illegal. Some of the great strain between the Raiffeisen and Schulze–Delitzsch branches reflected the former's efforts to reach out to rural households. Schulze–Delitzsch thought the cooperative model inappropriate in such circumstances, and viewed the Raiffeisen group's willingness to adapt his ideas as naïve. Some of the differences between the two groups were, at some level, simply ideological. Schulze–Delitzsch and his followers strenuously opposed any State involvement in the movement. They rejected all subsidies and resisted measures that would allow State entities to monitor the cooperatives. This reflected both a political orientation and their early bitter experience with the various German governments harassing their enterprises. Raiffeisen's group did not view the State in the same way and were more comfortable with accepting support that might come with some interference.

The Haas group, although it remained primarily rural, reflected a willingness to learn from the best-practice methods of both earlier strands. The national Haas organization tended to offer advice on cooperative organization, but rarely refused membership to cooperatives that refused to follow its advice. Thus, by the end of the 19th century, some credit cooperatives within the Haas organization could have switched to the Raiffeisen group without strain, while others closely resembled a Schulze–Delitzsch credit cooperative.

3 Cooperatives and Microfinance Today

German cooperatives grew and thrived. They made many millions of marks in loans, and got most of the money back. They needed little or no State assistance, and while they relied on volunteer labor, many also paid good dividends to their members. By all the criteria used to evaluate programs in developing countries today, the German credit cooperatives were a big success. No serious person would suggest that the success of German credit cooperatives in the 19th century automatically recommends this model to microfinance today. We need to acknowledge, up front, that the context for the German cooperatives was very different from that of most developing countries today. Usually this point brings to mind important differences in technology or the larger world economy. A cooperative leader in Germany in 1880 could not use a cell phone to confer with a subordinate elsewhere, nor could he log onto the Internet to exchange ideas with a leader in Africa. Similarly, improvements in health technology, both human and animal, have reduced many risks that plague lending.

But these comparisons can be misleading. In many important ways, Germany was *more* developed in the late 19th century than some developing countries today. Consider income; in 1914, according to Maddison, GDP per person in Germany was about US $3100 (1990 Geary–Khamis dollars). The poorest developing countries today have per capita incomes below or only slighty above that figure; for 2001, Maddison reports a figure of US $3100 for Peru, about US $2000 for India, US $900 for Bangladesh, and US $3500 for Sri Lanka.[3] Simple income comparisons cannot capture other differences that bear on the ability of an ordinary lender to give credit and get the money back. Many of these differences suggest that the German cooperators had it relatively easy. Although not a full parliamentary democracy, Germany had strong institutions protecting property rights and the rule of law, and the cooperatives benefited from a sophisticated business law and court system. The credit cooperatives did not make many mortgage loans, for example, but those that did could take advantage of a reliable and sophisticated mechanism for registering title to land and mortgages on land. The social insurance system Bismarck introduced in the 1880s meant that fewer and fewer Germans faced risks that might lead them to the credit market, risks that could also endanger repayment of loans taken for the education of children. Universal primary education meant that all potential borrowers could read simple loan documents, and there were many local people with the basic education necessary to become leaders of these enterprises. Cooperative practice emphasized making the organization's records public at set intervals, and this was no mere formality in a society where most adults could read and write. And while there were no cell phones, good

[3]Maddison (2003).

roads, an efficient post office and well-developed telegraph networks meant that communication to all parts of Germany was simpler than it is in some poor countries today.

The German cooperatives also benefitted from the development of the larger financial system, something few leaders at the time would cheerfully admit. Paralleling the growth of the cooperative movement was the growth of an extensive network of for-profit banks and related financial institutions. The German "Great Banks" are rightly famous, but equally deserving of attention are the many smaller banks that grew and developed alongside the credit cooperatives. By the outbreak of World War I, Germany had a dense and sophisticated banking system, one which many scholars think played an important role in the country's rapid rise to industrial leadership (Guinnane, 2002). These banks could and did provide services for cooperatives; the Dresdner Bank, one of the large, universal banks for which the period is famous, operated a special department that provided liquidity and payments services for Schulze–Delitzch cooperatives. More importantly, the broader infrastructure associated with this sophisticated financial system was available to cooperatives as well. The *Reichsbank* provided liquidity to cooperatives on the same terms as it did other firms; this did not mean much, because the cooperatives often did not have the right kind of assets to qualify, but the possibility was there. More concretely, when a cooperative made a loan, it did not send out two men on a motorbike with cash, as some other micro lenders today are forced to do. The cooperative could write the borrower a check drawn on a Central or a commercial bank. And if the borrower wanted cash in excess of what the cooperative had on hand, the cooperative could obtain the cash from its Central via Post Office money transfers. The economic issues facing lending to poor borrowers do not change, but, in some ways, the German environment in the 19th century was more hospitable to microfinance than is the environment in many poor countries today.

What is similar, I would argue, is the underlying economics that made it difficult for conventional banks to lend to many Germans, and the economics underpinning the institutional features of the German credit cooperatives that allowed them to step in where banks could not. The German cooperatives' success at lending in a difficult market reflected their ability to do things other lenders could not. What they did, simply put, was to harness the power of local ties to create information about potential borrowers and social pressure to repay that enabled them to do what a different kind of lender could not (Guinnane, 2001).

3.1 *Group lending*

The signature method of many early micro lenders such as Grameen was the group loan (or joint liability lending). Recent discussions have stressed the extent to which micro lenders should and have moved beyond group loans to offer a wider variety of loan products (Armendáriz de Aghion and Morduch, 2000). But it is still interesting to compare the elements of group lending in cooperative practice to those used by microfinance institutions today. Most cooperative loans in Germany, as noted, were secured by a co-signer. This practice differs from a Grameen-style group in that only one member of the "group" borrows. One can also view the cooperative membership as a whole in a group, in that they stand collectively liable for the depositor's funds. Again, this kind of group differs from what we see in most microfinance institutions, in that many cooperative members did not have a loan at a given time. Nonetheless, much of the economic analysis of group lending undertaken in the context of Grameen-style groups goes through (Besley and Coate, 1995; Ghatak and Guinnane, 1999; Armendariz de Aghion and Gollier, 2000; Ghatak, 2000). The cooperatives were indeed "screened by the company you keep", in that the identity of the co-signer could prove the difference between a positive and negative decision on a loan. A co-signer also acted as a monitor, and if the loan was not paid back, the co-signer was responsible. Other features of cooperative practiced diverged from the Grameen-style group. Not only was the cooperative "group" limited to two people, it was not formed as part of an explicit program in which each member would eventually both get credit and be responsible for others' loans.

The use of co-signers did not originate with credit cooperatives. Arrangements of this sort were central to for-profit banking long before cooperatives, and German cooperative manuals stress that, in making co-signer loans, the cooperatives benefited from the legal principles that shaped banking practice at the time. This observation cuts two ways. On the one hand, the credit cooperatives were, at some level, just small banks with an unusual ownership, lending and interest-rate policy. They had not hit upon some new model of lending. On the other hand, much can be said of group lending today; the *way* the Grameen Bank or other group-lending microfinance institutions employ the principle of joint liability may be new in itself, and certainly new to Bangladesh and other developing countries. But co-signing loans is a very old practice.

One important difference between the German cooperatives and the early group lending institutions such as Grameen concerns loan sizes. The size of loans made by the German cooperatives varied tremendously. The manuscript records included loans that we could compare to the tiny micro loans of today. One cooperative made loans of 50 marks; at prevailing wages for day labor, this would be about three weeks' wages. Loans of this size are well within the range of what we think of today as microcredit. But the mean German loan was larger, and even some rural cooperatives made loans of 10,000 marks on a fairly regular basis. Institutions such as Grameen tend to view their mission as service to a particular slice of the population: women, the poor, etc. Cooperative members saw their institution as serving the local populace, rather than being targeted at specific groups. This meant the cooperatives had to make loans that ranged widely in size.

Another important difference between the cooperatives and some micro lenders today concerns the sources of the funds they lent out. Although this is changing, until recently few microfinance institutions have tried to collect local deposits. The money they lent in a given place came from "somewhere else", as grants or loans from international agencies, foundations and governments. This was ordinarily not the case in Germany. Members *had* to be local. Most depositors were as well, although there was no requirement to that effect. The few credit cooperatives that were lending someone else's money were confined to those that started with a loan from a Central, a practice rare outside of some portions of far eastern Germany. This practice had two implications. The cooperative model was best suited to intermediating between *local* savers and *local* deposits. If a community was so poor that it had few savers, then, in theory, the cooperative could not provide credit. The cooperative model was also vulnerable to local shocks; a cattle plague, for example, would wipe out the assets of depositors at the same time as it increased the demand for loans. This was one reason for the Centrals. In theory at least, the Centrals afforded the chance to mitigate the impact of very local shocks by constructing channels for interregional lending within the cooperative movement. The Centrals also made better borrowers in the larger capital market; that is, their individual member cooperatives were rarely able to borrow from commercial banks, while some Centrals, presumably because of their greater size, better book-keeping and more socially prominent leadership, were sometimes able to do so.

Cooperative leaders in Germany were always clear that local depositors were in effect monitors who helped to make the entire system work. Conversely, the lack of local deposits in Ireland was a serious problem (Guinnane, 1994). A defaulting borrower was in effect stealing his neighbor's savings. And the cooperative membership knew that a poorly run cooperative was not endangering the assets of some faraway lenders, but their own neighbors. Some credit cooperatives viewed the promotion of savings as a goal in itself. This aim reflected the broader notions of the cooperative movement; by encouraging households to save, the argument went, the cooperatives would encourage practices of thrift and rational household economy.

A final important difference between the German credit cooperatives and microfinance institutions today concerns their goals. Some micro lenders today, such as the Grameen Bank, have complex goals, some of which are almost explicitly ideological. Most *members* of German cooperatives had fairly prosaic goals: they wanted access to cheaper credit, or to help foster an institution they thought would contribute to their community's broader economic development. The cooperative *leadership* often stressed grander aims. Raiffeisen's group thought that his form of cooperative was an expression of "Christian charity", and, at some level, he thought cooperatives important to provide a bulwark against the encroachment of market forces in rural life. Many cooperative leaders thought that taking local deposits would foster habits of savings, which they thought a good in itself; certainly the "penny accounts" that many cooperatives operated could not have been worth the bookkeeping they required on a strict commercial basis. And Schulze–Delitzsch, among others, stressed the importance of cooperatives in preserving a middle class in Germany that he thought was, as crucial as it was, under threat in his time.

Of course, larger goals can also be pragmatic. We see this most clearly in the effort to use cooperatives as training grounds for business and community leaders. The urban cooperatives tended to hire paid staff to run the actual operation, although their members were actively involved on the boards that made all decisions. Rural cooperatives were more nearly run by their membership; most had a single, part-time employee. Cooperative leaders stressed their movement not just as a way to improve the incomes of their members, but to educate a new generation of men to be better business people and citizens. Cooperative manuals stressed issues such as basic accounting, double-entry bookkeeping, etc. because the people who ran them had little formal business training. But these general skills were quite transferrable. The thousands of cooperatives that existed at the outbreak of World War I each had a treasurer capable of running a small business, most of them trained by their own cooperative. The auditing associations and Centrals were another avenue of advancement; it was not uncommon for a local treasurer to go on to work full-time for one of the regional institutions.

By the 1920s, the career of banker and cooperative manager overlapped considerably.

3.1.1 *Financial cooperatives*

Another class of microfinance institutions today more nearly resemble the original German credit cooperatives. This is not surprising, because they, too are cooperatives. Brief comparison with the financial cooperatives operating in west Africa today conveys a sense in which they have chosen similar or different solutions to the problems facing the Germans. With a few exceptions, the basic structure is the same: both sets of cooperatives combine local institutions with regional networks that provide services to their member cooperatives. Two exceptions are interesting. The African cooperative groups today do not include non-credit cooperatives, thus implying that any lending to other entities (as opposed to households or businesses directly) goes outside the system. The African cooperatives are also much more tightly connected to the State. The ministry of finance or the central bank audit the cooperatives, instead of the cooperatives themselves. Perhaps more importantly, the State remains a source of financial support for the cooperatives, which, in the past at least, has brought about the State control that the German cooperators feared.

Two aspects of the current African situation pose limits for cooperatives that the Germans never faced. German cooperatives competed in some cases, with other banking institutions (such as the *Sparkassen*). A cooperative close to a savings bank office might find it harder to collect deposits because the state-guaranteed deposit-taker was so close. Most rural cooperatives, however, enjoyed enough distance from any alternative to give them something like a monopoly on local deposits. Cooperatives in Africa face competition from a completely different animal, the NGO. NGOs there are legally forbidden to accept deposits, but they can make loans. Given their access to aid from abroad, the NGOs present a type of competition that can be tough to meet for an institution that has to at least break even. A second challenge facing African cooperatives is the specificity of the law that governs their operations. German cooperatives today fall under the general banking law and thus must have acceptable liquidity parameters, etc. But, in the 19th century, no law governed the structure of their balance sheets or any other financial matters. Thus, they could, in rural areas, fund long-term loans with short-term deposits. The law governing African cooperatives today forbids such practices, meaning that these financial cooperatives can really only make short-term loans until they can find a way to raise more long-term investments.

A final comparison brings us back to the pawnshop. One reason for pawnbroking's power in rural areas was the fact that with this model, the lender need not monitor the borrower. The lender is broadly indifferent to whether the lender repays the loan — he has the pawn as collateral. Some discussions of credit cooperatives in rural German noted that the system would only work if incentives could be created to have members monitor *each other.* No lender could make cheap, small loans if paid staff had to engage in extensive monitoring. This, again, is one reason that financial cooperatives have proven to be the better model in west Africa. The very low population densities there make it impractical to use lending models that require employees to monitor borrowers. This is an important contrast to Grameen and other group lending institutions. For all their talk about group members monitoring each other, these lenders still rely on expensive, intensive interaction between staff and borrowing groups. This works well when population density is high, but not when population density is low (as in west Africa) or where density is low and transportation systems are rudimentary (as in Germany).

4 Conclusions

The microfinance institutions that now occupy a prominent place in development policy have a long history. Sometimes that history has not been recognized, while, at other times, too simple comparisons have produced a misleading picture of how microfinance today differs from its historical antecedents. This paper has focused on two types of historical lending. Pawnshops, which few today view as a reasonable lending model, were the major source of credit for poor and working-class Europeans for centuries. They predated the later lending institutions such as credit cooperatives; to some extent credit cooperatives, loan funds and other later lending models reflected the limits of pawn-based lending. One of the most successful of the "new" microfinance institutions were the German credit cooperatives. These institutions became very successful in Germany, and their methods formed the basis for cooperative movements in many other countries. The German cooperatives succeeded by adapting standard banking practice to the needs of the markets in which they operated. The rural cooperatives especially drew heavily on the social ties that characterized the places in which they operated, and were able to make loans that bankers would not. Some of what is held to be "new" about modern microfinance was characteristic of the German cooperatives.

References

Armendáriz de Aghion, B and C Gollier (2000). Peer group formation in an adverse selection model. *The Economic Journal*, 119(465), 632–643.

Armendáriz de Aghion, B and J Morduch (2000). Microfinance beyond group lending. *The Economics of Transition*, 8(2), 401–420.

——— (2005). *The Economics of Microfinance*. Cambridge, MA: MIT Press.

Banerjee, A, T Besley and TW Guinnane (1994). Thy neighbor's keeper: The design of a credit cooperative, with theory and a test. *Quarterly Journal of Economics*, 109(2), 491–515.

Besley, TJ and S Coate (1995). Group lending, repayment incentives, and social collateral. *Journal of Development Economics*, 46(1), 1–18.

Busche, M (1963). *Öffentliche Förderung deutscher Genossenschaften vor 1914*. Berlin: Duncker & Humblot.

Carruthers, BG, TW Guinnane and Y Lee (2009). Bringing "Honest Capital" to Poor Borrowers: The Passage of the Uniform Small Loan Law, 1907–1930. Yale University Economic Growth Center Working Paper 971.

Fairbairn, B (1994). History from the ecological perspective: Gaia theory and the problem of cooperatives in turn-of-the-century Germany. *American Historical Review*, 99(4), 1203–1239.

Faust, H (1977). *Geschichte der Genossenschaftsbewegung*, 3rd Ed. Frankfurt a.M.

Ghatak, M (2000). Screening by the company you keep: Joint liability lending and the peer selection effect. *Journal of Development Economics*, 110(465).

Ghatak, M and TW Guinnane (1999). The economics of lending with joint liability: Theory and practice. *Journal of Development Economics*, 60, 195–228.

Guinnane, TW (1994). A failed institutional transplant: Raiffeisen's credit cooperatives in Ireland, 1894–1914. *Explorations in Economic History*, 31(1), 38–61.

——— (1997). Regional organizations in the German cooperative banking system in the late nineteenth century. *Ricerche Economiche*, 51(3), 251–274.

——— (2001). Cooperatives as information machines: German rural credit cooperatives, 1883–1914. *Journal of Economic History*, 61(2), 366–389.

——— (2002). Delegated monitors, large and small: Germany's banking system, 1800–1914. *Journal of Economic Literature*, 40, 73–124.

——— (2003). A friend and advisor: External auditing and confidence in Germany's credit cooperatives, 1889–1914. *Business History Review*, 77, 235–264.

——— (2009a). State policy and the German cooperative movement: It Really was Self-Help. Working Paper.

——— (2009b). What's So Bad About Pawnshops? Thoughts on Modern Microfinance. Working Paper.

——— (2010). New law for new enterprises: The development of cooperatives law in Germany, 1867–1914. Working Paper.

Guinnane, TW, R Harris, N Lamoreaux and JL Rosenthal (2007). Putting the corporation in its place. *Enterprise and Society*, 8(3), 687–729.

Guinnane, TW and I Henriksen (1998). Why credit cooperatives were unimportant in Denmark. *Scandinavian Economic History Review*, 46(2), 32–54.

Herrick, MT and R Ingalls (1915). *Rural Credits: Land and Cöoperative.* New York: Appleton and Company.

Hollis, A and A Sweetman (1998). Microcredit: What can we learn from the past? *World Development*, 26(10), 1875–1891.

—— (2001). The life-cycle of a microfinance institution: The Irish loan funds. *Journal of Economic Behavior and Organization*, 46, 291–311.

Maddison, A (2003). *The World Economy: Historical Statistics.* Paris: OECD.

Morduch, J (1999). The microfinance promise. *Journal of Economic Literature*, 37, 1569–1614.

Mushinski, D and RJ Phillipps (2007). The role of Morris Plan lending institutions in expanding consumer microcredit in the United States. In *Entrepreneurship in Emerging Domestic Markets: Barriers and Innovation*, G Yago, JR Barth and B Zeidman (eds.), pp. 121–139. New York: Springer.

Raiffeisen, FW (1951) (1866). *Die Darlehnskassen-Vereine as Mittel zur Abhilfe der Noth der ländlichen Bevölkerung sowie auch der städtischen Handwerker und Arbeiter.* Neuwied.

Schulze–Delitzsch, H (1897). *Vorschuss- und Kredit-Vereine als Volksbanken* (6th ed), H Crüger (ed.). Breslau.

Understanding the Diversity and Complexity of Demand for Microfinance Services: Lessons from Informal Finance

Isabelle Guérin

Institut de Recherche pour le Développement-UMR 201
Project Leader of RUME and CERMi*

Solène Morvant-Roux

Department of Political Economy, University of Fribourg
RUME and CERMi

Jean-Michel Servet

Graduate Institute (IHEID), Genèva,
Institut de Recherche pour le Développement-UMR 201 and CERMi

There is growing consensus that microfinance supply is too standardised, inflexible and inadequate given the diversity of financial needs. As a result, microfinance is a very partial substitute for informal financial services and their comparative advantages.

This paper aims to deepen understanding of financial service demand by learning from informal finance. Based on economic anthropology, our analysis shows that microfinance does not substitute informal finance for many reasons: because money and informal finance are multidimensional and context specific; because the boundary between saving and borrowing is blurred; because money circulates in small quantities and quickly in village economies; because informal finance is more flexible; and, last but not least, because informal finance is a vector of social inclusion.

---

* Rural Microfinance and Employment: Do processes matter? http://www.rume-rural-microfinance.org/

The first part proposes a general analytical framework for understanding the social dimension of money, debt and saving. The second part describes some fundamental mechanisms of informal finance, whilst the third part uses this analytical framework to understand how people appropriate microfinance.

1 The Social Meaning of Money, Debt and Saving

Money is the economic object of study *par excellence*; the great equalizer, money is considered a means of individualization, destroyer of hierarchies, obliterator of statutory privileges. The fundamental role of money, defined as a unit of calculation and a standardised means of payment, is ostensibly to create contractual relationships between equals. But ethnological and historical analysis of monetary practices reveals that money's impersonality and anonymity is illusory (Baumann *et al.*, 2008; Bazin and Selim, 2002; Guyer, 1995; Villarreal, 2004; Bloch and Parry, 1989; Zelizer, 1994, 2005; Servet, 1984, 2006). Money, and the practices stemming from it, are above all a social construct. Money is Embedded in preexisting relationships governed by rights and obligations; relationships it can influence, but never destroy.

1.1 *Money: A source of tension between the individual and the group*

Money and finance are social institutions in that their access and use depends on conventions, norms and formal rules (Commons, 1989; Polanyi, 1968; Servet, 1984, 2006). Consequently, money is characterised by a permanent tension between the individual and the group, between personal aspirations and collective responsibilities. This ongoing tension takes several forms:

— Although economists generally define saving and indebtedness in terms of time, with the purpose of securing material gain, finance is often*a means of relating to the group or creating interpersonal bonds of dependence and domination.* When individual behaviours are not reduced solely to their economic dimension, going into debt or lending money is a sign of social inclusion. *Indebtedness and saving reinforces a sense of social belonging, whether characterized by domination, dependence or equality.* As a result, in some societies, it is important for money to change hands quickly. The poor often accumulate debt and credit and repay loans according to their own informal hierarchies (Shipton, 2007) and frameworks of calculation (Villarreal, 2004). Such phenomena transcend material or self-centred motivations and reflect issues of status, honour, power, and individual and group identity.

— Hoarding goes directly against the rationale that money must change hands, which is why non-monetary saving practices are so common, whether in kind or in the form of exchanges or loans to others. This same rationale explains why people tend to rank savings possibilities not only in terms of security but social considerations.
— The social dimension of finance does not preclude financial reasoning, in the economic sense of the term. Quite the opposite. The poor more than anyone need to keep accounts, calculate and anticipate. But they are not necessarily sensitive to the same criteria, constraints or rationale that apply to the wealthy. Interest rates, for example, are often addressed in a Manichean manner ("Are the poor sensitive or not to high interest rates?"). In fact, there are many ways to interpret interest rates. Some vernacular languages have no specific terms to designate the surplus a debtor pays a lender. In such cases, debt is seen not in relationship to time but in terms of commercial margin (Baumann, 1998) or as a fee (Collins *et al.*, 2009).
— Financial transactions imply inclusion in one or more social groups, but the nature of this affiliation is far from simple. Not only can an individual belong to several social groups, ranging from the customary (family, ethnicity, caste, gender, religion) to the constructed (professional, neighbourhood, associative groupings), but membership is constantly evolving. The variety and vibrancy of financial practices reflect this diversity.
— Understanding financial behaviours requires a temporal perspective. There are immediate needs associated with daily survival, needs associated with life-cycle events, needs associated with social and religious rituals, and needs that are investments over a lifetime or even several generations.

The claim that microfinance clients are "financially excluded" and in need of financial inclusion and money management skills only holds true from a formal sector standpoint. Take into account informal finance, and it becomes altogether dubious.

1.2 *Informal finance: Diverse practices and landscapes*

Informal finance has kept pace with the monetarisation and financialisation of contemporary societies (Servet, 2006), remaining vibrant and extraordinarily diverse. Indeed, the term "informal finance" — with its monolithic connotation — is almost meaningless: it makes more sense to refer to *informal financial practices* instead. Because informal financial practices evolve with society,[1] they are as diverse as the social settings where they are found. Their social Embeddedness makes them consistently distinctive, their diversity a tribute to humankind's imaginative and adaptive capacities.

Informal finance takes many forms, both collective and individual. Examples include rotating savings and credit associations (ROSCAs) and community organisations designed to cover funeral costs, collective celebrations or large community projects.

A multitude of private intermediaries also exist. We now know that the cliché of exploitative and greedy usurers, a caricature much-favoured by the media, decision makers and many MFIs, does not stand up to factual analysis. Professional lenders are only one category of a mosaic of lenders. First, there is the inner circle of neighbours, friends and family, probably used everywhere to varying degrees. The principles of solidarity and reciprocity prevail in such exchanges, organised such that everyone takes their turn as debtor and creditor.

Next, there are individuals who lend by virtue of their status or privileged access to cash. These include private specialised lenders, pawnbrokers, shopkeepers who accord credit, traders who pay for harvests in advance, manual labourer employers or recruiters who advance payment, and salespeople who sell goods on credit and then immediately buy them back for less. Also in this category are wholesalers who sell on credit to small shopkeepers, artisans or travelling vendors, and employers who lend to former apprentices wanting to start their own activity. Local elites — landowners, employers, teachers, civil servants, migrants or migrants' wives, local elected officials, religious leaders, doctors — may also wish to invest liquidity surpluses and/or extend their social network.

There are also those who safeguard money. Some are mobile and make house calls. Others have shops or simply belong to the saver's social network. Often, savings collectors are a more secure alternative to hoarding.

The prevalence and complementarily of these informal practices varies across regions and cultures according to legal, technical, cultural and social

[1]Before almost universal salarisation took place, informal financial ties were extremely common in European societies (Fontaine, 2008).

constraints. Hence the expression 'financial landscape' (Bouman, 1994), which seeks to account for the diversity and interconnectedness of different practices even between the so-called formal financial sector and informal financial practices.

Indeed, most societies do not function in terms of financial dualism, with the formal sector on one side and the informal on the other. People often move fluidly between the two, not only the poor, but middle and high-income populations as well.

The diversity of so-called "informal financial practices" stems from all these elements combined: the social Embeddedness of money, multiple group affiliation, the permanent tension between the individual and the group, and evolution of financial needs throughout the life-cycle. These elements help better understand how people *perceive* finance in their daily life, whether in the context of credit, saving or risk management. They also shed light on how people appropriate financial services offered by outsiders, and in particular microfinance institutions.

2 In What Ways Do People Perceive and Experience Finance?

Analysing so-called informal finance practices brings to light *la pensée sauvage* (the savage mind) — to employ Lévi–Strauss's expression — with respect to money, debt and saving. It reveals conventions, habits and local categories of thought, i.e., the ways people perceive and use finance.

2.1 *Saving and credit: A false dichotomy*

For a long time, the "poor" were considered incapable of saving. While it is true that monetary hoarding is often limited, there is no doubt the poor do save to protect themselves from future risk and anticipate certain expenses (Collins *et al.*, 2009; Lelart, 1990; Rutherford, 2001; Servet, 1996). These include recurring expenditures (school fees, religious festivals) and life-cycle costs (housing, birth, coming of age ceremonies, marriages, funerals, pilgrimages, etc.). On the other hand, their savings options — and the criteria they use to assess them — vary. Reasons for saving are also diverse and sometimes contradictory, given the permanent tension between social obligations and individual desires. The result is a plethora of complementary practices, sometimes impossible to substitute.

What accounts for the decision to use a particular form of saving? The following list is neither exhaustive nor definitive, reflecting only tendencies observed in several regions of the world. The importance of each factor varies according to context, social groups and individual behaviours.

— **Security/thrift:** saving's primary function. Goods acting as a form of saving must be able to be stored safely without risk of degradation or depreciation.
— **Access to liquidity**: in urgent need, cash should be quickly and easily accessible.
— **Social identity**: some acts of saving are more an expression of one's social identity than an individual act.
— **Anonymity and discretion**: when saving is for a personal project, anonymity and discretion come into play. Even in families where individual members pool part of their income for common expenses, individuals often have savings practices and networks of their own. The desire for discretion is particularly great amongst women, who often seek to preserve a space, however tiny, for themselves, free from male intervention.
— **Illiquidity and incentives**: saving is difficult not only because cash is short and income irregular; the poor often face pressure to spend. Torn by the demands from family members and a constantly needy entourage, people often say that cash "burns their fingers". Given this pressure, families often look for mechanisms which incite, or even force them to save.[2] This need can be so pressing that people are prepared to *pay* to save: hence the success of itinerant savings collectors in many countries. The same logic holds true for ROSCA members who prefer to receive their sum at the end of the cycle. To account for the tensions created by the ongoing balancing act between liquidity and illiquidity, individualism and group responsibility, Shipton (1995) conceptualizes this mechanism as the "squawk factor" which he describes in the Gambian context: "[...] saving strategies are mainly concerned with removing wealth from the form of readily accessible cash without appearing antisocial" (Shipton, 1995: 257).

[2]This type of behaviour was studied by anthropologists in the 1980s and 1990s (see, for example, Guyer (1995), Shipton (1995). Over the last few years, an increasing number of economists have been looking at this "preference for illiquidity". See for instance Bauer *et al.* (2008). See also Collins *et al.* (2009), Vonderlack & Schreiner (2002), Guérin (2006).

— **Speculation**: "Money needs to multiply", declare Indian women, explaining their membership in *seetu* (ROSCAs) or gold purchases. Similar ideas can be found in the practices of Cameroonian *tontines* or Chinese *hui*. Speculation often explains the preference for saving forms likely to appreciate over time, such as precious metals, cereals or cattle.

While saving forms vary from one context to another, monetary hoarding is a rarity. This is as much a question of safety as it is an effort to resist the temptation to spend and to ward off requests from one's entourage; furthermore, immobilized money serves no purpose. In the English language and particularly in the work of David Ricardo, the term "circulation" is used in reference to money. Indeed in Senegal, money is often said to "burn", it circulates so quickly (Guérin, 2003). Women frequently joke about the way money circulates without stopping: "Money, yes, we see a lot of it, but it never stays still for long". "As soon as it arrives, it leaves." No sooner is it received, it is spent, released into the community as an "investment", — the women's choice of term — liable to be recovered at any moment in the case of "pressing need" or "problem". To the question "do you save?", it is common for people to sincerely reply that they lend; it is considered a form of savings. In the indigenous communities of Mexico, all forms of wealth (not only coins and notes but also bricks, food products or cattle) may be loaned if the owner does not have an immediate need for them (Morvant-Roux, 2009). Shipton (1995) has made the same observation in rural Gambia, where the slightest riches, whether in cash or in kind, are loaned to conceal ownership and cement social bonds.

The logic of constant circulation of debt and credit is neither exotic nor archaic and the blurring of savings and loans is found throughout the world (Guyer, 1995; Lont and Hospes, 2004). In fact, borrowing is simply a means to force oneself to save in the future (Rutherford, 2001), just as lending is a form of saving that presupposes the right to borrow later. Microfinance institutions are but one of many strategies clients use when juggling various formal and informal finance opportunities accessible.

2.2 *ROSCAs: Individual projects and collective constraints*

ROSCAs are a common financial form that exemplify the melding of saving and credit simultaneously. ROSCAs exist around the world, but their modalities, function and nomenclature are specifically local. A vast body of literature confirms their extraordinary diversity and capacity to adapt to very different and rapidly evolving environments (Ardener, 1964; Ardener and Burman, 1996; Bouman, 1977; Servet, 1995; Lelart, 1990, 2005). However, the success of ROSCAs probably stems largely from their ability to address individual financial constraints collectively (Servet, 1996). Hence the low rates of default as members force themselves to make regular payments.

Members who receive their sum early in the cycle essentially receive uncollateralized loans from the others. If a debtor stops paying his or her share, s/he may be banished from the community, thus the importance of carefully selecting members, or at least the organiser. The organiser is responsible for defaulting members, even if this means tracking down the defaulter, or calling on the police and courts. This is where group and individual rationales intersect. The organiser must ensure the ROSCA's proper functioning while exercising his/her power to ensure the defaulter eventually repays. The obligation to pay, to use Marcel Mauss's expression from his famous *Essay on the Gift* (1923–1924), is stronger than most legal constraints. Not honouring one's word would amount to social suicide. ROSCA members know they must respect their obligations if they want to participate in other tontines or simply extend to other contexts the benefits of solidarity and protection that come with being a member in good standing. In ROSCAs, the act of saving is not about an individual relationship to time but rather a social relationship where reciprocal obligations are bound and unbound (Lelart, 1990; Baumann, 2003).

The subtle balance between individual and group needs takes other forms. ROSCAs permit members to ward off loan requests from family members, whilst still allowing them, at least in some cases, to respect social obligations (pilgrimages, ceremonies, support family members, etc.). In broad terms, ROSCAs express and contribute to the restructuring of social relationships. Indeed, various case studies on ROSCAs show how family ties are sometimes used and reinforced, but also avoided, substituted or even weakened, depending on the region and community (Ardener, 1995; Guérin, 2006).

2.3 *The circulation of money and juggling practices*

Money is constantly "lacking", but it also circulates with astonishing intensity. The tendency to take on debt clearly arises from a mismatch between income and expenses, but it is also a matter of maintaining credibility, one's reputation and social networks. Lending presupposes the two parties already share a relationship of trust, but it also serves to maintain, reinforce and renew this relationship.

When describing their financial practices, Senegalese women state: "*Sab bukki, sulli bushidô*" (take a hyena, bury a hyena) or "*sab-sul*" (dig and bury), meaning they take new debt to pay off old debt. They also speak of "drawers", whereby all the people or groups they lend to or do a favour for represent a "drawer" they can pull at any moment. In Mexico, Magdalena Villarreal describes women's credit chains, in which any income is largely used to repay old debts, to maintain credibility and thus borrow again later (Villarreal, 2002). Morvant-Roux (2006) demonstrates how in rural Mexico, more than a third of 239 interviewees were concurrently indebted to at least two distinct financial sources.

Permanent juggling practices should not always be understood as a sign of over-indebtedness or poor management. In many cases, they reflect deliberate choices and strategies geared to multiply and reinforce social relationships and maintain a certain balance, considering the inherent ambiguity of all debt relations. Ambiguous, because while debt is a source of protection and solidarity, as well as a means of expressing reciprocal trust and respect, when it is not honoured or is too imbalanced, it can be a source of humiliation, shame, exploitation and servitude. It is both a lifeline and a death knot, to employ the expression of Charles Malamoud (1980). Marcel Mauss speaks of gift as the "poison", which he assimilates to a form of loan. Hence the subtle game to regularly reduce one's debt whilst taking on debt elsewhere.

"Saving-loans" are always reciprocated (the lender eventually becomes the borrower and vice versa) and address both short-term survival needs and long-term social ones, like religious rituals, marriage, puberty or godparenting ceremonies, annual festivals or funerals. The exchange may take the form of cash or goods with social and symbolic value: jewels, clothing (*pagnes* in Senegal, *sarees* in India) or animals (cows among the Fulbe in Sub-Saharan Africa, pigs in Papua New Guinea and also in certain tribes in India (Thanuja, 2005), turkeys in Mexico (Morvant, 2006)).

2.4 *Flexibility and negotiability*

Many studies on how populations compare financial services have highlighted the importance of "negotiability", defined as the possibility to negotiate transaction modalities and, particularly, defer repayment deadlines (Rutherford, 2001; Johnson, 2004; Servet, 2006).

Negotiability is important for two reasons. The possibility to adapt repayments to irregular incomes and expenses is a key advantage, particularly if income fluxes are seasonal and uncertain (as in agricultural production or migration). But negotiability is also a way to personalise a social relationship.

The principle of standardised prices and terms allows for a contractual relationship between equals. The principle of negotiability, in contrast, expresses a personal relationship: here, the nature of the relationship and the relative statuses of the two parties influence the terms of the exchange. Anthropological literature has shown the extent to which not fixing prices *a priori* is standard practice (Bloch and Parry, 1989). What at first glance appears to be a lack of transparency is ultimately a form of protection against the anonymity of a commercial relationship in which the same price and terms apply to everyone (Toren, 1989). In Africa, during the second half of the 20th, century, Sarah Berry (1995) demonstrates that negotiability responds to two sources of major uncertainties: uncertainty linked to economic crisis and hyperinflation, but also uncertainty linked to the redefinition of the notion of "value", status, hierarchies and identities as a result of monetarisation and "modernisation" (education, migration). There is no shortage of information regarding the allocation of resources and wealth creation; what is lacking is an understanding of the *meaning* behind this information; after all, the permanent negotiation of prices is first and foremost a negotiation of *value*.

In Southern India, a study on quality of financial services involving 170 families showed that "negotiability" is the most valued criteria (highlighted by over a third of those interviewed). Next was cost (26 percent) followed by "discretion" (17 percent). Negotiability is a major component of informal finance, and "contracts" between creditors and debtors are often flexible: cost and duration are not always specified at the outset and are likely to evolve over time. Repayment methods can be adapted to the borrowers' or lenders' constraints and the latter may reclaim their due in an emergency. In vertical or hierarchical financial relationships (for instance loans from an employer, a landowner or member of the local elite), the debt relationship is but one component of a larger relationship, which often resembles a form of patronage. The lender's generosity and flexibility demonstrates his or her role as protector, but this protection is "repaid" by material and symbolic compensations (favours or free assistance at a moment's notice, patronage of a shop controlled by the lender, recognition and gratitude). In the case of itinerant lenders, transaction terms vary greatly on the basis of loyalty and trust (not unlike commercial relationships in the West which employ client loyalty strategies). Regular clientele benefit from the best terms (such as low prices or greater flexibility), as do those who act as guarantor for other clients — a very common practice, as trust is the main collateral. Benefiting from the best terms is implicit compensation for favours accorded.

Negotiability also applies to the loan amount. Microcredit providers usually demand regular interest payments along with the principal. Some informal private lenders demand only regular interest payments, whilst retaining their rights over the principal. Such arrangements can last several years. The term "rent" is more fitting than "interest" in this kind of financial relationship. As a strategy, it compares to owners renting out a house that they have no interest in selling, even if they sometimes change tenants. What matters is that the balance is periodically paid off.[3] The way the debt is settled depends on the context, era and nature of the relationship between the creditor and the debtor. Sometimes the debt is never settled and is even passed on to the following generation. Sometimes, it is ultimately cancelled, if the debtor manages to show that the total interest paid is enough (in India, for example, some creditors cancel debt when interest payments represents two or three times the principal). In other cases, the principal is paid back after a few months or years.

Our purpose is not to idealise this personalisation of debt relationships, which can affirm solidarity but also reinforce subordination. Sometimes extreme flexibility or debt cancelation conceals relationships of subjugation and exploitation. Rather, we seek to demonstrate that people *perceive* finance and manage their finances in this way.

3 The Role of Informal Financial Practices in the Appropriation of Microfinance

Analysing informal finance gives us a better understanding of how microfinance is used. Interestingly, the fluid boundaries between saving and lending show up in loan use. For example, clients commonly put aside a portion of microcredit for saving (in the form of liquidity, gold purchases, or loans to others, etc.).[4] It is not surprising that some MFIs struggle to collect savings: in many cases, informal practices better correspond to people's constraints

[3]This analogy has basis in fact. In India, in Bolivia and in Morocco for example, it is possible for a tenant to pay an owner a large sum of money in exchange for the occupation of a house. The owner must return this sum when the tenant leaves the property. If he does not, the tenant can retain possession of the house and can sublet it until the owner repays the debt.

[4]This is common practice in southern India. Sebstad and Cohen (2000) point to the same phenomenon in several regions of the world.

and motivations. Some noteworthy innovations do exist. For short-term saving, SEWA's home savings programme in Gujarat, operating successfully since the 1970s, comes to mind, as does SafeSave in Bangladesh, betting on flexibility and proximity since the 1990s. For long-term saving, SEWA offers saving accounts remunerated in gold. There are probably other innovations worthy of documentation. But much remains to be done to design services adapted to how people perceive saving. Moreover, many informal saving practices are so much more advantageous, that the attempt to substitute is often in vain.

Analysing informal finance also reveals how *microcredit* is used. Clients do not passively consume microcredit services. They translate and interpret them according to their own frame of reference, adjusting and adapting them, often bypassing the rules to do so. A process of appropriation takes place, both at the individual and collective level (Morvant-Roux, 2006).

3.1 *Borrowing to onlend: Abuse or a normal part of the system?*

Some studies have found clients use microcredit for money lending. Instead of investing in a so-called productive activity or covering a family expense, clients onlend to their entourage, often with interest. MFIs antagonistic to usurers naturally condemn such practices. In our opinion, however, onlending should not be automatically judged as a digression or anomaly of the system, but rather a natural (even rational) outcome.

For example, Perry (2002) has shown that in some rural zones in Senegal, the major impact of microfinance has been to create a new category of informal private lenders: middle class and poor women. The zone studied is characterised by reduced availability of credit due to a slowdown of cooperative banks and landowners moving away from agriculture to go into business and who no longer have liquidity to lend. In contrast, for several years now, microfinance has targeted women. A large number of loans are in fact onlent locally, mostly to the borrowers' extended male kin. Several reasons explain this phenomenon. Productive opportunities are limited and risky (entry barriers, weak local demand, activities highly segmented along gender lines), whilst men's demand for credit is high. At the same time, the women explain that they are fulfilling a social obligation by helping their kin and maintaining bonds of reciprocity which they will be able to rely on in times of need. This type of activity is lucrative, but not considered "immoral" by the community.

In India, the principle of the *self-help group* also leads to parallel lending. Borrowing to onlend is relatively common, but difficult to quantify because women know that MFIs condemn this practice. Disbursement dates do not necessarily correspond to a precise need, however, and women clearly state that they do not know what to do with their money and that onlending is a way to put it to good use. Group leaders and loan officers are also active lenders, but their role is in fact much broader and includes a number of additional services. Clients use the term "adjustment" to refer to these additional services.

Adjustment is when the group leader or loan officer introduces a degree of negotiability. It is difficult to obtain reliable data on repayment rates but it is likely that on-time repayment rates are relatively low (around 50 percent), and readjustments the rule rather than the exception. Official rates of 95 percent refer to nine or 12 months. Loan officers and group leaders negotiate and jointly decide readjustments. Adjusting can involve helping clients find additional credit sources when microcredit is insufficient (in the case of certain investments or health/ceremonial expenses) or disbursement delays are too long. Adjustment may be necessary when clients have trouble repaying their loan. In the absence of an official grace period, the loan officer or group leader's occasional assistance helps the borrower "save face" and maintain credibility. This may involve facilitating access to other credit sources by acting as guarantor for dealings with private lenders or physically accompanying women to certain transactions. This assistance may also consist of direct loans. The source of funds is not clear, but it appears common that money comes from the group itself. What might appear an abuse of the system is deemed legitimate by group members as long as they have regular access to liquidity. Members even expect this practice: efficient group leaders and loan officers should be able to make loans; it is their duty!

3.2 *Group lending: Internal arrangements and the reproduction of pre-existing practices*

Once considered a major innovation, group lending is increasingly criticized as overly rigid, incapable of adapting to diverse needs, a source of hidden costs, and catering to the better-off.[5] Our purpose is not to compare

[5]See, for example, Coleman (2006); Harper (2007); Mayoux (2001); Molyneux (2002); Morvant-Roux (2007); Rankin (2002); Wright (2006).

individual and group loans. Either one is likely to prevail, depending on context, target population, and the objective. Instead, we aim to show how group members adjust to the group ethos and adapt it to their own habits.

In Mexico, a study of *Grameen*-type groups highlighted various arrangements between members (Morvant-Roux, 2007). Whilst officially individual loan amounts are determined by the MFI, the actual distribution is often very different. For example, clients tend to ask for the maximum amount even if they do not need it; the difference is given to another group member (who is in charge of repayment). "This amount must not be wasted", justify clients. In India, analyses of SHGs gave similar results: whether for internal or external loans, financial circulation within groups is more intense than the account books indicate. Such lack of transparency is deliberate: the women are all implicated in multiple and mutual debt relationships they prefer not to reveal, to avoid suspicion or jealousy.

These appropriation practices occur all the more readily, given some groups tend to mirror pre-existing social and therefore financial networks. In Mexico as in India, our observations show that borrower groups are grafted over existing debt and credit relationships. To form groups, leaders select members based on need and solvency — information only available to people already in similar financial circuits. Such mutual knowledge is exploited when the groups are created. The goal is not to contort financial supply, but rather to address the diverse needs within the same borrower group.

This appropriation process is not entirely surprising. After all, the principle of group lending is to exploit borrowers' mutual knowledge to compensate for information asymmetry. However, this process has two major implications. On the one hand, it renders financial service supply more flexible and adaptable through informal arrangements among group members. On the other, it has the potential to increase preexisting inequalities in terms of financial access. It is not unusual for group leaders themselves to be or to become moneylenders. Similarly, several quantitative studies indicate microfinance clients already have the best access to informal finance (see the example of Thailand [Coleman, 2006], Mexico [Morvant-Roux, 2006], Bangladesh [Sinha and Matin, 1998]). The ambivalence of group lending — flexibility and negotiability but also the reproduction of power relationships — is also highlighted by Susan Johnson (2007) regarding SHGs in Kenya.

3.3 *Substitution or leverage effect?*

Ample literature demonstrates that microfinance does not substitute informal finance. Not only are microfinance clients already well integrated into informal circuits, they are agile jugglers of various forms of financing and cross-financing: microfinance is used to pay back the informal, and vice versa (Sinha and Matin, 1998; Roesch and Héliès, 2007). In rural Mexico, juggling is the rule rather than the exception. Informal lenders regularly make "bridging loans" which clients reimburse with part of their microcredit (Morvant-Roux, 2006, 2009).

These various studies analyse cross-indebtedness and the coexistence of microfinance and informal finance from a predominantly economic and financial perspective (transaction costs, flexibility, risk). We would add two further arguments.

Firstly, substitution is limited for economic and financial but also social reasons: cutting oneself off from certain sources of indebtedness would amount to social suicide. Exclusive dependence on a single provider is unfeasible — especially when the provider is a foreign institution. Such dependence would require unlimited confidence in the institution's ability to satisfy all financial needs in the long-term.

Indebtedness can occur in response to a need, but can also serve to maintain, reinforce or create a social tie. The choice of creditor can partly be explained by the desire to maintain, reinforce or create a bond, sometimes regardless of the cost: for instance, being indebted to an employer or a labour recruiter as a guarantee of getting work; being indebted to a member of the local elite to facilitate access to various forms of assistance (like governmental programmes); becoming indebted to a itinerant lender because s/he favours loyal clients; or quite simply becoming indebted to maintain a desired link for what it is (and not for what it can bring). Conversely, refusing a loan with *a priori* advantageous terms to avoid dependence is also common practice, particularly amongst certain employers, suppliers or private lenders but also with respect to the entourage or family. Some people prefer to become indebted to a costly private lender rather than "beg" from family members.

Secondly, it is our hypothesis that in certain contexts and for certain clients, microfinance not only does not substitute the informal, but has a leverage effect and thus increases informal access. Our inquiries in Southern India indicate that clients do not think in terms of substitution, but rather multiplication of finance sources (Guérin *et al.*, 2009a, 2009b). Before microfinance, households juggled with two or three different options; now they have five, six or even more. There is a true leverage effect via various routes:

- The repayment of past debts (depending on the zone and population, this represents between a tenth and a quarter of microcredit use[6]) can lead to contradictory effects. Using microcredit to repay an informal lender can have a substitution effect, but it is often temporary. It also serves to preserve the borrower's reputation and recover jewels or land pledged, allowing him or her to borrow again later from the same creditor.
- Improved creditworthiness among potential creditors. The indirect role of microfinance is confirmed both by SHG members and informal financial providers. Some women say that they remain microfinance clients to maintain creditworthiness vis à vis other creditors. Even if amounts are limited compared to what they can obtain elsewhere, some women use their status as a SHG members to convince private lenders.[7] Some door-to-door moneylenders explicitly state that members of SHGs are privileged clients for two reasons. Firstly, they know that the clients can request a microcredit in the event of repayment difficulties; conversely, they know that some SHG members will require their services in order to pay into their obligatory savings or for loan repayment. Studies conducted in Kerala confirm these findings (Sunil, 2005). Some door-to-door lenders even choose to visit the village on the day of the SHG meeting.
- Improved understanding of local financial markets. The financial market is diversified and dynamic. But it is also segmented and opaque. Information circulates through the SHG. (For instance, who are the "good" and the "bad" lenders? What arguments should one use during negotiations?) Women who are mobile and accustomed to borrowing stand as guarantors for others (in the case of door-to-door lenders or pawnbrokers, for example) — thus increasing their access. While such mutual assistance is common in SHGs, repayment obligations and joint responsibility reinforce this type of practice.

[6]These figures come from various studies carried out by the Institut Français de Pondichéry team in 2006 and 2007, which covered 1395 families, clients of various microfinance organisations, and recipients of 3457 loans.
[7]In Orissa, David Mosse (2005) has observed exactly the same phenomenon.

4 Conclusion

The empirical results discussed in this article highlight the limits of the dichotomized approach to informal and formal finance based on economic criteria (transaction costs, risk, interest rates, etc.). The enmeshed relationship between informal and formal financial practices explains, in certain contexts, the overindebtedness of populations who juggle more or less deftly available finance sources. Understanding this relationship calls for studies that address all facets of finance: not just economic, but cultural, political and psychological as well.

Microfinance practitioners are not totally unaware of these practices. It is not uncommon for MFIs to use ROSCA-style expressions in advertising new products, to name their institution after the village granary, or use logos that evoke the idea of a "good" community finance institution that does its clients favours and builds relationships between individuals. At the same time, "bad finance", epitomized by "usurers" who are, incidentally, also community-based, is vilified. Many MFIs have the mission of eradicating this "bad finance", even when the latter are themselves very good MFI clients. This discourse has always resonated amongst decision makers (Bouman, 1989) and continues to do so today. For example, the World Bank report *Finance For All* considers financial inclusion a process that allows for the gradual suppression of informal finance, deemed both inefficient and unfair (World Bank, 2007: 66). It is true that some forms of informal finance are a source of poverty entrapment and servitude, and that microfinance can help reduce unhealthy dependency by offering contract-based working capital and risk coverage. But microfinance can also reproduce preexisting local hierarchies, for instance, when monopolized by the better-off.

More broadly, to truncate informal finance to the exploitative usurer or greedy landowner is extremely reductive. Moreover, it ignores the questions of social construction, social Embeddedness and social meaning of informal finance.

Microfinance and informal finance should be considered as complementary and not as substitute. One of the main challenges of the microfinance industry is to better identify market niches where informal finance is not competitive and produces social and financial exclusion. As we have seen, people are permanently borrowing and lending tiny amounts, both for economical and social reasons. If these transactions were to be intermediated by microfinance institutions, transaction costs would be astronomical, and interest rates would be even higher. In theory, microfinance is supposed to make money available for medium and long-term financial needs (especially "productive" investment). Some innovations are worth noting, such as contractual savings (Churchill, 2007), commitment saving plans (Collins *et al.*, 2009), rural leasing or warrantage (Morvant-Roux, 2009b; Bouquet *et al.*, 2009). However these services are more the exception than the rule. Microfinance's ability to deal with risk in the long run still remains to be proved (especially in rural areas). In many cases, microcredit is still mainly used for short-term financial needs. A lot remains to be done to design financial services that could better complement the weaknesses of informal finance. This volume will certainly help to move this forward.

References

Aglietta, M and A Orléans (eds.) (1998). *La monnaie souveraine*. Paris: Editions Odile Jacob.

Aglietta, M and A Orléan (eds.) (1995). *Souveraineté et légitimité de la monnaie*. Paris: AEF/CREA.

Ardener, S (1964). The comparative study of rotating credit associations. *Journal of the Royal Anthropological Institute of Great Britain and Scotland*, 94(2), 201–29.

Ardener, S and S Burman (eds.) (1996). *Money-Go-Rounds: The Importance of Rotating Savings and Credit Associations for Women*. Washington DC: Berg.

Bauer, M, J Chytilová and J Morduch (2008). Behavioral Foundations of Microcredit: Experimental and Survey Evidence From Rural India. IES Working Paper 28–2008. Institute of Economic Studies, Faculty of Social Sciences, Charles University in Pragu.

Baumann, E, L Barin, P Ould–Ahmed, P Phelinas, M Selim and R Sobel (eds.) (2008). *L'argent des anthropologues, la monnaie des économistes*. Paris: l'Harmattan.

Baumann, E (2003). "Vulnerability and micro-insurance. Reflections on post- adjustment Africa". In *Microfinance: From Daily Survival to Social Change*, Guérin I and J-M Servet (eds.), 27–43. Pondicherry: Pondy Papers in Social Sciences.

Baumann, E (1998). Chez nous, c'est 15% par mois. Coût du crédit et représentation du temps en milieu populaire à Dakar. In *Rapport Exclusion et liens financiers 1997*, Servet J-M and D Vallat (eds.). 35–41. Paris: AEF/Monchrestien.

Bazin, L and M Selim (2002). Monnaie: Pluralités — contradictions. *Special issue of Journal des anthropologues*, 90–91.

Berry, S (1995). Stable prices, unstable values: Some thoughts on monetization and the meaning of transactions in West African economies. In *Money Matters: Instability, Values and Social Payments in the Modern History of West African Communities*, Guyer J (ed.), 299–323. London/Portsmouth (NH): Currey/Heinemann.

Bloch, M and J Parry (eds.) (1989). *Money and the Morality of Exchange*. Cambridge: Cambridge University Press.

Bouman, F (1995). Rotating and accumulating savings and credit associations: A development perspective. *World Development*, 23(3), 371–384.

Bouman, F (1994). Roscas and Ascras: Beyond the Financial Landscape. In *Financial Landscape Reconstructed: The Fine Art of Mapping Development*, F Bouman and O Hospes (eds.), pp. 22/1–22/10. Boulder, CO: Westview Press.
Bouman, F (1989). *Small, Short and Unsecured. Informal Rural Finance in India.* New Delhi: Oxford University Press.
Bouman, F (1977). Indigenous savings and credit societies in the third world: A message. *Savings and Development*, 3(4), 181–218.
Bouman, F and O Hospes (1994). *Financial Landscape Reconstructed: The Fine Art of Mapping Development*, Boulder, CO: Westview Press.
Bouquet, E, B Wampfler and E Ralison (2009). Rice inventory credit in Madagascar: Diversity of rural household strategies around an hybrid financial and marketing service. *RUME Working Paper 2009–02.*
Churchill, C (ed.) (2006). *Protecting the Poor: A Microinsurance Compendium.* International Labour Office, Geneva.
Coleman, BE (2006). Microfinance in Northeast Thailand: Who benefits and how much? *World Development*, 34(9), 1612–1638.
Collins, D, J Morduch, S Rutherford and O Ruthven (2009). *Portfolios of the Poor: How the World's Poor Live on $2 a Day.* Princeton: Princeton University Press.
Commons, JR (1989). *Institutional Economics. Its place in Political Economy.* New Brunswick, London: Transaction Publishers.
Dichter, T and M Harper (eds.) (2007). *What's Wrong with Microfinance?* Warwickshire: Practical Action Publishing.
Fontaine, L (2008). *L'économie morale.* Paris: Gallimard.
Guérin, I (2006). Women and money: Multiple, complex and evolving practices. *Development and Change*, 37(3), 549–570.
Guérin, I, RM Venkatasubramanian and O Héliès (2009a). Microfinance, endettement et surendettement. *Revue Tiers Monde*, 197, 131–146.
Guérin, I and RM Venkatasubramanian (2009b). Microfinance and informal finance: Substitution or leverage effects? *RUME Working Paper 2009–01.*
Guyer, J (ed.) (1995). *Money Matters. Instability, Values and Social Payments in the Modern History of West African Communities.* London/Portsmouth (NH): Currey/Heinemann.
Harper, M (2007). What's wrong with groups? In *What's Wrong with Microfinance?* Dichter T and M Harper (eds.), pp. 35–49. Warwickshire: Practical Action Publishing.
Johnson, S (2007). Institutionalized suspicion: The management and governance challenge in user-owned microfinance groups. In *What's Wrong with Microfinance?* Dichter T and M Harper (eds.), pp. 61–72. Warwickshire: Practical Action Publishing.
Johnson, S (2004). Gender norms and financial markets: Evidence from Keyna. *World Development*, 32(8), 1355–1374.
Lelart, M (1990). Les circuits parallèles de financement: État de la question. In *L'entrepreneuriat en Afrique francophone: Culture, financement et dévelopement.* Hénault, G and M M'Rabat (eds.), 45–65. London/Paris: John Libbey/Aupelf-Uref.
Lelart, M (2005). *De la finance informelle à la microfinance.* Paris: AUF Editions, collection "Savoirs francophones".
Lont, H and O Hospes (eds.) (2004). *Livelihood and Microfinance. Anthropological and Sociological Perspectives on Savings and Debt.* Delft: Eburon Academic Publishers.
Malamoud, C (ed.) (1980). *La dette.* Paris: Ecole des Hautes Etudes en Sciences sociales (coll. *Purusartha*, Vol. 4).

Mauss, M (1993). Essai sur le don. In *Sociologie et anthropologie*, Mauss M (ed.), 145–272. Paris: PUF.

Mazzucato, V and D Niemeijer (2004). Saving arrangements in eastern Burkina Faso: An evolutionary perspective on institutional innovation. In *Livelihood and Microfinance. Anthropological and Sociological Perspectives on Savings and Debt*, Lont H and O Hospes (eds.), pp. 153–170. Delft: Eburon Academic Publishers.

Molyneux, M (2002). Gender and the silences of social capital. *Development and Change*, 33(2), 167–188.

Morvant-Roux, S (2009). Accès au microcrédit et continuité des dynamiques d'endettement au Mexique: Combiner anthropologie et économétrie. *Revue Tiers Monde*, 197, 109–130.

Morvant-Roux, S (ed.) (2009b). *Microfinance pour l'agriculture des pays du Sud, Rapport Exclusion et liens financiers 2008–2009*. Paris: Economica.

Morvant-Roux, S (2007). Microfinance institution's clients borrowing strategies and lending groups financial heterogeneity under progressive lending: Evidence from a Mexican microfinance program. *Savings and Development*, 2, 193–217.

Morvant-Roux, S (2006). Processus d'appropriation des dispositifs de microfinance: Un exemple en milieu rural mexicain. Thèse de doctorat en sciences économiques, Université Lumière Lyon 2.

Mosse, D (2005). *Cultivating Development. An Ethnography of Aid Policy and Practice.* London: Pluto Books.

Perry, D (2002). Microcredit and women moneylenders. The shifting terrain of credit in rural Senegal. *Human Organization*, 61(1), 30–10.

Polanyi, K (1968). *Primitive, Archaich and Modern Economies.* Boston: Beacon Press.

Rankin, KN (2002). Social Capital, Microfinance and the Politics of Development. *Feminist Economics,* 8(1), 1–24.

Roesch, M and O Helies (2007). La microfinance: Outil de gestion du risque ou de mise en danger par sur-endettement? *Revue Autrepart*, 44, 119–140.

Rutherford, S (2001). *The Poor and their Money.* Oxford: Oxford University Press.

Sebstad, J and M Cohen (2000). Microfinance, risk management and poverty. Washington DC, USAID AIMS Project.

Servet, JM (2006). *Banquiers aux pieds nus: La microfinance.* Paris: Odile Jacob.

Servet, JM (1996). Community relations, individual, social and economic constraints in the savings and loans associations. In *The Milano Papers*, Cangiani M (ed.), pp. 165–185. Montreal/London: Black Rose Books.

Servet, JM (ed.) (1995). *Épargne et liens sociaux. Études comparées d'informalités financières.* Paris: AEF/AUPELF–UREF.

Servet, JM (1985). Un système alternatif d'épargne et de prêt: Les tontines africaines. *Reflets et perspectives de la vie économique*, 24, 13–23.

Servet, JM (1984). *Nomismata. Etat et origines de la monnaie.* Lyon: Presses Universitaires de Lyon.

Shipton, P (2007). *The Nature of Entrustment. Intimacy, Exchange and the Sacred in Africa.* New Haven & London: Yale University Press.

Shipton, P (1995). How Gambians save: Culture and economic strategy at an ethnic crossroad. In *Money matters. Instability, Values and Social Payments in the Modern History of West African Communities*, Guyer J (ed.), pp. 245–277. London/Portsmouth (NH): Currey/Heinemann.

Shishir, S and S Chamala (2003). Moneylender's positive image. Paradigms and rural development. *Economic and Political Weekly*, 43(16), 1513–1519.

Sinha, S and I Matin (1998). Informal credit transactions of microcredit borrowers in rural Bangladesh. *IDS Bulletin*, 29(4), 66–80.

Sunil, R (2005). Microfinance, informal finance and empowerment of the poor. In: *Microfinance Challenges: Empowerment or Disempowerment of the Poor?*, Guérin, I and J Palier (eds.), pp. 173–182. Pondicherry: Editions of the French Institute of Pondicherry.

Thanuja, M (2005). Relevance of microfinance and empowerment in tribal areas: A case study of Konda Reddis. In: *Microfinance Challenges: Empowerment or Disempowerment of the Poor?*, Guérin, I and J Palier (eds.), pp. 63–81. Pondicherry: Editions of the French Institute of Pondicherry.

Toren, C (1989). Drinking cash: The purification of money through ceremonial exchange in Fiji. In *Money and the Morality of Exchange*, Bloch M and J Parry (eds.). 142–164. Cambridge: Cambridge University Press.

Villarreal, M (2004). Striving to make capital do "economic things" for the impoverished: On the issue of capitalization in rural microenterprises. In *Development Intervention: Actor and Activity Perspectives*, Kontinen T (ed.), pp. 67–81. Helsinki: University of Helsinki.

Villarreal, M (2000). Deudas, drogas, fiado y prestado en las tiendas de abarrotes rurales. *Desacatos* (3), 69–88.

Vonderlack, R and M Schreiner (2002). Women, microfinance, and savings: Lessons and proposals. *Development in Practice*, 12(5), 602–612.

World Bank (2007). *Finance for All? Policies and Pitfalls in Expanding Access.* A World Bank Policy Research Report. Washington DC: The World Bank.

Wright, K (2006). The darker side to microfinance: Evidence from Cajamarca, Peru. In *Microfinance. Perils and Prospects*, Fernando J (ed.), pp. 154–172. London: Routledge.

Zelizer, V (2005). *The Purchase of Intimacy.* Princeton: Princeton University Press.

Zelizer, V (1994). *The Social Meaning of Money.* New York: Basic Books.

Ethics in Microfinance

Marek Hudon
Solvay Brussels School of Economics and Management,
Université Libre de Bruxelles (U.L.B.), SBS-EM, Centre Emile Bernheim;
CERMi; Burgundy School of Business

1 Introduction

Microfinance is sometimes presented as an obvious ethical response to financial exclusion in developing countries. Since microfinance institutions (MFIs) target citizens excluded from the financial sector, presumably among the poor segment of the population, microfinance has been historically supported by donors. Later on, the sector has been praised as a socially responsible investment trying to fulfil its double bottom line: the social one, thanks to the poverty of the clientele and the financial one, thanks to the profits generated by the largest MFIs.

While recent evidence has raised major concerns in the microfinance sector, very little research is done on ethical issues in microfinance, contrary to research topics such as microfinance contracts or the efficiency of MFIs. Let us therefore start by defining the scope of this essay. Ethics is the discipline that studies the moral standards of a society. In line with traditional ethical analyses (Velasquez, 2006), we can distinguish three main kinds of ethical issues in microfinance in order to disentangle the moral responsibility of each actor.

The first is systemic issues questioning the economic, social, legal or political systems within which microfinance emerges. Some have pinpointed the impact of capitalism or neo-liberal policy reforms on microfinance activities (e.g., Weber, 2006). Due to the historical exclusion from credit in most developing countries and the very high rates charged by informal actors, microfinance proponents considered that microcredit may intrinsically bring social benefits since MFIs charge lower rates than moneylenders. For instance, the Microcredit Summit considers without restriction that "microcredit allows families to work to end their own poverty — with dignity". Moreover, simple participation in the group methodology was often considered a proxy for empowerment and assumed to always generate social capital (Rankin, 2006).

Microfinance has, however, been regularly criticised in the gender studies literature and sometimes considered as a way to put an additional burden on the women's shoulders. For example, Goetz and Sen Gupta (1996) report that only a minority of loans are either fully or significantly controlled by women, where "significant control" does not include control over marketing, and may thus imply little control over the income generated.

The second kind consists of individual issues raised about the behaviour of an individual, such as the nature of the pressure exerted by a credit officer to get the weekly instalment of a borrower. The third kind of ethical issues includes corporate or institution issues raised about a particular institution as it was the case in the debates around the Compartamos strategy. This paper will mainly focus on corporate issues, issues questioning the morality of these activities, policies or organisational structure of an enterprise as a whole (Velasquez, 2006). Most of these issues in microfinance are related to some strategy decisions such as the population targeted or the pricing. These three categories can be linked, since many individual cases are someway related or due to corporate decisions. Similarly, corporate issues, such as pricing, are related to more general norms of conduct in a sector.

Following this introduction, the next section will provide some basic ethical justification of microfinance. Many of these justifications are based on consequentialist arguments related to the activity and the management of MFIs: the relative poverty of the clientele, the intrinsic advantages of credit compared to other policies such as the grants or the additional margin due to cheaper rates in comparison to moneylenders.

In the third section, we will present some challenges of the intrinsic ethical dimensions of this sector. While some of the criticisms are related to corporate or individual cases, such as the behaviour of credit officers or managers, some others deeply challenge the whole sector and its impact, e.g., the recent studies on over-indebtedness.

Special attention will then be devoted to the debate concerning the level of microfinance interest rates since it is one of the most controversial issue in the sector. More specifically, we will present a few perspectives on what a just price would be when lending to the poor. In the fifth section, we will discuss Yunus's proposal of a right to credit as a radical solution to an ethical concern. He suggests a rights-based approach of microcredit that puts credit as part of a global rights-based approach, which is therefore a systemic issue. After an analysis of these ethical issues, we will finally show how new policies such as codes of conduct could help the sector to self-regulate, particularly to address corporate issues while limiting individual issues.

2 Ethical Justifications of Microfinance

Microfinance has almost simultaneously emerged in two very different areas in Asia and Latin America: Bangladesh on the one hand, and Brazil and Bolivia on the other. Even if these areas are very different, they, however, both share the characteristics that the innovation materialised from NGO-based projects. The sector has probably benefited from this link to civil society. While many state-owned programmes such as rural banks or credit projects had failed in the past, the development of a grassroots-level initiative has attracted attention from many donors. Moreover, the strong leadership of local microfinance actors such as Muhammad Yunus (Grameen) or Poncho Otero (Accion) has reinforced the legitimacy of the sector.

The primary ethical justification of microfinance comes from three majors arguments. The first one is directly related to the poverty of those financially excluded by traditional financial institutions. In many countries, financial institutions only target the wealthy, leaving behind the majority, or a large part, of the population. The originality of microfinance may be related to the double bottom line of MFIs including both social and financial performances. Very few MFIs pursue a narrow goal of profit maximization (Copestake *et al.*, 2005) and a vast majority focus on the poor, who are financially excluded by banks (Morduch, 1999). The poverty status of the clientele is a first normative justification of microfinance activity. Moreover, microfinance could bring about innovative contracts such as joint liability group lending and new attitudes towards the poor but also more care about the subsidies. It could therefore be a "win-win" policy where both clients and institutions profit (Morduch, 1999).

The second argument is partly related to the first one, and concerns the financial product itself: credit. Contrary to grants or direct subsidies, credit involves compensation and therefore responsibility and dignity in the use of the financial instrument (Armendariz and Morduch, 2005). Many practitioners argue that this compensation provides some dignity to the poor since they would become regular clients of a financial institution.

The third argument concerns additional financial margins gained with microfinance. These margins can come from profits generated, thanks to business growth and the fact that microcredit is normally cheaper than what they used before to finance their activity (McKenzie and Woodruff, 2006; de Mel *et al.*, 2008). Indeed, since most of the poor are not served by formal institutions, they have to use other sources of financing, notably cooperatives or very often informal lenders such as moneylenders or pawnbrokers. Since these lenders charge exorbitant rates, microentrepreneurs are either not able to develop their activities, or at least obliged to leave a large part of the surplus generated by their activity to these lenders. Microfinance offers cheaper funds and thus increases the potential for microentrepreneurs to diversify their business or simply scale up their activities. Recent surveys have for instance shown that access to credit is correlated with economic development (Beck *et al.*, 2006) and disproportionally helps the poor since their incomes grow faster than average per capita GDP growth (Beck *et al.*, 2006).

This argument, based on the direct impact of microfinance, uses a traditional consequentialist approach, which is probably the most frequent approach for microfinance practitioners. As explained by Sinnott–Armstrong (2006), consequentialism deems whether an act is morally right on the sole basis of its *consequences*. Fernando (2006a) pinpoints that most of the positive claims about microcredit are based on quantitative indicators such as the number of borrowers and lending institutions, and loan repayment rates. A good example of a consequentialist approach can be found in Dean Karlan's approach of microfinance as explained in the *Financial Times* in December 2008: "If you're trying to make the world a better place but you're not, that's bad. If you're trying to make profits and don't care about people, but make them better off anyway, that's good".[1] Consequentialism is therefore opposed to views concentrated on the "circumstances or the intrinsic nature of the act or anything that happens before the act" (Sinnott–Armstrong, 2006). For instance, the usury laws that fix high interest rates to protect very poor citizens, regardless of the impact of the credit, are a counter example of consequentialist thinking.

[1]Harford, T (2008). The battle for the soul of microfinance. *The Financial Times.* (6 December 2008).

3 Challenges of the Intrinsic Ethical Dimension of Microfinance

While microfinance has boomed during the last few years in terms of number of clients and number of loans or outstanding loans, the picture is not always as bright. In this section, we will give four examples of issues challenging the intrinsic ethical dimension of MFIs.

Firstly, microfinance has been occasionally criticised for the collection practices of MFIs or practices such as the public repayment of clients that can potentially stigmatise the very poor. Another concern is related to the lack of concern for those who stop being clients after having participated in microfinance programmes. For instance, Matin and Helms (2000) found that there are now more MFI dropouts in East Africa than there are active clients! Moreover, the reasons behind these dropouts are not always well understood. Since MFIs put more emphasis on standardisation than on the clients' needs, the mismatch between supply and demand is a potential explanation (Cohen, 2002).

Unethical practices have been denounced mostly since 2005. In 2006, district authorities in the Indian Andhra Pradesh State closed around 50 branches of two major MFIs. These criticisms relate to both corporate (ethical) issues, such as interest rates, and individual issues such as aggressive recovery practices. Other branches of large MFIs have been closed by authorities in Ecuador and Nicaragua since MFIs charged exorbitant rates, collected payments unethically, and hid rates from clients (Counts, 2008). These charges have been heavily contested in the sector, microfinance becoming a political tool of populist governments, according to local practitioners. Nevertheless, in light of such crackdowns, these ethical issues are now widely accepted by all as a major threat to the sustainability of the entire microfinance sector, what we can call the social sustainability of the sector.

Secondly, the interest rates and large profits of some major MFIs have refuelled an old debate in the sector on the trade-off between social and financial returns. There is, however, a fear that the commercialization of microfinance could lead to an over-preoccupation with profitability at the expense of poverty reduction and other development goals (e.g., Christen and Drake, 2002; Copestake, 2007). While new policies, such as a diminution in the costs of providing services, can simultaneously improve both financial and social performances, many management decisions entail a trade-off between them over time (Copestake, 2007). Commercialization and the related need to increase efficiency involve many risks and create a conflict between efficiency and outreach, implying that the strife to increase efficiency reduces the scope for lending to the poor (Hermes *et al.*, 2008). While the indicators used to measure financial performance are well-known, these indicators do, however, not reveal the institutional processes through which they have been achieved. In response to the push towards financial sustainability, microfinance NGOs are rapidly transforming their internal organizational practices and hiring professionals with high salaries. This has led to tensions between the various stakeholders of some NGOs (Fernando, 2006a). Similarly, there is a fear that financial sustainability imperatives could have led microfinance institutions to be less engaged in the time-consuming processes of consciousness and empowerment (Rankin, 2006).

A very notorious case related to this debate is Banco Compartamos in Mexico. Compartamos is well-known for its impressive growth rate, but also for its high interest rates. At the end of 2005, Compartamos was charging high interest rates of 86 percent p.a., net of taxes on its loans to the poor. These high interest rates were partly due to the low size of their loans and the related high transaction costs. Nevertheless, what seems to be low competition on price among Mexican MFIs allowed them to generate a high profit margin. Indeed, 23 percent of these 86 percent p.a. were pure profits, the result being that 40 percent of Compartamos assets came from retained benefits (Rosenberg, 2007). This policy, therefore, allowed for high profitability in comparison with traditional Mexican banks and for a booming book value of the shares that reached 21 times the paid-in capital by December 2006. In April 2007, Compartamos issued shares in a secondary offering IPO. Thirty percent of existing shares were sold at 12 times their book value to new investors, providing existing shareholders with a net profit of about 460 million dollars. The selling investors included NGOs such as Compartamos AC and ACCION, as well as IFC, the private lending arm of the World Bank group. Private individuals, who held a minority of shares, captured over $150 million from the sale (Ashta and Hudon, 2009). The backlash from Compartamos IPO was accusations on usurious interest rates and unfair policy favouring shareholders.

Finally, overindebtedness of vulnerable clientele has been recently denounced. Many worry that microcredit could push borrowers into debt beyond their repayment capacities and therefore leave them worse off (Hulme, 2000). Drawing on data collected in rural South India, Guérin *et al.* (2009) observe that microfinance "is a double-edged sword". Their data indicate that microfinance can indeed reduce the financial vulnerability of households, but can also push them further into debt. Overindebtedness of the clientele can also be due to multiple loans in various MFIs (or other informal and formal actors) or simply the incapacity of the client to repay the interest rates. Credit bureaus have been advocated so that MFIs share their databases to avoid overindebtedness. Nevertheless, credit bureaus are still exceptions in the microfinance world, probably because MFIs are sometimes reluctant to share information with competitors.

4 Fair Interest Rates in Microcredit

The debate on the importance of interest rates has long been a contested issue in both ethical and economic literature. It is well-known that comparing interest rate levels is very difficult. Many elements differ from one place or one situation to the other, such as the cultural and historical aspects, the lenders' social and economic environments, customs, taxes, currencies or laws (Homer and Sylla, 2005).

Egalitarian economists have always argued that interest rate levels matter since they represent a major mechanism of inequality in the distribution of income. This question certainly is relevant for the interest rates on loans since they are less equally divided than either aggregate incomes or employee compensations.

The appraisal of fair interest rates is even more complicated since interest rates are not the sole costs related to the microcredit. Microfinance borrowers must sometimes take other products, or respect some rules such as mandatory savings during a few months previous to the loan. Frequently, microfinance clients also have to pay some fixed fees on top of the interest rates that can represent a large part of the total costs.

Besides these costs, the most expensive charge is sometimes not related to the interest rate or to fees but to transaction costs due to the loan methodology (Collins *et al.*, 2009). Transaction costs are not always optimally lowered, even if the basic model of microcredit designed by Professor Yunus in Bangladesh emphasizes lowering transaction costs (thanks to the peer review of the members of the group). Many MFIs even experience an increase in transaction costs over time (Zeller, 2000). Moreover, the feeling of fairness, even if irrational, can play a major role in such a transaction.

While microfinance practitioners are used to the high interest rates of microcredit, these rates have always been debated by outsiders of the microfinance sector. While the clientele of MFIs is poor, average interest rates of 30 percent or 35 percent are very often described as usurious by people not active in the sector, particularly developmental NGOs, who regularly challenge the intrinsic assumptions behind high interest rates that most poor people would be able to generate this level of profits with their activity.

The sector has defended the interest rates policy with a few arguments. The high transaction costs related to the lending methodology and the small size of the loans are the most typical explanations given to the general audience. Many donors, experts or managers of MFIs also deemphasized the debate on interest rates, arguing that the access to credit is the most important issue, and that the high turnover of the activities of poor clients enables them to repay such high interest rates. For instance, Harper (1998) explains that the return on investment in larger businesses was generally lower than in smaller ones. In line with these arguments, Fernando (2006b) considers that the two main actions donors should conduct on interest rates are: promoting an enabling environment for MFIs, and encouraging the entry of different kinds of institutions to foster competitive markets. The rationale is that through the entry of new actors or increasing competition, interest rates would automatically decrease. Moreover, one should not forget the heated historical debates around interest rates of microfinance and the strong influence of Ohio School scholars. Representative of this debate is the seminal book *Undermining Rural Development with Cheap Credit* by Adams *et al.* (1984), written in response to the existing state of affairs in which the rural poor had access to low but highly subsidized interest rates. Therefore, they argued that cheap credit would destroy the incentive to save and, as a result, distort the way lenders look to allocate funds (Adams *et al.*, 1984, p. 75). The rationale was that "low interest rates on loans to rural people end, paradoxically, by restricting their access to financial services" (Von Pischke, 1983, p. 176).

Nevertheless, the current spread of interest rates in the sector, ranging from subsidised rates between 0 and 15 percent to more than 80 percent or 100 percent, show the diversity not only of environments where microfinance spreads, but also of appraisal of what interest rates should normatively be in microfinance. Moreover, the (financial) sustainability of the MFI, which would be the cheaper source of funds for the borrowers, would be more important than price since any collapse would leave the borrowers no other choice than to resort to moneylenders. "Access is more important than price" is therefore a very frequent argument. This position is often related to Adam Smith's position on the market. It is well-known that Adam

Smith considered the pursuing of one's own interest as a way of promoting the interests of civil society. In fact, he thought personal interest was more socially effective than premeditated social responses such as, for example, when one tries to promote social interest for its own sake (Smith, 1776, p. 400). Through the market and Smith's own "system of natural liberty", it appears that divergent interests actually end up synchronized. Smith was, however, in favor of the state restricting interest rates. Smith wanted a law in place that would fix interest rates in order to prevent the practice of extortion within usury (Smith, 1776, p. 376).

The question is then: To what extent do concerns about the institution's operation and sustainability come into conflict with the ideal of providing the lowest possible cost to the customer? As argued by Copestake (2007), raising microcredit interest rates may well improve financial performance, but it is likely to be at the expense of current social performance since net benefit per client will be reduced, as well as a possible short-term reduction in the breadth and depth of outreach. Nevertheless, the debate touches not only upon commercialization of the sector and, more particularly, the transformed and for-profit MFIs, but also upon NGOs. Indeed, MFIs registered as NGOs seem to offer more expensive interest rates than the other MFIs (Cull *et al.*, 2009), which represents a potential drawback, even if they are working with poorer clients that are more costly to reach and thus offer more expensive rates to poorer clients.

The debate on fair price when lending to the poor is central in microfinance since microcredit interest rates of sustainable MFIs will probably always be higher than traditional banks. E. Rhyne, vice-president of Accion, defines fair pricing as that which "allows the institution to operate as a (on)going concern, but at the same time is as low cost to the customer as possible" (Accion, 2004). The dominant concern in this definition is the institution's growth and profitability, while the fairness to customers comes second since, if there is a trade-off between the institution and the borrower, the interest rates must still be sufficient for the institution to operate sustainably.

Rosenberg *et al.* (2009) argue that an interest rate for microcredits is considered "unreasonable if it not only covers the costs of lending but also deposits 'excessive' profits into the pockets of the MFI's private owners". In this definition written after Compartamos's backlash of private profits, the rates must cover the costs (the operational sustainability) and yield a reasonable profit, but the way to assess it is not yet clear.

Laureate M. Yunus considers that microfinance institutions charging higher rates than the costs of funds plus a 15 percent margin should be considered as imitating money lending activity (RESULTS, 2006). He, therefore, restricts the spread of interest rate due to transaction costs to a maximum of 15 percent, which is likely to put many, if not most, MFIs among money lending activities if we look at databases such as the *Microbanking Bulletin*.

Other practitioners consider high repayment rates and repetitive loans as instrumental proxies of fairness. High repayment and constant demand would reflect the affordability of the loans and thus, its fairness. If a client decides to take these microcredit, repay them and often take additional loans, then the service must be very valuable to him (Hudon, 2007). Finally, Sandberg (2009) estimates that while it certainly would be preferable if MFIs could reduce their interest rates, the responsibility for creating an environment where microfinance interest rates could be lower should more fruitfully be said to rest on governments, the international political community, commercial banks or overseas investors.

All these definitions share a trade-off between the institutions' and the clients' interests. Moreover, they also imply a trade-off with the interest of other stakeholders. It could therefore be misleading to assess the fairness of interest rates without taking into account the net social benefits for all the stakeholders of the MFIs, and not only the shareholders and the clients but also the staff, for instance. We should indeed not forget that, for instance, for an institution that is not subsidized and which works in very competitive environments, very low interest rates could be beneficial for borrowers, but, in contrast, mean very low wages for its staff.

5 Rights-based Approach to Microfinance[2]

Rights are increasingly promoted in development discourses and microfinance makes no exception. They often question systematic ethical issues such as the socio-political framework of our societies. Economic and social rights have been established in an international covenant, which was adopted by the UN General Assembly in 1966.

In many of his speeches, Muhammad Yunus argues that credit should be a human right. He considers that self-employment and the liberty to

[2]This section draws on Hudon (2009).

unleash one's own potential is a fundamental human right. Peachey and Roe (2004) consider access to financial services to be on a similar level as access to basic needs such as safe water, health services, and education. Even if access to credit and savings schemes is sometimes quoted as a an instrumental measure to ensure some rights, no direct reference to access to the financial market is done in the International Covenant on Economic, Social and Cultural Rights or the Universal Declaration of Human Rights.

The basic argument when one wants to justify the formulation of an additional right is that by creating this new right, the holders of the right will be definitively better-off. Most proponents of a universal access to credit consider that credit is instrumental to create income and to get out of poverty, which is, again, a consequentialist approach. To justify an additional right, the instrumental argument is thus that the access to credit would specifically make a dent for the poor and not other elements related to the characteristic of the client.

Recent surveys have indeed shown that financial development disproportionately helps the poor, since their incomes grow faster than average per capita GDP growth. Furthermore, the use of financial services offered by traditional financial institutions is associated with the classic economic development indicators.[3] Recent research, however, shows that the impact of credit depends on a few elements, such as the credit use, the type of activity or the wealth of the borrower. In some instances, credit has not reduced the poverty level of the borrower but, on the contrary, put him in overindebtedness (Guérin *et al.*, 2009, Fernando, 2006a; Rahman, 1999).

In short, based on the condemnation of the social effects of financial exclusion, a right to credit has a potentially radical effect. It is, however, likely to be counterproductive and difficult to implement.

6 Policies and Practices Addressing Ethical Issues

Following major backlashes, such as in South India or in the Compartamos case, a few principles have been recently agreed as part of the social responsibility of MFIs. A major principle concerns pricing transparency. As many

[3] For economic data on these issues, see, for instance, Beck *et al.* (2006). A main limitation of existing evidence, however, is that they are all limited to banking institutions and ignore other financial service providers, such as microfinance institutions or cooperatives.

clients are illiterate or not always able to calculate the real costs of loans, there is a consensus that microcredit interest rates must be transparent and include hidden fees or any additional burden that the clients could not easily identify. Transparency of pricing is therefore not only an ethical imperative to avoid overindebtedness, but also essential to good management.

In order to avoid public intervention and regulation, MFIs leaders and some of their key donors have started to argue for codes of conduct. The most famous example is the Pocantico Declaration in May 2008 calling for standards on "consumer protection, social performance, pricing transparency, and promotion of financial literacy through client education". While the Pocantico Declaration emphasizes the need to develop a code of ethics for microfinance, it does not provide specifics on ethical principles that a code should embody, and does not offer a plan for how a code could be promoted to microfinance institutions. While this Declaration is certainly a first step in the right direction, it has been endorsed by only a minority of MFIs worldwide. Similarly, after the accusations of unethical practices in south India, some local microfinance actors decided to establish a self-governed five-point "code of conduct". Another example is the Accion consumer pledge, which states that "interest rates will not provide excessive profits, but will be sufficient to ensure that the business can survive and grow to reach more people" (Accion, 2004). A more recent example is the campaign for client protection in microfinance also launched by Accion. These pledges and campaigns are, of course, voluntary in nature and comprise a sort of gentleman's agreement, which could limit their efficiency.

More radical policies to protect the clients are usury laws. These laws that restrict interest rates often fix ceilings of maximum interest rates that the MFIs can charge. Many governments are introducing new usury laws or simply stronger usury laws in countries where they already exist, in order to protect poor citizens. Helms and Reille (2004) found that about 40 developing and transitional countries have introduced regulations of some kind about interest rate ceilings. Ceilings can certainly be instruments to protect clients against very high rates. The main criticism against them is that, although they define the maximum rates that can be charged, it is very difficult to take into account all environmental contexts into the law. The law will probably lack the required flexibility to consider all singular cases and might easily violate some privacy rights in order to do so correctly. Furthermore, if the maximum rate is fixed at too low a level, the institution's sustainability would be at risk, which might harm the least advantageous borrowers that have no other credit access. This is related to the fear of mission drift and the potential shift towards larger loans, leaving the poorest behind. This debate is still ongoing, with, for instance, Gosh and Van Tassel (2008) suggesting that MFIs shifting to larger loans do so only because it achieves a greater reduction in poverty.[4]

A final and still much debated topic is whether we should be more demanding with subsidised institutions. The Pocantico declaration says that "public money should be held to higher standards of accountability for achieving tangible social benefits with their use of public funds". Since donors have multiple bottom lines and must strive to fulfil them, it makes sense that fully subsidised institutions should be more accountable. While we know that a vast majority of MFIs have been created with subsidies, one could, however, deny the contribution of this principle. Nevertheless, the levels of subsidisation vary a lot among MFIs and should therefore be taken into account.

7 Conclusion

Microfinance is at a crossroads, not only in terms of growth and financial sustainability, but also for its social promises. If the sector wants to maintain its impressive growth rate, donors' money will certainly not be sufficient. Investors, particularly socially responsible investors, are therefore welcome to foster the sector. Nevertheless, recent experiences suggest that all practices of microfinance institutions do not always respect basic ethical standards and could put the whole sector at risk.

It is therefore likely that the sustainability of the microfinance sector will not only depend on the financial results achieved by the MFIs, which will facilitate the entry of new actors, but also on the social sustainability of microfinance. The ethical appraisal of microfinance practices by the general audience (the socio-political environment surrounding microfinance) and by clients is therefore crucial for the development of the sector. If these are not realised, new recoils, such as the closing of branches of MFIs or clients' protestation movements, are likely to be more frequent while the sector will not always be defended by regulators and governments.

Fearing over-regulation by local governments or new backlash, first initiatives to self-regulate the sector have been launched, such as the Pocantico Declaration. Codes of conduct or declarations are clearly a first step to

[4]See Armendariz and Szafarz's paper on mission drift in this Handbook.

address these concerns but it is still too premature to judge if they will be sufficient to avoid new regulations and raising ethical debates.

This self-regulation should aim at establishing a minimum level of ethical standards, denouncing unethical practices such as violent behaviour of credit officers. Donors and socially responsible investors should probably go further than this and impose limits on some key indicators related to the mission of the MFIs. To this end, tools such as the one currently developed to assess social performance should be generalised.

References

Accion (2004). Accion Consumer Pledge. Working Paper. Cambridge: Accion.

Adams, D, D Graham and JD Von Pischke (1984). *Undermining Rural Development with Cheap Credit.* Boulder: Westview Press.

Armendariz, B and J Morduch (2005). *The Economics of Microfinance.* Cambridge: MIT Press.

Ashta, A and M Hudon (2009). To Whom Should we be Fair? Ethical Issues in Balancing Stakeholder Interests from Banco Compartamos Case Study. Working Paper, CEB, Brussels.

Beck, T, A Demirguc–Kunt and MS Martinez Peria (2006). Reaching Out: Access to and use of Banking Services Across Countries. Policy Research Working Paper Series, 3754, World Bank, Washington DC.

Christen, C and R Drake (2002). Commercialization. The new reality of microfinance. In *The Commercialization of Microfinance Balancing Business and Development*, D Drake and E Rhyne (eds.), pp. 2–22. Bloomfield: Kumarian Press.

Cohen, M (2002). Making microfinance more client-led. *Journal of International Development*, 14(3), 335–350.

Collins, D, J Morduch, S Rutherford and O Ruthven (2009). *Portfolios of the Poor: How the World's Poor Live on $2 a Day.* Princeton: Princeton University Press.

Copestake, J (2007). Mainstreaming microfinance: Social performance management or mission drift? *World Development*, 35(10), 1721–1738.

Copestake, J, P Dawson, JP Fanning, A McKay and K Wright–Revolledo (2005). Monitoring the Diversity of the Poverty Outreach and Impact of Microfinance: A Comparison of Methods Using Data from Peru. *Development Policy Review*, 23(6), 703–723.

Counts, A (2008). Reimagining microfinance. *Stanford Social Innovation Review*, 46–53.

Cull, R, A Demirguc–Kunt and J Morduch (2009). Microfinance meets the market. *Journal of Economic Perspectives*, 23(1), 167–192.

De Mel, S, D McKenzie and C Woodruff (2008). Returns to capital: Results from a randomized experiment. *Quarterly Journal of Economics*, 123(4), 1329–1372.

Fernando, J (2006a). *Microfinance — Perils and Prospects.* New York: Routledge.

Fernando, N (2006b). *Understanding and Dealing With Interest Rates In Microcredit.* Manila: Asian Development Bank.

Ghosh, S and E Van Tassel (2008). A Model of Mission Drift in Microfinance Institutions. Working Paper 08003, Department of Economics, College of Business, Florida Atlantic University.

Goetz, A and R Sen Gupta (1996). Who takes the credit? Gender and power in rural credit programmes in Bangladesh. *World Development*, 27(1), 45–63.

Guérin, I, M Roesch, S Kumar, G Venkatasubramanian and M Sangare (2009). Microfinance and the dynamics of financial vulnerability. Lessons from rural South India. IRD Working Paper.

Harford, T (2008). The battle for the soul of microfinance. *The Financial Times*, (6 December 2008).

Harper, M (1998). *Profits for the Poor, Cases in Microfinance.* London: ITDG.

Helms, B and X Reille (2004). Interest Rates Ceilings and Microfinance: The Story So Far. CGAP Occasional Paper, 9. CGAP/ The World Bank Group, Washington DC.

Hermes, N, R Lensink and A Meesters (2008). Outreach and efficiency of microfinance institutions. Available at: http://ssrn.com/abstract=1143925.

Homer, S and R Sylla (2005). *History of Interest Rates* (4th ed.) Chichester: John Wiley & Sons.

Hudon, M (2009). Should access to credit be a right? *Journal of Business Ethics*, 84, 17–28.

Hudon, M (2007). Fair interest rates when lending to the poor. *Ethics and Economics*, 5(1), 1–8.

Hulme, D (2000). Is microdebt good for poor people? A note on the dark side of microfinance. *Small Enterprise Development Journal*, 11(1), 26–28.

Matin, I and B Helms (2000). Those Who Leave and Those Who Don't Join: Insights from East African Microfinance Institutions. CGAP Focus Note No 16, CGAP, Washington DC.

McKenzie, D and C Woodruff (2006). Do Entry Costs Provide an Empirical Basis for Poverty Traps? Evidence from Mexican Microenterprises. *Economic Development and Cultural Change*, 55(1), 3–42.

Morduch, J (1999). The microfinance promise. *Journal of Economic Literature*, 37, 1569–1614.

Peachey, S, A Roe (2004). *Access to Finance: A Study for the World Savings Bank Institute.* Oxford: Oxford Policy Management.

Rahman, A (1999). Micro-credit initiatives for equitable and sustainable development: Who pays? *World Development*, 27, 67–82.

Rankin, K (2006). Social capital, microfinance, and the politics of development. In *Microfinance — Perils and Prospects*, JL Fernando (ed.), pp. 89–111. Oxford: Routledge.

RESULTS (2006). *A Conversation with Muhammad Yunus.*

Rosenberg, R (2007). *CGAP Reflections on the Compartamos Initial Public Offering: A Case Study on Microfinance Interest Rates and Profits.* Retrieved from http://www.cgap.org/p/site/c/template.rc/1.9.2440.

Rosenberg, R, A Gonzalez and N Sushma (2009). The New Moneylenders: Are the Poor Being Exploited by High Microcredit Interest Rates? CGAP Ocassional Paper 15.

Sandberg, J (2009). *On Interest Rates, Usury and Justice.* Working Paper, University of Birmingham.

Smith, A (1776). *The Wealth of Nations.* New York: Dutton.

Sinnott–Armstrong, S (2006). *Moral Skepticisms.* Oxford: Oxford University Press.

Velasquez, M (2006). *Business Ethics. Case and Concepts* (6th ed.). London: Pearson.

Von Pischke, JD (1983). The Pitfalls of Specialized Farm Credit Institutions in Low-Income Countries. In *Rural Financial Markets in Developing Countries*, JD Von Pischke, D Adams and G Donald (eds.). Washington DC, World Bank Group.

Weber, H (2006). The global political economy of microfinance and poverty reduction: Locating local livelihoods in political analysis. In *Microfinance — Perils and Prospects*, JL Fernando (ed.), pp. 43–85. New York: Routledge.
Zeller, M (2000). Product Innovation for the Poor: The Role of Microfinance. Policy Brief No. 3, International Food Policy Research Institute, Washington DC.

PART II

Understanding Microfinance's Macro-Environment and Organization Context

Microfinance Trade-Offs: Regulation, Competition and Financing*

Robert Cull and Asli Demirgüç–Kunt
World Bank

Jonathan Morduch
Wagner Graduate School of Public Service, New York University

1 Introduction

Over three decades, microfinance has evolved, mutated and segmented. Microfinance started as a simple idea — to provide loans to poor entrepreneurs — but today it is a far ranging and dynamic sector, including institutions that provide savings and remittance services, sell insurance and offer loans for a wide range of purposes. The sector is bound together by a focus on bringing financial services to the underserved, but institutions vary in the income levels of the customers they serve, the use of subsidy, regulation and governance structures, and the breadth and quality of services offered. While lending remains a core activity, "providing microfinance" now entails a range of possibilities and a variety of models. In choosing strategies, microfinance providers face both new opportunities and trade-offs.

*The views are those of the authors and not necessarily those of the World Bank or its affiliate institutions. Morduch is grateful for funding from the Bill and Melinda Gates Foundation through the Financial Access Initiative. The Mix Market provided the data through an agreement between the World Bank Research Department and the Consultative Group to Assist the Poor. Confidentiality of institution-level data has been maintained. We thank Isabelle Barres, Joao Fonseca, Didier Thys and Peter Wall of the Microfinance Information Exchange (MIX). Sarojini Hirshleifer, Varun Kshirsagar, Mircea Trandafir provided expert assistance with the research on which we report. Catherine Burns assisted in writing and editing this paper. Any errors and views are ours only.

Economists have written extensively on the trade-offs that result from the combination of (i) customers' lack of assets which can serve as collateral, (ii) banks' lack of cost-effective monitoring and information gathering mechanisms. The combination has spawned much interesting work on the theory of contracts (Armendáriz and Morduch, 2010), particularly in the context of lending. While important, the focus ignores a broader set of challenges given by high transactions costs. These costs are of limited theoretical interest, but they can make all the difference to how the banks function and who they serve — and whether banks are even viable.

One can get a sense of the role of costs by examining different types of microfinance institutions. We show that the average loan size provided by the median nongovernmental organization (NGO) in our sample is less than a quarter the size of the average loan provided by the median commercial microfinance bank. That difference in loan sizes translates directly into differences in relative costs. While the NGOs in the sample economize on costs, their median operating costs are still roughly double that of the median commercial microfinance bank (when costs are taken as a share of loan value). Even if information asymmetries were not a major problem, the high transactions costs mean that reaching the very poor with small-scale services remains a tough business and often entails charging high fees or depending on steady subsidies.[1]

This structure of costs leads to practical trade-offs: Should the institution move upmarket to provide larger loans and improve financial performance? Is deposit taking feasible at such scales? Can socially-minded institutions survive commercial competition and regulation without re-defining their missions?

This paper describes our recent research on important trade-offs that microfinance practitioners, donors and regulators navigate (Cull *et al.*, 2007; 2009a; 2009b; 2009c). The evidence draws on large global surveys of microfinance institutions and complements the important body of studies on specific institutions (e.g., Rutherford, 2009; Rhyne, 2001). The findings establish quantitative benchmarks for conversations among practitioners, experts and regulators about ways to expand financial access.

[1]We know of no study that separates costs that are purely due to information problems from costs purely due to the lack of scale economies. Some of what are described as basic transaction costs are, at their root, surely due to information problems, but the basic costs of paperwork, risk appraisal and administration remain. One of the hopes of new technologies like mobile banking is to radically slash these kinds of costs, but it is too early to assess the promise and achievement.

Among the key findings are: (1) Raising interest rates improves profitability for many institutions but, after a point, higher rates are associated with increased loan delinquencies and diminished profits (unless contractual innovations are in place that limit delinquencies); (2) Financial self-sustainability and serving poor households are not, by definition, incompatible; (3) But most institutions serving the poorest customers earn profits too small to attract investors seeking purely commercial returns (rather than a blend of "social" and financial returns); still, (4), a substantial share of "non-profits" in fact earn profits, even if they are relatively small; (5) Non-profits do not duplicate the work of commercial lenders: non-profits tend to make far smaller loans on average and serve more women as a fraction of customers, relative to commercialized microfinance banks; (6) Rigorous and regular supervision is critical for deposit-taking institutions, but it is costly; regulatory supervision thus tends to push institutions to serve relatively better-off customers as a way to maintain profitability; and (7) competition, or potential competition from mainstream formal sector banks appears to steer microfinance institutions toward serving poorer customers.

The rest of this paper describes the data and key findings.

2 The MicroBanking Bulletin Data

In each of the four studies described below, we use cross-sectional data compiled by the Microfinance Information eXchange (the MIX). The MIX data are of unusually high quality, and we use the subset that is collected and standardized for the organization's biannual benchmarking report, the *MicroBanking Bulletin.* While the summary statistics are available in the *Bulletin* and on the MIX website, we were granted access to the more detailed underlying dataset. Starting with an original dataset on 124 institutions in 49 countries, we incorporated additional observations and data and variables, bringing the largest dataset to 346 institutions in 67 countries.

The data have important qualities. First, they provide multiple indicators to measure topics of interest; for example, the *Bulletin* includes three separate measures of customers' poverty levels. Second, the data are self-reported but are then independently verified to ensure coherence and consistency. Third, the data are adjusted to improve comparability across institutions using different reporting formats and the records are modified to account for implicit subsidies.

The data are not, however, representative of the full population of microfinance institutions. The data over-represent institutions that both have a commitment to financial sustainability and that are willing to comply with the MIX's relatively rigorous reporting standards. Because of this, the institutions are more likely to be industry leaders in terms of financial performance, and the data should be seen as giving a sense of best-case financial possibilities.

Bauchet and Morduch (2010) analyze differences between the MIX dataset and the larger database of the Microcredit Summit Campaign, a microfinance advocacy organization that promotes social change. As expected, they find that the MIX data are more heavily tilted toward financially sustainable institutions, and the latter toward institutions with strong social objectives. For example, the average operational self-sufficiency ratio of institutions reporting to the Microcredit Summit Campaign is 95 percent, compared to 115 percent for institutions reporting to the MIX. The MIX data also tilts more heavily toward Latin America and Eastern Europe, relative to the heavier Asia representation of the Microcredit Summit database.

On top of this general bias, the *MicroBanking Bulletin* adjustments to profit assume an implausibly low opportunity cost of capital. The calculations use a country's deposit rate (as reported by the International Monetary Fund) as the assumed benchmark cost that microfinance institutions would have to pay for capital in the open market. This choice exaggerates measures of profit and artificially shrinks measures of subsidy (Cull *et al.*, 2009a). As the price that deposit-taking institutions typically pay savers for capital, the deposit rate is a justifiable measure of capital costs in some contexts. Most microfinance institutions, however, do not count deposits as their most important source of capital. Moreover, the measure does not account for the transaction costs of servicing deposit accounts. Measures of trends are less clearly affected by this bias, and Cull *et al.* (2009a) show that the main conclusions here would be even stronger were the bias corrected.

Another issue is with the Financial Self-Sufficiency Ratio (FSS), our preferred metric for an institution's profitability. FSS incorporates figures adjusted to account for different kinds of subsidy to approximate an institution's returns in the absence of subsidized funding. However, FSS analysis captures a "snapshot" of current conditions at a given moment. It cannot indicate an institution's flexibility, nor what strategies its management would pursue if access to subsidized funding dried up. Ultimately, operating on commercial terms is tied to the ability to shift strategies as required. If the need arose, could the institution reallocate funds and find ways to operate more efficiently? The FSS ratio provides only a rough guide to this question. In this sense, the ratio usefully reveals circumstances at a given slice of time, but it gives only a limited perspective on what might be possible without subsidy.

It is also important to keep in mind that these studies are based on cross-country data, which allows us to draw conclusions about the microfinance landscape but which may offer an imperfect guide to possibilities in specific countries.

Finally, the papers map correlations and patterns in the data. For the most part, we are not making strong causal claims (the exception is in our work on regulation, and even there we tread lightly). Most progress in establishing causal relationships has been achieved in micro studies of the sort reviewed in Karlan and Morduch (2009), and World Bank (2008). Still, since many policy questions concern the working of institutions, analyzing institution-level data is critical.

3 Contracts

Economic theory details how problems arising from asymmetric information undermine economic incentives to such an extent that it may be impossible to serve the under-served (Akerlof, 1970; Stiglitz, 1974). The major contribution of microfinance has been to demonstrate innovative contracts that, both in practice and in theory, can make commercial lending to the poor viable. Gangopadhyay and Lensink (2009), for example, build on previous work on joint liability borrowing to show how contracts can mitigate adverse selection. Armendáriz and Morduch (2010) show how microfinance contracts reduce moral hazard.

In our 2007 analysis of the MIX data, we investigate the role of contracts empirically (Cull *et al.*, 2007). The study considers lenders that offer different kinds of contracts: conventional bilateral lending agreements, Grameen Bank-style group contracts, and "village banks" that also use group-based methods. Using one observation per institution from 1999 to 2002, we focus on qualitative information on institutions' lending style, range of services offered, profit status, ownership structure and source of funds. We include a "lending type" variable that categorizes institutions, separating individual-based lenders, group-based lenders, and village banks. For our profitability regressions, the primary dependent variable is the financial self-sufficiency ratio (FSS), a ratio of revenues and expenses adjusted to account for subsidies. We also regress two other measures of profitability, the operational self-sufficiency ratio (OSS) and return on assets (ROA). A second set of regressions uses "portfolio at risk" as the dependent variable, and a third investigates mission drift by regressing three outreach variables. In this third set, the dependent variables are average loan size over GNP, average loan size relative to the average per capita income of the bottom 20 percent for the country, and the share of borrowers that are women. While some observers define mission drift narrowly, in terms of the economic level of customers, here we are also concerned with shifts away from an orientation toward female customers. We control for institutional characteristics, including the institution's age, size, formal profit status, real gross portfolio yield (an approximation of the average interest rate charged by the institution), average loan size (only in the first set of profitability regressions) and region of operation. We also include four financial ratios: capital and labor costs relative to assets, loans to assets, and donations to loan portfolio.

The most telling sign of trade-offs emerges when we investigate how loan repayment rates vary with the interest rates that institutions charge borrowers. The patterns in the data generally line up with theoretical predictions: loan delinquency rates increase with interest rates for individual-based lenders. This pattern is also consistent with evidence from the field showing that demand for microcredit is sensitive to price.[2] We do not find this type of pattern for group lenders or village banks, however. The discrepancy is consistent with the claim that group-based contracts serve their intended purpose in these contexts, effectively mitigating information problems by taking the place of collateral as an incentive to repay loans (e.g., Gangopadhyay, Ghatak and Lensink, 2005). Lenders can then raise interest rates on loans without fearing a substantial weakening of portfolio quality.

We find mixed evidence for trade-offs between profitability and outreach. For both individual- and group-based lenders, serving poorer clients is associated with facing higher average costs. The finding follows from the observation that small loans are costlier to serve (per unit lent) relative to larger loans. After controlling for other factors, though, we find that this relatively large cost burden does not preclude profitability: higher costs are met with higher interest rates. Our results on the question of mission drift are promising: financially self-sustainable individual lenders tend to lend to

[2] Dehejia, Montgomery, and Morduch (2009) analyze data from a Bangladeshi lender and find that a 10 percentage point increase in the interest rate decreases the demand for credit by between 7.3 and 10.4 percent. Karlan and Zinman (2008) also study customers' sensitivity to interest rates, with data from South Africa. They find that demand for credit is "kinked": the customers are more sensitive to interest rate increases than to the lender's standard rates.

both relatively poorer clients and more women, suggesting that the pursuit of profit and social objectives are not incompatible. However, the typical larger and older institution in our sample does not achieve profitability and deep outreach simultaneously.

4 Commercialization

Commercialized microfinance has been an enduring promise in the field, but not without controversy (e.g., Morduch, 2000). Those who argue that commercialization should be *the* path for microfinance tend to dismiss concerns that commercialization can compromise social achievement — and tend to highlight the way in which commercialization can expand scale. Others argue that compromises between financial and social goals are manifest.

Cull *et al.* (2009a) use an updated and expanded version of the MIX dataset to explore questions around the commercialization of microfinance, jumping into the debate highlighted by the public offering of stock by Mexico's Banco Compartamos. Turning to the global landscape, we focus on eight questions: Who are the lenders? How widespread is profitability? Are loans in fact repaid at the high rates advertised? Who are the customers? Why are interest rates so high? Are profits high enough to attract profit-maximizing investors? How important are subsidies? And, how robust are the financial data?

For this and the other 2009 studies, we incorporate new data to bring the total number of institutions to 346, with at least one observation per institution from 2002 to 2004. For the 2009a paper on commercialization, we use the full dataset, which includes observations from institutions in 67 developing countries, looking for patterns in profitability and outreach related to institutional structure. We again use FSS as the primary measure of profitability. In addition to the variables listed in Section 3, we include the number of active borrowers,[3] operating cost as a percent of loan value, operating cost per active borrower (in PPP$), return on equity, subsidy per borrower (in PPP$), and the non-commercial funding ratio.

We show that, despite the attention generated by commercial microfinance, NGOs continue to dominate the sample of microfinance institutions

[3]In the *MicroBanking Bulletin*, "active borrowers" refers to "the number of borrowers with loans outstanding, adjusted for standardized write-offs" (*MicroBanking Bulletin*, 2005: 57).

collected for the *MicroBanking Bulletin*, accounting for 45 percent of institutions and 51 percent of borrowers. More than half of the institutions in the sample are profitable (defined as having a financial sustainability ratio above 1), including a large share of microfinance institutions with "non-profit" status. Although, unsurprisingly, a larger share of banks are profitable than of NGOs. Both commercial and non-commercial lenders do quite well in terms of repayment rates, with 30-day portfolio at risk below 4 percent at the median for all categories.

On average, commercial microfinance banks make loans that are about four times larger than loans from NGOs, suggesting that they tend to serve a substantially better-off group of borrowers.[4] We also find that as a group, NGOs charge interest rates roughly double the size of those charged by commercial microfinance banks.[5] Taken together, these last two findings suggest that the poorest customers tend to pay the most for loans. As surprising as this may be to outsiders, the equation is straightforward: as a group, NGOs make the smallest loans and, as a result, face the highest unit costs. To break even, NGOs must then charge the highest interest rates.

The first and fifth rows of data in Table 6.1 show that NGOs serve poorer clients than "non-bank financial institutions" (NBFIs) and banks, but they face significantly higher operating costs as a percent of loan value. The average loan size as a percent of income at the bottom quintile of the population is 48 percent for the median NGO, 160 for the median NBFI and 224 for the median bank, while operating cost as a percent of loan value is 26 for the median NGO, 17 for the median NBFI and 12 for the median bank. Hermes, Lensink, and Meesters (2008) also find evidence for a trade-off between a microfinance institution's outreach and efficiency. This trade-off is highlighted in Figure 6.1. To cover these relatively high operating costs, NGOs either have to charge higher rates of interest on loans or accept subsidy. Rows 4 and 6 in Table 6.1 show that they seem to be doing both (as noted above, the real gross portfolio yield approximates the average interest rate charged to customers). Figure 6.2 depicts the positive relationship between interest rates and costs.

Most institutions serving the poorest customers earn profits too small to attract profit-maximizing investors. This accounts for the continued

---

[4]In these analyses, the comparisons involve simple averages, not weighted by the size of institutions.

[5]There is much debate (and often confusion) around the prices charged for microfinance. Collins *et al.* (2009, Chapter 5) provide a discussion based on fieldwork in India, Bangladesh and South Africa.

Table 6.1: Performance indicators for NGOs, NBFIs and banks.

	Non-governmental organizations				Non-bank financial institutions				Banks			
	25th pctile (1)	Median (2)	75th pctile (3)	Median if profitable (4)	25th pctile (5)	Median (6)	75th pctile (7)	Median if profitable (8)	25th pctile (9)	Median (10)	75th pctile (11)	Median if profitable (12)
1. Average loan size/income at 20th percentile (%)	27	48	135	60	71	160	247	164	110	224	510	294
2. Active borrowers (thousands)	3.1	7.4	23.0	11.1	4.1	9.9	23.0	9.4	1.9	20.3	60.7	10.4
3. Women as a share of all borrowers (%)	63	85	100	86	47	66	94	67	23	52	58	49
4. Real portfolio yield (%)	15	25	37	26	12	20	26	20	9	13	19	14
5. Operating cost/loan value (%)	15	26	38	21	13	17	24	16	7	12	21	11
6. Subsidy/borrower (PPP$)	72	233	659	199	0	32	747	8	0	0	136	0
7. Non-commercial funding ratio	0.31	0.74	1.00	0.53	0.16	0.46	0.83	0.41	0.00	0.11	0.22	0.03

Source: Cull *et al.*, 2009a; *MicroBanking Bulletin* dataset. Subsidy per borrower numbers are donations from prior years plus donations to subsidize financial services plus an in-kind subsidy adjustment plus an adjustment for subsidies to the cost of funds.

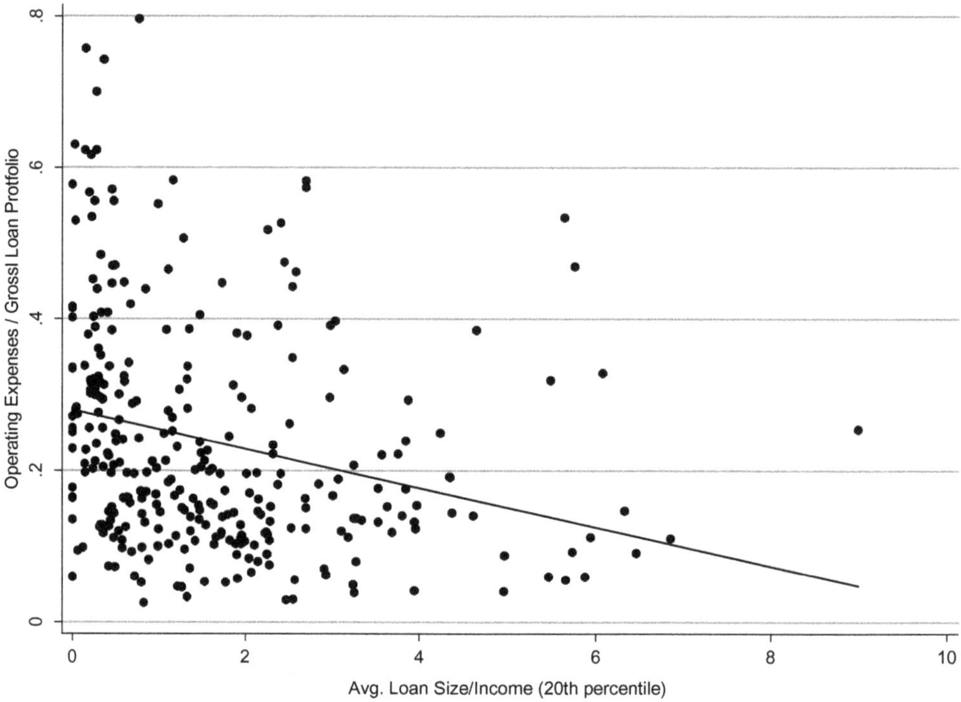

Figure 6.1: Average costs per dollar lent fall as loans get larger.

Source: Cull *et al.*, 2009a. Horizontal axis gives the average loan size as a fraction of the average income of households at the 20th percentile of the national income distribution.

importance of subsidies and non-commercial funding to NGOs, which receive 61 percent of all subsidies despite serving only 51 percent of all borrowers. For these NGOs, subsidization amounts to $233 per borrower at the median and reaches $659 at the 75th percentile. The data show that while programs reaching poorer clients can fully cover their costs, subsidization remains significant.

The study sharpens the evidence for a trade-off between pursuing profit and outreach by changing the focus from lending type to institutional structure. The findings suggest that a clear trade-off exists, where the depth of outreach is proxied by indicators of customers' poverty levels rather than direct evidence. (For an analysis along similar lines, see Galema and Lensink, 2009.)

Table 6.1 also shows that NBFIs and banks serve a smaller share of women than NGOs. For more than half of NGOs in our sample, 85 percent of clients are female, and at least a quarter of them serve women exclusively.

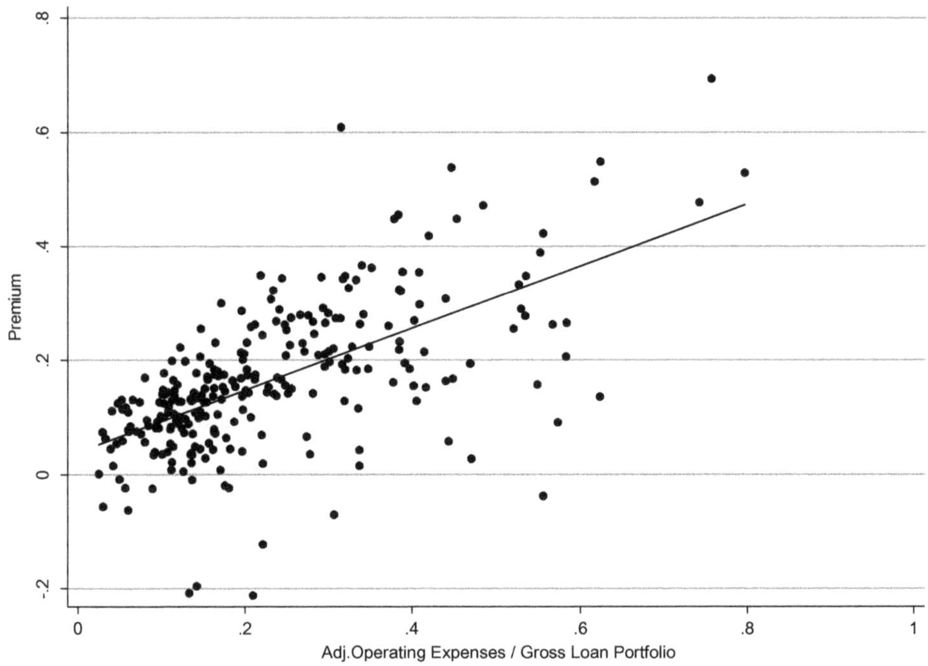

Figure 6.2: Interest rates rise with costs.

Source: Cull *et al.*, 2009a. The "premium" is the excess of the microlender's average interest rate charged to borrowers over the International Monetary Fund's inter-bank "lending interest rate" that banks in the given countries charge to prime customers (from IMF *International Financial Statistics*).

The median NBFIs and microfinance banks, on the other hand, serve only 66 percent and 52 percent women, respectively.

We recognize, though, that the issue of mission drift is complicated and poorly defined in terms of shifts in average loan size (a point made well by Dunford, 2002; and echoed by Armendáriz and Szafarz, 2009). Moving "upmarket" to serve more profitable customers may ultimately allow an institution to reach a larger absolute number of poorer customers and/or women through cross-subsidization, scale economies, or both.

Frank (2008) shows how this distinction matters. She analyzes the relationship between commercial transformation and outreach to women, showing that while commercialization is correlated with a decline in the fraction of female clients served (as a share of total clients), the institutions transformed from NGOs to commercial institutions within her dataset served twice as many women borrowers in absolute numbers relative to the non-transformed institutions.

Disaggregated data are necessary to take the conversation forward, and collecting more customer-level data on poverty levels and financial access remains a top priority. One piece of evidence that attenuates concern with the use of average loan size as a proxy for the poverty level of customers is provided by Gonzalez and Rosenberg (2006). They find a tight correlation between the fraction of smaller loans a lender provides and its self-reported fraction of poor borrowers served.

5 Regulation

In a third study, again using an updated MIX dataset, we examine the effect of regulatory supervision on the profitability of microfinance institutions (Cull *et al.*, 2009b). In particular, we investigate how regulated institutions manage the financial and administrative burdens of complying with regulation, looking at profits, business orientation, outreach and the share of employees who work in the field. We also look for evidence that regulation provides benefits by improving loan quality.

We conduct econometric analyses of the dataset described above, and of a subset, the 154 institutions that both reported detailed financial information and were subject to regulatory supervision (2009b). We estimate the impact of prudential regulation on profitability and financial self-sufficiency, using for the key regressors three dummy variables that summarize whether an institution faces prudential supervision and the intensity of that supervision. These dummy variables measure whether (1) an MFI faces a regular reporting requirement to a regulatory authority; (2) the MFI faces onsite supervision; and (3) onsite supervision occurs at regular intervals. We control for the same variables as in the 2007 study on contracts and added a measure of staff concentration and *Premium*, the difference between the interest rates an institution charges its borrowers and the "market" rate for capital. To account for country characteristics, we also include the growth rate of real GDP, the rate of inflation, and an index of institutional development developed by Kaufman, Kraay and Mastruzzi (2007).

We find that onsite supervision of microfinance institutions varies, even within the same country and among profit-oriented institutions. Whether an institution faces onsite supervision depends on its ownership structure, funding sources, activities, and organizational charter. In terms of trade-offs, we find that microfinance institutions subjected to more rigorous and regular supervision are as profitable as others, despite facing higher costs of supervision. This finding may in part reflect the fact that being regulated often permits institutions to collect deposits and thus gain a cheaper and/or more stable source of capital. For example, Ledgerwood and White (2006, pg. 174) draw on four to six years of data for nine microfinance institutions to report that "experience to date has shown that as transformed institutions mature, deposits as a percentage of funding liabilities increases".

However, supervision does have a significant impact on outreach. Regulatory supervision is associated with larger average loan sizes, a common proxy for the relative poverty of borrowers, and less lending to women. The finding is consistent with strategic choices by institutions facing high supervision costs to shift away from serving more cost-intensive segments of the population. We also find that supervision is associated with having a higher share of staff concentrated in the head office, a natural response to reporting requirements and formalization.

Mersland and Strøm (2009) also conduct an econometric analysis of the impact of regulation with cross-institution data. In line with our findings on regulation and profitability, they find that regulation does not have a significant impact on financial performance. They do not find evidence for the trade-off with outreach, however. Hartarska and Nadolynk (2007) also show that regulation does not directly affect the performance of microfinance institutions, either in terms of operational self-sustainability (OSS) or outreach. They find that deposit-taking institutions have broader outreach though, suggesting that regulation may offer an indirect benefit by permitting institutions to expand. The innovation in Cull *et al.* (2009b) is use of the *MicroBanking Bulletin* data and, importantly, use of an indicator for on-site supervision.

Taken together, the evidence underscores the need to take more seriously the "regulator's dilemma", a notion developed by David Porteous (the studies are available at http://www.financialaccess.org; see also Jay Rosengard's contribution to this volume).

6 Competition

Our 2009c study turns to the "industrial organization" of the microfinance sector. We investigate the effects of competition on the profitability and outreach of microfinance institutions, focusing on competition from mainstream commercial banks. Here, we combine the MIX dataset with data on bank penetration from 99 developed and developing countries from Beck, Demirgüç–Kunt, and Martinez Peria (2007). Missing data for some of the control variables and imperfect overlap between the datasets reduce the final number of observations to 342, from 238 microfinance institutions in 38 developing countries for our largest regressions incorporating bank penetration variables. The Beck *et al.* (2007) data provide measures of bank penetration that serve as the key explanatory variables in this analysis: the number of bank branches in a country per capita and the number of branches per square kilometer. We also add banking sector ownership and concentration variables, and two more country-characteristic variables: the share of the population residing in rural areas and rural population growth.

We start from the observation that commercial banks initially were deterred from entering the microfinance niche by the small scale of the transactions that define it, but that the commercialization of microfinance has started to change that mindset. A growing number of commercial banks are downscaling their operations, opening up services to poorer segments of the population, and competition is emerging as a result. Increased competition could change the industry in a number of ways, some for the better and others less favorably. We again look at MIX data, in search of evidence on where the balance between these competing effects rests.

We look for a relationship between competition and a profitability-outreach trade-off. There are plausible explanations for both a positive and negative relationship. If microfinance institutions facing greater competition from commercial banks attempt to compensate by shifting their loan portfolios away from segments of the population that are perceived as being more costly to serve — i.e., the relatively poor and women — competition may hinder outreach. However, competition could support the financial self-sufficiency of microbanks if the benefits of agglomeration effects and a stronger regulatory environment outweigh negative spillovers, and could lead to deeper outreach.[6]

We find that greater competition, as indicated by greater bank penetration in the overall economy, is associated with deeper outreach by the microfinance institutions, suggesting that competition pushes microbanks toward poorer markets, as reflected by smaller average loans sizes and greater outreach to women. However, in this sample, competition seems to have little effect on the profitability of microbanks. This is a useful finding, as it complements analyses of competition between different microfinance institutions

[6]Microfinance experience to date shows competing impacts on costs from serving poorer customers and women. On the one hand, women are relatively more reliable borrowers than men. On the other, women tend to request smaller loans on average, which increases average costs (Armendáriz and Morduch, 2010, Chapter 7).

(in contrast to the competition analyzed here, between microfinance institutions and commercial banks). When analyzing competition between microfinance institutions, Armendariz and Morduch (2010, Chapter 5) argue that competition can undermine the "dynamic incentives" that are so critical to achieving high loan repayment rates — i.e., customers may be less willing to repay loans if they know that other reliable loan sources are available. Credit bureaus can help here (e.g., de Janvry, McIntosh, and Sadoulet, 2008).

7 Conclusion

Microfinance promises improvements in both the efficiency and fairness of capital markets. It promises to correct market failures by improving the allocation of capital and by expanding opportunities for the poor (World Bank, 2008). Advocates also aim to reach some of the world's poorest citizens and help lift them from poverty (Daley–Harris, 2009). But the global evidence shows that it is hard to do all things simultaneously. In practice, microfinance often entails distinct trade-offs between meeting social goals and maximizing financial performance.

The four studies highlighted here examine trade-offs that arise in the context of the choice of contracting mechanisms, level of commercialization, rigor of regulation and extent of competition. Our focus is on both the profitability and outreach of microfinance. The results suggest that developing meaningful interventions requires making deliberate choices — and thus embracing and weighing trade-offs carefully. The analyses here provide a global picture. The exact nature of these trade-offs differs across regions, but meaningful trade-offs need to be recognized and weighed everywhere.

References

Akerlof, G (1970). The market for lemons: Quality uncertainty and the market mechanism. *Quarterly Journal of Economics*, 84, 488–500.

Armendáriz, B and J Morduch (2010). *The Economics of Microfinance* (2nd ed.). Cambridge, MA: MIT Press.

Armendáriz, B and A Szafarz (2009). On Mission Drift in Microfinance Institutions. Working Paper, WP–CEB 09–05. Centre Emile Bernheim, Brussels Solvay Business School of Economics, Business and Management, Université Libre de Bruxelles, Belgium.

Bauchet, J and J Morduch (2010). Selective knowledge: Reporting bias in microfinance data. *Perspectives on Global Development and Technology*, 9(3–4), 240–269.

Beck, T, A Demirgüç–Kunt and MS Martinez Peria (2007). Reaching out: Access to and use of banking services across countries. *Journal of Financial Economics*, 85(1), 234–266.

Collins, D, J Morduch, S Rutherford and O Ruthven (2009). *Portfolios of the Poor: How the World's Poor Live on $2 a Day*. Princeton, NJ: Princeton University Press.

Cull, R, A Demirgüç–Kunt and J Morduch (2007). Financial performance and outreach: A global analysis of leading microbanks. *Economic Journal*, 117(517), F107–F133.

Cull, R, A Demirgüç–Kunt and J Morduch (2009a). Microfinance meets the market. *Journal of Economic Perspectives*, 23(1), 167–192.

Cull, R, A Demirgüç–Kunt and J Morduch (2009b). Does regulatory supervision curtail microfinance profitability and outreach? *World Development*, forthcoming.

Cull, R, A Demirgüç–Kunt and J Morduch (2009c). Banks and micro-banks. Working Paper.

Daley–Harris, S (2009). State of the Microcredit Summit Campaign Report 2009. Washington, DC: Microcredit Summit Campaign.

de Janvry, A, C McIntosh and E Sadoulet (2008). The supply- and demand-side impacts of credit market information. Working Paper, University of California–Berkeley and University of California–San Diego.

Dehejia, R, H Montgomery and J Morduch (2009). Do interest rates matter? Credit demand in the Dhaka slums. Working Paper, Financial Access Initiative.

Dunford, C (2002). What's wrong with loan size? Unpublished manuscript. Freedom From Hunger.

Frank, C (2008). Stemming the tide of mission drift: Microfinance transformation and the double bottom line. Women's World Banking Focus Note.

Galema, R and R Lensink (2009). Microfinance commercialization: Financially and socially optimal investments. Working Paper, University of Groningen.

Gangopadhyay, S, M Ghatak and R Lensink (2005). On joint liability and the peer selection effect. *Economic Journal*, 115, 1012–1020.

Gangopadhyay, S and R Lensink (2009). Symmetric and asymmetric joint liability lending contracts in an adverse selection model. Working Paper, University of Groningen.

Gonzalez, A and R Rosenberg (2006). The state of microfinance — Outreach, profitability, and poverty (findings from a database of 2600 microfinance institutions). Presentation at *World Bank Conference on Access to Finance*.

Hartarska, V and D Nadolnyak (2007). Do regulated microfinance institutions achieve better sustainability and outreach? *Applied Economics*, 39, 1207–1222.

Hermes, N, R Lensink and A Meesters (2008). Outreach and efficiency of microfinance institutions. Working Paper, Centre for International Banking, Insurance and Finance.

Karlan, D and J Morduch (2009). Access to finance. In *Handbook of Development Economics*, D Rodrik and M Rosenzweig (eds.), pp. 4703–4784. Amsterdam: Elsevier.

Karlan, D and J Zinman (2008). Credit elasticities in less-developed economies: Implications for microfinance. *American Economic Review*, 98(3), 1040–1068.

Kaufmann, D, A Kraay and M Mastruzzi (2007). Governance Matters VI: Governance Indicators of 1996–2006. World Bank Policy Research Working Paper 4280. Washington DC.

Ledgerwood, J and V White (2006). *Transforming Microfinance Institutions: Providing Full Financial Services to the Poor.* Washington DC: World Bank.

Mersland, R and R Øystein Strøm (2009). Performance and governance in microfinance institutions. *Journal of Banking and Finance*, 33(4), 662–669.

MicroBanking Bulletin (2005). *The MicroBanking Bulletin* 10.

Morduch, J (2000). The microfinance schism. *World Development*, 28(4), 617–629.
Rhyne, E (2001). *Mainstreaming Microfinance: How Lending to the Poor Began, Grew, and Came of Age in Bolivia.* West Hartford, CT: Kumarian Press.
Rosengard, J (2010). Oversight is a many-splendored thing: Choice and proportionality in regulating and supervising microfinance institutions. In *The Handbook of Microfinance*, B Armendáriz and M Labie (eds.). Singapore: World Scientific Publishing.
Rutherford, S (2009). *The Pledge: ASA, Peasant Politics, and Microfinance in the Development of Bangladesh.* New York: Oxford University Press.
Stiglitz, JE (1974). Incentives and risk sharing in sharecropping. *Review of Economic Studies*, 41, 219–256.
World Bank (2008). *Finance for All.* Washington DC: World Bank.

Oversight is a Many-Splendored Thing: Choice and Proportionality in Regulating and Supervising Microfinance Institutions

Jay K. Rosengard*
John F. Kennedy School of Government, Harvard University

1 Introduction

Just as there are many different types of microfinance institutions (MFIs), there are also many options for regulating and supervising MFIs. Oversight is a many-splendored thing, with a long menu of options from which to formulate an appropriate mixture of MFI regulatory and supervisory regimes — one size certainly does not fit all.

The objective of this essay is to highlight the many choices available for regulating and supervising MFIs, and to provide guidance in judicious application of the proportionality principle to make prudent selections among these choices.

To make the case for choice and proportionality in MFI regulation and supervision, this essay is organized around the following five key questions:

- Why regulate and supervise financial institutions?
- Why distinguish between regulation and supervision?
- What is so special about microfinance institutions?
- What are our main alternatives for MFI oversight?
- How can we balance conflicting objectives?

Each question will be addressed in sequence, so that by the end of the essay, the reader might fully appreciate the complexity of MFI regulation

*Lecturer in Public Policy and Director of the Financial Sector Program.

and supervision, as well as the opportunities that MFI diversity offers to effectively meet oversight needs creatively.

2 Lest We Forget: Why Regulate and Supervise Financial Institutions?

The financial sector is among the most regulated and supervised part of a nation's economy around the world, regardless of a country's stage of economic development or the nature of its political system. This is not accidental or coincidental. The functions performed by financial institutions, particularly banks, are unique, and thus, the risks entailed in undertaking these functions are also unique.

The first principal group of financial institution functions revolve around the mobilization of savings and the allocation of credit, or financial intermediation; the second main set of functions are related to the provision of liquidity and payment services, or facilitation of financial transactions. The risks associated with these financial functions are twofold: macroeconomic market failures and microeconomic institutional collapses.

There are four macroeconomic market failures related to financial institutions. First, not only do financial services have a high intrinsic value, but they are also perceived as *quasi-public goods*, essential components and basic needs of an efficient and equitable economy that should be available to all. Second, financial sector difficulties are therefore seen as imposing costs on society far in excess of the cost to any single financial institution or to the customers of that institution, commonly referred to as *negative externalities*. Third, today's global economic crisis is a vivid example of the tremendous havoc that these negative externalities can wreak by causing massive *macroeconomic disequilibrium*. Fourth, financial sector weaknesses are heightened by *asymmetries of information*, or unequal distribution of information — savers generally lack the capacity to assess the soundness of depository institutions, while lenders find it difficult to assess the willingness and capacity of borrowers to repay their loans.

These four macroeconomic vulnerabilities are further exacerbated by two unique risks associated with the microeconomic transmission mechanisms of financial institution failure: they start with bank runs for individual institutions, due to the *sequential servicing of customer claims* and resultant loss of customer confidence; they spread throughout the financial system and later the real economy via *the contagion effect*, like a viral disease, ultimately resulting in systemic collapse.

The purpose of financial institution regulation and supervision is thus to maintain confidence in the financial system and protect consumers of financial services, by mitigating these risks associated with both macroeconomic market failures and microeconomic institutional collapses. The primary objective is to avoid a banking crisis, where one or more bank failures can lead to systemic collapse, thereby threatening depositors with loss of their savings, depriving creditworthy businesses and households of access to loans, and compromising the viability of the entire payments system.

3 Terminology Check: Why Distinguish Between Regulation and Supervision?

Regulation entails setting standards and determining rules of the game; supervision is monitoring and enforcing compliance with these regulations. It is important to distinguish between the two because they are both distinct from each other and symbiotic. Understanding the differences between financial regulation and supervision, as well as their interactions with each other, should help countries to articulate highly focused and specific objectives, and thus apply the most appropriate tools to achieve these objectives.

As indicated in Figure 7.1 below, there are two basic types of financial regulation: those related to financial soundness, or prudential regulation,

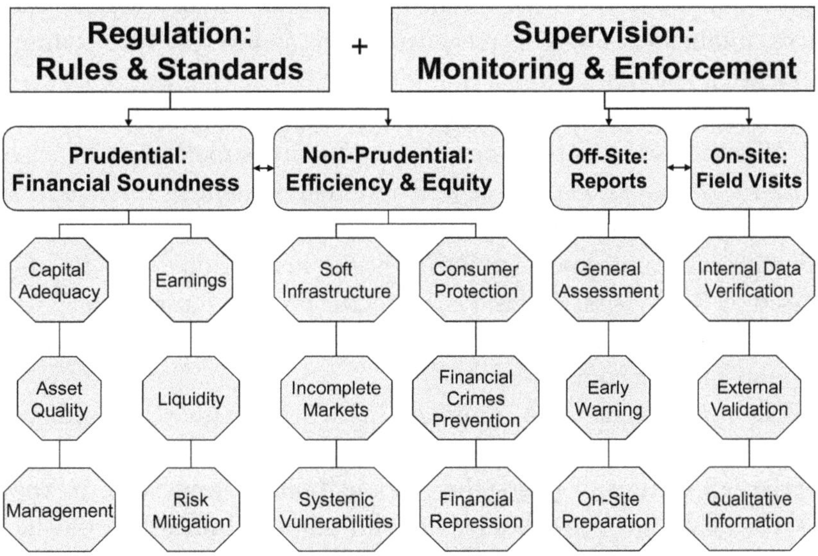

Figure 7.1: Oversight of microfinance institutions.

and those related to market efficiency and market equity, or non-prudential regulation.

The purpose of prudential regulation is to determine the health of financial institutions, particularly to ensure that they are liquid and solvent, and are usually based on some variation of the CAMEL-Plus rating system: **C**apital Adequacy, **A**sset Quality, **M**anagement, **E**arnings, **L**iquidity, and **Risk** Mitigation. This is the main preventative measure to guard against financial institution failure.

The purpose of non-prudential regulation is to improve the quality of the markets in which financial institutions operate. The most extensive of these is sometimes referred to as "soft infrastructure" regulation, and is comprised of legal and judicial protocols for secured transaction, contract enforcement, and bankruptcy procedures; tax and accounting treatment of financial institutions and products; authority to grant permission to undertake financial activities, as well as establish and transform financial institutions; and credit bureau operating parameters.

Other components of non-prudential regulation include requirements to serve incomplete markets, such as the Community Reinvestment Act in the United States; measures to reduce system vulnerabilities, such as controls over hot capital; consumer protection laws to promote transparency and accountability, such as requiring common presentation of effective interest rates and full disclosure of the risks of financial instruments; financial crimes prevention, particularly money laundering and the funding of terrorist operations; and although often well-intentioned but usually counterproductive, financial repression measures, such as interest rate ceilings and credit allocation quotas.

Supervision of financial institutions is commonly divided into two components: off-site and on-site supervision. Off-site supervision is based on reports, and is designed to provide a general assessment of financial institution soundness, give supervisors an early warning of potential problems and help field supervisors prepare for their on-site inspections. On-site supervision is based on field visits, and is conducted to provide internal data verification, external data validation, and qualitative information on management, customer and market conditions.

Given the many elements of financial institution regulation and supervision, the fundamental challenge for governments is to determine the most cost-effective allocation of oversight responsibilities, especially in the context of MFIs. It is not self-evident that all responsibilities should lie with the central bank or national superintendency.

4 The Informal Economy: What Is So Special About Microfinance Institutions?

Most of the preceding discussion has been focused on regulation and supervision of financial institutions in general. However, microfinance has special features that pose unique oversight challenges, the most important of these being:

- Client base — Microfinance clients are low-income households and informal family businesses, so while they still require the same financial services as higher income households and formal enterprises, the design and delivery of these products must be adapted to their specific household finances and business needs. For example, the priority for savings services might be safety and access rather than return, while the primary consideration for loans might be matching repayment schedules with the timing and amount of anticipated cash flows.
- Lending methodology — Most microenterprises do not keep formal financial records and their owners do not possess conventionally accepted collateral, so loan appraisal is often based on a qualitative assessment of character and a rough estimate of cash flow from a reconstructed income statement, while items such as movable assets or group guarantees are accepted as collateral.
- Transaction costs — Although the cost of loanable funds might not be much higher than the cost for other markets and microcredit risk might actually be lower, the transaction costs for microfinance are extremely high due to the small value of each transaction and the necessity of reducing client transaction costs by bringing microfinance services as close to clients as possible. This means that interest rates on loans must be at the high end of market rates to cover all lending costs.
- Portfolio composition — In contrast to small and medium enterprise lending and corporate lending, microcredit is comprised of very small, quite short-term loans, and one of the keys to MFI financial sustainability is to generate an extremely high volume of microloans as efficiently (low unit costs) and effectively (low number of non-performing loans) as possible.
- Structure and governance — Most MFIs have a relatively decentralized structure and weak governance practices, often making conventional institutional assessment inappropriate for determining financial soundness.

Failure to adapt standard financial oversight metrics to these special attributes of microfinance can result in problematic microfinance regulations, for example:

- *Application of standard prudential norms and ratios* that in many respects are not demanding enough for MFIs. The most common example of this practice is loan classification, provisioning, and write-off requirements — given the short-term nature of microloans, the aging and write-off of microcredit arrears should be faster than conventional loans. Likewise, given the remote location of many MFI branches, it might be more prudent to require higher liquidity ratios for MFIs than for mainstream commercial banks. On the other hand, unreasonably high minimum capital requirements often serve as barriers to entry for new MFIs without contributing significantly to MFI financial soundness.
- *Mandatory bank consolidation and rationalization programs* in the belief that larger financial institutions and conventional financial products are safer than community-based financial institutions offering customized products for local markets. However, these programs often increase financial sector vulnerabilities through the concentration of credit risk by location, product and market.
- *Rejection of non-conventional collateral for microloans* and treating the entire microcredit portfolio as unsecured, thus requiring capital at the highest risk weighting and adding considerably to the MFI's cost of making microloans. In addition, *imposition of formal collateral registration requirements* further increase the expense of microcredit by adding to borrower transaction costs.
- *Imposition of extensive formal loan documentation requirements* for microcredit borrowers when such financial records simply do not exist for microenterprise, as well as *imposition of nominative loan portfolio documentation requirements* for MFIs when aggregate portfolio documentation would be more practical and appropriate to monitor loan portfolio quality and assess MFI credit risk exposure.
- *Imposition of interest rate ceilings* too low for MFIs to cover all of their lending costs, forcing MFIs to either seek subsidies or resort to non-transparent means of increasing effective interest rates such as special fees and commissions.
- *Imposition of individual legal lending limits* rather than by portfolio composition, which would be a more effective way of mitigating risk of credit concentration.

- *Imposition of operational efficiency measures* that are often too lax for MFIs, such as number of loans per loan officer — this number is usually much higher for MFIs than mainstream commercial banks.
- *Imposition of organizational structure, staffing, and physical office requirements* more appropriate for large commercial banks than MFIs.

These regulations are usually promulgated with good intentions: to mitigate the most critical vulnerabilities in financial institutions. However, while MFIs, especially microfinance banks, do indeed have risks similar to other financial institutions, measurement of these risks must be adapted to the special characteristics of microfinance.

This does not entail leniency in standards. A bank, even a microfinance bank, is still a bank, and one that accepts savings from low-income families should be even more careful in protecting these savings than banks serving wealthier clients, as the poor often have nothing else to fall back on should their savings be wiped out.

Thus, as noted above, sometimes MFI regulations should be stricter than the norm. What is required, though, is flexibility in calibration: equally rigorous requirements for the same regulatory objective measured differently.

The special nature of microfinance also requires adaptation of MFI supervision.

For off-site supervision, reporting systems must be more frequent than conventional bank reports, given how quickly things can go bad with high-volume, small-scale, short-term lending — timing is critical in microfinance supervision. Microcredit reports must also be more consolidated than conventional loan reports to reflect portfolio condition and trends, as loan by loan reporting for microcredit can be overwhelming in volume while adding little of value for supervisory purposes. To be frequent, timely, and easily consolidated, MFI reports must also be relatively short and simple.

For on-site supervision, MFI field inspections must also be more frequent than for conventional banking, and should go beyond typical audit functions to include external data validation via customer interviews and technical support if required. The high intensity of MFI on-site supervision, coupled with the rapidly expanding number of MFIs in many countries and the need for a large cadre of specially designated and trained field supervisors dedicated exclusively to MFIs, usually creates overwhelming oversight demands for central banks or national superintendencies. Hence the need for allocation of MFI regulatory and supervisory responsibilities among a variety of institutional alternatives, as discussed in the next two sections of this essay.

5 Menu of Choices: What Are Our Main Alternatives for MFI Oversight?

The key to cost-effective allocation of MFI regulatory and supervisory responsibilities is matching the most appropriate MFI oversight model with each segment of the MFI market. This entails clear identification of MFI oversight alternatives, together with conceptually credible disaggregation of the microfinance sector by both MFI characteristics and the nature of microfinance services offered by each type of MFI.

As noted in Table 7.1, the subjects of MFI oversight can be grouped together into six general categories:

- conventional banks, which generally offer a full range of microfinance credit, savings, and payment services;
- branchless banking, which, in its most mature form, can also offer microfinance services comparable to conventional banks;
- special license banks, which can vary from full-service banks to banks with selected restrictions on their services, the most common of these being geographic limitations, prohibition on foreign exchange transactions, and exclusion from national payment and clearing systems;
- finance companies, which can either provide credit to a variety of sectors or be specialized lenders (i.e., auto loans or home loans), but in either case must usually raise their funds from financial or capital markets — in most countries, they are not allowed to accept deposits from the public;
- client-owned MFIs such as credit unions, cooperatives, and *mutuelles*, which typically can only collect savings from, and make loans to, their members; and
- other non-bank MFIs such as leasing, insurance, and wire transfer companies.

There are also five basic alternatives for MFI oversight, noted in Table 7.1 as well:

- direct regulation and supervision by a central bank or bank superintendency;
- central bank/bank superintendency delegated regulation and supervision, perhaps to a state-owned bank on behalf of the central bank/bank superintendency;

Table 7.1: Regulation and supervision alternatives for microfinance institutions.

Alternative	Conventional bank	Branchless banking	Special license bank	Finance company	Client-owned MFI	Other non-bank MFI
Central Bank/ Bank Superintendency	Credit/Savings/ Payments	Credit/Savings/ Payments	Credit/Savings/ Payments			
Delegated Regulation/ Supervision			Credit/Savings/ Payments			
Other Regulatory/ Supervisory Agency				Credit	Credit/Member Savings	Credit, Leasing, Insurance, Payments
Self-Regulation/ Supervision				Credit	Credit/Member Savings	Credit, Leasing, Insurance, Payments
Unregulation/ Unsupervised				Credit	Credit/Member Savings	Credit, Leasing, Insurance, Payments

- a regulatory/supervisory agency other than a central bank/bank superintendency, such as a unit in the ministry of finance in charge of non-bank financial institutions, another ministry such as the ministry of cooperatives, or a semi-autonomous agency such as an insurance regulatory commission;
- MFI self-regulation and supervision, for example a cooperative or credit union association overseeing its member institutions; and
- essentially unregulated and unsupervised MFIs.

As indicated in Table 7.1, when MFI oversight alternatives are matched with types of MFIs, the results fall into two groups based on MFI product lines.

The determining factor that distinguishes these two groups from each other is whether or not the MFI accepts deposits from the public. If the answer is potentially yes, as in the first three types of MFIs, then a central bank or bank superintendency is usually responsible for MFI regulation and supervision, either directly or via a proxy such as a state-owned bank acting on its behalf. If the answer is absolutely not, as in the latter three types of MFIs, then alternative MFI regulatory and supervisory models are utilized.

The market segmentation presented in Table 7.1 is simplified and stylized to provide a comprehensive conceptual framework and accompanying general policy guidelines based on this framework. In practice, situations are often more complicated and ambiguous. For example, although client-owned MFIs such as credit unions, cooperatives, and *mutuelles* are usually formally restricted to receiving deposits from members only, the larger they become, the smaller their community of common interests and the more they begin to look like banks — sometimes the only thing members have in common is payment of a pro-forma membership fee. In addition to being *de facto* banks without the oversight that *de jure* banks have, giving them unfair competitive advantage, these client-owned MFIs might grow to become among the largest financial institutions in a country as well, and thus, also too big to ignore from a regulatory and supervisory perspective.

Thus, determination of the appropriate regime for regulating and supervising MFIs must go beyond simple application of the guidelines presented in Table 7.1. While a useful point of departure, they should be accompanied by a cost-benefit analysis, typically implicit rather than explicit, of proportionality in reconciling conflicting policy objectives in an environment of severe resource constraints, as described in the next section.

6 The Proportionality Principle: How Can We Balance Conflicting Objectives?

A common dilemma faced by central banks and bank superintendencies around the world is that they simply do not have the resources to effectively regulate and supervise all financial institutions in their country. So what is the best allocation of their scarce resources, particularly in respect to MFIs, given their mandate to protect consumers of financial services and to maintain confidence in their financial system?

The principle of proportionality is a helpful way to prioritize and allocate regulatory and supervisory responsibilities for MFIs, in three distinct but interrelated dimensions.

The first of these is proportionality in the *probability* an MFI will fail versus the *potential impact* of that failure. For example, if there is a high probability of failure but the impact is local rather than systemic, it should be low public priority. In contrast, if there is relatively low probability of failure but this failure can potentially undermine a significant part of the financial system, it should be a high public priority.

The second is proportionality in the estimated *total and distributional cost* of preventing an MFI failure versus the likely *total and distributional benefit* of preventing the failure. For example, if regulatory and supervisory costs are high and borne by the state while significant benefits accrue to donor agencies sponsoring MFIs, it should be a low public priority — let the sponsors lose their investment or find another way of protecting it against failure of their MFI NGO. In contrast, if oversight costs are moderate and borne by the state while significant benefits accrue to low-income third-party savers, it should be a high public priority, perhaps delegated, if direct oversight it too costly.

The third is proportionality in *risk mitigation* versus *stifling of financial sector innovation*. This dimension is more functional than institutional. For example, standard prudential norms greatly reduce risk without smothering initiative. In contrast, over-reactive re-regulation after a financial crisis, such as forcing consolidation or prohibiting customized microfinance products, tends to be counterproductive in two ways — it both increases risk and stifles innovation.

In determining the regulatory and supervisory priorities of a central bank or bank superintendency, policy makers should therefore ask themselves:

- If a microfinance institution fails, who are the winners and who are the losers?

- How much are they estimated to win or lose if the MFI collapses, and what is the likelihood of collapse?
- Is there an acceptable balance between MFI oversight costs and benefits?
- Are these costs and benefits fairly distributed?
- Will problems with an individual MFI spread throughout the microfinance industry, or even worse, the entire financial sector?
- Could too much risk aversion in the design of preventive measures kill incentives to innovate?

These questions do not imply that all MFIs not regulated or supervised by the central bank or bank superintendency should be left to the whims of market forces in fanatical adherence to laissez-faire ideology.

Rather, they suggest criteria for determining operational parameters in the selective utilization of scarce public resources — Table 7.1 provides institutional alternatives for the regulation and supervision of MFIs that fall outside the scope of MFI oversight that can be provided cost-effectively by central government banking authorities.

7 Conclusion

Diversity in MFIs requires corresponding diversity in the regulation and supervision of these MFIs. The rapidly growing, quickly evolving MFIs around the world have a plethora of different institutional structures, products and markets, and thus, have significantly different vulnerabilities that pose a wide variety of risks to their customers and their markets. At the same time, central banks and bank superintendencies do not have the capacity to cost-effectively regulate and supervise all of these MFIs. This essay summarizes the principal alternatives for oversight of MFIs, and applies the proportionality principle as a framework for making prudent selections among the main MFI regulatory and supervisory options.

Appendix: A Note on Key References

This essay focuses on fundamental policy questions in the regulation and supervision of MFIs from a strategic and tactical perspective.

Few specific examples are provided for two main reasons:

- the field is changing so quickly that many of the examples would probably be obsolete by the time this handbook is published; and

- others have already exhaustively documented current MFI regulatory and supervisory practices.

In July 2003, The Consultative Group to Assist the Poor (CGAP) published *Microfinance Consensus Guidelines: Guiding Principles on Regulation and Supervision of Microfinance*, which provides a glossary of many of the terms and concepts summarized or adapted in this paper, as well as a description of "best practices" for both prudential and non-prudential regulation and supervision of microfinance, based on the collective experience of CGAP's 29 donor member agencies.

In addition, CGAP, together with The Iris Center at the University of Maryland, jointly created the "Microfinance Regulation and Supervision Resource Center", which is accessible via http://www.microfinanceregulationcenter.org.

The Resource Center provides a worldwide comparative database on microfinance regulation and supervision. To quote from the website:

> Use the Comparative Database to get a snapshot of the regulatory environment for microfinance in 52 different countries. From individual country profiles to comparisons across countries, institution types and topics, the Comparative Database quickly and easily provides a comprehensive overview of regulation and supervision around the world.

The Resource Center also provides a short guide to the basic issues and alternatives in microfinance regulation and supervision in a framework that is a somewhat simplified version of the framework presented in this essay.

Finally, branchless banking is mentioned briefly in this essay, but is a rapidly growing industry that has created unique challenges in microfinance regulation and supervision. CGAP, together with the United Kingdom's Department for International Development (DFID), published *Regulating Transformational Branchless Banking: Mobile Phones and Other Technology to Increase Access to Finance* (CGAP Focus No. 43) in January 2008; this provides extensive documentation of branchless banking trends to date, together with a detailed analysis of the implications for microfinance regulation and supervision.

The Performance of Microfinance Institutions: Do Macro Conditions Matter?

Niels Hermes*

Faculty of Economics and Business, University of Groningen

Aljar Meesters

Faculty of Economics and Business, University of Groningen

This paper analyzes whether the performance of microfinance institutions (MFIs) is associated with the macro conditions these institutions are confronted with. The analysis focuses on the macroeconomic, financial development, institutional and political variables as potentially important features of the macro conditions influencing the performance of MFIs. We measure performance in terms of the cost-efficiency of MFI operations. We find that economic growth and financial development are clearly and robustly associated with MFI efficiency. For institutional and political conditions, the picture is less obvious: while some dimensions of the institutional and political environment seem to be associated with efficiency, the general conclusion is that we cannot find a clear relationship between the two dimensions and the efficiency of MFIs.

1 Introduction

Lack of finance is generally acknowledged as being an important impediment to economic activity. Especially in less developed economies, many investment projects of micro- and small-scale entrepreneurs may therefore remain unrealized because there is no finance available. Microfinance institutions (MFIs) provide loans to borrowers who have no or very limited access to other sources of finance. In this way, potentially profitable projects allow small-scale entrepreneurs to generate a stable and, possibly, even a growing income.

*Corresponding author: Faculty of Economics and Business, University of Groningen, PO BOX 800, 9700 AV Groningen, the Netherlands. Tel.: +31-50-363-4863; Fax: +31-50-363-7356; e-mail: c.l.m.hermes@rug.nl

Microfinance has received a lot of attention as an important instrument to combat poverty. The UN declared 2005 to be the international Year of Microcredit. In 2006, the attention for microfinance and its role in reducing poverty was further increased when Mohammad Yunus received the Nobel Peace prize. These developments have led to high expectations among policy-makers and aid organizations about the potential poverty-reducing effects of microfinance. Yet, in order to be able to make a significant and long-term contribution to reducing worldwide poverty, MFIs need to be successful in extending loans to poor borrowers, while at the same time being able to at least cover the costs of their lending activities, i.e., they may need to focus on being financially sustainable in the long run. An important question, however, is what conditions are important for explaining the success of microfinance institutions in terms of developing cost-efficient lending practices. Several studies have been focusing on this issue, using micro-level and institutional-specific data, to establish why MFIs perform differently in this respect.

Another approach to answering this question is to investigate what macro conditions are important in moderating the performance of MFIs. Does the macroeconomic situation have an impact on MFIs? Is the institutional environment important? Are political aspects relevant to explain why MFIs are successful in containing lending costs? In general, this approach allows investigation into whether country-specific factors explain MFI performance. Such an analysis allows investigating why MFIs from one country on average perform better than those located in another country. Yet, the literature on the macro determinants of MFI performance has only recently started to emerge, which means that there are only a few studies that have investigated this issue.

This paper aims at contributing to the discussion on the macro determinants of MFI performance, and in particular with respect to the cost efficiency of their lending practices. In Section 2, we first review the existing literature on this issue and subsequently provide new empirical evidence on whether, and to what extent the macro environment influences MFIs and their outcomes. In the review, we focus on economic growth, financial development, the formal institutional environment in terms of existing regulatory policies, the quality of rule of law, the quality of the bureaucracy and the existence of corruption, and political (in-)stability, referring to factors such as political rights and civil liberties, etc. In Section 3, we discuss the measurement of cost efficiency of the lending practices of MFIs. Section 4 continues with a discussion of the data we use, after which we describe the empirical methodology in Section 5. In Section 6, we discuss the results of our empirical analysis. Finally, Section 7 provides a summary of the findings, their policy relevance and a research agenda for the future.

2 Macro Conditions and MFI Performance: A Review of the Literature

In this section, we review the literature on the macro conditions influencing MFI performance. In particular, we discuss the role of macroeconomic conditions, the domestic financial system, the overall (formal) institutional environment and political factors.

2.1 *Macroeconomic conditions*

Macroeconomic performance may affect MFI performance in many different ways (Ahlin, Lin and Maio, 2008). On the one hand, a growing economy may increase incentives of small-scale entrepreneurs to invest in and extend existing projects and business opportunities. Moreover, if the economy is experiencing growth, this allows these entrepreneurs to develop new profitable investment projects. This, in turn, will lead to higher demands for MFI loans and/or improving repayment performance of MFI borrowers. Both higher loan demand and improved repayment performance may also help MFIs to increase their cost efficiency. Whereas increased demand may lead to lower costs per borrower and/or loan due to economies of scale, improved repayment performance reduces costs related to recovering loans and/or reduces the costs of holding loan loss reserves. Yet, a growing economy could also lead to less growth (or even a decline) in the demand for loans as entrepreneurs are able to finance projects from the profits they generate and/or access finance from formal channels, such as banks. Consequently, MFI performance, also in terms of their cost efficiency, may be hurt.

On the other hand, if the economy is slowing down, or is even experiencing stagnation or crisis, one could argue that this leads to a rise of demand for loans from MFIs, due to the fact that in a crisis situation, people may lose their jobs in the formal economy and turn to developing activities in the informal economy. It is well-known that many MFI loans are taken up for activities carried out in the informal economy. Also, as the economy is slowing down and incomes decrease, this reduces demand for more expensive imported goods and people substitute these goods by demanding cheaper alternatives produced by domestic small-scale enterprises. This substitution effect may both raise demand for MFI loans and increase the repayment performance of MFI borrowers. In contrast, however, a slowing down of the economy may also deteriorate incomes, leading to less demand for loans as business opportunities are scarce. Moreover, with deteriorating incomes accompanying the crisis, borrowers may have more difficulties to repay their loans to the MFI.

Finally, the performance of MFIs may be unrelated to macroeconomic conditions. This is the case if most clients of MFIs concentrate their activities in the informal economy and the formal and informal economies are unrelated. In such a situation, no matter what happens in the formal economy, the business activities of MFI borrowers, and thus also the performance of MFIs (among which is also their cost efficiency), may be unaffected by macroeconomic events.

The above discussion clearly shows that the relationship between MFI performance and macroeconomic conditions is undetermined *ex ante*. Perhaps surprisingly, until now only a few studies have investigated this relationship. The importance of macroeconomic conditions has been mentioned in several impact studies. Woller and Woodworth (2001) discuss a large number of these studies and show that one of their main conclusions refers to the importance of stable economic growth, low levels of inflation and fiscal discipline as poor macroeconomic conditions hurt the viability of small-scale entrepreneurs and the MFIs that lend money to them. In a recent case study, Fernando (2003) concludes that MFIs have not been very successful in Brazil due to the high levels of inflation. In another recent case study, Sharma (2004) compares the success of microfinance in India and Nepal and concludes that the growth of MFIs in India was mainly related to the country's positive macroeconomic conditions, whereas the lack of successful growth of Nepalese MFIs was due to political instability following the Maoist insurgency in 1996.

One of the first academic papers linking macroeconomic conditions to MFI performance is a paper by Patten, Rosengard and Johnston (2001), in which they describe how Bank Rakyat Indonesia performed during the East Asian crisis of 1997–1998. Bank Rakyat Indonesia is a large commercial bank.[1] The bank provides microloans to small-scale business, next to its retail banking and corporate banking activities, which are directed

[1]Bank Rakyat Indonesia has been a state-owned bank until November 2003 when it became a listed company. The government sold 30 per cent of its shares to the public. As of the end of 2008, 43 per cent of the bank's shares were in the hands of the public. http://www.bri.co.id/TentangKami/Sejarah/tabid/61/language/en-US/Default.aspx (accessed 8 July 2009).

towards larger clients and businesses. The analysis shows that while retail and corporate banking were adversely affected by the crisis, especially in terms of credit repayment, microbanking activities thrived relatively well. Repayment of microloans remained strong and the portfolio of loans outstanding actually increased, albeit slowly, during the period from December 1996 until March 2000.

Patten *et al.* (2001) explain these positive results for the microbanking division of Bank Rakyat during the crisis by pointing out that microloans were more compatible with the cash flows generated by the small-scale borrowers, as compared to the loans extended by the corporate division to large companies. Moreover, small-scale enterprises were less affected by the Asian crisis. First, small-scale borrowers were more engaged in domestically produced goods instead of import-based goods. Consequently, they were less struck by the price increases of imports due to the crisis. Second, as many of these microloan borrowers were active in rural areas, they were also more insulated from the crisis as compared to the corporate loan borrowers in the urban areas. Finally, Patten *et al.*, argue that microloan borrowers were keener on keeping access to loans from the Bank Rakyat, perhaps because this was their only option of accessing external finance, thus making sure they repaid their loans even during the crisis.

A second academic study, by Marconi and Mosley (2006), reviews the performance of MFIs in Bolivia during the economic crisis of 1998–2004. In Bolivia, the relationship between macroeconomic conditions and MFI performance seemed to be in contrast to the Indonesian experience. Here, adverse macroeconomic conditions led to falling lending activities and increasing loan defaults. In several cases, MFIs even went bankrupt. Marconi and Mosley argue that the adverse impact of macroeconomic trends mainly affected MFIs that were profit-driven and were focused on extending consumer credit, whereas MFIs that provided additional services, such as savings, training, etc., next to issuing loans, were the ones that survived and did relatively well. Marconi and Mosley also argue that the structure of demand and government policies regarding the microfinance market may have played a role with respect to the relationship between the macro economy and MFIs. The MFIs that performed badly were the ones that had extended a large part of their loan portfolio to the services sector (particularly retail and wholesale); the service sector was hit hardest by the crisis. Moreover, the government bailed out MFIs that had debt repayment problems, thereby creating moral hazard behavior.

These two studies show that country-specific conditions may influence the relationship between macroeconomic conditions and MFI performance.

But what is the general picture? Do MFIs play the role of shock absorbers, which seems to have been the case in Indonesia, or do they accelerate the adverse impact of macroeconomic decline, which is what happened in Bolivia, at least to some extent? One recent study by Ahlin, Lin and Maio (2008) investigates the question of macro determinants of MFI performance in a broader context, using panel data (with four to 11 years of observation) for 329 MFI from 70 countries. They focus on several indicators of MFI performance, such as financial sustainability measures; default risk measures, such as write-off and portfolio-at-risk ratios; costs per borrower and growth of number of borrowers, which is an indicator of outreach. Their empirical investigation shows a number of interesting results. First, economic growth has a positive impact on MFI performance. In particular, it seems that growth is associated with the growth of the MFI loan size: higher macroeconomic growth correlates with MFIs lending larger amounts to their clients. At the same time, however, they also find that the degree of formalization and industrialization of the economy is associated negatively with MFI performance, especially when it comes to measures of their outreach. This suggests that MFI performance may be associated both positively and negatively with macroeconomic conditions.

Two other recent papers have also investigated the relationship between macroeconomic conditions and MFI performance, albeit less rigorously from an econometric point of view. Gonzalez (2007) relates economic growth to measures of MFI performance in terms of their portfolio default, using panel data (1999–2005) for 639 institutions from 88 countries. He finds no evidence that economic growth and portfolio at risk of MFIs are related and concludes that MFIs appear to be resilient to economic shocks. Strictly speaking, this conclusion is somewhat stretched, as Gonzalez does not really measure the effect of shocks, but more generally looks at economic conditions, which can be either positive or negative. Vanroose (2008) investigates a slightly different, but related issue. In her paper she asks the question whether MFIs reach out more in poorer countries, using GNI per capita as an indicator of the level of income. She uses data for one year (2004) for over 3,000 institutions from 115 different countries. In contrast to what was expected, MFIs in richer countries appear to have higher levels of outreach. According to Vanroose, this result shows that a country must have reached a threshold level of development before MFIs are able to reach out to a significant number of clients.

In conclusion, the empirical evidence on the relationship between macroeconomic conditions and MFI performance is rather scarce. Moreover, available studies provide contrasting answers and outcomes. Finally, no study has investigated the relationship between macroeconomic conditions and the cost efficiency of MFIs. Thus, a clear picture of the nature of the link between MFI performance and macroeconomic conditions is still hard to give.

2.1.1 *The domestic financial system*

MFI performance may also be related to the characteristics of the financial system of a country. The domestic financial system consists of financial institutions such as commercial banks, development banks, stock exchanges, pension funds, etc., regulatory and supervisory institutions such as central banks; and financial instruments such as debt and equity. Does the existence of a well-developed financial system affect the operations and performance of MFIs in a country? There are good reasons to believe there is a connection between the two. First, in a more developed financial system, commercial banks may become engaged in offering microloans, especially if these activities have been shown to be profitable for MFIs. In the literature, this process is referred to as "downscaling". The growth of microloan activities of commercial banks may confront MFIs with increased competition for borrowers. This may force them to reduce costs and improve the quality of services delivered. Second, the presence of commercial banks may lead to positive spill-over effects in terms of modern and more efficient banking techniques that may be copied by MFIs. Moreover, it may improve the skills of loan officers and managers working at MFIs, since it enlarges the pool of financially educated people. Third, if the domestic financial system is more developed, MFIs themselves may have better opportunities to have access to financial services, such as saving, borrowing, refinancing loans, transferring funds between branches, hedging for specific risks (such as exchange rate risk), etc. All these arguments suggest there may be a positive relationship between MFI performance and the level of development of the financial system in which they are embedded.

The relationship may also be negative, however. First the presence of commercial banks may lead borrowers to substitute their loans from MFIs for loans from commercial banks for various reasons, such as lower borrowing costs, more flexibility with respect to borrowing options and larger amounts that can be borrowed. Moreover, competition may have an adverse effect on the repayment performance of MFI borrowers, if they take up multiple loans from different financial institutions (McIntosh, De Janvry and Sadoulet, 2005). Finally, the development of the domestic financial system and MFI performance may be correlated negatively when these institutions complement the low level of financial development in these countries. A high demand for MFI services in environments in which financial services are scarce may help increase the efficiency of MFI activities.

Only two studies have explicitly investigated the relationship between financial system development and MFI performance. Vanroose and D'Espallier (2009) find that MFIs have higher outreach and are more profitable when access to the formal financial system is low. They argue that this result supports the so-called market-failure hypothesis, i.e. MFIs perform better in environments where the formal banking sector fails. At the same time, however, they also find evidence that MFI performance and formal financial sector development are correlated positively. First, MFIs are less profitable when interest rates are high, which they interpret as for the fact that MFIs depend upon the domestic banking system for external funding. Second, they show that MFIs are less profitable when inflation is high. This may suggest that MFIs benefit from a stable formal financial system. Hermes, Lensink and Meesters (2009) focus on analyzing the relationship between MFI efficiency and measures of financial system development. They find evidence that MFI efficiency and domestic financial system development are positively correlated. They interpret this result as evidence for the fact that more developed financial systems create more efficient MFIs. More specifically, they claim that in an environment with more developed bank markets, increased competition provides incentives for MFIs to improving the efficiency of their activities. Ahlin *et al.* (2008) also look at the impact of the financial system on MFI performance, but take this as one of several aspects of the macroeconomic context. Their results corroborate those of Hermes *et al.* (2009) as they also find evidence that competition is beneficial for MFIs' performance. In particular, they show that deeper financial markets are associated with lower costs, lower interest rate margins and lower default rates. Moreover, they relate information on credit rights and credit information availability to performance and show that especially credit information availability is associated positively to lower operating costs of MFIs.

Overall then, the few available empirical studies on the relationship of the characteristics of the domestic financial system and MFI performance provide mixed results.

2.1.2 *Formal institutions*

A third class of macro conditions that may influence MFI performance relates to the existence (or absence) and quality of formal institutions.

With respect to formal institutions, we focus on measures of the rule of law, the establishment of property rights, regulatory quality, government effectiveness and control of corruption. In the literature, these aspects of the institutional environment have been studied extensively, in particular due to the work of Kaufmann, Kraay and Mastruzzi (2008). In their work, they have developed several measures of the institutional quality per country in terms of the perceptions of individuals regarding different aspects of the country's institutional environment. To be more specific, Kaufmann *et al.* (2008) collected data on the rule of law, which is measured as perceptions of individuals regarding the confidence they have in the quality of contract enforcement, property rights, the police and the courts. Government effectiveness measures perceptions of individuals regarding the quality of public services, the quality of the civil service and the degree of its independence from political pressures, the quality of policy formulation and implementation, and the credibility of the government's commitment to such policies. Regulatory quality focuses on the measurement of perceptions regarding the ability of the government to formulate and implement sound policies and regulations permitting and promoting private sector development. Finally, Kaufmann *et al.*, collected data on the control of corruption, which is measured as perceptions regarding the extent to which public power is exercised for private gain.[2]

In theory, the institutional environment may be an important determinant of the possibilities and/or restraints entrepreneurs are confronted with when operating existing or starting new business activities. As was the case with macroeconomic growth and financial system variables, the institutional environment may affect MFI performance in both directions. On the one hand, well-developed institutions such as clear property rights, strong rule of law and a well-functioning and effective government that is able to formulate business-friendly policies and to reduce the use of corruption, may be important prerequisites for small-scale business to thrive. If this is the

[2]In our analysis, we do not explicitly take into account measures of the regulatory frameworks of countries as one of the formal institutional factors. Two recent papers by Hartarska and Nadolnyak (2007) and Cull *et al.* (2009) focus on regulatory frameworks and MFI performance, showing mixed results. Both papers use time invariant indicators of the regulatory framework of a country. In our paper, we decided to leave out these measures, because we have a panel dataset for 11 years, but we have no panel data on the regulatory frameworks per country and on the question whether MFIs are regulated yes or no. The MixMarket data does provide information with respect to whether an MFI is regulated yes or no, but this information is invariant over time, i.e., it does not indicate when the MFI became regulated.

case, then the demand for loans and other services of MFIs will rise, leading to better performance of these institutions. On the other hand, however, well-developed institutions may also make doing business more difficult. For example, an effective government may also mean a large amount of rules and regulations which entrepreneurs have to obey. The costs of these rules and regulations may be especially burdensome for small-scale entrepreneurs due to the fixed cost character. As another example, if corruption is reduced effectively, this may reduce possibilities of especially small-scale business to avoid all kinds of costly government rules and tax payments and/or may make it more difficult to get access to government services that are difficult to obtain without paying bribes. If this is the case, then institutional quality may actually hinder rather than accommodate private initiative, leading to less demand for MFI services and thus, also lower performance (including cost efficiency) of these institutions.

The importance of formal institutions for microfinance has been mentioned in various studies. Hubka and Zaidi (2005) stress the importance of facilitating the formalization of small-scale business activities in the informal sector, for example by simplifying the process to establish property rights. Ledgerwood (1999), in her book, also emphasizes the importance of having strong property rights. Zeller and Meyer (2002) argue that government interventions lead to high administrative costs and distorted pricing systems, which hurt the performance of MFIs. Yet, although these studies mention the importance of institutional factors, they do not explicitly measure their impact on MFI performance.

Ahlin *et al.* (2008) provide one of the very few systematic analyses of the relationship between formal institutions and MFI performance. They use the Kaufmann indicators and link them to different measures of MFI performance. In general, the study shows that there is some evidence that MFI performance (especially in terms of operating costs) is worse when institutions are stronger. Moreover, Ahlin *et al.* used data from the Doing Business survey of the World Bank. This survey includes information on institutional barriers business may be confronted with, such as how difficult it is to officially start a business, how long it takes to enforce a written contract, and indicators of labor-related regulations. Ahlin *et al.* find supportive evidence for the fact that indicators of starting a business are positively related to smaller loan sizes, which they interprete as evidence that difficulties in officially starting a business pushes small-scale entrepreneurs towards borrowing from MFIs. Moreover, they find indications that higher barriers to official contract enforcement are associated with smaller loans and lower costs, which again is interpreted as evidence that small-scale entrepreneurs are borrowing from MFIs due to these insitutional restrictions. Finally, labor market rigidities are negatively associated with MFI performance: these rigidities make doing business more difficult leading to less demand for loans from MFIs, thus reducing their performance.

Crabb (2007) provides another empirical investigation of the relationship between the institutional environment and MFI performance. His analysis is based on data for 511 MFIs of 90 countries for the period 2000–2004. Crabb focuses on measures of financial sustainability of MFIs and relate these to measures of economic freedom, provided by the Heritage Foundation. These measures include the quality of property rights, the extent of government intervention, the extent to which the government interferes with the financial sector, regulations regarding labor markets, and an overall measure of the extent of regulations that may affect doing business in a country. Of these measures, only the extent of government regulations and the extent to which the government interferes with the financial sector adversely affect the financial sustainability of MFIs.

To conclude, the scarce evidence on the relationship between institutional quality and MFI performance seems to suggest that the relationship is generally negative, meaning that better institutions are costly for MFI clients. Thus, improving institutional quality raises the cost of operations of MFIs.

2.1.3 *Political factors*

Finally, we focus on how political factors may influence MFI performance. Political factors may first of all cover the type of political system of a country. This may be measured by the extent to which society is able to raise its voice with respect to political decisions and/or the extent to which politicians can be held accountable, for example, through regular elections. Moreover, the role of freedom of the press is an important dimension of the accountability of policymakers. Political systems in which politicians can be held accountable and where the population may influence decision-making can be either positively or negatively related to economic activity (Przeworski and Limongi, 1993). On the one hand, if politicians can be held accountable and the population can raise its voice, this may lead to a more open society and to the development of policies that are supportive to doing business in general. This may also support the growth of small-scale entrepreneurship, leading to higher demand for MFI services, thus increasing the performance of these institutions.

In contrast, it may also be argued that once the political system is less transparent, politicians are unaccountable and the population has no possibilities to raise its voice, economic activity may be adversely affected. One consequence may be that economic actors turn to the informal sector for their business and since many MFIs focus on financing activities in the informal sector, this may lead to a negative association between political accountability and MFI performance, i.e., the lower the political accountability, the higher the performance of MFIs.

A second important political factor may be the stability of the political system. This can be measured in terms of the extent of cross-border, civil and/or ethnic conflicts, number of assassinations, coups, etc. A fair amount of empirical studies have shown the existence of a negative association between political instability and macroeconomic growth (Alesina, Ozler, Roubini and Swagel, 1996). Generally speaking, in politically instable environments, doing business becomes extremely difficult, as it may disrupt economic activity in general. Access to inputs may become difficult; infrastructure such as roads, telephone and internet facilities may be destroyed or at least function far from optimal; and opportunities to sell output may have reduced substantially. Moreover, entrepreneurs may wait until political stability has been reestablished before undertaking costly and irreversible investment projects. Finally, domestic savings may fall, as risk-averse individuals may put their money on foreign banks outside the reach of the government. However, MFIs may also show increased performance in times of war and political unrest. This may be the case the moment they are used as one of the solutions to reduce the impact of war and unrest on the population. Actually, in some cases, microfinance has been used as an instrument for conflict and post-conflict resolution. Examples of MFIs that have been established during and after domestic political conflicts can be found in, for example, Bosnia, Kosovo, Liberia and Uganda (Doerring *et al.*, 2004).

The relationship between political variables and the performance of MFIs is shortly discussed in Ahlin *et al.* (2008). They use a measure of voice and accountability from the Kaufmann dataset defined as the extent to which the population is able to participate in selecting the government, the extent of the freedom of expression, freedom of association and a free media. For this variable, they find a positive association with the costs per dollar lent. They argue that this may indicate that in countries with higher levels of voice and accountability, costs of lending are higher due to the fact that MFIs' feedback, responsiveness and transparency are expected to be better developed. Sometimes, in qualitative case studies, the role of political factors is discussed. As was mentioned above, Sharma (2004) argues that the lack of successful growth of Nepalese MFIs was due to political instability following the Maoist insurgency in 1996.

2.1.4 *Concluding remarks*

In this section, we have discussed the relationship between various macro conditions and MFI performance. The discussion made clear that the relationship may go both ways. Either these macro conditions provide a solid basis for stimulating private small-scale entrepreneurship and initiative, subsequently leading to more demand for loans and other services from MFIs, as well as better repayment performance; or they reduce repayment performance and/or reduce the demand for these services, for example, due to the substitution of MFI borrowing by formal bank borrowing, or by hindering private initiative. Changes with respect to the demand for MFI services and/or the repayment performance of existing clients also affects the cost structure of MFIs, i.e., their cost efficiency may change as well. Moreover, changing competition in microfinance markets directly affects cost structures and cost efficiency. Since, on theoretical grounds, it is impossible to conclude whether the relationship between the two is positive or negative, we need empirical analysis to draw conclusions. In the next section, we provide new empirical evidence that should help to evaluate the direction of the relationship between the macro conditions and MFI performance. Our empirical analysis adds to existing work because we focus on explaining differences in cost efficiency due to differences in the macro conditions MFIs are confronted with. To the best of our knowlegde, this is the first study investigating the relationship between cost efficiency of MFIs and various macro conditions.[3]

3 Methodology

As has been discussed extensively in the literature, financial sustainability may be a prerequisite for microfinance in making a significant and long-term

[3]In the discussion on the relationship between macro conditions and MFI performance we assume that causality runs from the macro conditions to MFI performance. Admittedly, MFI performance may, at least in theory, also affect macro conditions, such as macroeconomic performance and financial system development. However, since the size of the MFI activities is considered to be relatively small relative to the size of a country's economic activities and the domestic formal financial market, we rule out the possibility that MFI performance drives macro conditions.

contribution to poverty reduction. Financial sustainability is determined by the extent to which MFIs are efficient in using resources and turning them into services. Knowing the determinants of MFI efficiency helps us understand what determines financial sustainability, which in turn increases our understanding of the potential of microfinance in making a contribution to poverty reduction. This is why, in our analysis, we focus on cost efficiency as our measure of MFI performance, i.e., providing services at the lowest possible cost.

We measure cost efficiency in terms of how close the actual costs of the lending activities of an MFI are to what the costs of a best-practice MFI would have been when producing identical output under the same conditions. In order to be able to know what the costs of a best-practice MFI in producing its services are, we need to estimate a so-called efficient cost function or efficient cost frontier. This frontier shows the combinations of output volumes and related minimum levels of inputs costs. If an MFI is cost-efficient, it is located somewhere on the frontier. In this case, the MFI is said to be both technically efficient (meaning that it maximizes available production-given inputs) and allocatively efficient (i.e., it uses the optimal mix of inputs given the relative price of each input). If an MFI is located somewhere below the efficient cost frontier, however, it is producing its services (technically and/or allocatively) inefficiently. The distance between the location below the frontier and the frontier is a measure of the extent to which the MFI is considered to be inefficient. Figure 8.1 illustrates this point.

There are several methodologies that allow for determining the efficient cost frontier and inefficiencies (i.e., distances to the frontier) for

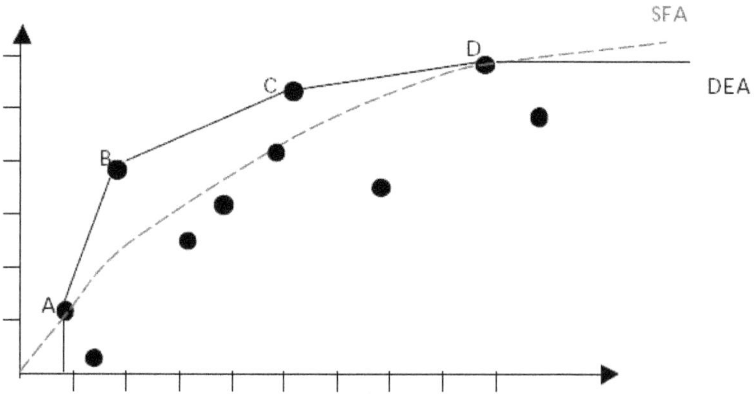

Figure 8.1: Efficient cost frontier.

individually-producing units (in our case MFIs). The two most often used methodologies are the data envelopment analysis (DEA) and the stochastic frontier analysis (SFA). Both methods use the observed data on input prices and output of producing units as their information set. DEA determines the frontier as the curve linking output levels for which costs are minimized (see Figure 8.1). SFA estimates the efficienct cost frontier, rather than deterministically establish its position, as is the case for DEA. In technical terms, DEA is a non-parametric approach, whereas SFA is a parametric approach.[4] SFA allows for taking into account several factors that may determine the position of the cost frontier, next to output levels and input prices. It also allows for measurement errors in the underlying information set. Non-parametric techniques do not allow for measurement errors. These techniques attribute any deviation from the best-practice MFI to inefficiency. When SFA is used, however, some combinations of output levels and input prices may lie above the efficient cost frontier, i.e., when the measurement error is substantial. In the analysis, we use a specific version of SFA, allowing us to simultaneously estimate the cost frontier and the equation specifying the determinants of the distance between realized costs and output levels for each individual MFI (i.e. the inefficiency equation). As explained, this distance is our measure of inefficiency.[5] Both equations are estimated using the maximum likelihood technique.

For the specification of the cost function of an MFI, we use the model developed by Sealey and Lindley (1977), who state that a bank acts as an intermediary between funders and borrowers. In their model, loans are defined as the output of a bank, whereas deposits are taken as inputs. Following their approach, we use total expenses per unit of labor and the interest expenses per unit of deposits held as input prices, whereas we use the gross loan portfolio of an MFI as our measure of output. The cost function has a translog specification to allow for maximum flexibility when determining the shape of the frontier. This means that our specification takes into account the individual input and output variables, the square of these

[4]For a more extensive review of the differences between the non-parametric and the parametric approach, see Matousek and Taci (2004). The contribution of Gutierrez-Nieto *et al.*, in this volume applies DEA in the context of MFI efficiency.

[5]See Battese and Coelli (1995) and Wang and Schmidt (2002) for more details about this approach to SFA, and why estimating the frontier and inefficiency equation simulataneously is preferred as compared to estimating both equations separately in two subsequent steps.

variables, as well as combinations of these variables. We use the following specification of the cost function:

$$\begin{aligned}\ln(TC_{i,t}) = {} & \beta_0 + \beta_1 \ln(LABOR_{i,t}) + \beta_2 \ln(CAPITAL_{i,t}) \\ & + \beta_3 \ln(LOANS_{i,t}) + \beta_4 \ln(LABOR_{i,t})^2 \\ & + \beta_5 \ln(CAPITAL_{i,t})^2 + \beta_6 \ln(LOANS_{i,t})^2 \\ & + \beta_7 \ln(LABOR_{i,t}) \ln(CAPITAL_{i,t}) \\ & + \beta_8 \ln(LABOR_{i,t}) \ln(LOANS_{i,t}) \\ & + \beta_9 \ln(CAPITAL_{i,t}) \ln(LOANS_{i,t}) + \beta_{10} YEAR_t \\ & + \beta_{11} YEAR_t^2 + \beta_{12} YEAR_t(LABOR_{i,t}) \\ & + \beta_{13} YEAR(CAPITAL_{i,t}) + \beta_{14} YEAR(LOANS_{i,t}) \\ & + \sum_{m=15}^{18} \beta_m MFITYPE_{i,t} + \beta_{19} EQ_{i,t} + \beta_{20} LLR_{i,t}. \qquad (1)\end{aligned}$$

In equation (1), TC represents total costs MFI i faces at time t and is measured as the total expenses of an MFI; $LABOR$ represents the price of a unit of labor for one year and is measured as the total operating expenses per employee of an MFI; $CAPITAL$ is the interest expenses per unit of deposits held and is measured as the MFI's total financial expenses per US dollar of deposits; and $LOANS$ is the gross loan portfolio. All input and output variables and the dependent variable in equation (1) are taken in logs. We also include a year dummy ($YEAR$), which runs from 1 to 11, the square of the year dummy, and its interactions with the input variables to account for technology changes over time.

In order to control for the fact that different types of MFIs may have different cost functions, we add a vector of dummies for the type of MFI ($MFITYPE$). In particular, cost functions may differ between types of MFI due to differences in the levels of subsidies these institutions receive from outside.[6] We have dummy variables for banks ($BANK$), cooperatives ($COOP$), non-bank financial institutions ($NBANK$) non-governmental organizations (NGO), rural banks ($RBANK$) and other organizations

[6]The data we use (discussed in more detail below) do not provide detailed information about subsidies received. By adding dummies for different types of MFIs, we assume that subsidy levels are similar for the same type of MFIs.

(*OTHER*).[7] Finally, we add two control variables measuring differences in risk-taking strategies among MFIs. These variables are the equity to total assets ratio (*EQ*) and the loan loss reserves divided by gross loans outstanding (*LLR*).

As explained above, the focus of our analysis is on establishing the determinants of MFI inefficiency. For this, we specify the inefficiency equation in which measures of macro conditions are included, as it is the aim of this paper to analyze whether macro conditions are related to the efficiency of MFIs. Next to a set of macro variables, we include two MFI-specific control variables, which may also influence the inefficiency of MFIs. Following the discussion on macro conditions and MFI performance in Section 2, the inefficiency equation is specified as follows:

$$\begin{aligned} INEFF_{i,t} = {} & \gamma_0 + \gamma_1 GROWTH_{i,t} + \gamma_2 INCOME_{i,t} \\ & + \gamma_3 CREDIT_{j,t} + \sum_{4}^{7} \gamma_{n=4\ldots7} INSTIT_{j,t} \\ & + \sum_{8}^{14} \gamma_{n=8\ldots14} POLIT_{j,t} + \gamma_{15} AGE_{i,t} \\ & + \gamma_{16} LSIZE_{i,t}. \end{aligned} \tag{2}$$

In equation (2), $INEFF_{i,t}$ is a measure of inefficiency for MFI i at time t, determined by the distance between the observed output-input combination of MFI i at time t and the efficient cost frontier. The first five (sets of) independent variables relate to the four classes of macro conditions discussed in Section 2. $GROWTH_{j,t}$ is the annual growth rate of GDP per capita of country j at time t, which is our measure of the macroeconomic conditions an MFI is confronted with. *INCOME* is the log of GDP per capita. This variable is included to control for the fact that MFIs in more developed countries may generally be more efficient. *CREDIT* measures the private credit to GDP ratio, which is a generally accepted measure of the development of the domestic financial sector of a country (King and Levine, 1993; Levine, 2005). *INSTIT* is a vector of measures of institutional quality, generally known as the Kaufmann indicators (Kaufmann *et al.*, 2008).[8] It includes measures of

[7] The dummy variable *OTHER* is left out of the empirical analysis for reasons of singularity.

[8] We do not use the Doing Business database of the World Bank to measure institutional quality. Although this database provides important information with respect to the institutional barriers related to starting a business, enforcing contracts, etc., the information is only available from 2003, which would seriously reduce the number of observations in the analysis.

government effectiveness (*GOVEFF*), regulatory quality (*REGQ*), rule of law (*RULE*) and control of corruption (*CORRUPT*). Finally, *POLIT* is a vector of variables related to the political system and political stability of a country. This vector includes a measure of the extent to which the population is able to participate in political decision-making (*VOICE*), which is one of the Kaufmann indicators. The vector also includes six measures of political instability, measuring the extent to which a country has been involved in or confronted with international violence (*INTVIOL*), international war conflicts (*INTWAR*), domestic violence (*CIVVIOL*), civil wars (*CIVWAR*), ethnic violence (*ETHNVIOL*) and/or ethnic wars (*ETHNWAR*). The political instability variables are taken from the *POLITY IV* data set. The two MFI-specific control variables are *AGE* and *LOAN*. *AGE* measures the number of years since the MFI was established, controlling for the possibility that older MFIs may be more experienced and therefore more efficient; or, alternatively, that younger MFI are more efficienct. The inclusion of this variable is based on Alexander Gerschenkron's (1962) notion of the advantages of backwardness. *LSIZE* is the average loan size per borrower (in logs), which is added to control for the possibility that MFIs with larger clients/loans are also more efficient due to economies of scale.

4 Data

For our analysis, we use data from the MixMarket™, a global web-based microfinance information platform. From this dataset, we obtain information for 435 MFIs in 63 countries over a period of 11 years (1997–2007). These MFIs have been selected based upon data availability with respect to the variables we need for the estimation of the cost frontier and the efficiency equation. Our full sample consists of 1,304 observations. For many MFIs, we have only one or two years of observation, and we do not have information for all 11 years for any institution.[9]

We acknowledge that the dataset we have created may be biased towards the larger and more profitable MFIs, since participation by these institutions in the MixMarket database is voluntary. This also means that the MFIs in

[9]Data requirements regarding the costs and output of MFIs are quite demanding, which results in the loss of a relatively large number of MFIs for which this type of data is not available in the MixMarket dataset. Still, our sample of 435 MFIs and more than 1,300 observations allows us to come up with robust estimations of the cost frontier and the inefficiency equation.

Table 8.1: Descriptive statistics.

Variable	Observations	Mean	Std. Dev.	Min	Max
TC	1,304	14.01	2.12	7.42	20.54
LABOR	1,304	8.96	1.02	5.77	11.16
CAPITAL	1,304	−2.05	1.80	−8.95	5.94
LOANS	1304	15.25	2.17	8.08	21.83
BANK	1,304	0.18	0.38	0	1
COOP	1,304	0.31	0.46	0	1
NBANK	1,304	0.25	0.43	0	1
NGO	1,304	0.15	0.36	0	1
RBANK	1,304	0.10	0.31	0	1
LLR	1,304	0.04	0.05	−0.07	0.81
EQ	1,304	0.27	0.23	−1.43	0.96
YEAR	1,304	7.91	1.95	1	11
AGE	1,304	12.24	12.33	1	111
LSIZE	1,304	6.09	1.30	2.40	10.01
INCOME	884	6.45	0.90	4.74	8.73
GROWTH	884	0.03	0.03	−0.15	0.25
CREDIT	861	24.32	15.14	3.43	120.33
VOICE	1,228	−0.36	0.56	−1.82	1.21
GOVEFF	1,222	−0.50	0.42	−1.59	1.35
REGQ	1,221	−0.40	0.48	−2.33	1.48
RULE	1,225	−0.64	0.43	−2.07	1.20
CORRUPT	1,225	−0.64	0.42	−1.54	1.48
INTVIOLl	1,218	0.02	0.12	0	1
INTWAR	1,218	0.04	0.36	0	5
CIVVIOL	1,218	0.07	0.38	0	4
CIVWAR	1,218	0.05	0.31	0	3
ETHNVIOL	1,218	0.22	0.67	0	4
ETHNWAR	1,218	0.61	1.42	0	5

our sample are probably also more cost-efficient on average. At the same time, however, we do not have access to other more comprehensive data that allows us to analyze the efficiency of MFIs, leaving us no other option than using the current dataset. Table 8.1 provides the descriptive statistics of the variables we have used in the empirical analysis.

Table 8.2 provides information on the average inefficiency of MFIs at the country level. The variable *INEFF* is 1 if the MFI is at the cost frontier, i.e., it is technically and allocatively efficient. If *INEFF* has a value of 2, this means that the MFI produces output (loans) at cost levels that are twice the level of a cost-efficient MFI located at the cost frontier. Thus, the higher the value of *INEFF*, the more inefficient the MFI is. The table shows that the most efficient MFIs can be found in Bulgaria (with MFIs

Table 8.2: Inefficiency of MFIs: Country averages.

Country	INEFF	Country	INEFF	Country	INEFF
Bulgaria	1.19	Benin	2.09	Mozambique	2.51
Azerbaijan	1.24	Mexico	2.09	Moldova	2.53
Namibia	1.25	Nicaragua	2.15	Rwanda	2.56
Georgia	1.31	Panama	2.17	Nigeria	2.63
Brazil	1.32	India	2.17	Pakistan	2.69
Dominican Rep.	1.35	Zambia	2.21	Tanzania	2.70
Chad	1.44	Niger	2.21	Vietnam	2.73
Guatemala	1.45	Kenya	2.22	Ghana	2.75
El Salvador	1.52	Togo	2.23	Sri Lanka	2.77
Chile	1.55	Philippines	2.25	Kazakhstan	2.80
Bosnia and H.	1.56	Burkina F.	2.25	Costa Rica	2.83
Bolivia	1.58	Ethiopia	2.27	Bangladesh	2.85
South Africa	1.58	Angola	2.28	Honduras	2.94
Romania	1.61	Mali	2.30	Malawi	3.03
Ecuador	1.67	Indonesia	2.31	Colombia	3.11
Peru	1.79	Mongolia	2.33	Madagascar	3.19
Tajikistan	1.80	Nepal	2.34	Uganda	3.20
Senegal	1.88	Lebanon	2.36	Guinea	3.38
Albania	1.94	Paraguay	2.45	Uruguay	3.72
Ukraine	1.99	Cameroon	2.46	Haiti	3.76
Armenia	2.08	Cambodia	2.47	Zimbabwe	4.71

in Azerbaijan and Namibia close by), whereas the most inefficient MFIs are located in Zimbabwe. Whereas in Bulgaria, MFIs seem to be close to the efficient cost frontier (*INEFF* is 1.19), in Zimbabwe MFIs on average produce at cost levels that are 5 times those of a cost-efficient MFI.

Table 8.3 shows average inefficiency values at the regional level. The general picture seems to be that MFIs in Eastern European and Latin American countries are relatively less inefficient, whereas MFIs in Africa and South Asia are relatively more inefficient. Finally, if we look at inefficiency from the perspective of the type of MFIs (also shown in Table 8.3), it appears that MFI banks are most cost-efficient, whereas NGOs are most inefficient.[10] This outcome may not be surprising, as NGO generally are less focused on producing services at the lowest cost, whereas MFI banks, which are active in competitive markets, need to care about their cost efficiency more, because otherwise they run the risk of being pushed out of the market.

[10] A similar result was found in a recent study by Gonzalez and Rosenberg (2006).

Table 8.3: Inefficiency of MFIs: regional averages and averages per MFI type.

Country region	INEFF	MFI Type	INEFF
Africa	2.47	*BANK*	1.92
East Asia	2.37	*COOP*	2.18
Eastern Europe	1.75	*NBANK*	2.44
Latin America	1.86	*NGO*	2.78
South Asia	2.89	*RBANK*	2.14
Average	2.29	Average	2.29

5 Results

Tables 8.4 and 8.5 provide the estimation results of the relationship between macro conditions and the cost efficiency of MFIs. Table 8.4 discusses the results regarding macroeconomic, financial system and institutional conditions and the results regarding the political system; Table 8.5 shows the results for the political instability factors. Panels 4A and 5A show the results of the efficient cost frontier; panels 4B and 5B show the results for the inefficiency equation. As was explained in Section 3, both equations are estimated simultaneously using SFA. Since our data have a panel structure, all estimations have been carried out using pooled regressions.

Panel A of Table 8.4 refers to the estimation results of the cost frontier. A positive coefficient implies an outward shift of the cost function, and hence — *ceteris-paribus* — higher costs. The estimation results are as expected in most cases: the coefficients for *LABOR* and *LOANS* are always significant and positive. The coefficient for *CAPITAL* is not significant, implying that the cost of capital for the MFI does not influence its costs. Yet, the interaction term with *LABOR* and the quadratic term for *CAPITAL* are significant and always positive, which suggests that interest costs are an important factor explaining total costs of MFIs. All dummy variables for the type of MFIs, as well as the variables *EQUITY* and *LLR* are statistically significant in all specifications in Table 8.4A, indicating that the type of MFI and the risk-taking strategy of an MFI indeed affect the cost frontier. Finally, the year dummy (*YEAR*) is always negative and statistically significant, suggesting that total costs have reduced over time, possibly due to technological changes. Based upon the results reported in Table 8.4 we conclude that we are able to specify a cost frontier that fits theory reasonably well.

Table 8.4A: Results of the estimations — The cost frontier, part 1.

	[1]	[2]	[3]	[4]	[5]	[6]
LABOR	1.604***	1.367***	1.282***	1.303***	1.301***	1.300***
	[0.233]	[0.242]	[0.242]	[0.242]	[0.241]	[0.241]
CAPITAL	−0.122	−0.111	−0.129	−0.139	−0.14	−0.137
	[0.101]	[0.103]	[0.106]	[0.105]	[0.105]	[0.105]
LOANS	0.733***	0.746***	0.773***	0.765***	0.766***	0.768***
	[0.090]	[0.092]	[0.092]	[0.092]	[0.092]	[0.092]
*LABOR*CAPITAL*	0.025**	0.019*	0.018*	0.019*	0.019*	0.019*
	[0.010]	[0.011]	[0.011]	[0.011]	[0.011]	[0.011]
*CAPITAL*LOANS*	−0.005	−0.003	−0.001	−0.001	−0.001	−0.001
	[0.006]	[0.006]	[0.006]	[0.006]	[0.006]	[0.006]
*LABOR*LOANS*	−0.01	−0.007	−0.008	−0.008	−0.008	−0.008
	[0.009]	[0.009]	[0.009]	[0.009]	[0.009]	[0.009]
$LABOR^2$	−0.062***	−0.051***	−0.046***	−0.048***	−0.047***	−0.047***
	[0.015]	[0.016]	[0.016]	[0.016]	[0.016]	[0.016]
$LOANS^2$	0.006*	0.005	0.005	0.005	0.005	0.005
	[0.003]	[0.003]	[0.003]	[0.003]	[0.003]	[0.003]
$CAPITAL^2$	0.005**	0.005*	0.004*	0.004*	0.004*	0.004*
	[0.002]	[0.002]	[0.002]	[0.002]	[0.002]	[0.003]
BANK	−0.713***	−0.688***	−0.695***	−0.695***	−0.695***	−0.695***
	[0.159]	[0.160]	[0.159]	[0.160]	[0.160]	[0.160]
COOP	−1.296***	−1.297***	−1.297***	−1.300***	−1.300***	−1.300***
	[0.158]	[0.159]	[0.159]	[0.159]	[0.159]	[0.159]
NBANK	−0.971***	−0.975***	−0.988***	−0.992***	−0.994***	−0.992***
	[0.161]	[0.162]	[0.162]	[0.162]	[0.162]	[0.162]
NGO	−1.052***	−1.047***	−1.049***	−1.053***	−1.054***	−1.053***
	[0.163]	[0.164]	[0.164]	[0.164]	[0.164]	[0.164]
RBANK	−1.276***	−1.272***	−1.275***	−1.274***	−1.274***	−1.273***
	[0.166]	[0.168]	[0.167]	[0.167]	[0.167]	[0.167]
LLR	2.515***	2.487***	2.466***	2.470***	2.471***	2.468***
	[0.221]	[0.221]	[0.219]	[0.219]	[0.219]	[0.220]
EQ	−0.269***	−0.259***	−0.257***	−0.261***	−0.263***	−0.260***
	[0.069]	[0.071]	[0.071]	[0.071]	[0.071]	[0.071]
YEAR	−0.187**	−0.157*	−0.163*	−0.167*	−0.168*	−0.166*
	[0.088]	[0.089]	[0.089]	[0.089]	[0.089]	[0.089]
$YEAR^2$	0.008**	0.010***	0.010***	0.010***	0.010***	0.010***
	[0.003]	[0.003]	[0.003]	[0.003]	[0.003]	[0.003]
*LOANS*YEAR*	0.001	0.000	0.000	0.000	0.000	0.000
	[0.005]	[0.005]	[0.005]	[0.005]	[0.005]	[0.005]
*LABOR*YEAR*	0.007	0.003	0.004	0.005	0.005	0.005
	[0.009]	[0.009]	[0.009]	[0.009]	[0.009]	[0.009]
*CAPITAL*YEAR*	0.002	0.002	0.002	0.002	0.002	0.002
	[0.005]	[0.005]	[0.005]	[0.005]	[0.005]	[0.005]
Constant	−5.821***	−4.891***	−4.769***	−4.818***	−4.811***	−4.817***
	[1.044]	[1.076]	[1.069]	[1.067]	[1.067]	[1.069]
Observations	884	848	848	848	848	848
Number of MFIs	339	324	324	324	324	324

Note: Standard errors are between brackets; *, ** and *** refer to levels of significance at 10, 5 and 1 per cent.

Table 8.4B: Results of the estimations — The inefficiency equation, part 1.

	[1]	[2]	[3]	[4]	[5]	[6]
INCOME	−0.043*	0.001	−0.012	−0.003	−0.005	−0.005
	[0.024]	[0.028]	[0.029]	[0.030]	[0.027]	[0.028]
GROWTH	−2.089***	−2.309***	−2.051***	−1.964***	−1.953***	−1.975***
	[0.590]	[0.601]	[0.594]	0.578]	[0.580]	[0.577]
CREDIT		−0.006***	−0.006***	−0.006***	−0.005***	−0.006***
		[0.002]	[0.002]	[0.002]	[0.002]	[0.002]
GOVEFF			0.048			
			[0.058]			
REGQ				−0.009		
				[0.049]		
RULE					−0.014	
					[0.050]	
CORRUPT						0.000
						[0.053]
AGE	0.008***	0.008***	0.007***	0.007***	0.007***	0.007***
	[0.002]	[0.002]	[0.002]	[0.002]	[0.002]	[0.002]
LSIZE	−0.211***	−0.209***	−0.205***	−0.207***	−0.208***	−0.207***
	[0.025]	[0.025]	[0.025]	[0.024]	[0.025]	[0.025]
Constant	2.168***	2.001***	2.100***	2.028***	2.039***	2.044***
	[0.208]	[0.216]	[0.224]	[0.229]	[0.214]	[0.218]
Observations	884	848	848	848	848	848
Number of MFIs	339	330	324	324	324	324

Note: Standard errors are between brackets; *, ** and *** refer to levels of significance at 10, 5 and 1 per cent.

Panel B of Table 8.4 refers to the estimation of the inefficiency equation, focusing on the impact of macro conditions on MFI efficiency. The results in columns [1] through [6] suggest the following. First, we find strong evidence that macroeconomic conditions are positively related to the efficiency of MFIs (columns [1] to [6]). The coefficient of the variable *GROWTH* is negative and highly significant, indicating that if per capita growth increases, the inefficiency of MFIs goes down. The results also show that MFI inefficiency does not vary with the level of economic development: *INCOME* is never significant (except in column [1]). Second, the development of the domestic financial system is also positively associated with the efficiency of MFIs, as the coefficient of the variable *CREDIT* is very significant and negative in all specifications (columns [2] to [6]). Thus, macroeconomic and financial system conditions very clearly have an impact on the efficiency of MFIs. This corroborates the findings reported in Ahlin *et al.* (2008), but contrasts the results found by Gonzalez (2007).

The results for the institutional environment are far less satisfying. None of the four variables we include in our analysis is statistically significant (see

Table 8.5A: Results of the estimations — The cost frontier, part 2.

	[7]	[8]	[9]	[10]	[11]	[12]	[13]
LABOR	1.322***	1.353***	1.321***	1.326***	1.317***	1.328***	1.301***
	[0.241]	[0.240]	[0.241]	[0.241]	[0.241]	[0.241]	[0.242]
CAPITAL	−0.151	−0.164	−0.152	−0.152	−0.134	−0.157	−0.144
	[0.104]	[0.104]	[0.104]	[0.104]	[0.105]	[0.104]	[0.105]
LOANS	0.766***	0.770***	0.765***	0.753***	0.774***	0.770***	0.777***
	[0.091]	[0.090]	[0.091]	[0.092]	[0.091]	[0.091]	[0.092]
*LABOR*CAPITAL*	0.019*	0.022**	0.019*	0.020*	0.018*	0.021*	0.018*
	[0.011]	[0.011]	[0.011]	[0.011]	[0.011]	[0.011]	[0.011]
*CAPITAL*LOANS*	0.000	0.000	0.000	−0.001	0.000	0.000	0.000
	[0.006]	[0.006]	[0.006]	[0.006]	[0.006]	[0.006]	[0.006]
*LABOR*LOANS*	−0.008	−0.009	−0.007	−0.007	−0.007	−0.009	−0.007
	[0.009]	[0.009]	[0.009]	[0.009]	[0.009]	[0.009]	[0.009]
$LABOR^2$	−0.049***	−0.049***	−0.049***	−0.049***	−0.050***	−0.048***	−0.048***
	[0.016]	[0.016]	[0.016]	[0.016]	[0.016]	[0.016]	[0.016]
$LOANS^2$	0.005	0.005*	0.005	0.005	0.005	0.005	0.004
	[0.003]	[0.003]	[0.003]	[0.003]	[0.003]	[0.003]	[0.003]
$CAPITAL^2$	0.005*	0.005**	0.005*	0.005*	0.005*	0.005**	0.004*
	[0.002]	[0.002]	[0.002]	[0.002]	[0.002]	[0.002]	[0.002]
BANK	−0.699***	−0.710***	−0.698***	−0.700***	−0.693***	−0.705***	−0.702***
	[0.160]	[0.160]	[0.160]	[0.159]	[0.160]	[0.160]	[0.160]
COOP	−1.298***	−1.305***	−1.298***	−1.295***	−1.299***	−1.301***	−1.304***
	[0.159]	[0.159]	[0.159]	[0.158]	[0.159]	[0.159]	[0.159]
NBANK	−1.006***	−1.023***	−1.007***	−1.008***	−1.008***	−1.014***	−1.013***
	[0.162]	[0.162]	[0.162]	[0.161]	[0.162]	[0.162]	[0.162]
NGO	−1.057***	−1.075***	−1.057***	−1.052***	−1.056***	−1.062***	−1.063***
	[0.163]	[0.163]	[0.163]	[0.163]	[0.164]	[0.164]	[0.164]
RBANK	−1.276***	−1.289***	−1.275***	−1.267***	−1.278***	−1.283***	−1.278***
	[0.167]	[0.167]	[0.167]	[0.167]	[0.167]	[0.168]	[0.167]
LLR	2.479***	2.524***	2.478***	2.481***	2.473***	2.509***	2.478***
	[0.217]	[0.219]	[0.217]	[0.217]	[0.217]	[0.219]	[0.217]
EQ	−0.277***	−0.269***	−0.277***	−0.268***	−0.283***	−0.283***	−0.284***
	[0.071]	[0.071]	[0.071]	[0.072]	[0.071]	[0.071]	[0.072]
YEAR	−0.177**	−0.133	−0.177**	−0.175**	−0.196**	−0.178**	−0.179**
	[0.089]	[0.090]	[0.089]	[0.089]	[0.090]	[0.089]	[0.089]
$YEAR^2$	0.010***	0.009***	0.010***	0.010***	0.010***	0.010***	0.010***
	[0.003]	[0.003]	[0.003]	[0.003]	[0.003]	[0.003]	[0.003]
*LOANS*YEAR*	−0.001	−0.002	−0.001	−0.001	−0.001	0.000	0.000
	[0.005]	[0.005]	[0.005]	[0.005]	[0.005]	[0.005]	[0.005]
*LABOR*YEAR*	0.007	0.005	0.007	0.007	0.008	0.006	0.006
	[0.009]	[0.009]	[0.009]	[0.009]	[0.009]	[0.009]	[0.009]
*CAPITAL*YEAR*	0.002	0.000	0.002	0.003	0.001	0.002	0.002
	[0.005]	[0.005]	[0.005]	[0.005]	[0.006]	[0.005]	[0.005]
Constant	−4.914***	−5.264***	−4.913***	−4.864***	−4.852***	−4.983***	−4.870***
	[1.066]	[1.066]	[1.066]	[1.066]	[1.066]	[1.066]	[1.067]
Observations	848	848	848	848	848	848	848
Number of MFIs	324	324	324	324	324	324	324

Note: Standard errors are between brackets; *, ** and *** refer to levels of significance at 10, 5 and 1 per cent.

Table 8.5B: Results of the estimations — The inefficiency equation, part 2.

	[7]	[8]	[9]	[10]	[11]	[12]	[13]
INCOME	0.012	0.014	0.010	0.009	0.011	0.013	0.011
	[0.028]	[0.028]	[0.029]	[0.028]	[0.028]	[0.028]	[0.028]
GROWTH	−1.897***	−1.933***	−1.906***	−1.929***	−1.891***	−1.856***	−1.845***
	[0.560]	[0.552]	[0.560]	[0.558]	[0.558]	[0.558]	[0.562]
CREDIT	−0.005***	−0.004***	−0.005***	−0.005***	−0.005***	−0.005***	−0.005***
	[0.002]	[0.002]	[0.002]	[0.002]	[0.002]	[0.002]	[0.002]
VOICE	−0.070*	−0.062*	−0.070*	−0.073*	−0.069*	−0.067*	−0.059
	[0.038]	[0.037]	[0.038]	[0.038]	[0.038]	[0.038]	[0.040]
INTVIOL		0.327***					
		[0.105]					
INTWAR			−0.028				
			[0.071]				
CIVVIOL				0.049			
				[0.042]			
CIVWAR					−0.155		
					[0.131]		
ETHNVIOL						0.03	
						[0.022]	
ETHNWAR							−0.013
							[0.014]
AGE	0.007***	0.007***	0.007***	0.007***	0.007***	0.007***	0.007***
	[0.002]	[0.002]	[0.002]	[0.002]	[0.002]	[0.002]	[0.002]
LSIZE	−0.209***	−0.204***	−0.208***	−0.207***	−0.209***	−0.207***	−0.213***
	[0.024]	[0.024]	[0.024]	[0.024]	[0.024]	[0.024]	[0.025]
Constant	1.931***	1.882***	1.941***	1.939***	1.941***	1.898***	1.958***
	[0.221]	[0.221]	[0.222]	[0.221]	[0.221]	[0.223]	[0.222]
Observations	848	848	848	848	848	848	848
Number of MFIs	324	324	324	324	324	324	324

Note: Standard errors are between brackets; *, ** and *** refer to levels of significance at 10, 5 and 1 per cent.

columns [3] to [6]). This suggests that the institutional environment does not affect the efficiency of MFIs. To some extent, this is in line with what Ahlin *et al.* (2008) found; in their analysis, only one of the Kaufmann institutional variables appeared to be associated with MFI performance (*REGQ*). Perhaps, the result that institutions do not seem to matter for MFI efficiency is due to the fact that the positive and negative consequences institutions may have for MFI efficiency cancel each other out. On the one hand, institutions may help create an environment that is conducive to doing business; at the same time, however, institutions may create rules and regulations that hinder business and/or that are costly (see Section 2).

The results in panel A of Table 8.5 again refer to the efficient cost frontier. These results are very much in line with the results found in Table 8.4A, suggesting once again that also for the specifications in which we include the political variables, we are able to specify a cost frontier that fits the theory reasonably well.

Panel B of Table 8.5 reports the estimation results regarding the inefficiency equation including the political variables. First, the political system appears to have a positive association with MFI efficiency (column [1]). The coefficient of the variable *VOICE* is negative and significant, albeit only at the 10 per cent level. This suggests that the extent to which the population is able to participate in political decision-making positively affects MFI efficiency. As explained in Section 2, this may be explained by the fact that if politicians can be held accountable and the population can raise its voice, this may lead to a more open society and to the development of policies that are supportive to doing business in general. This may support the growth of small-scale entrepreneurship, leading to higher demand for MFI services, which may help increase their efficiency.

With respect to the political instability variables, the results are much less supportive. On the one hand, for the variables *INTVIOL* we find a positive and highly significant coefficient, suggesting that in countries that are confronted with and/or involved in international violence, MFI efficiency is negatively affected. For all other political instability variables, however, we find no significant results. The overall conclusion, therefore, must be that at least based upon the analysis in this paper, there seems to be no clear relationship between political instability and the efficiency of MFIs.

As a final remark on the results, we observe in Tables 8.4B and 8.5B that the coefficients for the two MFI-specific variables *AGE* and *LSIZE* are highly significant and show the expected results. The coefficient for *AGE* is always positive, indicating that older MFIs are less efficient, which is in line with the notion of the advantage of backwardness. The coefficient of *LSIZE* is always negative, which implies that economies of scale are important for efficiency, as MFIs that provide larger loans to their clients are more efficient.

6 Conclusions

As was discussed in the introduction, if microfinance aims at making a significant and long-term contribution to reducing worldwide poverty, MFIs need to be successful in extending loans to poor borrowers, while at the same being able to develop cost-efficient lending practices. Knowing the determinants of cost efficiency, therefore, is an important issue. While some papers have focused on MFI-specific determinants, we have taken a different approach in this paper, i.e., whether MFI efficiency is related to macro conditions. The academic literature on the relationship between MFI performance and macro conditions have emerged only recently. We are the first to link these conditions to MFI efficiency. We have looked at macroeconomic, domestic financial system, institutional and political conditions, and find fairly strong evidence that macroeconomic conditions and the development of the domestic financial system are associated positively with MFI efficiency. We also find some evidence for a positive relationship between the political system and efficiency. With respect to political instability and institutional quality, however, we find hardly any evidence for a relationship between these conditions and MFI efficiency.

The results of this study show that if we want to evaluate the performance of MFIs, we should also take into account the macroeconomic, financial system and to some extent also political conditions. Thus, MFI-specific factors do not tell the whole story when looking at MFI outcomes and/or comparing results of different MFIs working in different macro environments. This is important information for policymakers, donors and investors who are increasingly willing to put their money into these institutions.

The results may also be important in light of the current global economic and financial crisis. If, as is shown in this paper, macroeconomic growth is an important determinant for MFI efficiency, the global crisis may have a major adverse impact on MFIs in the near future. Policymakers, donors and investors may therefore have to consider one of the following two choices. Either MFIs are left on their own, muddling through the crisis years, which reduces their potential positive contribution to reducing poverty, at least in the short run. Or MFIs are financially supported so as to reduce the negative impact of the global crisis on their activities as much as possible. The possibilities that the second option will be chosen seem rather dim, given the fact that the crisis is hurting everyone, including the large donor countries and Western investors. This suggests that MFIs may have no other option than to muddle through the crisis on their own.

References

Ahlin, C, J Lin and M Maio (2008). Where Does Microfinance Flourish: Microfinance Institution Performance in a Macroeconomic Context. Unpublished Working Paper.

Alesina, A, S Ozler, N Roubini and P Swagel (1996). Political instability and economic growth. *Journal of Economic Growth*, 1, 189–211.

Battese, GE and TJ Coelli (1995). A model for technical inefficiency effects in a stochastic frontier production function for panel data. *Empirical Economics*, 20, 325–332.

Crabb, P (2007). Economic freedom and the success of microfinance institutions. *Journal of Developmental Entrepreneurship*, 13.

Cull, R, J Morduch and A Demirguc–Kunt (2009), Does Regulatory Supervision Curtail Microfinance Profitability and Outreach? World Bank Policy Research Working Paper No. 4948.

Doerring, L, D Larson, C Miller, D Norell, T Nourse, R Reynolds, M Stephens and K Tilock (2004). Conflict and post-conflict environments: Ten short lessons to make microfinance work. SEEP Network Progess Note, 5.

Fernando, N (2003). *The Changing Face of Microfinance: Transformation of NGOs into Regulated Financial Institutions.* Manila: Asian Development Bank.

Gerschenkron, A (1962). *Economic Backwardness in Historical Perspective: A Book of Essays.* Cambridge, Mass: Belknap Press.

Gonzalez, A (2007). Resilience of microfinance institutions to national macroeconomic events: An econometric analysis of MFI asset quality. MIX Discussion Paper 1.

Gonzalez, A and R Rosenberg (2006). The state of microfinance — outreach, profitability and poverty: Findings from a database of 2300 microfinance institutions. Unpublished Working Paper. Available at SSRN, WPS 1400253.

Gutierrez–Nieto B, C Serrano-Cinca and C Mar Molinero (2010). Social and financial efficiency of microfinance institutions. In *The Handbook of Microfinance*, B Armendáriz and M Labie (eds.). Singapore: World Scientific Publishing.

Hartarska, V and D Nadolnyak (2007). Do regulated microfinance institutions achieve better sustainability and outreach: Cross-country evidence. *Applied Economics*, 39, 1207–1222.

Hermes, N, R Lensink and A Meesters (2009). Financial development and the efficiency of microfinance institutions. Unpublished Working Paper (available at SSRN, WPS 1396202).

Hubka, A and R Zaidi (2005). Impact of government regulation on microfinance. Paper prepared for the World Bank Development Report 2005: Improving the investment climate for growth and poverty reduction.

Kaufmann, D, A Kraay and M Mastruzzi (2008). Governance matters VII: Aggregate and individual governance indicators 1996–2007. World Bank Policy Research Working Paper 4654, Washington DC: World Bank.

King RG and R Levine (1993). Finance and growth: Schumpeter might be right. *Quarterly Journal of Economics*, 108, 717–737.

Ledgerwood, J (1999). *Microfinance Handbook: An Institutional and Financial Perspective.* Washington DC: World Bank.

Levine, R (2005). Finance and growth: Theory and evidence. In *Handbook of Economic Growth.* P Aghion and S Durlauf (eds.), pp. 865–934. Amsterdam: Elsevier Science.

Marconi, R and P Mosley (2006). Bolivia during the global crisis 1998–2004: Towards a "macroeconomics of microfinance". *Journal of International Development*, 18, 237–261.

Matousek, R and A Taci (2004). Banking efficiency in transition economies: Empirical evidence from the Czech Republic. *Economics of Planning*, 37, 225–244.

McIntosh, C, A de Janvry and E Sadoulet (2005). How competition among microfinance institutions affects incumbent lenders. *Economic Journal*, 115, 987–1004.

Patten, RH, JK Rosengard and D Johnston Jr (2001). Microfinance success amidst macroeconomic failure: The experience of Bank Rakyat Indonesia during the East Asian crisis. *World Development*, 29, 1057–1069.

Przeworski, A and F Limongi (1993). Political regimes and economic growth. *Journal of Economic Perspectives*, 7, 51–69.

Sealey, CW Jr and JT Lindley (1977). Input, output, and a theory of production and cost at depository financial institutions. *Journal of Finance*, 32, 1251–1266.

Sharma, MP (2004). Community-driven development and scaling-up of microfinance services: Case studies from Nepal and India. Discussion Paper 178, Washington DC: International Food Policy Research Institute.

Vanroose, A (2008). What macro factors make microfinance institutions reach out? *Savings and Development*, 32, 153–174.

Vanroose, A and B D'Espallier (2009). Microfinance and financial sector development. Working paper CEB 09-040. RS, Brussels: Université Libre de Bruxelles.

Wang, HJ and P Schmidt (2002). One-step and two-step estimation of the effects of exogenous variables on technical efficiency. *Journal of Productivity Analysis*, 18, 129–144.

Woller, G and W Woodworth (2001). Microcredit as a grass-roots policy for international development. *Policy Studies Journal*, 29, 267–283.

Zeller, M and RL Meyer (eds.) (2003). *The triangle of microfinance: Financial sustainability, outreach and impact.* Baltimore: International Food Policy Research Institute.

Microfinance in Bolivia: Foundation of the Growth, Outreach and Stability of the Financial System

Claudio Gonzalez-Vega and Marcelo Villafani-Ibarnegaray*

The Ohio State University

Our goal is to analyze the evolution of Bolivian microfinance from a system's perspective. While individual microfinance institutions (MFIs) have indeed shown an outstanding performance, our focus is — rather — on the development of the whole sector (namely, the set of regulated and non-regulated MFIs) and on its influence on the progress of the aggregate Bolivian financial system. To achieve this purpose: (i) we describe key dimensions of the

*Claudio Gonzalez-Vega is Professor of Agricultural, Environmental and Development Economics and Director of the Rural Finance Program at The Ohio State University (OSU). Marcelo Villafani-Ibarnegaray is Post-Doctoral Researcher at OSU. Over the years, their research on Bolivian microfinance has been funded by the OARDC at OSU, USAID, ECLAC (Santiago), and several Bolivian and international agencies. Among co-authors in these broader efforts, they want to acknowledge Franz Gómez-Soto, Adrián González, Jorge H. Maldonado, Rodolfo Quirós, Jorge Rodríguez-Meza, and Vivianne E. Romero. The research outcomes owe much to the advice and collaboration of numerous colleagues in Bolivia including, among many others, José Auad-Lema, Pedro Arriola, Eduardo Bazobery, Néstor Castro, Gonzalo Chávez, Eduardo Gutiérrez, Evelyn Grandi, Hans Hassenteufel, Julio César Herbas, Miguel Hoyos, Luis Carlos Jemio, Kurt Koenigsfest, Marcelo Mallea, Reynaldo Marconi, Misael Miranda, Fernando Monpó, Juan Antonio Morales, Elizabeth Nava, Sergio Navajas, Silvia Palacios, Fernando Prado, María Elena Querejazu, Pilar Ramírez, Carlos Rodríguez, Antonio Sivilá, Jacques Trigo, and Carmen Velasco and, in general, feedback from Juan Buchenau, Robert P. Christen, Richard Meyer, María Otero, Richard Rosenberg and Mark Schreiner as well as many participants in the OSU projects and seminars and comments from Beatriz Armendáriz and Marc Labie, the editors of the *The Handbook of Microfinance*. The authors thank all the institutions that provided data for their research, in particular, ASOFIN, the Central Bank of Bolivia, FINRURAL, the National Statistics Institute (INE) and the Authority for the Supervision of the Financial System (ASFI), previously the Superintendency of Banks and Financial Institutions (SBEF). Other data came from OSU surveys and specific financial institutions.

successful evolution of microfinance in this country and compare them to the performance of other types of financial intermediaries, (ii) we identify potential determinants of these exceptional outcomes, and (iii) we derive lessons about combinations of circumstances that favor a substantial expansion of the outreach of a financial system in a low-income country with incomplete institutions.

In Bolivia, a confluence of supply-side (leadership, governance and institutional design, and ceaseless innovation), demand-side (blooming informal sector), and market circumstances (intense competition, appropriate prudential regulation) have contributed to this exceptional outcome. Over time, dynamic interactions and externalities have sustained the sector's healthy growth, even in the presence of major systemic shocks. Given these virtuous combinations of circumstances, microfinance has become the most vibrant and a major segment (indeed, the engine and the anchor) of the Bolivian financial system. We explain how and why.

1 Background

At each stage of its evolution, since its emergence a little over two decades ago, the performance of the Bolivian microfinance sector has been outstanding. In part, these admirable results have reflected features shared by other celebrated examples of the global microfinance revolution. These dimensions have responded, in particular, to key innovations in lending and deposit mobilization technologies, many of them originating in Bolivia and then replicated elsewhere. In part, these surprising outcomes have reflected Bolivian idiosyncrasies.

Key lessons about the development of more inclusive financial systems have emerged from this experience. These lessons have highlighted promising characteristics of: (i) processes of innovation in financial technologies that expand outreach, (ii) institutional designs that promote sustainability, and (iii) regulation frameworks that encourage stability and efficiency. These lessons also suggest that technologies, institutions and regulations must evolve and adapt to changing circumstances. Thus, rather than adopting a fixed set of "best practices", practitioners and regulators should identify the determinants of dynamic paths for the "most appropriate practices for the times".

In evaluating options for the future, as during these times of global crisis, the lessons from history matter. It would not be possible, however, to write the global history of microfinance without acknowledging the substantial contributions of the Bolivian experience, given the wealth of lessons that have emerged both from the nature of the challenges faced and from the variety of approaches and progression of stages in successfully addressing these challenges. Moreover, it would neither be possible to write the recent socioeconomic history of Bolivia, without highlighting the significant influence of microfinance on its path of development. Among this broader set of impacts, however, and building on Gonzalez–Vega and Villafani–Ibarnegaray (2007), here we focus on the specific influence of microfinance on the evolution (growth, outreach, and stability) of the aggregate financial system of Bolivia.

Somehow, that Bolivia has become the source of major lessons in financial deepening is surprising. Just over two decades ago, as the country emerged from a dramatic hyperinflation and negative economic growth, few would have imagined the range and the scale of the microfinance blossoming that the country was about to experience and, even less, the substantial ways in which microfinance was to influence the Bolivian process of financial deepening. At that time, any trust in financial contracts and institutions had been eroded by inflation, while the state-owned banks — closed after the fiscal crisis in the mid-1980s — had only succeeded in politicizing loan portfolios and in destroying the culture of repayment (Trigo Loubière, 2003). In every possible way, Bolivia was a fragmented economy, fractured by geography, language and ethnicity, and endowed with a minimal and fragile physical and institutional infrastructure. Overcoming these obstacles —in any attempt to promote a vigorous process of financial deepening — had to be a formidable task. Microfinance was the engine that made it possible.

Both the swelling of the urban informal sector — and possibly some cultural traits that encouraged peer cooperation — as well as the rapid economic growth and absence of inflation that followed the policies of macroeconomic stabilization and financial liberalization — post-1986 — contributed to this success (Morales and Sachs, 1990). These necessary but not sufficient conditions offered fertile ground for the innovations in financial technologies, institutional design, and regulation frameworks — driven by a group of outstanding local non-government leaders — that explain the exceptional outcomes. Once the process of innovation was triggered, moreover, learning by doing, demonstration and imitation effects, and numerous positive externalities — mostly through human capital mobility — pushed the microfinance sector along a virtuous path of expansion.

In turn, towards the end of the century, negative externalities (contagion), from the swift emergence and collapse of the non-bank financial intermediaries (e.g., Acceso FFP and Fassil FFP) that had deployed consumer lending technologies (in contrast to microfinance) and from equivalent downscaling commercial bank efforts (e.g., Banco Union's *CrediÁgil*, Banco Económico's *Presto*, and Banco Santa Cruz' *Solución* products), did test and strengthen the robustness of the MFIs and encouraged further innovations in financial technologies and institutional designs. This continued ability to innovate helped in preparing the MFIs to successfully withstand the systemic macroeconomic shocks that followed soon afterwards.

Born after the collapse of the private commercial banks and the demise of the state-owned banks, Bolivian microfinance was a child of the macroeconomic crisis of the 1980s. These origins may have endowed the sector with the resilience that has underpinned its unusual performance for over two decades, even in the presence of major adverse shocks. The earlier success encouraged, in turn, the prudential authorities to approve the creation, in 1992, of BancoSol — the first private commercial bank fully specialized in microfinance in the world — and the search for a non-bank charter — eventually that of the *fondo financiero privado*, FFP — that would provide an appropriate framework for the prudential regulation and supervision of microfinance (Gonzalez–Vega *et al.*, 1997). This bold policy decision of the Superintendency of Banks and Financial Institutions (SBEF) triggered, in turn, a dialectic process, with microfinance innovations leading the way and the prudential framework adjusting to and supporting the evolution of the sector, by allowing enough room for innovation while safeguarding the stability of the system.

The substantial pay-offs from this regulatory gamble were a consequence of: (i) the wide-ranging preparedness of the MFIs; (ii) the technical expertise of the SBEF, accumulated through sustained investments in human capital, with assistance from various international organizations; and (iii) the fruitful interaction of the two parties in the regulation process. In few other countries has an accommodating and yet so rigorous framework for the prudential regulation of microfinance been adopted so early in the evolution of the system. Thus, from the start, the Bolivian MFIs both sought — given their focus on sustainability as a necessary condition for permanent outreach — and were induced to adopt a strict financial discipline.

The transformation of several of the original microfinance NGOs into prudentially regulated institutions (Caja Los Andes FFP, which turned into Banco Los Andes ProCredit in 2005, FIE FFP (which turned into Banco FIE in 2010), PRODEM FFP, and EcoFuturo FFP), in addition to BancoSol, bolstered the expansion of the sector. While BancoSol received — because of its early banking status — much international attention, it soon faced the vigorous competition from other, equally robust, regulated MFIs. A world leader in innovation in *group* credit technologies and a member of the ACCION International network, BancoSol had to face Caja Los Andes, a member of the German IPC network, as well as the local maverick FIE, both leaders in innovation in *individual* credit technologies. Bolivia thus became "the arena" where some of the best experiments with these two lending technologies were being tested and contrasted, in keen — both market and intellectual — competition (Rhyne and Otero, 1994; Gonzalez–Vega *et al.*, 1996; Schmidt and Zeitinger, 1998). In turn, PRODEM, given the original terms of its participation in the creation of BancoSol, was becoming a leading innovator in rural financial products and deposit mobilization (Frankiewicz, 2001). Further, the success of microfinance — in its clash with the consumer credit FFPs at the end of the century, to be discussed below — encouraged two other regulated non-bank intermediaries to eventually revamp their financial technology and transform into microfinance institutions (Fassil FFP and Fortaleza FFP). Their data are included with those of the regulated MFIs since 2004.

This process has led to two important lessons. First, rather than holding outreach back, a rigorous set of prudential norms — which demanded substantial institution-building efforts and financial discipline from the organizations — actually allowed the provision of a broader range of services as well as considerable expansion toward the target clientele, way beyond what would have been otherwise possible (Trigo Loubière, Devaney and Rhyne, 2004). In contrast to countries where the regulation of microfinance was either non-existent or more lax, Bolivian MFIs grew rapidly, at all margins, and became more robust than elsewhere (Jansson, Rosales and Westley, 2003). This early comparative success of Bolivian microfinance regulation reflected both the initial pre-regulation strength of the MFIs (which offered a demonstration of their ability to operate under rigorous norms) and the role of visionary prudential authorities. Once, however, the superior performance of the MFIs had become evident, even during the macroeconomic crisis, the adoption of differential prudential norms, which would have acknowledged critical differences in risk profiles between banks and MFIs, in contrast to the uniform (pooling) and at times the even more restrictive rules actually adopted in recent times, might have further promoted the efficient and stable expansion of the Bolivian financial system (Villafani–Ibarnegaray, 2008).

Second, the upgrading of microfinance performance that accompanied the transformation into regulated institutions has spilled over into the non-regulated sector. There, some of the not-for-profit organizations (e.g., CRECER, FADES, FONDECO, Pro Mujer) that, for different reasons, had chosen not to adopt the FFP charter became, over time, outstanding performers — among the best in the world in their own category. The interaction between these two (regulated and non-regulated) sectors has led, in turn, to a healthy process of institution-building by imitation, complementation (including some strategic alliances), competition and accommodation, which has given the Bolivian microfinance sector the opportunity to build a broader and stronger umbrella for the efficient and specialized provision of financial services to marginal clientele. In evaluating the outcome of this process, therefore, it is critical to consider the system as a whole, in all of its interactions and complementarities, rather than just look at individual organizations.

Further, the *de facto* strengthening of the non-regulated microfinance institutions — with recent guidance from FINRURAL's self-regulation program — encouraged the prudential authorities to start the process of approval, by 2008, of yet another charter — that of the *instituciones financieras de desarrollo*, IFD — to allow the regulated operation of *not-for-profit* microfinance organizations that may, in addition,combine financial intermediation with the delivery of training, health and other non-financial services (Zabalaga, 2009). In the midst of the current crisis, the implementation of this bold and promising initiative might create unusual opportunities at the same time that it faces considerable threats. On the one hand, the IFDs have specialized in reaching poorer clienteles and they may be more inclined toward expanding into the rural areas, where deposit facilities have been extremely scarce. On the other hand, both the prudential authorities and the organizations have been strained during the recent global crisis, given slower rates of portfolio growth and higher rates of arrears. Strong competition in a shrinking market has caused some over-indebtedness, while the sector faces growing political threats.

In summary, Bolivian microfinance has grown in stages, from its non-government origins — and, except for prudential regulation, with no state intervention whatsoever — to a staggered transformation into a sector of regulated financial intermediaries (Wiedmaier-Pfister, Pastor and Salinas, 2001; Ledgerwood and White, 2006). Major adjustments in prudential norms and operational practices have taken place along the way, in the shape of flexible responses to the numerous challenges faced by the sector — such as the asymmetric competition from the consumer credit FFPs (Rhyne, 2001), the earlier absence of information-sharing mechanisms (Rosenberg, 2008), a deep recession at the end of the past century (Jemio, 2001), socio-political instability in the new century (Evia, Laserna and Skaperdas, 2008), and the threats and opportunities from the more recent global crisis. In contrast to other country experiences, where fairly rigid and slowly changing models have been implemented (frequently based more on ideological beliefs than on market realities), a central feature of the Bolivian evolution has been the vast creative flexibility of both the MFIs and the prudential authorities.

Thus, from the humble beginnings of a few microfinance NGOs, born in the second-half of the 1980s, the microfinance sector has grown to become a sizeable and the most dynamic component of the Bolivian financial system. Indeed, the country's process of financial deepening has been driven, particularly during this century, by the evolution of the microfinance sector. In this sense, microfinance has become both the engine and the anchor of the evolution of the financial system, to such an extent that the future of finance in Bolivia will be mostly governed by the performance of microfinance and by the reactions of other actors (in particular, banks and government agencies) to its progress. Here, we evaluate this evolution and suggest how this outcome has emerged. While an impact of this magnitude has been achieved in few, if any, other countries, the Bolivian microfinance experience is a story about "what may be possible", along the path toward increased financial inclusion.

2 Financial Deepening

The impact of microfinance in Bolivia has reached well beyond the valuable inclusion — into formal financial markets — of large segments of the population, until then excluded from access to institutional financial services. The breadth of this impact has encompassed influences on both financial and non-financial outcomes. In particular, the performance of the microfinance sector has critically influenced the evolution of the entire Bolivian financial system, our focus here. On the one hand, the microfinance sector has drastically offset the weak performance and decline of the commercial banks and other regulated intermediaries, especially during the last decade. On the other hand, the challenges from the MFIs have recently provoked reactions and revisions of behavior even among the banks, and these changes — in their attempts to imitate microfinance — have been at the roots of the banks' slow recovery.

In a variety of ways, therefore, the microfinance sector has made substantial contributions to the country's process of financial deepening, in its own right (by expanding the frontier of institutional finance along several margins where it had been missing), while at the same time helping to contain the process of disintermediation that has afflicted the rest of the financial system (Gonzalez–Vega and Villafani–Ibarnegaray, 2007). Thus, even if the banks had not shrunk, the sector would have added new dimensions of supply to a highly undeveloped market. Further, given the decline of the banks, the rapid growth of microfinance has become even more critical in preventing, in recent years, a severe financial crunch. In view of this experience, it would be fair to claim that towards the future — unless the process is interrupted by a political shock — the MFIs will determine the pace and style of financial development in Bolivia.

To evaluate these impacts, we use the concept of *financial deepening* introduced by Shaw (1973), defined as an increase in the volume of financial transactions (financial wealth) with respect to real levels of economic activity (total wealth). This indicator matters, because it highlights the various roles of financial *intermediation* in improving the allocation of resources, facilitating the management of risk, and encouraging innovation and growth in an economy (McKinnon, 1973; Fry, 1994; Levine, 2005). The proxies typically used to measure deepening are ratios of financial magnitudes (e.g., loan portfolios or deposits mobilized) with respect to the GDP (Levine, 1997). In turn, this indicator must be distinguished from changes in the *depth* (as contrasted to the *breadth*) of the *outreach* of financial institutions among different segments of the population (Navajas *et al.*, 2000; Schreiner, 2002). Here, we evaluate the performance of Bolivian microfinance from both perspectives.

During their earlier stages, regulated MFIs in Bolivia mostly focused on the development of their credit portfolios. Over time, however, the mobilization of deposits from the public also became an important dimension of their operations. Indeed, their success in delivering valuable services to depositors — and not just credit — and their ability to fund most of their loan portfolios with deposits mobilized from the public has been one of the distinguishing features of the Bolivian MFIs. This progression — from microcredit providers to full-fledged microfinance institutions — enhanced their key role in the process of financial intermediation (Gómez–Soto and Gonzalez–Vega, 2007b).

As a result, their target clientele has enjoyed not just access to a widening menu of credit services, but also access to convenient deposit facilities and other financial services previously unavailable to these segments of the population — payments, remittances, insurance — that also contribute to enhanced productivity and household welfare. In addition, the successful mobilization of deposits from the public — both from their traditional credit clients as well as from other segments of society — has increased their lending capacity in the target market segment, facilitated their management of liquidity risk, improved client loyalty, and strengthened institutional robustness. This broader service offer has apparently generated economies of scale and of scope, and the accompanying reductions in operating costs have benefitted all — but mostly the smallest — clients.

Further, both the theoretical and the empirical literature suggest that financial deepening (as well as an increased breadth of outreach, through which larger segments of the population are incorporated into the market economy) contribute to improved resource allocations and pro-poor economic growth (Beck, Demirgüc–Kunt, and Levine, 2004). While a few empirical exercises have encountered mixed results in attempts to link financial development with long-term aggregate economic growth in Bolivia (Morales, 2007), microfinance has certainly contributed to more broadly-based income growth and consumption smoothing — since poor Bolivian clients had previously been both severely credit-constrained and highly vulnerable to risk — and, in particular, it may be contributing to higher future welfare, through the observed impact of microfinance on human capital formation (Maldonado and Gonzalez–Vega, 2008).

The role of MFIs in expanding the frontier of finance in Bolivia has reflected aggregate and substitution effects. Among the former, an *incorporation* effect has reflected the market access gained by segments of the population that had not used financial services before, except perhaps informal transactions with friends and relatives. In addition, a *widening* effect has reflected the — broader — market offer, to those segments of the population that had already had some access to credit, of financial services beyond short-term loans for working capital. This broader menu of services has supported investment (including housing improvements) and more efficient strategies (in particular, safe and convenient deposit facilities) for the accumulation of precautionary wealth (Gómez–Soto and Gonzalez–Vega, 2007a).

In addition, there have been several *substitution* effects. First, there has been a — partial — replacement of informal by institutional financial services. This *formal-informal* substitution has meant a substantial improvement in the terms and conditions of loan contracts, including much lower interest rates, larger loan sizes, and longer terms to maturity. The availability of the institutional financial services has also broken the local covariance and wealth constraints associated with informal sources of finance. This substitution has thus been a component of the process of market integration and modernization of the Bolivian economy. For some (in particular, the poorer) clients, however, microfinance services have been a complement of the informal liquidity and risk-management tools already at their disposal (Collins *et al.*, 2009). By enhancing the set of financial instruments available to poor households, access to institutional services has improved their consumption-smoothing outcomes, livelihoods, and welfare. On average, across the set of formal and informal tools, the costs and the risks (mostly from the lack of reliability and the strong covariance of informal sources) have declined.

Thus, through a combination of substitution and complementation effects, microfinance has improved the aggregate financial management of poor households. Moreover, given the breadth of outreach and the variety and appropriateness of the financial services supplied by regulated Bolivian MFIs, formal-informal substitution effects may have been stronger in Bolivia than in other places, where microfinance organizations have offered a more limited range of products. In addition to various types of loan products, the regulated Bolivian MFIs had offered a broad range of non-credit financial services, while the non-regulated IFDs have offered preferred tools for risk management, such as the internal account of village banks, as well as non-financial services (Gonzalez–Vega and Maldonado, 2003). Nevertheless, during periods of severe distress (as with the crisis at the turn of the century), the incidence of access to informal finance has resurged among some MFI clients. The proportion of microfinance clients who also used informal credit (namely, a combination of formal and informal loans) in a given year increased from 17 percent in 1998 to 72 percent in 2001, and it then declined again (González and Gonzalez–Vega, 2003).

Second, there has been a gradual shift from *non-regulated to regulated* microfinance and a sustained *institutionalization* of all financial transactions. Originally crafted by non-regulated NGOs, the sector is now dominated by regulated intermediaries (specialized banks and FFPs), while the prudential authorities have recently embarked in an innovative process of regulation of the IFDs, in reflection of a determined concern for the safety and soundness of all financial intermediaries, even in these market segments. Once the latter effort concludes, all microfinance in Bolivia will be regulated.

Nevertheless, these prudential interventions have not been accompanied by repressive interest rate controls — of any kind — or by mandated portfolio requirements. Rather, this path towards institutionalization has contributed to the strengthening of *institutions* (namely, the organizations themselves, the delivery of ancillary services, such as credit bureaus, and the rules of the game). Within a stronger institutional framework, MFIs have been able to buttress the role of *contracts*, build the confidence of their clients, and sharply broaden the range of their services. The shifting perceptions, from a concept of credit as a policy (political) tool towards the idea of credit as a contract (a valuable agreement among the parties involved) have contributed to the strengthening of the culture of repayment as a component of Bolivia's social capital (Gonzalez–Vega, 2003).

Third, there has been a sharp gain in the market share of MFIs, at the expense of other financial intermediaries. After two decades, regulated and non-regulated MFIs now account for a substantial and growing share of the assets (in particular, of the loan portfolio) of the Bolivian financial system, while regulated MFIs — those with the authorization to mobilize funds from the public — now account for a growing share of the liabilities (deposits) of the system. The gains in MFI shares in the total number of clients of the financial system have been even more spectacular, as reported below. These gains have been a consequence of the differential performance of the various types of institutions, particularly during periods of adverse systemic shocks. They have also resulted from a clash of financial technologies, from which microfinance institutions have emerged victorious (Navajas, Conning and Gonzalez–Vega, 2003; Villafani–Ibarnegaray and Gonzalez–Vega, 2007; Villafani–Ibarnegaray, 2008).

In particular, a comparison with the behavior of banks, credit unions and cooperatives, savings and loan associations (*mutuales*), and the short-lived episode of consumer finance FFPs reveals a more robust performance and less *pro-cyclical* behavior of the regulated and non-regulated MFIs than for any other type of financial intermediary. This differential performance has resulted in significant changes in the market structure of the Bolivian financial system and in its ability to reach broader segments of the population (Gonzalez–Vega and Rodríguez–Meza, 2003).

3 Differential Performance

Ever since their earlier days and for over two decades now, the credit portfolios of the Bolivian MFIs have grown along an almost exponential path. The only exception has been a slight deceleration at the end of the past century, mostly as a consequence — but not only — of the country's macroeconomic crisis. Interestingly, such a sustained deceleration has not taken place, at least not yet, during the current global crisis.

The rapid and sustained growth of microfinance portfolios has been reflected by a host of diverse indicators of lending activity. For details and sources of the data presented here, see Gonzalez–Vega and

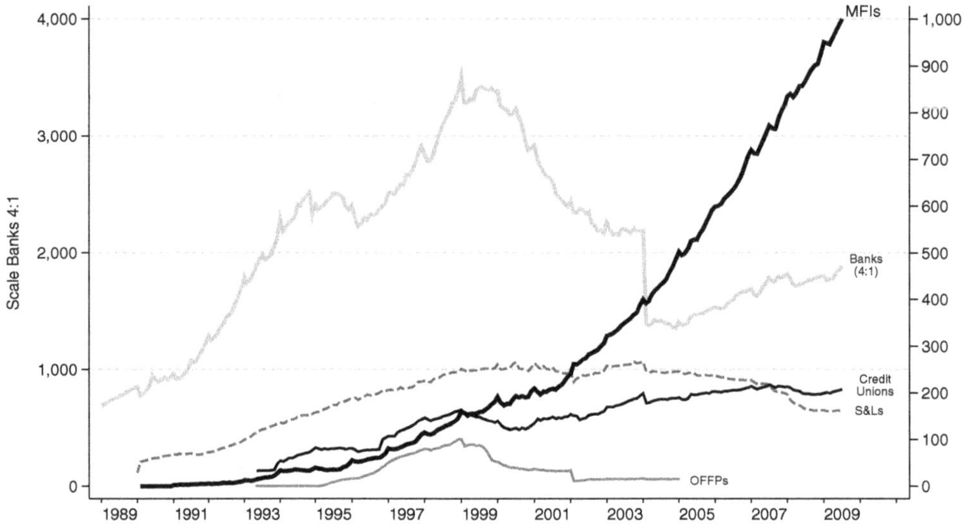

Source: Gonzalez–Vega and Villafani–Ibarnegaray (2010).

Figure 9.1: Performing loan portfolio of the Bolivian financial system.

Note: By type of institution (banks, credit unions, savings and loan associations, microfinance institutions and consumer FFPs) from December 1988 to June 2009 (in the million dollar equivalent of real bolivianos, as of December 2005).

Villafani–Ibarnegaray (2007, 2009). In particular, Figure 9.1 shows the evolution of the performing loan portfolio of the regulated and non-regulated MFIs, in contrast to the evolution of the loan portfolios of other types of financial intermediaries. The *performing* loan portfolio excludes, from the *gross* portfolio, the outstanding balances of loans with at least one payment in arrears. All nominal figures have been deflated, to first express them in bolivianos of constant purchasing power — as of December of 2005 — in order to account for domestic inflation, and then they have been converted into US dollars — at the exchange rate as of the same date, of eight bolivianos per dollar. They represent, therefore, the US dollar equivalent of boliviano figures in real terms. Unless otherwise noted, all figures below are computed in these units.

The sustained growth of microfinance loan portfolios stands out, in sharp contrast to the dramatic decline that followed the initial expansion of the aggregate portfolio of the financial system. Once hyperinflation was swiftly conquered and in response to Bolivia's financial reforms, adopted since the mid-1980s, the gross loan portfolio of the financial system grew rapidly from almost nothing to reach a historic peak of US$ 4.5 billion, in real terms, by July of 1999. The Bolivian macroeconomic crisis — at the turn of the century — induced, however, a sharp portfolio decline followed, since 2004, by a slow and very unstable recovery path. Thus, by December of 2008, the gross loan portfolio of the Bolivian financial system had climbed back to just US$ 3.4 billion, in real terms.

To be sure, the performance of the various types of financial intermediaries during this critical episode has not been homogeneous. Particularly dramatic has been the collapse of the loan portfolio of the commercial banks. After a slight recovery, since 2004, by December 2008 their gross portfolio amounted to US$ 1.7 billion less than its value a decade earlier. This is equivalent to a loss of 45 percent of its former value. Credit unions, savings and loan associations, and consumer credit FFPs also experienced major portfolio reductions. In contrast, by December of 2008, the gross loan portfolio of the MFIs amounted to US$ 963 million. This is equivalent to 464 percent of its value, in real terms, a decade earlier. In other words, over a decade, the real value of the gross loan portfolio of the commercial banks was cut almost in half, while the gross loan portfolio of the MFIs experienced almost a five-fold increase.

The seeds of this differential performance were sown during the 1990s. The rapid expansion of the loan portfolios of the commercial banks reflected, at first, substantial gains in *financial deepening*, as Bolivia emerged from the inflationary debacle of the early 1980s — and as it regained its macroeconomic stability — and as prudent monetary policies encouraged depositor confidence. Particularly since 1997, however, the banks used foreign borrowing at an increasing pace, in order to keep expanding their loan portfolios. The rate of portfolio growth was no longer compatible with the rates of real economic growth, domestic deposit mobilization, and the ongoing process of financial market integration. The over-indebtedness associated with a typical credit boom began to build up (Gavin and Haussman, 1996). Further, a weak framework of prudential regulation and very low capital adequacy requirements (which, between 1994 and 1998, allowed the banks to leverage their assets over 15 times the value of their equity) encouraged the opportunistic behavior of the commercial banks, mostly grounded on expectations of a likely government bailout, if needed, given the banks' political influence (Trigo Loubière, 2003).

When the exogenous recessive shock — a contagion of the international crisis — hit Bolivia in 1999, a banking credit crunch followed the boom and loan default rates increased. In response, the commercial banks rescheduled many delinquent loans. Further, to make actual riskiness more transparent, the prudential authorities required a separate reporting of rescheduled loans.

This change in reporting standards explains the sharp drop — by January of 2004 — in the banks' *performing* portfolio, as shown in Figure 9.1. Both the deteriorated portfolio health and the revelation of — until then — hidden risks introduced a growing wedge between the gross and the performing loan portfolios of the banks. This change in prudential norms also revealed an important clue about the contrasting evolution of banks and MFIs. While the commercial banks had to immediately reclassify — into the riskier category — 36 percent of their gross loan portfolios, this proportion was only 3 percent for the MFIs. This is astounding, as the MFIs had to deal, not just with the systemic macroeconomic shocks, but also with the deterioration of the culture of repayment that had resulted from the aggressive attempt of some consumer credit FFPs to expand into their market segment.

The short episode of rapid expansion and decline of the consumer credit FFPs deserves special attention. In the second-half of the 1990s, a number of financial intermediaries obtained the FFP charter, which allowed them to mobilize deposits from the public, and then introduced a *consumer* lending technology, mostly based on credit-scoring tools. The performing portfolio of these consumption FFPs grew from US$ 16.2 million (December of 1995) to US$ 100.3 million (December of 1998). As of the same date, the performing portfolio of the MFIs was slightly larger (US$ 119.3 million). By December of 2002, however, the portfolio of these consumer lenders had sharply declined, back to US$ 14.6 million, in real terms (OFFPs in Figure 9.1). In the process, some of them declared bankruptcy, under the guidance of the SBEF (e.g., Acceso FFP), while others abandoned their consumer credit technology and became micro and small enterprise lenders (e.g., Fassil FFP and Fortaleza FFP). For their operations, the consumer FFPs had mobilized deposits from the public (95 percent of their total funding), by offering high interest rates on term deposits, sometimes twice the level of those offered by the banks. It seems that they were unsuccessful in persuading other financial intermediaries to lend to them. When, eventually, Acceso FFP went bankrupt, the SBEF forced the (Chilean) owners to cover all of the deposit liabilities.

The distinction made here between microfinance and consumer-lending institutions does not reflect differences in the actual use of the loan funds. Given the fungibility of funds, consumption is almost always one of the various (marginal) uses undertaken with the increased liquidity allowed by a loan (Von Pischke and Adams, 1983). Rather, the critical distinction here is the lending technology. A *lending technology* is the set of procedures, steps, criteria and actions taken by a lender in order to decide if the loan will be granted or not and to determine the loan size and conditions attached

(Navajas and Gonzalez–Vega, 2002). It is the production function of the loan, and it involves screening, monitoring, and contract enforcement tasks. Modern information and communication tools (such as hand-held computers or smart phones) may be an input into the lending technology, but the critical components are the collection, interpretation and use-in-decisions of information (in order to determine the applicant's ability and willingness to repay) and the design of contracts (in order to create incentives to repay). Consumer lending technologies largely rely on wages from secure salaried employment — as the main source of repayment — and the expectation that borrowers will repay in order to avoid the garnishment of their wages. In contrast, microfinance lenders evaluate income and cash flows from self-employment, microenterprises, and household-firm portfolios of diversified activities, while the value of reputation, either in the relationship with the lender or with peers in a credit group, is the main incentive to repay (González, 2009).

In the case of Bolivian microfinance, applicants were being screened on the basis of a direct and detailed assessment of risk, *in situ*, by experienced loan officers (or from the direct knowledge of peers within a credit group), and incentives to repay relied mostly on the value of the relationship with the MFI. In contrast, before failing, the other FFPs implemented a consumer lending technology that relied on: (i) lax screening — in part based on credit-scoring tools (adapted from other countries) not appropriate for the Bolivian self-employed informal sector — and the door-to-door marketing of loans by a "sales" force, (ii) abusive loan recovery by a separate collection team (whose tough practices provoked the formation of delinquent borrower associations); and (iii) high interest rates and penalties for arrears, designed to cover for the high expected losses from default. These features were in sharp contrast with: (i) the personal knowledge of peers or loan officers (in screening) and the direct interaction, associated with a strong client *relationship*, that built compatible incentives between borrower and lender; (ii) the full accountability of loan officers, from screening to collection (supported by performance-based remunerations); and (iii) a zero tolerance of arrears, all of which have characterized microfinance transactions in Bolivia. This episode thus highlighted the importance of *appropriate technology* in determining the performance of the loan portfolios generated by different types of intermediaries, to be discussed below (Gonzalez–Vega and Villafani–Ibarnegaray, 2007).

This differential evolution of the various types of financial intermediaries, and — in particular — the contrast when comparing banks and MFIs, has

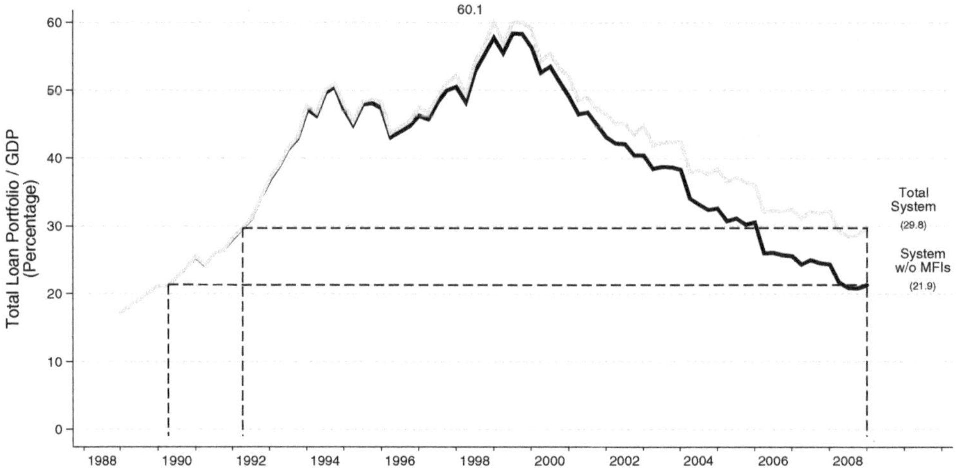

Source: Gonzalez-Vega and Villafani-Ibarnegaray (2010).

Figure 9.2: Financial deepening: Gross loan portfolio of the Bolivian financial system with respect to GDP, with and without microfinance.

Note: The data are in percentages, for December 1988 to December 2008.

had major consequences on the country's financial deepening achievements. In Figure 9.2, ratios of the gross loan portfolio of the financial system with respect to the GDP are used as a proxy for financial deepening. By December 1998, this ratio had increased — from 0.171 as of December of 1988 — to a peak of 0.601, at twice the average level for Latin American countries in the 1990s. Ten years later, the level of this indicator (0.298) was less than one-half of its level a decade earlier. A similar decline is revealed by the ratio of the performing loan portfolio with respect to the GDP, which dropped from 0.568 in 1998 to 0.271 in 2008 (not shown in the graph). This process of disintermediation pushed Bolivia back about 17 years in its financial deepening attainments.

This setback would have been even worse, however, in the absence of microfinance. By the end of 2008, the ratio of the system's loan portfolio — with respect to the GDP — would have been only 0.219 (gross) or 0.193 (performing), if microfinance were ignored. That is, microfinance loan portfolios are now equivalent to about 8 percent of Bolivia's GDP. Without microfinance, Bolivia would have lost 19 (rather than 17) years of financial progress in the last decade, returning to levels of financial deepening already achieved by the end of 1989, and Bolivia would have ranked 13th among 18 Latin American countries in this respect (Rojas–Suárez, 2008). In turn, if only the commercial banks, then the dominant presence in the financial system, were considered, at least two full decades of portfolio gains with respect to the GDP would have been lost, as a result of the crisis. From this perspective, one key role for MFIs in Bolivia has been to curb the loss of financial deepening suffered by the country.

This differential evolution has resulted in a deep transformation of the financial system, as shown by major changes in the shares of the various market participants. Most striking have been the loss of market share of the commercial banks (from 83.8 to 60.6 percent of the system's performing loan portfolio, between 1998 and 2008) and the gain of market share of the MFIs (from 2.8 to 30.5 percent, in the same period). This combined share of microfinance institutions reflects 26.9 points corresponding to seven regulated MFIs and 3.7 points corresponding to 16 unregulated IFDs. Some degree of *de-formalization* of credit transactions has been implicit in this market transformation, given the less rigid requirements introduced by the microfinance innovations in lending technologies. Rather than using the audited financial statements, mortgage pledges, and court foreclosures of delinquent loans typical of banking technologies, MFIs have been able to determine creditworthiness with less formality and in a more cost-effective fashion.

Moreover, the commercial banks have recently attempted to hold back their loss of market share, by rapidly expanding their own microcredit transactions. Strong *imitation* effects may be allowing this downscaling effort for some banks, which currently accounts for the most dynamic portion of their portfolio, but their success is yet to be seen. In particular, the learning-by-doing and accumulated knowledge of the MFIs — which can be only acquired over a long time and over many transactions — represent sunk costs that have given the MFIs an unusual advantage in this market segment. Moreover, the commercial banks have encountered some difficulties in organizing their microfinance initiatives within their traditional corporate banking culture.

In general, furthermore, the financial market has been characterized by a strong competition among diverse intermediaries, as reflected by a Herfindahl–Hirschman index of 724. While the benefits — from intense competition — for the clients have been evident, as shown below, strong competitive pressures during the current global crisis may eventually contribute to higher default rates. Indeed, access to a broader set of suppliers, combined with the lower present value of client relationships (given, in part, by the expectation of more limited business opportunities), may increase the opportunistic behavior of borrowers, whose repayment capacity has also been declining (as it did, in large part, because of a 28 percent increase in the price of food in 2008). Nevertheless, in contrast to the earlier experience of over-indebtedness, triggered by the consumer lending FFPs at the end of the century, information-sharing through a credit bureau that includes both regulated and non-regulated institutions may help in somewhat containing this more recent threat (de Janvry *et al.*, 2003).

Indeed, before the consumer credit episode, only regulated intermediaries had had access to the credit rating system (*Central de Riesgos*) run by the SBEF. While this mechanism, managed in an objective and professional way, had created trust in information-sharing arrangements, it did not cover the many clients of the then non-regulated institutions. The crisis episode softened, however, the political objections that may have blocked the development of credit bureaus in other countries and, with active participation of both regulated and non-regulated MFIs, a private credit bureau has been operating since that time. This institutional arrangement has helped to constrain some opportunistic behavior in the presence of intense competition and adverse systemic shocks (Haider, 2000).

Eventually, the Bolivian MFIs also became very successful in the mobilization of deposits. The swift expansion of the credit assets of the MFIs preceded, however, the expansion of their deposit liabilities by about a decade. On the one hand, in the non-regulated segment, the IFDs have not yet had the authorization to mobilize deposits from the public, while other regulatory constraints may have piled on the inherent difficulties and costs associated with the development of facilities for the mobilization of very small and liquid deposits. On the other hand, access to funding from alternative sources (mostly their own equity and funds from international donors) may have discouraged the mobilization of deposits even by the regulated MFIs. Further, once the initial efforts and the accompanying learning had been focused on building a loan portfolio, the MFIs may have sought the full consolidation of their lending operations before turning their attention to savings mobilization. Once they did, however, the outcome of their deposit activities has been as spectacular as their performance on the lending side (Gómez–Soto and Gonzalez–Vega, 2007).

Indeed, microfinance has also induced a transformation of the market for *deposits* in Bolivia. In the decade following the macroeconomic and financial reforms of the mid-1980s and until 1998, the deposits mobilized by the Bolivian financial system grew rapidly, first exponentially — as depositor trust was regained — and then at a declining rate after 1994 when the country was already reaching levels of financial deepening above those of its peers and as more demanding prudential requirements (which allowed the banks less leveraging) were being introduced. Over a decade, the deposits of the system grew sevenfold, from US$ 509 million (1988) to US$ 3.6 billion (1998) in real terms. With the crisis at the end of the century, however, these deposits experienced a stagnant and, at times, declining trend accompanied by exceptional volatility. For example, while the stock of deposits had reached a peak of US$ 3.9 billion, in real terms, by January 2002, this was followed by a sharp decline, to US$ 3.2 billion, by July of the same year, mostly as a consequence of political shocks.

Stagnation and much volatility continued through mid-2006 when the deposits of the public regained a rapid upward trend, with some but less severe volatility. Thus, aggregate deposits grew only 12 percent for the whole decade (1998–2008), in sharp contrast to the sevenfold increase of the previous decade (1988–1998), and they reached US$ 4.1 billion, in real terms, by December 2008. During their most recent expansion, these deposits grew from US$ 3.4 billion (June 2006) to US$ 4.5 billion (June 2009). Exceptionally high export prices and values, growing remittance levels, and the apparent increase in cocaine traffic (UNODC, 2009) may have contributed to this recent but difficult-to-sustain deposit expansion, given the impact of the current global crisis. Further, the shift of the system's liabilities towards dollar-denominated accounts and towards the most liquid among the deposit instruments available to the public may signal a gradual loss of depositor confidence. Expectations may change, if the exceptional growth of export earnings and government revenues of recent years is not repeated in the future and as the stock of public domestic debt keeps accumulating.

The evolution of the deposits mobilized by the Bolivian financial system has reflected a swing in *financial deepening* equivalent to that observed with respect to credit portfolios. The ratio of the deposits mobilized with respect to the GDP reached a peak of 0.517, by September 1999, more than 10 percentage points above the Latin American average at that time. Almost a decade later and after some recovery, by December 2008 this ratio was only 0.353. Here, again, the reversion in financial deepening would have been even worse in the absence of microfinance. If the deposits mobilized by the MFIs — a good portion of them from segments of society never reached with this financial service before — were ignored, the ratio would have been 0.304 by the latter date. This would imply a setback of more than 16 years, almost two years more than when the MFIs are included in the figures.

The differential performance observed with respect to the evolution of their loan portfolios is also reflected by the evolution of the mobilization

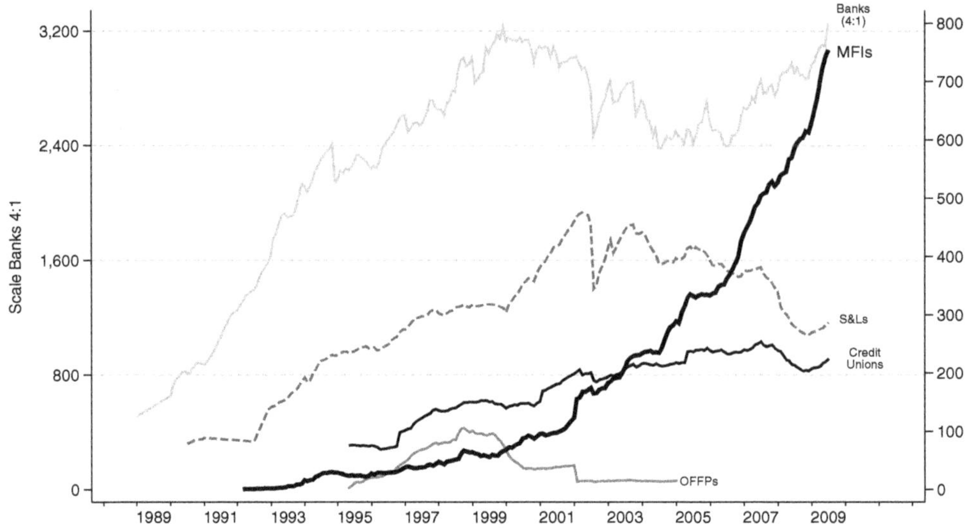

Source: Gonzalez–Vega and Villafani–Ibarnegaray (2010).

Figure 9.3: Deposits of the public in the Bolivian financial system.

Note: The data are by type of institution: banks, credit unions, savings and loan associations (S&Ls), regulated microfinance institutions (MFIs) and other FFPs (OFFPs), for December 1988 to June 2009 (in the million dollar equivalent of real bolivianos, as of December of 2005).

of funds from the public by the different types of financial intermediaries. Figure 9.3 illustrates the unstable deposit mobilization by the commercial banks and the recent losses of deposits by the credit unions, savings and loan associations, and consumer credit FFPs. The sharply exponential increase in the deposits mobilized by the regulated MFIs stands in indisputable contrast. MFI deposits increased almost tenfold over a decade, from US$ 64 million (December 1998) to US$ 628 million (December 2008) and they reached US$ 756 million by June 2009 — therefore accounting for a good portion of the US$ 1,021 million of their gross loan portfolio. Thus, having initially built a portfolio without any funding from deposits, the savings mobilized from the public by the MFIs now fund three-quarters (74 percent) of their loan volume. Rather than being a conduit for government funds, the MFIs have been substantially contributing to the country's process of financial *intermediation*.

Moreover, by June 2009, credit from other financial institutions, including foreign and domestic commercial banks as well as several international agencies, represented only 22 percent of the funding — different from their equity — of the regulated MFIs. The difference (78 percent) had been mobilized as deposits from the public. These deposits have represented more than

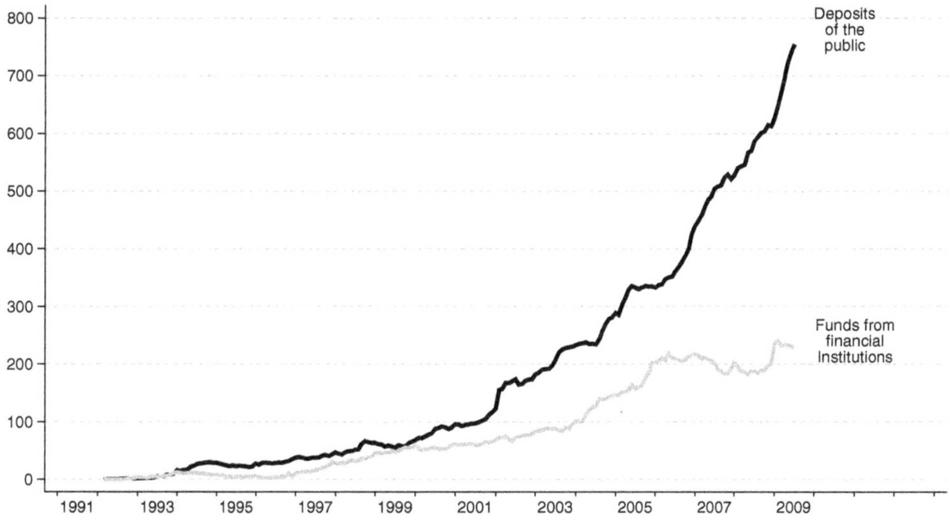

Source: Gonzalez–Vega and Villafani–Ibarnegaray (2010).

Figure 9.4: Funding from foreign and domestic financial institutions and deposits of the public in the Bolivian regulated microfinance institutions.

Note: The data are for February 1992 to June 2009 (in the million dollar equivalent of real bolivianos, as of December 2005).

half of this funding ever since 1993, when they had accounted for 56 percent. The relative importance of deposits increased to 93 percent, by March of 1996, and it then declined to 54 percent of non-equity funding by the end of 1999 (Figure 9.4). In the new century, however, there has been a sustained increase in the share of deposits in this funding. Moreover, by June of 2009, credit from (cheaper) foreign sources represented 63 percent of the funding from financial institutions, in reflection of the strong creditworthiness of the MFIs, while domestic sources accounted for 37 percent. Among these domestic sources, loans from banks represented only 4 percent of the non-equity funds used by the MFIs. Therefore, by being able to rely mostly on the deposits mobilized from the public — and on their own equity — as well as on their access to foreign funding (given their recognized strength), for their loanable funds, the contraction of bank lending — during the crisis — does not seem to have affected the growing ability of the MFIs to lend.

Further, as explained below, their clients much valued the deposits held with the MFIs as an important risk management tool — particularly during the crisis — and this behavior favored the continued expansion of MFI deposits. In turn, in the case of the non-regulated IFDs, which do not yet have the authorization to mobilize deposits, they typically use the infrastructure of the banks to allow their clients access to banking windows. Also, the contractual savings mobilized by village banking programs have been held in accounts with regulated intermediaries (where these savings have exceeded any loans to the IFD from these institutions). Further, some IFDs have engaged in strategic alliances that induce regulated institutions to open windows in their own branches (e.g., FIE windows in the Pro Mujer focal centers) and to offer other financial services for which the IFD has not yet been authorized (Miller Wise and Berry, 2005; Gonzalez–Vega and Quirós, 2008).

In this intermediation task, the deposits mobilized by the regulated MFIs are equivalent to 5 percent of the GDP. This lower contribution to financial deepening (compared to 8 percent of the GDP, in the case of the loan portfolio) reflects, in part, the advantage that banks have in offering checking accounts. In Bolivia, checking accounts are used mostly by corporations and high-income urban households subject to tax liabilities, and these accounts allow the banks, therefore, to mobilize substantial amounts from a few depositors. For other segments of the population, a developed market of online transactions and trust in checks is almost inexistent, and they prefer to use passbook savings accounts as their tool for liquidity management.

The contrast between banks and MFIs — in the intermediation role — also reflects a key difference in their asset-holding behavior. While, by December 2008, the banks devoted 34.3 percent of their assets to holdings of Central Bank short-term securities (performing, thereby, a *quasi-fiscal* function) and only 49.4 percent of their assets to their gross loan portfolio, the regulated MFIs kept just 11.0 percent of their assets in Central Bank securities and 75.9 percent in their loan portfolio. Moreover, the non-regulated IFDs held 84.8 percent of their assets as a loan portfolio and only 3.2 percent in Central Bank securities. The difference with total assets, in all cases, represents liquidity holdings. In their intermediation function of transforming deposits from the public (surplus units) into loans to enterprises and households (deficit units), the MFIs have been more effective than the banks. In this role, the contribution of MFIs to resource allocation through financial intermediation has been substantial.

This extraordinary expansion — on the deposit side — has reflected key innovations in savings mobilization (including new types of debit cards and ATM services, based on biometrics and indigenous languages), available in a rapidly expanding network of branches and other delivery points, where the services offered have been appropriate for the circumstances of marginal clienteles (Hernandez and Mugica, 2003). This progress has also been facilitated by more flexible prudential norms (including those that regulate locations, days and hours of service) and by the strengthened image of the MFIs — given the quality of their portfolios, the behavior of their managers during political shocks that induced runs on deposits (in protecting the trust placed on them by the depositors), and a quality of services that has encouraged client loyalty (Gómez–Soto and Gonzalez–Vega, 2007).

The expansion has also been a result of a valuable learning process, during which the Bolivian MFIs have recognized that a perfect matching between their borrowing and their depositing clienteles is not necessarily optimum. Thus, while still offering valuable services to small depositors in their target market, the regulated MFIs have also attracted wealthier depositors and other surplus units (including some cooperatives and non-regulated IFDs) and this has allowed them to offer better loan contracts to poorer borrowers (deficit units). In bringing together these different actors, the MFIs have increased both the participation in markets of the target population and the level of intermediation in the economy and have also enhanced opportunities for risk-pooling.

In the process, the share of the commercial banks in the market for deposits from the public declined from almost 100 percent at the end of 1988 and 82.6 percent at the end of 1998, to 72.8 percent at the end of 2008. In turn, the share of the regulated MFIs increased from 1.7 percent (December 1998) to 15.4 percent (December 2008) and 16.7 percent (June 2009). The still big share of the commercial banks has been largely influenced by their near monopoly of checking accounts, in large part because of prudential regulation constraints on the MFIs. These current accounts, mostly from corporations, represent the largest share of the amounts captured by the banks from the public. In contrast, by December 2008, the banks' share of the value of savings accounts — the preferred instrument of middle- and low-income households — was 69.8 percent and it was only 58.2 percent in the case of time deposits. In turn, the shares of the regulated MFIs had grown to 14.8 percent of the value of savings accounts and 26.8 percent of the value of time deposits. The high share in the market for time deposits signals the strong confidence that the public has on the long-term robustness of the regulated MFIs. As their image with savers has gained strength, the MFIs have been able to offer smaller premiums in their deposit interest rates, than initially, in order to attract funds from the public.

4 Instability: Credit and Liquidity Risks

The analysis of the growing contributions of the regulated and non-regulated MFIs to the loan portfolio and deposit mobilization outcomes of the Bolivian financial system has suggested that, increasingly, microfinance has been the *engine* moving the country's process of financial deepening. In this section, we will show that microfinance has also been an *anchor*, whose evolution has reduced the instability that has characterized the system during this period. Indeed, when contrasted to other types of financial intermediaries, the loan portfolios of MFIs have shown much lower default rates (less credit risk) and the deposits mobilized from the public have shown less volatility in the presence of systemic shocks (less liquidity risk).

By December 2008, the *portfolio at risk* rates of the Bolivian financial system (outstanding balances for loans with at least one day of arrears) reached a historic low of 3.7 percent of the gross loan portfolio. This average indicator of delinquency conceals, however, two significant features. The portfolio at risk rate has experienced large swings over time and there have been recurrent differences in the performance of the various types of financial intermediaries, in their control of credit risks. On the one hand, despite some major fluctuations (particularly in early 1996 and mostly driven by the banks), during most of the 1990s delinquency rates rapidly declined. By December 1998, the system's portfolio at risk rate was as low as 5.3 percent, although the swift increases in the volume of loans were already hiding the accumulating portfolio weakness. Inevitably, the systemic crisis at the end of the century sharply increased the portfolio at risk rate, to a peak of 18.4 percent of the system's gross portfolio (by April 2003). Thereafter, delinquency rates steadily declined again. It seems, however, as if the system may have been at the bottom of this swing by the end of 2008. Delinquency rates are slowly creeping up again, maybe in reflection of intense competition, in a market that may be shrinking from the impact of the global crisis, political uncertainty and the deceleration of the Bolivian economy.

On the other hand, there have been sharp differences regarding the timing, the length, and the depth of the delinquency problems suffered by the commercial banks (and the other financial intermediaries) and those experienced by the MFIs. Actually, the superior portfolio quality of the MFIs has surprised many who, *a priori*, had judged microcredit transactions to be intrinsically riskier than other loans. However, the Bolivian experience suggests that, even if the *ex ante* risks were (which may not necessarily be the case) higher, the superiority of the innovations in microfinance lending technologies — in successfully addressing these risks — has actually resulted in lower *ex post* delinquency outcomes, compared to other components of the financial system's loan portfolio (including those loans that had been guaranteed with mortgages and other types of hard collateral). Again, these accomplishments have resulted from the development of microfinance — non-mortgage-based — lending technologies that, in their appropriateness for the particular market segment, have led to a superior loan portfolio performance in Bolivia.

Moreover, many (including some prudential supervisors) still believe that microfinance loan portfolios are inevitably more vulnerable to systemic shocks than regular banking portfolios. The Bolivian experience demonstrates the likelihood of the opposite result. Microfinance portfolios not only are (in their growth behavior) less pro-cyclical than the portfolios of other financial intermediaries; they actually represent — because of the lower incidence of default that they experience during periods of adverse shocks, compared to other portfolios — a diversification tool, which partially protects financial intermediaries during systemic crises. That is, in the case of MFIs, the risk of default appears to be less covariant with adverse systemic shocks than for banks (unless a particular shock is directly related to this market segment, as might have been the case with the recent food price crisis). Thus, the greater presence of microfinance transactions in the portfolios of financial institutions (or as a component of a financial system) may be expected to be related to more resilience and to less portfolio at risk, in the presence of macroeconomic and political systemic shocks (Villafani–Ibarnegaray and Gonzalez–Vega, 2007; Villafani–Ibarnegaray, 2008). In this sense, the substantial presence of microfinance in Bolivia has actually improved the quality and reduced the instability of the aggregate financial system's loan portfolios. Microfinance has been an anchor in these turbulent times.

In effect, from the time of their creation (except briefly in 1999), MFIs have shown lower portfolio at risk rates than all other types of financial intermediaries (and this ranking has been order-preserving). In particular, up to 1999, these rates were always lower than those for the commercial banks (Figure 9.5). The portfolio at risk rates for savings and loan associations (almost always above 10 percent) and for cooperatives (frequently above 15 percent) were even higher than for the banks, and the unfortunate episode of the consumer credit FFPs led to portfolio at risk rates above 30 percent (not shown in the graph). Moreover, while, during the crisis, all delinquency rates increased, those for all other financial intermediaries increased well above those for the MFIs. Eventually, these rates declined for all institutions and, by December 2008, the portfolio at risk rate for MFIs

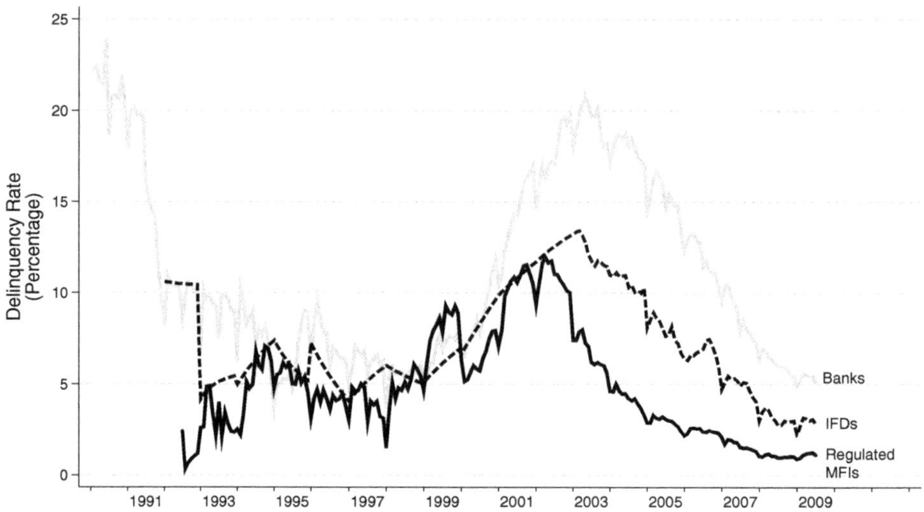

Source: Gonzalez–Vega and Villafani–Ibarnegaray (2010).

Figure 9.5: Portfolio at risk in the banks, regulated microfinance institutions and non-regulated development finance institutions of Bolivia.

Note: Portfolio at risk is measured as the non-performing portfolio as a percentage of the gross portfolio. The data are from December 1990 to June 2009.

was 1.1 percent of their gross loan portfolio (the lowest rate historically observed for any type of financial intermediary in Bolivia), in contrast to 4.9 percent for the banks, 5.0 percent for the savings and loan associations, and 2.5 percent for the cooperatives. In turn, the combined indicator for the MFIs resulted from a portfolio at risk rate of 0.9 percent for the regulated and 2.2 percent for the non-regulated microfinance institutions.

There have been important differences, not only in the level but also in the timing and the duration of these delinquency problems. First, during the crisis, the maximum portfolio at risk rate for MFIs (11.2 percent, by September 2001) was below the maximum for cooperatives (17.9 percent, by February 2002), savings and loan associations (18.1 percent, by February 2002) and commercial banks (20.8 percent, by April 2003). This ranking, with the banks at the top of the delinquency rates, has been mostly preserved every year thereafter. Moreover, in the case of the banks, the delinquency rates would have been much higher than those actually recorded, if it were not for their massive rescheduling of delinquent loans and substantial write-offs. When, in January 2004, the prudential authorities required the explicit accounting of *rescheduled* loans — and assuming that these loans represented a higher risk than performing loans — the "contaminated" portfolio of the commercial banks would have increased from 18.1 to 46.2 percent, while the "contaminated" portfolio of the MFIs would have increased from 4.8 to just 8.3 percent. From this other perspective, therefore, the actual differences in portfolio quality were more pronounced than those shown by the portfolio at risk indicator. That the MFIs had to reschedule so many fewer loans reveals how their clients were making a stronger repayment effort — under the initial contract conditions — than the commercial bank clients.

Moreover, the MFIs were able to turn around their delinquency rates — from the peak — quite early (about a year-and-a-half earlier than the banks and half-a-year earlier than other intermediaries) and these institutions rapidly gained control of their portfolio quality (Gonzalez–Vega and Villafani–Ibarnegaray, 2010). This control of default came sooner for the regulated MFIs than for the IFDs (with the exception of Crecer and Pro Mujer, two village banking programs that experienced the least delinquency problems among all Bolivian financial institutions). In contrast, the other intermediaries found it harder to halt the growth of their portfolios at risk, which kept increasing for additional periods and then reached higher levels. There were also important differences, among intermediaries, in the length of the delinquency episode. While, after the peak, it took the MFIs three months to get their portfolio at risk rates at the one-digit level (December 2001), this achievement took the banks several years (not attained until December 2006). Similarly, while MFIs managed to lower their portfolio at risk rates below 5 percent by December 2003, this achievement took the banks five additional years (not attained until December 2008).

A key determinant of the superior performance of microfinance credit portfolios has been the *appropriateness* of the *lending technology* for the target clientele. In general, microfinance technologies have been very effective in addressing information, incentives and contract enforcement problems, in their specific market segment (Navajas and Gonzalez–Vega, 2002; Armendáriz and Morduch, 2010). In Bolivia, despite the small country size, several types of lending technologies have been developed and have been implemented in particularly cost-effective ways (Quirós–Rodríguez, Rodríguez–Meza and Gonzalez–Vega, 2003; Rodríguez–Meza and González, 2003; Rodríguez–Meza and Gonzalez–Vega, 2003; Rodríguez–Meza and Quirós–Rodríguez, 2003). As a result, the steady decline in operational costs (which has allowed sharp reductions in interest rates) and the low portfolio at risk rates have marched hand in hand. That is, the Bolivian MFIs have been able to strictly contain default while incurring declining operational costs in the expansion of their outreach.

Some of the major innovations of the microfinance revolution have buried deep roots in Bolivia. Critical, from the start, has been the *signal* that a loan is a *contract*, which creates rights and responsibilities for both parties. This has been in sharp contrast with the earlier top-down notion of credit as a policy (political/electoral) tool (Gonzalez–Vega, 2003). Interestingly enough, the recently created state-owned bank (*Banco de Desarrollo Productivo*) has faced major difficulties in expanding its loan portfolio, in part due to the limited credibility of its offer and to the fears of some MFIs, as potential borrowers, that the requirements that they on-lend the funds at subsidized interest rates and to specific clienteles may create negative demonstration effects with their traditional clientele. What is clear is that, in a scenario without microfinance, small entrepreneurs and peasants would have been marching, as is usual in Bolivia, to demand access to credit, particularly during the current crisis. That this has not been the case implicitly reveals the success of the new contractual relationships. Further, the MFIs' pursuit of sustainability has sealed their promises of future service with the credibility needed to induce compatible incentives among their borrowers.

Thus, at the core of the new lending technologies has been the development, *in situ*, of credible *relationships* that are mutually valuable. The resulting structures of incentives have encouraged investment, by all parties, in these relationships, and the present value of these relationships — for both borrowers and lenders — has nurtured repayment. Different variations of these lending technologies have relied on complementary relationships: among the members of a village bank or a solidarity group, between individual borrowers and their lenders or between borrowers and the loan officers that operate as surrogates of the MFIs, and between the MFIs and their loan officers. The relationships have been more valuable when attractive productive opportunities have been available to the borrowers (given Bolivia's rapid economic growth), when the MFIs' services have assisted households in consumption smoothing, when their services have matched the demand of clients, and when the MFIs have been perceived as sustainable. In turn, the resulting client "loyalty" has lowered the costs and risks of the MFIs.

Not all lending technologies, however, have been equally robust in the presence of systemic shocks. Given the inherent inability of the members of credit groups to self-insure against systemic risks, the joint liability group lending technologies of BancoSol and PRODEM collapsed during the crisis, and these MFIs had to embark in a painful transition toward individual loan methodologies. In contrast, the market share of the MFIs that, from the start, had delivered individual loans to the same target population — such as FIE and Caja los Andes — sharply increased. These organizations were better able to tailor their individual loan contracts (as they had learned much about specific clients), an advantage not possessed by institutions that delegated screening and monitoring to groups (Gonzalez–Vega and Villafani–Ibarnegaray, 2007). Thus, the Bolivian experience during systemic shocks questions *a priori* assumptions about the riskiness of group versus individual credit contracts (Stiglitz, 1990; Ghatak and Guinnane, 1999).

Moreover, while, for the lenders, the (fixed) costs per loan of the group credit and village banking programs have been lower than the operational costs of individual loans, the suppliers of individual loans have been able to offer substantially larger loans — to the same type of clients — without increasing the risk of default. This has resulted from the greater differentiating power of their screening efforts. As a consequence of these larger loan sizes, *ceteris paribus*, the individual-loan MFIs have enjoyed cost advantages over other MFIs (Rodríguez–Meza and Gonzalez–Vega, 2003). Moreover, particularly in the case of village banking, the opportunity costs of frequent and prolonged group meetings have exceeded the transaction costs of individual borrowers. When offered the opportunity to access an individual loan, most MFI clients have shown a strong preference, thereby revealing the lower transaction costs that they perceive.

In addition to differences in lending technologies, dimensions of organizational design also explain the observed differential performance between MFIs and other types of intermediaries, particularly banks. Banks had shown less prudence when building their loan portfolios, relying on their political clout and on perceptions of "too big to fail" in their anticipation of a government bailout (which actually took place). Smaller in size and with less political connections, the behavior of the MFIs had been less opportunistic. Moreover, opportunistic behavior among the microfinance clients did not emerge for a long time, in contrast with the loan pardoning expectations harbored by (particularly the large) clients of the commercial banks (who were frequently also linked to the owners of the banks). Further, the challenge of the consumer credit FFPs had forced MFIs to fine-tune their risk management skills, just before the macroeconomic and political shocks took place. This challenging episode had thus stimulated a valuable learning process among MFI managers, which assisted in their greater ability to control their portfolios during the crisis. In turn, the consumer credit FFPs (and some commercial bank microcredit programs) gambled on charging interest rates high enough to cover the high rates of default expected from their more lax screening and weaker client relationships. They lost their bet and had to exit the market.

Finally, the superior performance of microfinance loan portfolios has reflected key client characteristics. Several of the weaknesses that some (including prudential authorities) usually attribute to microfinance clients — and that also represent barriers to the production of financial transactions, when using traditional banking technologies — actually represent a strength during periods of systemic shocks (Gonzalez–Vega, 2003). Central to these features is the informality of clients, particularly in the labor market. Operations in the informal economy endow these household-firms with flexibility (in terms of the deployment of the household's labor supply), versatility (in terms of the range of occupations and diversification of household portfolios), and mobility (both geographic and occupational). These features bestow microfinance borrowers with great resilience and broader opportunities, including international migration, to diversify against various types of shocks. These characteristics protect the microfinance borrower's *ability* to repay (González and Gonzalez–Vega, 2003).

Further, the high present value of client relationships bolsters *willingness* to repay. This high value responds, in part, to the limited options (previously) available to these household-firms and, in part, to the quality and appropriateness of the services offered by the MFIs. Thus, borrowers are willing to incur high costs, in order to protect their credit history with particular lenders. As revealed by a survey of clients of financial intermediaries, during the crisis at the end of the century, microfinance borrowers were willing to undertake (in 76 percent of the cases) exceptional actions — beyond those expected at the time of the contract — in order to repay. These actions included working more than the ordinary schedules (66 percent), using financial savings (47 percent), receiving specific remittances (29 percent), selling productive assets (23 percent), and borrowing from other sources (10 percent). In a simulation of what might have happened, in the absence of these exceptional actions, 44 percent (rather than 12 percent) would have been in arrears for over 30 days, 41 percent (rather than 38 percent) would have been in arrears for less than 30 days, and only 15 percent (instead of 49 percent) would have repaid on time (González, 2008). The high costs implicit in these exceptional actions reveal the high value of these relationships and the associated lower risks of moral hazard faced by MFIs. The MFIs can count on a limited extent of opportunism, however, only as long as they build value in these relationships. This dimension was missing, however, in the contracts written by the consumer lending FFPs in the late 1990s, and this was reflected by portfolio at risk rates above 30 percent, which eventually resulted in the failure and exit from the market of some of these intermediaries.

The MFIs' superior ability in the management of credit risk has been mirrored — and not as a coincidence — by their superior ability in the management of liquidity risk. In the past decade, Bolivia has experienced a succession of major systemic shocks, including the macroeconomic crisis at the end of the century, severe political instability (as reflected by the stay in power of six presidents in a six-year period), and frequent social disturbances. These shocks have induced, at different times and to a different extent, temporary runs on deposits. There have been major differences, across financial intermediaries, in the severity of these runs.

Figure 9.6 reports the month-by-month reductions in the deposits of the public, by type of institution. One critical episode took place in July 2002, given acute uncertainty about the outcome of the presidential election. In a few days, the savings and loan associations lost 24 percent of their deposits, and they lost another 7 percent in the following weeks. While the deposit losses of the commercial banks amounted to 12 percent in that month and another 14 percent in the following months, given their dominance in the system this represented substantial amounts in absolute terms. In contrast, the cooperatives lost 8 percent and the MFIs lost only 6 percent of their deposits (mostly deposits from other financial institutions), which the latter

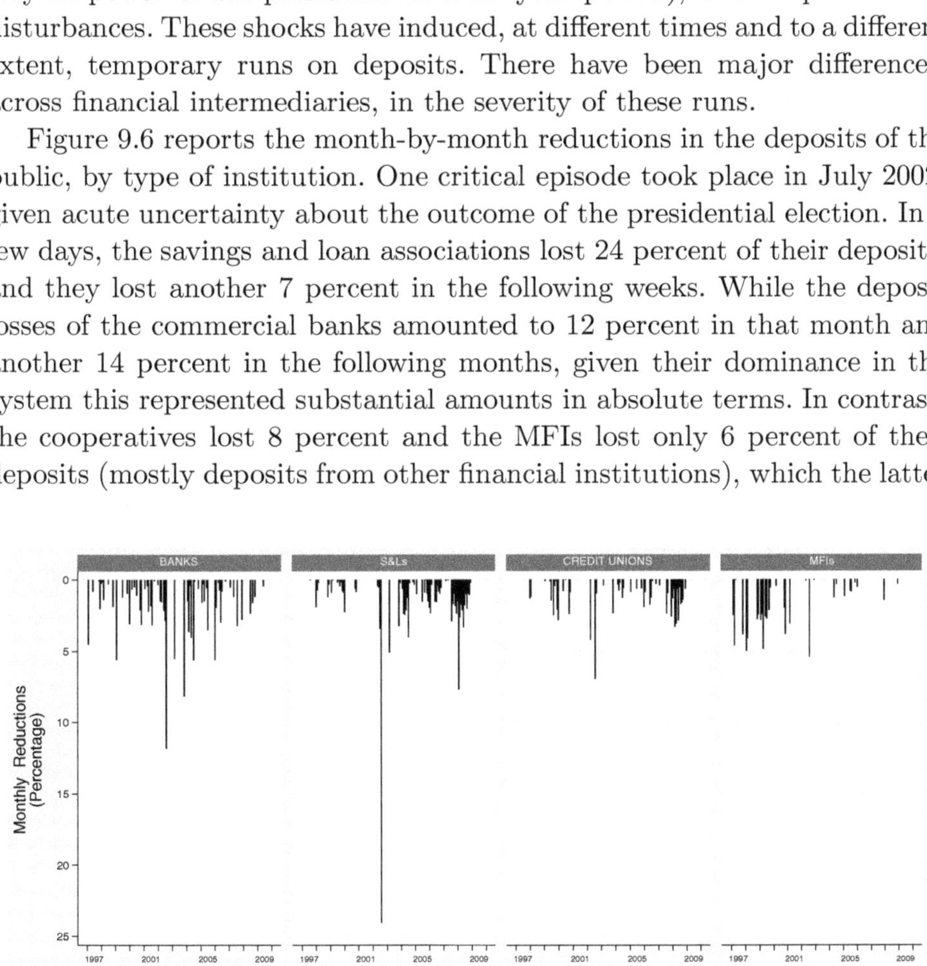

Source: Gonzalez–Vega and Villafani–Ibarnegaray (2010).

Figure 9.6: Monthly reductions in the volume of deposits of the public in Bolivia.

Note: Data are by type of financial institution (banks, savings and loan associations, credit unions, microfinance institutions). Monthly reductions are in percentages, for December 1989 through June 2009.

managed to recover very quickly. The experience has been repeated several times. For instance, in February 2003, the army and the police fought each other in the streets of La Paz, and the runs on deposits returned. The savings and loan associations lost 5.5 percent and the banks lost 5.3 percent, while the MFIs lost only 1.7 percent of their deposits. By October 2003, when President Sánchez de Lozada was deposed, all other intermediaries continued to lose deposits while the MFIs actually gained deposits. This outcome (the loss of deposits by other intermediaries at the same time that the MFIs gained deposits) has been repeated with additional crises ever since (Gómez–Soto and Gonzalez–Vega, 2007).

A number of circumstances have contributed to this favorable outcome. The deposits of MFI clients seem to be mostly precautionary reserves. These reserves are particularly important among the poor, and their propensity to accumulate reserves increases during periods of uncertainty. This hypothesis seems to be confirmed by the much greater increase in the deposits with balances below US$ 1,000, during these episodes, compared to losses among large-amount deposits. In addition, it seems that depositors trusted MFIs even during moments of stress (rioters had actually destroyed some MFI branches). To a large extent, keeping their deposits at the MFI may have been part of the reciprocity implicit in a strong client *relationship*. Controlling for the structure of deposits (currency, terms to maturity, and depositor characteristics), Gómez–Soto and Gonzalez–Vega (2003) show that, if the MFIs had had the same structure of deposits as the banks, the volatility of their deposits would have been much less (for example, they would have lost only 4.6 percent of their deposits, compared to 12.5 percent for the banks, in July 2002). This behavior reflects both perceptions about the sustainability of the MFIs (as reflected by their lower portfolio at risk rates) and economies of scope from the client relationship with the institution. Moreover, the MFI managers demonstrated extreme diligence in contacting depositors during the shocks and reassuring them.

5 Exceptional Outreach

Microfinance matters for financial development. In Bolivia, microfinance has played critical roles as the engine and the anchor of the recent evolution of the financial system. From this perspective, it has contributed to the process of financial deepening in a country characterized by very low incomes and incomplete institutions. Furthermore, several dimensions of *outreach* — forces of financial inclusion — matter for the clients (welfare) and for society (broad-based development) as well (Littlefield, Morduch and Hashemi, 2003; Christen, Rosenberg and Jayadeva, 2004). Frequently acknowledged and sometimes even challenged, the Bolivian microfinance achievements, in terms of outreach, have been outstanding. These outreach outcomes have been exceptional along several margins: breadth, depth, value (quality and cost of services to clients), variety, and the permanence guaranteed by sustainability (Schreiner, 2002).

The gains in *breadth* of outreach (inclusion) have been astonishing. In a country of 9.2 million inhabitants, 1.1 million borrowers had outstanding balances, by December 2008, with some institution of the Bolivian financial system. This is equivalent to 28 percent of the Bolivian labor force (a historic peak for this ratio). In contrast, by February 1992, when BancoSol was created, there were only 76,000 borrowers in the entire Bolivian financial system. Moreover, at the peak of their operations, the borrowers of the Bolivian state-owned banks never surpassed the 1992 numbers for the whole system (Trigo Loubière, 2003).

Thus, with the addition of over one million borrowers in 17 years (1992 to 2009), the breadth of outreach of the financial system has increased almost 15 times. By the end of 2008, of these new borrowers, 849 thousand (77 percent of the total) were clients of a microfinance institution. Of these, 501,000 were borrowers of regulated MFIs and 348,000 were borrowers of non-regulated IFDs. Thus, the outstanding breadth of outreach owes much to both regulated and non-regulated MFIs. In contrast, by the end of 2008, the banks had 159,000 borrowers (14 percent of the total). These data do not fully correct, unfortunately, for clients that held loans from more than one institution. Based on earlier information from credit bureaus, however, on average the borrowers in the system may have about 1.25 client relationships, and these numbers must be discounted accordingly (Villafani–Ibarnegaray, 2003).

The number of borrowers in the financial system had grown rapidly, to 808 thousand (September 2002), and it then declined, with the crisis, to 563 thousand (May 2003). Thus, for the system as a whole, the number of borrowers experienced a deep swing, equivalent to the swing observed in the loan portfolio. Figure 9.7 tells, however, two contrasting stories. Indeed, with the crisis, the number of microfinance borrowers also experienced a (much milder) swing and, in this respect, microfinance was not able to offset the sharp decline in the breadth of outreach of the other financial intermediaries. After a virtual stagnation in the number of microfinance borrowers between

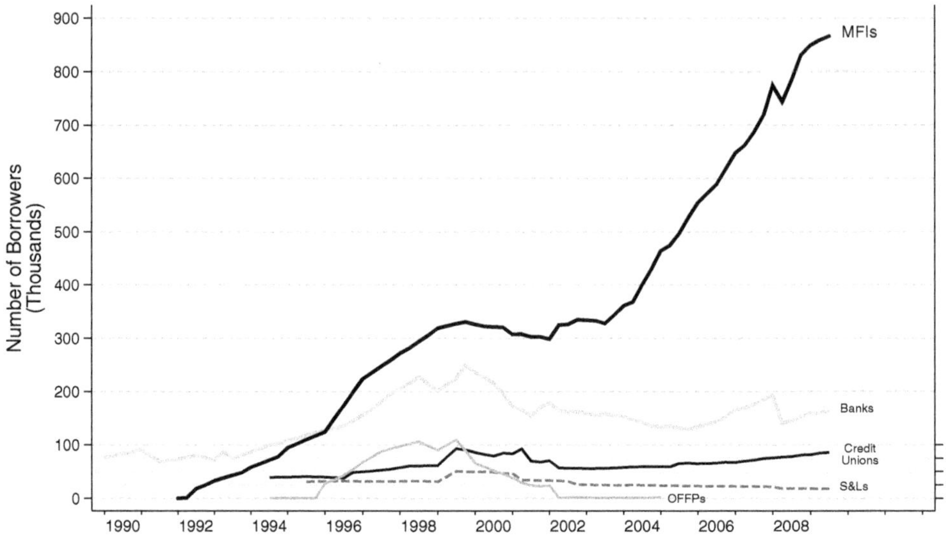

Source: Gonzalez–Vega and Villafani–Ibarnegaray (2010).

Figure 9.7: Number of borrowers in the Bolivian financial system.

Note: Data are by type of financial institution (banks, credit unions, savings and loan associations (S&Ls), microfinance institutions (MFIs) and other FFPs (OFFPs), in thousands, from December 1989 to June 2009).

1999 and 2002 (mostly because of the demise of the group lending technologies), their number exploded, from 298,000 (December 2001) to 867,000 (June 2009). In contrast, all of the other types of financial intermediaries have still not been able to get back to the number of borrowers they had before the crisis. As a consequence, the gap between microfinance and the rest — in their breadth of outreach — continues to increase.

Figure 9.7 also shows that the number of microfinance borrowers has exceeded the number of bank borrowers since March 1996. Moreover, just the regulated MFIs have had more borrowers than the banks since 2002. Also, just the non-regulated IFDs have had more borrowers than the banks since 2002. Amazingly, just two village banking programs (Crecer and Pro Mujer) have had more borrowers than the banks since 2007. However, the average loan size at the banks (US$ 13,000) has been about 60 times the average size of loans (US$ 224) for these village banking organizations (Gonzalez–Vega and Villafani–Ibarnegaray, 2009). Also, nine out of the ten Bolivian financial institutions with the largest numbers of clients are MFIs (five of them regulated and four non-regulated).

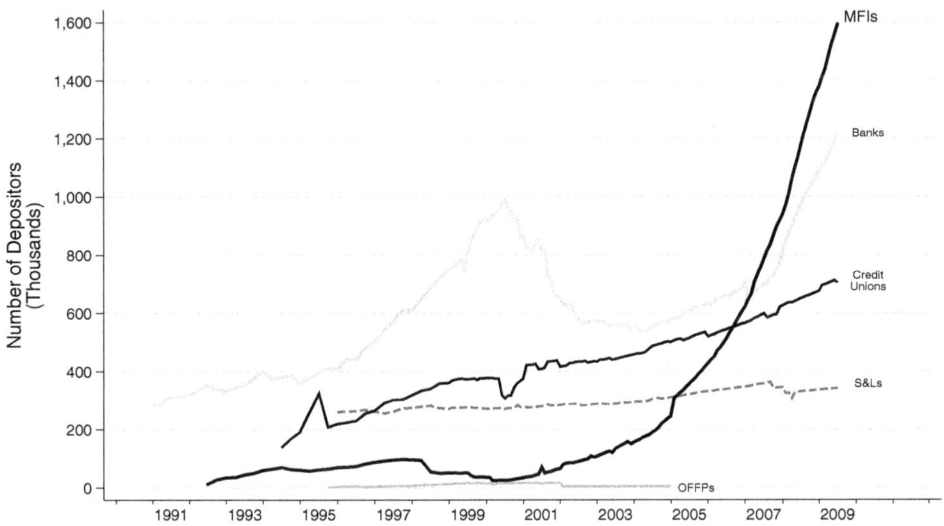

Source: Gonzalez–Vega and Villafani–Ibarnegaray (2010).

Figure 9.8: Number of depositors in the Bolivian financial system (thousands).

Note: The data are by type of intermediary (banks, credit unions, savings and loan associations (S&Ls), regulated microfinance institutions (MFI) and other FFPs (OFFPs), in thousands, from December 1990 to June 2009).

With a lag of about a decade, the evolution of the deposits of the Bolivian financial system tells a similar story (Figure 9.8). At the time of the creation of BancoSol (March 1992), there were 334,000 depositors at the banks. In the following years, the number of bank depositors increased to a peak of 990,000 (June 2000), but this number sharply declined with the crisis and the subsequent political shocks, to 540,000 (March 2004). By that time, just before the explosive growth in their numbers, there were 171,000 depositors in the regulated MFIs (less than one-third than at the banks). The number of depositors in the regulated MFIs surpassed the number of bank depositors, however, in early 2007, and by the end of 2008 it reached 1.4 million (1.6 million by June 2009, mostly with passbook savings accounts). In turn, after a rapid recuperation, particularly in the most recent years, the number of bank depositors reached 1.1 million by the end of 2008. Thus, the regulated MFIs are the largest savings mobilization force in Bolivia and they now attract almost 1.5 times more depositors than the banks. Further, despite the small size of Bolivia, four Bolivian MFIs are among the top 10 Latin American MFIs with the largest number of depositors — PRODEM FFP (4th), Banco Los Andes Procredit (5th), FIE FFP (8th) and BancoSol

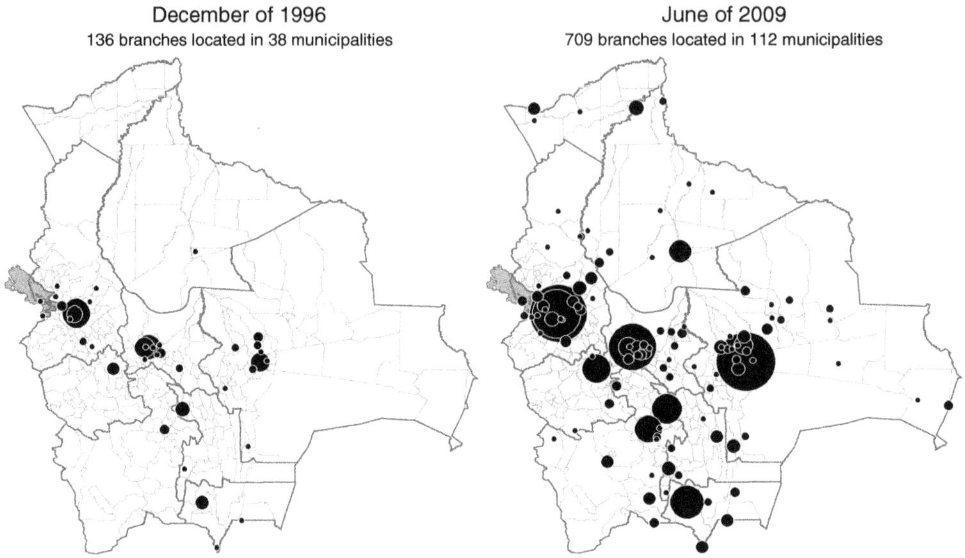

Source: Gonzalez–Vega and Villafani–Ibarnegaray (2010).

Figure 9.9: Branch locations of the Bolivian microfinance institutions, by municipalities, 1996 and 2009.

Note: The number of branches in a municipality is represented by the diameter of the circle.

(9th), according to the Multilateral Investment Fund of the InterAmerican Development Bank (2009).

The successful mobilization of deposits by the regulated MFIs has been an achievement both in terms of the breadth (numbers) and variety of outreach (menu of services). The broader delivery of deposit, credit and other financial services has been made possible, in turn, by a dramatic increase in the microfinance sector's physical infrastructure, as shown in Figure 9.9. In large part, this expansion was facilitated by more flexible prudential norms for the creation and operation of branches. By December 1996, the MFIs operated out of 136 branches in 38 municipalities, in contrast to 229 bank branches in 30 municipalities. By June 2009, however, there were only 206 bank branches (after some mergers) in 48 municipalities compared to 709 branches of MFIs in 112 municipalities (out of 327 municipalities in the country, of which 85 have less than 5,000 inhabitants). That is, while the geographic outreach of the banking infrastructure has remained basically unchanged, since 1996 there has been a five-fold increase in the number of locations where microfinance services are delivered. As shown in Figure 9.9, by reaching into remote areas — in a country with a rugged topography and little infrastructure — and where financial services had not been available before, this spatial expansion has facilitated the microfinance achievements in depth of outreach.

There has been much controversy, however, about the *depth* of outreach of Bolivian microfinance. First, information on the poverty of clients is, unfortunately, scarce and scattered. The available data suggest that most clients are in the top 50 percent of households below the poverty line (Navajas *et al.*, 2000; González, 2002). Second, with women borrowers still representing over two-thirds of the total by the end of 2008, and from other pieces of evidence, gender differences in access do not seem to be an issue in Bolivia. Third, microfinance average loan sizes have consistently been the lowest among the various types of financial intermediaries. Moreover, after increasing between 1995 and 2003, the average size of loans for MFIs has remained essentially constant. By March of 2009, loan size amounted to US$1,141, almost the same as in 2004. This combined average concealed, however, substantial differences in loan size between the two types of MFIs. While average loan size was US$339 for the non-regulated IFDs, it was US$1,695 for the regulated institutions (up from US$326 in June of 1995).

Several authors have questioned if changes in loan size can be interpreted as *mission drift* (Armendáriz and Szafarz, 2010). To explore this issue, we look at the evolution of the composition of the clientele of the regulated MFIs, by size of loan. Similar information is not available for the non-regulated IFDs. Most of their borrowers, however, get very small loans. Further, rather than increasing, for these institutions, since 2003 the average loan size has been rapidly declining. In large part, this has been due to the swift expansion of Crecer and Pro Mujer, which supply the smallest loans in the system.

Figure 9.10 shows the evolution of the number of borrowers of the regulated MFIs for six classes of loan sizes. Since the creation of BancoSol in 1992, the number of borrowers of the regulated MFIs with loans of US$ 500 or less steadily climbed to 125,000 (September 2000). After substantial volatility during the crisis, this number declined to 50,000 (December 2001). This decline was not a consequence, as some have argued, of the transformation of MFIs into regulated institutions (Mosley, 1996). Rather, it was mostly a consequence of the failure of group lending in the presence of systemic shocks (Gonzalez–Vega and Villafani–Ibarnegaray, 2007). MFIs engaged in group lending lost borrowers, while those (also regulated) offering individual loans gained borrowers. Moreover, during the crisis, the borrowers who lost their access to BancoSol and PRODEM, because of the failure of credit groups, almost immediately swelled the numbers of clients of non-regulated microfinance institutions, particularly the village banking

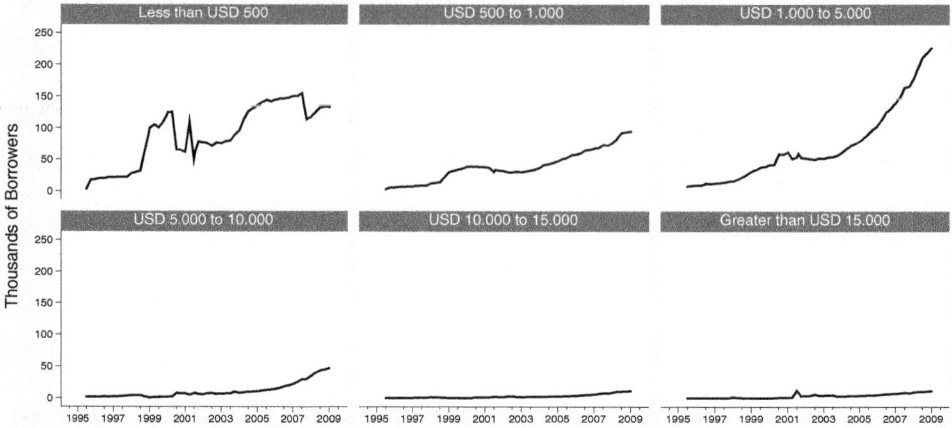

Source: Gonzalez–Vega and Villafani–Ibarnegaray (2010).

Figure 9.10: Number of borrowers for each class (by size of loan) of the regulated microfinance institutions from December 1995 to June 2009.

Note: The data are in thousands, for December 1995 to June 2009.

programs (Gonzalez–Vega and Maldonado, 2003). This episode highlighted the complementary role of various types of MFIs in offering a broad umbrella to the target population in Bolivia.

Once the adjustments in lending technologies took place, in the regulated MFIs the number of borrowers with loans of US$ 500 or less increased again, to 155,000 (December 2007). The recent crisis (in particular, the sharp increase of food prices during 2008) may have hurt this segment of borrowers again, and their number reached 133,000 by the end of 2008. Moreover, most of the 348,000 borrowers of the IFDs, at the end of 2008, would fall in this size category as well. Combined, there would be about 491,000 borrowers (58 percent of the total for the microfinance sector) with loans of less than US$ 500. This undoubtedly is an impressive achievement in depth of outreach. Figure 9.10 also shows the rapid increase in the number of clients with loans above US$ 500 and up to US$ 1,000. The number of these similarly small borrowers reached 93,000, by the end of 2008. After the crisis, however, the fastest increase took place among the group of borrowers with loans of more than US$ 1,000 and up to US$ 5,000. For Bolivia, these borrowers are still in the relevant range for microfinance. Their number reached 226,000. Therefore, 449,000 (88 percent) of the borrowers of the regulated MFIs had loans of less than US$ 5,000. If the borrowers of the non-regulated IFDs are added to this total, 797 thousand microfinance borrowers in Bolivia (94 percent of the total) have loans below US$ 5,000.

In turn, the number of borrowers from the regulated MFIs with loans larger than US$ 5,000 increased, to reach 64,000 by the end of 2008. In this process, the regulated MFIs have been adding a thin layer of larger borrowers to their clientele, without abandoning their traditional target group. Because these larger borrowers receive 56 percent of the gross portfolio, however, their presence in large part explains the increases in average loan size for the regulated MFIs. Averages can be deceiving, nevertheless, and the evolution of the size distribution of the number of borrowers tells a more accurate and complete story, in terms of depth of outreach. Moreover, changes in loan size may respond to numerous factors, including the successful evolution of the businesses of some borrowers as well as learning by MFIs that has allowed them to offer loan sizes that more closely reflect the client's "true" repayment capacity (Gonzalez–Vega *et al.*, 1996).

Further, this loan-size creep strategy, which leads to the *layering* of the number of borrowers by loan size, also helps explain the success of Bolivian microfinance in terms of the *value* (quality and cost) of outreach. Indeed, the presence of a variety of clients (by loan and deposit size, regionally, and by sector of economic activity) has both allowed the regulated MFIs to dilute their substantial fixed costs (through the generation of economies of scale and economies of scope) and to diversify their risks. The resulting dramatic reductions in costs, combined with intense competition, have allowed a substantial fall in interest rates, which has benefited, in particular, the smaller borrowers (who, in any case, represent 88 percent of the clientele). These MFIs would not have been able to sustainably offer the highly-personalized, high quality of credit services to small borrowers, if it were not for these cost reductions. This was particularly critical during the crisis, given the higher portfolio at risk rates and the high costs of revamping lending technologies.

The most extraordinary dimension of outreach in the Bolivian microfinance story has been the *value* of the services offered. Not only have the terms and conditions of loan and deposit contracts carefully responded to the actual demands of clients, but also the costs of these services — for the clients — have appreciably declined in the past two decades. In particular, this has been a story about how the cost of credit was dramatically reduced for sizeable segments of the population. This spectacular *cheapening* of credit has combined several dimensions. First, if lack of access (namely, a missing market) is equivalent to being asked an arbitrarily high price, as economists like to claim, then the massive inclusion of (first-time) borrowers who had never had access to credit is a basic dimension of this cheapening.

Second, if transaction costs are the most relevant dimension of the costs of borrowing, particularly for those with small loans, then the extent to which Bolivian innovations in lending technologies have substantially reduced these costs has actually made credit cheaper, particularly for the poorer borrowers. These innovations have, among other things, (i) allowed the MFIs to get closer to their clients, thereby reducing the influence of distance on borrower transaction costs; (ii) sharply reduced the waiting time for loan disbursements, with the associated lower opportunity costs; and (iii) substantially simplified procedures and requirements. By offering larger loan sizes than similar organizations would supply to "identical" applicants in other places (given the exceptional expertise in screening that they have developed — after intense learning — and the strength of the incentives to repay they have created), the transaction costs per dollar borrowed have been lower than elsewhere. Further, borrowers with access to the individual loans that have been displacing group loans, at all levels, have saved in the transaction costs associated with group meetings and in the risks of joint liability. In turn, depositors have faced less strict requirements to open an account and have enjoyed access to ATM innovations. Indeed, because borrower and depositor transaction costs are mostly independent of loan or deposit size, they disproportionately burden clients with small transactions (Gonzalez–Vega, 2003; Gonzalez–Vega and Villafani–Ibarnegaray, 2007). By reducing the (geographic, ethnic, cultural, linguistic, social) *distance* between clients and institutions, by valuing the time of clients and the timing of transactions, and by building on client relationships rather than on traditional collateral, Bolivian microfinance has drastically reduced borrower transaction costs.

Third, the success of microfinance has led to a huge reduction of interest rates in Bolivia. For those borrowers who have substituted microfinance providers for their earlier informal moneylenders, there has been an immediate and substantial decline in effective interest rates. The most surprising and promising dimension of credit cheapening, however, has been the sustained reduction in the effective interest rates charged by the MFIs themselves. Figure 9.11 shows the evolution of the interest rates charged on loans by the regulated MFIs and other financial intermediaries, since the time of creation of BancoSol (February 1992). These rates are computed as the effective financial earnings on the gross loan portfolio. They incorporate, therefore, any fees and commissions charged in addition to interest payments and are independent of the way in which interest is computed in a particular loan transaction. Unfortunately, a similar series is not available for the non-regulated IFDs.

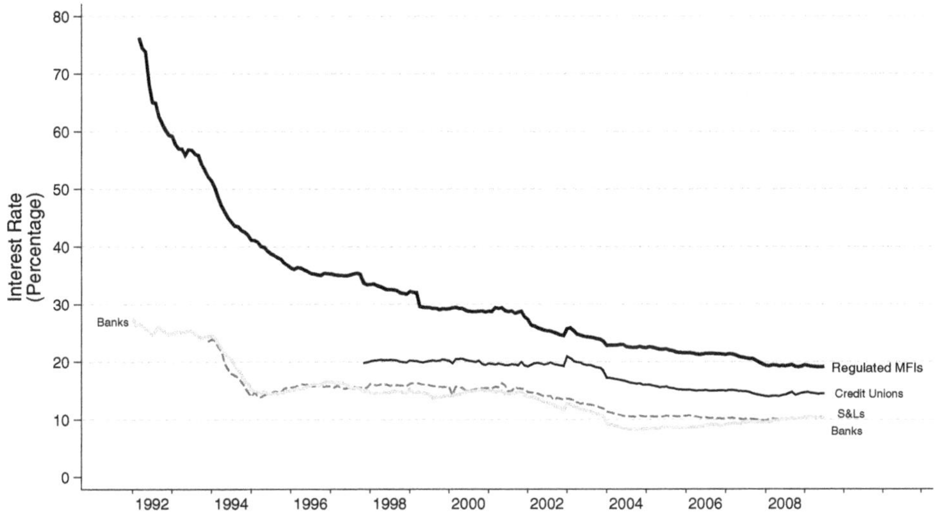

Source: Gonzalez–Vega and Villafani–Ibarnegaray (2010).

Figure 9.11: Effective nominal loan interest rates (percentages per year).

Note: Rates are expressed as percentages per year, by type of institution: banks, credit unions, savings and loan associations (S&Ls), and regulated microfinance institutions (MFIs), for December 1991 to June 2009.

As of February of 1992, there were major differences in the nominal annual interest rates charged by banks (26.5 percent) and those charged by the regulated MFIs (76.2 percent) — BancoSol at that time. Mostly driven by reductions in the international cost of funds, the interest rates charged by the banks declined rapidly in about a couple of years, to 15.2 percent, by December of 1994. The initial decline also reflected a reduction in commissions, when the authorities forced the banks to make them transparent. These rates then remained almost unaltered (within a range of about one percentage point above and one percentage point below), for a long time. Indeed, by December 2001, bank loan interest rates were still at 14.0 percent per year. The rates charged by the savings and loan associations had followed the bank loan rates very closely and, by December 2001, they stood at 14.8 percent. In turn, the rates charged by the credit cooperatives had been systemically higher but also markedly stable and stood at 19.2 percent. In contrast, even with new organizations joining the ranks of regulated institutions over the years, the interest rates charged by the MFIs declined by 48.9 percentage points since 1992, to stand at 27.4 percent per year by the end of 2001. If the drop of 12.5 percentage points in the bank interest rates could be assumed to have mostly responded to the evolution of the market for funds, an additional reduction of 36.4 percentage points may be attributed to increases in the efficiency of the MFIs.

After 2001, bank interest rates gradually declined again, to stand at 10.6 percent by June 2004, and they essentially remained at this level thereafter. Throughout, inflation rates were very low and fairly constant. Although the nominal interest rates charged by banks were still 10.5 percent by December 2008, however, the higher rates of inflation experienced in that year may have pushed them into negative levels, in real terms. In turn, during this century, the interest rates charged by MFIs continued to steadily drop, to 19.4 percent by December 2008. Thus, over a period of 17 years since the creation of BancoSol, the difference in interest rates between the banks and the MFIs declined from 49.7 percentage points (1992) to 9.0 percentage points (2008). The current interest rate differential seems quite narrow, given the substantial differences in client characteristics, contract conditions and loan size between these two types of institutions. Given these differences in loan products, the narrow interest rate differential suggests the presence of intense competition, at some margin, between the banks and MFIs.

Moreover, the interest rates charged by the regulated MFIs dropped by 56.8 percentage points (from 76.2 to 19.4 percent per year) over the same period from 1992 to 2008. Indeed, this has been an extraordinary achievement in making credit cheaper. However, it has not been accomplished by decree, interest rate ceilings or any other form of government intervention (Gonzalez–Vega, 2003). Rather, it has been a consequence of continued innovation and learning, economies of scale and of scope, the cost advantages obtained from the layering of different loan sizes, more effective portfolio diversification, appropriate structures of incentives for staff and managers, and additional drivers of efficiency. In a fiercely competitive market, efficiency became a necessary condition for institutional survival. Virtues of organizational design provided the additional conditions needed.

In contrast, the interest rates charged by the banks declined only 16.1 percentage points during the same period, and most of these reductions took place in the earlier years of the series. To a significant extent, therefore, these differences reflect the diverse strength of innovation and of incentives for cost and default containment between the two types of institutions. In particular, sharp differences in the search for efficiency have been reflected by the evolution of the operational costs of the various financial intermediaries. By February 1996, the operational costs of banks — as a proportion of their gross loan portfolio — amounted to 5.8 percentage points. By the same date, the operational costs of MFIs amounted to 29.4 percentage points. Thereafter, the operational efficiency of the banks remained essentially unaltered, and these costs amounted to 7.7 percentage points by the end of 2008. For the MFIs, operational costs were 11.9 percent. This represents the outstanding reduction of 17.5 percentage points, a major force in the reduction of microfinance interest rates.

6 Concluding Comments

The performance of Bolivian microfinance has been outstanding, in terms of both its contributions to financial *deepening* and to the *outreach* of institutional finance. It would be impossible, however, to identify one single determinant of this Bolivian microfinance success. Rather, there has been a virtuous convergence of numerous circumstances, which have mutually reinforced each other, along a dynamic path.

In this *virtuous convergence* of circumstances, innovation and institutional design have been the central pillars. While many of the innovations in lending technologies have been tried out in several other places as well, Bolivia has been exceptional in the variety of experiments and in the flexibility of approaches. These MFIs have shown an extreme willingness to learn by trial and error, leave behind what does not work, and continue searching for new products and procedures. They have been willing and able to adjust and adapt to changing circumstances over time as well as in response to the detailed demands of specific clienteles, particular competitive threats, or systemic adverse shocks. The diversity of approaches present from the very beginning and a favorable environment, where all of these approaches — several modalities of individual loans, group credit, and village banking — managed to flourish, did create *initial conditions* that may explain the particular creativity and dynamism of the innovation process observed in Bolivia. Because learning-by-doing and the accumulation of situation-specific knowledge do take time, given these initial conditions, the evolution of Bolivian microfinance followed a *path* shaped by the accumulation of experience (that is, with a strong dependence on history).

Thus, because each one of the different approaches was able to achieve considerable success in the earlier days, Bolivia enjoyed quite a broad laboratory for testing the effectiveness of particular dimensions of the different technologies. Moreover, an environment of intense competition forced all the MFIs to "keep on their toes" all the time. Because they were competing in close proximity, all kinds of synergies and externalities emerged. Good practices were imitated and soon afterwards even improved by a competitor. Substantial labor mobility across the MFIs allowed the system, as a whole, to benefit from the aggregate stock of human capital that had been accumulated in the process. These staff movements, at all levels, allowed a cross-fertilization that facilitated the broad implementation of the innovations.

Several dimensions of organizational design also played a key role: (i) incentive-compatible property rights structures where, among other things, local individual leaders behaved as daring and yet prudent "owners"; (ii) very horizontal management structures, which allowed learning across broad segments of the staff and a quick feedback on challenges and outcomes; (iii) the feeling of the organizations of being "outsiders", which would not be bailed out by the state; (iv) the constant "need" to demonstrate their value, both in the market and for society, and to protect their sustainability, in order to survive; (v) the virtual absence of government intervention in the sector, which allowed the emergence of organizational structures where innovation would not be curtailed by bureaucratic, rent-seeking, or political maneuvering; and (vi) in some but not all of the cases, the ability to learn from the rest of the world through their connections to some of the best international networks. Bolivia then became the arena where an implicit contest among microfinance approaches was being played in earnest.

Building on these two key sources of strength (technology and organization), prudential regulation responded to the revealed strong institutional capacity and it reinforced the process. As in the case of the MFIs, visionary authorities created something close to the right balance of quite demanding prudential requirements — to protect stability — with opportunities for innovation. In turn, this expansion of microfinance supply met the largely unsatisfied demand for financial services of a vigorous informal sector, which emerged after the structural reforms of the mid-1980s, where a fairly agile, flexible, hard-working population found these services to be extremely valuable for their diversified livelihoods. Emerging from the shock of hyperinflation, the non-politicized offer from the microfinance NGOs was a welcome novelty for this segment of the population. Thus, a combination of a huge demand (in a rapidly growing economy) with the delivery of high-value services helped cement a culture of repayment — where relationships became very valuable — which would not be challenged for over a decade.

In summary, technologies, institutions, and regulation frameworks dynamically evolved and dialectically interacted, in response to particular challenges, and the resilience of the Bolivian microfinance sector allowed it to flourish even in the midst of major systemic crises, along numerous dimensions and in ways that few would have imagined a couple of decades ago. As a result, microfinance has been the engine and the anchor for the recent evolution of the Bolivian financial system and, in this role, both regulated and non-regulated MFIs have incorporated substantial segments of the excluded population under a broad umbrella of high-quality, low-cost financial services.

References

Armendáriz, B and J Morduch (2010). *The Economics of Microfinance* (2nd ed.) Cambridge, MA: The MIT Press.

Armendáriz, B and A Szafarz (2010). On Mission Drift in Microfinance Institutions. In *The Handbook of Microfinance*, B Armendáriz and M Labie (eds.). Singapore: World Scientific Publishing.

Beck, T, A Demirgüc–Kunt and R Levine (2004). Finance, Inequality and Poverty. World Bank Policy Research Working Paper 3388, Washington DC.

Christen, RP, R Rosenberg and V Jayadeva (2004). Financial Institutions with a Double Bottom Line: Implications for the Future of Microfinance. *Occasional Paper 8*, Washington DC: Consultative Group to Assist the Poor.

Collins, D, J Morduch, S Rutherford and O Ruthven (2009). *Portfolios of the Poor: How the World's Poor Live on $2 a day*. Princeton: Princeton University Press.

de Janvry, A, E Sadoulet, C McIntosh, B Wydick and J Luoto (2003). Credit Bureaus and the Rural Microfinance Sector: Peru, Guatemala and Bolivia. BASIS Report, University of California at Berkeley.

Evia, JL, R Laserna and S Skaperdas (2008). Socio- Political Conflict and Economic Performance in Bolivia. CESifo Working Paper Series. Available at: http://papers.ssrn.com/sol3/papers.cfm?abstract_id=1104954

Frankiewicz, C (2001). *Building Institutional Capacity: The Story of PRODEM, 1987–2000*. Toronto: Calmeadow.

Fry, M (1994), *Money, Interest and Banking in Economic Development*. Baltimore, MD: Johns Hopkins University Press.

Ghatak, M and TW Guinnane (1999). The economics of lending with joint liability: Theory and practice. *Journal of Development Economics*, 60(1), 195–228.

Gavin, M and R Hausmann (1996). The roots of banking crises: The macroeconomic context. In *Banking Crises in Latin America*, R Hausmann and L Rojas-Suarez (eds.). Washington DC: Inter-American Development Bank.

Gómez–Soto, F and C Gonzalez–Vega (2007a). Precautionary wealth of rural households: Is it better to hold it at the barn or at the bank? Paper presented at the *International Conference on Rural Finance Research: Moving Results to Practice*. Food and Agriculture Organization, Rome.

Gómez–Soto, F and C Gonzalez–Vega (2007b). Determinantes del riesgo de liquidez y volatilidad diferenciada de los depósitos en el sistema financiero boliviano. Desempeño de las entidades de microfinanzas ante múltiples shocks sistémicos. *Latin American Journal of Economic Development*, 8, 53–86.

González, A (2002). Crecer and Pro Mujer poverty profiles. Poverty is complex and there are no simple indicators. Working Paper of the Rural Finance Program, The Ohio State University, Columbus, Ohio.

González, A (2008). Microfinance, incentives to repay, and overindebtedness: Evidence from a household survey in Boliva. Ph.D. dissertation, The Ohio State University, Columbus, Ohio.

González, A (2009). Consumption, commercial or mortgage loans: Does it matter for MFIs in Latin America? MIX Data Brief 3.

González, A and C Gonzalez–Vega (2003). Sobreendeudamiento en las microfinanzas bolivianas, 1997–2001. Working paper of the Rural Finance Program, The Ohio State University. Available at: http://aede.osu.edu/programs/Rural Finance/bolivia.htm.

Gonzalez–Vega, C (2003). Deepening rural financial markets: Macroeconomic, policy and political decisions. Paper presented at the International Conference on *Paving the Way Forward for Rural Finance*, Washington DC. Available at: http://aede/osu.edu/programs/RuralFinance/publications.htm

Gonzalez–Vega, C and JH Maldonado (2003). Profundización crediticia entre los clientes de Crecer y de Pro Mujer. Working paper of the Rural Finance Program, The Ohio State University, Columbus, Ohio. Available at: http://aede.osu.edu/programs/RuralFinance/Bolivia

Gonzalez–Vega, C and R Quirós (2008). Strategic alliances for scale and scope economies: Lessons from FADES in Bolivia. In *Expanding the Frontier in Rural Finance. Financial Linkages and Strategic Alliances*, M Pagura (ed.). Rugby, England: Practical Action Publishing.

Gonzalez–Vega, C and JL Rodríguez–Meza (2003). Importancia de la macroeconomía para las microfinanzas en Bolivia. *Cuaderno de SEFIR* 15, La Paz, Bolivia. Available at: http://www.aede.ag.ohio-state.edu/programs/ruralfinance/bolivia

Gonzalez–Vega, C and M Villafani–Ibarnegaray (2007). Las microfinanzas en la profundización del sistema financiero. El caso de Bolivia. *El Trimestre Económico*, 74(1), 5–65.

Gonzalez–Vega, C and M Villafani–Ibarnegaray (2010). *Las microfinanzas en el sistema financiero de Bolivia. Evolución, situación actual y perspectivas.* Santiago de Chile: Sección de Estudios del Desarrollo, CEPAL.

Gonzalez–Vega, C, M Schreiner, RL Meyer, J Rodriguez and S Navajas (1997). The challenge of growth for microfinance organisations: The case of Banco Solidario in Bolivia. In *Microfinance for the Poor?* H Schneider (ed.). Paris: Organisation for Economic Co-operation and Development.

Gonzalez–Vega, C, RL Meyer, S Navajas, M Schreiner, J Rodriguez–Meza and GF Monge (1996). Microfinance market niches and client profiles in Bolivia. Economics and Sociology Occasional Paper 2346, The Ohio State University.

Haider, E (2000). Credit bureaus: Leveraging information for the benefit of microenterprises. *Microenterprise Development Review*, 2(2), 1–8.

Hernandez, R and Y Mugica (2003). What works: Prodem FFP's multilingual smart ATMs for microfinance. Innovative solutions for delivering financial services to rural Bolivia. World Resources Institute. Available at: http://www.digitaldividend.org/pdf/prodem.pdf.

InterAmerican Development Bank. Multilateral Investment Fund (2009). *Microfinanzas Americas: Las cien mejores, 2009.* Available at: http://www.iadb.org/micamericas

Jansson, T, R Rosales and G Westley (2003). *Principios y prácticas para la regulación y supervisión de las microfinanzas.* Washington DC: Banco Interamericano de Desarrollo.

Jemio, LC (2001). Macroeconomic Adjustment in Bolivia since the 1970s: Adjustment to what, by whom and how? Analytical insights from a SAM model. Kiel Working Paper 1031, The Kiel Institute of World Economics.

Ledgerwood, J and V White (2006). *Transforming Microfinance Institutions. Providing Full Financial Services to the Poor.* Washington DC: The World Bank.

Levine, R (1997). Financial development and economic growth: Views and agenda. *Journal of Economic Literature*, 35(2), 688–726.

Levine, R (2005). Finance and growth: Theory and evidence. In *Handbook of Economic Growth*, P Aghion and S Durlauf (eds.), 865–934. Boston, MA: Elsevier Science.

Littlefield, E, J Morduch and S Hashemi (2003). Is Microfinance an Effective Strategy to Reach the Millennium Development Goals? Focus Note 24, Consultative Group to Assist the Poor (CGAP).

McKinnon, RI (1973). *Money and Capital in Economic Development.* Washington DC: Brookings Institution.

Maldonado, JH and C Gonzalez–Vega (2008). Impact of microfinance on schooling. Evidence from poor rural households in Bolivia. *World Development*, 36(11), 2440–2455.

Miller Wise, H and J Berry (2005). Opening markets through strategic partnerships: An analysis of the alliance between FIE and Pro Mujer. USAID: MicroReport 23.

Morales, JA (2007). Financial deepening and economic growth in Bolivia. Working paper, La Paz, Bolivia: Universidad Católica Boliviana.

Morales, JA and JD Sachs (1990). Bolivia's Economic Crisis. In *Developing Country Debt and Economic Performance*, Vol. 2, JD Sachs (ed.). Chicago: Chicago University Press.

Mosley, P (1996). Metamorphosis from NGO to commercial bank: The case of BancoSol in Bolivia. In *Finance Against Poverty*, D Hulme and P Mosley (eds.). London: Routledge.

Navajas, S and C Gonzalez–Vega (2002). Innovación en las finanzas rurales: Financiera Calpiá de El Salvador. In *Prácticas prometedoras en finanzas rurales. Experiencias de América Latina y el Caribe*, MD Wenner, J Alvarado and F Galarza (eds.). Washington, Banco Interamericano de Desarrollo, Instituto Peruano de Estudios Sociales y Academia de Centroamérica.

Navajas, S, J Conning and C Gonzalez–Vega (2003). Lending technologies, competition and consolidation in the market for microfinance in Bolivia. *Journal of International Development*, 15, 747–770.

Navajas, S, M Schreiner, R Meyer, C Gonzalez–Vega, and J Rodriguez–Meza (2000). Microcredit and the poorest of the poor: Theory and evidence from Bolivia. *World Development*, 28(2), 333–346.

Quirós-Rodríguez, R, J Rodríguez–Meza and C Gonzalez–Vega (2003). Tecnología de crédito rural de Crecer en Bolivia. *Cuaderno de SEFIR* 9. La Paz, Bolivia. Available at: http://www.aede.ag.ohio-state.edu/programs/ruralfinance/bolivia

Rhyne, E (2001). *Mainstreaming Microfinance: How Lending to the Poor Began, Grew, and Came of Age in Bolivia.* Bloomfield, Connecticut: Kumarian Press.

Rhyne, E and M Otero (1994). Financial services for microenterprises: principles and institutions. In *The New World of Microenterprise Finance: Building Healthy Financial Institutions for the Poor*, M Otero and E Rhyne (eds.), 11–26. West Hartford, Conn.: Kumarian Press.

Rodríguez–Meza, J and C Gonzalez–Vega (2003). La tecnología de crédito rural de Caja Los Andes en Bolivia. *Cuaderno de SEFIR* 7, La Paz. Bolivia. Available at: http://www.aede.ag.ohio-state.edu/programs/ruralfinance/bolivia

Rodríguez–Meza, J and A González (2003). La tecnología de crédito rural de Prodem FFP. *Cuaderno de SEFIR* 8. La Paz, Bolivia. Available at: http://www.aede.ag.ohio-state.edu/programs/ruralfinance/bolivia

Rodríguez–Meza, J and R Quirós–Rodríguez (2003). Tecnología de crédito rural de FADES en Bolivia. *Cuaderno de SEFIR* 10. La Paz, Bolivia. Available at: http://www.aede.ag.ohio-state.edu/programs/ruralfinance/bolivia

Rojas-Suárez, L (2008). La bancarización en América Latina: obstáculos, avances y la agenda pendiente. Sao Paulo: FELABAN Annual Meetings.

Rosenberg, R (2008). Should governments regulate microfinance? In *Microfinance: Emerging Trends and Challenges*, S Sanduresan (ed.). Northampton, MA: Edward Edgar Publishing.

Shaw, E (1973). *Financial Deepening in Economic Development.* Oxford: Oxford University Press.

Schmidt, RH and CP Zeitinger (1998). Critical Issues in microbusiness finance and the role of donors. In *Strategic Issues in Microfinance*, MS Kimenyi, RC Wieland and JD Von Pischke (eds.). Aldershot, England: Ashgate.

Schreiner, M (2002). Aspects of outreach: A framework for discussion of the social benefits of microfinance. *Journal of International Development*, 14(5), 591–603.

Stiglitz, JA (1990). Peer monitoring and credit markets. *The World Bank Economic Review,* 4(3), 351–366.

Trigo Loubière, J (2003). Crises in the Bolivian financial system: Causes and solutions. In *Financial Crises in Japan and Latin America*, E Demaestri and P Masci (eds.). Washington DC: Inter-American Development Bank.

Trigo Loubière, J, PL Devaney and E Rhyne (2004). Supervising and regulating microfinance in the context of financial sector liberalization. Lessons from Bolivia, Colombia and Mexico. Report to the Tinker Foundation. Boston, MA: Accion Internacional.

UNDOC (2009). Estado Plurinacional de Bolivia. Monitoreo de Cultivos de Coca. Junio 2009. La Paz, Bolivia: Oficina de las Naciones Unidas contra la Droga y el Delito and Gobierno del Estado Plurinacional de Bolivia.

Villafani–Ibarnegaray, M (2003). Evolución de la cartera de los Fondos Financieros Privados y BancoSol: Mirando las cifras desde una nueva perspectiva. Cuaderno de SEFIR No. 14, La Paz, Bolivia. Available at: http://www.unodc.org/documents/crop-monitoring/Bolivia_Coca_Survey_for2008_ES.pdf

Villafani–Ibarnegaray, M (2008). Pooling versus separating regulation: The performance of banks and microfinance in Bolivia under systemic shocks. PhD dissertation, The Ohio State University, Columbus, Ohio.

Villafani–Ibarnegaray, M and C Gonzalez–Vega (2007). Tasas de interés y desempeño diferenciado de cartera de las entidades de microfinanzas ante múltiples shocks sistémicos. Se cumple el teorema de Stiglitz-Weiss en las microfinanzas bolivianas? *Latin American Journal of Economic Development*, 8, 11–52.

Von Pischke, JD and DW Adams (1983). Fungibility and the design and evaluation of agricultural credit projects. *American Journal of Agricultural Economics*, 62, 719–726.

Wiedmaier-Pfister, M, F Pastor and L Salinas (2001). From financial NGO to private financial fund: The formalization process in the Bolivian financial sector and its impact. La Paz, Bolivia: Rural Finance System Project (FONDESIF GTZ), Technical Bulletin 1.

Zabalaga, M (2009). Regulación y políticas públicas en microfinanzas. La experiencia de Bolivia. Presentation, Foro Latinoamericano de Marcos Regulatorios y Políticas Públicas para las Microfinanzas. Managua: REDCAMIF.

Microfinance — A Strategic Management Framework

Guy Stuart*
John F Kennedy School of Government, Harvard University

The Mulkanoor Women's Thrift Cooperative (WTC) in the Karimnagar District of Andhra Pradesh in India started life in 1990, at the prompting of the Cooperative Development Foundation (CDF), which introduced its early members to the idea of a cooperative. CDF helped the cooperative work out how to mobilize savings, which it then on-lent to its members. The Mulkanoor WTC was one of the first in over 400 women's and men's cooperatives founded by the CDF, which, almost 20 years later, have a combined membership of over 150,000. As it grew these cooperatives village by village, the CDF trained the cooperatives' leaders and accountants and worked with them to refine their product offerings. At the same time, the CDF actively fought for the reform of the Andhra Pradesh cooperative law to minimize political interference in their functioning, gaining passage of the Mutually Aided Cooperative Societies Act in 1995 and defending it against efforts to undermine it ever since.

BancoCompartamos started life as a division of a non-profit organization making small loans to the people of the southern states of Mexico. In less than 20 years, it grew to an organization serving over 800,000 people through thousands of village banks without itself developing an extensive brick and mortar network. Instead it developed partnerships with mainstream banks through which it distributed its loans and collected its repayments, maintaining contact with the village banks through its *promotores* (promoters). Along the way it converted itself from a division of a non-profit

*Lecturer in Public Policy, Harvard's Kennedy School

to a "limited objective" finance company (SOFOL is the Spanish acronym) to a fully licensed bank, raised money from bi-lateral organizations, foundations and the bond market to finance its lending, and then sold shares to the public. The sale of these shares resulted in huge returns for the initial investors in the organization, and a flurry of debate within the microfinance field about the actions of the managers and owners of the bank.

What do these very different stories have in common? They demonstrate the multifaceted skills managers or promoters of microfinance organizations (MFOs) must have: a devotion to mission, the ability to get things done, and political skills. Like the managers of all other organizations, MFOs must build efficient and effective operational systems, place their organizations in a strong strategic position within a complex and dynamic environment, while ensuring that they continue to fulfill their stated mission, in this case providing financial services to the poor. When employing all their skills in ways that align their organization's mission, operations, and environment, managers of MFOs are engaging in strategic management.

Moore (2000) builds a framework for understanding the concerns of managers of non-profit and public sector organizations that encompasses their concerns with mission, operations, and environment. He argues that the mission of organizations is to create "public value" — value that benefits customers directly, and benefits other stakeholders indirectly. He further argues that effective managers deploy resources efficiently and effectively to ensure the delivery of public value, while managing their "authorizing" environment to ensure that they receive the legitimacy and support necessary to do their work.

Though many MFOs are for-profit entities, this framework makes sense for analyzing the strategic management choices facing managers of all MFOs, regardless of ownership, because of the type of work they do. I explain this in more detail in the next two sections, in which I describe how MFOs create value and how they manage their authorizing environment to allow them to do their work. I then revisit Moore's framework to discuss how MFOs have sought to align their value proposition with their operations and authorizing environment, and use this idea of alignment to analyze an important debate within microfinance: the debate about sustainability and reaching the very poor. In analyzing the debate, I hope to show the utility of the strategic management framework for analyzing the challenges facing MFOs. I argue that taking the "manager's eye-view" provides valuable insights that connect broad policy questions with the strategic challenges of MFOs. I end with recommendations for further research.

1 Creating Value

MFOs create value by providing financial services to the poor. They do so in a market already populated by a wide variety of indigenous, informal organizations, such as money-lenders, deposit collectors, various forms of savings and insurance clubs, and a wide variety of rotating savings and credit associations (ROSCAs) (Rutherford, 2000: 31). What distinguishes MFOs from these indigenous providers is that they deliver financial services to the poor through formal organizational mechanisms. MFOs have numerous formal policies and procedures regarding client interactions, product parameters, human resources, cash handling and accounting, to name a few. These formal mechanisms result in equal access to financial services for the poor, regardless of their position within local social networks. They also give the poor a sense of fair treatment. And the formality enables the MFO to offer a variety of products, because the information and governance systems that enable an organization to manage the complexity of providing more than one product are best built on formal service provision mechanisms. These formal mechanisms succeed, in part, because they take advantage of the existing social relations within which MFOs' clients are embedded, and, as such, avoids one of the pitfalls of formalization — the inability to meet the particular needs of a diverse client base. It is this combination that enhances the ability of the poor to gain access to the financial services on offer.

2 Authorizing Environment

MFIs do not engage in their value-creating activities in a vacuum. Beyond the indigenous providers, with whom MFOs compete, there are a number of stakeholders in the operations of MFOs that seek to have a say in how MFOs go about their business. They vary along two key dimensions. First, they vary by their location. A stakeholder can be an actor within the local environment in which the MFO operates, or it can be an external actor, either national or international. Second, they vary by the type of control they exercise. The stakeholder can be in a position to influence the MFO either by dictating what it can and cannot do or by controlling the flow of resources to it.

External stakeholders who can exercise control over what the MFO can and cannot do include regulators and lawmakers who set the rules within which MFOs must operate. Stakeholders who exercise control over what an MFO can and cannot do from within the local environment include the MFO's clients themselves and local community leaders. Stakeholders who are external actors who control resources flowing to MFOs include grant donors, socially responsible lenders and investors and profit-maximizing lenders and investors. They can be both national and international, and they can be government, civil society, or private sector organizations. Finally, stakeholders who control resources flowing to MFOs from within the local environment are clients who, through their savings activities, determine how much capital an MFO has to on-lend, and, through their loan repayments, determine the earned revenue stream of the MFO and its capital recapture. There can also be local donors who either contribute money or their time and effort to the MFO.

In addition, the particular stakeholder configuration an MFO manager faces is contingent on the nature of their own organization, and the local and national context in which they are operating. With respect to the nature of the organization, two key variables are important. First, the ownership structure of the organization: whether it is a for-profit, non-profit, or cooperative organization, and whether or not it is a subsidiary of another organization. Second, the products the MFO offers: whether it is a credit-only or a savings and credit financial institution. This latter variable interacts strongly with the national context in which MFOs operate because governments are far more likely to want to regulate savings mobilization than they are the extension of credit. As a result, because countries vary considerably in how and the extent to which they regulate microfinance savings mobilization, as an activity that is separate from mainstream banks' savings mobilization, the ability of an MFO to mobilize savings is highly contingent on its national context — credit-led MFOs operate throughout the developing world, but savings and credit MFOs do not, for want of an appropriate regulatory environment in many countries.

Given the number of different variables with which they must contend, managers of MFOs face very different authorizing environments. By way of examples, Boxes 10.1A and 10.1B provide partial accounts[1] of the very different authorizing environments facing Compartamos in Mexico and the WTCs in Andhra Pradesh. And Tables 10.1A and 10.1B summarize the stakeholder configurations of each organization along the dimensions of location and control.

[1]These accounts are partial, limited by the sources to which this author had access at the time of writing. The Compartamos account relies heavily on the audited financial statements available on MixMarket.org, and on Rosenberg (2007) and Schaffer and Stuart (2004). The Women's Thrift Cooperatives account depends on a more comprehensive set of data including interviews with staff at CDF, interviews with women leaders and ordinary members of the cooperatives, annual reports, and a detailed analysis of accounts databases. These are all reported in more detail in Stuart (2003 and 2007).

Box 10.1A: Compartamos in Mexico

Compartamos has evolved from a non-profit division within a larger social service organization to a for-profit bank. Throughout its life it has largely offered one product through one delivery channel — microcredit through village banking. The village banking model depends on social ties within the communities in which it operates to manage the disbursement and collection of loans. As such, a key stakeholder in Compartamos is the community of clients it serves (not just the clients as individuals), and the organization explicitly acknowledges this in the title it gives its field workers — they are not credit or loan officers but "promoters".

While their local authorizing environment has had some consistency due to the consistency in the product and delivery channel, other parts of the authorizing environment have changed as Compartamos has evolved. In the mid-1990s, Asociacion Programa Compartamos, I.A.P. (Institución de Asistencia Privada; The Mexican designation for non-profit organizations) had three direct service programs, one of which was the microcredit program. The income and expenses of the microcredit program were part of those of the organization in general, and the audited financial statements suggest that the microcredit program shared its management with the other programs. But a loan from CGAP in 1993 required that the organization report separately on its microcredit activities, showing a separate balance sheet, income and expenses statement, and cash flow statement. Furthermore, the auditors checked to see if Compartamos had met its contractual obligations to CGAP with respect to three targets: number of active clients (32,254 vs. target of 28,000), loan default rate (−0.206 percent vs target of 10 percent), and rate of return on assets (10.43 percent vs. target of −10 percent). In contrast, a Mx$175,000 loan from the federal government as part of an agreement to do work in the south of Mexico and the Yucutan Peninsula did not require any special audit statements.

In 2000, Compartamos became a separate, regulated, for-profit finance company, with a "limited objective" of providing microenterprise credit. As such, it now had its own separate audit, and an increasingly complicated set of financial and regulatory stakeholders. The 2001/2 audit reveals that it had issued stock exchange certificates, a type of bond, and that it had multiple bank and aid agency loans, as well as retirement reserve requirements set by Mexico's labor laws, minimum capital requirements set by the Treasury (SHCP), accounting requirements set by the Comision Nacional de Bancarias y Valores (CNBV), and tax obligations. The conversion to a bank in May 2006 brought Compartamos under the additional supervision of the Bank of Mexico. And the 2005/6 audit reveals that the organization was required to present its financial statements with a new level of detail. Finally, when Compartamos went public in 2007, it opened itself up to a new set of stakeholders — shareholders who could publicly trade the bank's shares on a daily basis.

Sources: Compartamos (1996, 2002, 2006); Rosenberg (2008)

Box 10.1B: Women's Thrift Cooperatives in Andhra Pradesh

In 1981, a group of reform-minded advocates of economic cooperatives created the Cooperative Development Foundation, which focused on, among other things, creating women's financial cooperatives and reforming the state cooperative laws. After some false starts, which included trying to integrate women into existing financial cooperatives and trying to work through another organization in founding new cooperatives, the CDF founded its first women's thrift cooperative in 1990. In founding these cooperatives, the CDF had to work within the existing social structure of rural Andhra Pradesh. To gain the trust of the village women they hoped would become members and owners of the cooperatives, they sought legitimacy from local community leaders. As a result, the cooperatives' leadership was more likely to be from the higher caste groups in the village.

Once in place, the leaders of the cooperatives operated in a multilevel authorizing environment. The leaders were subject to elections every three years, with the president being elected from a 12-person board. Each cooperative was part of an association of cooperatives requiring monthly meetings, and the associations were part of a confederation coordinated by the CDF. The associations created a system of mutual accountability among the cooperative leaders, and enabled deposit-rich cooperatives to lend to those with excess loan demand. And the confederation served as a forum in which leaders could come to a consensus on the rules that each individual cooperative adopted and implemented.

The CDF's relationship with the cooperatives extended beyond its role in coordinating the work of the confederation. It trained the leaders in cooperative management, trained the cooperatives' paid accountants, and set up an audit system for the cooperatives. Furthermore, it managed the regulatory environment in which the cooperatives were operating. Like many other microfinance organizations, the WTCs started life outside of any regulatory structure. The CDF had not been successful in changing the state's cooperative laws and the cooperatives founded in 1990 were not registered under the existing law. But in the early 1990s, the CDF changed tactics and sought the passage of a "parallel law", that was more liberal and ensured less government intrusion into the workings of the cooperatives than did the existing law. In 1995, the CDF was successful, with the passage of the Mutually Aided Cooperative Societies (MACS) Act. The cooperatives the CDF promoted quickly registered under the MACS Act, and since then their number has grown rapidly. As of 2009, there were over 400 thrift cooperatives that had been assisted by the CDF.

Sources: Stuart and Kanneganti (2003) and Stuart (2007)

Control/ Location	Over activities	Over resources
Local	• Clients (due to village banking model). • Parent organization (to 2000).	• Clients (loan repayments). • Parent organization (to 2000).
External	• SHCP (after 2000). • CNBV (after 2000). • Tax authorities (after 2000). • Bank of Mexico (after 2006).	• IADB, CGAP, Accion, USAID and other donors and lenders. • Bond market (after 2005). • Stock exchange (after 2007).

Table 10.1A: Compartamos Stakeholders.

Control/ Location	Over activities	Over resources
Local	• Members. • CDF. • Local community leaders. • Village norms with regard to caste.	• Members (as savers and loan repayers). • Other cooperatives within association (through inter-cooperative loans).
External	• State registrar of cooperatives.	• CDF (in-kind training and support). • CDF's funders who allow CDF to provide the cooperatives support free of charge.

Table 10.1B: WTC Stakeholders.

3 Public Value: A Strategic Management Framework

The previous two sections describe the major concerns facing the manager of an MFO. They have to work out how they can create value by delivering financial services to the poor in competition with local indigenous providers, and in cooperation with the local community. In addition, they have to be sensitive to the expectations of stakeholders and manage those expectations so that they can retain the authority to provide financial services to the poor.

Moore describes these sets of activities as creating *public* value. What makes the value that MFOs create *public* is the fact that they do more than just create value for the poor, who pay for this value through interest payments on loans and other fees, and investors, who receive a return based on the difference between what the poor pay and what it costs to serve them. In the discussion of the authorizing environment, we saw that there are other stakeholders who receive value from the activities of the MFO. Those who provide subsidies to the MFOs get a social return. Regulators, politicians and community leaders get the assurance that the organization is operating in a legal and legitimate manner. In satisfying the concerns and expectations of these stakeholders, the MFO is creating *public* value in addition to the private value it creates for its customers and investors.[2]

Once we understand that MFOs are in the business of creating public value, a number of strategic elements fall into place. First, and foremost, the concept forces an MFO to consider whether what it creates is valuable to all its stakeholders. For instance, are the terms on the loans it originates ones that funders and local politicians are willing to accept as legitimate? If not, what should be done? Can the MFO create the same value for its customers through loans with different terms, or does it have to develop a strategy for gaining the support of funders or local politicians? Or, another example, can MFOs that require compulsory savings satisfy the regulatory requirements of the banking authorities? Do they need to become fully licensed banks? Can they rename the compulsory savings something else? If they do, how will their clients react? Or can they come to some sort of compromise with the regulators?

[2]Note here that public value is not simply a management theorist's translation of the economists' public good. What distinguishes public value from private value is that it is paid for by someone other than the direct recipient of the good or service. They receive value, but not the value inherent in the good or service being delivered, but, rather, the value in having it be delivered to someone else and in a particular way.

These questions point to the fact that MFOs have to align the value they create for customers and stakeholders. They also have to align operations and the authorizing environment, and operations and the value proposition. For example, as discussed above, MFOs create value by introducing formal systems into the local financial services market. Such systems create value for customers, but also value for other stakeholders like grant funders, investors, and regulators who value an organization's ability to produce intelligible accounts and reports. In this case, operations are aligned with the value proposition of the organization and the requirements of the authorizing environment. That MFOs have fallen short on their accounting and reporting over the years is testament to the fact that the formality required to create value for customers falls short of, or is different from, the formality other stakeholders require. And what we have seen over the years have been efforts by MFOs to improve their accounting and reporting systems in response to stakeholder demands.

An easy way to picture this framework is as a "strategic triangle", with the vertices holding the three elements that a manager must pay attention to, and the lines connecting the vertices representing the fact that the elements are supposed to be related to each other in a well-run organization (Figure 10.1). To make the triangle less abstract, I have listed some core activities, conditions and structures that connect each element to its neighbor. As a first cut at strategic management, those activities, conditions and structures should make sense. But there is more. The challenge for the manager is to make sure that all three elements are aligned with each other, requiring that the activities, conditions and structures on each line are consistent with each other.

I suggest in Figure 10.2 that there is such consistency by, for example, noting that "formal systems" are a feature of MFOs that are both operationally important in creating value — formal systems help the MFO get its work done, and something that the authorizing environment expects from an MFO. One could also argue that the regulators' (authorizing environment) demand for safety and soundness in a savings-led organization is consistent with an MFO's need to gain the reputation of trustworthiness if it is to deliver value to its savings customers. A potential inconsistency in the triangle, as I have drawn it, is between the local knowledge capture activities of an MFO and regulators' concerns with safety and soundness.

In sum, the public value strategic framework makes explicit the challenge an MFO manager faces. They have to align their public value proposition, authorizing environment, and operational capacity. The reality of

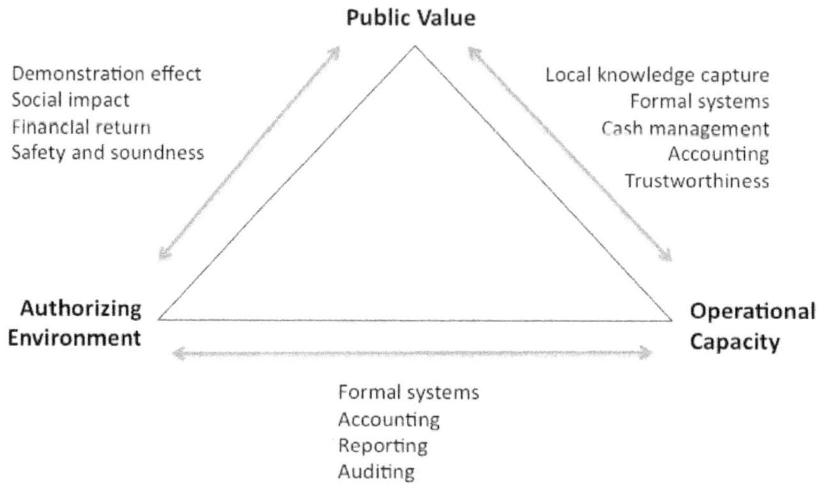

Figure 10.1: A strategic triangle of a management framework.

day-to-day management of an organization suggests that this alignment will never be perfect, and that a manager will spend their time on one vertex of the triangle more than the others at any particular point in the evolution of the organization. Nevertheless, the public value framework gives managers a simple and useful way to think about their strategic concerns.

4 A Manager's Eye-View of a Policy Question: Sustainability and the Creation of Public Value for all the Poor

Beyond its utility to managers, the public value strategic management framework is a useful means of analyzing broad policy questions and debates in the microfinance field, from the point of view of an MFO manager — the manager's eye-view. Inherent in the idea of public value is the idea that the creation of value includes considerations that go beyond the concerns of the people directly receiving the service. The need to consider other stakeholders implies a need to consider other definitions of what is valuable, and how best to create that value. These are what policy questions and debates are about. To give a sense of how a manager's eye-view might inform a policy debate, let us look at the debate about whether MFOs should receive subsidies to help them provide financial services to the very poor.

There has been considerable public and philanthropic investment in MFOs over the past 30 years, because almost all MFOs had to start from scratch, and there was almost no interest from commercial investors or banks in financing the activities of MFOs. But today, many MFOs have shown they are capable of covering their operational and financial costs with the revenues they earn from their customers.[3] This ability to cover costs with customer-generated revenues has made popular the idea that MFOs can be completely self-sustaining and should eschew subsidies of any sort. Advocates of a strong emphasis on sustainability argue that the focus on sustainability itself improves the management of MFOs because it forces the MFO to operate in a cost-effective, customer-focused manner. Furthermore, they argue that it is only through the self-sustainability of MFOs that we can be assured that the poor will continue to receive microfinance services in the long run. And finally, they argue that it is only through self-sustainability that MFOs can attract the large amounts of for-profit capital necessary for the full scale-up of an industry that has only just begun to reach its full market potential, and that when the industry does fulfill its potential it will be serving far more of the poor than it otherwise would.

In contrast, there are those who argue that subsidies are still necessary. In particular, those who focus on outreach to the very poor worry that a strong focus on financial sustainability causes MFOs to drift away from the very poor towards the more affluent poor from whom they are able to earn more profits. The debate suggests an inherent trade-off between serving all segments of the poor population, while subsidies last, on the one hand, and serving the more affluent poor on a sustainable, permanent basis, on the other.

The idea of such a trade-off makes sense. The very poor have smaller-sized transactions with higher administrative costs relative to the income they generate. Furthermore, the very poor are more likely to have irregular income streams. As a result, they are not able to make regular payments of a fixed amount, which MFOs favor because they are administratively less costly to service and help them with risk mitigation (Rutherford, 2004). Finally, the very poor are likely to live in more remote, rural areas, which are harder for an MFO to reach and raise the transactions costs associated with serving them. In sum, serving the very poor generates less revenue per transaction, and may involve higher relative and absolute costs.

The public value framework recasts the debate over sustainability and outreach to the very poor by rejecting the narrow definition of sustainability.

[3]For the sake of convenience, I will refer to the people who receive services from an MFO directly and pay for them through interest and fee payments as customers.

The framework takes a broader view of sustainability: a public manager intent on creating public value can run a sustainable organization so long as s/he can secure revenues from a variety of sources, including non-customers. To do so the manager must have the capacity to produce something of value for their authorizing environment — she or he must pay attention to the three vertices of the strategic triangle. In the context of microfinance, a manager of an MFO can run a sustainable MFO by generating revenues from its customers and receiving support from donors who value the MFO's work. As a result, serving the very poor can be a sustainable enterprise even if the MFO loses money on each transaction with the very poor, because serving the very poor is something that donors value and for which they are willing to pay.

The purpose of recasting the debate in this way is not to rehabilitate subsidies for their own sake, but to use the broader definition of sustainability to raise questions about the inherent bias that the narrower definition brings to the debate about sustainability and outreach to the very poor, and explore fully the justifications for donor money in the sustenance of MFOs, especially for the purpose of reaching the very poor.

As stated above, the argument for the narrow approach to sustainability rests on the vision of an efficient, large-scale, permanent industry funded by the international capital markets that serves more of the less poor than it might otherwise, but still serves more of the very poor. Using a simple formal model, Ghosh and van Tassel (2008) show that the entry of profit-oriented funders (they use the word "donors" but that implies a grant element given the meaning of the related word "donation"), sets off a dynamic process whereby MFOs with heterogeneous capabilities react to each other's strategies in trying to secure increased funding from for-profit investors. The reactive equilibrium they identify is a situation in which the MFOs serve more of the very poor, but do so while serving a larger number of the less poor, thus diluting the overall impact of their much larger-scale activities. Furthermore, the most efficient and effective MFO (the most "capable" in their words) gets the for-profit funding, while the less capable continues to rely solely on donor funding targeted at serving very poor customers.

The model from which this formal result is derived is purposefully simple, but it is a good starting point for an elaboration of a strategic management perspective, which puts the model into the context of the reality of managing an MFO. First, Ghosh and van Tassel treat MFOs as unitary actors making adjustments to the actions of other MFOs' decisions on an ongoing basis.

But MFOs are organizations that have to be actively managed. If an MFO changes its portfolio mix to attract investor funding, it has to change the incentives it provides its credit officers and manage the change process, which will likely be plagued by confusion among the employees about the direction of the organization. In addition, management will have to develop a nuanced set of incentives that either enable individual credit officers to manage a mixed portfolio, or they will have to segregate the credit officers into those that serve the very poor and those that serve the less poor. There is no reason that this cannot be done, but it illustrates the fact that the vision of the advocates of the narrow definition of sustainability (and the formal model's results) are contingent on an adept manager aligning their organization's operational capacity with the demands of the authorizing environment to maintain and grow the delivery of services to a heterogeneous market of poor households.

Second, the model mirrors an assumption that the advocates of a narrow definition of sustainability hold, namely that MFOs have the willingness and capacity to take on external funding beyond that available from donors and funders who are not solely profit-oriented, and that it is only through for-profit funders that MFOs will achieve their large-scale potential. The empirical evidence for this is weak because the pool of available funding has grown not only due to the emergence of for-profit funders but also due to the emergence of social investors, with an interest in a double bottom line, and a new focus on savings mobilization, which offers the opportunity for MFOs to raise some of their own loan capital from their customers. And the assumption is especially weak in the current economic crisis when private capital flows of all sorts have dried up.

This last point raises an additional question about external funding: which funder is more reliable? There are fears that donors interested in MFOs serving the very poor will lose interest and move on to something else that promises to improve the lives of the poor more effectively than the provision of financial services. But there is also the possibility that private capital will dry up due to events in the capital markets or in response to problems that MFOs encounter in generating revenue from their customers.

In sum, MFOs interested in serving the very poor have more choices than advocates of the narrow definition of sustainability assume. Furthermore, the smart choice may be to take funds from sources that have an interest in microfinance beyond the profit it generates because they will be less swayed in their funding decisions by the vicissitudes of the international capital markets, and more interested in the long-term work of improving the lives of the very poor, though more empirical work needs to be done to work out which is the smart choice.

Finally, Ghosh and van Tessel's model provides an interesting insight into the question of whether access to private capital prompts greater efficiency and effectiveness among MFOs. In their model, it is the more capable MFO that attracts for-profit funding, rather than the for-profit funding resulting in improvements in the operations of the MFO. The empirical evidence on the association between private capital investments in MFOs and efficiency is weak. Hudon's (2006) analysis of 100 MFOs suggests that unsubsidized MFOs are no more efficient than their subsidized counterparts. More work needs to be done to examine what drives managers towards greater efficiency and effectiveness, but one simple hypothesis is that managers increase their external funding options, whether they be donor subsidies, social investors, or for-profit investments, by continuously improving their internal operations.

In sum, advocates of the narrow definition of sustainability envision a world in which microfinance reaches its full potential through the investor-funded scale-up of efficient, profitable operations that serve a heterogeneous market of poor people that includes the very poor, but is not solely focused on them. The Ghoshen and van Tassel model formally explains the role that for-profit funders might play in bringing about this world. But the realities of microfinance funding are more complex, and a more nuanced, manager's eye-view approach to the question of sustainability points the manager towards a strategy that aligns their internal operational capacity with its authorizing environment. Fortunately for the managers of MFOs, there are numerous funding sources from which to choose that vary in the extent to which they require a market-rate return, including the mobilization of savings. As a result, a manager can strategically choose when and how to use subsidies based on the answers to the following questions:

(i) Is there an activity that our MFO wishes to engage in that is consistent with our mission, but cannot be paid for with revenues raised from customers, and is the type of activity that some external funder is willing to pay for?
(ii) Does using such external funding make the organization more or less vulnerable to future financial difficulties?
(iii) Will this new activity disrupt our existing operations to the point that the viability of our current activities is undermined?

If the answers are "yes", "less vulnerable" or "no more vulnerable", and "no", then it is appropriate for the MFO to engage in a new, subsidized activity. If one of these answers is different, then the MFO needs to either abandon the idea or work out how to address the problem they will be creating for themselves. As a result, the policy debate about sustainability, narrowly defined, and subsidies should not be in terms of the stark choice between one or the other, but rather in terms of whether managers are making smart use of the various types of subsidized funding available to them, and whether funders are aiding those smart uses.

5 Conclusion and Suggestions for Further Research

Microfinance creates public value by providing financial services to the poor in a manner that gains legitimacy and support from its authorizing environment. This framework for understanding the challenges MFOs face provides practitioners with an explicit guide to what many of them have already been doing implicitly. This guide should help them to anticipate future problems and develop a strategy for their organization that makes it less vulnerable.

The framework also provides a useful way to present a "manager's eye-view" of policy debates in the microfinance field. In this paper, I have looked at one such debate from this view — the debate about subsidies and sustainability. There are other debates that are easily amenable to similar analysis: credit-first vs. savings-first microfinance initiatives; finance only vs. finance plus; and the merits of transforming MFOs into publicly-traded companies. In most cases, the framework will show that there is no right answer, that "it depends", due in part to the fact that a key variable in the framework, the authorizing environment, is highly context-specific.

The framework also has the potential to frame future research. There are few case studies of MFOs tracking their evolution from start-ups to large-scale organizations. Such case studies can give us insights into the general validity of the framework: Is it the case that MFOs really have to align their mission, operations, and authorizing environment or do they just have to have managers who can manage a misalignment? They can also reveal the dynamics of an MFO's growth, with some lessons about what parts of the strategic triangle need the most attention when. With the increasing availability of organizational field data such as those on MixMarket, or those of rating agencies, there are also new opportunities to conduct cross-organizational studies that test whether strategy matters to the success of an MFO. Operationalizing strategy as an independent variable will be a challenge, but not one that is insurmountable. Such an analysis could be extremely useful for rating agencies trying to assess the long-term viability of an MFO.

Finally, there needs to be more specific analyses of organizational questions. For example, we know little about the conditions under which a finance plus strategy succeeds. The analysis in Hudon (2006) on the impact of subsidies on efficiency is preliminary, and more work needs to be done on this question. And there are interesting questions to be answered about the long-term viability of the savings groups being promoted by OxfamUSA and CARE, which are exploding in number with little regard for the potential reaction of the authorizing environment.

References

Compartamos (1996). Audited Financial Statements, 1995/6. Available at http://www.mixmarket.org/mfi/compartamosbanco/files

Compartamos (2002). Audited Financial Statements, 2001/2. Available at http://www.mixmarket.org/mfi/compartamosbanco/files

Compartamos (2006). Audited Financial Statements, 2005/6. Available at http://www.mixmarket.org/mfi/compartamosbanco/files

Ghosh, S and E Van Tassel (2008). A Model of Mission Drift in Microfinance Institutions. Working Paper.

Hudon, M (2006). Financial Performance, Management and Ratings of the Microfinance Institutions: Do Subsidies Matter? Working Paper, Solvay Business School, University of Brussels.

Moore, MH (1995). *Creating Public Value: Strategic Management in Government.* Cambridge, MA: Harvard University Press.

Moore, MH (2000). Managing for Value: Organizational Strategy in For-Profit, Nonprofit, and Governmental Organizations. *Nonprofit and Voluntary Sector Quarterly*, 9(1), 183–204.

Rosenberg, R (2007). CGAP Reflections on the Compartamos Initial Public Offering: A Case Study On Microfinance Interest Rates and Profits. CGAP Focus Note 42.

Rutherford, S (2000). *The Poor and their Money.* New Delhi, India. Oxford India Paperbacks.

Rutherford, S (2004). GRAMEEN II at the End of 2003: A 'Grounded View' of how Grameen's New Initiative is Progressing in the Villages. Dhaka, Bangladesh: MicroSave.

Schlefer, R and G Stuart (2004). Corporate Values and Tansformation: The Microlender Compartamos. Kennedy School of Government, Case No. 1706.1.

Stuart, G and S Kanneganti (2003). Embedded Cooperation: Women's Thrift Cooperatives in Andhra Pradesh. Kennedy School of Government Working Paper Series, RWP03–026.

Stuart, G (2007). Organizations, institutions, and embeddedness: Caste and gender in savings and credit cooperatives in Andhra Pradesh, India. *International Public Management Journal*, 10(4), 415–438.

What External Control Mechanisms Help Microfinance Institutions Meet the Needs of Marginal Clientele?

Valentina Hartarska*
Auburn University and CERMi

Denis Nadolnyak*
Auburn University

1 Introduction

Well run microfinance institutions (MFIs) make better use of scarce funds by providing better financial services and reaching more poor clients. Microfinance practitioners have argued that governance and control mechanisms are critical for the success of an MFI (Campion, 1998; Rock, Otero and Saltzman, 1998). This paper studies how external governance, defined as the control exercised by stakeholders and markets, and accountability mechanisms that operate to enforce internal governance, affect MFIs' outreach directly and indirectly via their impact on MFIs' sustainability.

Microfinance is a growing industry and MFIs control significant private and development aid resources. Until a few years ago, annual funding for microfinance activities worldwide was US $1–1.5 billion with about 90 percent coming from developed countries' taxpayers (CGAP, 2004). A 2008 survey by the Consultative Group to Assist the Poor (CGAP) reports that the assets under management by various Microfinance Investment Vehicles, which intermediate between foreign investors and MFIs, has grown significantly to $5.4 billion at the end 2007, or some 78% increase from 2006.

*Author Contact Information: Valentina Hartarska, Associate Professor, Department of Agricultural Economics and Rural Sociology, 210 Comer Hall, Auburn, Al 36830. Tel.: (334) 844-5666, Fax: (334) 844 5639; E-mail: hartarska@auburn.edu

Most of the growth has come from private institutional investors such as TIAA–CRAFT and ABP. Higher stakes for private investors suggest that it will become increasingly important to understand what external control mechanisms work and how they may affect MFI performance in terms of outreach and sustainability.

MFI-specific characteristics such as stakes held by a regulator or a donor may affect the ability of market forces to discipline MFIs. This paper summarizes several recent cross-country studies exploring the joint and separate impact of regulation, information disclosure, microfinance rating, credit bureaus, and competition on MFI's ability to reach poor borrowers as well as on MFI sustainability as only sustainable MFIs have the chance to maintain a long-term presence in the market and reach poor borrowers.

The rest of the paper is organized as follows. Part two presents a general framework for analysis. Part three presents evidence on the impact of regulation; part four summarizes the evidence on the impact of rating; part five discusses evidence on credit bureaus, competition and information disclosure. Part six offers conclusions and suggestions for future research.

2 Framework for a Cross-Country Analysis

Microfinance Institutions are remarkably diverse. They operate as Non-Governmental Organizations (NGOs), banks or rural banks, cooperatives, or non-bank financial institutions. Most MFIs focus on lending but others offer payment facilities and about a third also mobilize deposits (authors' calculations based on the MIX market database). MFIs face various degrees of market-based discipline because some MFIs are regulated and may be subject to different degrees of ongoing supervision by an independent banking authority and because some are organized as not-for-profit or membership-based cooperatives. The asset base of most MFIs was built with grant money and most MFIs do not have widely held equity and are not publicly-traded companies. These characteristics, combined with various degrees of regulation, underline the need to understand how regulation and market forces affect MFIs' ability to reach marginal clientele.

Like other organizations, MFIs can function and expand if they have sufficient liquidity to meet current obligations and can raise funds from outside sources. Therefore, donors' and creditors' willingness to continue support is important. At present, these MFI stakeholders base their decisions on information on the performance of MFIs from audited financial statements, from information provided by regulators, credit and global risk ratings by independent raters, and by comparing an MFI's performance with that of the competition. A regulator or a major donor can affect the degree of efficiency of market forces, and may interfere with the mission of an MFI. Empirical work, therefore, must control for these factors to identify the correct impact of a single control mechanism.

Most empirical studies follow cross-country banking studies where performance is specified as a function of bank-specific (or MFI-specific) variables and country specific macroeconomic and institutional factors (Barth *et al.*, 2004; Hartarska, 2005; Hartarska and Nadolnyak, 2007 and 2008; Hartarska, 2009). Empirical banking and MFI papers focusing on external governance augmented this basic model by introducing another vector of explanatory variables to capture the impact of external governance framework (Barth *et al.*, 2005; and Barth *et al.*, 2007). Specifically, the model is:

$$P_{it} = \text{constant} + \alpha' EG_{it} + \beta' \mathrm{MS}_t + \varphi' \mathrm{M}_t + \varepsilon_{it} \tag{1}$$

where P_{it} denotes a performance indicator for an MFI i at time t and $EGit$ is a vector of variables that capture the impact of the external governance framework. The model also includes measure(s) of whether the MFI was regulated or the stringency of regulation, one or several variables that measure the use of rating agencies and credit bureaus, competition and, in earlier studies, audit. MSt is a vector of MFI-specific variables such as age, size, quality of the portfolio, type of organization, etc. Mt are macroeconomic country-specific variables such as inflation, GDP and GDP per capita, and ε_{it} is an error term.

Careful selection of variables to measure performance and to control for differences in MFI-specific and region- and country-specific conditions is crucial for successful empirical studies. Measurements of MFI financial performance in the work reviewed here include operational and financial self-sustainability, ROA, and ROE. Measurements of the breadth of outreach include mostly the number of active borrowers or clients (borrowers and savers). Measures of depth of outreach are used less often because appropriate measures are rarely available and recent theoretical work demonstrates that easily available measures such as the average loan size used to measure clients' poverty level as well as possible mission drift are problematic (Armedariz and Szafarz, 2009). Some newer work incorporates both the outreach and the sustainability missions in a classical cost minimization context where while cost minimization is pursued, the objective to serve many clients is captured by measuring output in the cost function by the number of clients rather than volume of loans and deposits (Caudill *et al.*, 2009; Hartarska and Mersland, forthcoming).

3 Regulation and Its Impact on MFI Performance

Regulation of MFIs is expected to allow them to offer a wider range of financial services and access to more funds through deposits, equity and commercial borrowings (Arun, 2005; Gallardo, 2001; Lauer, 2008).[1] One expected consequence, so far not supported by empirical results, is that regulation can lower the costs of funds (Rosemberg *et al.*, 2009; Hartarska, Parmeter and Mersland, 2009). The consensus on MFI regulation is that deposit-taking MFIs should be subject to prudential regulation, MFIs not mobilizing deposits should not, and MFIs that fall in between should have some form of targeted regulation with licensing and monitoring linked to the sources of funds and the clients served (Hardy *et al.*, 2003). Currently, MFIs are subject to either mandatory entry regulation, prudential supervision, or some sort of entry regulation and consequent monitoring (tiered regulation). Data collected by the Mixmarket in 2006 show that there were countries where regulated MFIs collect deposits, countries where unregulated MFIs can offer savings products and countries where MFIs are regulated but do not necessarily collect deposits (mixmarket.org data summarized in Table 1, Hartarska and Nadolnyak, 2007).

[1]Regulation in financial intermediaries is justified by market failure arising from market power, negative externalities and asymmetric information (Freixas and Rochet, 1997). MFIs operate as local monopolies but, in the past, policies such as interest rate ceilings and targeted credit used to affect loan disbursement by monopolistic agricultural development banks have proven ineffective and rural banks ended up lending not to poor but to wealthy farmers (Gonzalez–Vega, 1977). Thus, regulatory framework supportive of competition may be a better strategy than regulating local monopolies. While MFIs provide payment facilities, they work in niche markets and do not have the market penetration necessary to cause systemic risk (negative externality) in the financial system, at least not in every country (Wright, 2000). Thus, regulating for the sake of preventing systemic risk does not have much support.

Information asymmetry inherent in the transaction between a financial intermediary and its depositors justifies prudential regulation and supervision because the regulator can protect the interest of small and dispersed depositors (Dewatripont and Tirole, 1994). Inadequate regulation of deposit-taking microfinance institutions has been costly. For example, in Bangladesh, many poor people lost their savings due to fraud by little known, unregulated institutions (Wright, 2000).

Typical banking regulations do not cover microfinance activities and changes in laws and regulations to accommodate microfinance activities have resulted from active promotion by large microfinance networks or after the MFI sector becomes visible to the regulator. Less attention by a regulator has had both negative and positive aspects. Regulatory ambiguity leaves MFI vulnerable to regulatory discretion in the interpretation of the legal basis for lending activity, as in Russia prior to 1999 (Safavian *et al.*, 2001).

Relative noninvolvement, however, made the establishment and operating of MFI easier in some Latin American countries (Christen and Rosenberg, 2000). Early non-regulated incumbents' desire for regulation and commercialization may be motivated by expected rents from preventing entry by new competitors and thus may limit the outreach potential of the industry (Stigler, 1971).[2]

A negative consequence from regulatory involvement could be that a regulated MFI can have a mission drift, that is, it may be more likely to change its clientele to include less poor borrowers to satisfy various stakeholders' preferences. Empirical work explores the impact of regulation on outreach directly and indirectly via its impact on sustainability. Studies make different assumptions about regulation depending on the data available, but reach similar results. In a study that focuses on the impact of both internal and external governance mechanisms on the performance of MFIs in Eastern Europe and Central Asia, Hartarska (2005) uses survey data for major MFIs and finds that MFIs supervised by an independent banking authority in the year of the survey do not differ in terms of breadth of outreach (measured by the number of borrowers), but also finds some weak evidence that supervised MFIs have lower ROA and serve richer borrowers.

Hartarska and Nadolnyak (2007) use the Mixmarket panel data and an empirical model that corrects for endogenous regulatory status. This is necessary because MFI performance and its status as a regulated or unregulated organization are likely to be affected by unobserved individual characteristics such as quality of its management. Fixed effect panel method is the preferable method to account for this unobservable individual MFI

[2]Examples of MFIs starting as non-regulated and transforming into commercial, regulated MFIs include PRODEM, established in Bolivia in 1986 as NGO and transformed into BancoSol in 1992; Mibanco, with microfinance operation dating back to 1982, transformed into a bank in 1998; and AMPES (Asociacioń de la Mediana y Pequenã Empresa) with microfinance operations (The ServicioCrediticio of AMPES) dating back to 1988, which transformed into Financiera Calpia, chartered as a bank.

heterogeneity, which is important in an organizationally diverse industry. However, fixed effects panel estimation cannot be used when the policy variable of interest is a dummy variable for regulatory status which does not change over time. To correct for this problem, the authors use a Hausmann–Taylor IV method which accommodates an endogenous regulation dummy within the fixed effects model. The number of funding sources the MFI uses and the number of competitors are used as instruments for regulation and non-profit status, which were shown to be endogenous. The results show that regulation does not affect outreach measured by the number of borrowers nor does it affect sustainability measured by operational self-sustainability. The results show, however, weak evidence that regulated MFIs serve richer borrowers and, in this sense, are consistent with the findings in Hartarska (2005), Demirgüç–Kunt *et al.* (2008), as well as Cull *et al.* (2009) who find evidence of negative impact of stringency of regulatory enforcement on depth of outreach, measured by average loan size.

More recently, Mersland and Strom (2009) find no impact of regulation measured by an index of financial sector maturity on MFI performance within an endogenous equations context. Caudill *et al.* (2009) find that, in the ECA region, efficiency improves over time for regulated MFI banks with efficiency measured by the estimated technical efficiency from a mixture model with a translog cost function. Hartarska and Mersland (forthcoming) use a similar methodology to analyze a sample of rated MFIs and find that MFIs regulated by an independent bank authority are more efficient at reaching more clients when including both savers and borrowers, but not more efficient at reaching borrowers only. However, MFIs operating in countries with more mature regulatory systems are less efficient in reaching more clients so the impact on efficiency seems to be driven by the number of depositors. This suggests that, in countries with a mature regulatory environment, MFIs find it more difficult to attract savers, perhaps because other banks already collect deposits.

4 The Impact of Rating

From a theoretical perspective, rating has value if it produces information which market participants do not already have. The new information plays a disciplining role by affecting security prices and the funding decisions of donors, creditors, and investors. The effectiveness of rating, furthermore, depends on market participants' perception of the extent to which a particular donor and, in MFIs collecting deposits, a regulator may dilute market signals because of implicit guarantees to rescue an MFI in trouble. The empirical literature suggest that the main contribution of rating banks may be to help regulators identify problem banks and take the necessary measures to strengthen them (Morgan, 2002; Morgan and Stiroh, 2000).

The asset base of most MFIs is built from grants, and equity is not widely held. Moreover, few MFIs can issue bonds, less than a third collect deposits, and may or may not be regulated. Nevertheless, just like other organizations, MFIs need adequate access to funds to meet current obligations or to expand. Credit and global risk rating by independent raters could play a disciplining role by affecting donors' and increasingly investors' decisions to fund a particular MFI.

Rating for MFIs was supported by the Microfinance Rating and Assessment Fund co-founded in 2001 by the Inter-American Development Bank and the Consultative Group to Assist the Poor, and by the European Union after 2005. This Fund offered tiered subsidies for up to three ratings from preapproved microfinance rating agencies but started phasing out its subsidies at the end of 2007 as it became clear that the demand was weakening and the effectiveness of the mainstream rating agencies started to be questioned.

Typical credit rating is the evaluation of an organization's probability of default on its debt. Originally, microfinance rating agencies did not rate exclusively debt but developed methodologies to evaluate the overall performance of the organization in terms of both outreach and sustainability. Under pressure to offer easier to interpret reports, in late 2004, rating agencies pioneered a single overall letter grade.

The direct impact of rating on MFI outreach has not been explored. The evidence available is on the indirect impact of rating on MFIs' ability to raise funds and thus maintain their outreach. Hartarska and Nadolnyak (2008) analyze this issue for the period prior to the letter grading. They survey five major rating agencies by which MFIs were rated and match the rating data with pre-and post-rating individual financial and outreach data from the MIX Market database.

First, Hartarska and Nadolnyak investigate which MFIs sought rating and rating subsidy using logistic regressions. They find that the probability of being rated is not affected by performance indicators like outreach or financial performance but increased with size, and with age for up to nine years. MFIs with higher focus on lending (higher loan-total assets ratio) were also more likely to obtain rating and to get a rating subsidy. Less leveraged

MFIs sought subsidy for their rating and the Rating Funds encouraged the use of rating for such purposes. Relatively younger MFIs aged up to 14 years were more likely to have received a subsidy, but size did not affect the probability of subsidies for rating.

Next, Hartarska and Nadolnyak study what factors affect the amount of equity and non-deposit liability raised by specifying changes in equity (liability) as a function of a dummy for rating, and previous period MFI-specific and macro indicators to correct for possible endogeneity. Models with data for all MFIs and two subsamples for MFIs in Eastern Europe and Central Asia (ECA), and Latin America were included.[3] The results show that rated MFIs are no better at fundraising. MFIs with subsidized rating did not raise more or less funds according to most of the regression results, except in the case of equity in Latin America, suggesting that MFIs there were using subsidized rating to improve their equity positions consistent with the request of major donors to get rating prior to equity injections.

Hartarska and Nadolnyak (2008) also analyze whether rating by an individual rater affected fundraising and find some evidence that not all rating agencies have the same impact. Specifically, MFIs rated by Planet Rating were able to borrow more in the period following rating mostly in the ECA region but also worldwide, and MFIs rated by ACCION raised more equity in Latin America. The results are interpreted to mean that there is a trade-off between raising debt and equity, perhaps influenced by the choice of the rater or requested by a potential funding source. Contrary to the expectations, MFIs rated by the Microfinanza with subsidy covered by the Rating Fund had lower credit in the period following rating. Some managers from the region have noted that rating is useful as a substitute for external consultants to identify problems such as the need to improve capitalization.[4]

Finally, this paper provides evidence that rating may be producing new information because ratings dummies are statistically significant even after controlling for numerous lagged performance indicators. The results also show that MFIs in the ECA region with better outreach characteristics were more likely to raise additional equity but less likely to raise extra debt, perhaps reflecting policies of major donors/creditors to support MFIs serving more clients with grants rather than with loans. Donors' preferences are

[3]Observations from other regions of the world were too few to investigate separately.
[4]Authors' interviews with managers from the ECA region.

also reflected in the finding that MFIs in Latin America with higher proportion of deposits to total liability were more likely to have raised additional debt and MFIs in the ECA region with less emphasis on collecting deposits were less likely to increase their equity positions.

One more interesting result is that other external variables, such as deposit insurance, also affect fundraising in a different way across regions. For example, MFIs in countries with deposit insurance in the ECA region were more likely to have attracted additional debt, while MFIs in countries with deposit insurance in Latin America were less likely to attract additional debt but more likely to attract additional equity, again reflecting regional donors' preferences for MFI support which suggest a lesser role for rating.

The results from this paper are valid for the period prior to letter grading but other studies also do not find robust impact of rating. Wang (2007) uses a larger sample of 315 MFIs from 63 countries operating pre- and post-letter grading, namely between 1999 and 2006. Wang uses lagged explanatory variable model to control for endogeneity in the MFI-specific variables, as well as a two-stage least squares procedure. The results are consistent with those in Hartarska and Nadolnyak (2008) in that she also identifies differential impact by individual raters but no impact with 2SLS. Wang also finds that rating updates and subsidized rating do not affect fundraising.

With a larger dataset and higher quality data, Gonzalez and Hartarska (2007) investigate the relation between MFI access to different sources of capital, especially commercial funds (thus, indirectly, the cost of funds) and rating and rating grade. A major part of that study is the assembly of a database containing information from all ratings performed by major microfinance rating agencies and MFI performance information from publicly available data from the MIX Market and confidential MBB data from 1,046 MFIs for the period 2000–2006. Gonzalez and Hartarska use fixed effects models because tests showed they were preferable to random effects. The analysis includes regressing several dependent variables, such as change in liability (net of savings), change in equity, and the ratio of commercial funding to liability, on rating variables measuring rating, letter grade value, subsidized rating dummy, and MFI–specific characteristics such as size, age, legal status, capital structure, and repayment history, and also country-specific and regional variables. Since raters use different letter grading methodologies, MFIs were classified in four groups based on the relative letter grade they received compared to their peers in a rating scale standardized across raters, i.e., MFIs in higher tercile, middle tercile, lower tercile, and MFIs rated without a grade.

Overall, Gonzalez and Hartarska do not find statistically significant evidence suggesting that grade ratings have a positive or negative effect on the variables of interest. They note, however, that this and related studies should be interpreted with caution because data do not permit controlling for several factors that the literature suggest may affect results. For example, it is not possible to collect data on whether the rating was voluntary or requested by a don, or whether it was a rating of the credit risk or a global rating. Furthermore, rating and letter grades were introduced relatively recently and post-rating MFI performance data were unavailable at the time of the study, thus limiting the ability to pick up impact.

It is very important to note that the above studies do not look exclusively at the impact on outreach and that outreach is only indirectly accounted for since sustainable MFIs are able to serve marginal clientele. Hartarska (2005) finds evidence that rated MFI operating in the ECA region in 1999–2002 had better outreach than unrated MFIs but Hartarska (2009) does not find similar evidence for the rest of the world. Moreover, Gutierrez–Nieto and Serrano–Cinca (2007) find that factors unrelated to social objectives affect the rating grade, since larger, more profitable, and less risky MFIs achieved better ratings. They conclude that, given MFIs' important social mission, agencies should develop ratings that accurately reflect the achievement of social goals. Indeed, a new development in microfinance rating has been the attention to social rating, and various initiatives to offer social rating products and to unify standards are underway (e.g., Social Performance Map and Common Social Rating Framework, by SEEP Network Social Performance Working Group, 2008). Preliminary results in Auklah, Hartarska, and Nadolnyak (2009) suggest that rating did not affect outreach of MFIs during the 2003–2005 period.

Overall, the empirical evidence on effectiveness of microfinance rating does not seem to show the impact that donors and rating agencies have hoped for but is consistent with empirical evidence from the banking literature showing that, in the US, credit rating needs to co-exist with regulation (Flannery, 1998; Morgan and Stiroh, 2000; Berger, Davis, and Flannery, 2000). Recent cross-country studies show that, while information disclosure measurement in general is associated with better performing banks, rating may be the least effective of all methods (Barth *et al.*, 2005; and Barth *et al.*, 2007).

5 Other Control Mechanisms

External reporting and audit requirements reduce information asymmetries between stakeholders and the firm which usually translates into lower cost of funds (Healy and Palepu, 2001). In two separate studies of banks from over 70 countries for the periods 1999–2001, and 2000–2002, Barth *et al.* (2005, 2007) investigate the role of external governance mechanism by constructing indexes capturing various aspects of the control mechanisms affecting commercial banks. They find that financial statement transparency, the strength of external audit, and international accounting standards improve bank profitability and efficiency.

However, MFIs with audited financial statements do not have better outreach or sustainability than MFIs without audited financial statements (Hartarska, 2005; Hartarska and Nadolnyak, 2007). Some preliminary results show that MFIs in the ECA countries with higher coverage by private credit bureaus have higher average loan balances suggesting possible mission drift away from the poorest marginal clientele (Auklah, Hartarska and Nadolnyak, 2009).

More intense competition may act as a substitute for strong internal governance and, in mission-driven organizations, may improve overall efficiency (Hart, 1983; Schmidt and Tyrell, 1997; Besley and Ghatak, 2004). However, competition may also undermine institution-customer long-term relationships and, among non-profit lenders, exacerbates asymmetric information problems and leads to worse loan contracts for all borrowers (Gorton and Winton, 2003; McIntosh and Wyndyck, 2005). Evidence from competitive microfinance markets such as Bolivia and Uganda indicates that too much competition may decrease profitability (as in the case of Bolivia), although it may lower interest rates that borrowers are charged (as in Uganda and Bangladesh), and thus affect outreach (Porteous, 2006).

Cross-country studies provide mixed evidence. Mersland and Strøm (2009) find no impact on performance using a sample of rated MFIs while Hartarska and Nadolnyak (2007) find weak evidence of positive impact on outreach for a sample of Mixmarket data.

Hartarska and Mersland (forthcoming) focus on the impact of various internal and external governance mechanisms on MFI efficiency for a sample of rated MFIs while controlling for the impact of competition. They find that MFIs in more competitive environments are less efficient, but this effect disappears after internal governance variables are included. These results are consistent with those from a country-level study by McIntosh and Widyck

(2005), which show negative impact of competition. Hartarska and Mersland (forthcoming) argue that since competition is measured by an index based on raters' opinions, the lack of impact by this competition index may suggest that raters are not as well-informed about the market as expected, consistent with Hartarska and Nadolnyak (2008) and Gonzalez and Hartarska (2007).

6 Conclusions

Empirical work focusing on the role of external mechanisms of control is only emerging. The main conclusions are that regulation does not seem to have direct impact on financial performance or the number of borrowers reached but there is some evidence that it may lead to a mission drift. So far, the evidence suggests that rating with a letter grade does not improve fundraising and may be an unproductive expense that shifts resources away from the focus on outreach. Microfinance rating has not been informative of the success of the outreach mission of each MFI and has not provided the quality information it was expected to provide, which is consistent with problems in the wider credit rating industry. Competition may hurt outreach in the absence of effective internal control mechanisms, and preliminary results point to a possible negative link between credit bureau use in a country and may shift lending away from the poorest borrowers.

The evidence is somewhat inconclusive because the data and methods used vary. Empirical work adapts banking studies and applies various estimation techniques to address methodological challenges. The main challenge is the endogeneity of some of the explanatory variables, which is usually addressed by using lagged dependent variables in a panel setting, a system of endogenous equations, panel instrumental variables, or stochastic frontier analysis.

In addition, results depend on the datasets analyzed and these vary. Currently, there are three major datasets used in cross-country studies. The most accessible dataset is that assembled by the MIXMARKET, which contains the widest population of MFIs and is the largest. These data are self-reported and may be less precise than what is necessary for sophisticated analyses. Another dataset widely used is assembled from rating agencies' reports but contains a subset of possibly financially constrained MFIs in need to raise capital. Therefore, in some cases, selection issues may be important. The dataset compiled by the MBB, which includes but does not entirely overlap with that of the MIXMARKET, is large and consists of high quality data. This dataset, however, is not available to external researchers, and is only used for internal WB research which may or may not be affected by current policy priorities and needs. Some of the papers reviewed employed a combination of these datasets and other data such as survey data (e.g., from rating agencies and from bank regulators), and seem the most reliable.

Finally, since researchers are starting to pay attention to this type of analysis, the hope is that high quality data, preferably regional in nature, will be collected and shared. One such dataset is that by the Microfinance Center for Central and Eastern Europe and the Newly Independent States in Poland. As data become more widely available, independent researchers would be able to apply ever more sophisticated methods in analyzing the impact of market mechanisms of control and answering other important questions with which not only microfinance institutions, but also the wider financial intermediation industry, struggle.

References

Auklah, J, V Hartarska and D Nadolnyak (2009). What External Mechanisms of Control Work Best for MFIs in the ECA Region. Working Paper, Auburn University.

Barth, J, M Burtus, V Hartarska, D Nolle and T Phumiwasana (2007). External governance and bank performance: A cross-country analysis. In *Corporate Governance in Banking: An International Perspective*, B. Gup (ed.). Edward Elgar Publishing.

Barth, J, V Hartarska, D Noelle and T Phumiwasana (2005). A cross-country analysis of external governance and bank profitability. In *Regulation of Financial Intermediaries in Emerging Markets*, T Mohan, R Nitsure and M Joseph (eds.), pp. 46–86. New Delhi, India: Response Books, A Sage Publications Division.

Barth, JR, G Caprio and R Levine (2004). Bank regulation and supervision: What works best? *Journal of Financial Intermediation*, 13, 205–248.

Barth, J, D Noelle, T Phumiwasana and G Yago (2003). A cross-country analysis of the bank supervisory framework and bank performance. *Financial Markets, Institutions & Instruments*, 12, 67–120.

Berger, A, S Davies and M Flannery (2000). Comparing market and supervisory assessments of bank performance: Who knows what and when? *Journal of Money, Credit & Banking*, 32, 641–667.

Besley, T, and M Ghatak (2004). Competition and Incentives with Motivated Agents. Working Paper, London School of Economics.

Campion, A (1998). Current governance practices of microfinance institutions. Occasional Paper 3, The Microfinance Network, Washington DC.

Caudill, S, D Gropper and V Hartarska (2009). Which microfinance institutions are becoming more cost-effective with time? Evidence from a mixture model. *Journal of Money, Credit, and Banking*, 41(4), 651–672.

Christen, RP and R Rosenberg (2000). The rush to regulate: Legal frameworks for microfinance. CGAP Occasional Paper, Washington DC.

CGAP (2004). Foreign Investment In Microfinance: Debt and Equity from Quasi-Commercial Investors. Focus Note 25.

Cull R, A Demirguc–Kunt and J Morduch (2009). Does regulatory supervision curtail microfinance profitability and outreach? Policy Research Working Paper Series 4948, The World Bank.

Demirgüç–Kunt, A, E Detragiache and T Tressel (2008). Banking on the principles: Compliance with Basel core principles and bank soundness. *Journal of Financial Intermediation*. 17(4), 511–542.

Dewatripont, M and J Tirole (1994). *The Prudential Regulation of Banks*. Cambridge, Massachusetts: MIT Press.

Flannery, M (1998). Using market information in prudential banks supervision: A review of the US empirical evidence. *Journal of Money, Credit & Banking*, 30(3), 273–305.

Freixas, X and J Rochet (1997). *Microeconomics of Banking*. Cambridge, Massachusetts: MIT Press.

Gonzalez–Vega, C (1977). Interest rate restrictions and income distribution. *American Journal of Agricultural Economics*, 59, 973–6.

Gorton, G and A Winton (2003). Financial intermediation. In *Handbook of the Economics of Finance*, G Constantinides *et al.* (eds.). Elsevier Science.

Gutierrez–Nieto, B and C Serrano–Cinca (2007). Factors explaining the rating of microfinance institutions. *Nonprofit and Voluntary Sector Quarterly*, 36(3), 439–64.

Hardy, D, P Holden and V Prokopenko (2003). Microfinance institutions and public policy. *Journal of Policy Reform*, 6, 147–58.

Hart, O (1983). The market mechanism as an incentive scheme. *Bell Journal of Economics*, 14, 366–382.

Hartarska, V (2009). The impact of outside control in microfinance. *Managerial Finance*, 35(12), 975–989.

Hartarska, V (2005). Governance and performance of microfinance institutions in central and eastern Europe and the Newly Independent States. *World Development*, 33(10), 1627–1643.

Hartarska, V and R Mersland (*forthcoming*). What governance mechanisms promote efficiency in reaching poor clients? Evidence from rated MFIs. *European Financial Management*.

Hartarska, V and D Nadolnyak (2007). Do regulated microfinance institutions achieve better sustainability and outreach? Cross-country evidence. *Applied Economics*, 39(10–12), 1207–1222.

Hartarska, V and D Nadolnyak (2008). Does rating help microfinance institutions raise funds? Cross-country evidence. *International Review of Economics and Finance*, 17, 558–571.

Healy, PM and GP Krishna (2001). Information asymmetry, corporate disclosure, and the capital markets: A review of the empirical disclosure literature. *Journal of Accounting & Economics*, 31, 405–440.

McIntosh, C and B Widyck (2005). Competition and microfinance. *Journal of Development Economics*, 78, 271–98.

Mersland, R and O Strøm (2009). Performance and governance in microfinance institutions. *Journal of Banking and Finance*, 33(4), 662–669.

Morgan, D and K Stiroh (2000). Bond Market Discipline of Banks: Is the Market Tough Enough? Federal Reserve Bank of New York Staff Report, 95.

Morgan, D (2002). Rating banks: Risk and uncertainty in an opaque industry. *American Economic Review*, 92(4), 874–889.

Porteous, D (2006). The Enabling Environment for Mobile Banking in Africa. Report commissioned by DFID. Available at: http://www.infodev.org/en/Document.171.pdf

Rock, R, M Otero and S Saltzman (1998). *Principles and Practices of Microfinance Governance*. Washington DC: ACCION International.

Safavian, MS, DH Graham and C Gonzalez–Vega (2001). Corruption and microenterprises in Russia. *World Development*, 29(7), 1215–24.

Schmidt, RH and M Tyrell (1997). Financial systems, corporate finance and corporate governance. *European Financial Management*, 3(3), 333–61.

SEEP Network Social Performance Working Group (2008). *Social Performance Map*. Washington DC: The SEEP Network END NOTES.

Stigler, G (1971). The economic theory of regulation. *Bell Journal of Economics and Management Science*, 2, 3–21.

Van Greuning, H, J Galardo and B Randhawa (1999). A Framework for Regulating Microfinance Institutions. The World Bank Policy Research Working Paper 2061, The World Bank, Washington DC.

Wang, Q (2007). Does Rating Help Microfinance Institutions Raise Funds? Analysis of the Role of Rating Agency Assessments' in Microfinance. MS thesis, Auburn University.

Wright, G (2000). *Microfinance Systems: Designing Quality Financial Services for the Poor*. London: Zed Books.

Corporate Governance Challenges in Microfinance

Marc Labie
*Warocqué Business School,
Université de Mons (UMONS), and CERMi*

Roy Mersland
University of Agder (Norway) and CERMi

1 Introduction

Good corporate governance can improve firm performance and help assure long-term firm survival (Thomsen, 2008). Most providers of microfinance struggle to become financially self-sufficient and to achieve their social objectives of servicing with quality the poorest clientele possible. The issue of corporate governance has therefore been of increasing interest for microfinance as it is today considered to be one of the weakest areas in the industry (CSFI, 2008). This paper aims to (i) inform the reader about what constitutes governance in relation to microfinance; (ii) identify the reasons why it is of such high importance for the industry; (iii) review existing academic research on microfinance governance; and (iv) highlight ideas on how to tackle corporate governance issues in microfinance properly. Moreover, a new research agenda is proposed.

Recent research by Mersland and Strøm (2009a) and Hartarska (2005) have found that best practice governance mechanisms for firms in mature markets generally have little influence on the MFIs. Therefore, there is a need for a different and more specific approach to identifying and understanding the governance system better, which can help MFIs to reach their goals and enhance their long-term survival. However, searching for a "one-size-fits-it-all" solution will certainly be of little use. Rather than looking for standard best practices, it may thus be more rewarding to identify a general framework that can be adapted to different situations and different types of MFIs, and that can inform policymakers and other stakeholders in their respective microfinance markets.

In order to contribute to this debate, this paper is structured as follows. Section 2 introduces the topic of corporate governance and identifies the various reasons why it deserves attention in the microfinance industry. Section 3 reviews the literature on microfinance governance and argues that there is a need to move beyond the traditional agency theory and board management best practices in this industry. Section 4 lays out the need for a broader and deeper approach to microfinance governance. Section 5 proposes a new framework for the analysis of microfinance governance. Finally, Section 6 concludes and presents a new agenda for researchers who are interested in exploring the complex issue of microfinance governance.

2 Why Governance Matters for the Microfinance Industry

Microfinance, which is understood as the means and institutions created in order to provide financial services to people excluded from traditional banking, has a long history. Modern microfinance in particular, which has emerged since the 1970s, owes much to the cooperative movement and to traditional "informal" financial practices — for instance, Rotating Savings and Credit Associations (ROSCAs) — that have been popular for centuries across the world (Lelart, 1990; Bouman, 1995). From an international development perspective, microfinance has attracted increasing interest due to a wide variety of new institutions. Some of these have directly emerged from the credit unions movement (such as the major credit and saving cooperatives networks in Africa); some have their roots in NGOs (such as the seminal cases of the Grameen Bank in Bangladesh, Prodem–Bancosol in Bolivia and the K–Rep Bank in Kenya); while others have emerged from public bank restructurings (such as the emblematic case of Bank Rakyat in Indonesia). Together these initiatives, along with hundreds more, have received a great deal of attention from national authorities, as well as from international donor and development communities. During the last decade, we have also seen increased interest from the international banking and investment communities (Reille and Foster, 2008). The wide variety in origins and the many different stakeholders, with their often competing interests and competencies, together form one of the reasons why corporate governance in microfinance is an interesting research area, but remains demanding in terms of formulating public policy.

There are several reasons for governance to be at the forefront of the microfinance policy debate. Among the major ones are: firstly, the tremendous growth in service providers of various types translates to a greater number of clients and assets, as well as more elaborate structures to manage. Secondly, there have been numerous institutional and legal changes, with credit unions building more and more elaborate networks and many NGOs turning into (shareholder-owned) regulated financial institutions. Thirdly, institutions are evolving, from focussing mostly on a single product (usually credit) to becoming more complete banking institutions that provide not only credit, but also savings, and sometimes other types of financial services such as money transfers, remittances, payment systems and insurance, therefore reinforcing the risks assumed by these institutions. Fourthly, liabilities management, which had not received much attention at first, when donors were often the main source of funds, is now increasingly important. Local depositors, national public funds and the many international Microfinance Investment Vehicles (MIVs) spur on microfinance growth and are becoming important stakeholders of MFIs. Fifthly, the behaviour of public authorities towards microfinance is also changing. Their original neglect is being replaced by more proactive policies that create regulatory and supervisory frameworks supposed to favour a sound development of the industry. Sixthly, the international attention given to microfinance has been incredible, culminating with the United Nations naming 2005 as the "Year of Microcredit" and the Nobel Peace Prize being awarded to the Grameen Bank and Mohammad Yunus in 2006. Today, most people in Europe and the US know about microfinance, and thousands of international NGOs, politicians and celebrities have joined in extolling microfinance, motivating more actors to become involved.

Without doubt, these changes have been significant. However, critical voices are being raised that question the impact, efficiency and ethics of microfinance,[1] the business models that are used and favoured by the international community and the long-term survival and apparently noble objectives of microfinance providers (e.g., Dichter and Harper, 2007). This is

[1]We will not discuss these issues here, as they are clearly central to some other papers in this handbook. For instance, on impact, see Karlan and Goldberg's contribution; on efficiency, see Cull *et al.*'s, Galema and Lensink's, Hudon and Balkenhol's, and Serrano-Cinca *et al.*'s contributions; and on ethics, see Hudon's contribution.

where the corporate governance debate comes in. Basically, corporate governance in microfinance is about assuring the long-term survival of service providers without them losing track of their missions. Some institutions have experienced major crises, showing the high importance of controlling institutional development. This can be illustrated by the much cited case of Corposol/Finansol, now better known as Finamerica, in Colombia. This was created as an entrepreneurial NGO, dominated by a CEO who was strongly supported by the chairman of a passive board. At its conception, the NGO culture and cross-control between the different members of the staff allowed for great success. Later on, the organisation got into trouble because of a more pyramidal and bureaucratic organisational structure, setting wrong incentives to the staff and being weakly controlled by the board and stakeholders (international cooperation agencies and microfinance networks on the one hand, private banks providing debt on the other) (Austin, Gutierrez, Labie and Ogliastri, 1998). Other more recent crises are happening in major institutions in countries like Benin or Morocco.

Corporate governance is typically defined as a system, or a set of mechanisms, by which organisations are directed and controlled (OECD, 1999). Governance mechanisms can be defined internally by the MFI itself (boards, auditing, CEO characteristics and incentives, etc.) or externally (through market competition, public regulation, etc.). Two major points should be highlighted in this definition. Firstly, the idea that "corporate governance is a system" means that it involves a variety of mechanisms that act together in directing and controlling the firm. There is thus no single relationship based on a single tool, as is advocated by many experts when they focus exclusively on the role of boards. Secondly, the definition stresses the fact that governance is not just about "*ex-post* controls", but also about how organisations are directed. In a way, this comes close to Gérard Charreaux's definition of corporate governance as "*the set of mechanisms that aim at limiting the discretionary power of the executives*"[2] (Charreaux, 1997:1). However, one point remains poorly defined in these definitions: the ultimate aim of the control — the objective of the firm. Indeed, in a field like microfinance, where organisations are usually characterised by multiple objectives (mostly financial and social), it is not always clear where the priorities should lie. This is why, by modifying slightly the phrasing of the OECD, we suggest the following definition: "*corporate governance is a*

[2]The sentence was translated from French into English by the authors.

system, or a set of mechanisms, by which an organization is directed and controlled in order to reach its mission and objectives". The advantage of this slightly expanded definition is that it provides a benchmark for strategic planning and control (i.e., the objectives), and it provides a specific benchmark for each institution rather than "a standard for the industry". After all, as illustrated by Mersland (2009) for example, microfinance is practiced by a wide variety of organisations, not all of whom have the same priorities. Not only are MFIs different in terms of their organisational forms, but they are also different in terms of products, methodologies, social priorities and profit-seeking behaviour, not to mention subsidy dependence and historical roots. It can thus be argued that microfinance governance does not only need an industry-specific approach (Mersland and Strøm, 2009a), but also an ownership-specific, objective-specific and even a situation-specific approach.

3 Reviewing the Literature on Microfinance Governance

Most of the literature on corporate governance in the microfinance industry consists of consultancy reports and guidelines on how to regulate the industry, how to structure boards and board procedures and warnings against the "weak governance structures" found in cooperatives and non-profit organisations like NGOs (Campion and Frankiewicz, 1999; Council of microfinance equity funds, 2005; Rock *et al.*, 1998; Otero and Chu, 2002; Jansson *et al.*, 2004; Clarkson and Deck, 1997). What these reports have in common is their point of departure, which seems to be that MFIs are not greatly different from western firms. Governance recommendations from regular firms in mature markets are thus "translated" to the microfinance industry, and are, in most cases, supported by limited empirics.

Theoretically, banking governance is generally studied from four perspectives: ownership control, board management, regulation and supervision, and market pressure (Adams and Mehran, 2003). Recently, a few specific studies regarding microfinance governance have been conducted. As with the consultancy reports, these have taken a traditional approach in "translating" banking governance, and, to some degree NGO-governance, to microfinance governance. The aim of these studies is, first and foremost, to identify those governance mechanisms that influence the financial or social performance of MFIs. Interestingly, the studies struggle to identify important mechanisms, and those that are recommended in the industry guidelines are often not important.

For example, Hartarska (2005) and Mersland and Strøm (2009a) explore the effect of traditional governance mechanisms such as board composition and size, managerial incentives, ownership type and regulation. However, consistency in the findings both within and across the two studies is rare, and both studies struggle to identify significant governance influence. Mersland and Strøm (2009a) found that having a female CEO and an internal auditor reporting to the board is associated with better financial performance, while international directors on the board increase costs and reduce operational self-sufficiency. Other governance variables were judged insignificant or inconsistent. Hartarska (2005) found support for independent boards with limited employee participation. None of the variables that were deemed significant in the two studies were explored in both.

Two non-findings in these studies are actually the most interesting. Hartarska (2005) and Mersland and Strøm (2009a) both found that neither regulation nor a for-profit ownership structure advanced the performance of MFIs. Hartarska and Nadolnyak (2007) confirmed the finding that regulation has no effect, while Mersland and Strøm (2008) confirmed that ownership of MFIs is not greatly significant. Both Hartarska (2005) and Mersland and Strøm (2009a) concluded that governance does matter, but found that traditional governance mechanisms seem to matter less in MFIs compared to firms in mature markets. They called for better data and a study of alternative governance mechanisms in order to better understand the effect of corporate governance in the microfinance industry.

Two recent studies that have taken an original approach are particularly interesting. Firstly, Hartarska and Mersland (2010) evaluate the effectiveness of several governance mechanisms by taking into account *the dual objectives* of MFIs simultaneously. While other studies estimate the impact of governance separately for social and financial dimensions, they use stochastic cost frontier analysis to capture the duality of objectives in MFIs. This study is thus the first that adapts to the overall mission of most MFIs — the struggle to reach both social and financial objectives simultaneously. Their findings indicate that MFIs are less efficient in reaching the dual objectives when the positions of the CEO and the board chair are combined, and when MFIs have a larger proportion of insiders (employees) on the board. They also find that the efficiency of boards is non-linear, and is best between eight and nine members. These findings confirm some of the advice that have been provided by the consulting reports already mentioned, but with a stronger theoretical academic base. However, Hartarska and Mersland (2010) do not find consistent evidence that product market competition improves efficiency, although they do find weak evidence that MFIs in countries with mature regulatory environments could reach more clients by operating as a unit that is regulated by the banking authorities.

Another recent study was conducted by Mersland and Strøm (2009b), with the assumption that governance mechanisms may act as substitutes for or may complement each other (Demsetz and Lehn, 1985). They thus search for any interconnection between governance mechanisms and assume that they will find different governance set-ups in non-profit and for-profit MFIs. The findings confirm their assumptions. Board and CEO characteristics act as substitutes and complements in the formation of board composition and size, the existence of external governance mechanisms influence the set-up of internal mechanisms and the type of ownership influences the set-up of internal governance. They conclude that researchers should include interaction effects when studying the effect of governance on microfinance performance.

4 Beyond Agency Theory and Board Management

Although the aforementioned studies represent a step forward, there remains considerable ground to cover and a need to broaden the theoretical perspectives. Most MFIs operate in markets with limited competition, where the manager labour market is thin and very few MFIs are publically quoted. These facts limit the possibility of "market discipline", an underlying mechanism in traditional governance studies. In addition, the influence of regulators, which is normally strong in the banking industry, is limited in the microfinance industry because of inadequate regulation and/or a huge gap between the regulations and the ability of the regulator actually to supervise what is being regulated.

"Market discipline" and regulation are seldom part of the microfinance governance "toolbox", which is generally limited to boards and "professional" owners (Campion and Frankiewicz, 1999; Council of microfinance equity funds, 2005; Jansson *et al.*, 2004). We argue that this is short-sighted. The real effect of the corporate governance impact of boards often turns out to be minor in most industries (Thomsen, 2008), and type of ownership tends to be a poor predictor of bank (Altunbas *et al.*, 2001) and MFI (Mersland and Strøm, 2008) performance. For example, a case study by Labie and Sota (2004) is interesting in this respect. Analysing a Colombian microfinance NGO, they show that, even in an organisation where the board is highly active and supportive, strategic direction and control may come more from a fine-tuning balance between key executives than from board supervision. This indicates again the need for a more integrative approach to the governance of MFIs.

How can the approach to microfinance governance be broadened? There are at least three ways that may be used. Firstly, we propose *taking a historical perspective and looking for lessons to learn.* Microfinance is not a recent phenomenon. Several pro-poor banking systems have been around for centuries (Hollis and Sweetman, 1998). In a recent study by Mersland (2010), he reviews historical literature to identify the governance mechanisms that enabled the survival of the 19th century savings banks in Europe and the USA. The findings in this paper indicate that boards did not have much influence. What mattered were bank associations (similar to, but more advanced than, the MFI networks today), mismatches in liability/asset maturity (deposits that could be withdrawn on demand) that forced managers to manage the banks well, local communities monitoring "their banks", and donors risking their own personal reputations. Boards, regulation and market discipline were less important.

Secondly, we propose *focussing on risk analysis.* Institutional governance issues often receive a large amount of attention when a crisis is emerging or unfolding. Indeed, when everything seems to be running smoothly, there is usually little concern about ways of improving governance. But when balance sheets, access to funds, shareholders' value and staff are at stake, governance rises higher on the agenda. This should lead us to the following consideration: for many stakeholders, governance is first and foremost a "crisis avoidance tool". In this regard, a recent paper by Galema *et al.* (2009) helps to set the agenda. The dependent variable in this paper is the *variability* of performance. The assumption is that, for many MFI stakeholders such as the employees, one main objective is to avoid going out of business. Galema *et al.* (2009) show that having a powerful CEO is risky because it increases performance variability.

Thirdly, *adopting a real stakeholder approach could help broaden the perspective.* Paying attention to all of the potential stakeholders in the MFIs (and there are usually many) may give a broader vision of what the most influential governance mechanisms can be. As part of this, a clear focus on where "real authority" stands — to use the term suggested by Aghion and Tirole would clearly contribute to a wider understanding of how MFIs are really managed (Aghion and Tirole, 1997). A first step in this direction is to be found in the type of analysis promoted by CERISE.[3] This proposes a framework that is based on the idea that good governance should not only be based on its ability to ensure financial sustainability and regulatory fitness, but also on a clear strategic vision and a high level of transparency. All of this would appear easier in a stakeholder approach that includes all of the key actors of an organisation (workers, elected representatives, clients, communities, fund providers and/or shareholders) (Lapenu, 2002). Based on this, CERISE suggests that analysing governance may be done through three steps. The first consists of finding out who really has the power in the organisation based on two major criteria (who is the owner and who makes the decisions). The second step focuses on the way that power is exercised, looking at the information that is provided in order for a decision to emerge. The third step focuses on dysfunctions and risk analysis.[4]

The CERISE framework is certainly interesting as it focuses on questions (regarding power, transparency and stakeholder participation) which can be considered as relevant to MFIs. Indeed, microfinance methodologies are normally based on highly decentralised procedures, which supports the idea that transparency and stakeholder participation make sense for this type of organisation. As a broad approach, it is therefore useful. Nevertheless, we may wonder whether it is possible to suggest a more detailed framework that would allow us to identify what the prime mechanisms are for each type of microfinance organisation at each stage of its existence (Labie, 2001).

5 A New Framework for Microfinance Governance

Charreaux (1997) suggests an analysis framework which classifies the corporate governance mechanisms. Altough this was not established for microfinance, it can be used as a first approach to identify a broad list of potential governance mechanisms.

Charreaux's framework is based on two criteria: the intentionality of the mechanism, and its specific or non-specific character. A mechanism is said to be "intentional" if it was originally designed to improve corporate governance. A mechanism is said to be spontaneous if its role in governance

[3]CERISE (Comité d'échanges, de réflexion et d'information sur les systèmes d'épargne-crédit) is a group of French research centers (CIDR, CIRAD, GRET & IRAM).

[4]This last step allows for a parallelism with the second approach previously mentioned.

Table 12.1: A classification of corporate governance mechanisms.

	Specific Mechanisms	Non-Specific Mechanisms
Intentional Mechanisms	• Direct shareholders control (assembly) • Board of directors • Salary and bonus mechanisms • Formal structure and organization chart • Internal auditors • Ownership structure	• Legal environment (Regulation and supervision procedures) • Legal auditors • Consumer associations • National and international associations and networks
Spontaneous Mechanisms	• Informal (relationship) networks • Managers cross-control • Corporate culture • Reputation (among the employees)	• Depositors • Financial providers (MIVs and others) • Labour market • Political market • Media environment • Business culture

Source: Adapted from Charreaux (1997: 427).

Note: "Specific mechanisms" refer to those created for a "specific firm" whereas "non-specific" are created for a whole set of similar firms (for instance all the MFIs or all the cooperatives). "Intentional mechanisms" are created for a corporate governance purpose whereas "spontaneous mechanisms" exist but were not established with a "corporate governance" goal in the first place.

is an "indirect effect" of this mechanism, rather than being a prime reason for its existence. In terms of being specific or non-specific, a mechanism is said to be "specific" if it was "designed for a specific firm", while it is considered "non-specific" if it was created for a whole set of institutions.

Of course, Table 12.1 does not suggest that all mechanisms are relevant in all cases. On the contrary, Charreaux (1997) favours looking through the whole table in order to identify the key mechanisms for any given organisation. It is thus possible to use the framework to understand how corporate governance is structured for a specific organisation.

In our opinion, this type of framework constitutes an interesting first step for the following three reasons. Firstly, the governance mechanisms which are often advocated, such as boards and market competition, are only part of the whole set. Secondly, the mechanisms that are usually analysed in literature and advocated by policy makers are intentional ones such as regulation and supervision (non-specific but intentional) or board management (specific and intentional). There is thus a whole set of mechanisms that may (and do) play a role that are widely underestimated — the so-called "spontaneous mechanisms", those whose role is not intentional but rather derives from unplanned externalities.

Thirdly, although the framework does not mention this explicitly, the results may show that some mechanisms are highly relevant at certain stages (e.g., the birth and infancy of an organisation), while others may only play a role further down the road. This framework of analysis could therefore create a potentially dynamic perspective. For instance, after its conception, an NGO may rely on spontaneous and specific mechanisms (such as corporate culture or cross-control between managers); later on, as it grows and develops a more elaborate structure, intentional and specific mechanisms may play a greater role; further down the road, when local competitors and regulations have emerged, non-specific mechanisms may be of more importance.

Adapting Charreaux's (1997) framework can help to obtain a better view of the mechanisms that have the potential to provide good governance to the various types of MFI. A first attempt has already been made in the case of credit unions, showing the importance of network management (Labie and Périlleux, 2008; Périlleux, 2008). However, this still lacks one dimension: a way of identifying the key stakeholders at certain times in order to identify the type of mechanism most likely to play a major role in maintaining good governance over time.

Identifying the key stakeholders is therefore fundamental. Indeed, without this, there is a risk of free riding, where everyone joins a bandwagon in believing that someone else is monitoring whatever is happening. This is one of the lessons learned from the Corposol saga, where many actors were involved (microfinance international networks, major donors, banks, Colombian authorities, wealthy businessmen, academics), giving everyone a sense of confidence (Labie, 1998; Austin *et al.*, 2000). In order to avoid this situation, it is important to identify at each stage the type of stakeholder that may be the most efficient for ensuring good governance and, from then on, to pay specific attention to the type of mechanism usually associated with this type of stakeholders.

This could be achieved by analysing the surplus distribution (rent extraction) in the organisation. Indeed, property theory states that the true owner (and therefore the stakeholder to whom governance should matter most) is the one who benefits from the residual earnings (Hansmann, 1996). Some research is in progress using this approach, but it is not yet clear the extent to which it will help in identifying key mechanisms for good governance (Hudon and Périlleux, 2008).

Another method would be to rely on Mintzberg's framework of analysis (Mintzberg, Quin and Ghoshal, 1995). In Mintzberg's model, the key to analysing an organisation is identifying where the true power for decision-making lies. Mintzberg suggests considering the organisation as a balance between an internal and an external coalition of interests. He identifies categories of stakeholders that may be susceptible to assuming power in the organisation. For the internal coalition, five types of stakeholders are identified: the strategic apex (top management team), the middle line (the intermediary staff), the operating core (the people actually in charge of operations), the techno-structure (the specialists in charge of planning and organising) and the support staff.[5] Mintzberg shows that the actor or stakeholder who is dominating the organisation plays a major role in imposing the type of supervision mechanism and the level of centralisation or decentralisation that will maintain their control on the organisation. For the external coalition, he lists a whole series of potential stakeholders, the main ones being the different types of publics addressed by the organisation, the different levels of public authority and the more direct "partners" of the organisation (clients, suppliers, associates, trade unions, competitors). Mintzberg suggests that the external coalition may be either *passive* (leaving the power to the internal coalition), *dominated* (by one of the actors of the external coalition) or *divided* (when various actors of the external coalition tries to dominate the organsation). Therefore, using the categories suggested by Mintzberg, it may be possible to identify, for any type of organisation at any stage of its life, who are the stakeholders dominating the organisation and, from this, to question the type of mechanism that should help to ensure good governance.

6 A New Research Agenda

The purpose of this paper is to outline microfinance governance and to stimulate a broader search for the mechanisms that actually control and

[5]Please note that Mintzberg's framework also mention a sixth element that Mintzberg calls the 'ideology', which is the whole set of values that organisation members may share. We do not mention this in our list because it does not match a category of individuals.

direct MFIs. Based on the analysis of the former sections, we suggest a new research agenda. This agenda should be driven by a multi-theoretical approach and move beyond agency theory (Dennis, 2001). The following eight patterns may help to stimulate new research:

First, we suggest historical studies. What were the governance mechanisms that helped prior microfinance systems to survive and what were the ones that failed when systems disappeared (Hollis and Sweetman, 2001)? By identifying these historically important mechanisms, researchers can study their influence in MFIs today. For example, following Mersland (2010), it is time to investigate how MFI networks today influence the governance of MFIs, how depositor monitoring and liability maturity discipline managers, whether MFIs that are more embedded in their communities are different from other MFIs and whether MFIs with donors who take a more active governance role perform differently from other MFIs.

Second, there is a need to understand governance in relation to risks. A natural step in this would be to identify the various risks (performance, survival, environmental) of an MFI, and to search for governance mechanisms that can help to control or alleviate each of these risks.

Third, because of their nature and the fact that MFIs generally operate in contexts with limited "market discipline" and public regulation, we believe that MFIs should be analysed from the stakeholders' points of view. Microfinance corporate governance is more than simply a question of good board management, or having the right shareholders providing the right incentives to the right staff. Microfinance corporate governance is a complex issue because microfinance institutions are diverse, multipurpose organisations. However, they are also organisations in which many people put their trust. There is thus a need to understand better which are the stakeholders who truly influence the governance of MFIs.

Fourth, as illustrated in Charreaux's (1997) framework, there is a need to look at microfinance governance as *a set* of mechanisms that can substitute for and/or complement one another. Which mechanisms substitute for and which are those that complement one another?

Fifth, also using Charreaux's (1997) framework, we need to know more about the specific and spontaneous governance mechanisms, such as corporate culture or the cross-control of managers. These remain, to a large extent, unexplored in the literature on microfinance governance. This may be combined with Mintzberg's organisational framework.

Sixth, MFIs differ greatly in terms of ownership structures, legal incorporations and organisational objectives. There is definitely a need to better understand how the differences between MFIs influence their governance structures. This could be further broadened through studying what are the most efficient mechanisms for the different types of institutions at the different stages of their lives.

Seventh, studies may help to understand how local contexts and institutions influence the governance of an MFI. For example, a paper by Seibel (2009) shows that the governance of an MFI depends on the local culture. Similar papers are needed, as are papers studying the effects of other institutional/contextual factors, identifying what key contingencies should be taken into consideration when analysing the corporate governance of MFIs.

Eighth, and finally, microfinance is an international business, where alliances and cooperation across borders is common. Greater efforts are needed to understand how international actors such as donors, networks, investors and policy advocates influence the governance of MFIs.

References

Adams, RB and H Mehran (2003). Is corporate governance different for bank-holding companies? *Economic Policy Review*, 9, 123–142.

Aghion, P and J Tirole (1997). Formal and real authority in organizations. *Journal of Political Economy*, 105(1), 1–29.

Altunbas, Y, L Evans and P Molyneux (2001). Bank ownership and efficiency. *Journal of Money, Credit, and Banking*, 33, 926–954.

Austin, J, R Gutierrez, M Labie and E Ogliastri (1997). Finansol: Financiera Para Microempresas. Harvard Business School Case, Harvard University, N9-398-073 (en español).

Austin, J, R Gutierrez, M Labie and E Ogliastri (1998). Finansol. Harvard Business School Case, Harvard University, N9-398-071 (in English).

Austin, J, R Gutierrez, M Labie and E Ogliastri (2000). Dos casos colombianos de gerencia social: La Corporación de Acción Solidaria Corposol y la Compañía de Financiamiento Comercial Finansol. Universidad de los Andes, Monografías de Administración, Serie Casos, 55.

Bouman, FJA (1995). Rotating and accumulating savings and credit associations: A development perspective. *World Development*, 23, 371–384.

Campion, A (1998). Current Governance Practices of Microfinance Institutions. Microfinance Network, Washington.

Campion, A and C Frankiewicz (1999). Guidelines for the Effective Governance of Microfinance Institutions. Microfinance Network, Occasional Paper No. 3.

Campion, A and V White (1999). Institutional Metamorphosis: Transformation of Microfinance NGO into Regulated Financial Institutions. Microfinance Network, Occasional Paper No. 4.

Charreaux, G (1997). Le gouvernement des entreprises. *Economica*. Paris.

Churchill, CF (1997). Establishing a Microfinance Industry, Governance, Best Practices, Access to Capital Markets. Microfinance Network, Washington.

Churchill, CF (ed.) (1998). Moving Microfinance Forward: Ownership, Competition, and Control of Microfinance Institutions. Microfinance Network, Washington.

Clarkson, M and M Deck (1997). Effective Governance for Micro-Finance Institutions. *Focus*, No. 7. CGAP.

Council of Microfinance Equity Funds (2005). The Practices of Corporate Governance in Shareholder-Owned Microfinance Institutions: Consensus Statement of the Council of Microfinance Equity Funds. *Microfinance Network*, Washington.

CSFI (2008). Microfinance Banana Skins — Risks in a Booming Industry. Centre for the Study of Financial Innovation, London.

Demsetz, H and K Lehn (1985). The structure of corporate ownership: Causes and Consequences. *Journal of Political Economy*, 93(6), 1155–1177.

Denis, DK (2001). Twenty-five years of corporate governance research ... and counting. *Review of Financial Studies*, 10, 191–212.

Dichter, TW and M Harper (eds.) (2007). *What's Wrong with Microfinance*? Essex: Practical Action Publishing.

Duca, DJ (1996). *Nonprofit Boards, Roles, Responsibilities and Performance*. New York: John Wiley & Sons.

Galema, R, R Lensink and R Mersland (2009). Do Powerful CEOs Have an Impact on Microfinance Performance? *First European Research Conference on Microfinance*, Brussels.

Hansmann, H (1996). *The Ownership of Enterprise*. Cambridge, Massachusetts: The Belknap Press of Harvard University Press.

Hartarska, V (2005). Governance and performance of microfinance institutions in central and eastern Europe and the newly independent states. *World Development*, 33, 1627–1643.

Hartarska, V and R Mersland (2010). What Governance Mechanisms Promote Efficiency in Reaching Poor Clients? Evidence from Rated Microfinance Institutions. *European Financial Management*. doi: 10.1111/j.1468-036X.2009.00524.X

Hartarska, V and D Nadolnyak (2007). Do regulated microfinance institutuions achieve better sustainability and outreach? Cross-country evidence. *Applied Economics*, 39, 1–16.

Hollis, A and A Sweetman (1998). Microcredit: What can we learn from the past? *World Development*, 26, 1875–1891.

Hollies, A and A Sweetman (2001). The life cycle of a microfinance institution : The Irish loan funds. *Journal of Economic Behavior & Organization*, 46, 291–311.

Jansson, T, R Rosales and G Westley (2004). *Principles and Practices for Regulating and Supervising Microfinance*. Washington DC: Inter-American Development Bank.

Labie, M (1998). La pérennité des systèmes financiers décentralisés spécialisés dans le crédit aux petites et micro-entreprises — étude du cas "Corposol-Finansol" en Colombie. Thèse de doctorat, Université de Mons Hainaut.

Labie, M (2001). Corporate governance in microfinance organizations: A long and winding road. *Management Decision*, 39(4), 296–301.

Labie, M and J Sota (2004). Gobernabilidad y organizaciones de microfinanzas: la necesidad de delimitar las funciones de una Junta Directiva. *Revista española de Desarrollo y Cooperación*, Instituto Universitario de Desarrollo y Cooperación, Universidad Complutense de Madrid, No.13, otoño-invierno, 135–148.

Labie, M and A Périlleux (2008). Corporate Governance in Microfinance: Credit Unions. Working Paper No.08/003, Centre Emile Bernheim, Solvay Business School. Université libre de Bruxelles.

Lapenu, C (2002). La gouvernance en microfinance: grille d'analyse et perspectives de recherche. *Revue Tiers Monde*, 43(172), 847–865.

Lelart, M (1990). La tontine, pratique informelle d'épargne et de crédit dans les pays en voie de développement. *AUPELF–UREF*, John Libbey Eurotext, Paris.

Mersland, R (2009). The cost of ownership in microfinance organizations. *World Development*, 37, 469–478.

Mersland, R (2010). The governance of non-profit microfinance institutions — lessons from history. *Journal of Management and Governance.* doi: 10.1007/S10997-009-9116-7

Mersland, R and RØ Strøm (2008). Performance and trade-offs in microfinance institutions — does ownership matter? *Journal of International Development*, 20, 598–612.

Mersland, R and RØ Strøm (2009a). Performance and governance in microfinance institutions. *Journal of Banking and Finance*, 33, 662–669.

Mersland, R and RØ Strøm (2009b). What Explains Governance Structure in Non-profit and For-profit Microfinance Institutions? *First European Research Conference on Microfinance:* Brussels.

Mintzberg, H, JB Quin and S Ghoshal (1995). *The Strategy Process* (European Ed.). London: Prentice Hall.

OECD (1999). *OECD Principles of Corporate Governance.* Paris: OECD Publications.

Oster, SM (1995). *Strategic Management for Non-Profit Organizations. Theory and Cases.* New York and Oxford: Oxford University Press.

Otero, M and M Chu (2002). Governance and Ownership of Microfinance Institutions. In *The Commercialization of Microfinance*, D Drake and E Rhyne (eds.). Bloomfield: Kumarian Press.

Périlleux, A, E Bloy and M Hudon (2009). Productivity surplus distribution in microfinance: Does ownership matter? Working Paper 2009/8, Warocqué Research Center, Warocqué Business School, Université de Mons (UMONS).

Périlleux, A (2008). Les coopératives d'épargne et de crédit en microfinance face aux problématiques de gouvernance et de croissance. Working Paper No. 08/007, Centre Emile Bernheim, Solvay Business School. Université libre de Bruxelles (ULB).

Reille, X and S Foster (2008). Foreign Capital Investment in Microfinance. Focus Note. Washington, CGAP.

Rock, R, M Otero and S Saltzman (1998). Principles and Practices of Microfinance Governance. *Microenterprise Best Practices.* Development Alternatives.

Seibel, HD (2009). Culture and Governance in Microfinance: Desa Pakraman and Lembaga Perkreditan Desa in Bali. *2nd International Workshop on Microfinance Management and Governance*, Kristiansand, Norway.

Thomsen, S (2008). *An Introduction to Corporate Governance — Mechanisms and Systems.* Copenhagen: DJØF Publishing.

PART III

Current Trends Toward Commercialization

Corporate Responsibility Versus Social Performance and Financial Inclusion

Jean-Michel Servet

Graduate Institute (IHEID), Geneva

Institut de Recherche pour le Développement-UMR 201 and CERMi

For many stakeholders and observers, the inclusion of microfinance[1] in the social and solidarity-based economic sector has been obvious since a long time. Its main objective was to "combat poverty". During a discussion with Muhammed Yunus, organized by the World Microfinance Forum Geneva in 2008, Michael Chu, the former president of Accion International, and head of microfinance investment funds in Latin America, excluded half of the billion or so poor families living on the planet who, according to him, are not able to take advantage of the available financial services.[2] Even so, microcredit can still be considered as an instrument contributing to the Millenium Development Goal of reducing world poverty by half by 2015, in particular through national strategic plans.

However, from an analysis of the clientele, especially with regard to their social composition, it does not seem as if they belong to the poorest sections of the population. Microfinance activities are conducted in areas with a high percentage of low-income and often marginalized groups (peri-urban

[1]The institutions considered here as "microfinancial" can have various statuses: they are private or public financial establishments, with or without banking status, such as non-governmental organisations whose activity is in fact primarily, or even exclusively, financial (Servet, 2006).

[2]"It does not take stretching the definition of poverty too much to think that 4 billion people of the 6.5 billion in the world live in unsatisfactory conditions. If you assume an average family of four, that means 1 billion families. If you assume that half of them would benefit from microcredit (because not everyone benefits from financial services), that leaves 500 million families". (M. Chu, in: *World Microfinance 2008*).

and, to a lesser extent, rural). Mostly it is the groups with the highest capacity in these zones that constitute the clientele, as they have the most potential for making profit. Let us also mention that impact studies do not conclusively prove the globally positive role of credit on income,[3] so great is the fungibility of the financial resources of households. Microcredit funds are often used to better manage resources and expenditure over a period of time rather than to increase investment significantly for productivity purposes.[4] As a result, over-indebtedness appears to be a recurrent problem.

Gradually, the objectives of offering microfinance services to the masses (mostly short-term microcredit) and the marketing conditions of their distribution have positioned this sector under new terms (Guérin, Lapenu, Doligez, 2009). Over and above the issue of the war against poverty, the question of a generalized financial inclusion is increasingly cropping up.

1 Microfinance Subject to a Twofold Ambiguous Movement

A dual movement has come about.

Firstly, in their dealings with clients, a subsidy-free risk cover was sought. Barring exceptional circumstances (related, for instance, to population density), this is only possible when interest rates are high. The other option is that often cooperative or mutual-type organizations harness low-yielding savings. But this financial equilibrium is more a strategy imposed by donor agencies than an objective that has been really and fully achieved. Public or private funds at preferential interest rates make it possible to meet this constraint of financial sustainability. External support in the main finances research, innovation and training activities. It should be noted that the transformation of non-governmental organizations or unregulated financial institutions into fully-fledged financial organizations has often been linked to their desire to consolidate their projects, thus enabling them to harness savings for re-lending. On the basis of this initial transformation, the conditions for their mutation into profit-making organizations were set up.

Secondly, microfinance institutions have become centres of profit-making investment. With regard to international funding, the search for

[3] Armendariz and Morduch, 2005; Roodman and Morduch 2009; Servet, 2006.

[4] The critique of a comprehension of the working of artisanal and peasant units (unsalaried) using economic categories by Chayanov (1925, trans. 1966) is still extraordinarily relevent.

diversification of portfolios has led to a growing interest in them. It is recommended that these investments not exceed 5 percent of the portfolio and that they be of mixed composition in order to reduce risk. International investments in microfinance in the form of loans or equity infusion into microfinance institutions tripled between 2004 and 2006 and continued to grow until 2008 at a rate higher than 25 percent per year. Assets increased from 4 billion dollars in 2006 to 7 billion in 2008 split between 104 funds (Lutzel, 2009), to which should be added the contributions of major commercial banks and institutional investors.

This quest for profitability of microfinance, offering its facilities to the public at large, and the development of financial investments in the sector are linked. Evolution implies the professionalisation of the major non-governmental organizations. Many of them have gone beyond their field of action and their various statuses and switched to consultancy and brokerage development. To this end, they considered the provision of microfinance services as an opportunity. This enabled non-governmental organizations and development projects specializing in microfinance to become banks. Bancosol Bolivia, Equity in Kenya, ACLEDA in Cambodia, SKS Microfinance in India, and Financiera Independencia and Compartamos in Mexico are frequently cited. The last example of the commercialization of a microfinance institution is often contested. In 2007, the public issue of 30 percent of the Banco Compartamos shares, which then went on to lend to its 600,000 customers at an effective interest rate of approximately 100 percent per annum, and the sharp rise in its share prices (over 20 percent in one day) was staggering. This triggered a global shock in view of the ongoing transformations and especially with regard to the future of some prominent microfinance institutions. Many players in this sector wondered how an organization which was an NGO until 2000, and as such had benefited from public subsidies and foundation funds for its development, could permit a small number of shareholders (including the founders) to amass so much wealth and in such a short time.

More and more stakeholders and researchers have questioned the compatibility between the simultaneous large-scale growth of financial performance and social performance. There is no consensus of opinion on this compatibility (Balkenhol, 2007). The situation is further confused by the fact that profitability is not only the due of profit-making organizations and that in the allegedly private investments of the microfinance sector, public institutions are very much present (especially with the support of German Development Aid).

2 Recognition of Social Responsibility

In the UNDP and the World Bank Reports of the last five years, "social responsibility" is a quasi new term, which since then is increasingly being used.[5] Donor agencies supporting private and public funds as well as civil society organizations that invest in microfinance expect more and more information on the outcome of their assistance (Audran, 2008; Lutzel, 2009).

In fact, private investments in microcredit institutions are at the mercy of the negative information that is being circulated, which is in direct contradiction to the microcredit mania of recent years in the press (France 24; Kholiquzzaman, 2007; Fouillet, 2006; France 2, 2009; Fubini, 2009). An economic downturn also leads to a decrease in the reimbursement rate of borrowers, and therefore of profitability. The overall collapse of the various stock exchanges and the fall in the share price of some microcredit institutions (such as Compartamos) have led to a loss of interest in such issues. Compartamos shares that were quoted at US $6.5 in June 2007 fell to US $1.5 in March 2009. The share price of the Equity Bank (Kenya) moved up from 5 in autumn 2006 to 30 plus in July 2008, only to drop to 9 in early March 2009, then climb up to 18 in early April 2009. That of BRI (Bank Rakyat Indonesia) quoted on the Jakarta Stock Exchange, from 2000 in 2004 moved up to 8000 in autumn 2007, then fell to 2,800 in December 2008 and settled at 5,000 in early April 2009. However, we can point out that the share price of the principal microfinance banks fell relatively less than that of the major international banks, or even of the stock exchanges of these countries... As a result, there were still investment opportunities in this field.

Some reservations against the supposedly *always* positive effects of microfinance (especially microcredit) have led to an increasing sensitivity towards social responsibility in the microfinance sector, both with regard to multilateral and bilateral cooperation as well as international finance. The NGO ActionAid Bangladesh and Bangladesh Unayan Parishad, for example, have backed the report prepared under the guidance of Professor Ahmad Qazi Kholiquzzaman, which gives an accurate picture of the impact of microcredit on the country both from a scientific perspective and because of its severity (Kholiquzzaman, 2007). As for the economic effect, it is limited: "*Microborrowing does not usually provide the borrowers with an economic base to break out of income poverty and move on to significantly higher levels of income and living standard. Moreover, many get caught up in an increasing*

[5]Cf. Benedict XVI, 2009.

debt-syndrome and slide further into poverty". The reasons for this low impact and negative effect are due to the considerable weight of funded activities, which are not productive but commercial in nature (37 percent of the loans taken by the borrowers). The trap of economic underdevelopment is precisely because of the importance of margins and the many unproductive intermediations. Land rents account for 13 percent, rickshaw transport activities for 8 percent and cattle breeding for only 7 percent. One also has to take into account the cost of education and the marriage of children (7 percent). In addition, previous loans have to be repaid (6.4 percent). One should also note that the actual cost of microcredit is much higher for the borrowers than that posted by the institutions. This leads to a significant reduction in the family's income: the interest rate is actually 30.5 percent instead of the 10 percent quoted by the Grameen Bank, 44.8 percent instead of 15 percent quoted by BRAC and also ASA and 42.3 percent instead of 14 percent by PROSHIKA. The report emphasises: "*The respondents taking micro-credit have generally remained tied to rudimentary economic activities, many of which do not have much prospect of expanding into sustainable growth either because of market saturation (most of the products and services are directed to local markets) and/or limited scope of productivity improvement....*"

If one goes beyond these dimensions linked to production and exchange systems, to focus on dimensions that are considered non-economic, the findings are also negative. Among the clients (essentially women), microcredit counts for only 16 percent as one of the factors leading to an increase in school enrollment; similarly three-fourths of those who have improved their lot in life attribute it to causes other than microcredit. Apparently, it is public policies and the effort put in by civil society organizations that have made all the difference in the field of education and health. Let us just add that only one borrower in ten says that microcredit has enabled her to undertake an activity independently. What is more disturbing, 82 percent of the women interviewed said that the dowry amount has increased and 60 percent of those subjected to moral and physical violence within the family (27.8 percent of the respondents) said as far as they were concerned, violence had increased since they had become recipients of a microcredit. This stems from their new economic and financial status in the family. Only 27.3 percent of the women said that the violence against them had decreased. However, one of the positive results has been that only 28 percent of the women stated that the recognition of their viewpoint in the management of the microcredit had not changed.

It took 10 years to set up a financial rating for financial organizations. Social rating is much more recent, but it has grown very rapidly over the last two to three years (Guérin, Lapenu, Doligez, 2009; Lutzel, 2009). Some experts, who before were shocked when people doubted the positive effects of microfinance on poverty levels and on the rise in the income level of clients, as well as on the capacity of the alleged beneficiaries, and who refused all public discussion on the matter, unashamedly and adeptly adapted themselves very quickly and offered their services for this kind of evaluation. It turned out to be a juicy affair for them. It also illustrates their effectiveness as development brokers. It is difficult to separate their positive contributions from their parasitism in a context where the financial flows in the South-North sense henceforth prevail over the reverse flows (Gutner, 2007).

However, it is necessary for a reflection on the social responsibility of institutions not to confuse it with ethics. The task of the latter is to establish the norms that determine the choices and hierarchies among the objectives that those in charge of the institutions have set for themselves. Ethics or ideology can commission a study on a particular type of performance by an institution: the choice can be in the social or environmental field, in work relations or the internal governance of an organization, on the impact on clients and local communities in particular. On the one hand, ethics is based on moral norms (Labie, 2007; Some, 2008; Marek in this Handbook), for example, limiting the interest rate, and even replacing it by integrating the risk pertaining to a self-financed activity, as in the case of Islamic finance. This includes a ban on financing certain activities such as piggeries or alcoholic beverages for Muslim associations, arms, pornography, tobacco for some and genetically-altered organisms for others). On the other hand, ethics implies consistency between the goals pursued (both local and global) and the means employed to achieve them. Social responsibility can therefore be addressed differently.

These approaches in terms of ethics or social responsibility overlap partially. This overlapping creates confusion, which we propose to clarify here while emphasizing the ideological and practical implications.

The first viewpoint takes into account various performances whose common feature is that they are not immediately financial. These performances could be social, primarily the war against poverty and against discrimination towards specific categories of the population in view of a socially sustainable development. They can also focus on the environment by supporting an environmentally sustainable growth. The SIPEM in Madagascar, for example, refuses to fund activities that use charcoal, as this would lead to the deforestation of the *Grande Ile*.

The second viewpoint places the social and moral responsibility of institutions at the centre of their particular field of activity. Therefore, the social responsibility of a financial institution should be to promote the financial inclusion of all groups. More precisely, financial services should be tailored to meet the needs of the target groups and their cost should be such as to enable them to avail the services being offered.

Let us note that there are different types of investors: individuals, foundations, denominational organizations, public institutions operating mainly under market modalities. Hence, one can find different types of investment motivations, ethical, moral, social, etc. Different indicators should correspond to these various motivations. A fresh assessment on the basis of social and environmental performance, sharing or strictly ethical behavior (these four can overlap and be the subject of a synthetic index) are ways of attracting investors who want to make meaningful investments, but at the same time would like a certain level of remuneration. Fortunately, there is also a market for such investments and some players are involved in developing new types of products and quotations. M. Yunus (2007), for example, proposed the creation of a stock market in order to facilitate social business investments and the listing of such enterprises. Similarly, companies are subjected to stock price valuations and positive or negative media images that influence certain clients who may or may not go in for hiring new employees. Much of the aid given to microfinance is based on such procedures.

3 Civic Responsibility as the Benchmark for Social and Environmental Performance

Diversification of investments of an individual's capital can assume a civic dimension by making social investments or investing in sustainable development. The same goes for certain corporate activities, directly or through foundations which they create and sustain. While drawing up a list of the sponsors of microfinance institutions, we realize that behind such foundations are companies whose activities are very far removed from finance. A commercial group such as Carrefour supports microfinance. Such an involvement can make sense for a distribution company if the support is specific to areas where hypermarkets are established; for example, it would mean promoting the growth of small service providers in the vicinity or encouraging the professional advancement of certain employees who would hence become micro-entrepreneurs. The social responsibility of hypermarkets can be fully justified and effective, for example, in the sectors of fair trade, public health and environment. Similarly, an automobile insurance group can encourage its customers not to use their cars by subsidizing the purchase of season tickets for public transport. There are many other instances when support to microcredit projects has no connection with the sponsor's own activity. Thus we have Accor Hotels, the Italian brand Benetton, the cement manufacturer Lafarge, agrofood groups such as Nestlé and Danone, a consultant in management and information technology Capgemini Sogetis or an automobile manufacturer like Ford. Among the many sponsors of the best known French microfinance organization, PlanetFinance, we find financial groups (Axa, Citigroup, Credit Agricole Private Equity) and a large number of firms whose links with microfinance can be quite surprising: Microsoft, Peugeot, Orange, SFR, Suez, Accor Hotels, the travel agency Directours, a glass manufacturer Glaverbel, Bombardier Transportation, and even Damas, The Art of Beauty...

The Netherlands Development Finance Company (FMO) has published, for example, under the title *Social and Environmental Field Guide for Micro Finance Institutions*, a guide to good practice in microfinance with a view to applying the standards set by the International Labor Organization. This document has been translated into French with the support of a bank, the Société Générale. The search for non-financial performances is one of the specificities of microfinance, in the sense that it has been defined, as we have seen, on the basis of the criterion of poverty or the alleged marginality of the target audience. We note the client's objectives with regard to the percentage of women (considered to be poorer than the men), refugees, those living in remote areas, etc. In order to understand poverty, simple criteria can be defined for surveys on the basis of the active assets owned by the person, housing, travel and mobility (empowerment), the consumption of certain food items, utilization of medical facilities, and access to education. The problem is that categorizing the poor and women from their capacity to access a particular good or service does not necessarily improve their well-being. On each occasion, it is necessary to contextualize the representativeness of the various criteria and not think that there exists a universal definition of poverty. The MDGs, the Millennium Development Goals, are only one symbol out of a multitude of hierarchies of possible values.

Providing microcredit to a particular group considered economically disadvantaged does not necessarily produce a positive effect. The causes for the deterioration in their well-being could be:

- Over-indebtedness, understood not by the failure to pay off a debt but first and foremost as being impoverished by a credit and the payments arising from it,[6]
- Heavy workload (involving mainly women; apart from purely productive work, it could be other duties that are their lot in life ranging from forms of forced participation to regular meetings),
- Deteriorating working conditions (hazardous, unhealthy and injurious to health, child labor and deschooling),
- Monetary outflows (and therefore of income) from the production systems and local trade which ultimately lead to the impoverishment rather than the enrichment of communities, because of the financial charges levied as opposed to the returns on funded activities (Morvant-Roux, 2009). This question is even more relevant at the macro-level. As a public and private development aid tool, microfinance should be subject to the same scrutiny as other external support interventions. These seem to be highly useful in post-natural catastrophe and post-conflict humanitarian emergencies.[7] As a permanent structural support however, over half a century of development aid has failed to prove their worth as a dynamic in effective and permanent autonomous growth. There is rapid considerable dependence on aid, and the effect of projects and programmes supported in this way are exceptionally long-lasting when they subsequently become autonomous, unless, as demonstrated by the policies of a number of South East Asian countries, there is a strong will on the part of the state to control and manage these external supports. Worldwide, the greatest limitation of the negative impact of external aid is due to changes in modes of consumption and dependence on imports and external businesses. Moreover, historically we can see that countries begin to truly develop not when capital compensates for insufficient internal

[6]This is notably the consequence of resorting to several sources of debt at the same time, some of which are informal (see the article by Guérin, Morvant–Roux and Servet in this Handbook).
[7]See the bibliographic review by Agbodjan (2007).

> saving, but when the countries themselves become net exporters of capital.[8]

There could also be a problem with regard to the compatibility of the chosen objectives. This raises the issue of arbitration. Can one, for example, aim at both job creation and income-generating activities and ensure, in any place and at any time, that they are not responsible for pollution or over-exploitation of land, which would result in the destruction of the environment (often the case with tanneries)? They can also help companies whose employment conditions do not meet the standards set by international organizations for "decent work" (in their fight against child labor and debt bondage)?

Moreover, some forms of microcredit can augment the average income of a section of the population, while income disparities, vulnerability and insecurity of the majority continue to grow. An increase in average income is only beneficial for all if the growth in the income of the rich automatically leads to an improvement in the condition of the poor.

It is not enough to record the presence of microfinance activities and an improvement in the situation on the basis of certain criteria and attribute it to the former. Direct interventions in health, education, and for ending isolation may be the real reason. Bangladesh's example is a case in point.

Lastly, it is not enough to set noble objectives for oneself; one has to also have the necessary wherewithal for verifying that they have more or less been achieved. Good intentions are not to be confused with the good itself. The moral responsibility of institutions is not only to defend positive goals, but also to provide the means to monitor the impact and effects of their financing activities.

---

[8]Mende (1973; pp. 13–14, 170–171, 182–183) reveals the damaging impact of external aid. For more on this matter, see also Myrdal (1968), Robinson (1962) and Amin (1970). Keith Griffin has done much work on this topic using the example of Latin America; see Griffin (1969) and Griffin (1970).

At the same time, these arguments refute Nurske's theory (1953) regarding the positive role of external aid to compensate for a weakness in internal savings. For more critiques of external aid, see also Ayres (1962), which draws heavily on Gordon's (1961) historical study. Along the same lines, see especially Bairoch (1996).

4 Social Responsibility in Microfinance at the Centre of the Business of Financial Institutions

Civic responsibility strategies of companies, which we have just briefly described, induce them to favor a particular need of the society in general or a specific performance by the projects they support. But this approach carries the risk of the privatization of the collective's organization, whereas the basic needs are neglected. The risk is that of a plutocratic regime where those who can contribute decide the happiness of the others, without involving the alleged beneficiaries in the definition of these objectives. Civic responsibility can be the cause of a dangerous drift that democratic societies can take (Servet, 2007a; Servet, 2010).

From a financial perspective, we define *social responsibility* in microfinance through its direct contribution to the financial inclusion of people. It must be understood as the available financial services that effectively and efficiently meet the needs of the different categories of the population at a price that is compatible with their ability to meet it and in forms that are culturally accessible. From this point of view, social responsibility does not cover all of the multiple social engagements an organization may fix for itself. As previously discussed, this can be in relation to its clients, employees, communities in which its activities are undertaken and in various fields, which include tackling poverty, bringing about empowerment through notably the involvement of a particular population category in decision-making, and the preservation of the environment. These multiple engagements can make possible cobweb diagrams (see Figure 13.1) which allow one to visualize the relative weight of a given possible engagement. It is possible, as in the case of Symbiotics SA, to propose a synthetic indicator for the totality of the engagements, allowing investors to hedge their choice of investment and the risk undertaken (which more classically gives a synthetic financial indicator).

Taking into account the degree of banking inclusion is essential, for inequalities are rife across the globe. Depending on the country, access to formal financial services ranges from 1 percent to almost 100 percent of households.[9] There are huge disparities between continents, as well as between regions and localities. In Latin America, the national rates vary

[9] Claessens (2006), Demirgüç–Kunt (2007), Morvant-Roux (2007).

from 5 percent in Nicaragua to 60 percent in Chile, while generally fluctuating between 25 percent and 40 percent. In Africa, the inclusion rate is usually below 20 percent, particularly in East Africa. In South Asia, Pakistan and Bhutan access ranges from 12 percent to 16 percent respectively, while in India and China the rates are above 40 percent. We are talking about national averages. However, the latter mask the massive regional disparities found in the country. Thus, in most so-called "developing" countries, people with an average income, who therefore cannot be classified as "poor" and certainly not "very poor", have no access to basic financial services (Demirgüç–Kunt, 2007). This limited access is not only due to legal restrictions or regulatory barriers, but also because of the physical absence of institutions in certain areas. It is also due to the high level of financial illiteracy which renders the use of certain financial services virtually impossible as they are inappropriate.

It is therefore necessary to define, in different financial contexts, the relevant factors which help us to understand this responsibility which is specific to institutions whose principal activity is to create and offer microfinance

Figure 13.1: Cobweb diagrams to visualize the relative weights of a given possible engagement.

Dimensions	MFI	Bench.	Comments / Rationals
SOCIAL RATING			Higher/same/lower score than the benchmark; Main strengths and weaknesses.
OVERALL GRADE	..%	..%	Very strong/ strong/ satisfactory/ moderate/ weak in: Social governance; Labor climate; Financial inclusion; Client protection; Product design; SR to Community; Environment.
Social Governance	..%	..%	Social orientation of shareholders; Social commitment of the board of directors; Institutionalization of the social mission.
Labor Climate	..%	..%	Employment conditions; Labor/ management relations; Diversity and equal opportunity; Training and education; Occupational health and safety.
Financial Inclusion	..%	..%	Proactive and innovative financial inclusion strategy; Target of financially-excluded people; Removal of barriers to financial inclusion.
Client Protection	..%	..%	Avoidance of over-indebtedness; Transparency on investments terms; Ethical staff behavior; Quality of client relationship; Compliance with regulations & voluntary codes.
Products	..%	..%	Market research and segmentation strategy; Diversity, cost and adaptation of Credit products, Savings products, Insurance products, Money transfer services and Non-financial services.
Community	..%	..%	Impact on employment creation; Social screening of activities financed; Integration into local and international communities.
Environment	..%	..%	Environmental policy directed at the MFI (Use of electricity, fuels, water & paper); Environmental policy directed at financed clients (environmental screening).

Source: Symbiotics SA, Genève (2009).

Figure 13.1: (*Continued*)

services. This responsibility applies not only to the result but also to the processes (inclusive and not exclusive) by which these institutions produce and distribute financial services to their customers or users. This responsibility is to their customers and users. It also applies to their relations with other players in the microfinance sector with whom they compete or cooperate.

To assess the degree of financial inclusion, it is not enough to know about the distribution of services (number of loans and bank accounts in a population) in order to pronounce financial inclusion successful or not. It is also necessary to assess the degree of adaptation and quality of services (mainly via the non-monetary costs of obtaining credit).

Many discussions have recently focused on the interest rate levels, particularly in view of the Compartamos example in Mexico, whose rates approximate to 100 percent per annum. A study released by the CGAP (Rosenberg, 2009) can be understood as projecting the viewpoint of the lenders, in the sense that the question of the profitability of operations and the use to which funds have been put (whether revenue has been generated or not) is not seen as central to the deliberations, no matter how useful and well documented they are. It is assumed that the returns obtained from the activities are higher than the interest rates paid and that there is greater investment in the micro-enterprises. This still remains to be proved. A 100 percent level may suggest that microcredit providers have become a new brand of usurers. Moreover, a high interest level does not exist by itself. If we lend 100 percent for an activity that brings us 150, then it leaves a margin of about 50 percent for the borrower. If the effective interest rate on the loan is only 30 percent, but the activity leaves a lower overall margin of 20 percent for example, the borrower is impoverished by the loan, whatever the good intentions of the lender. It is a delusion to believe that the borrower can always refuse the loan. If he is waiting for money to come in, in a pre-harvest period for instance, he is forced to borrow in the interim. In countries where competition among institutions based on interest rates is slight, it leads to deductions by the formal financial sector on the wealth created through loans, or worse, in the daily intertemporal management of income and expenditure. One might think that before the development of microcredit institutions, similar charges were levied by private lenders or "loan sharks". However, in this case, in view of their local origins and involvement in the local communities that enable them to make a proper estimation of the risks involved and the pressure they can exert on debtors, we have strong reasons to believe that consequently there was an "endogenisation" of expenses. This is not the case with capital borrowed from external sources. A movement has emerged in microfinance which refuses to take at face value the rates posted by organizations and instead computes the actual cost of loans. This includes non-remunerative or low-yielding deposits, locked-in contributions, the calculation of interest not on the remaining capital balance but on the originally borrowed sum, etc. It is advisable that in-depth studies on profitability comparisons between activities, and interest rates be conducted in order to determine whether the interest rate level is sustainable or not for the borrower.

To determine whether needs are being met, one has to consult with clients (especially in order to identify the gap between demand and needs).[10] The straitened circumstances in which many sections of the population find themselves with regard to access to financial services, forces them to resort to them even when it is not their most pressing need. For example, a funding offer is often chosen whereas savings, insurance and remittances would be more useful to deal with insecurity and vulnerability. We thus note that productive funding possibilities are encouraged whereas a loan leads to over-borrowing due to poor returns from the little diversified activities; the need is for swingline credits at specific periods of the year or in case of illness (to avoid decapitalization which would shrink future incomings).

As it happens, despite very limited financial inclusion across the planet, no global indicator of access and use[11] of financial services figures among the indicators adopted under the Millennium Development Goals.[12] The same applies to the human development criteria fixed by the United Nations Development Program, and more surprisingly still, to the World Development Report released by the World Bank. The omission of financial indicators among the ones retained to gauge human development, contrasts more and more with the increasing exposure received by microcredit in the media since the first Microcredit Summit in 1997 and up to 2006, when the Nobel Peace Prize was awarded to Muhammad Yunus and the Grameen Bank. However, the indicators proposed by the various multilateral organizations in the field of development are diversified, and go beyond the strict economic level. One can find references to health, education, environment, women's participation in community life and housing conditions. These indicators primarily highlight people's capacity to be more productive in the accelerated process of privatisation and commodification of human activity (Appadurai, 1986; Servet, 2007b). It results in companies expanding and intensifying their financialization. Admittedly, all human societies follow highly varied financial practices and through institutions that are very

[10]To have a better understanding of the needs of borrowers, it is useful to concentrate not on success stories but to analyze the reasons for dropping out and failing to pay off their debts.

[11]For an in-depth analysis of this difference and their advanced definition in the *Rapports Exclusion et liens financiers* (Trans: Exclusion relations and financial links) (Paris, Economica), First Report (1997), Eighth report (2009), see the thesis of Gloukoviezoff (published in 2010).

[12]See the targets and objectives at http://millenniumindicators.un.org/unsd/mifre/mi_goals.asp.

different in nature.[13] But because of the increasing rate of dependency on these financial operations and the use of monetary instruments for improving the daily lot of a vast majority of the population, we can affirm that human societies have, from this point of view, experienced a qualitative change during the second half of the twentieth century. These changes in dependency through finance have brought about changes in the organization of societies due to finance (Servet, 2006).

In the present context of a more and more pressing, and even oppressive, financialization of such limited formal financial inclusion across the planet, how can one interpret this omission of the capacity to operate in the financial domain? This inattention results in the international community not feeling obligated to act quickly and universally in order to fight for financial inclusion. Although we can see the expansion and intensification of financialization that has occurred in all modern societies, including among low-income groups, access to financial services is not (yet) generally deemed a fundamental human right. The use of monetary and financial instruments is not considered a factor of identification of groups and individuals. However, the ability to cope with the risks of existence, seize opportunities to achieve a higher income and manage resources and expenses over time, is increasingly centred around the use of financial instruments. Access to financial services is vital in contemporary societies. It is simply essential in our day to day activities.[14]

Financial services are seen as a means of action, but are not in themselves really a need or a factor of identity of individuals and groups. They are more in the nature of a vehicle. Microcredit, by far the most recognized among microfinance services, is generally seen as a tool to promote the emergence of income-generating activities, especially programmes aimed at the facilitation of the MDGs. In developing countries, unlike the microcredit which is built into the labor policies of countries with a high average per capita income, it is exceptional for microcredit to finance new businesses. While microcredit is seen primarily as an economic means of action, its income multiplier effects are not clearly identified and especially not quantified with a high degree of accuracy, except for some case studies, to enable us to generalize at the macroeconomic level. It is not considered a requisite for managing vital social resources and expenditure flows in the long

[13]Cf. the example of payments by mobile phone in Servet (2009).

[14]On this approach to monetary and financial relations and bonds, see Aglietta and Orlean (1998), Servet (1998), Théret (2008) and Zeliser (1994).

run. As a result, the reflection on the social responsibility of the different stakeholders in a society for a generalized financial inclusion, and the political commitments that it entails, is more exceptional than the thinking on other needs such as food, access to water, health, education, housing and environment. These requirements are considered fundamental in themselves for the survival of human beings in an intendedly democratic society (by extending it to an equitable political representation, including in gender terms). Finance is not so yet.

5 Conclusion

We started from investors. Our analysis then focused mainly on the social responsibility of microfinance institutions operating in the field. The social responsibility of investors is not only dependent downstream of the sum total of the immediate and indirect consequences of the choices made by the service providing institutions, which they support. A part of the responsibility lies with the lenders and investors of the institutions. In a non-limitative sense, we can cite certain options:

- The option of loaning in the local currency rather than in a foreign currency;
- The option of mobilizing local financial resources (for example through a guarantee fund) in order to steer clear of a potent exogenous effects;
- The option of targeting those sectors which employ a large section of the poor who, in some countries, have no access to financial services: agriculture rather than trade, even though the rate of returns on investment in the latter is usually much higher and quicker, but the effect on the economic take-off is practically nil;
- The option of geographical zones deemed difficult and largely cut off from international funding (mainly sub-Saharan Africa);
- The option of supporting newly emerging organizations in the microfinance sector in order to further their development (a higher risk as compared to supporting well documented institutions);
- The option of taking into account all the contextual factors when posting results considered as positive. This should help to prevent creating damaging illusions vis-à-vis competitors and set goals for them only within the context of their field of action (population density, insecurity, average income, etc.), which would otherwise be impossible for them to achieve;

- The option of helping in the dissemination of information through participation in networks, seminars, group discussions, etc., in order to contribute via participative competition towards general improvement in the performance and innovation of the microfinance sector.

In so doing, the issue of social responsibility does not only involve institutions and stakeholders, with diverse statuses and levels of intervention, who either procure funds or provide financial services to the people. This issue also involves technical outsourcers (experts and evaluators), public authorities (at the local, national and international levels), non-governmental organizations (which are very active in the sector), and researchers (Wampfler, 2006). Experts have their specific social responsibility. The current crisis has highlighted the dangers of conformism. This shows that it is difficult to make oneself heard if we take a heterodox stand with respect to common beliefs.

Not only financial institutions, but also players in the production and delivery of microfinance services are involved through the issue of social responsibility in a particular field of activity. Indeed there arises the question of the capacity of access and use by groups that are currently facing social exclusion and financial marginalization. It also applies to the conditions of production and delivery of these services and their overall impact. Such services can be exploited for the sole benefit of the suppliers and thus jeopardise the socially sustainable development of societies.[15]

It is naive to believe that there exist in the microfinance services field, categories of stakeholders who, because of their position, would be the good players, while others (e.g. financial intermediaries or a particular category among them such as commercial banks) would be harmful or would corrupt the good intentions of others. Microcredit is not in itself a good or bad form of intervention. It is a financing technique which could, if used in a particular context and aimed at a specific public, improve or, on the contrary, embrittle or even weaken (sometimes rather drastically) the situation of a particular section of the population (Fernando, 2006; Kholiquzzaman, 2007; Servet, 2006). A particular form of intervention through microfinance might, depending on the context, turn out to be positive, neutral or detrimental for certain sections of the population and encourage, or on the contrary, slow down (or hinder) the progress of the developmental dynamics of these

[15]See the use of mobile phones to make payments in Servet (2009).

activities at a macroeconomic level. A clarification of the effective role of various stakeholders in the financial operations, over and above their particular status, is therefore necessary.

Reflection as to the social responsibility of the various microfinance actors indicates that the sector is increasingly mature. In the past, questions were raised as to what positive aspects microfinance, in general, could bring to its clients and local communities, or more generally for development. If today it is recognized as neither a bad or good thing in itself, but according to the context of its use and the actors involved, it is on this question that the investigation should focus.

From this point of view, a final remark is to emphasize that it would be wrong to simplistically oppose financial performance to other performances (social and environmental). It is not systematically a matter of additional cost. This approach can, for example, improve the repayment rate of loans, build customer loyalty through greater involvement, reduce the cost of certain transactions, etc. An organization which espouses the line of social responsibility has, in general, a clearer vision of the future and is therefore in a better position to cope with possible external as well as internal shocks. This applies to preventing over-borrowing, which can eventually lead to a sharp reduction in reimbursements. But also to the establishment of micro-insurance systems that can enhance clients' well-being. The promotion of the social responsibility of organizations is not a new form of compassion. It can be a medium or long-term contribution to their financial performance. An initial approach to interpreting corporate social responsibility is to think of it as a cost to be made good and a loss to be sustained. A second approach sees it in the light of a risk to be assumed as part of a healthy long-term organization. Placing the social responsibility of an enterprise within its line of activity can help to anticipate possible legal proceedings, or public bashing by civil society organizations, local communities, activist groups, foreign governments, etc. This happens when an activity is found to negatively affect a section of the population in a particular place, in the aftermath of a sectoral crisis or a deterioration of the physical and cultural environment. In financial matters, this risk is much more contained than in others. However, it provides a general framework for the development of social responsibility actions in the overall business activity. A third approach considers social responsibility as an investment due to the positive image of the business which is thereby reinforced or created. The first two interpretations deal with the risk to be assumed. They are defensive in nature. The third approach is positive. We are even tempted to label it as offensive. It turns social responsibility into an opportunity for institutions who have decided to adhere to it. Thus, it mobilises particular interests in the search for a common good.

References

Agbodjan, ED (2007). L' usage de la microfinance dans les situations de post-conflit: une revue de la littérature. *Autrepart*, 44, 227–240.
Aglietta, M and A Orléan (eds.) (1998). *La Monnaie Souveraine.* Paris: Odile Jacob.
Amin, S (1970). *Accumulation on a World Scale: A Critique of the Theory of Underdevelopment* (tr. from the French). New York: Monthly Review Press.
Appadurai, A (ed.) (1986). *The Social Life of Things: Commodities in Cultural Perspective.* Cambridge: Cambridge University Press.
Armendariz, B and J Morduch (2005). *The Economics of Microfinance.* Cambridge, MA: MIT.
Audran, J (2008). Microfinance, Inclusion financière et création de valeur sociale. Au-delà des bonnes intentions, la gestion de la performance sociale dans les véhicules d'investissement en microfinance. Mémoire Master IHEID.
Ayres, CE (1962). *The Theory of Economic Progress.* New York: Schocken Books.
Bairoch, P (1996). Globalization, myths and realities: One century of external trade and foreign investment. In *States Against Markets: The Limits of Globalization*, R Boyer and D Drache (eds.), pp. 128–142. London: Routledge.
Balkenhol, B (ed.) (2007). *Microfinance and Public Policy, Outreach, Performance and Efficiency.* London: Palgrave–Macmillan/ILO.
Benedict XVI (2009). *Caritas in Veritas.* Libreria Editrice Vaticana.
Chayanov, A (1925, trad. 1966). *The Theory of Peasant Economy.* London: Irwin.
Claessens, S (2006). Access to Financial Services: A Review of the Issues and Public Policy Objectives. *The World Bank Research Observer*, 21(2): 207–240.
Demirgüç–Kunt, A, T Beck and P Honohan (eds.) (2007). *Finance for All? Policies and Pitfalls in Expanding Access.* Washington DC: BIRD.
Dialogue européen n°1, novembre 2008, European Microfinance Platform, *Le rôle des investisseurs dans la promotion des performances sociales en microfinance*, 121 p.
Fernando, JL (ed.) (2006). *Microfinance. Perils and Prospects.* London: Routledge.
Fontaine, L (2008). *L'économie morale.* Paris: Gallimard.
Fouillet, C (2006). La microfinance serait-elle devenue folle? Crise en Andhra Pradesh. *Bulletin d'information du Mardi*, CIRAD/GRET, Espace Finance.
France 2 (2009). Envoyé Spécial, *Banquier des pauvres.* 14 mai 2009. http://www. dailymotion.com/playlist/x9afce_banquier-des-pauvres-2-2-envaye-spe_news
France 24 (2008). Reportage. http://www.france24.com/fr/20080324-le-magazine-laction-humanitaire-humanitaire?q=node/1078209.
Fubini, F (2009). Microcredito: Ora I poveri si ribellano. *Corriere della Sera.*
Gloukoviezoff, G (2006). From financial exclusion to over-indebtedness: The paradox of difficulties of people on low income? In *New Frontiers in Banking Services*, L Anderloni, MD Braga and EM Carluccio (eds.). 191–212. Springer.
Gloukoviezoff, G (2010). *L'exclusion bancaire.* Paris: Puf.
Gordon, W (1961). The contribution of foreign investments: A case study of United States foreign investment history. *Inter-American Economic Affairs*, Spring Issue.
Griffin, K (1969). *Underdevelopment in Spanish America.* London: Allen and Unwin.

Griffin, K (1970). Foreign capital, domestic savings and economic development. *Oxford Bulletin of Economics and Statistics*, 32(2), 99–112.

Guérin, I, C Lapenu and F Dolingez (2009). La microfinance est-elle socialement responsable? *Tiers Monde* (197) Jan–Mar.

Gurtner, B (2007). Un monde à l'envers: le Sud finance le Nord. In *Financer le développment par la mobilisation des ressources locales, Annuaire suisse de politique de développement*, 26(2): 57–80. Genève, IUED.

Kholiquzzaman, AQ (ed.) (2007). *Socio-Economic and Indebtedness-Related Impact of Micro-Credit in Bangladesh.* Dhaka: The University Press Limited.

Labie, M (2007). Réflexions préliminaires pour une approche éthique de la gestion des organisations en microfinance. *Ethics and Economics*, 5(1): 1–8.

Lutzel, E de, B Coupez and N Reille (2009). Paradoxes et défis de la microfinance: Une industrie qui résiste à la crise, une nouvelle classe d'actifs. In *Rapport sur l'argent dans le Monde 2009*, Paris, Association d'economie financière.

Mende, T (1973). *From Aid to Recolonization: Lessons of a Failure* (tr. from French). New York: Pantheon Books.

Morvant–Roux, S (ed.) (2009). Microfinance et Agriculture, *Rapport Exclusion et Liens Financiers 2009*, Paris: Economica.

Morvant–Roux, S and JM Servet (2007). De l'exclusion financière à l'inclusion par la microfinance. *Horizons Bancaires*, 334: 23–35.

Myrdal, G (1968). *Asian Drama: An Inquiry Into the Poverty of Nations.* New York: Pantheon.

Nurske, R (1953). *Problems of Capital Formation in Underdeveloped Countries.* Oxford: Basic Blackwell.

Robinson, J (1962). *Economic Philosophy.* Chicago: Aldine Pub. Co.

Roodman, D and J Morduch (2009). The Impact of Microcredit on the Poor: Revisiting the Evidence. Working Paper, No. 174, Center for Global Development.

Rosenberg, R, A Gonzalez and S Narain (2009). The New Moneylenders: Are the poor being exploited by high microcredit interest rates? CCAP Occasional Paper No. 15.

Servet, JM (1998). *L'euro au quotidien, une question de confiance.* Paris, Desclée de Brouwer, collection sociologie économique.

Servet, JM (2006). *Banquiers aux pieds nus, La microfinance.* Paris: Odile Jacob.

Servet, JM (2007a). Au-delà du trou noir de la financiarisation. In *Annuaire suisse de politique de développement*, 26(2): 25–56. Genève, IUED.

Servet, JM (2007b). Les illusions des objectifs du Millénaire. In *Institutions et développement: La fabrique institutionnelle et politique des trajectoires de développement*, Lafaye de Michaux, E, E Mulot and P Ould–Ahmed (eds.). 63–88. Rennes: Presses universitaires.

Servet JM (2009). Responsabilité sociale versus performance sociale en microfinance. *Revue Tiers Monde*, No. 197.

Servet, JM (2010). *Le Grand renversement. De la crise au renouveau solidaire.* Paris: Desclée de Brouwer.

Somé, Y (2008). La responsabilité sociale des organisations de microfinance: Quels critères pour une meilleure contribution de la microfinance à l'inclusion financière? l'exemple du Burkina Faso. Mémoire Master IHEID.

Tiers Monde (2009). La microfinance est-elle socialement responsable? 197 (Jan–Mar).

van Oosterhout, H (2005). *Where Does the Money Go? From Policy Assumptions to Financial Behaviour at the Grassroots.* Utrecht: Dutch University Press.

UNCDF (2005). *Microfinance and the Millennium Development Goals.* International Year of Microcredit 2005.

Wampfler, B, I Guérin and JM Servet (2006). The Role of Research in Microfinance. *European Dialogue*, 36: 7–21.

World Bank (2007). *World Development Report 2008: Agriculture for Development.* Washington: World Bank.

World Microfinance Forum (2008). Is it fair to do business with the poor? *Symposium Special Issue.* Geneva.

Yunus, M and K Weber (2007). *Creating a World Without Poverty, Social Business and the Future of Capitalism.* New York: Public Affairs.

Zeliser, V (1994). *The Social Meaning of Money. Pin Money, Paychecks, Poor Relief and Other Currencies.* New York: Basic Books.

The Importance of the Link Between Socially Responsible Investors and Microfinance Institutions

Erna Karrer–Rüedi*

Credit Suisse

Banks are essential intermediaries for the sound development of an economy, functioning as the Link between those who provide capital and those who need to borrow. This is a core task and the current crisis has provided a wake-up call about the role and importance of this Link. This core function is also at the heart of microfinance; thus, between capital providers, here referred to as socially responsible investors (SRIs) and Microfinance Institutions (MFIs) which in turn reach out to microentrepreneurs; thus, the underserved people who want to invest in potentially profitable projects of their choice.

In this paper, we first discuss the relevance of the Link between socially responsible investors and MFIs. Second, we address the extent to which the Link fosters social impact investment illustrated by the examples of women's empowerment, better health and education. Third, the critical role of achieving sustainability is highlighted. Fourth, the need for increased efficiency throughout the microfinance value chain, hence from SRIs to lending to microentrepreneurs, is discussed. Fifth, as particularly critical for the Link, we consider the commitment to the microfinance mission, especially in the light of the socially responsible investors. Last but not least, we discuss two current challenges, both having the potential to destabilize the Link at the macroeconomic level: Does microfinance lead to a boost of the informal economy rather than sustainable development? What if the international capital flow is significantly reduced in the coming years due to the 2008 financial crisis?

*The author is a specialist in socially responsible investment and microfinance in particular at Credit Suisse. The views and opinions expressed herein are those of the author and do not necessarily represent those of Credit Suisse. Email: e.karrer-rueedi@alumni.ethz.ch
A special thank you goes to Dr. Arthur Vayloyan, Private Banking, Global Head of Investment Products and Services, Credit Suisse, whose inspiring, insightful and forward looking thoughts about microfinance I had the opportunity to widely draw from in this paper.

1 The Link between Socially Responsible Investors and the Microfinance Sector

Microfinance is a powerful tool for financial inclusion and eradication of poverty in the world; in other words, it has proven itself to be an effective catalyst for many individuals throughout the world in overcoming poverty (Yunus, 2007; Iskenderian, 2008; Sachs, 2006; Easterly, 2007). Microcredit is then the major element of microfinance which also comprises microsaving, microtransfers and microinsurance. Microcredit allows microentrepreneurs to have access to credit which they would normally not access through the banking system.

Contributing to a solid development of microfinance in a global society where more than four billion people still live on less than US $4 per day is therefore important (International Finance Corporation, 2008; Prahalad, 2006). Microfinance aims to provide access to financial services to underserved but economically active people. To ensure access to capital and availability, a strong Link is needed between socially responsible investors (SRIs) and microfinance institutions (MFIs), hence microentrepreneurs.

As of 2008, over US $11.7 billion have been committed to microfinance by 54 donors and investors (Littlefield, 2009). Donors currently provide 53 percent of funding and investors 47 percent. Microfinance investment vehicles (MIVs) continue to grow despite the crisis; as of December 2008, there were 103 MIVs with estimated assets under management of US $6.6 billion (Reille, 2009). The MIVs have attracted a large pool of socially-oriented investors, including public, institutional, and retail investors. Elizabeth Littlefield of the Consultative Group to Assist the Poor (CGAP) emphasizes that retail investors have continued to fuel the growth of microfinance funds in 2008, reaching about 34 percent of MIV funding sources (Littlefield, 2009).

This trend can be highlighted by looking at Credit Suisse's engagement in microfinance. The firm launched, together with partner firm responsAbility, a microfinance fund in 2003 whose main purpose is to Link the needs of the microfinance sector with those of socially responsible investors. The latter seek an investment with a dual return, i.e., a financial and a social return, while MFIs need capital to provide small loans to microentrepreneurs.

In fact, the explicit request by some of Credit Suisse's clients to invest in microfinance was a critical factor in considering the launch of the MIV. It goes hand in hand with the bank's commitment to focus on client needs and to exceed their expectations — in true and long-term partnerships (Vayloyan, 2008). In addition, we must remember that in the early 2000s, the microfinance sector was highly non-transparent and very few commercially-oriented MIVs were available on the market. Even the concept of microfinance was largely unknown. Investments in individual microfinance institutions would not have allowed for a highly diversified offering across various MFIs and geographical areas. Thus, building a Link was primarily about developing a mutual understanding of the emerging microfinance sector, its aims and efforts, and, gradually, its social impact, expected returns, and related risks (INSEAD, 2009).

The groundwork for the launch of the responsAbility Global Microfinance Fund (rAGMF) was laid. However, it was only over time that a larger group of investors did want to do good with their investments. The first three years showed a slow increase of inflow, reaching less than US $100 million by the end of 2006. Only in the last two and a half years have socially responsible investors felt more broadly confident about investing in microfinance, lending to a sector known for providing unsecured loans to underserved people with no credit history and, in most cases, with no collateral. The rAGMF has certainly established a track record of its own, with no defaults of MFIs, steady financial return, and low volatility. By the end of September 2009, the Link between Credit Suisse's socially responsible investors and the microfinance sector had generated a capital flow of about US $884 million, as seen in Figure 14.1 — a Link between socially responsible investors and, ultimately, microentrepreneurs who gained access to financial services.

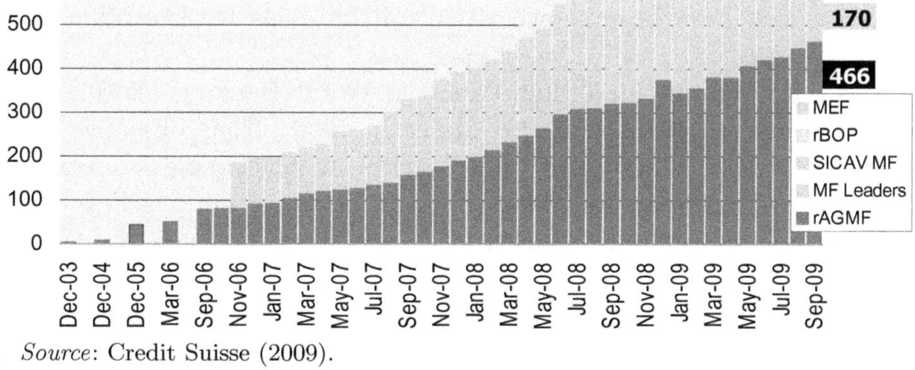

Source: Credit Suisse (2009).

Figure 14.1: Volume of responsAbility microfinance funds.

rAGMF is one of about 100 MIVs through which the inflow of capital to microfinance institutions has been established.

What are the driving forces behind this fund's success? One of the critical factors is the aforementioned solid relationship with investors established over time. Another relevant factor is that more and more people as well as institutions around the globe use profit-seeking investment to generate social and environmental good in moving from a periphery of activist investors to the core of mainstream financial institutions. These impact investors actively seek to place capital in businesses and funds that can provide solutions at a scale that purely philanthropic interventions usually cannot reach (Freireich, 2009).

Therefore, the commitment of top management at Credit Suisse to embrace the concept of microfinance as a way of impact investment, and thus as a response to SRIs' need to find a solid Link to a vertically diversified microfinance sector striving for financial access and outreach, is crucial for its success.

2 The Link Fosters Social Impact

Microfinance provides access to financial means, supports people who want to help themselves, take initiatives to secure a better life and attempt to leave poverty behind for themselves and for their families (Velasco, 2009; Counts, 2009). Poor women, in particular, find hope in the idea of microfinance. Women's status, both in their homes and in their communities, is elevated when they become responsible for managing loans and savings. The ability to generate and manage their own income can further empower poor women. Research shows that credit extended to women has a significant impact on their families' quality of life, especially their children. Poor women also tend to have "the best credit ratings". In Bangladesh, for example, women have been shown to default on loans far less often than men (Yunus, 2008).

It was with this in mind that Women's World Banking (WWB) was founded in the late 1970s and Pro Mujer in 1990. Their objective is to improve the economic status of poor families in developing countries by unleashing the capabilities inherent in women, helping them to access financial services and information. Already back then, it was believed that when a woman is given the means to develop a small business, build assets and take preventive measures against catastrophic loss, she is empowered to change her life and that of her family; hence, to climb out of poverty.

One may hypothesize that a thorough commitment and dedication to microfinance exists among women investors. Socially responsible investment is very often seen as a soft topic and thus more associated with women. Our initial analysis into investors in microfinance reveal and confirm exactly that — women support women!

The empowerment of women and poverty reduction are two Millennium Development Goals (MDGs) that socially responsible investors subscribe greatly to. Small loans allow poor but economically active people to start their own businesses. This results, among other things, in raising standards of living and helps to transform the local economy. Credit Suisse clients show a solid commitment to socially responsible investments and, thus, microfinance in particular across all investor "lifestyles", among women in particular. For example, about 70 percent of private clients' microfinance investment in Switzerland, measured by volume, has been made by women (Credit Suisse, 2008). Many of these women investors tell us that they themselves had to work very hard to grow into their current positions under difficult and sometimes discriminating working environments. Others appreciate the empowered positions they now are in and want to make sure that women around the world get a chance to achieve equality as well. They are committed to making their investment work toward providing other women access to financial means so that they get the chance to make use of their skills and work their way out of poverty.

rAGMF provides loans to both men and women. However, over the many years that it has been in operation, the majority of loans have gone to women, i.e., about 55 to 60 percent. Eligibility criteria based on a predetermined percentage of women clients do not exist in selecting MFIs for funding. Although it is considered important in the widening gap between women and men, and this aspect is highly relevant for social indicators, it is not a criteria for exclusion (responsAbility, 2008).

We should keep in mind that, according to the World Bank's International Finance Corporation (IFC), women still have the hardest time gaining access to financial means. As Muhammad Yunus, founder of the Grameen Bank and a Nobel Prize winner, whose bank only lends to women, noted recently that the current financial crisis would almost certainly not have happened if women had shaped world financial practices: "Women are more cautious; they would not have taken the enormous types of risks that brought the system down".

As microfinance provides access to financial means, the gender aspect cannot be underestimated and is one of the crucial factors of microfinance. As a next aspect, we discuss the importance of the Link's role in achieving sustainability.

3 The Link Plays a Critical Role in Achieving Sustainability

Microfinance is often perceived as a unique amalgamation of public sector interests and private sector principles. This development can be viewed as a tremendous opportunity for achieving sustainability, especially when it comes to offering continuous and increasing capital flows, as well as keeping the mission of microfinance true to its principles. Let me elaborate on the capital need for microfinance and how it copes with the need to support sustainable growth and avoid major disruptions that could threaten the continuity of microfinance.

As mentioned earlier, about US $6.6 billion capital have been provided by the international capital market to the microfinance sector in 2008. It is obvious that only big capital flows can match a US $300 billion investment need (Dieckmann, 2007). To respond to this challenge, the microfinance sector is in the process of transforming itself from a sector dominated by a mission-driven self-conception to one that responds to the needs and interests of private capital. The sector must do this if it is to provide an ever larger number of poor people with access to financial services. Given the US $300 billion demand for microfinance credit products alone, it also becomes obvious that a shift from depending on public money to providing private capital (Marc de Sousa Shields, 2007) needs to occur in parallel.

In the process of growing from a microfinance community to a veritable microfinance sector, microfinance institutions and their stakeholders have struggled and will always be challenged, to find a balance between their social and development objectives and the need to achieve a financial return. Although a financial return was not a goal in itself for most institutions during their initial stages, many have begun to accept by now that it is a requirement for self-sustainability, because they want to see their institutions survive in the market beyond an initial period of public subsidy (Steidl, 2007).

The development of a quasi-commercial approach to microlending has been a crucial factor in the success of early MFIs, e.g., Pro Crédito (now Banco Los Andes) and Prodem (the incubator of Banco Sol and Prodem FFP) in Bolivia, and Servicio Crediticio AMPES (the latter changed its name first to Financiera Calpià and now to Banco ProCredit) in El Salvador, and has proven that microlending can be managed on a sustainable and profitable basis.

With this in mind, rAGMF includes microfinance institutions that are eligible for funding only if they can show a successful track record of at least three years as well as audited annual reports and a business plan. Of course, there are many other aspects, such as the portfolio quality, balance sheet analysis, etc., that are also taken into consideration.

Back in the 1980s and 1990s, the most visionary MFIs knew that the flow of subsidies would eventually stop, and that commercial sources of capital would have to step in (Steidl, 2007). While many of the large MFIs have achieved a significant degree of commercial success, not many of the estimated 10,000 MFIs are at that stage today. In 2001, only 64 out of 124 that reported to the *MicroBanking Bulletin* (MBB) were fully sustainable financial institutions. The Kreditanstalt für Wiederaufbau (KfW) reports of approximately 100 to 200 MFIs that are considered economically viable. An analysis of the data of 1,100 MFIs listed on the MIX Market reveals that about 60 percent of these MFIs showed a positive return in 2006.

The increased pressure from private capital providers investing in sustainable MFIs certainly accelerates this process. However, sustainability also has to be looked at from the quality of management and governance at MFIs, among others (Banana Skins, 2009). This is why Credit Suisse has established the capacity building initiative in 2008, a long-term philanthropic microfinance platform awarding several million US dollar grants through the Credit Suisse Foundation. The initiative works with microfinance networks like ACCION, FINCA, Opportunity International and SwissContact in order to provide management training to microfinance institutions around the world and to facilitate access to financial services through research, systematically foster innovation, as well as constructive dialogue and new solutions (Buholzer, 2008).

The Link can play a critical and multifaceted role in reaching sustainability; continuous capital flow and investing in the skills and knowledge of people working in the sector are certainly two of them; but it is still a long way to go.

In the following three sections, we consider three aspects that are particularly relevant for the further development of the microfinance Link: efficiency throughout the microfinance value chain, commitment to the mission, and investors' changing attitudes to socially responsible investments.

4 The Link Increases the Efficiency of the Microfinance Value Chain

It has been observed that the interest rates charged to borrowers of microloans are quite high. The rates are often decried as being exorbitant and usurious, when, in fact, they are the product of some of the most fundamental principles of economics and are advantageous not only for the lender, but for the borrower as well. Interest rates charged for lending are a function of a number of factors, including but not limited to transaction costs, agency problems, and moral hazard (Armendariz and Morduch, 2005). In addition, micro-lenders are subject to significantly higher transaction costs than banks in the developed world, both in absolute and in relative terms.

The success of microfinance, in this case microcredit in particular, is based on microentrepreneurs who pay back their loans with interest reliably and on time. Because microentrepreneurs often know relatively little about finances, let alone the financial system, MFIs have a huge responsibility to assess the credit-worthiness of potential micro-borrowers. Close cooperation between a credit advisor and the borrower constitutes a critical success factor in the microfinance business; it helps to prevent clients from getting over-indebted.

Credit Suisse signed the CGAP's Microfinance Client Protection Investor Initiative about one year ago, i.e., it is committed to the principles set forward in it and, thus, to controlling the interest rate charged to the MFI carefully. More specifically, one of the six principles — transparent pricing — requires that the pricing, terms, and conditions of financial products (including interest charges, insurance premiums, all fees, etc.) are transparent and are adequately disclosed in a form that is understandable to clients.

The increased demand for transparency is coupled with on-going benchmarking and therefore ultimately putting pressure on the costs of funding, presumably resulting in continuously increasing efficiency. Looking at the three main drivers of funding costs associated with the lending process, we can distinguish the cost of funds for on-lending, the cost of risk (e.g., loan loss), and operational costs such as identifying and screening clients, processing loan applications, disbursing payments, collecting repayments, and following up on late or non-repayment. With regard to loan administration, microcredit is an industry that is heavily dependent on personal contacts. This is very time-consuming and resource-intensive, and allows each loan officer to reach only a limited audience of potential borrowers. By contrast, the credit lending process for commercial banks is supported by sophisticated technology, e.g., for computerized credit scoring, communication with clients, and payment processing. Not only is the very same process much less efficient for a micro-lender on a loan-for-loan basis mainly due to manual operations and lack of technology, but the problem is compounded further by the fact that, while a developed commercial institution may lend a large sum of money to one borrower, a micro-lender will by definition lend very small amounts to many borrowers, thereby multiplying the total operational costs on average by the factor of the number of borrowers.

Together, these factors contribute to a higher absolute transaction cost per loan relative to the loan size, compared to commercial banks. It is a simple fact of sustainability that business costs must be covered in order to continue operations. For instance, responsAbility seeks a 5 percent profit contribution for the microfinance institution; this after deducting 19 percent for credit analysis, processing, and monitoring; a provision rate of 3 percent; and an average refinancing cost rate of 7 percent; (responsAbility, 2008). This makes it possible to set up a viable business model without being dependent upon subsidies in the longer run.

However, based on economic principles, it is expected that transaction costs and, thus, interest rates will decrease over time. The use of new technologies in the front office and in the field as well as in the back office enables transaction costs to be reduced by a multiple. Let us take the example of an open source technology-based initiative for microfinance (Mifos), an industry-wide effort which aims to increase access to technology for all microfinance institutions, ultimately enabling them to extend their reach to the world's poor and reducing transaction costs at the same time.

In the front office and in the field, the opportunities for leveraging technology in order to reduce transaction costs seem almost infinite. Improvement areas include low-fee checking accounts, money orders, remittances, and payroll cards. Another opportunity lies in mobile phone banking; mobile subscriptions are expected to grow from three billion subscriptions worldwide today to about five billion by 2015. Partnering with mobile services operators provides MFIs with the best opportunity to penetrate remote areas. Also, other technology solutions and innovations can help to tap into remote, so far underserved markets in the developing world and reduce transaction costs, including point-of-sale terminals, smart cards, biometrics, etc. (*The Banker*, 2008).

To conclude, it is important to keep in mind that despite these high interest rates, micro-loans still can provide positive marginal benefits for borrowers today. Moreover, the potential exists to increase these benefits as the capabilities of the microfinance industry grows, which will contribute to lowering costs, which in turn may also help to reduce the interest rates charged to borrowers.

5 The Link Enhances the Microfinance Mission

Improving the efficiency of the microfinance value chain is one factor; the commitment to its mission is another critical factor for the microfinance Link. MFIs can shine a powerful and positive light on the financial services sector by demonstrating that combining social and financial returns is a business model that works. It appears obvious that poor people who need very small loans are unlikely to be serviced simply because very small loans are more costly than larger ones, as discussed above. But if the focus is on social impact while realizing sufficient financial return to attract the capital needed for growth, a trade-off is necessary.

Let us take another look at the rAGMF. The portfolio of the fund is regularly assessed with respect to its social impact. This information is retrieved to a large extent directly from the MFIs, quarterly or annually. For example, the MFI client segment is classified based on the *MicroBanking Bulletin* (MBB) methodology. Similarly, the types of MFIs based on the amount borrowed and the portfolio at risk (PAR) are assessed based on sources such as MBB. UNDP or World Bank data are used to estimate MFI outreach and demographic development, always calculated in conjunction with the data collected by the MFIs themselves (responsAbility, 2009).

As explained earlier, poor people often lack access to financial services, such as credit, savings, and insurance. In Sub-Saharan Africa, only 4 percent of the population has a bank account. There are several reasons for the lack of access to financial services. Foremost is the fact that banks have no branches in rural areas of developing countries. Formal financial institutions prefer urban areas due to higher incomes, lower costs and risks. With the absence of these financial services in non-urban areas, rural populations are deprived of a coping mechanism. Exclusion from credit and insurance also reduces their ability to survive income or price shocks, and to keep food consumption at adequate levels. Access to financial services plays an important role in reducing and transferring the manifold risks poor people have to deal with. The microfinance revolution has generated a stream of innovations in the area of financial services, addressing widespread market failures and providing financial services to poor households (Sheeran, 2008).

Historically, the demand for microfinance services has been attributed to the inability and unwillingness of the formal financial sector to serve the needs of low-income clients. In recent years, however, the microfinance industry has evolved to include MFIs operating under a wide range of legal structures, including a growing number of Regulated Financial Institutions

(RFIs) in addition to traditional NGOs. WWB, like many others in the industry, is concerned whether the influx of private capital causes a "mission drift", whereby the poverty-alleviation focus of transformed MFIs is diluted in the face of increased pressure to generate profits.

In response to the dearth of available information about the impact of formalization on individual MFIs, WWB tracked and analyzed indicators for a control group of approximately 25 microfinance institutions in an effort to put a quantitative framework around the question of whether mission drift occurs in formalizing MFIs. The study analyzed both the financial and non-financial trends, including client and portfolio growth, average loan size, profitability, savings mobilization, and the shareholding structure that emerged when a select set of transformed MFIs were compared against non-transformed institutions.

A broad range of perspectives on the question of the inevitability of mission drift for formalized institutions does exist. Not surprisingly, the opinions of leaders from transformed and non-transformed institutions favored the legal status of the institutions they represented. Those that had taken the decision to transform argued that, with appropriate checks and rigorous oversight, institutions can successfully manage the balance of double bottomline objectives; those leaders who had explicitly chosen not to formalize saw a strong correlation between commitment to the MFI's mission and the MFI's status as a nonprofit institution (Frank, 2008).

The microfinance industry can harness market forces and thus enhance and expand the sector on solid grounds. As long as investors have a long-term view, the social and financial mission of microfinance intertwines. And increasingly, more and more investors are looking for these dual bottomline returns as discussed earlier.

Nevertheless, some challenges remain. For example, does microfinance lead to a boost of the informal economy rather than sustainable development? What if the international capital flow is significantly reduced in the coming years due to the 2008 financial crisis?

6 Challenges and Misconceptions

6.1 *Microfinance and the informal economy*

Given the focus on pro-poor growth and poverty reduction, the role of the informal sector in the process of economic development has gained quite a lot of attention. Does microfinance contribute significantly to the informal sector without contributing to the formal economy, and what are its implications? It is of crucial importance to understand the linkages between the formal and the informal sector.

For more than a year, critics have argued that — perhaps no coincidence after a highly successful phase of outreach and volume growth — microfinance funding supports the informal sector including "the very tiniest and least sustainable of micro-businesses" (Bateman, 2009). Instead, so the critique goes, new microenterprises mainly displace existing jobs and income streams in non-client microenterprises. In addition, Milford Bateman states, many of the new microfinance-supported microenterprises collapse after a short period of time.

Microfinance has to address the informal sector specifically or, if the informal sector evolves like the rest of the economy, whether accepted formal growth policies are also accepted informal sector policies. It is, therefore, of crucial importance to understand the linkages — in quality and magnitude — between the informal sector and the rest of the economy.

Maloney (2003) shows that the informal sector size, depending on the country studied, might react both pro-cyclically as well as anti-cyclically to average informal earnings diminishing or growing independent of the evolution of the informal sector size. In addition, recent empirical evidence of urban labor markets in developing countries has also contradicted earlier concepts of the informal sector labor size and earnings, and, thus, its relationship to the formal sector.

The most important criticism of earlier studies is that the heterogeneity of the informal sector is not appropriately taken into account. Many households in developing and emerging countries are engaged in both the formal and informal sector (Blunch, Canagarajah, and Raju, 2001), and the sector of employment of the household head might have a high influence on the labor supply and sector choice of other household members. However, even more important than household decisions concerning collective labor supply is the household as an observation unit for standards of living and with that the importance of intra-household transfers. For the case of west Africa, Azam (2004) finds some evidence for high investments of formal sector employees in informal enterprises. For instance, he claims that on average 40 people are supported by one formal sector income. Hence, given that labor supply decisions and the generation of income by individuals happen within their respective households and simultaneously with the decisions of other household members, the notion of "dichotomy" between the formal and informal sector loses some of its significance and the value of an assessment of the relationship between the informal and formal sector based on an analysis of individuals or enterprise surveys becomes questionable (Lachaud, 1990).

Therefore, the notion that microfinance is not sustainable because of the informal sector may be a premature conclusion. Next, we take a look at the continuity of the international capital flow to MFIs in emerging markets given the financially and economically challenging times.

6.1.1 *Stability of the link in economically challenging times*

According to a recent IMF study about the economic crisis, US banks suffered 57 percent of the financial sector losses on US-originated securitized debt, and European banks suffered 39 percent, but Asian institutions took only a 4 percent hit (International Monetary Fund, 2009). Once considered an European and United States phenomenon, it is apparent today that GDP growth is declining sharply in all regions of the world. The decoupling hopes were put to rest with the latest financial crisis and its consequences for capital markets. Emerging and developing markets were almost immediately hit by the sharp rise in risk aversion and the resulting sudden halt to capital inflows.

The Institute of International Finance (IIF) based in Washington DC projects a collapse of private sector financial flows to the world's emerging market economies (mainly middle income countries such as Morocco in north Africa), from US $928.6 billion in 2007 to just US $165.3 billion in 2009 (see Figure 14.2). International commercial banks are expected to reduce their loans to middle income countries by around US $60 billion, compared with a net loan increase of US $410 billion in 2007 (Institute of International Finance, 2009).

We have to assume that 2008 marked the end of a growth cycle in global foreign direct investment (FDI) with worldwide flows down by more than 20 percent. Due to the global financial crisis, the capacity of companies to invest has been weakened by reduced access to financial resources, both internally and externally, and their propensity to invest has been severely affected by collapsed growth prospects and heightened risks. Because they were at the epicenter of the crisis, developed countries suffered from a one-third contraction in total FDI inflows in 2008. Developing economies started to feel the impact later, but with more to come eventually (UNCTAD, 2009).

Moreover, current account deficits, reflected by the disparity between savings and investments in an economy, need to be financed in international

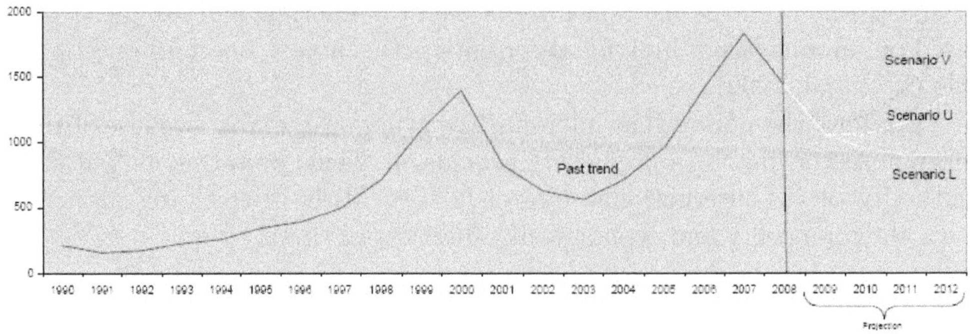

Source: UNCTAD, based on FDI/TNC database and UNCTAD's own estimates.

Figure 14.2: Global FDI inflows, 1990–2008, and three scenarios for the period 2009–2012.

financial markets. The current distressed situation in international capital and money markets is thus penalizing countries that are running a deficit compared to surplus countries. Taking a closer look at the current account balance adjusted for net direct investments in terms of GDP (see Figure 14.3) — adjusted because these flows are judged to be long-term in nature and are thus less prone to quick reversal — countries like Romania, the Baltic states, Bulgaria, South Africa, Turkey, and Hungary are more vulnerable than many Asian and Latin American countries and Russia in periods of declining risk appetite (Credit Suisse, 2009). We recognize that the global slowdown and financial market stresses may also impact global FDI flows negatively in upcoming quarters.

International capital flow is needed in developing and emerging markets, aggravated by plummeting remittances from expatriates to their families in poor countries, and millions of workers returning home after losing jobs, work permits, and visas.

Looking at the current situation in microfinance capital flow, we see basically two developments: one that shows a yet unbroken stream of capital into MFIs (Symbiotics, 2009) and another — and we probably see a precautionary approach here — that sees the launch of, for example, Microfinance Enhancement Facilities (MEFs) providing capital for continuous growth, especially in the case of a shortage of capital for refinancing at MFIs.

The capital flow of the Luxembourg registered MIVs shows a continuous volume growth since early 2006; however, we also notice a flatter curve since October 2008, which is, nevertheless, still increasing slightly over time. The rAGMF reveals a similar pattern. The volume more than tripled in the past

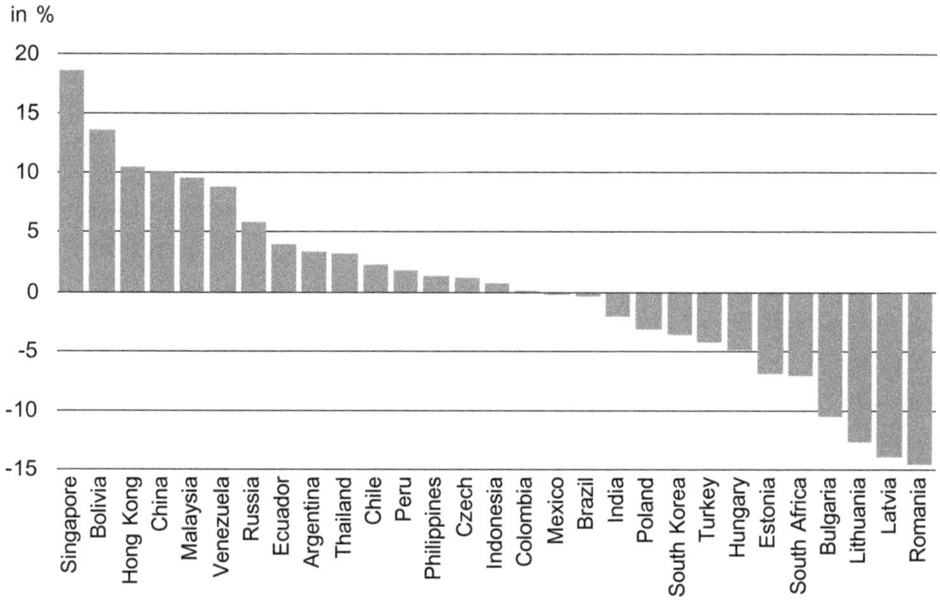

Source: Credit Suisse (2009).

Figure 14.3: Account balance adjusted for net direct investments in terms of GDP 2008.

two years, and we see a continuous inflow even though reduced net new assets led to a flattened curve toward the end of 2008.

However, in the survey published by CGAP in March 2009 covering over 400 MFIs across the world, respondents reported that the current economic situation adversely affected MFI clients' loan repayments. The survey showed that the quality of MFI portfolios was deteriorating, with 69 percent of respondents reporting an increase in portfolio at risk (PAR). Loan growth, after a decade of exceptional growth, had also stalled: 65 percent of respondents reported that their gross loan portfolios were either flat or had decreased over the previous six months (Reille, 2009).

We therefore cannot assume that Microfinance operates without corelation to the global economy and with the financial markets being truly international, an increasing interdependency of the microfinance sector and the rest of the economies seems rather evident.

7 Conclusions

Many of the topics and aspects around microfinance as discussed in this paper are seen as controversial. However, this paper has shown that socially responsible investors provide valuable capital through the Link so that underserved people have access to financial means in order to pursue business activities of their choice. Without this Link, resources outside their villages would not be available and therefore the base of the pyramid would have no or very limited access to financial services, or the outreach would be much more limited to an exclusive and small number of entrepreneurs.

We are convinced that a well-established Link, even in difficult times, allows the furthering of microfinance outreach while, at the same time, still providing a unique opportunity for investors to do good.

References

Armendariz, B and J Morduch (2005). *The Economics of Microfinance.* Cambridge MA: MIT.

Azam, JP and F Gubert (2004). *Those in Kayes: The Impact of Remittances on their Recipients in Africa.* IDEI Working Paper, Institut d'Economie Industrielle, Toulouse.

Banana Skins (2009). Microfinance Banana Skins 2009: Confronting Crisis and Change. Centre for the Study of Financial Innovation, New York.

Banker (2008). *The Right Tool for the Unbanked.* Available at: http://www.thebanker.com/news/fullstory.php/aid/5567/The_right_tools_for_the_unbanked.html

Bateman, M (2009). Three Perspectives on the Achievements, Challenges and Future of Microfinance. *Research Quarterly.* Credit Suisse, Zurich.

Blunch, NH, S Canagarajah and D Raju (2001). The informal Sector revisited: A Synthesis across Space and Time. Social Protection Discussion Paper Series, 0119, World Bank, Washington DC.

Buholzer, R (2008). *Launch of the Microfinance Capacity Building Initiative.* Zurich: Credit Suisse.

Counts, A (2009). Three Perspectives on the Achievements, Challenges and Future of Microfinance. *Research Quarterly.* Credit Suisse, Zurich.

Credit Suisse (2008). *Microfinance.* Zurich.

Credit Suisse (2009). *Global Research.* Zurich.

De Sousa Shields, M (2007). Challenges in the Transition to Private Capital. In *From Microfinance to Small Business Finance.* B Leleux and D Constantinou (eds.). England: Palgrave Macmillan Publishers.

Dieckmann, R (2007). *Microfinance: An Emerging Investment Opportunity.* Frankfurt am Main: Deutsche Bank Research.

Easterly, W (2007). *The White Man's Burden: Why the West's Efforts to AID the Rest have done so much Ill and so little Good.* USA: Penguin Books.

Economist (2009). *Microfinance — Sub-par but not Subprime.* London.

Elmer, P (2009). How to build your own MFI. In Credit Suisse Salon Credit Suisse, Zurich.

Emling, D, J Tobin and R Buholzer (2009). Mikrofinanz — Werkzeug zur Armutsbekämpfung. *Schweizer Monatshefte*. No. 967, Einsiedeln.

Frank, C (2008). *Stemming the Tide of Mission Drift: Microfinance and the Double Bottomline*. Women's World Banking Focus Note, New York.

Freireich, J and K Fulton (2009). *Investing for Social & Environmental Impact*. Cambridge, MA: Monitor Institute.

Golstein Brouwers Van, M (2008). *The Crisis in the Financial Sector: Opportunities for Change?*. The Netherlands: Triodos Bank.

Hechler-Fayd'Herbe, N and Y Luescher (2009). Microfinance after the Global Crisis. Research Quarterly. Credit Suisse, Zurich.

Institute of International Finance (2009). *2009 to see sharp declines in Capital Flows to Emerging Markets*. Geneva.

International Finance Corporation (2008). *Frontier Focus: IFC in the World's Poorest Countries*. Washington DC.

International Monetary Fund (2008). *Reshaping the Global Economy*. 46(1). Washington DC.

Insead (2009). Microfinance at Credit Suisse: Linking the TOP with the BOP. Case Study. Fontainbleau.

Iskenderian, ME (2008). Investing in Empowerment for the Benefit of Society. In *Insights into Microfinance — The goal of social businesses is the maximization of social benefit*. T Eigenmann, E Karrer-Rueedi *et al.* (eds.). Zurich: Credit Suisse Salon.

Karrer-Rueedi, E (2009). Microfinance in the Spotlight. In *Credit Suisse Salon*. Credit Suisse, Zurich.

Lauchad, JP (1990). *Urban informal Sector and the Labor Market in the Sub-Saharan Africa*. D Turnham *et al.*, OECD Development Centre, Paris.

Littlefield, E (2009). Three Perspectives on the Achievements, Challenges and Future of Microfinance. *Research Quarterly*, June 22 2009, 1–6. Zurich: Credit Suisse.

Maloney, W (2003). Informal Self-Employment: Poverty Trap or Decent Alternative. In *Pathways out of Poverty — Private Firms and Economic Mobility in Developing Countries*. G Fields and G Pfeffermann (eds.). Boston: Kluwer Academic Publishers.

Prahalad, CK (2006). *The Fortune at the Bottom of the Pyramid: Eradicating Poverty Through Profits*. New Jersey: Wharton School Publishing.

Reille, X *et al.* (2009). MIV Performance and Prospects: Highlights from the CGAP 2009 MIV Benchmark Survey. CGAP Brief, Washington DC.

ResponsAbility (2008). *Social Performance Report*. Zurich: ResponsAbility Social Investments AG.

ResponsAbility (2009). Mission and Performance. ResponsAbility Social Investments AG, Zurich.

Sachs, J (2006). *The End of Poverty: Economic Possibilities for our Time*. Penguin Books.

Sheeran, J (2008). The Silent Tsunami: The Role of Microfinance in the Global Food Crisis. *Microfinance Insights*. 9.

Steidl, M (2007). Challenges in the Transition to Private Capital. In *From Microfinance to Small Business Finance*. B Leleux and D Constantinou (eds.). England: Palgrave Macmillan Publishers.

Symbiotics (2009). Luxembourg Microfinance Investment Vehicles. In http://www.syminvest.com/microfinance-investment-vehicle/luxembourg.

Tobin, J *et al.* (2009). Microfinance Roundtable: Wherever there's a Will, there is a Way. *Credit Suisse Bulletin*. Zurich.

Unctad (2009). *Global FDI flows halved in 1st Quarter of 2009.* Geneva.
Vayloyan, A (2008). Microfinance, Innovation and Client-Centricity. In *Insights into Microfinance — The Goal of Social Businesses is the Maximization of Social Benefit.* T Eigenmann, E Karrer–Rueedi *et al.* (eds.). Zurich: Credit Suisse Salon.
Velasco, C (2009). Interview with Carmen Velasco, Pro Mujer International. *Women's Forum Newsletter.* Zurich: Credit Suisse.
Yunus, M (2007). *Creating a World Without Poverty: Social Business and the Future of Capitalism.* New York: Public Affairs.
Yunus, M (2008). Consigning Poverty to the Museum. In *Insights into Microfinance — The Goal of Social Businesses is the Maximization of Social Benefit.* T Eigenmann, E Karrer–Rueedi *et al.* (eds.). Zurich: Credit Suisse Salon.

On Mission Drift in Microfinance Institutions*

Beatriz Armendáriz
Harvard University, University College London, and CERMi

Ariane Szafarz
Université Libre de Bruxelles (ULB), Solvay Brussels School of Economics and Management, Centre Emile Bernheim, and CERMi

This paper sheds light on a poorly understood phenomenon in microfinance which is often referred to as "mission drift": A tendency reviewed by numerous microfinance institutions to extend larger average loan sizes in the process of scaling–up. We argue that this phenomenon is not driven by transaction cost minimization alone. Instead, poverty-oriented microfinance institutions could potentially deviate from their mission by extending larger loan sizes neither because of "progressive lending" nor because of "cross-subsidization" but because of the interplay between their own mission, the cost differentials between poor and unbanked wealthier clients, and region-specific clientele parameters. In a simple one-period framework we pin down the conditions under which mission drift can emerge. Our framework shows that there is a thin line between mission drift and cross-subsidization, which in turn makes it difficult for empirical researchers to establish whether a microfinance institution has deviated from its poverty-reduction mission. This paper also suggests that institutions operating in regions which host a relatively small number of very poor individuals might be misleadingly perceived as deviating from their social objectives. Because existing empirical studies cannot differentiate between mission drift and cross-subsidization, these studies can potentially mislead donors and socially responsible investors pertaining to resource allocation across institutions offering financial services to the poor. The difficulty in separating cross-subsidization and mission drift is discussed in light of the contrasting experiences between microfinance institutions operating in Latin America and South Asia.

*We thank Claudio Gonzalez-Vega, Marek Hudon, Marc Labie, and Jonathan Morduch for their very helpful comments on an earlier draft. We are grateful to Annabel Vanroose for her expertise and technical support.

1 Introduction

What is "mission drift"? In answering this question from a microfinance standpoint, we must start by looking into how the microfinance institutions (MFIs) advertize themselves. What is their main mission? Suppose for a moment, and for the sake of argument, that a particular MFI states that its main objective or mission is poverty reduction.[1] Let us assume again, for the sake of argument, that a good proxy for poverty is average loan size — the smaller the average loan size, the greater the depth of outreach, to use the microfinance parlance.[2] Then, instead of asking what is mission drift, we could simply ask: What prompts an MFI to increase its average loan size over time, thereby lowering outreach depth? There are two straightforward answers to this question. First, progressive lending, which, in the microfinance jargon, pertains to the idea that existing clients can reach up to higher credit ceilings after observing a "clean" repayment record at the end of each credit cycle.[3] Second, cross-subsidization, which entails reaching out to unbanked wealthier clients in order to finance a larger number of poor clients whose average loan size is relatively small. These two explanations are in line with the MFI social objective.

Rather, mission drift relates to a phenomenon whereby an MFI increases its average loan size by reaching out to wealthier clients neither for progressive lending nor for cross-subsidization reasons. Mission drift in microfinance arises when an MFI finds it profitable to reach out to unbanked wealthier individuals while at the same time crowding out poor clients. According to this definition, mission drift can only appear when the announced mission is not aligned with the MFI's average loan size minimization. Because this is often the case, our definition has the advantage of being a rather easily observable outcome, which can be measured empirically.

Building on a comprehensive literature review from individual MFI experiences by Fidler (1998), on pioneering theoretical work by Copestake (2007) and Ghosh and Van Tassel (2008), and on recent empirical work by Cull *et al.* (2008), this paper sheds light on a poorly understood phenomenon

[1]This is not an unrealistic assumption as shown in Section 2 of this article.
[2]See, for example, Mosley (1996), Armendáriz and Morduch (2010), and Cull *et al.* (2008). For a detailed discussion on the merits of this definition of poverty, see Schreiner (2001).
[3]See Armendáriz and Morduch (2010) for a more complete explanation on progressive lending and the rationale behind it.

in microfinance which is often referred to as "mission drift": A tendency reviewed by numerous microfinance institutions to extend larger average loan sizes in the process of scaling-up. We argue that this phenomenon is not driven by transaction cost minimization alone. Instead, poverty-oriented microfinance institutions can deviate from their mission by extending larger loan sizes neither because of "progressive lending" nor because of "cross-subsidization" but because of the interplay between their own mission, the cost differentials between poor and unbanked wealthier clients,[4] and region-specific parameters pertaining MFIs' clients.[5] Christen (2000) lists several factors such as strategy, and portfolio maturity. These may indeed make the loan size larger without MFIs necessarily deviating from their poverty-reduction.[6]

In a simple one-period framework, we pin down the conditions under which mission drift can emerge. The main point resulting from our framework is that there is a thin line between what constitutes mission drift and cross-subsidization, which in turn makes it difficult for empirical researchers to establish whether a microfinance institution has indeed deviated from its poverty-reduction mission.[7] This paper also suggests that institutions operating in regions which host a relatively small number of very poor individuals might be misleadingly perceived as deviating from their mission. Because existing empirical studies cannot differentiate between mission drift and cross-subsidization, these studies can mislead donors and socially responsible investors. The difficulty in separating cross-subsidization and mission

[4]Agency problems might also enter the picture (see Aubert *et al.*, 2009; Labie *et al.*, 2010).

[5]While the focus of this paper is on microfinance institutions which "drift" away from their poverty-reduction mission, where poverty is proxied by average loan size, we could also think of situations where such a drift is triggered by profit-oriented donors. As discussed below, the latter scenario has been analyzed by Ghosh and Van Tassel (2008). Mission drift could also be rooted in shareholders' pursuit of a self-sustainability objective which might take priority over their poverty-reduction objective (Hermes and Lensink, 2007).

[6]Henceforth, we use outreach maximization and poverty reduction mission/objective interchangeably.

[7]One way to assess empirically whether an institution has deviated from its mission is the following: In its growth process, does the MFI crowd out the poor as the size of its portfolio grows? However, a clean empirical analysis on this requires a well-defined notion of poverty, which further complicates the picture. Empirical researchers tend to associate mission drift with larger average loan size. As we will argue below, this is potentially misleading to begin with. This paper can thus be viewed as a "warning" on further empirical research without theoretical and empirically sound underpinnings.

drift is discussed in light of the contrasting experiences between microfinance institutions operating in Latin America and South Asia.

While our model is static for the sake of simplicity, it does shed light on the profitable scaling-up process whereby, in their efforts to avoid loan arrears and monitoring costs, MFIs tend to target better-off clients in priority. Simply put: relative to poor clients, unbanked wealthier clients cost less. MFIs' excessive focus on (relatively costless) unbanked wealthier clients might be motivated by profit-oriented donors, and drifting from their mission might be the only way to attract more resources, in the model by Gosh and Van Tassel (2008). Alternatively, the motivation for MFIs to drift from their mission might be because such institutions wish to attract socially responsible investors. Commercial MFIs are a typical example, which is often invoked in the empirical literature. This literature generally uses as a proxy of mission drift the larger loan sizes that commercial MFIs offer relative to the size of the loans offered by non-governmental organizations (NGOs), for example. In recent empirical work by Cull *et al.* (2009) across different MFIs operating in different regions, the proxy for poverty is average loan size, suggesting that mission drift results from the recent microfinance commercialization trend.

Taking average loan size as a proxy for poverty is gaining increasing empirical popularity. This paper will focus on the merits of this approach in the hope of offering some guidance for empirical researchers. Our main argument is closest in spirit to what Gonzalez-Vega *et al.* (1997) describe as a "loan size creep". That is, creeping up to larger loans to wealthier clients, rather than growing a larger numbers of small-loan customers. A straightforward interpretation of the loan size creep idea is that increased profitability by MFIs tapping wealthier clients — who typically request a larger loan size — is triggered by these institutions' efforts to minimize the transaction costs involved in dealing with small loans, which in turn hinders self-sustainability. In this paper, we dispel this view by showing that transaction cost minimization alone is not at the root of a mission drift phenomenon. Instead, MFIs serving the poor might be constrained by the number of poor clients that can potentially be served in a particular region, as well as other region-specific parameters. This, in turn, makes empirical efforts to detect mission drift across MFIs exceedingly difficult, if not impossible. From a policy standpoint, donors and socially responsible investors should be cautious in taking existing empirical efforts suggesting mission drift. These results might bias donors and socially responsible investors' decisions against funding organizations that offer good financial prospects for the poor via cross-subsidization.

The paper is structured as follows. Section 2 describes some basic stylized facts on the top 10 MFIs worldwide, ranked from top to bottom in terms of clients reached, and their various missions. Four poverty-reduction mission-driven institutions are in Asia. The three MFIs which are based in Latin America do not advertise themselves as poverty-reduction mission-driven institutions. Nevertheless, social orientation is clearly there. Section 3 briefly discusses the theoretical concept of mission fulfillment in microfinance. Section 4 displays the basic model showing that a mission drift theory based on transaction cost minimization alone can be misleading. Section 5 shows that the most important region-specific parameters, which might differ quite widely across MFIs, are at the root of a potential mission drift. These parameters are decisive in any attempt to distinguish cross-subsidization from mission drift. In particular, this section shows that heterogeneity across MFIs and regions might explain why some institutions are more prone to deviate from their poverty-reduction/outreach maximization objectives. While it remains true that some institutions might give more weight to serving the poor, we show that there are at least two parameters which play an important role, namely, the relative cost of serving the poor relative to that of serving the unbanked wealthier on the one hand, and the scope for serving larger numbers of poor individuals on the other. The interplay of these key parameters can predict which MFIs will be more prone to deviate from their outreach maximization/poverty reduction objective. Section 6 discusses the model in light of the contrasting experiences in South Asia and Latin America. Section 7 concludes and opens avenues for future research.

2 The Poverty Reduction Mission in Perspective

Table 15.1 displays the top 10 microfinance institutions (MFIs) ranked by the Microfinance Information Exchange (MIX) market from highest to lowest in terms of number of clients reached. The second column delivers a proxy for outreach as a percentage of the total population which is being served by the MFI in question in a particular country. Bangladesh's Grameen Bank and Vietnam's VBSP rank highest in terms of outreach, most likely because the number of poor in those countries is the highest, a parameter to which

Table 15.1: Missions of the 10 largest microfinance institutions worldwide.

Institution	Outreach (as a percentage of country's population)	Country	Legal Status	Main Mission	Other Mission(s)
Grameen Bank	4.43	Bangladesh	Regulated Bank.	Poverty Reduction.	Focus on women.
ASA	3.31	Bangladesh	NGO.	Income Generation.	Integrate women.
VBSP	5.43	Vietnam	State-Owned Regulated Bank.	Poverty Reduction.	Low interest rates.
BRAC	2.92	Bangladesh	NGO.	Poverty Reduction.	Literacy & Disease.
BRI	1.44	Indonesia	Regulated Bank.	Wide Financial Services to small entrepreneurs.	Best Corporate Governance & Profits for Stakeholders.
Spandana	.08	India	Regulated Financial Institution.	Leading Financial Service Provider.	Marketable & Equitable Solutions for Benefit of Stakeholders.
SHARE	.07	India	Regulated Financial Institution.	Poverty Reduction.	Focus on Women.
Caja Popular Mexicana	.58	Mexico	Regulated Cooperative.	Cooperative for Improving Quality of Life of Members.	Offer Competitive Financial Products to its Members.
Compartamos	.55	Mexico	Regulated Bank.	Create Development Opportunities.	Develop "trust relationships".
BCSC	1.34	Colombia	Regulated Bank.	Leading in "popular" banking.	To develop social objectives among community members.

Source: Mix Market 2007 Report and Grameen Foundation.

we shall come back in greater detail later in the analysis as it captures the notion of poverty in a controversial manner, namely, via average loan sizes.[8]

The last two columns show the main mission of each MFI as well as other missions, as stated by the profile of each MFI by MIX.[9] At one end of the spectrum, we find institutions such as Bangladesh's BRAC, whose main mission is not just poverty reduction via the provision of financial services for income-generating activities, but also that of fighting illiteracy and diseases.[10] These three objectives accord well with a more comprehensive notion of poverty, as captured by the Human Development Index (HDI).[11] At the other end of the spectrum, we observe South Asian seemingly for-profit MFIs such as India's Spandana, whose main mission is to become the largest provider of financial services and to maximize stakeholders' welfare — poor clients could be potentially included as stakeholders but their welfare might be equally valued relative to that of wealthier clients. This simple comparison between two Asian MFIs takes us to the bottom of more serious empirical findings: BRAC's average loan size for the year 2007 is US$188, Spandana's $199. Can a difference of US$11 make Spandana a mission-drifting institution relative to BRAC?

Somewhat related and contrary to the "received wisdom", MFIs' legal status does not seem to appear as an important determinant of a poverty-reduction mission. The institutional characteristics are shown in column four. A case in point is the well-known Grameen Bank of Bangladesh, which does not advertise itself as an NGO despite the fact that its main mission is to alleviate poverty. In theory, the Grameen Bank is a cooperative, although

[8]Note, however, that outreach numbers can be misleading. While they deliver some indication of the number of clients served by institution, those numbers hide market structure considerations. For example, the Grameen Bank, ASA, and BRAC are the three main institutions serving nearly 20 million clients in Bangladesh. Compartamos, on the other hand, faces little competition, and does not even serve 600 thousand clients in Mexico, in the year 2007, according to the data provided by MIX.

[9]A notable example is that of the Grameen Bank, whose mission statement, as reported by MIX is N/A. The mission statement for this particular institution was obtained from the website of Grameen Foundation, headquartered in the United States.

[10]Our argument at this stage is on the main missions, as advertized by the institutions themselves, not on the means to attain those objectives. In the particular case of BRAC, the main mission is poverty reduction. The other missions are however advertized by BRAC itself even though it uses affiliates like Self-Employed Women's Association (SEWA).

[11]The Human Development Index (HDI) delivers a broader notion of poverty involving income, health, and education. For more on how this index is derived, see the Human Development Reports, published annually by the United Nations.

the bulk of the funds it mobilizes does not come from its members.[12] The Grameen Bank, quite independently of its legal status, is not the only MFI advertising itself as having poverty-reduction as its main mission. In particular, four out of the top 10 MFIs state quite explicitly that exact same poverty reduction mission. Interestingly, the four of them are located in South Asia. In particular, and according to recent estimates by the World Bank, South Asia continues to host the largest number of individuals living in poverty, and this fact alone should in principle attract massive numbers of poor into the microfinance industry. On the other hand, poor and middle-income countries in, for example, Latin America are known to have underdeveloped financial systems making MFIs an attractive source of funding for unbanked wealthier clients.

Identifying the notion of poverty with average loan size dates back to Mosley (1996) who explains that Bolivia's Bancosol deviates from its mission by serving larger loans to wealthier clients for the sake of self-sustainability, but at the expense of deviating resources away from the poor who request smaller loans.[13] Ever since, average loan size has become the most widely used proxy in quantitative studies showing that some MFIs like Bancosol might prioritize self-sustainability at the expense of their poverty-reduction or outreach maximization mission. Moreover, MFIs often advertize small average loan sizes as an important indicator pertaining to outreach, and as a reinforcing signal for their main mission. Mix (2008), for example, reports that the average loan size for the four poverty-reduction MFIs displayed in Table 15.1 for the year 2007 was estimated to be of around USD 175 compared with USD 1,065 for the remaining six.[14]

---

[12] We should note that the case of the Grameen Bank is rather peculiar in that it advertizes itself as a fully-regulated bank. In reality, however, while the Grameen Bank belongs to its members and can therefore be defined as a cooperative, the little savings it mobilizes from its members makes it look like a "hybrid", that is, a bank-cooperative institution.

[13] More precisely, the ratio of average loan size and per capita GDP. For a very comprehensive discussion on this, see Schreiner (2001) and Dunford (2002).

[14] Clearly, a per capita comparison is more meaningful. Mix does not report per capita average loan size for the year 2007. For the year 2006, however, percentage average loan size per capita for the four poverty-reduction MFIs was 24.94 compared to 34.6 for the remaining six. This approximation shows that while the gap is reduced, as expected, the 10 percentage points higher for the non-poverty reduction MFIs is not negligible. Interestingly, region-wise, the percentages for the year 2006 show consistency. In particular, the four poverty-reduction MFIs shown in Table 15.1, all in Asia, review an average per capita loan size of 23.94 compared to 28.31 for their non-poverty reduction counterparts, also in Asia. Not surprisingly, the average for three Latin American MFIs, namely, 40.89, is the highest of all.

Somewhat surprisingly, the literature on mission drift leaves aside interest rate considerations.[15] Even though interest rate considerations are beyond the scope of this paper, note that in Table 15.1, the four poverty-reduction-driven MFIs review an estimated average interest rate of approximately 17 percent, while the remaining six charge an average of 28 percent.[16] Out of these six, four are commercial MFIs.[17]

Thus, assuming that a good proxy of mission drift relates to the tendency by MFIs to serve unbanked wealthier clients who request relatively large average loan sizes can be a bit of a stretch indeed, but this is what empirical researchers do. And they might not be totally wrong. Table 15.1 appears to strengthen what empirical researchers might have in mind. At one extreme is Bangladesh's ASA, which reviews an average loan size (the lowest among all 10) of about US$ 67 which has remained pretty stable over the past four years. At the other extreme is Mexico's Banco Compartamos which is above average in terms of average loan size set at US$ 450. Banco Compartamos is often portrayed as an example of a mission-drifting MFI. ASA, on the other hand, is often praised as a cost-minimization institution, which has managed to be highly efficient while serving massive numbers of poor clients.

The above example illustrates rather well the meaning of mission drift so far. Generally speaking, mission drift is observed when an MFI transits from being a NGO to a commercial for-profit bank, and during this process it increases its average loan size.[18] A typical case in point is Banco

---

[15]For a comprehensive review on interest rates, see Hudon (2007).

[16]The proxy for interest rates was obtained from MIX MFIs profile. It is stated as "financial revenue ratio". This is roughly cash financial revenue divided by average gross portfolio, which is the proxy for average interest rate use by, for example, Cull *et al.* (2008). We should note, however, that unlike the MFIs that state poverty reduction as their main mission, the interest rate range for the remaining six is huge (16.12 percent for Caja Popular Mexicana to 68.48 percent for Compartamos).

[17]Cull *et al.* (2008) distinguish commercial MFIs and NGOs, however, showing that the latter charge higher interest rates. Their explanation relies on the fact that NGOs face higher costs while serving a relatively poorer clientele. In contrast, Ghosh and Van Tassel (2008) suggest that NGOs charge higher interest rates because these type of MFIs are funded by profit-oriented donors.

[18]The passage of an MFI from a NGO to a fully-regulated bank is not a necessary condition for an institution to deviate from its mission. As documented by González and Rosenberg (2006), and Cull *et al.* (2008), relative to fully-regulated commercial MFIs, NGOs often charge higher interest rates. Interest rate considerations should indeed be part of a more comprehensive notion of mission drift, as suggested by Ashta and Hudon (2009) in their work on Banco Compartamos. From a purely theoretical standpoint, and for the sake of simplicity, however, interest rate considerations are beyond the scope of our analysis. We nevertheless raise this important issue in the conclusion of this paper.

Compartamos (Ashta and Hudon, 2009). The question as to why Banco Compartamos and, more generally, Latin American MFIs have a tendency to be more commercially-oriented relative to those MFIs which are based in Asia, has never been raised in scholarly articles. We will try to elaborate on this question in Section 6.[19]

Column six in Table 15.1 shows that MFIs might have other missions, such as prioritizing women clients. This fits well with UNDP reports showing that women in developing economies are the poorest of the poor.[20] Thus, yet another indicator to assess if MFIs are being faithful to their poverty-reduction mission is related to gender. Both average loan size and gender are being considered in Cull *et al.*'s empirical investigation (2009) on the commercialization of microfinance, and its effects on poverty reduction. The authors conclude that recent commercialization trends are "bad" news for the poor because commercialization is being accompanied by larger loan sizes and less focus on women.

Cross-MFI empirical studies such as the Cull *et al.* (2009) study should be taken with a great deal of caution. To make our point, let's go back for a moment to Table 15.1 where outperformers are located in either South Asia or Latin America, with the former generally considered a low-income region while the latter a middle-income region. Both regions are thick in microfinance relative to, say, Sub Saharan Africa (Armendáriz and Vanroose, 2009). Average loan sizes are not surprisingly different in both these regions. However, common sense indicates that this is normal. In particular, according to the recent OECD report, average GDP per head in Latin America is nearly three times higher than its Asian counterpart. The main point of this article is that, whatever the interpretation of that such cross-MFIs regressions, researchers remain unable to distinguish whether higher average loan sizes are due to cross-subsidization or to mission drift.

Ghosh and Van Tassel (2008), on the other hand, suggest that the most accurate approach to deal with the mission drift issue is neither loan size nor gender, but the poverty gap ratio. Their model is most adequate for clarifying the notion of poverty reduction and mission drift. Their approach, however, delivers little guidance for empirical researchers, if only because poverty is more difficult to measure in practice, and because the poverty

[19] A notable example can be found in Rhyne (2001). However, her historical analysis focuses mostly on Bolivia on the one hand, and is not viewed through the lens of theory, on the other hand.

[20] See, for example, Armendáriz and Vanroose (2009) and Agier and Szafarz (2010).

gap ratio is based on poverty line estimates which are already controversial among econometricians.[21]

Another difference between the Cull *et al.* (2009) and the Ghosh and Van Tassel (2008) articles deserves attention. The former emphasizes commercial MFIs, and suggests that mission drift takes place because these institutions desire to attract more socially-responsible investors. The latter emphasizes for-profit NGOs, and suggests that mission drift results from MFIs' efforts to attract more capital from profit-oriented donors. In both papers, mission drift is perceived as a device for attracting more capital to fund MFIs. In both instances, the presence of a third party socially-responsible investors in the case of Cull *et al.* (2009), and for-profit donors in the case of Ghosh and Van Tassel (2008) is key. In what follows, we will argue that there is no need to complicate the picture by including donors or socially-responsible investors in order to explain why MFIs may deviate from their poverty-reduction mission. Simply put, the rather obscure notion of mission drift can be elucidated without the presence of a "third party" — be these donors or socially responsible investors.

3 Mission Drift from a Theoretical Standpoint

Somewhat surprisingly, the notion of "mission" in economics is rarely used and studied in great detail. Instead, the literature tends to identify mission with objective. A notable exception is a distinguished tradition in public policy, first started by Wilson (1989). His work focuses on incentives for government officials to adhere to an institution's mission. Following Wilson's tradition, Dewatripont *et al.* (1999) use a principal-agent model *à la* Holmstrom and Milgrom (1991) where agents pursue multiple missions. They show that while organizations might gain from pursuing multiple missions, they can lose focus leading to less autonomy being delegated to government officials (or agents).

From a purely theoretical standpoint, and with the notable exception of Ghosh and Van Tassel (2008), modeling MFIs' objective function adopts a principal-agent approach to highlight adverse selection and moral hazard issues, which can be potentially circumvented via contract design between an MFI and peer groups. Examples of this approach abound. See, for example, Stiglitz (1990), Banerjee *et al.* (1994), Besley and Coate (1995), Armendáriz

[21]For an in-depth discussion, see Blundell and Preston (1998).

(1999), Conning (1999), Ghatak (1999), Ghatak (2000), Armendáriz and Gollier (2000), Jain and Mansuri (2003), and Tedeschi (2006), Labie *et al.* (2010), and many others.

Without underestimating the merits of the principal-agent approach adopted by the vast majority of authors who have written sophisticated models in order to gain important insights into optimal financial contracting in the absence of collateral, our approach in this article differs widely in three important ways. First, and in contrast with Ghosh and Van Tassel (2008), our focus is in just one mission or objective to be maximized, and this maximizing objective function involves one and only one entity, namely, the MFI itself.[22] Second, that particular mission or objective is well-defined: a representative MFI is assumed to have a poverty reduction mission (henceforth: the representative MFI is assumed to maximize outreach).[23] Last but not least, our model shows that mission drift is the result of an optimization process by an outreach-maximizing MFI facing different costs while serving a heterogeneous clientele of poor and wealthier borrowers.

4 The Absence of a Transaction Cost-Driven Mission Drift

Transaction costs are typically at the heart of most discussions on mission drift. Using loan size as a proxy for the poverty level of clients, Cull *et al.* (2008)'s recent findings indicate that MFIs with the highest profit levels perform the weakest in terms of outreach. Also, larger loan sizes are associated with lower average costs, which supports the idea that those institutions that target poorest borrowers struggle in pursuit of financial sustainability. Do transaction costs play a crucial role at explaining why MFIs might drift from their outreach maximization objective? In what follows, we will show

---

[22]Simply put, donors or socially responsible investors do not play any role in our framework. While introducing them might help us gain important principal-agent insights in microfinance, our conjecture is that our main results will remain fundamentally the same.

[23]Outreach and poverty are different notions. However, we use these two terms interchangeably for two reasons: First, the notion of outreach is closely related to microfinance while poverty is much more general, and we wish to derive some testable implications which are simpler to deal with using the notion of outreach. Second, entering into a discussion on what is the most accurate definition of poverty and measures relying on fussy concepts such as the poverty line are beyond the scope of this paper. For a discussion, see Sen (1999).

that a mission drift phenomenon, which is solely based on transaction costs, lacks theoretical support, and is therefore misleading.

Consider an MFI which is endowed with an amount of capital, K, as its only source of funds for extending loans to poor clients. Suppose that the MFI serves N clients via loans of an identical amount s. Assume that the MFI faces fixed costs F (with $F < K$) and variable transaction cost $T(N)$. It follows that the MFI's total cost is given by:

$$C = F + T(N) = f(N), \quad \text{with } f(0) = F \quad \text{and} \quad f'(.) \geq 0 \tag{1}$$

Assume that the MFI's objective is to maximize outreach via micro-loans, that is, the MFI maximizes outreach, N, by controlling the loan size, s, subject to a budget constraint. Specifically, the MFI's maximization program is:

$$\begin{aligned} &\underset{s\geq 0}{\text{Max}}\, N \\ &\text{s.t. } K = sN + f(N) \end{aligned} \tag{2}$$

In the absence of costs, $f(N) = 0$, and the MFI's optimization function is simply:[24]

$$\underset{s\geq 0}{\text{Max}}\, \frac{K}{s} \tag{3}$$

and the trivial solution, for all possible values of K, is a corner solution: $s^* = 0, N^* = +\infty$.

Clearly, when $f(N) \neq 0$, total costs increase and, all things equal, higher costs reduce the amount of resources that the MFI can use for serving its clientele. Consider, for example, the case where transaction costs are linear, that is: $f(N) = F + yN, y > 0$. Then, the MFI's objective function becomes:

$$\underset{s\geq 0}{\text{Max}}\, \frac{K - F}{s + \gamma} \tag{4}$$

And the optimal solution is again reached at $s^* = 0$. We should note, however, that under this particular scenario, as $K = sN + F + \gamma N$, the number of (tiny) loans is finite.[25] In particular: $N^* = \frac{K-F}{\gamma}$. Thus, while linear transaction costs reduce outreach, such costs alone do not alter the optimal loan size. Moreover, as we show in the Appendix, this result is robust for

[24]Note that even if the MFI is a NGO receiving grants with amount linked to the size of its loans: $K = K(s)$, $K'(.) \leq 0$, the solution remains the same.

[25]The capital available for loans, K, is exogenous. Moreover, we ignore the repayment probability which, in the steady-state, could increase the value of K. Actually, at the optimum; we have a finite number of infinitesimal loans resulting in negligible repayments.

quadratic and other types of transaction cost functions. We thus have the following:

Result 1: *When all loans are identical, transaction costs reduce the number of loans but do not increase their size. Therefore, the standard argument that a mission drift phenomenon is a direct consequence of transaction costs alone does not seem to be supported by theory.*

Now suppose that the MFI can choose between two types of clients or, equivalently, between two types of financial products, 1 and 2, respectively. Product 1 is available to the poor, its size, $s_1 \geq 0$, which is assumed to be chosen by the MFI.[26] Product 2, on the other hand, is made available to unbanked wealthier clients. Assume that the latter clients require a minimal size: $s_2 \geq \underline{s}$ to start up an investment project which can only be financed by the MFI.[27] The cost function $f(N_1, N_2)$ now depends on the number of loans for each product: N_1 for type 1 clients, and N_2 for type 2 clients. The MFI's objective function in this case is:

$$\begin{aligned} &\underset{s_1, s_2 \geq 0}{\text{Max}} (N_1 + N_2) \\ &\text{s.t. } K = s_1 N_1 + s_2 N_2 + f(N_1, N_2) \\ &\quad\;\; s_2 \geq \underline{s} \end{aligned} \tag{5}$$

As in the previous case, when $f(N_1, N_2) = 0$, the MFI's optimal solution is reached via extending an infinite number of tiny loans. But as type 2 loans are bounded by $\underline{s}$, the MFI will only serve type 1 clients, i.e., the poor. Note that in this setting outreach is being maximized, and that the optimal solution regarding loan size results from the model, and not from the MFIs' mission as such.[28]

The one reason which is often invoked to justify the existence of a shift from type 1 to type 2 clients seems to be intimately related to cost considerations. We consider here an asymmetric cost function making the clients

---

[26]Implicit in this assumption is that the MFI has all the bargaining power. This might be true for several large MFIs that enjoy monopoly power. An alternative justification to this assumption is that the size of the loan offered by the MFI is incentive-compatible.

[27]Implicit in this assumption is that there is only one MFI serving all clients in the loan market. Our results will not be altered if we were to assume that the MFI is perfectly competitive and, as long as the loan contract is incentive-compatible, both types of clients will face the exact same loan contract from all MFIs operating in the market.

[28]It could not be otherwise because mission drift (larger loans) is only conceivable when the optimization is held on another objective function.

of type 2 less costly to the MFI. We formalize this argument by assuming an additive cost function which gives more weight to loans of type 1.[29]

$$f(N_1, N_2) = \gamma_1 N_1 + \gamma_2 N_2, \qquad \gamma_1 \geq \gamma_2 > 0 \tag{6}$$

And the objective of the MFI in this case is:[30]

$$\begin{aligned} &\underset{s_1, s_2 \geq 0}{\text{Max}} (N_1 + N_2) \\ &\text{s.t. } K = (s_1 + \gamma_1)N_1 + (\gamma_2 + s_2)N_2 \\ &\quad s_2 \geq \underline{s} \end{aligned} \tag{7}$$

The MFI now faces a trade-off: it can benefit by adhering to its mission via the provision of a large number of tiny loans to the poor clients at a unit cost γ_1 on the one hand, and it can profitably serve a clientele of unbanked wealthier clients who require larger loans at a lower unit cost γ_2 at the expense of drifting from its poverty reduction mission on the other. Serving clients of type 1 only will deliver, as before, a situation where s_1 is infinitesimal and $N_1 = \frac{K}{\gamma_1}$. At the other extreme, focusing on clients of type 2 only will result in $s_2 = \underline{s}$ (the threshold required by wealthier borrowers) and $N_2 = \frac{K}{\gamma_2 + \underline{s}}$. In this simple linear set-up, either solution is optimal, depending on the value of the parameters. In particular, if $\frac{K}{\gamma_2 + \underline{s}} > \frac{K}{\gamma_1}$, or equivalently $\gamma_2 + \underline{s} < \gamma_1$, then, the MFI will only serve clients of type 2:

$$N_1^* = 0, \quad N_2^* = \frac{K}{\gamma_2 + \underline{s}} \tag{8}$$

Clearly, this case results from a situation where serving poor clients is exceedingly expensive. The number of unbanked wealthier clients served, on the other hand, decreases with the cost of serving these borrowers, and with the start-up cost that each better-off borrower requests to make a profitable investment. But serving unbanked wealthier clients increases with the amount of capital that the MFI can raise from donors and/or socially-responsible investors.

[29]What we have in mind here is that serving the poor is more costly because more monitoring effort is needed, and this additional effort is costly for the MFI. More generally, this assumption may summarize all the reasons that make poorer clients less lucrative; i.e., the poor are financially illiterate, healthwise are less productive, have limited business savvy, require training sessions, etc. Because our model does not explicitly spell out loan — repayments, a simple and realistic way of interpreting this assumption is that the additional cost incurred by an MFI that serves the poorest comes at the expense of less capital for financial intermediation.

[30]In order to avoid cumbersome notations, we assume here that $F = 0$, or alternatively, that K stands for $K - F$.

When $\gamma_2 + \underline{s} > \gamma_1$, that is, when serving the poor is not too costly, we have:

$$N_1^* = \frac{K}{\gamma_1}, \quad N_2^* = 0 \tag{9}$$

The number of poor clients that the MFI will serve at the optimum will again decrease with the cost of serving the poor, but increase with the amount of capital that the MFI can raise. This analytical exercise delivers the following:

***Result 2*:** *In the presence of two types of clients, poor clients and unbanked wealthier clients, an MFI facing different transaction costs, high for the poor and low for the unbanked wealthier, will end up serving either the poor or the unbanked wealthier, but not both. Thus, MFIs that are faithful to their outreach maximization objective, do not derive any benefit from having a portfolio of poor and unbanked wealthier clients. Quite simply, MFIs do not gain anything from serving poor and unbanked wealthier clients simultaneously. Note that, when* $\gamma_2 + \underline{s} = \gamma_1$, *the MFI might be indifferent between serving either type of clients, but serving the unbanked wealthier might be detrimental to its poverty reduction mission. Hence, mission drift cannot result from just transaction cost differentials between the poor and the unbanked wealthier clients.*

5 MFI Heterogeneity-Driven Mission Drift

In the previous model, the two types of clients were identified with two different cost functions (high for the poor and low for the unbanked wealthier), but both type of clients' contributions to outreach maximization is identical. In other words, in the scenario described in the previous section, the MFI does not resolve its trade-off between serving poor and unbanked wealthier clients by having a "mixed" portfolio. While wealthier clients are cost-effective, these clients do not tangibly contribute *less* to the MFI's outreach maximization objective. Now suppose that unbanked wealthier clients weight less in a particular MFI's objective function. Then, unbanked wealthier customers are more cost-effective and therefore more profitable in that $\gamma_2 + \underline{s} < \gamma_1$ but they are also burdensome. As we shall soon show, this simple characterization of the MFI objective function can lead to mission drift and to cross-subsidization. Moreover, such an objective function is deliberately constructed with the use of quantifiable and observable variables such as the number of clients and average loan size. Specifically, the MFI maximization program is:

$$\begin{aligned} &\underset{s_1,s_2\geq 0}{\text{Max}}\,(N_1+\delta N_2),\ 0\leq\delta\leq 1\\ &\text{s.t. } K=(s_1+\gamma_1)N_1+(\gamma_2+s_2)N_2\\ &\qquad s_2\geq \underline{s} \end{aligned} \tag{10}$$

where parameter δ captures *the degree of concern that the MFI has as it deviates from its mission* via the inclusion of wealthier clients. While this concern is MFI-specific, it can be easily captured by differences in MFIs' profiles (see Table 15.1). Clearly, (10) is equivalent to (7) if one replaces N_2 by $\tilde{N}_2=\delta N_2$. Then: $(\gamma_2+s_2)N_2$ is to be replaced by $\frac{(\gamma_2+s_2)}{\delta}\tilde{N}_2$, which boils down to increasing the cost that the MFI incurs as it includes wealthier clients in its portfolio. In the particular case where δ is chosen such that $\frac{\gamma_2+\underline{s}}{\delta}=\gamma_1$, then both types of clients may coexist. And our main point here is that one might find it difficult in practice to distinguish if such co-existence of poor and unbanked wealthier clients is due to cross-subsidization or to mission drift.

If, on the other hand, we allow for unbanked wealthier clients to be less costly, that is, if $\gamma_2+\underline{s}<\gamma_1$ the inequalities linking the cost function parameters become $\gamma_1\geq 0, \gamma_1>\gamma_2$, and the sign of $\gamma_2+\underline{s}$ can be negative.[31] When $\gamma_2+\underline{s}<0$, then cross-subsidization is indeed possible. So, a plausible explanation of what is referred to as "cross-subsidization" for an outreach maximizing MFI could be attributed to a deliberate bias in favour of unbanked wealthier borrowers as these borrowers are *de facto* creating a positive externality on poor borrowers.

Typically, relative to rural clients, urban poor are more literate, fill in paperwork on their own more easily, and can even offer some form of collateral when requesting a loan to the MFI (Armendáriz and Morduch, 2000). Because their presence is not burdensome to the institution's mission, an overwhelming representation of unbanked wealthier borrowers in, for example, urban areas might not necessarily mean that urban MFIs deviated from

[31]This could well be the case if the credit risk is negligible because the borrowers are wealthy enough and the bank officers do not even bother spending time screening or monitoring their actions. In that case, these clients offer benefit to the MFI rather than costs. More generally, as our simplistic model considers K as a fixed exogenous budget, one can interpret γ_1 and γ_2 as net costs, i.e., the costs minus the benefits associated to expected reimbursements in a steady-state risk-neutral perspective. According to that view, assuming $\gamma_1\geq 0$ and $\gamma_2+\underline{s}<0$ means that the very poor clients are costly and served solely because of the MFI social mission while less poor clients are profitable to the MFI.

their poverty reduction mission. Distinguishing between mission drift and cross-subsidization in practice, however, might be difficult, if not impossible.

From a theoretical standpoint, however, we have just argued that cross-subsidization is only possible when unbanked wealthier clients are profitable. Moreover, it can also be the case that the population of potential clients that are very poor and unbanked is relatively small. Then, when looking at an MFI's profile which is serving a large number of unbanked wealthier clients does not necessarily mean that such an MFI is drifting from its mission. It may well be the case that, cost-wise, there is an upper bound to the number of poor that the institution can serve. Unbanked wealthier are relatively more abundant than unbanked poor in many middle-income regions too, which in turn justifies further the contrast between Asia and Latin-America discussed in greater detail below.[32]

Now consider the limit case where $\delta = 0$, that is, a situation where the MFI's objective is serving the poor only. Then, either the unbanked wealthier represent a profitable side business ($\gamma_2 + \underline{s} < 0$) that does not contribute to the mission, but offers additional capital for reaching the poor. Or, the unbanked wealthier clients are not profitable ($\gamma_2 + \underline{s} > 0$) and are simply neglected. In the polar case where $\delta = 1$, the MFI gives equal weight to both types of clients. This brings us back to equation (7). For intermediate cases, $\delta \in (0,1)$, the MFI decision pertaining to the type of clients to be served depends on the direction of the inequality between the weight δ attributed to wealthier clients in the MFI's objective function, on the one hand, and on the cost ratio $\frac{\gamma_2+\underline{s}}{\gamma_1}$, on the other.

For any given value of $\delta \in (0,1)$, in populations with a relatively large number of poor people, the size of an MFI's clientele in terms of depth of outreach can be potentially large indeed. In contrast, in regions where the number of unbanked poor is relatively small, depth of outreach is limited, and the poor can be more costly to reach, particularly in areas where population densities are low. Consequently, the threshold required to move from poor to unbanked wealthier clients may be region-specific. On the

[32]In particular (see Table 15.1), at the one end of the spectrum, we have low-income countries like Bangladesh where income per head in 2007 was US$1400. At the other end of the spectrum, there are upper middle-income countries like Mexico where income per head in 2007 was US$14,500. Not surprisingly, and according to the data published by MIX for that particular year, Grameen Bank Bangladesh alone had over six million active clients compared to just over eight hundred thousand for the case of Banco Compartamos in Mexico. Average loan size for the Grameen Bank was US$79, and for Compartamos was $450. (As explained in footnote 9, MIX does not publish data on average loan size in per capita for the year 2007 and beyond.)

Table 15.2: Possible outcomes depending on MFIs' concerns and region-specific parameters.

	$\gamma_2 + \underline{s} < 0$	$\gamma_2 + \underline{s} = 0$	$0 < \gamma_2 + \underline{s} < \gamma_1\delta$	$\gamma_2 + \underline{s} = \gamma_1\delta$	$\gamma_2 + \underline{s} > \gamma_1\delta$
$\delta = 0$	$N_1 = +\infty$ $N_2 = +\infty$ Cross-subsidization.	$N_1 = \frac{K}{\gamma_1}$ N_2 undeterm. Possible mission drift (up to discretion).	Impossible.	$N_1 = \frac{K}{\gamma_1}$, $N_2 = 0$ No mission drift.	$N_1 = \frac{K}{\gamma_1}$, $N_2 = 0$ No mission drift.
$0 < \delta \leq 1$	$N_1 = +\infty$ $N_2 = +\infty$ Cross-subsidization.	$N_1 = \frac{K}{\gamma_1}$ $N_2 = +\infty$ Mission drift.	$N_1 = 0$ $N_2 = \frac{K}{\gamma_2 + \underline{s}}$ Full mission drift.	$N_1 \in \left[0, \frac{K}{\gamma_1}\right]$ $N_2 = \frac{K - \gamma_1 N_1}{\gamma_2 + \underline{s}}$ Possible mission drift (up to discretion).	$N_1 = \frac{K}{\gamma_1}$, $N_2 = 0$ No mission drift.

surface, outreach penetration looks considerably larger in countries such as Bangladesh where the Grameen Bank alone reaches out to over six million clients whose average loan size is small, relative to, for example, Banco Compartamos in Mexico, which reaches at most 10 times *less* clients with an average loan size which is three times larger. Thus, if we are to take at face value the idea that a good proxy for an institution being faithful to its mission is given by average loan size alone, then all MFIs, except for those operating in South Asia and Sub-Saharan Africa, have deviated from their mission, which is confusing at best, misleading at worst.[33]

Table 15.2 summarizes the results. A good benchmark is provided by the set of points where the MFI is indifferent between its two types of clients: $\gamma_2 + \underline{s} = \gamma_1 \delta$. In this set, when δ increases, the cost for the MFI as it deviates from its mission is offset by its gain in terms of the number of poor whose investment projects can be financed. For a given δ, increasing γ_1 (or alternatively, decreasing $\gamma_2 + \underline{s}$) makes the MFI deviate from its mission to finance the increasing costs of serving the poor.

What Table 15.1 shows is that the interplay between the weight that the MFI gives to serving the poor, as captured by δ, which is MFI-specific, the cost parameters γ_1, γ_2, and $\underline{s}$ which are region-specific, deliver myriad outcomes. Chief among these are (a) mission drift, (b) no mission drift, and (c) cross-subsidization.

Figure 15.1 represents the three possible outcomes of the model. In this figure, the parameter γ_1 has a fixed positive value while $\gamma_2 + \underline{s}$ can take any

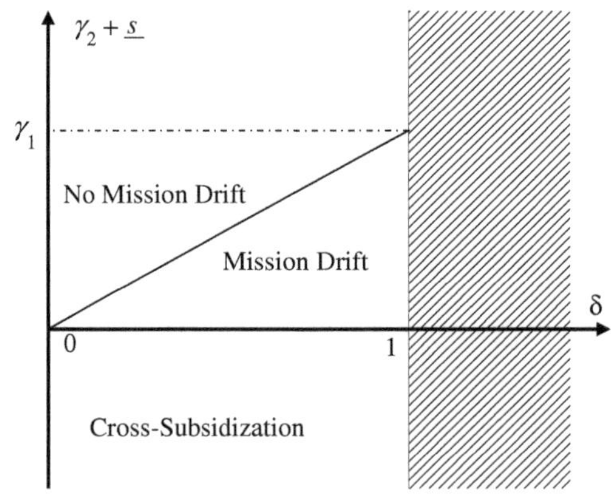

Figure 15.1: A representation of the possible outcomes.

[33]Pro Mujer in Latin America, for example, is one of the most poverty-oriented MFIs in the world.

real value, positive or negative, and δ varies in $[0, 1]$. The cost of burdensome wealthier clients ($\gamma_2 + \underline{s}$ on the vertical axis) is a crucial determinant of how far the MFI can continue serving the poor. The cross-subsidization zone corresponds to negative values of $\gamma_2+\underline{s}$, or "profits" which the MFI can extract from unbanked wealthier clients. With the exception of the indifference line $\gamma_2 + \underline{s} = \gamma_1\delta$, the cross-subsidization zone is the only place in the graph where the two types of clients can coexist. An important prediction of our model can therefore be stated in the following:

Result 3: *Microfinance institutions which serve a significant number of unbanked poor and unbanked wealthier clients are not necessarily mission-drifting institutions. These institutions' commitment to contribute to poverty reduction may be compatible with having a side business with unbanked wealthier clients, as these clients allow for cross-subsidization for the sake of MFIs' outreach maximization objective.*

6 Contrasting Latin America and Asia

Microfinance started in the mid-1970s from parallel movements in sparsely populated Latin America and densely-populated Asia (Armendáriz and Morduch, 2010). It has recently been established that the two regions where microfinance activity is the highest are also Latin America and Asia (Armendáriz and Vanroose, 2009). This is somewhat captured in Table 15.1 above where the top 10 MFIs in terms of number of clients served are all located in either Asia or Latin America.[34] Regarding poverty, recent estimates by the World Bank (2004) suggest that South Asia hosts approximately 31 percent of the world's poor while a similar estimate for Latin America is only eight percent.

As seen in the previous section, if serving the poor is not too costly, an outreach-maximizer MFI is unlikely to drift from its mission. This might be the case of densely-populated South Asia where, relative to Latin America, the poor can be more easily served, if only because the number of individuals considered to be poor are four times larger.[35] The relative abundance of

---

[34]Christen (2000), however, point out that there is a huge difference across the very diverse Latin-American countries; some, like Nicaragua and Haiti, might be just as poor as some of their Asian counterparts.

[35]Vanroose (2009) finds a population density coefficient which is positive and significant in determining outreach.

poor individuals make γ_1 to be considerably smaller in Asia relative to the γ_1 in Latin America. This means that for the same δ, an MFI in Asia will find it easy to portray itself as an MFI with a considerably higher depth of outreach penetration.

On the other hand, the scope for cross-subsidization in Latin America is much higher, because all countries in Latin America (with the exception of Haiti and Nicaragua) have a GDP per head which is, on average, three times higher than the one observed in South Asia (OECD Report, 2005). Latin America as a whole remains a middle-income region. Its banking sector, however, is highly underdeveloped. Hence, our conjecture is that the relatively wealthier but unbanked individuals in Latin America are, by and large, being served by MFIs. And the prediction of our model is that if serving the unbanked wealthier individuals is profitable, there is ample scope for cross-subsidization, a conjecture worth exploring empirically. This conjecture suggests that judging an institution as having mission-drifted by looking at the average loan size alone is misleading indeed. More information is needed. Are such institutions *a priori* labeled mission-drifted institutions keeping an important number of poor clients in their portfolio? Are poorer clients being crowded out by wealthier clients? These are real challenges for empirical researchers.

However, a dynamic analysis would be needed in order to assess empirically if MFIs in Latin America are scaling up *and* crowding out poor clients as per González-Vega *et al.* (1996)'s definition. We strongly believe that this observation is worth exploring. As this paper goes to press, Armendáriz *et al.* (forthcoming) are making further inquiries in this direction. These inquiries should further guide empirical analysis, and deliver a clearer picture of whether MFIs are indeed deviating from their missions. Important questions are up for grabs here: Is the current commercialization of microfinance truly biased against the poor as the recent Cull *et al.* (2009) paper suggests?

7 Concluding Remarks

In this paper, we have delivered a very simple model where outreach-maximizing MFIs can deviate from their mission. The model predicts that mission drift will result from the interplay of MFI-specific parameters, such as the weight that the MFI gives to serving the poor, and from country-specific parameters pertaining to the cost of reaching the poor. From a policy standpoint, our model highlights that donors and socially responsible investors can be easily misled by MFIs which are serving unbanked wealthier populations. This prediction is thought-provoking as retaining unbanked wealthier might represent a challenge for MFIs to better serve the poor. While our model is purposely simple to guide future empirical research on the subject, a more complete picture of mission drift should include interest rates and market structure considerations. However, data constraints are a major challenge here.

Besides, interest rates might be relatively high due to country-specific considerations as well. The fact that Sub-Saharan countries host a much larger population of poor individuals relative to Latin America, and that outreach is higher in the latter is a clear example. This might call for subsidies for MFIs which are operating in those sparsely-populated regions where access to poor households is time-consuming, where the scope for profitable projects is limited, and where microfinance expertise is lacking. Again, these region-specific considerations might offer crucial guidance for donors that prioritize social over self-sustainability objectives.

But interest rates might be also high due to monopoly power. And this raises the question as to whether the notion of mission drift is, once more, misleading empirical research. Monopolistic interest rates *together* with low average loan size can deliver a more transparent picture of what mission drift really means. This notion of mission drift merits further scrutiny. Ethical considerations aside, monopolistic pricing of microfinance products creates adverse selection and moral hazard inefficiencies. Shouldn't this be part of our notion of mission drift? From an empirical standpoint, going beyond average loan size as a proxy for mission drift by at least integrating interest rates into the picture while controlling for market structure is a step in the right direction.

Last but not least, insights can be gained by constructing a dynamic model. In a dynamic model, key questions as to why MFIs transit from being NGOs prioritizing poverty to commercial MFIs prioritizing profitability can be tackled. Is this truly the case? Is client heterogeneity a necessity that emerges over time? Why do MFIs wish to scale up in the first place if they risk deviating from their poverty-reduction objective? Region-specific considerations aside, should MFIs deliberately tap wealthier clients in their scaling-up process? Is this a viable solution for outreach growth for MFIs to fence themselves off from a situation where donor aid dries up? Is donor aid itself a variable which depends on outreach growth?

References

Aniket, K (2007). Does Subsidising the Cost of Capital Really Help the Poorest? An Analysis of Saving Opportunities in Group Lending. ESE Discussion Paper No. 140.

Armendáriz, B (1999). On the design of a credit agreement with peer monitoring. *Journal of Development Economics*, 60(1), 79–104.

Armendáriz, B and C Gollier (2000). Peer group formation in an adverse selection model. *Economic Journal*, 110(465), 632–643.

Armendáriz, B and J Morduch (2000). Microfinance beyond group lending. *The Economics of Transition*, 8(2), 401–420.

Armendáriz, B and J Morduch (2010). *The Economics of Microfinance*, 2nd ed. Cambridge, MA: MIT Press.

Armendáriz, B and A Vanroose (2009). Uncovering three microfinance myths: Does age matter? *Reflects et Perspectives de la Vie Economique*, 48(3), 7–17.

Armendáriz, B, B d'Espallier, M Hudon and A Szafarz (forthcoming). Subsidy Uncertainty and Microfinance Mission Drift. Center for European Research in Microfinance (CERMi), ULB.

Ashta, A and M Hudon (2009). To Whom Should we be Fair? Ethical Issues in Balancing Stakeholder Interests from Banco Compartamos Case Study. Manuscript, Center for European Research in Microfinance (CERMi), ULB.

Aubert, C, A de Janvry and E Sadoulet (2009). Designing credit agent incentives to prevent mission drift in pro-poor microfinance institutions. *Journal of Development Economics*, 90(1), 153–162.

Banerjee, A, T Besley and T Guinnane (1994). Thy neighbor's keeper: The design of a credit cooperative with theory and a test. *Quarterly Journal of Economics*, 109(2), 491–515.

Besley, T and S Coate (1995). Group lending, repayment incentives and social collateral. *Journal of Development Economics*, 46(1), 1–18.

Christen, RP (2000). *Commercialization and Mission Drift: The Transformation of Microfinance in Latin America.* Consultative Group to Assist the Poor (CGAP), Washington DC.

Conning, J (1999). Outreach, sustainability and leverage in monitored and peer-monitored lending. *Journal of Development Economics*, 60, 51–77.

Copestake, J (2007). Mainstreaming microfinance: Social performance management or mission drift? *World Development*, 35(10), 1721–1738.

Cull, R, A Demirgüç-Kunt and J Morduch (2007). Financial performance and outreach: A global analysis of leading microbanks. *Economic Journal*, 117(517), 107–133.

Cull, R, A Demirgüç-Kunt and J Morduch (2009). Microfinance meets the market. *Journal of Economic Perspectives*, 23(1), 167–192.

Dewatripont, M, I Jewitt and J Tirole (1999). The economics of career concerns, Part II: Application to missions and accountability of government agencies. *Review of Economic Studies*, 66(1), 199–217.

Dunford, C (2002). What's wrong with loan size? Freedom from Hunger. http://www.ffhtechnical.org/publications/summary/loansize0302.html.

Fidler, P (1998). *Bolivia: Assessing the Performance of Banco Solidario.* Case Studies in Microfinance, Sustainable Banking with the Poor. Washington DC: World Bank.

Foster, J, J Greer and E Thorbecke (1984). A class of decomposable poverty measures. *Econometrica*, 52(3), 761–766.

Ghatak, M (1999). Group lending, local information and peer selection. *Journal of Development Economics*, 60, 27–50.

Ghatak, M (2000). Screening by the company you keep: Joint liability lending and the peer selection effect. *Economic Journal*, 110(465), 601–631.

Ghosh, S and E Van Tassel (2008). A Model of Microfinance and Mission Drift. Department of Economics, Florida Atlantic University.

González, A and R Rosenberg (2006). *The State of Microfinance — Outreach, Profitability, and Poverty: Findings from a Database of 2600 Microfinance Institutions.* Washington DC: Consultative Group to Assist the Poor (CGAP).

González-Vega, C, M Schreiner, RL Meyer, J Rodriguez-Meza and S Navajas (1996). *BANCOSOL: The Challenge for Growth for Microfinance Organizations.* Ohio State University, Columbus, Ohio: Economics and Sociology Occasional Paper 2332.

Hermes, N and R Lensink (2007). The empirics of microfinance: What do we know. *Economic Journal*, 117(517), F1–F10.

Holmstrom, B and P Milgrom (1991). Multitask principal-agent analyses: Incentive contracts, asset ownership and job design. *Journal of Law, Economics and Organization*, 7, 24–52.

Hudon, M (2007). Fair interest rate when lending to the poor. *Ethics and Economics*, 4(2), 1–8.

Jain, S and G Mansuri (2003). A little at a time: The use of regularly scheduled repayments in microfinance programs. *Journal of Development Economics*, 72, 253–279.

Labie, M, PG Méon, R Mersland and A Szafarz (2010). Discrimination by Microcredit Officers: Theory and Evidence on Disability in Uganda. WP–CEB: No. 10-007, ULB.

McIntosh, C and B Wydick (2005). Competition and microfinance. *Journal of Development Economics*, 78, 271–298.

Mosley, P (1996). Metamorphosis from NGO to commercial bank: The case of Bancosol in Bolivia. In *Finance Against Poverty*, D Hulme and P Mosley (eds.). London: Routledge.

Navajas, S, M Schreiner, RL Meyer, C Gonzalez-Vega and J Rodriguez-Meza (2000). Microcredit and the poorest of the poor: Theory and evidence from Bolivia. *World Development*, 28(2), 333–346.

OECD Development Centre (2005). *Report.* Paris, France: OECD Publications.

Rhyne, E (2001). *Mainstreaming Microfinance: How Lending to the Poor Began, Grew and Came of Age in Bolivia.* New York: Stylus Publishing.

Sen, A (1999). *Development as Freedom.* New York: Random Publishers.

Schreiner, M (2001). Seven Aspects of Loan Size. Typescript, Center for Social Development, Washington University in Saint Louis.

Schreiner, M (2002). Aspects of outreach: A framework for discussion of the social benefits of microfinance. *Journal of International Development*, 14, 591–603.

Stiglitz, JA (1990). Peer monitoring and credit markets. *The World Bank Economic Review*, 4(3), 351–366.

Tedeschi, GA (2006). Here today, gone tomorrow: Can dynamic incentives make microfinance more flexible? *Journal of Development Economics*, 80, 84–105.

Vanroose, A (2008). What factors influence the uneven outreach of microfinance institutions? *Savings and Development*, 32(2), 153–174.

Wilson, JQ (1989). *Bureaucracy: What Government Agencies Do, and Why Do It?* New York: Basic Books.

World Bank (2004). *Annual Report 2004.* Washington DC: The World Bank.

Appendix

We consider the problem:

$$\begin{aligned}&\max_{s\geq 0} N\\&\text{s.t. } K = sN + f(N)\end{aligned}$$

The equation $G(s, N) = K - sN - f(N) = 0$ implicitly defines the function g such that: $N = g(s)$ that is to be maximized. Therefore, thanks to the theorem of implicit functions:

$$g'(s) = -\frac{\frac{\partial G}{\partial s}}{\frac{\partial G}{\partial N}} = \frac{N}{s + f'(N)} > 0$$

Consequently, for the maximization problem, the solution will always be the corner solution $s^* = 0$ leading to:

$$K = f(N) \Rightarrow N* = f^{-1}(K).$$

For example, with a quadratic transaction cost, $f(N) = F + \alpha N^2, \alpha > 0$, the optimum is obtained for $s^* = 0$ and $K - F = \alpha N^2 \Rightarrow N^* = \sqrt{\frac{K-F}{\alpha}}$.

Social Investment in Microfinance: The Trade-Off Between Risk, Return and Outreach to the Poor

Rients Galema

University of Groningen

Robert Lensink

University of Groningen, Wageningen University, and CERMi

1 Introduction

Access to finance is a crucial mechanism for generating persistent economic growth and for reducing worldwide poverty. Although data on access to financial services is still limited, it is clear that there is a huge unmet demand for financial services by the poor. Beck *et al.* (2007), for instance, estimate that about 40 to 80 percent of the populations in developing economies lack access to the formal banking sector. The access to financial services differs considerably between developing countries. According to the World Bank (2008), less than 50 percent of the population in most developing countries has a bank account, whereas in most Sub-Saharan African countries, more than 80 percent of the population lack a bank account.

The limited access to financial services by the poor is due to many reasons, such as a lack of education, a lack of collateral, and the small transactions leading to high costs for financial institutions. Since the late 1970s, however, specialized microfinance institutions serving the poor have tried to overcome these problems in innovative ways e.g., by using group-lending schemes, dynamic incentives and by hiring local loan officers. The microfinance movement has been impressive, both in terms of new programmes introduced and in terms of the number of clients that are reached. Nowadays, more than 10,000 MFIs in more than 85 countries serve over 100 million micro-entrepreneurs. Driven by increasing access to commercial funding sources, the volume of microfinance loans has risen sharply in recent years, from an estimated US$4 billion in 2001 to approximately US$25 billion in 2006. However, according to Dieckman (2007), the microfinance sector still faces a US$250 billion funding gap, implying that the potential microfinance market is huge.

Currently, non-governmental organizations serve about half of all microfinance customers, whereas commercial institutions serve less than 20 percent (Cull *et al.*, 2009). As non-governmental organizations receive about 40 percent of their funding from subsidies, the question arises whether non-governmental organizations will be able to raise enough subsidies to serve the potential market. Instead, many agree that commercial microfinance, which is the for-profit part of the microfinance sector, is necessary to fund the potential untapped demand for microfinance. Indeed mainstream financial institutions e.g., commercial banks and private and institutional investors are becoming interested in the market for microfinance. Pension funds especially are willing to invest in microfinance. Still, the current proliferation of non-profit organizations and the limited profitability of the very small loans they provide to the poorest borrowers suggest that subsidies and social investment will continue to be important (Cull *et al.*, 2009).

In this paper, we focus on social investors, which are investors that next to financial performance also value the social performance of their investments. They have started to invest substantially in microfinance: by 2007 they have invested US$4 billion in microfinance (CGAP, 2008). Social investors value both the financial and the social returns of microfinance. They are willing to invest in microfinance institutions (MFIs) that are possibly less profitable and more risky, but reach poorer borrowers, i.e., have higher outreach.

One of the most controversial questions about investing in microfinance is whether there exists a trade-off between risk and return on the one hand, and outreach to the poor, on the other. Moreover, if there appears to be such a trade-off, what is the extent to which social investors are willing to accept a decrease in returns and/or an increase in riskiness in order to achieve a higher outreach. In this paper, we add to the growing evidence that outreach and returns of MFIs are negatively correlated. Moreover, and more importantly, for the first time ever, we try to quantify the trade-off between financial returns of investing in MFIs and outreach to the poor. More specifically, the paper aims to derive the price of increasing portfolio outreach, which investors in microfinance have to pay in terms of accepting lower returns or higher risk. The results in this paper will help social investors to evaluate the trade-offs between financial and social returns.

In terms of the methodology we use, we assume that social investors construct a portfolio of different MFIs and we adapt the mean-variance framework of Markowitz (1958) to construct mean-variance-outreach optimal portfolios. Specifically, we incorporate outreach as an additional constraint in the portfolio optimization procedure to obtain mean-variance efficient portfolios for different degrees of outreach. This paper proceeds as follows. Section 2 presents our data. Section 3 discusses whether there is a risk-return-outreach trade-off and supports this with some descriptive statistics. Section 4 shows how we quantify the risk-return-outreach trade-off and Section 5 concludes.

2 Data

We use a version of the MixMarket dataset, which covers the period 1997 to 2007, to attempt to quantify the trade-off social investors face between return, risk and outreach. The MixMarket dataset is publicly available from www.mixmarket.org. All numerical data are converted to US dollars at contemporaneous exchange rates. The number of MFIs has grown explosively over the last 11 years. In 1997, there were only about 25 MFIs in our dataset; while in 2006, there were already 800 MFIs in our portfolio. MFIs can voluntarily participate in the MixMarket database, but data entry is closely monitored by MixMarket. Participants have to enclose documentation that supports the data, such as audited financial statements and annual reports. In order to be able to provide such data, reporting MFIs should have an adequate information infrastructure. Therefore, the MixMarket database probably represents a random sample of the best managed MFIs in the world (Kraus and Walter, 2009; Gonzalez, 2007). The data reported by MixMarket are not adjusted for subsidies. These subsidies can be seen by investors as shielding a bank from bankruptcy, similar to a too-big-to-fail (TBFT) support for commercial banks (Kraus and Walter, 2009). Nonetheless, the frequency and size of subsidies is not certain and thus constitutes an investment risk. Unfortunately, we are not able to account for this risk in the present study.

3 The Risk-Return-Outreach Trade-Off

Before turning to the analysis, we first consider to what extent there is a trade-off between return and outreach, and risk and outreach. Considering the trade-off between return and outreach, it is generally agreed that it is more costly to reach poorer borrowers than it is to reach richer borrowers. Obviously, it will be more costly to administer and monitor 1000 loans of US$200 than doing the same for a single loan of US$200,000. To some extent, the increased costs of providing small loans can be covered by economies of scale; although after 2000 clients, MFIs tend to have captured most scale benefits (Rosenberg *et al.*, 2009). This is probably due to the labor-intensive nature of microfinance in which operating expenses consist mainly of salaries, compared to fixed costs which are relatively low (Rosenberg *et al.*, 2009). The academic literature also finds evidence of a trade-off between performance and outreach. Hermes *et al.* (2011) find in a stochastic frontier analysis that efficiency decreases with outreach and Cull *et al.* (2007) find that operating expenses decrease with average loan size.

To cover the higher costs of providing small loans, MFIs set higher interest rates (Rosenberg *et al.*, 2009). Due to these higher interest rates, MFIs that also offer relatively small loans are able to make a small profit (Cull *et al.*, 2009). Still, the profit is modest compared to MFIs that offer larger loans. To illustrate, in our dataset, the average return on assets for an average loan size below US$1,000 is −0.08 percent, while it is 1.8 percent for loans above US$1,000. This difference in performance of small and larger loans, which is statistically significant at 1 percent, implies that investing in MFIs that offer small loans is probably only of interest to social investors.

Considering the trade-off between risk and outreach, one of the main success stories of microfinance is that very poor lenders also have very high repayment rates. In addition, poor lenders typically operate in the informal sector, which tends to be less correlated to the economy as a whole (Ahlin and Lin, 2006), such that poor borrowers face less macroeconomic risk. This would imply that there is no trade-off, i.e., reaching poorer borrowers is not necessarily more risky. Investors are, however, not so much interested in borrower risk as in MFI risk, which differs among different types of MFIs. Cull *et al.* (2009) show that the type of organization that typically serves the richer segment of poor borrowers is different from the type of organization that serves the poorer segment. MFIs that serve the richer borrowers typically have a for-profit status, employ an individual lending method, have lower operating costs per loan, are more profitable and rely less on subsidies. By contrast, MFIs that serve the poorest borrowers typically have a non-profit status, employ a group lending method, have higher operating costs per loan, are less profitable and rely more on subsidies.

There are a number of reasons why the latter types, which are typically non-profit organizations, could be more risky. First, although they do make a profit, their after-subsidy profit depends on the amount of subsidies they receive, which creates a subsidy risk. Second, non-profit organizations are typically smaller than other MFIs: in our dataset their median amount of assets is US$1.7 million, whereas the median amount of assets of all other MFIs is US$3.7 million. In the advent of financial setbacks, these smaller institutions may have less deep pockets to cushion adverse shocks, like credit contraction or a system-wide decrease in repayment rates. That is, smaller institutions face higher liquidity risk. Third, non-profit organizations usually lack a broad base of deposits, such that they are more exposed to refinancing risk. In most countries, MFIs need a bank status to be allowed to take deposits. Indeed, for many non-governmental organizations that want to expand their business, this is an important reason to become a regulated institution.

Figure 16.1 illustrates why MFIs that serve poorer borrowers are more risky. It shows a scatter plot of MFI return on assets versus average loan size below US$2,000. Clearly, return on assets is much more dispersed for smaller average loan sizes, especially for average loan sizes below US$500. Consistent with Cull *et al.* (2009), who show that most customers are served by non-governmental organizations who serve the poorest borrowers, 2,579 MFIs have an average loan size below US$1,000, whereas 828 MFIs have an

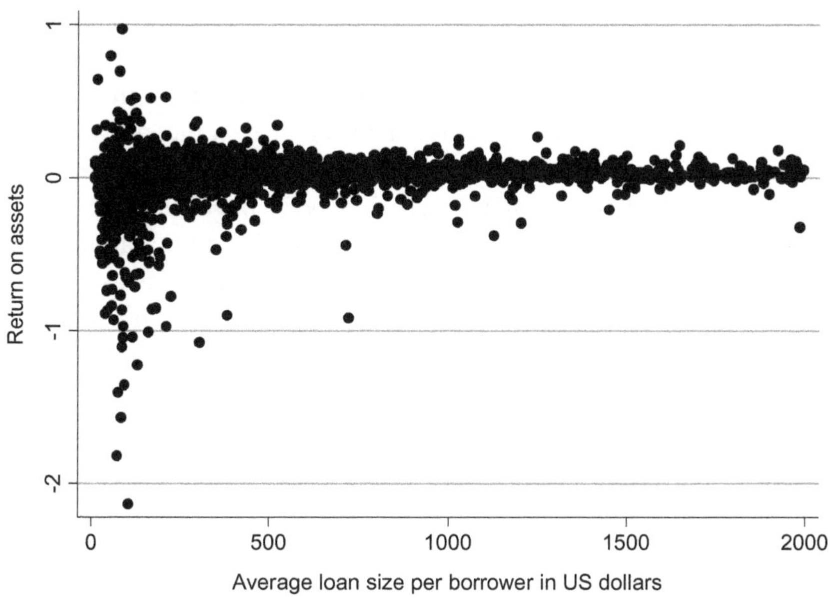

Figure 16.1: Scatter diagram of return on assets versus average loan size per borrower.

average loan size between US$1,000 and US$2,000. Although we expect that a larger group has higher dispersion, merely due to its size, an unreported variance test also shows that MFIs with an average loan size below US$1,000 have significantly higher return on assets variability than those with an average loan size between US$1,000 and US$2,000.

4 Quantifying the Risk-Return-Outreach Trade-Off

Now that we have identified there is a trade-off between risk, return and outreach, we are ready to quantify this trade-off. In mainstream finance, the trade-off faced by investors in terms of risk and return is usually expressed in the portfolio optimization framework of Markowitz (1958). According to this framework, investors choose optimal portfolio weights to maximize their mean portfolio return and minimize their portfolio standard deviation (from now on, expected return and standard deviation, respectively). Optimal portfolios can be depicted as lying on a concave curve, the mean-variance frontier, where each point on the curve is an optimal portfolio. The mean-variance frontier can be drawn in a space with expected return on the y-axis and standard deviation on the x-axis. Portfolios on the mean-variance frontier are optimal in the sense that expected return can only be increased by also increasing risk along the frontier. That is, investors cannot obtain portfolios that lie above the frontier.

To quantify the risk-return-outreach trade-off, we adapt the Markowitz framework to include outreach. In particular, we draw a mean-variance frontier for each value of expected average loan size. We do this by constraining the portfolio optimization problem such that each portfolio on the frontier has a particular expected average loan size, which is the portfolio-weighted average of MFIs' average loan sizes. In this way, we create one mean-variance frontier for each level of expected average loan size, where frontiers with a lower expected average loan size lie below those with a higher expected average loan size. By progressively lowering the expected average loan size, we try to find the price of increasing portfolio outreach, which investors pay by accepting lower returns or higher risk. A formal discussion of this methodology is presented in the Appendix.

For portfolio optimization, we need relatively long time spans of data, but on Mixmarket, there are only a few MFIs that report returns for a sufficient number of years. Therefore, we choose a sample of MFIs with nine years of returns, which includes 19 MFIs over the period 1998–2006. To construct the frontiers, we use return on equity, although using return on assets yields comparable results. Table 16.1 reports summary statistics. It shows that the majority of MFIs come from Latin America and the Caribbean and have a non-profit status. In general, non-profits appear to have lower average loan sizes and returns than banks, although there are exceptions and there is considerable heterogeneity in the sample.

For each expected average loan size, we construct a mean-variance frontier to obtain Figure 16.2. In Figure 16.2, mean-variance frontiers that have a higher expected average loan size are located above frontiers that have a lower expected average loan size. We see that for high values of expected average loan size, the constraint is not very restrictive; but for lower values, it becomes rapidly more restrictive. This is apparent from the fast downward shift of the mean-variance frontiers for the lower values of expected average loan size.

To quantify the trade-off between return and outreach, we plot the relationship between expected returns and expected average loan size for different standard deviations, which are vertical cross-sections of Figure 16.2. For instance, to find out how much return decreases for a standard deviation of 6.5 percent when we decrease expected average loan size, we can draw a vertical line at 6.5 percent on the x-axis, which intersects all mean-variance frontiers. At each intersection, we find a value for expected return and average loans size from which we can construct a plot of expected return versus expected average loan size, i.e., a return-outreach curve. To obtain plots for multiple portfolio standard deviations, we let the standard deviation run from 3 percent to 10 percent and take 0.5 percent as step size.

Figure 16.3 shows the resulting return-outreach curves. For a standard deviation of 10 percent, we obtain the highest return-outreach curve and we obtain the lower return-outreach curves as we incrementally lower the standard deviation to 3 percent. The highest return-outreach curve shows the steepest drop as we lower average portfolio loan size. As we draw curves for lower standard deviations, the drop becomes less steep. So to obtain a lower expected average loan size, expected returns have to fall much more for high standard deviation portfolios than for low standard deviation portfolios. This is due to the fact that the number of assets to choose from with a certain average loan size is much smaller for high standard deviation, high return portfolios.

In Figure 16.3 and Table 16.2 we can also see that for an investor who prefers a standard deviation of 6.5 percent, which is the seventh curve from below, a decrease in expected average loan size from US\$179.36 to US\$138.89

Table 16.1: Summary Statistics.

	MFI	Region	Type	Return on assets		Return on Equity		Average loan size	
				Mean	Std.Dev.	Mean	Std.Dev.	Mean	Std.Dev.
1	Asociación de Consultores para el Desarrollo de la Pequeña, Mediana y Microempresa	Latin America and The Caribbean.	Non-profit.	0.05	0.04	0.19	0.16	347.22	63.71
2	Association Al Amana for the Promotion of MicroEnterprises Morocco	Middle East and North Africa.	Non-profit.	0.00	0.15	0.05	0.19	254.67	128.27
3	Association pour la Promotion et l' Appui au Développement de MicroEntreprises	Africa.	Non-profit.	0.07	0.06	0.14	0.13	693.11	270.47
4	Banco Compartamos, S.A., Institución de Banca Múltiple	Latin America and The Caribbean.	Bank.	0.26	0.12	0.49	0.10	264.00	123.35
5	BancoSol	Latin America and The Caribbean.	Bank.	0.02	0.01	0.14	0.10	1375.78	259.08
6	D–miro	Latin America and The Caribbean.	Non-profit.	0.05	0.08	0.08	0.11	334.89	183.03
7	FINCA Peru	Latin America and The Caribbean.	Non-profit.	0.05	0.04	0.06	0.04	143.22	18.27
8	Fondation Zakoura	Middle East and North Africa.	Non-profit.	0.04	0.05	0.10	0.10	138.89	53.64
9	Fondo Financiero Privado PRODEM	Latin America and The Caribbean.	Non-bank Fin.	0.02	0.02	0.11	0.09	1555.22	778.26

Table 16.1: (*Continued*).

	MFI	Region	Type	Return on assets		Return on Equity		Average loan size	
				Mean	Std.Dev.	Mean	Std.Dev.	Mean	Std.Dev.
10	Fundación Mundo Mujer Popayán	Latin America and The Caribbean.	Non-profit.	0.15	0.04	0.24	0.05	366.89	108.99
11	Fundación WWB Colombia — Cali	Latin America and The Caribbean.	Non-profit.	0.06	0.04	0.17	0.12	580.22	193.80
12	Fundación para el Apoyo a la Microempresa	Latin America and The Caribbean.	Non-profit.	0.08	0.03	0.14	0.05	458.89	72.90
13	Hattha Kaksekar Ltd.	East Asia and the Pacific.	Non-bank Fin.	−0.01	0.06	0.01	0.10	275.33	137.68
14	KSK RPK	Eastern Europe and Central Asia.	COOP.	0.01	0.01	0.02	0.02	5361.44	2504.00
15	MIKROFIN Banja Luka	Eastern Europe and Central Asia.	Non-bank Fin.	0.05	0.08	0.12	0.49	1524.89	656.72
16	MiBanco	Latin America and The Caribbean.	Bank.	0.04	0.02	0.20	0.13	902.11	377.43
17	Programas para la Mujer — Bolivia	Latin America and The Caribbean.	Non-profit.	0.06	0.02	0.08	0.03	147.22	20.09
18	SHARE Microfin Ltd.	South Asia.	Non-bank Fin.	−0.01	0.05	0.06	0.16	83.78	14.47
19	Women's World Banking — Medellín	Latin America and The Caribbean.	Non-profit.	0.06	0.01	0.16	0.04	444.67	158.92

In this table, we report summary statistics for the 19 MFIs in our sample. We selected MFIs that have at least nine years of returns and for which the covariance matrix is positive definite. The type of MFI can be Non-profit (NGO), Bank, Non-bank financial institution and COOP/Credit union (Cooperative/Credit union).

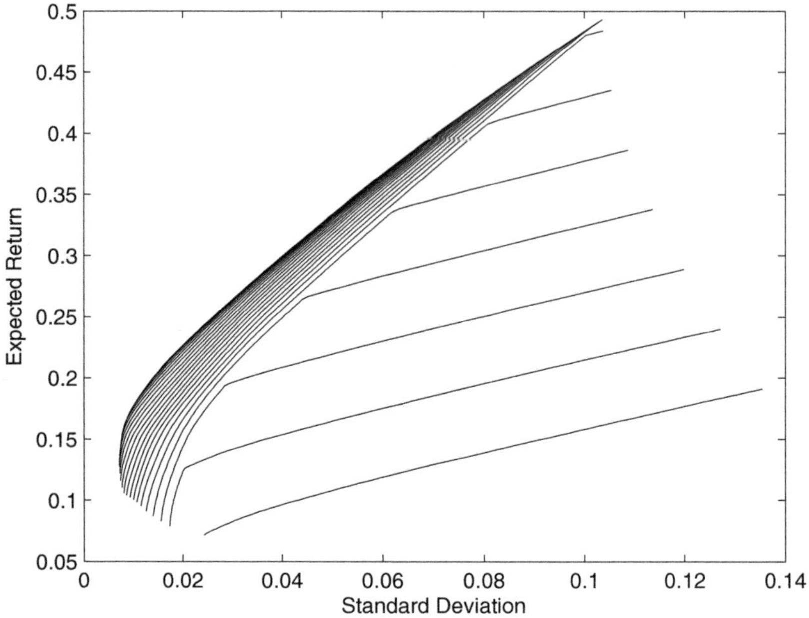

Figure 16.2: Mean-variance frontiers for different expected loan sizes.

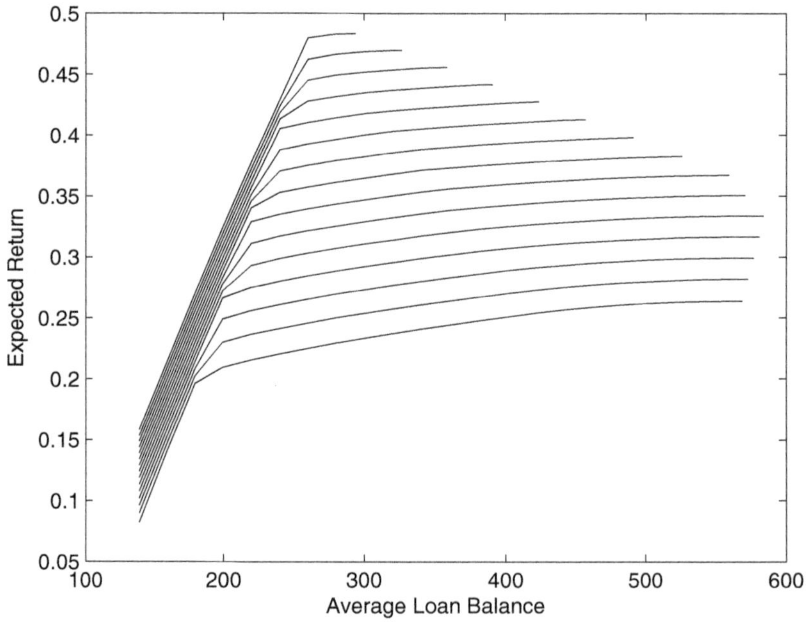

Figure 16.3: Return-outreach curves for different standard deviations.

Table 16.2: The risk-return-outreach trade-off.

Average Loan Size	Expected return	Arc Elasticity (%)
Panel A: Average Loan Size — Expected Return		
Standard Deviation = 0.03		
\$138.89 → \$179.36	0.083 → 0.196	320.8
\$179.36 → \$568.91	0.196 → 0.264	28.3
Standard Deviation = 0.065		
\$138.89 → \$199.59	0.124 → 0.289	222.2
\$199.59 → \$526.12	0.289 → 0.383	31.2
Standard Deviation = 0.1		
\$138.89 → \$240.06	0.158 → 0.430	172.9
\$240.06 → \$294.24	0.430 → 0.483	58.1

Average Loan Size	Standard deviation	Arc Elasticity (%)
Panel B: Average Loan Size — Standard Deviation		
Return = 0.15		
\$138.89 → \$179.36	0.091 → 0.021	−495.7
\$179.36 → \$462.62	0.021 → 0.008	−104.9

This table presents the risk-return-outreach trade-off. The arrows are used to indicate the decrease in Average Loan Size and the corresponding change in Expected Return or Standard deviation. The Arc Elasticity indicates the average percentage change in expected return or standard deviation when we decrease Average Loan Size with one percent. This estimator of the actual elasticity, which we cannot measure since we have no functional form, is defined as:

$$AE_{x,y} = \frac{(x_2 - x_1)/((x_1 + x_2)/2)}{(y_2 - y_1)/((y_1 + y_2)/2)}$$

where x indicate either Expected return or standard deviation and y indicates Average Loan Size. Subscript 1 indicates the value to the left-hand side of the arrow and subscript 2 that to the right-hand side.

costs 11.3 percent in return on equity. For the same investor, a decrease in portfolio average loan size from US\$568.91 to US\$179.36, will only cost about 6.8 percent in ROE. As shown in Table 16.2, in terms of arc elasticity, a percentage decrease in outreach leads to a 320.8 percent increase in percentage returns in the first case, whereas a percentage increase in outreach only leads to a 28.3 percent increase in percentage returns in the second case. So a social investor faces a much starker trade-off between returns and average loan size for portfolios that have a lower average loan size.

Next, we quantify the trade-off between risk and outreach by taking a horizontal cross-section of Figure 16.2. That is, for an expected return of 15 percent, we draw a horizontal line at 15 percent on the y-axis, which

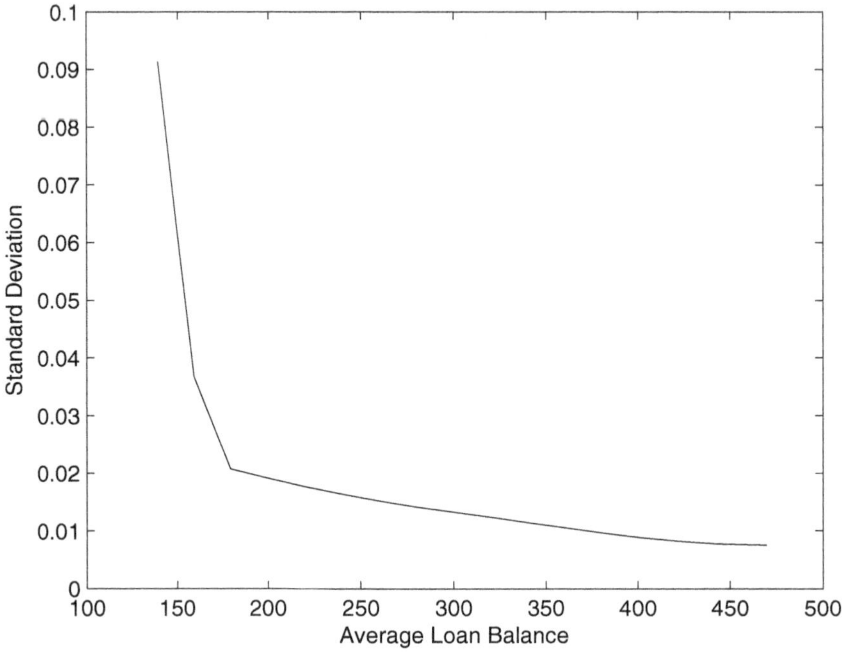

Figure 16.4: Risk-outreach curve for an expected return of 15 percent.

intersects all mean-variance frontiers. At each point where this line intersects a mean-variance frontier, we obtain a different standard deviation and expected average loan size. This yields a plot of the standard deviation against expected average loan size for a return of 15 percent, which allows us to find out how much the standard deviation increases when we decrease average loan size. We only plot the standard deviation against expected average loan size for one return level, since the range of return values that intersects all mean-variances curves is very small. Similar to our previous figures, the kink in the graph in Figure 16.4 shows that there is a very strong trade-off between outreach and risk for low average loan sizes. Specifically, keeping returns constant at 15 percent, to lower average loan size from US$179.36 to US$138.89 on has to accept an increase in standard deviation of 7 percent, which corresponds to an arc elasticity of −495.7 percent.

5 Conclusion

In this paper, we have shown that social investors in microfinance face a trade-off between, risk, returns and outreach. They face a trade-off between returns and outreach, since it is more costly to lend to very poor borrowers. They also face a trade-off between risk and outreach, since it is typically more risky to finance the types of MFIs that serve the poorest borrowers. These types of MFIs are typically small non-profit institutions, which are more subject to subsidy, liquidity and refinancing risk than their larger for-profit counterparts. Yet, social investors are willing to accept these trade-offs, i.e., they are willing to give up some returns or to bear more risk to obtain a portfolio of MFIs that, on average, reduces poverty more.

To quantify how much return investors have to give up, or how much more risk they need to bear to obtain more outreach, this paper uses the portfolio optimization framework of Markowitz (1958). We find that the trade-offs are not very large for reasonably large average loan size, i.e., average loan sizes above US$180. Yet, for average loan sizes lower than US$180, the trade-off is very pronounced: to lower expected average loan size, an investor has to accept a decrease in return on equity of 11 percent or alternatively an increase in standard deviation of 7 percent.

We realize that our results are specific to our small sample and cannot be generalized to the entire population of MFIs. Also, using average loan size as a proxy for outreach is problematic in several ways. A first problem concerns outliers. A MFI can appear to have less outreach, when it has just a few very large borrowers that distort average loan size upward. Second, cross-subsidization of smaller loans with larger loans can increase total outreach. Armendáriz and Szafarz (2009) argue that in richer regions like Latin America, there is actually more scope for cross-subsidization, which implies that the higher average loan size observed in this country are not necessarily a sign of mission drift. Third, comparing average loan size across countries is problematic since different countries are in different stages of development, such that a large loan in one country can be a small loan in another.

Nevertheless, we believe that the approach presented in this paper clearly illustrates the trade-offs between the financial and social returns of investing in microfinance. While additional research has to be done, and much more data collection is needed before any solid conclusion can be reached, we hope that the techniques presented in this paper will be valuable for Microfinance investors to evaluate the trade-offs between financial and social returns.

References

Ahlin, C and J Lin (2006). Luck or Skill? MFI Performance in Macroeconomic Context. BREAD Working Paper, 132.

Armendáriz, B and A Szafarz (2009). On mission drift in microfinance institutions. CEB Working Paper, 9.

Beck, T, A Dermirgüç-Kunt and M Soledad Martinez Peria (2007). Reaching out: Access to and use of banking services across countries. *Journal of Financial Economics*, 85: 234–266.

Consultative Group to assist the Poor (CGAP) (2008). Foreign capital investment in microfinance: Balancing social and financial returns. Focus Note 44.

Cull, R, A Dermirgüç-Kunt and J Morduch (2009). Microfinance meets the market. *Journal of Economic Perspectives*, 23(1), 167–192.

Cull, R, A Demirgüç-Kunt and J Morduch (2007). Financial performance and outreach: A global analysis of leading microfinance banks. *Economic Journal,* 117: F107–F133.

Dieckmann, R (2007). Microfinance: An emerging investment opportunity. Deutsche Bank Research.

Gonzalez, A (2007). Resilience of microfinance institutions to national macroeconomic events: An economic analysis of MFI asset quality. MIX discussion paper no. 1.

Hermes, N, R Lensink and A Meesters (2011). Outreach and efficiency of microfinance institutions. *World Development*, forthcoming.

Krauss, N and I Walter (2009). Can microfinance reduce portfolio valatility? *Economic Development and Cultural Change*, 58(1), 85–110.

Markowitz, H (1958). *Portfolio Selection: Efficient Diversification of Investment.* New Haven, Conn: Yale University Press.

Rosenberg, R, A Gonzalez and S Narain (2009). The new moneylenders: Are the poor being exploited by high microcredit interest rates? Consultative Group to assist the Poor (CGAP) occasional paper.

World Bank (2008). *Finance for All? Policies and Pitfalls in Expanding Access.* A World Bank Policy Research Report. Washington DC: The World Bank.

Appendix: Methodology

We assess the effect of constraining the mean-variance optimization for different degrees of outreach. We plot the mean-variance frontier by solving the following quadratic program for 100 different expected portfolio returns, $E[R]$:

$$\begin{aligned} &\min_{\mathbf{x}} \mathbf{x}'\boldsymbol{\Omega}\mathbf{x} \\ &\text{s.t. } \mathbf{x}'\bar{\mathbf{r}} = E[R]_j \qquad j = 1, \ldots, 100 \\ &\qquad \mathbf{x}'\boldsymbol{\iota} = 1 \\ &\qquad \mathbf{x} \geq \mathbf{0} \end{aligned} \tag{1}$$

where $\mathbf{x}$ is a vector of weights, $\boldsymbol{\Omega}$ is the variance-covariance matrix of returns, $\bar{\mathbf{r}}$ is vector of expected returns of the assets included in the optimization and $\boldsymbol{\iota}$ indicates a vector of ones.

We can further constrain this optimization by demanding that the optimal portfolio's average loan balance should be smaller than some pre-specified amount $E[ALS]$. The lower $E[ALS]$ is, the more constrained the optimization is. In this way, we can plot a mean-variance frontier for each $E[ALS]$ by solving the following quadratic program:

$$\begin{aligned}
&\min_{\mathbf{x}} \mathbf{x}'\boldsymbol{\Omega}\mathbf{x} \\
&\text{s.t. } \mathbf{x}'\bar{\mathbf{r}} = E[R]_j \qquad j = 1, \ldots, 100 \\
&\qquad \mathbf{x}'\boldsymbol{\iota} = 1 \\
&\qquad \mathbf{x} \geq \mathbf{0} \\
&\qquad \mathbf{x}'\overline{\mathbf{ALS}} \leq E[ALS] \quad E[ALS] = \min(\overline{\mathbf{ALS2}}), \ldots, \max(\overline{\mathbf{ALS2}})
\end{aligned} \tag{2}$$

where $\overline{\mathbf{ALS}}$ is a vector with expected ALS's of the assets and **ALS2** is the same vector, only with the maximum and minimum value excluded.[1] Obviously, frontiers plotted for higher values of $E[ALS]$ will lie above frontiers plotted for lower values of ALS.

[1]Note that we do this to prevent portfolio formations based on one asset.

Efficiency

Bernd Balkenhol
International Labour Organization, and Université de Genève

Marek Hudon
Université Libre de Bruxelles (U.L.B.), SBS-EM, Centre Emile Bernheim; CERMi; Burgundy School of Business

1 Introduction

Microfinance has been praised during the last 20 years as a new development policy strategy serving people who have been excluded from the formal banking system. The sector has spectacularly developed during the last 10 years and is now offering financial services to nearly 150 million poor who were previously excluded from the traditional banking institutions.

Nevertheless, even if microfinance has been constantly presented as a new sustainable development policy, one must recognize that very few MFIs have reached independence from donors' funds. Dozens of institutions that claim to make profits still rely on subsidies in order to cover their seemingly high transaction costs (Armendariz and Morduch, 2005).

Moreover, MFIs have received a lot of subsidies to develop their activity. A survey from the CGAP estimates that, over the last 20 years, the sector has attracted a remarkable US$ 1 billion per year, in subsidies from private and public donors (CGAP, 2005). Hence, the microfinance promise that it would create a more inclusive financial sector, increasing the efficiency and professionalism in delivering financial services to poor clients (CGAP, 2004) has been challenged, with donors and microfinance managers being the first to be questioned. While donors mostly focus on financial sustainability or social performance, as part of the double bottom line, efficiency indicators have been recently introduced in the public policy debate in microfinance

(Balkenhol, 2007). Similarly, while little research was done before 2005 on efficiency,[1] it is currently an emerging topic in the academic sector.

We will argue in this paper that efficiency is a key criterion for donors and managers that helps discriminate with greater accuracy than financial performance alone between support-worthy and underperforming MFIs, irrespective of the emphasis placed by each MFI on commercial success versus impact on poverty. A MFI can be more or less efficient in reaching many poor people with small average transactions, as a MFI can equally be more or less efficient if it seeks positive financial results in the shortest term possible. Both are support-worthy as long as they are on or near the efficiency frontier or moving towards it, for a given production function and in a given operating environment. Finally, we will argue for a new paradigm of efficiency in microfinance, taking into account the implications for public policy, the varieties of actors and the challenges the actors face to reach more difficult populations.

After this short introduction, this paper will present the debates and pinpoint the trade-offs between theory and practice. Third, we will define the notion of efficiency in microfinance and provide some of its key drivers. Fourth, we will present different indicators used in the sector and their measures. Before drawing some conclusions, we will sequentially present some recent trends and insert efficiency in the public policy debate.

2 Efficiency in the Theory and Practice of Microfinance

Performance in microfinance is a matter of financial results as much as of social impact. All MFIs combine these two goals in their mission and strategy, but each one places its own individual emphasis on one or the other. Some MFIs are more commercial than others, some MFIs are more keen on client service than others that prefer to ensure first their own institutional sustainability. Thus, both profitability and poverty impact are legitimate and essential dimensions of performance in their own right, but giving preference to one over the other seems to clash with the whole idea of microfinance. This dilemma has led to a renewed interest in efficiency as a third performance dimension. Regardless of the goal mix in individual MFIs, efficiency is a dimension of performance common to all MFIs, because it measures simply the maximisation of outputs for a given set of inputs, respectively the minimisation in input use for a given set of outputs.

[1]Exceptions are for instance, Bazoberry (2001), Brand (2000) or Christen (2000).

The growing interest in efficiency stems from the conceptual and practical difficulties to rationalize public support to institutions providing microfinance. This is particularly challenging if MFIs cater to the poor, provide socially useful services but are at pains to become fully financially self-sufficient; it just does not seem appropriate to let commercial success alone be the yardstick to decide whether a MFI merits public support including subsidies. Inversely, evidence of social improvements alone cannot suffice to qualify a MFI as performing, it also needs to show some business acumen towards sustainability.

In order to balance these different combinations of social and financial goals in microfinance, efficiency comes in handy, especially for donors that have to decide whether to continue subsidizing MFIs despite an overrun of the 10-year period considered necessary to allow a MFI to mature to full financial sustainability. Subsidizing an efficient MFI that is on the way towards financial self-sufficiency is obviously preferable to subsidizing an inefficient MFI, or even continuing to subsidize a MFI that is already financially self-sufficient.

However, the measure of efficiency is not the same across all MFIs, as MFIs differ by their production function and their outputs and inputs are not the same across all MFIs: some provide just loans, other also take deposits and most offer a range of outputs. At the same time, the inputs used by MFIs differ as well: IT is an input, but not consistently used across all MFIs; voluntary labour is another input available to some cooperatively organized MFI, but not to NGO or non-bank MFIs. The same applies to the inputs used by microfinance institutions: loans on market terms, soft loans, grant/equity, client deposits and other financial resources are used by different MFIs in different proportions. As a result, there is not just one production function possible in microfinance, but several.

3 Efficiency Definition and Drivers

In microeconomics, efficiency relates quantities and costs of inputs to quantities and revenues on outputs. A firm is efficient if it maximizes the quantity/revenue an output for given quantities/costs of inputs, alternatively, it is efficient if, for a given output, it operates with the least quantity or least costs of inputs.

In microfinance, efficiency is a matter of transforming inputs such as staff, funds and equipment into loans, deposits, other financial and non-financial services at least costs. "Technical" efficiency measures are ratios relating the number of clients to loan officers. Measures of "allocative" efficiency relate output prices (interest rates, fees) to input prices (wages, capital costs, rental cost of equipment). While preliminary indicators of efficiency were related to staff (mainly the loan officers for staff productivity), we will see that the new indicators have slightly modified the focus on more general management. New efficiency indicators provide a broader perspective on the performance of the institution than the sole staff productivity.

The choice of the output variable has implications for the performance-ranking of MFIs. In their assessment of 30 Latin American MFIs, Nieto, Cinca and Molinero (2004) show that performance in efficiency depends on the specification of the input and output variables chosen. For instance, FIE, Los Andes and FONDESA, three major MFIs in Latin America, achieve high efficiency values when measuring efficiency with the output variable "average loan", whilst two Women's World Banking (WWB) affiliates in Colombia come out best when efficiency is measured in terms of the output variable of number of client borrowers (von Stauffenberg, 2002).

Some MFIs score high on efficiency because of superior technical efficiency or productivity values (number of loans per loan officer), others score high because of the maximization of revenues for a given level of operating expense, i.e., because of the efficient use of operating expense (allocative efficiency).

The selection of a particular variable as 'input' or 'output' depends on how financial transactions are interpreted: in the intermediation model, the input 'deposits' is transformed into an output 'loans'; in the production model, deposits are seen as an output — a financial service — produced by inputs such as labour, financial resources and information technology and communication (ITC) equipment (Nieto, Cinca and Molinero, 2004).

Since financial performance is easier to measure than impact on poverty, there are more efficiency ratios using financial aggregates on both the outputs and inputs sides. The social outcomes of microfinance are less frequently factored into efficiency indicators. The next section will explain the main drivers of efficiency.

Efficiency in microfinance is defined mostly as "operating expenses/ average gross loan portfolio". The value of this ratio is determined by three drivers:

- average loan balances,
- staff costs,
- staff productivity.

The first one, average loan balance (expressed as a percentage of GDP) is a common poverty indicator: it reflects the debt absorption capacity of clients and the MFI's poverty focus. When a MFI decides to set itself up in a particular location, it can no longer freely vary its clientele. The average loan balance in this location may be too low for compressing administrative expenses, but this is a deliberate choice on the part of the MFI. Such a MFI cannot be labelled 'inefficient' only because its average loan balances are small. Within any given market segment, some MFIs can be efficient and others not, average loan balance on its own has little to do with efficiency. This poverty indicator has been criticised a few times by practitioners and academicians. For instance, Dunford (2002) argues that while it is clear only better-off clients apply for larger loans, there is no corresponding evidence showing that only the very poor apply for small loans. Moreover, the credit scarcity in many areas of intervention for microfinance could force even better-off people to compete for small loans. Nevertheless, despite its approximations, average loan balance remains the most commonly used indicators because of the lack of an alternative indicator that could be as easily calculable.

The second efficiency driver is staff costs. Salaries and other labour costs reflect supply and demand in a particular labour market for a given level of skills, experience and trustworthiness. Of course, it is possible that a MFI may end up with high staff costs because it did not look carefully enough on the local market for loan officers, but high staff costs can also be the result of an objective scarcity of skills and experience. Hence when comparing the wages paid by MFIs, one should group MFIs facing similar local labour markets and using similar delivery techniques, that is, production functions. The lower ratio of wages to GNP per capita in poverty-focused MFIs must not necessarily reflect inflated pay rates or unsatisfactory staff productivity. In fact, unsustainable MFIs appear to pay lower wages per head and have identical levels of staff productivity (Christen, 2000). Their high level of operating costs is due to other factors, rooted in different production functions: their operations are more labour-intensive.

The third driver is staff productivity. Efficiency has long been mainly analysed through staff productivity. For instance, the 6th issue of the *MicroBanking Bulletin*, published in April 2001, focused on productivity. Since most microfinance institutions originally offered mostly group lending, it was one of the key indicators. Nevertheless, it is difficult to compare staff productivity between institutions since many factors can influence it, on top of the managerial structure. Staff productivity is determined by organization and management but also depends on location and delivery methodology: MFIs in rural areas using an individual client approach are likely to show lower staff productivity than MFIs operating in urban areas with a mix of group lending and individual lending. Staff expenses are higher if transactions are small and frequent, as they require the same staff-time screening, negotiating, controlling and monitoring larger transactions. Cost-reducing delivery techniques, such as joint liability, can help here, but again not systematically, because they are not universally accepted: they may work wonders in Bangladesh, but not necessarily elsewhere.

Differences in staff productivity can be attributed to inefficiency of managers, but also to differences in context. The Caisses Villageoises in Mali, for example, relied on volunteers for up to two-thirds of its staff. As competition increased with other MFIs in Mali, the Caisses Villageoises found it difficult to retain these volunteers and were obliged to recruit salaried staff. This drove up operating expenses and affected adversely its compliance with financial performance benchmarks.[2]

These three drivers of efficiency in microfinance are thus partly under and partly beyond the control of MFI managers. The exogenous drivers constrain pricing at full cost and cost reduction through externalisation. Put differently, pricing financial services at fully cost-covering levels may be feasible for some, but not *all* MFIs. After having studied the key drivers of efficiency, we can now turn to the concrete indicators used in the sector. Even if all indicators can be useful to assess a MFI, we will see that some indicators might be more valuable for certain kinds of institutions, such as the minimalist institutions, those specializing just on two or three loan products, while others are more appropriate for the other institutions.

4 Efficiency Indicators and their Measures

The Microfinance Consensus Guidelines (CGAP, 2003) present nine ratios for efficiency. Two of these relate an output to another output (value of

[2] As one MFI staff member commented, "Initially it was normal for everyone to work for the community without being paid; unfortunately, lately the competition with other NGOs that pay their staff is making things more difficult for the CV. As a result many cashiers who had been trained by our extension service leave and work in other NGOs where they get better wages... These NGOs also compere with unrealistically low interest rates, because they get a lot of funding from donors"(GLAN survey questionnaire response, translated from French).

loans disbursed to total number of loans disbursed), two ratios relate an output (the number of active borrowers/clients) to an input (number of loan officers/staff). Four ratios relate operating expenses (or a subset of this) to an output (either average gross loan portfolio or number of active borrowers/clients). Of all these indicators of efficiency one ratio is singled out as the "most commonly used efficiency indicator for MFIs": operating expense/average gross loan portfolio or total assets.[3]

Since 2005 the *MicroBanking Bulletin* lists 5 indicators:

• Operating expense/ Loan portfolio.	Adjusted operating expense/Adjusted average gross loan portfolio.
• Personnel expense/Loan portfolio.	Adjusted personnel expense/Adjusted average gross loan portfolio.
• Average salary/GNI per capita.	Adjusted average personnel expense/GNI per capita.
• Cost per borrower.	Adjusted operating expense/Adjusted average number of active borrowers.
• Cost per loan.	Adjusted operating expense/Adjusted average number of loans.

The most commonly used indicator of efficiency, operating costs/gross loan portfolio, is more appropriate for "minimalist" MFIs. Savings-based MFIs would claim that their first output is a range of deposit products, so the denominator would need to be different. Yet another complication arises with MFIs that provide, in addition to financial services, a range of literacy courses, sensitisation on HIV/AIDS, legal advice and a host of other non-financial services. Strictly speaking, these are also "outputs" and would need to be factored into the efficiency indicator.

Can one specify the efficiency of MFIs with which techniques? In other economic sectors where profit-maximising units compete with double bottomline units, like labour exchanges, sport facilities, old folks' homes or health insurance, linear programming techniques like data envelopment

[3]The Consensus Guidelines warn that this indicator may lead to misinterpretations: "MFIs that provide smaller loans will compare unfavorably to others, even though they may be serving their target market efficiently... likewise MFIs that offer savings and other services will also compare unfavorably to those that do not offer these services".

analysis (DEA) have been applied with good results. Many recent publications have used the DEA methods in microfinance, such as Nieto *et al.* (2004).

The interest in applying DEA to MFI performance measurement lies in three particularities that fit the real-life situation of MFIs: first, DEA requires that the entities whose performance is assessed relative to each other must be homogeneous; that is, "use the same resources to procure the same outcomes, albeit in varying amounts" (Thassoulis, 2001: 21). This is meaningful in an environment with different types of MFIs operating side by side, where, for example, credit-based NGOs compete with other types of MFIs such as savings and credit cooperatives, and where each can be constituted as a reference group.

DEA also differentiates between performance drivers that the management of a firm can influence and other uncontrollable variables. This makes sense in microfinance because of differences in market and regulatory contexts: some countries have interest rate ceilings, others not; some prohibit deposit-taking, others not; some governments are actively involved in retail microfinance, others stay out.

Thirdly, DEA accommodates the fact that a unit uses several inputs and produces several outputs: measurement takes into account whether the output mix is modified as a result of an increase or reduction in input uses. Again, considering the modifications over time in product range and use of different kinds of labour and capital that one finds in microfinance, this is an appealing feature of DEA to measure efficiency.

The efficiency of a MFI can be expressed as economies in input use that it could achieve if it produced on the efficiency frontier instead of on its current location. A 0.79 figure, for example, signals that a MFI could save on 21 percent of inputs, such as loan officer staff-time, if it operated on the frontier. The value can also be expressed as a percentage inefficiency, in this case 27 percent: $(1 - 0.79)/0.79$. The next section will present the recent trends on efficiency in the microfinance sector.

5 Efficiency and Financial Sustainability: Recent Trends

According to the MBB data, the efficiency in MFIs measured as operating expense/loan portfolio has on the whole improved from 2004 to 2006: down from 23 percent in 2004 to 19.2 percent in 2006. There are important variations, though: efficiency in 2006 is superior in mature (18.4 percent) than in young institutions (27.8 percent); it is better in rural banks (7.8 percent) than in NGOs (27.1 percent); it is better in savings-based MFI (15.6 percent) than in other MFIs (22.6 percent); MFIs with individual lending (15.4 percent) do better than group-based MFIs (34.4 percent). Scale effects are likely to explain also the higher average efficiency of large-scale MFIs (16.4 percent) compared to small-scale MFIs (29.1 percent). Also, as could be expected, financially sustainable MFIs are on the whole more efficient than not yet sustainable MFIs: 17.8 percent compared to 27 percent. Using a more complex methodology — a semi — parametric smooth coefficient model to correct for potential bias, Hartaska *et al.* (2009) find significant scope economies which for the sample amount to 22 percent on average. They, however, also find about a fifth of the MFIs have diseconomies of scope.

Surprisingly, though, there is hardly a difference between for-profit and not-for-profit MFIs: 18.3 percent and 19.8 percent respectively. Africa is the only region where efficiency dropped on average from 27.7 percent to 29.5 percent, whilst the other regions have seen more or less marked improvements, most strikingly in the MENA region.

Efficiency and financial sustainability are related, but distinct dimensions of institutional performance in microfinance. In a perfect market environment, it may make sense to equate efficiency with yield and operating costs relative to the loan portfolio, but in a market where many operators are not profit maximizing units, this indicator fails to fully capture performance. Two, not uncommon, scenarios illustrate this. In the first, a MFI may operate in an environment that may constrain economies of scale, like rural and remote areas which would lead to prohibitively high interest rates if the high unit transaction costs were passed on fully to the client. Another scenario is that an already financially sustainable MFI continues to receive grants and subsidies because the donors want the MFI to distribute non-financial services without charging the full costs to the client.

MFIs that are, for exogenous reasons, unable to further compress costs and unwilling to charge fully cost-covering interest rates to their clients cannot be generally considered "inefficient". In fact, poverty-focused MFIs that engage in very small transactions already tend to set their interest rates comparatively high; compared to other MFIs, they also tend to have the highest staff productivity in their respective regions and delivery techniques and compressed staff pay (Christen, 2000). In terms of allocative and technical efficiency, they seem to operate already fairly close to their efficiency frontier. They appear to have pushed managerial efficiency to the limit: to obtain full financial sustainability, they would thus have to raise the average loan size and go up-market.[4]

In a recent empirical paper based on a database of 435 MFIs, Lensink *et al.* (forthcoming) have found through a stochastic frontier analysis (SFA) that outreach and efficiency of MFIs are negatively correlated. The increasing competition between MFIs may also affect the social bottomline of the sector. McIntosh *et al.* (2005) have indeed empirically shown that wealthier borrowers are likely to benefit from increasing competition among MFIs, but that it leads to lower levels of welfare for the poorer borrowers.

Hartaska *et al.* (2009b) use a cost function to determine whether MFIs active in Eastern Europe and Central Asia are becoming more cost-effective over time. Their results indicate that about half of the MFIs in the region are becoming more cost-effective over time and about half are showing no improvement. This first type of MFIs would be less reliant on subsidies and more reliant on deposits.

6 Efficiency and Public Policy: Which Incentives?

For growth and competitiveness in microfinance markets, donors and governments need to look beyond financial performance and poverty outreach and consider more systematically a dimension that has so far been largely overlooked: efficiency. Surprisingly, evidence on the impact of subsidies on the performance of MFIs is scarce.

Hudon and Traca (2009) provide some preliminary evidence on the impact of subsidies on MFIs efficiency. The effect of subsidies on efficiency is a topic of intense debate in academic and policy circles. On one hand, some are afraid that excessive subsidization will decrease the incentives for productivity and end up inhibiting the promise of sustainability in the provision of financial services to the poor. Subsidies would distort the market by favouring more inefficient institutions and undercut both scale and efficiency within the MFI. Using a cross-section regression, Hudon and Traca (2009) find that MFIs that receive subsidies are more efficient than those

[4]According to CGAP (2001). Commercialization and Mission Drift — the Transformation of Microfinance in Latin America, Occasional Paper No. 5: 16, seven out of nine leading MFIs in Latin America, for example, saw an increase in their average real outstanding loan balance as a percentage of per capita GNP from 1990–99, remaining, though, still below poverty parity. Only two (Procredito Caja de los Andes and ADEMI) ended up with a portfolio that was clearly no longer poverty-focused.

that do not until a treshold. These results reinforce the notion of small ("smart") subsidies allowing MFIs to increase the productivity of their staff, but beyond a certain threshold, subsidies lower productivity at the margin, in line with the moral hazard arguments raised in the literature.

Some of the determinants of efficiency can be influenced by MFI management like the choice of delivery technique, collateral requirements, graduation lending, etc; others escape its control and for these determinants like client density, scope of clients' viable income-generating activities, etc., managers cannot be held accountable. A third category of efficiency drivers cannot be qualified as clearly endogenously or exogenously attributed, for example, the wages paid to loan officers. For reasons of fairness, only endogeneous efficiency drivers should be used by governments and donors to fix, modify or phase out a subsidy for performance.

To qualify a MFI as more or less efficient requires information on a batch of comparable MFIs. Comparability is based on several criteria: where a MFI positions itself on the poverty–profitability continuum, whether it operates in rural or urban areas, whether it is a monopolist or not. It is also based on similarity of output mixes and production functions (technology, delivery technique like group vs. individual lending, or collateral-based vs. collateral-free lending). Efficiency measurement of MFIs is thus relative to one institution that is closest to the efficiency frontier: the "best in class". Rather than focus on the most efficient institution without considering the particularities, the "best in class" enables consideration of the various missions and organisational forms of MFIs in the evaluation.

Different production functions define clusters of MFIs; they differ by the degree to which MFI management can influence the quantity and price of labour, capital and other inputs, as well as the quantity and price of the output mix. Cluster analysis and other multivariate techniques determine types of MFIs in a given country. Cluster formation takes into account the orientation and mission of the MFI, as it groups together distinctly poverty-focused MFIs, commercial MFIs and others in between. Linear programming techniques like DEA capture the distance from the frontier and help determine how far a MFI is still removed from the efficiency frontier and whether, over time, it is making progress getting there. Comparisons of the efficiency of MFIs are best done within a single country context to control for a number of exogenous factors.

The absolute level of efficiency can be established on the basis of input and output variables; namely, number of clients, number of loan officers, number of staff members, administrative expenses (or the subset "staff expenses"), number of loans and overall loan portfolio. Applying DEA systematically across all countries with a certain density of MFIs and repeating this every two years would show which MFI is best in class. This could be updated regularly to allow managers of MFIs as well as donors to track the movement of MFIs towards the efficiency frontier.

In order to meet the efficiency targets, clear incentive-based contracts are needed. Performance-based contracts between donor agencies and MFIs should contain efficiency targets that differentiate between areas for which MFI managers can be held accountable and other contextual factors beyond their control. In addition, the performance contract could specify the period over which progress should be achieved, given benchmark data established on the basis of the above-mentioned efficiency indicators and the norms of the reference MFI ("best in class"). The performance contract should spell out the consequences for failure to progress in efficiency if the MFI management can be held accountable; in other words, managers of the MFI should be able to anticipate the cost of non-compliance, in the form of a reduced or cancelled subsidy.

Most importantly, the contract should signal the rewards and incentives that the MFI can expect if it progresses in efficiency. This accommodates a variety of MFI types in a single country; the more homogeneous the domestic microfinance market, the easier it is to define the rewards and incentives. Ultimately, a more rational and transparent system of allocating subsidies to MFIs should, instead of favouring one type of MFI at the expense of another type, gear aid resources towards greater efficiency in each type, working towards a more economic resource use in all MFI configurations and allowing for a broad, competitive and varied supply of financial services to the poor.

Taking these methodological considerations into account, another policy issue concerning the timing of the performance should be stressed. Donors should look at institutional performance in a dynamic perspective, i.e., progression of an individual MFI towards a higher level of efficiency matters as much — if not more — as its position relative to the ranking of other MFIs.

The second issue concerns the limitation to the assessment of efficiency. We have already given the examples of institutions that would be very close to the efficiency frontier and therefore appear to have pushed managerial efficiency to the limit leaving them few other options outside of cost reduction to obtain full financial sustainability, like raising the average loan size and going upmarket. If some minimum standards are reached, donors may well favour a more social institution than another one. Of course, these minimum standards must be demanding for institutions.

7 Conclusion

The efficiency of MFIs is a topic of intense debate in academic and policy circles. While very little was known on their efficiency five years ago, many authors now include efficiency indicators in their publications. In parallel to this academic interest, the drivers and indicators have rapidly evolved during the last few years. While the operation expense ratio and staff productivity were originally the most frequent indicators, new surveys are increasingly comparable with the efficiency analyses in the banking sector, for instance with the DEA or SFA approach.

Recent figures show an increase of efficiency in microfinance, partly due to economies of scale. They, however, often suggest that the efficiency indicators vary according to the methodology, the region and probably to the poverty-focus of the institution. We have argued in this paper that instead of expecting that all institutions reach the same efficiency levels while they serve very different clients in different environments, one requires information on a batch of comparable MFIs. The "best in class" approach offers this possibility since it takes into account some key external factors influencing efficiency that escapes the control of the managers.

References

Armendáriz, B and J Morduch (2005). *The Economics of Microfinance.* Cambridge, Mass.: The MIT Press.

Balkenhol, B (ed.) (2007). *Microfinance and Public Policy.* Basingstoke: Palgrave Macmillan and ILO.

Bazoberry, E (2001). We aren't selling vacuum cleaners: PRODEM's experience with staff incentives. *MicroBanking Bulletin*, 6, 11–13.

Brand, M (2000). More bang for the buck: Improving efficiency. *MicroBanking Bulletin*, 14, 13–18.

Caudill, S, D Gropper and V Hartarska (2009). Which microfinance institutions are becoming more cost-effective with time? Evidence from a mixture model. *Journal of Money, Credit, and Banking*, 41(4), 651–672.

CGAP (2003). Phase III Strategy 2003–2008. Available at: http://www.cgap.org/assets/images/CGAP%20III%20Stragery_forWeb.pdf.

CGAP (2005). CLEAR Report on Madagascar.

Christen, R (2000). Bulletin highlights. *MicroBanking Bulletin*, 4, 41–47.

Dunford, C (2002). What's Wrong with Loan Size? Unpublished paper. Davis: Freedom from Hunger. www.freefromhunger.org.

Gutiérrez Nieto, B, C Serrano Cinca and C Mar Molinaro (2004). *Microfinance Institutions and Efficiency.* Discussion papers in Accounting and Finance, AFO4-20. University of Southampton.

Hartarska, V, C Parmeter and R Mersland (2009). Economies of Scope in Microfinance: Evidence from a Group of Rated MFIS. Working Paper.

Hartarska, V, NV James and R Mersland (2009). *Scale Economies and Input Price Elasticities in Rated MFIs.* Aubum University Working Paper.

Hartarska, V and R Mersland (2009). What governance mechanisms promote efficiency in reaching poor clients? Evidence from leading MFIs R&R. *European Financial Management.*

Hudon, M and D Traca (forthcoming). On the efficiency effects of subsisidies in microfinance: An empirical inquiry. *World Development.*

Lensink, R, N Hermes and A Meesters (forthcoming). *World Development*, 39.

McIntosh, C, A de Janvry, E Sadoulet (2005). Flow rising competition among microfinance institutions affects incumbent leaders. *The Economic Journal*, 115, 984–1004.

Thassoulis, E (2001). *Introduction to the Theory and Application of Data Envelopment Analysis.* Norwell: Kluwer Academic Publishers.

Von Stauffenberg, D (2002). *Latin America's Top MFIS.* Available at: http://www.iadb.org/features-and-web-stories/2007-12/english/latin-americas-top-mfis-4305.html.

Social and Financial Efficiency of Microfinance Institutions

Carlos Serrano-Cinca
Universidad de Zaragoza

Begoña Gutiérrez-Nieto
Universidad de Zaragoza and CERMi

Cecilio Mar Molinero
University of Kent

The performance of Microfinance Institutions (MFIs) is examined in this paper. MFIs have a double aspect: financial and not-for-profit. It is, therefore, appropriate to assess their performance by means, not only of financial ratios, but also by means of social indicators. We propose the use of Data Envelopment Analysis (DEA) as a way of assessing the relative efficiency with which an institution uses inputs in order to generate outputs. The outputs can be either financial or social. We also study the relationship between financial and social efficiency, and between these and other indicators. We have used Principal Components Analysis, Cluster Analysis, and Multivariate Regression as analysis tools. The results show that it is possible to explain the performance of a MFI by means of a reduced set of variables. The paper ends by discussing the need to extend the use of social efficiency indicators, as we consider that they are appropriate in the assessment of the performance of MFIs.

1 Introduction

When compared with traditional international banks, many Microfinance Institutions (MFIs) operate under very high intermediation margins. Fernando (2006), in a study of MFIs in the Asia and Pacific region, found that most MFIs charged nominal interest rates ranging from 30 percent to 70 percent per year. But we need to point out that these interest rates are much lower than those charged by local moneylenders, whose percentage rates can be up to 10 times higher. The high percentage rates charged by

MFIs may be caused, at least in part, by the fact that the costs of making a small loan are higher, in percentage terms, than the costs of making a larger loan (Goodwin-Groen, 2002). MFIs have a double objective. From the social point of view, they are required to make loans to the poor. MFIs are valued according to their outreach, and the smaller the loan, the higher the outreach. But they are also required to be self-sufficient and financially efficient; this means that their income must cover their expenditure or, at least, most of it. In this paper, we study this double aim of outreach versus efficiency. We suggest the use of performance indicators that measure efficiency, concentrating on social efficiency. From our point of view, a good MFI should lend to the poor but in an efficient way; this is to say, it should optimise the use of inputs. In this we follow an idea proposed by Gutiérrez-Nieto *et al.* (2009).

The assessment of MFIs has traditionally been done using Yaron's (1994) approach which takes into account outreach and sustainability. There is a long debate on whether one should concentrate on the financial aspects or on the social aspects, and on whether these are mutually compatible; see Conning (1999), Woller *et al.* (1999), Copestake (2007) and Cull *et al.* (2007). The "institutionalist" point of view emphasises sustainability, and argues that MFIs should be able to survive on their own resources, and should not depend on external donors. "Welfarism" sustains that social aspects come first, and that the role of MFIs is to support the poor. Both points of view can coexist (Morduch, 2000).

MFIs are financial institutions: they collect money and make loans. They differ from traditional banks in that they lend to the poor, and their loans are for small amounts. The collateral that back these microcredits differ from the collateral required by traditional banks, but default rates are normally low (Morduch, 1999). However, even if MFIs operate differently from traditional banks, one should still be interested in measuring their performance. The tools used to measure the performance of traditional banks may be appropriate, but they need to be adapted to the microfinance context. CGAP (2003) provides microfinance consensus guidelines, and lists a set of financial ratios that are specific to microfinance. These are divided into four categories: sustainability/profitability, assets/liability management, portfolio quality, and efficiency/productivity.

A further difference between banks and MFIs is that MFIs do not only receive deposits but also grants. The bodies that make the grants value the social aspects of the MFI as well as the financial aspects. It follows that, in order to assess the performance of MFIs, we need to take into account their social aspect, their outreach work. Outreach has been defined as "the social value of the output of a microfinance organization in terms of depth, worth to users, cost to users, breadth, length, and scope" (Navajas *et al.*, 2000: 335). To these six dimensions of outreach, we add a further one: outreach efficiency. We suggest that social outputs should be studied within an efficiency context; this is to say, that MFIs should provide the maximum amount of social outputs compatible with the resources at their disposal.

The objective of this paper is to offer a global overview of the assessment of microfinance institutions taking into account such aspects as profitability, productivity, sustainability, outreach, financial efficiency, and social efficiency. We have used Data Envelopment Analysis (DEA) as a tool for efficiency analysis. We propose an efficiency index that combines social and financial aspects, and that makes it possible to analyse MFIs' social and financial performance. We have studied the relationship between indicators in an empirical study. The mathematical tools used are multivariate statistics, principal components, cluster analysis, and multivariate regression.

2 Measuring MFI Performance

In this section, we discuss some popular indicators used to measure MFI performance. When assessing the performance of a firm, financial analysts concentrate on aspects such as profitability, solvency, or debt structure. In the case of financial institutions, the key concepts are risk and efficiency. It is common wisdom that a financial institution should never externalise risk, and the 2008 banking crisis demonstrates the consequences for those institutions that lost control of the risk inherent to their operations. We will not deal in this paper with risks such as assets and liability management, or portfolio quality, interesting as these might be. Disaster risk management has been studied by Pantoja (2002) in the context of microfinance.

2.1 *Efficiency*

Efficiency is a key characteristic for every financial institution. Efficiency is normally studied by means of financial ratios (Brownlow, 2007). The ratio that is used most often is non-interest expense (staff expenditure) divided by total revenue less interest expense. The lower this ratio, the more efficient is the institution. A decrease in this ratio is associated either with a decrease in operating costs, or with an increase in revenues, making the institution better prepared to face a situation of falling margins or reduced income. Were, for example, this ratio to take the value 40 percent, it would mean that for every monetary unit that comes in, the institution spends 40 cents. However, this ratio is not without problems in the case of MFIs, since, for some of them, income is smaller than expenditure, and the ratio takes a negative value.

Besides, we are reluctant to analyse MFI performance by means of a single ratio, since we think that efficiency is a multidimensional concept. Given that MFIs employ several inputs such as labour, capital, or technology, it is possible for an MFI to be efficient in the use of labour, but inefficient in the use of technology (or the other way round). The intensive use of information technology, for example, is affecting competition in the financial sector. Another aspect is employee efficiency, normally referred to as productivity. Finally, was an institution to opt for outsourcing as a strategy, some indicators would improve — such as staff efficiency — but others would worsen.

There are other techniques, besides financial ratios, that allow us to calculate efficiency on the basis of various inputs and outputs. Berger and Humphrey (1997) classify 130 papers on efficiency in financial institutions according to the technical approach employed. They listed the following techniques: Stochastic Frontier Approach (SFA), Distribution Free Approach, Thick Frontier Approach, Free Disposal Hull, Index Numbers, Mixed Optimal Strategy, and Data Envelopment Analysis (DEA). They found DEA to be the most popular technique, which was used in 62 of the papers they reviewed. DEA can be used to compare homogeneous units, such as bank branches, which share common inputs and common outputs. It performs multiple comparisons using Linear Programming. An advantage of DEA is that inputs and outputs do not need to be measured in the same units.

DEA calculates "relative efficiencies". They are relative in the sense that a value of 1 is assigned to the best possible result. As a technique, it is suited to the analysis of non-for-profit entities, such as MFIs, since it can be applied when conventional objectives, such as cost and profit, are not suitable. For an introduction to DEA, see, for example, Thanassoulis (2001); Charnes *et al.* (1994) or Cooper *et al.* (2000). But DEA imposes conditions on homogeneity, and one has to be cautious when establishing comparisons between institutions located in different countries since margins can be affected by the different market conditions. Examples of such conditions are different market regulations, infrastructures, or even population density.

DEA has been used to analyze efficiency in MFIs; see, for example, Gutiérrez-Nieto *et al.* (2007), Flückiger and Vassiliev (2008), or Gutiérrez-Nieto *et al.* (2009). Other authors have used SFA to analyze MFIs efficiency, for example Caudill *et al.* (2009), Hartarska and Mersland (2009), or Hermes *et al.* (2009).

Two distinct approaches to modelling efficiency in financial institutions are prevalent in the literature. These depend on whether institutions are seen as intermediaries in financial markets, or are seen as production units; see Athanassoupoulos (1997) and Camanho and Dyson (2005). Under the intermediation model, institutions collect deposits and make loans in order to make a profit. Deposits and acquired loans are inputs. Institutions are interested in placing loans, which are traditional outputs in studies of this kind; see, for example, Berger and Humphrey (1991). Under the production model, a financial institution uses physical resources such as labour and plant in order to process transactions, take deposits, lend funds, and so on. In the production model, manpower and assets are treated as inputs and transactions dealt with — such as deposits and loans — are treated as outputs. See, for example, Vassiloglou and Giokas (1990), and Soteriou and Zenios (1999). In our opinion, the production model is best suited to MFIs, as the emphasis is in the granting of loans. In fact, many MFIs do not even collect deposits, a crucial aspect of the intermediation model, but receive donations and subsidies.

2.2 *Profitability and sustainability*

When analysing the performance of an industrial firm, analysts tend to use profitability ratios. However, this is not the preferred approach in the case of financial institutions, where efficiency ratios are considered to be more important than profitability ratios. There is an explanation for this difference. Take, for example, the ratio "returns on assets" (ROA), defined as total profit divided by total assets. ROA makes sense in the context of industrial firms, which use assets such as plant and equipment to generate profit. However, the turnover of a financial institution is not necessarily related to total assets. Financial institutions thrive on margins; they buy and sell money, it is more relevant to study the surplus that such transactions generate. This makes efficiency ratios, which relate income to expenditure, more revealing than profitability ratios. Indeed, improving efficiency may be a way of reducing nominal interest rates. In this context, for example, Goodwin-Groen (2002) mentions the case of the Bolivian BancoSol that, over the last 10 years has lowered its nominal interest rates from 50 percent to about 24 percent as a result of improvements in efficiency. Unfortunately, generalizations cannot be made from this example. Microfinance is important in developing financial deepening. Bolivia has one of the more developed microfinance markets, where margins are narrowing and this is resulting in mergers and acquisitions within the MFI industry (Silva, 2003, González-Vega and Villafani-Ibarnegaray, 2007).

Other ratios that are important in the cases of MFIs relate to self-sufficiency. Operational self-sufficiency (OSS) measures how well an MFI covers its costs through operating revenues. It is defined as financial revenue/(financial expense + impairment losses on loans + operating expense). Financial self-sufficiency (FSS) is similar, but it takes into account a number of adjustments to operating revenues and expenses, to model how well the MFI could cover its costs if its operations were unsubsidized. Woller and Schreiner (2009) see financial self-sufficiency (FSS) as the non-profit equivalent of profitability; it is to be noted that FSS is basically the inverse of an efficiency ratio.

MFIs have been engaging in many improvements in terms of self-sufficiency. A simple examination of the data that Mixmarket.org provides reveals that, in 1998, 42 out of the 95 institutions included in its database (44 percent) operated with an OSS ratio lower than 100, implying that income was lower than expenditure. Five years later, the percentage had decreased to 35 percent. In the most recent dataset, corresponding to 2006, it has further declined to 26 percent: 226 out of 853. Cull *et al.* (2007) found that more than half the MFI institutions that they examined were profitable, and that the rest were approaching profitability and financial sustainability.

2.3 *Social performance*

Although MFIs carry out many of the functions that traditional banking institutions perform, their social work makes them clearly different. MFIs lend to the members of society who would otherwise be excluded from financial services. Besides, the money that they lend proceeds in part from customer deposits, but also from grants and donations. Donors value the financial side of MFIs and also the social side. Given this dual orientation, MFIs are assessed on the basis of a double bottomline: financial and social. At the moment, no universally agreed standards exist to measure the social side; see Zeller *et al.* (2002), Navajas *et al.* (2000), and Cull *et al.* (2007) for a discussion on this subject.

Social performance is currently assessed by means of indicators of outreach that emanate from the Yaron (1994) perspective. Hulme (2000) has studied their methodological aspects, identifying three paradigms in the assessment of MFIs's social aspects. He names them as scientific paradigm, humanistic paradigm, and participative learning paradigm. Navajas *et al.* (2000) give a list of outreach proxies. The number of customers is taken as an indicator of the breath of outreach; the higher the number of customers, the higher the breath of outreach. Average loan per customer is usually taken as an indicator of depth of outreach; see, for example, Cull *et al.* (2007) or Copestake (2007). Anyway, there is a huge controversy over the use of average loan size as a social indicator, see, for example, Armendáriz and Szafarz (2009). MFIs that make small loans are understood to have more depth of outreach. But what is meant by "small" depends on the context. In order to make international comparisons possible, this ratio is normally divided by the per capita gross national income (GNIpc). Other common indicators are the number, or percentage, of clients below the poverty line, or whose income is lower than one dollar a day.

The percentage of women borrowers is also often used as a social indicator, since many MFIs have the support of women as a stated aim. UNDP shows that women are the poorest of the poor, and it is believed that women are the main providers of health and education in the family. On the other hand, there is evidence suggesting that microfinance does not necessarily empower women. See, for example, Goetz and Gupta (1996), Rahman (2001), Mayoux (1999) and Armendáriz and Roome (2008). Other possible outreach indicators are provided by Cull *et al.* (2007).

We think that it is very important to calculate indicators of social efficiency. These indicators would relate financial inputs to social outputs. A possible indicator would be the ratio of borrowers per staff member, defined as the ratio between active borrowers and staff numbers. This ratio measures the efficiency with which members of staff manage clients. One can think of other such ratios by including in the numerator variables such as the number of loans granted, the number of women clients, or the number of very poor customers.

As it is the case with financial efficiency, DEA can be used to calculate social efficiency (Gutiérrez-Nieto *et al.*, 2009). In this approach, inputs could be the same ones used to calculate financial efficiency, but outputs could take into account the objectives of the MFI: the number of loans made to women, the number of customers below the poverty threshold, or the impact on the community as measured by the number of people in the community who benefits from an MFI loan.

3 Empirical Study

3.1 *Sample and data*

For the purposes of this study, we have used the Microfinance Information eXchange (MIX) database, which is available in the web address Mixmarket.org. MIX publishes data that has been standardised across the industry, so as to make comparisons and benchmarking possible. Rhyne and Otero (2006) highlight that the MIX gathers data from MFIs "that are able to produce and willing to release complete financial statements". Mersland and Strøm (2009) affirm that "the third-party and standardised collected MFI data must be judged better than self-reported data, as found for instance in the Mixmarket database". In one previous study (Gutiérrez-Nieto *et al.* 2008) we found that large MFIs with a high degree of Internet public exposure disclose greater amounts of information on the Internet than smaller and less visible MFIs. We also found that for-profit MFIs disclose more financial information on the Internet, while MFI NGOs reveal more social information. Zacharias (2008), using data from Mixmarket, confirms the previous insights on self-reporting bias. Anyway, he concludes by saying that Mixmarket data has greatly improved the traditional lack of powerful data in microfinance studies.

The financial information published by MIX includes balance sheet accounts, and profit and loss accounts. For each MFI it also publishes social information on outreach and impact. The data used in this study is for the year 2003 and includes 89 MFIs for which full information was available. This data set was used previously in Gutiérrez-Nieto *et al.* (2009) but, in that earlier study we analysed the social efficiency of the MFI institutions, and here we look at all the indicators using multivariate statistical techniques. In the present study, we have used seven financial ratios and three social indicators. Furthermore, we have calculated seven DEA efficiency models that include financial and social outputs. The variables included in the study are listed in Table 18.1.

The seven financial ratios were taken from CGAP (2003) classification. The first four ratios belong to the category sustainability/profitability comprising: return on equity (ROE), return on assets (ROA), operational self-sufficiency (OSS), and profit margin (MARGIN). The next three are

Table 18.1: Variables used in the study and their definitions.

Financial ratios	ROA	Return on assets. (Net operating income, less taxes)/ Total assets.
	ROE	Return on equity. (Net operating income, less taxes)/ Total equity.
	MARGIN	Profit margin. Net operating income/Financial revenue.
	OSS	Operational self-sufficiency. Financial revenue/ (Financial expense + loan loss provision expense + operating expense).
	PERS_PROD	Borrowers per staff member. Number of active borrowers/Number of personnel.
	C/B	Cost per borrower. Operating expense/Number of active borrowers.
	OE/L	Operating expense/Gross loan portfolio.
Social indicators	AVG_L	Average loan balance per borrower. Gross loan portfolio/Number of active borrowers.
	AVG_Lpc	Average loan balance per borrower/Gross national income per capita.
	%W	Percentage of women borrowers. Number of female borrowers/Number of active borrowers.
DEA efficiencies	DEA_L	DEA efficiency model with gross loan portfolio (L) as an output.
	DEA_R	DEA efficiency model with financial revenue (R) as an output.
	DEA_LR	DEA efficiency model with L and R as output.
	DEA_W	DEA efficiency model with active women borrowers (W) as an output.
	DEA_P	DEA efficiency model with a Proxy for the Number of poor (P) as an output. See the explanation in the text.
	DEA_WP	DEA efficiency model with W and P as output.
	DEA_LRWP	DEA efficiency model with L, R, W and P as output.

efficiency/productivity ratios: personnel productivity (PERS_PROD), operating expense ratio (OE/L), and cost per borrower (C/B).

We have also used three social indicators: average loan balance per borrower (AVG_L), average loan balance per borrower divided by GNIpc (AVG_Lpc), and percentage of women borrowers (%W). The first two are indicators of depth of outreach; the higher the values, the lower the depth of outreach.

The seven DEA efficiency measures were calculated with the EMS (Efficiency Measurement Software) software. This is a freely available package distributed by Holger Scheel, University of Dortmund. We used the CCR model for constant returns to scale (Charnes *et al.* 1978). Following the findings of a literature review on the subject of efficiency in financial institutions, we settled for three inputs and four outputs. The three inputs are quite standard in the financial literature: total assets, operating costs, and number of employees. The selection of outputs is based on Yaron's (1994) views on outreach and sustainability. Two outputs are financial: gross loan portfolio (L), and revenues (R); the other two outputs are social: the number of women borrowers (W), and an index that takes into account the number of clients who are poor and relative poverty (P). We now explain how P was calculated.

Taking into account that not all the customers of an MFI are poor, we have attempted to create an indicator (P) that can be a proxy for the prevalence of poor customers in the institution. Full details of P's calculation can be seen in Gutiérrez-Nieto *et al.* (2009). In broad lines, we multiplied the number of customers in the institution by the percentage of poor customers in the institution. This percentage was estimated by comparing the average loan size corrected for per capita income in the sample used, with the average loan size corrected for per capita income (AVG_Lpc) in the institution under examination. AVG_Lpc was first transformed to the 0-1 range using:

$$\frac{AVG\_Lpc_i - \min(AVG\_Lpc_i)}{\max(AVG\_Lpc_i) - \min(AVG\_Lpc_i)}$$

Dividing by a constant (the range of values in AVG_Lpc) is just a change of variable that does not affect the statistical properties of the data. It is, in this sense, equivalent to standardisation, which divides by the standard deviation of the data. The removal of a constant from all the data- min(AVG_Lpc) is a change in origin that does not affect the statistical properties of the data either. But this transformation has, over the more usual statistical standardisation method, the advantage that all the values of the index are positive, and DEA, in the form that was used here, requires all inputs and outputs to be positive.

Seven DEA efficiency measures were obtained. All of them included the same inputs: total assets, operations cost, and staff numbers. We will distinguish them by indicating the outputs that were included in the specification. For example, DEA_L contained a single output, the gross loan portfolio (L); DEA_LRWP contained as outputs gross loan portfolio (L), financial revenues (R), women borrowers (W), and poverty (P); the remaining specifications are DEA_R, DEA_LR, DEA_W, DEA_P, and DEA_WP.

3.2 *Results*

In order to explore the data, we have calculated Pearson Correlation coefficients, and we have performed a series of analyses: cluster analysis, principal components analysis, and a regression-based technique known as property fitting, which is used to interpret the results of Principal Components Analysis.

3.2.1 *Correlation analysis*

Table 18.2 contains the values of Pearson's correlation coefficients between ratios and DEA efficiencies. These will now be discussed.

1. *Reliability of indicators that belong to the same category.* Reliability implies consistency amongst the indicators that measure the same concept. We understand that results are reliable when correlations between indicators that belong to a given category are high. It is found here that there is high significant positive correlation between sustainability/profitability ratios. Just to give an example, the correlation between OSS and ROA is 0.72. There are also positive correlations between the indicators of financial efficiency.

If we now look at social indicators, the correlation between the percentage of women clients (%W) and AVG_Lpc is negative. This is consistent with small loans being made to women, which makes sense, since many MFIs lend to poor women. Typically, women in microfinance engage themselves in home-stay activities and divide their working day between income-generating activities from microfinance and household chores.

We also find reliability amongst social efficiency indicators. The value of the correlation coefficient between DEA_P and DEA_W is 0.87. This is what would be expected, as it has been argued that the empowerment of women is an effective weapon in the fight against poverty (Premchander, 2003) and this finding means that the institutions that are efficient in fighting poverty are also efficient in supporting women. We also find significant positive correlation between "borrowers per staff member" (PERS_PROD) and social efficiency indicators; for example, the correlation between PERS_PROD and DEA_P is 0.72. Again, this is what would be expected, as both PERS_PROD and DEA_P measure the ability that staff members have in dealing with customers.

2. *Positive correlation between social efficiency and financial efficiency.* The correlation between social efficiency (DEA_WP) and financial efficiency

Table 18.2: Pearson's correlation coefficients.

	ROA	ROE	MARGIN	OSS	PERS_PROD	C/B	OE/L	DEA_L	DEA_R	DEA_LR	DEA_W	DEA_P	DEA_WP	DEA_LRWP	AVG_Lpc	%W	AVG_Lpc
ROA	1	0.77 (0.00)	0.82 (0.00)	0.72 (0.00)	0.10 (0.34)	−0.07 (0.50)	−0.75 (0.00)	0.36 (0.00)	0.25 (0.02)	0.34 (0.00)	0.09 (0.38)	0.11 (0.30)	0.12 (0.28)	0.31 (0.00)	0.20 (0.06)	−0.10 (0.36)	0.08 (0.48)
ROE		1	0.62 (0.00)	0.65 (0.00)	0.12 (0.26)	−0.11 (0.28)	−0.55 (0.00)	0.38 (0.00)	0.25 (0.02)	0.37 (0.00)	0.15 (0.16)	0.21 (0.05)	0.21 (0.05)	0.37 (0.00)	0.15 (0.16)	−0.09 (0.39)	−0.02 (0.86)
MARGIN			1	0.72 (0.00)	0.13 (0.22)	−0.02 (0.82)	−0.67 (0.00)	0.42 (0.00)	0.26 (0.01)	0.41 (0.00)	0.10 (0.37)	0.12 (0.27)	0.12 (0.25)	0.36 (0.00)	0.18 (0.09)	−0.10 (0.37)	0.09 (0.43)
OSS				1	0.21 (0.05)	0.00 (1.00)	−0.46 (0.00)	0.52 (0.00)	0.32 (0.00)	0.50 (0.00)	0.14 (0.19)	0.20 (0.07)	0.19 (0.07)	0.43 (0.00)	0.25 (0.02)	−0.10 (0.36)	0.01 (0.96)
PERS_PROD					1	−0.40 (0.00)	−0.19 (0.07)	0.27 (0.01)	0.17 (0.12)	0.26 (0.01)	0.56 (0.00)	0.72 (0.00)	0.72 (0.00)	0.54 (0.00)	−0.20 (0.06)	0.11 (0.29)	−0.36 (0.00)
C/B						1	0.29 (0.01)	−0.14 (0.20)	0.24 (0.02)	−0.19 (0.07)	−0.46 (0.00)	−0.51 (0.00)	−0.51 (0.00)	−0.32 (0.00)	0.66 (0.00)	−0.32 (0.00)	0.44 (0.00)
OE/L							1	−0.53 (0.00)	−0.24 (0.02)	−0.53 (0.00)	−0.12 (0.26)	−0.18 (0.09)	−0.19 (0.08)	−0.46 (0.00)	−0.16 (0.14)	0.13 (0.24)	−0.12 (0.26)
DEA_L								1	0.33 (0.00)	0.90 (0.00)	0.14 (0.19)	0.24 (0.02)	0.26 (0.02)	0.80 (0.00)	0.38 (0.00)	−0.07 (0.49)	0.12 (0.26)
DEA_R									1	0.50 (0.00)	0.12 (0.28)	0.15 (0.17)	0.15 (0.16)	0.45 (0.00)	0.55 (0.00)	−0.06 (0.55)	0.08 (0.46)
DEA_LR										1	0.21 (0.05)	0.31 (0.00)	0.32 (0.00)	0.83 (0.00)	0.30 (0.00)	−0.04 (0.68)	0.07 (0.51)
DEA_W											1	0.87 (0.00)	0.89 (0.00)	0.59 (0.00)	−0.33 (0.00)	0.62 (0.00)	−0.46 (0.00)
DEA_P												1	0.99 (0.00)	0.67 (0.00)	−0.33 (0.00)	0.30 (0.00)	−0.49 (0.00)
DEA_WP													1	0.68 (0.00)	−0.33 (0.00)	0.34 (0.00)	−0.48 (0.00)
DEA_LRWP														1	0.17 (0.10)	0.20 (0.06)	−0.15 (0.16)
AVG_Lpc															1	−0.37 (0.00)	0.50 (0.00)
%W																1	−0.55 (0.00)
																	1

(DEA_LR) is significantly different from zero, but low (0.32). If the original data is examined, it is found that social efficiency is higher than financial efficiency in only 13 out of the 89 MFIs. This is consistent with the interpretation that, in order to be socially efficient, an MFI has to be financially efficient, since financial efficiency ensures future institutional viability. It is, however, possible for an institution to be financially inefficient but surviving, thanks to the support of external donations. Finally, we cannot neglect the effect of transaction costs in more socially-driven MFIs: for example, Paxton *et al.* (2000) affirm that there is a trade-off between serving the poor and financial viability, because transaction costs of smaller loans are high compared with transaction costs of larger loans.

3. *Significant correlation between profitability and financial efficiency.* The value of the correlation between ROA and OE/L is −0.75. This was clearly to be expected, since it indicates that where it is expensive to place loans — a high value of OE/L — profitability is low. Furthermore, we find positive correlation between profitability and DEA financial efficiency, but the correlations are not very high; the highest correlations are found between the OSS ratio and DEA financial efficiencies, the highest of which is 0.52 between OSS and DEA_L. We have already pointed out that the definition of OSS has much in common with efficiency ratios.

4. *There is no significant positive correlation between profitability ratios and social indicators, or indicators of social efficiency.* In general, empirical studies that relate outreach to self-sufficiency find mixed results; Woller and Schreiner (2009), Cull *et al.* (2007), and Copestake (2007). Our study does not produce any significant relationship in this context: the correlation coefficient between self-sustainability (OSS) and depth of outreach (AVG_Lpc) is 0.01. We do not find any significant correlation between financial efficiency and outreach either: the correlation between DEA_R and AVG_Lpc is 0.08.

Finally, we do not find any significant correlation between profitability and social efficiency; for example, the value of the correlation coefficient between ROA and DEA_W is 0.09. It can be said that profitability and social efficiency follow their own track. There are some facts that can change this trend, for example, the entry of for-profit external donors, which lead MFIs to charge higher interest rates, and thus, to a mission drift (Ghosh and Van Tassel, 2008). One might well argue that a MFI has to be profitable in order to survive, and that they are profitable because they manage well their investments, lending to profitable projects. However, the results reveal that MFIs, whilst understanding their social work, have not directed their efforts to profit maximisation.

3.2.2 *Principal components analysis*

The values of all the indicators in Table 18.1 were calculated for all the MFI institutions and treated as a table of variables (indicators) by cases (MFIs). We performed a Principal Components Analysis of this data set. Four components were found to be associated with eigenvalues greater than 1. The first component accounted for 35.7 percent of the variance, the second component accounted for 25 percent, the third for 10.8 percent, and the fourth one for 6.7 percent.

Component loadings, normally used to attach meaning, are shown in Table 18.3. The 89 institutions have been plotted on the first two principal components in Fig. 18.1, and have been identified by means of their acronyms. Since the first two principal components account for almost 61 percent of the variance in the data, this graph is a good representation of the MFIs and will be discussed next.

A variant of the biplot, used to represent variables in the same space as cases, known as Property Fitting has been used to interpret Figure 18.1. Property Fitting represents a variable as a normalised oriented vector from the centre of coordinates, pointing in the direction in which the value of the

Table 18.3: Factor loadings.

	PC1	PC2	PC3	PC4
Variance explained:	35.7%	25.0%	10.8%	6.7%
DEA_LRWP	0.883	−0.029	0.383	−0.120
DEA_LR	0.738	0.310	0.370	−0.309
DEA_WP	0.731	−0.584	0.124	0.081
DEA_P	0.722	−0.581	0.118	0.077
DEA_L	0.699	0.365	0.331	−0.364
OSS	0.654	0.441	−0.237	0.201
OE/L	−0.651	−0.394	0.306	0.261
DEA_W	0.637	−0.626	0.072	0.244
ROE	0.613	0.378	−0.418	0.170
MARGIN	0.612	0.485	−0.419	0.125
ROA	0.610	0.493	−0.524	0.161
PERS_PROD	0.609	−0.408	0.152	−0.018
AVG_L	0.036	0.752	0.487	0.250
AVG_Lpc	−0.253	0.668	0.177	−0.244
C/B	−0.428	0.558	0.313	0.495
DEA_R	0.414	0.362	0.486	0.423
%W	0.184	−0.594	−0.054	0.306

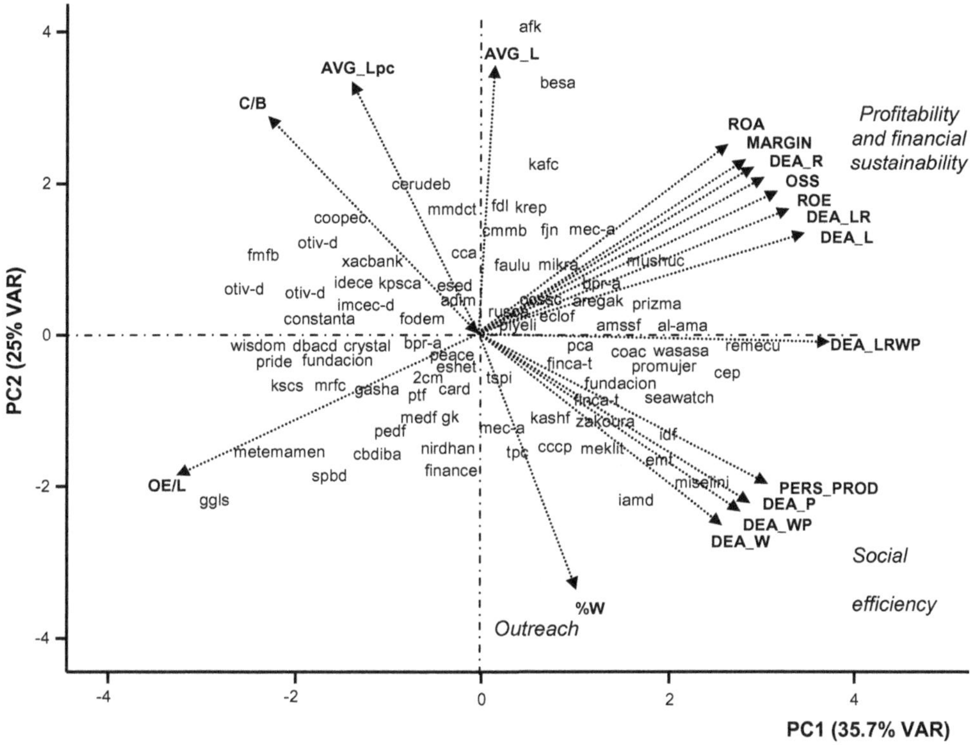

Note: Arrows represent property-fitting directional vectors.

Figure 18.1: PC1 versus PC2.

variable increases. The calculation of the direction in which the vector points is made using multiple regression analysis. All 17 variables are represented in Fig. 18.1, something that required 17 regressions. In the regressions, an MFI was an observation, the dependent variable was the value of the variable for the MFI, and the independent variables were the coordinates of the MFIs in the plot, i.e., the component loadings for each MFI. The vectors were normalised to common length and plotted in the four dimensional space. In this way, the length of the vector on the representation is associated with its relevance in the interpretation of the representation. The vectors can be seen in Fig. 18.1, together with the name of the variable associated with each one of them.

The directional cosines between the vectors that represent the variables and the axes of the representation can be seen in Table 18.3. The nearer a directional cosine is to unity, the more relevant it is to the interpretation of an axis. Taking this into account, and observing Fig. 18.1, it is possible to interpret the loading on the first principal component as an overall performance measure for each institution. We see in Fig. 18.1 that all efficiency indicators, as well as all profitability/sustainability indicators, point towards the right hand side, in the direction of the first principal component. The full DEA model, which includes three inputs and four outputs, is the one that most closely matches the horizontal axis.

The percentage of women borrowers (%W) is close to the vertical axis in the lower direction. This is a measure of outreach. In the upper direction, close to this second principal component, we find AVG_L and AVG_Lpc. The higher the value of these two indicators, the lower the depth of outreach. We, therefore, interpret the second principal component as "outreach".

Having interpreted the meaning of the first two principal components, we have acquired a compass that allows us to make sense of the figure, and to discover the strong and the weak points of each MFI from its position on the map. It is to be noticed that the vectors that point towards the upper right hand side are associated with profitability and financial efficiency ratios. From this we deduce that institutions located in the upper right hand side of the map are salient in their profitability and financial efficiency. In the lower right hand side of the map, we find institutions in which social efficiency is prominent. The institutions that are located in the middle of the right hand side perform well in both social and financial efficiency; they are the best from the global performance point of view. Institutions located in the left hand side present problems due to their low relative efficiency but we must be careful not to express value judgements without having carefully studied the causes of such inefficiency. One should also take into account the country effect and the conditions imposed by operating in different countries, as is done in Gutiérrez-Nieto *et al.* (2009).

We will not discuss the remaining principal components in depth, but we will mention that the third component is a contrast between profitability and efficiency ratios. The fourth component is well explained by the ratio C/B (cost per borrower).

3.2.3 *Cluster analysis*

We will now concentrate on the relationships between the various ratios and efficiency indicators, and will perform a Cluster analysis in order to produce a taxonomy of such variables. The analysis starts by standardising the variables to zero mean and unit variance, since they are measured in different units. As a clustering algorithm, we used hierarchical cluster with the

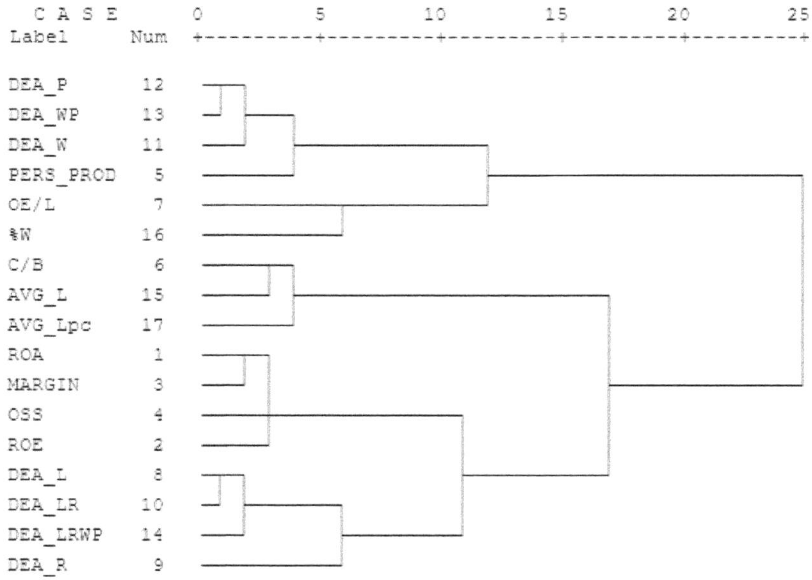

Figure 18.2: Dendrogram using Ward method.

Ward measure of distance, which maximises the homogeneity within groups and the heterogeneity between groups. Figure 18.2 shows the dendrogram obtained. We identify four well-defined clusters in this dendrogram.

The first cluster contains indicators of social efficiency, both in the form of DEA efficiencies and through the ratio PERS_PROD. This cluster contains the vectors that point towards the lower right hand side of Fig. 18.1. Other members of this cluster are %W, the percentage of women customers, and the ratio OE/L, but they cluster at a higher level, and may well have been identified as a different cluster. In the second cluster, we find C/B and the social indicators AVG_L and AVG_Lpc. Their associated vectors are situated towards the top of Fig. 18.1. The third cluster contains profitability ratios (ROA, ROE, MARGIN, and OSS). The fourth cluster groups DEA efficiency with a financial output.

We conclude from our studies that, if we had to choose an overall measure of performance, the preferred one would be DEA_LRWP. This measure describes best the first principal component. Since it includes financial and social outputs, it can be described as an overall efficiency measure. However, we do not recommend the use of a single indicator. Perhaps 17 indicators are too many, but we should be using at least four when assessing the performance of a MFI: a profitability ratio, a financial efficiency ratio, a social efficiency ratio, and a social indicator.

4 Final Thoughts

MFIs perform an important social task by granting loans to people who would otherwise be excluded from conventional financial systems. We must not forget, however, that MFIs deal in financial products, and this requires the assessment of both their financial and their social performance.

Being financial institutions, MFIs deal in money, the most standardised product that exists. To buy and to sell money is a business of margins, and it is extremely important to operate efficiently, so that nominal interest rates charged by MFIs can be low. Not all institutions are equally efficient, and it becomes important to study their relative efficiency. This has been the aim of the present paper.

We have used DEA in order to assess relative efficiencies for MFIs. DEA has been extensively used in the assessment of the efficiency of financial institutions. This technique performs multiple comparisons using a Linear Programming-based approach, and answers the question of whether the resources that have been allocated to a particular institution would have been better used allocating them to the rest of the system. We have carried out an empirical study with data from 89 MFIs. The models have included both the study of financial efficiency and the study of social efficiency. We used financial outputs (loans and income) and social outputs (number of women clients, and a proxy for the number of poor customers) as well as a set of financial ratios and social indicators. The total number of variables included in the study was 17.

An exploratory data analysis found significant correlations between financial efficiency and profitability ratios. We also found a positive, but low, correlation between social and financial efficiencies. The correlation between efficiency in the support of women clients and support for the poor was found to be positive and significant. We did not find a relationship between social efficiency and profitability. We did not find statistically significant correlations between sustainability ratios and outreach either.

We carried out a principal component analysis and a cluster analysis in order to further understand the relationships that may exist between the various indicators. If we had to choose a single indicator, the choice would be one with social and financial outputs, a highly correlated one with the first principal component which explains most of the variance in the 17 variables data set. But, judging from the results of the dimensionality reduction techniques that have been applied, it would not be wise to settle for a single indicator. It would be necessary to keep at least four: a profitability ratio, a financial efficiency indicator, a social efficiency indicator, and an outreach indicator.

We must not forget that this study has been based on a limited number of variables and MFIs. It would be wise to extend it by adding further variables that measure other aspects of the way in which MFIs work, and by extending the number of MFIs included and the number of years covered. The data is not disaggregated enough to deliver other conclusions. The Mixmarket database employed has currently certain shortfalls, such as the shortage of social data and the profitability bias of the MFIs self-reporting to the Mixmarket. Another remark is the fact that different countries were analyzed, which made it necessary to standardize the data.

Although MFIs have been continuously increasing their efficiency, they are still far from reaching the same levels attained by conventional banking. Most experts in the matter coincide in thinking that this efficiency improvement must continue, and that the method to achieve this improvement is to increase staff productivity, or to cut operating costs. A way of improving efficiency is to invest on technology, and many MFIs are considering this course of action. Another way of improving efficiency is to create more financial products such as, for example, collecting savings by opening deposit accounts. Deposits have a lower financial cost, from the institution point of view, since deposits are rewarded at a lower price than borrowing in the inter-banking markets. Anyway, the administrative cost cannot be neglected, especially for MFIs entering the savings market. This, however, would require further regulation of MFIs, an important issue to be debated.

If it were the case that all microfinance institutions had implemented management cost accounting systems, and that costs and income could be assigned to each one of their activities, it would be possible to analyse the efficiency with which each one of these activities is conducted. In this way we would be able to calculate financial and social efficiencies for each one of their activities. We have to take into account that, beyond their principal task of granting micro-credits, some MFIs engage in other business activities such as collecting deposits, accepting donations, dealing with emigrant funds transfer, and selling insurance. We could calculate the efficiency of each one of these activities.

Finally, in this paper, we have proposed the use of indicators that measure MFI's social efficiency, and are defined in such a way that they contain social outputs. From our point of view, the "best" MFIs perform a social task by lending to the poor and to women, but they do so efficiently, i.e., optimising the use of inputs. We consider that it is important for analysts, donors, and rating agencies to make special efforts in collecting, documenting, and valuing the social achievements of MFIs. They should also take into account the efficiency — outreach efficiency — with which MFIs achieve these social goals.

References

Armendariz, B and N Roome (2008). Empowering women via microfinance in fragile states. Working Papers CEB 08–001.RS. Solvay Brussels School of Economics and Management, Centre Emile Bernheim (CEB). Université Libre de Bruxelles.

Armendariz, B and A Szafarz (2009). On Mission Drift In Microfinance Institutions. Working Papers CEB 09–015.RS. Solvay Brussels School of Economics and Management, Centre Emile Bernheim (CEB). Université Libre de Bruxelles.

Athanassopoulos, AD (1997). Service quality and operating efficiency synergies for management control in the provision of financial services: Evidence from Greek bank branches. *European Journal of Operational Research*, 98(2), 300–313.

Berger, AN and DB Humphrey (1991). The dominance of inefficiencies over scale and product mix economies in banking. *Journal of Monetary Economics*, 28, 117–148.

Berger, AN and DB Humphrey (1997). Efficiency of financial institutions: International survey and directions for future research. *European Journal of Operational Research*, 98, 175–212.

Brownlow, D (2007). Bank Efficiency: Measure for measure. *International Banking Systems Journal* 16, http://www.ibspublishing.com/index.cfm?section=features&action=view&id=10065.

Camanho, AS and RG Dyson (2005). Cost efficiency, production and value-added models in the analysis of bank branch performance. *Journal of the Operational Research Society*, 56, 483–494.

Caudill, S, D Gropper and V Hartarska (2009). Which microfinance institutions are becoming more cost-effective with time? Evidence from a mixture model. *Journal of Money Credit and Banking*, 41(4), 651–672.

CGAP (2003). *Microfinance consensus guidelines. Definitions of selected financial terms, ratios and adjustments for microfinance* (3rd ed.). Washington DC, USA: Consultative Group to Assist the Poor.

Charnes, A, WW Cooper and E Rhodes (1978). Measuring the efficiency of decision-making units. *European Journal of Operational Research*, 2, 429–444.

Charnes, A, WW Cooper, YA Lewin and ML Seiford (1994). *Data Envelopment Analysis: Theory, Methodology and Applications.* Dordrecht, The Netherlands: Kluwer Academic Publishers.

Conning, J (1999). Outreach, sustainability and leverage in monitored and peer-monitored lending. *Journal of Development Economics*, 60, 51–77.

Cooper, WW, LM Seiford and K Tone (2000). *Data Envelopment Analysis: A Comprehensive Text with Models, Applications, References and DEA-Solver Software.* Dordrecht, The Netherlands: Kluwer Academic Publishers.

Copestake, J (2007). Mainstreaming microfinance: Social performance management or mission drift? *World Development*, 35(10), 1721–1738.

Cull, R, A Demirgüç-Kunt and J Morduch (2007). Financial performance and outreach: A global analysis of leading microbanks. *Economic Journal*, 117(517), 107–133.

Fernando, NA (2006). *Understanding and Dealing with High Interest Rates on Microcredit. A Note to Policymakers in the Asia and Pacific Region.* Manila: Asian Development Bank. http://www.adb.org/Documents/Books/interest-rates-microcredit/Microcredit-Understanding-Dealing.pdf.

Flückiger, Y and A Vassiliev (2008). Efficiency in Microfinance Institutions: An Application of Data Envelopment Analysis to MFIs in Peru. In *Microfinance and Public Policy: Outreach, Performance and Efficiency*, B Balkenhol (ed.). Houndsmill, UK: Palgrave, McMillan Publishers, pp. 89–109.

Ghosh, S and E Van Tassel (2008). A Model of Mission Drift in Microfinance Institutions. Working Papers 08003, Department of Economics, College of Business, Florida Atlantic University, USA.

Goetz, AM and RS Gupta (1996). Who takes the credit? Gender, power, and control over loan use in rural credit programs in Bangladesh. *World Development*, 24(1), 45–63.

González-Vega, C and M Villafani-Ibarnegaray (2007). Las microfinanzas en la profundización del sistema financiero. El Caso de Bolivia. *El Trimestre Económico*, 293, 5–65.

Goodwin-Groen, RP (2002). Making Sense of Microcredit Interest Rates (Donor Brief'06), Consultative Group to Assist the Poor, Washington DC, USA.

Gutiérrez-Nieto, B, C Serrano-Cinca and C Mar-Molinero (2007). Microfinance Institutions and Efficiency. *Omega*, 35(2), 131–142.

Gutiérrez-Nieto, B, Y Fuertes-Callén and C Serrano-Cinca (2008). Internet reporting in Microfinance Institutions. *Online Information Review*, 32(3), 415–436.

Gutiérrez-Nieto, B, C Serrano-Cinca and C Mar-Molinero (2009). Social efficiency in microfinance institutions. *Journal of the Operational Research Society*, 60(19), 104–119.

Hartarska, V and R Mersland (2008). What governance mechanisms promote efficiency in reaching poor clients? Evidence from rated MFIs. *European Financial Management*, forthcoming.

Hermes, N, R Lensink and A Meesters (2008). Efficiency and outreach of microfinance institutions. Centre for International Banking, Insurance and Finance Working Paper.

Hulme, D (2000). Impact assessment methodologies for microfinance: Theory, experience and better practice. *World Development*, 28(1), 79–98.

Mayoux, L (1999). Questioning virtuous spirals: Microfinance and women's empowerment in Africa. *Journal of International Development*, 11, 957–984.

Mersland, R, RO Strøm (2009). What Explains Governance Structure in Non-Profit and For-Profit Microfinance Institutions? http://ssrn.com/abstract=1342427.

Morduch, J (1999). The microfinance promise. *Journal of Economic Literature*, 37, 1569–1614.

Morduch, J (2000). The microfinance schism. *World Development*, 28(4), 617–629.

Navajas, S, M Schreiner, RL Meyer, C González-Vega and J Rodríguez-Meza (2000). Microcredit and the poorest of the poor: Theory and evidence from Bolivia. *World Development*, 28(2), 333–346.

Paxton, J, D Graham and C Thraen (2000). Modeling group loan repayment behavior: New insights from Burkina Faso. *Economic Development and Cultural Change*, 48(3), 639–655.

Pantoja, E (2002). *Microfinance and Disaster Risk Management. Experiences and Lessons Learned.* Washington DC: World Bank.

Premchander, S. (2003). NGOs and local MFIs — how to increase poverty reduction through women's small and micro-enterprise. *Futures*, 35(4), 361–378.
Rahman, A (2001). *Women and Microcredit in Rural Bangladesh: An Anthropological Study of Grameen Bank Lending*. Boulder, USA: Westview Press.
Rhyne, E and M Otero (2006). *Microfinance through the Next Decade: Visioning the Who, What, Where, and How*. Boston, USA: ACCION.
Silva, S (2003). Microfinance institutions win a coveted seal of approval. *Microenterprise Americas*, Autumn, 12–17.
Soteriou, A and SA Zenios (1999). Operations, quality and profitability in the provision of banking services. *Management Science*, 45(9), 1221–1238.
Thanassoulis, E (2001). *Introduction to the Theory and Application of Data Envelopment Analysis*. Dordrecht, The Netherlands: Kluwer Academic Publishers.
Vassiloglou, M and D Giokas (1990). A study of the relative efficiency of bank branches: An application of data envelopment analysis. *The Journal of the Operational Research Society*, 41, 591–597.
Woller, G, C Dunford and W Woodworth (2002). Where to microfinance? *International Journal of Economic Development*, 1(1), 29–64.
Woller, G and M Schreiner (2009). Poverty lending, financial self-sufficiency, and the blended value approach to reconciling the two. *Journal of International Development*, forthcoming.
Yaron, J (1994). What makes rural finance institutions successful? *The World Bank Research Observer*, 9(1), 49–70.
Zeller, M, M Sharma, C Henry and C Lapenu (2002). An operational tool for evaluating poverty outreach of development policies and projects. In *The Triangle of Microfinance*, M Zeller and RL Meyer (eds.). Baltimore and London: John Hopkins University Press, pp. 172–195.

PART IV

Meeting Unmet Demand: The Challenge of Financing Agriculture

Is Microfinance the Adequate Tool to Finance Agriculture?

Solène Morvant-Roux
Department of Political Economy,
University of Fribourg, Switzerland,
Rural Microfinance and Employment (RUME), and CERMi

Agriculture has already started to become a primary global concern. Prices of agricultural goods are characterized by a high degree of volatility. Food security is no longer guaranteed and high food prices are a short-term problem for the poor in many countries. This situation gives peasants who are struggling to survive in Southern countries a chance to earn a decent living. Thus farmers still need to invest and increase production; access to finance is therefore decisive. The new rural finance paradigm has redefined the roles of the various actors involved in providing financial services, especially governments. Public subsidies have been redirected towards creating new microfinance institutions (MFIs) to enhance *financial inclusion*. The focus is now towards financial inclusion and depth of outreach while achieving financial sustainability thanks to cost-covering interest rates. This emphasis on financial inclusion instead of financing a specific economic sector has led to a low interest of microfinance towards agriculture and in rural areas, a low adaptation of financial services to small farmers' financial needs.

Yet despite a renewed and more promising approach based on financial markets construction in comparison to the "old rural finance paradigm" based on public intervention in credit markets, the majority of peasants in developing countries are still excluded from access to financial services.

1 Introduction

Seventy five percent of the world's poor live in rural areas where their survival depends mainly on agriculture (food producing agriculture and cash crop production) that is exposed to the risks of climate and changes in the market, and characterized by relatively weak profitability (World Bank, 2007). To develop their productive activities, agricultural households face numerous constraints including access to finance. Most of the farmers in developing countries are actually excluded from the banking systems.

The number of people in Africa or South Asia working in agriculture and possessing bank accounts does not exceed 5 or 6 percent, whereas in the developed countries, agriculture banks early on played a major role in modernizing agriculture and incorporating farmers into the banking system.

In the countries of the southern hemisphere, the interventionist logic that prevailed during the 1960s and 1970s, ("the old rural finance paradigm") has been broadly criticized for its inability to consider the realities of a situation, its costs and finally its ineffectiveness in dealing with real needs. The trend toward market regulation as the best vector for social justice was naturally adopted by public policy. However, the results of years of financial liberalisation and the strong growth of microfinance over the past 30 years raise questions regarding what had appeared to be a universal solution: financing structured and offered to poor and marginalized populations, particularly those living in rural areas, is still insufficient. Despite the importance of growth in the agriculture sector for reducing poverty,[1] more often than not the sector has only marginally enjoyed access to financial services (credit, savings, insurance, etc.). In this context and to fill the gap microfinance has not been able to do, a new grouping of players in civil society, the private sector and government has emerged.

Given the uniqueness of agricultural finance, the current trend is toward a less dualist approach that does not disavow the basis for the change in the paradigm, and particularly the goal of sustainability of the sector; what needs to be identified are intermediate approaches that allow a number of diverse public and private players to interact. The approach which was developed in the 1990s, and is based principally on contractual innovations, has given way to innovations in terms of products but also of governance schemes. The dynamics of restructuring public financing institutions in various regions, particularly in Latin America, have shown promise. Accordingly, the effectiveness of public policy can be improved through the establishment of innovative partnerships linking the public and private sectors, as numerous encouraging examples in the agricultural system have shown.

This paper will show evidence of a shift in the scope of the new rural finance paradigm towards financial inclusion instead of the financing of a specific sector of activity whereas during the old paradigm, agriculture was at the center of the scope. We will then show evidence of insufficient supply

[1] "*(...) GDP growth due to agriculture contributes at least twice as much to the reduction of poverty as does GDP growth from the non-agricultural sector*" (summarized from WDR, 2008: 7).

and a poorly adapted financial offer to agriculture. Finally, we will describe different categories of innovations: product innovations and institutional ones.

2 From the Old to the New Paradigm in Rural Finance

2.1 *From the failure of the interventionist approach to the promises of the new paradigm in rural finance*

The old rural finance paradigm of the 1960s and 1970s was based on public authorities' desire to facilitate access to rural finance. The objective was to promote agricultural development by modernizing agriculture. The most common approach involved direct government intervention via state-owned development banks and direct donor intervention in credit markets with favorable terms and conditions like soft interest rates or lenient guarantees. However, this system was costly and unsustainable, due to poor repayment, and ultimately did not have the desired effect on the development of agriculture production (Nagarajan and Meyer, 2005). What Dale Adams calls "Agricultural Credit I" was thus typified by bank-contracted, agriculture-focused credit combined with a push for modernisation of the agricultural systems (green revolution). The many well-known failures of this approach (short-term handout solutions, loan defaults, corruption, etc.) led to a complete denial not only of public intervention, but also of agriculture itself. The paradigm that has been in place from 1980 to the present called "Agricultural credit zero" by D. Adams was born out of this. Development financing in this system is limited to microfinancing, a useful but limited instrument not aimed at financing agriculture since microfinance has mainly focused on urban areas, women, short-term loans, regular repayments, consumption smoothing and high interest rates, etc.

The new paradigm for rural finance is based on an approach of promoting financial inclusion instead of encouraging investments in a specific economic sector. For example, in Mexico, the public programme Patmir (Programa de asistencia técnica al microfinanciamiento rural) implemented by Sagarpa in early 2000's, the Mexican ministry of agriculture, to provide support to financial intermediaries in rural areas aims at financial inclusion through massification of access to financial services. This objective in turn has led to a standardized approach as well as the development of financial products that are easiest to implement than financial services for agriculture.

All these specificities of the new paradim are hardly compatible with agricultural financing.

Moreover, the roles of the different stakeholders have been redefined, particularly that of public intervention. Above and beyond the support provided in the form of public subsidies when rural credit institutions are being created (in particular for microfinance), public institutions have been structured with an emphasis on sector regulation, with legal frameworks specific to microfinance gradually being developed. In terms of targeting, public intervention has mainly focused on medium-sized farm and not on smallholdings considered as a non-profitable segment of the population.

2.2 *Supply continues to be insufficient or not adapted to smallholders' financial needs*

Despite the hopes raised by this new approach to rural finance in developing countries, and in particular the emergence and strong growth of the microfinance sector,[2] we must admit that the supply of financial services to the agriculture sector has remained inadequate and most often only imperfectly meets the needs of small farms.

If we look at microfinance, it is characterized by large disparities among countries and even within the territory of certain nations. Some countries attain very high degrees of penetration, (the case of Bangladesh) while other regions (in particular Sub-Saharan Africa) show much lower rates. Moreover, major disparities exist within countries, between urban zones and outlying suburbs and the rural areas which more often than not remain marginalized. Microfinance is mainly concentrated in urban areas and outlying suburbs which are easier to serve: among rural institutions, the part of the loan portfolio intended for financing agricultural activities varies greatly. In India, in 2006–2007, 8 percent of the loans granted by the microfinance sector directly financed agriculture and 14 percent went to animal husbandry. The remaining 78 percent was distributed for household consumption, funding microenterprises and commerce. Moreover, microfinance

[2]Annual growth of the sector between 1997 and 2005 was over 30 percent (Daley–Harris, 2006). However, this figure hides large disparities between countries and within the territory of individual nations.

provided practically no credits for agriculture, mechanization, irrigation and land development (Pillarisetti, 2007).[3]

The revolution in microfinance that emerged during the 1980s and 1990s was thus generally limited to urban areas in most of Africa and South America. Even when it did reach rural areas, as in certain regions of Asia, it was generally reserved for rural microenterprises. The approach was driven by diversification of income sources rather than helping farmers investing in crop production. The rural and urban clients of microfinance are generally located in densely populated, low-income areas, and where the economic activity is not agriculture. We have recognized that some microfinance institutions such as CECAM in Madagascar or Kafo jiginew in Mali were started in order to target smallholder farmers and to meet their financial needs. But the vast majority did not aim at targeting farmers.

At the same time, with the liberalisation of the banking sector, the removal of government has not been compensated by growth of the commercial banking sector in rural areas and even less toward increased financing of agriculture. On the contrary, many banks have even closed their rural branches (Zeller, 2003). Thus, despite the available data, which is relatively general and mixed and only concerns certain geographic areas, we have to admit that agriculture remains inadequately funded or that supply most often meets the needs of agricultural producers[4] only imperfectly. This situation is essentially due to the fact that the financing of these activities is on the whole more costly, riskier, and less profitable above and beyond the difficulties that are usually pointed out when financial services are to be established in rural areas. Agriculture presents a certain number of specificities that financing schemes must understand and take into consideration.

---

[3]However, it should be emphasized that certain networks adopt can-do approaches to cover the financial needs of farmers. Such is the case of the Confederation of Financial Institutions (CFI) in West Africa. An analysis of loan terms granted by the network over three sample years (1998, 2001 and 2004) shows a considerable change in medium-term loans (those maturing between 12 and 36 months) from 5 percent in 1998 to 36 percent in 2004. Even if the issue of covering needs is still current and significant regional disparities persist, these results are encouraging.

[4]Data provided by the CIF network once again goes against the trend observed in numerous contexts, since 40 percent of the loans granted by institutions in the network in 2006 were for financing agricultural and fishing activities. The rest of the portfolio was divided between crafts (8 percent) and trade and services (52 percent). These results are encouraging despite the significant regional disparities. Indeed, within the WAEMU, the figures are 19 percent, 21 percent and 60 percent for trade (Ouedraogo and Gentil, 2008).

Agriculture is distinct from other sectors of economic activity in several respects. The factors that hinder the development of financial services made accessible to family agriculture are numerous and have been well identified. The location of these activities in isolated areas are characterized by low population density and lack of infrastructure;[5] a dependence on climatic conditions and the temporality of production cycles; the seasonality of income and, in a more general manner, the limited proportion of monetary revenue; the volatility of prices for agricultural products; less reliable guarantees from both the legal and economic perspectives; etc. Efforts needed to better understand the financial needs of farmers combined with the risks associated with these activities thus constitute additional obstacles to establishing a financing package for agriculture. In addition, the interest rates applied by financial intermediaries to cover the costs engendered by the services they offer and to protect themselves against risks have often been incompatible with the low profitability level associated with most agriculture productions.

It is not an accident that faced with these constraints, institutions established in rural areas experience greater difficulty in being financially profitable and must often resort to public subsidies. Pressure on profitability imposes strategic choices on these institutions which generally lead them to neglect rural areas and agriculture, preferring to establish themselves in urban areas and the outlying suburbs where they are exposed to strong competition from for-profit organisations (Servet, 2008). The logic of the market, combined with the many contractual innovations that have been promoted by the new paradigm, have not fulfilled all the promises to the rural world and more particularly to agriculture that finance would be forthcoming.

3 Financing Agriculture: the Need for Innovations

In order to develop agricultural finance, different kinds of innovations regarding products and services as well as institutional aspects are very important. The challenge is twofold: improve financial inclusion through better outreach of marginalized populations as well as financial services that fit the diversity of financial needs.

---

[5]Current experiments using new information and communication technologies can provide a certain number of solutions to the problem of geographic isolation and low population density (Ivatury, 2006).

3.1 *Product innovations*

While classic microcredit is often limited to small amounts, short-term leasing has shown to be a promising tool not only for investment, but also for other expenses at the household level. Using the good as collateral reduces the risk for both the borrower and the lender (Nair *et al.*, 2004). Another innovation that is promising, even if some conditions are required, deals with experiences of wharehouse receipt systems. By allowing producers to deposit their production and obtain a receipt, the lender can mitigate credit risk by using stored commodity as collateral. In contexts of seasonality of prices, experience shows that this mechanism not only improves the selling prices for farm households, but also contributes to food security (food storage). Although the system faces many implementation challenges, it is quite promising to help farmers gain access to financial services (Coulter and Onumah, 2002).

Other solutions to promote efficient, sustainable and accessible financial services for smallholder farmers are being found in terms of institutional organization such as portfolio diversification between urban and rural borrowers or between agricultural activities and less risky economic activities within rural areas in order to mitigate risk. In various contexts (Mali, Madagascar, Peru, etc.), microfinance institutions that were implemented to reach rural areas and to meet farmers' financial needs, have adopted portfolio diversification strategy in order to reduce their dependency on crop production and to improve risk management. These institutions started to implement activities in urban areas. Besides governance and mission drift issues, we recognize that this strategy implies capacity building costs for skills acquisition since urban and rural development of financial products require different expertise. Skills acquisition is highly challenging in rural areas but it is crucial to develop specific expertise adequate to agricultural activities financing. One possibility could be that public support goes to cover the costs associated with the acquisition of such expertise.

Agriculture output is highly dependent on weather conditions. Evidence is growing of connections between climate change, and the increasing incidence of crop-damaging weather of extreme severity. Thus, the question of risk management and climate risks in particular are considered an essential condition for developing agricultural financial services.

The solutions are therefore to be found in climate insurance and loans coupled with insurance. The question is how low-income farmers can be indemnified against agricultural losses from severe weather conditions and how such schemes can be made profitable. Actually, the implementation is quite challenging due to the necessity of available weather time-series data in order to create index-based weather insurance products, due to loss assessment issues, etc. (FAO, 2005). The specificities of the risk level of agricultural production make insurance schemes unprofitable and explain why premiums only make up 0.4 percent of the value of global agricultural production. In most countries without public subsidies, insurers would simply be unable or unwilling to provide agricultural insurance (Roth and McCord, 2008).

This calls for partnerships between governments and private insurance companies (Pagura, 2008).

Moreover, in this context and faced with the specific characteristics of financing agriculture, the current trend is beginning to take a less dualist approach. Without abandoning the fundamental reasons for changing the paradigm, the current trend actually stresses the limits of a monolithic theory of division between public and private, and encourages a redefinition of the scope of action and the respective roles of government, the private sector and civil society (Bouquet, 2007). The microfinance movement which was based mainly on contractual innovations (required collateral, ways to encourage repayment and financial products) and upon which the new paradigm for rural finance has been developed, has left room for innovation in terms of governance. Above and beyond the institutional model, a certain equilibrium among the various players is sought. This balance should help to avoid the errors of the past.

3.2 *Development banks converted to engines of agricultural development*

Faced with this new paradigm for rural finance, public financial institutions initially lost all legitimacy in terms of participating in the structuring of a financial package in developing countries (Gonzales–Vega, 2003). However, in contrast with the dominant ideology, the debate in Latin America and in certain Asian or African countries no longer consists simply of questioning the relevance of creating or maintaining public financial institutions, but trying to make them work more effectively and ensuring that they best serve the development goals entrusted to them.

3.2.1 *Experiences from Latin America*

In Latin America, there are 108 Development Financing Institutions (DFI), 32 of which offer loans for agriculture, either because they were established with this objective or because they usually finance various sectors of economic activity. Recent changes in some of these institutions have taught us some interesting lessons. The issue of the effectiveness of these organisations has actually led to the promotion of private sector participation through governance that aims at limiting political interference, a factor that renders these institutions fragile.[6]

The experience of Banrural S.A. in Guatemala is interesting from two perspectives: the innovative character of its governance structure matched with financial performance goals. Banrural S.A. resulted from the restructuring of Bandesa, the Guatemala public bank for agricultural development. The most credible alternative at the time (first half of the 1990s) and the one supported by several multilateral agencies was the outright privatization of Bandesa. However, the restructuring of Bandesa by local players caused other options to emerge aimed at creating a new model, while at the same time preserving certain characteristics inherited from Bandesa which were conducive to its mission of promoting development; this mission would have been compromised if the privatization option had been chosen.

The model of governance at Banrural SA is original in several respects. In the first place, Banrural SA is a mixed-capital bank in which the public sector holds 30 percent of the shares, with the remaining 70 percent held by private shareholders: the cooperative movement (20 percent), farmer organisations (20 percent) and various private shareholders (NGOs, micro-entrepreneurs, etc.) hold the last 30 percent. This model allows each of the shareholder categories to elect their leaders during general meetings. Each group can sell stock only to other members of the group. The composition of the management committee thus remains representative of the different categories of shareholders. The result is a system that requires permanent negotiation and a search for consensus among the shareholders. At an operational level, the bank works at two levels: either directly through its branches located in almost all the major cites of the country (its primary business); or indirectly through a refinancing line of credit which targets those entities involved in microfinance (NGOs or cooperatives) operating in isolated areas (its secondary business). The loan officers visit all clients and decisions are based on evaluation of business and household income flows.

[6]The analysis of Latin American experiences of development banks are based on Trivelli and Venero, 2007.

Thanks to an important growth in point of services mainly in rural areas, Banrural has been able to develop its offer towards rural areas and agriculture. The good quality of the financial services offered has also played a central role. Since it began to offer this line of credit, Banrural SA has managed to serve more than 75,000 rural clients through over 150 local financial organisations. The share of its portfolio towards agriculture was of 12 percent in 2006, but the objective was to increase it. The interest rate is quite low (16 percent per year) thanks to a cheap credit line and low level of operational costs whereas the default rate of agricultural credit is 1 percent.

Of all the original characteristics of this model, we draw attention to two: on the one hand, the possibility given to civil society organisations to invest in the new bank, thereby offering these entities greater opportunities to be considered and recognized in the public sphere. On the other hand, the possibility for the State through the executive branch — as shareholder — to share its ideas for rural development strategy with the management committee, and to promote the work of the bank as a way to support and enhance government programme initiatives. Overall, Banrural S.A. appears to be an exemplary institution from a profitability and coverage perspective, and it provides for balance between the various shareholders — the State, cooperatives, indigenous or farmer organisations and non-profit organisations.

The profile of the development bank in Latin America in which the public sector still plays a significant role has thus changed a great deal during recent years. There are now various formulae for development banks in the agricultural sector, ranging from exclusively public entities specialising in agriculture, to refinancing, mixed capital or multi-sector institutions. This multiplicity of potential responses to the obstacles limiting finance in the agricultural sector reveals a number of attractive alternatives. Between institutions controlled by the public sector which are generally dependent on the current administration in power, and privatisation, there are various alternatives for reform that can bring about change within the governing structures of those entities dedicated to financing development. These alternatives allow the best advantages of private initiative to be enhanced while preserving the positive aspects of those entities involved in development that are supported by the power of the State (which we differentiate from the government in place at any particular time).

It should be pointed out, however, that in terms of the participation of clients/members of these financing institutions, where they are involved in governance (which is not the case in Chile, Argentina, Peru or Colombia), their role in determining the kind of financial services offered is more often than not marginal. In Mexico, agricultural representatives play a political role but are not involved in determining what financial services are offered. Once again, the experience of Banrural S.A. Guatemala is an exception with its real convergence of, on the one hand, the participation of customers of the institution in its governing body, and on the other hand, managers who are convinced of the importance of responding in the best possible way to the needs of customers in order to ensure the viability of its services.

3.2.2 *Experiences in Asia and Africa*

Other experiences of restructuring financial institutions which have aimed at creating a financial product adapted to the constraints of the agricultural sector have occurred in a number of Asian countries. We cite the example of the BAAC (Bank for Agriculture and Agricultural Cooperatives), in Thailand. Governance of the BAAC with majority ownership controlled by members of the government (99 percent of the shares are in the hands of the Ministry of Finance, and the remaining 1 percent is held by agricultural cooperatives) does not shield it from emphasising those short-term strategies that may characterize governmental institutions and which may go against a medium-to-long-term stability essential for constructing a sustainable product. On the other hand, the restructuring has concentrated more on business profitability, and the emphasis placed on attracting savings has considerably reduced the dependence of the institution vis-à-vis external sources of finance. In 2003, the BAAC reached 5.3 million households or close to 92 percent of all agricultural households in Thailand.

In India, the NABARD (National Bank for Agriculture and Rural Development) initiated its institutional development from below, through a DAP (Development Action Plan) prepared for each category of rural financial institution (RFI) — cooperative banks, regional rural banks, etc. These reforms of the financial sector through the DAPs also led a large number of institutions to change their systems and procedures, their credit and deposit programmes as well as their methods for managing human resources, all in the interest of improving their profitability while ensuring that their credit programmes were broadly distributed. Even if the initial results were not particularly successful, a large number of these institutions (district central cooperative banks as well as regional rural banks) managed to be profitable while maintaining loans for agriculture (Pillarisetti, 2007).

The linkage between national banks dedicated to agriculture and microfinance institutions also proved to be productive in Mali where support of the National Bank for Agricultural Development (Banque Nationale de Développement Agricole — BNDA), in the form of a refinance facility, allowed these institutions to reduce their liquidity risks. A study carried out by D. Seibel showed that Kafo Jiginew, the network of savings and loan cooperatives, used lines of credit and savings accounts from the BNDA or from other commercial banks to reduce annual cash flow fluctuations due to the seasonality of agricultural activity (Seibel, 2008). As a general rule, we should underline the preponderant place of producers' organisations as the favoured interlocutors in the process of establishing financial schemes for funding agriculture in the countries of the southern hemisphere. Their participation in the governance of financial institutions could be encouraged.

The Federation of NGOs in Senegal (FONGS) has encouraged participation in the governance of the National Bank for Agricultural Credit of Senegal (Caisse Nationale de Credit Agricole du Senegal — CNCAS) due to an acquisition of 4 percent of the bank's capital which allowed it to have a seat on the bank's board of directors in order to secure the only instrument of agricultural finance. An additional goal was to influence the rural finance policy of the CNCAS and in particular to ensure the development and sustainability of finance in rural areas. This strategy has led to notable advances in the area of rural and agricultural finance:

- Expansion of CNCAS's network and increased proximity to rural producers,
- Reduction of interest rates from 18 percent to 7.5 percent,
- The beginning of a dialogue regarding linkages between CNCAS's network and decentralized endogenous savings and credit cooperatives.

The examples presented above, however, illustrate that the idea of a unique organisational model adapted to the specific characteristics of financing agriculture does not correspond to reality as we know it. Selecting the institutional model in strategies for accessing financial services is not the sole determinant.

But what emerges is that the forms of governance of development financial institutions, as seen particularly in Latin America, bring the private sector together with civil society in the governing structures; they combine to provide support (principally in the form of refinance facilities) and to structure the financial sector; this interesting compromise strengthens and stabilises the sources of finance for agriculture. These experiences have led to a better coverage of the needs of this economic sector by emphasizing the demands of short-term profitability that are compatible with the agriculture sector. The role of the State in financing agriculture is therefore bound to change. Beyond the functions related to sovereignty, which confine its action to developing a legal and regulatory framework,[7] its intervention is always justifiable, especially when there is concern for equity among the different categories of the population.

However, in most contexts, public intervention has focused on promoting private sector development to reduce financial exclusion. This approach of financial inclusion has not led to a leading role played by the private sector in agriculture. This is supported by Burgess and Pande (2005). The authors show that in India, the expansion of the rural bank network between 1977 and 1990, thanks to the social banking program, increased non-agricultural sectors' growth but not agricultural growth. These results strongly support the fact that the private sector doesn't substitute for the state's leading role in agriculture. It is interesting to notice that in Mexico state intervention has given up support to small farms through subsidized credit whereas commercial farming still benefits from this kind of state support (Morvant-Roux *et al.*, 2009).

In fact, research has identified the advantages associated with public banks in emerging economies. What we see is a greater involvement in those sectors which traditionally have not benefited from the services offered by commercial banks (such as small farms, women and small businesses) as well as a greater stability and permanence of their commitment to these sectors of economic activity or segments of the population compared to private banks (See, *inter alia*, Voguel, 2005, and Micco and Panizza, 2005). Public subsidies also allow the most disadvantaged groups to be reached (Balkenhol, 2007). More generally, to the extent that the problem of agricultural finance consists of uniting proximity, innovation and diversification, and risk reduction, other methods of interaction have been experimented in the agricultural sector.

From this viewpoint, the fact that not only financial institutions, but also all the players in the industry (producers, suppliers, buyers, processors) face numerous risks justifies efforts at coordination in order to reduce these risks. Consequently, through strategic alliances, we are now witnessing more reflective thinking by all parties aimed at bringing together the comparative

[7]There is much reticence about direct public intervention in the financial market; some fear market distortion and its negative repercussions on the private sector of associations and cooperatives, which voluntarily try to cover the demand for financial services in rural disadvantaged areas.

advantage of each category, stimulating mutual dynamics and reducing risks for all players.

Several initiatives aiming to strengthen interaction between these two sectors are underway. The objective is to build long-term relationships and reduce risk for the different actors: producers, borrowers, buyers and processors.

These partnerships come in different forms.

- Some focus on one link in the value chain (for instance, partnerships between MFIs and storage facilities or MFIs and exporters).
- Others address the chain as a whole (Danone's business model in Bangladesh).
- Partnerships may be direct or indirect, i.e., incited by a third party, such as an NGO, who plays the role of catalyst, facilitator and sometimes service provider.

There are recent examples of value chain actors playing the limited role of "virtual guarantor", in which case a producer's mere association with a large buyer or processor, for instance, serves as a sign of creditworthiness in the eyes of financial institutions. The value chain actor may also be directly involved in financial transactions, providing producers with credit services in a more traditional approach (Gonzales-Vega *et al.*, 2006).

Entrusting the financing of development to private resources and players should not totally supplant public action which alone is capable of promoting a certain level of collective consistency indispensable for these operations and for the development goals they claim to serve (Servet, 2008).

4 Conclusion

Given the limits of the two models — State and market — alternative approaches have emerged and should be looked at more closely. Parallel to this, the international economic situation is bringing agriculture, particularly in developing countries, back to the centre of the world's concerns. In this context, the major problem of meeting the food needs of developing countries must be ensured by regional producers. But under what conditions could rural areas meet this growing demand? For developing countries' farmers, this context offers opportunities but in order to seize this historic good fortune, they need to invest in and increase their production. That implies having access to the appropriate credit and insurance systems. Faced with these challenges, the State has a strong role to play in supporting schemes for financing agriculture.

So far, in the context of liberalization, governments in many countries have given priority to financial inclusion. This laid aside the priority of the 60s given to financing a strategic economic sector, namely agricultural production. Moreover, with the financial inclusion trend has come the income-generating activities diversification: in rural areas, where agriculture is mostly unprofitable, rural populations are encouraged to invest microcredit into new productive activities. This income sources diversification is supposed to reduce households' vulnerability. In that context, few microfinance institutions have developed an offer for farmers' financial needs (Morvant-Roux *et al.*, 2009).

However, among the current initiatives that we have highlighted, some are promising but we still need time to evaluate the effectiveness of the new forms of partnerships as well as the public policy tools to meet the diverse financial needs of agricultural producers. Research and analyses carried out to date have been specific and do not lend themselves to generalities. The studies devoted to the role of the State rarely take into account the specificities of agriculture, so their scope is therefore limited. Cross analyses at a regional level are of great value because, without being prescriptive, they lead to the identification of experiences that offer solutions and can thus guide the decisions of the different players.

References

Balkenhol, B (ed.) (2007). *Microfinance and Public Policy: Outreach, Performance and Efficiency.* London: Palgrave MacMillan.

Bouquet, E (2007). Construir un sistema financiero para el desarrollo rural en México. Nuevos papeles para el Estado y la sociedad civil. *Revue Trace*, 52.

Burgess, R and R Pande (2005). Can rural banks reduce poverty? Evidence from the Indian social banking experiment. *American Economic Review*, 95(3), 780–795.

Coulter, J and G Onumah (2002). The role of warehouse receipt systems in enhanced commodity marketing and rural livelihoods in Africa. *Food Policy*, 27, 319–337.

Daley-Harris, S (2006). *State of the Microcredit Summit Campaign, Report 2006.* Washington: Microcredit Summit Campaign.

González-Vega, C (2003). Deeping Rural Financial Markets: Macroeconomic Policy and Political Dimensions. Paper Presented at the Conference *Paving the Way Forward: An International Conference on Best Practices in Rural Finance*, Washington DC.

González-Vega, C, G Chalmers, R Quiros and J Rodriguez-Mega (2006). Hortifruti in Central America: A Case Study About the Influence of Supermarkets on the Development and Evolution of Creditworthiness Among Small and Medium Agricultural Producers. *microREPORT* 57, AMAP Publication. Development Alternatives Inc. and The Ohio State University.

Ivatury, G (2006). La technologie au service de systèmes financiers inclusifs. CGAP, Focus note 32.

Micco, A and U Panizza (2005). Public Banks in Latin America. Background Paper Prepared for the Conference. *Public Banks in Latin America: Myth and Reality*, IDB, Washington.

Morvant-Roux, S (2008). What Can Microfinance Contribute to Agriculture in Developing Countries? *Proceedings of the International FARM Conference.*

Morvant-Roux, S (ed.) (2009). *Microfinance pour l'agriculture des pays du Sud, 8ième rapport, Exclusions et liens financiers.* Paris: Economica, pp. 458.

Morvant-Roux, S, I Guérin, M Roesch and J–M Servet (2009). Politiques d'inclusion financière et financement de l'agriculture. Le cas de l'Inde et du Mexique. *Mondes en Développement*, 38-2010/3-n° 151.

Nagarajan, G and RL Meyer (2005). Rural Finance: Recent Advances and Emerging Lessons, Debates, and Opportunities. Working Paper AEDE-WP-0041-05, Department of Agricultural, Environmental, and Development Economics, The Ohio State University.

Nair, A, R Kloeppinger-Todd and A Mulder (2004). Leasing: An Underutilized Tool in Rural Finance. World Bank Agricultural and Rural Development, Discussion Paper 7.

Ouedraogo, A and D Gentil (eds.) (2008). *La microfinance en Afrique de l'Ouest: Histoires et innovations.* Paris: CIF-KARTHALA.

Pagura, M (ed.) (2008). *Expanding the Frontier in Rural Finance: Financial Linkage and Strategic Alliances.* Rugby: Practical Action Publishing.

Pillarisetti, S (2007). Microfinance for Agriculture: Perspectives from India. Paper for the International Conference. *What Can Microfinance Contribute to Agriculture in Developing Countries*? Paris.

Seibel, D (2008). Self-Reliance vs. Donor Dependence: Linkages Between Banks and Microfinance Institutions in Mali. In *Expanding the Frontier in Rural Finance: Financial Linkage and Strategic Alliances*, M Pagura (ed.), pp. 147–168. Rugby: Practical Action Publishing.

Servet, J–M (2008). Inclusion financière et responsabilité sociale: Production de plus values financières et de valeurs sociales en microfinance. *Revue Tiers-Monde* 2009/1 (197).

Trivelli, C and H Venero (2007). *Banca de desarrollo para el agro: experiencias en curso en América Latina*, Lima (Perú): Instituto de Estudios Peruanos.

Voguel, R (2005). Costs and Benefits of Liquidating Peru's Agricultural Bank. USAID–EGAT–AMAP.

World Bank (2007). *World Development Report 2008: Agriculture for Development.* Washington DC.

Zeller (2003). Models of Rural Financial Institutions. Paper Presented at *Paving the Way Forward: An International Conference on Best Practices in Rural Finance*, Washington DC.

What is the Demand for Microcredit? The Case of Rural Areas in Serbia

William Parienté

IRES, Université Catholique de Louvain, JPAL

Interventions in the credit market, such as microcredit programs, are developed under the assumption that low-income individuals are credit-constrained and have a positive demand for credit which is left unsatisfied by existing credit sources. Although there has been a significant expansion of microcredit programs in the world, there is still important potential for low-income individuals that remain credit-constrained, especially in rural areas.

This article contributes to the analysis of the gap between supply and demand of credit using empirical results from a study carried out in rural areas of Serbia where there is a combination of substantial credit constraints and a low overall demand for microcredit services.

Without directly analyzing household's credit behavior, we evaluate credit demand from rural households through the analysis of consumer preferences, using choice-based conjoint (CBC) methods, commonly used to analyze demand for products that have many attributes. Interestingly, we also find very low demand for credit products that have the conventional attributes of microcredit. We then look at the household characteristics that affect demand for microcredit.

From the results of this study, we elaborate on the factors that impede the development of microcredit.

1 Introduction

Financial services are essential for various reasons, such as for the accumulation of physical or human capital as well as for consumption smoothing in the absence of insurance markets. The lack of access to credit may therefore have significant consequences on the economic productivity and mobility of households. Credit constraints, in an agricultural context, may lead for instance to the choice of low risk-low return production or asset portfolios (Rosenzweig and Biswanger, 1993).

Interventions in the credit market, such as microcredit programs, are developed under the assumption that low-income individuals are credit-constrained and have a positive demand for credit which is left unsatisfied by existing credit sources. Although there has been significant expansion of microcredit programs in the world, their outreach is, in some rural contexts, still limited, and there is still much potential for improving the availability of microfinance services for low-income individuals that remain credit-constrained.

The extent of access to credit and the existence of credit constraints result from the confrontation of credit supply and demand. Although much has been written on credit market imperfections and their implications in terms of credit rationing, there is very little empirical evidence of measures[1] of credit demand. Evaluating credit demand is complex for several reasons, the main one being that financial demand depends on the various terms of credit transactions: interest rate, maturity, frequency of repayment instalments, grace period, timing of disbursement, transaction costs, and so on. The second reason is that, because of credit constraints, observing an absence of credit transactions does not imply an absence of financial demand. This would only be the case if there were no credit transactions and no credit constraints as well. Thirdly, evaluating demand for credit for a specific use, like financing agricultural production, is difficult if credit can be used for various purposes.

Although several studies have attempted to estimate credit demand in developing countries, the estimates are often biased. In fact, it is difficult to distinguish between demand and supply factors, and data is often truncated by omitting non-borrowers (David, 1979; David and Meyer, 1980).

Thus, there is an overall lack of rigorous methods to evaluate how credit demand varies across credit contract parameters. One of the most successful attempts to analyze credit demand sensitivity comes from a randomized experiment in South Africa (Karlan and Zinman, 2008) where interest rates and loan maturities are randomly assigned to a pool of former clients of

[1]The measurement of credit constraint has been subject to different methods within various theoretical frameworks. Empirical studies have treated credit constraint at different levels. Several works attempt to evaluate the constraint via consumption outcomes (Japelli, 1990; Zeldes, 1989). Some studies (Godquin and Sharma, 2005) attempt to evaluate production and consumption constraints in an agricultural model framework. Still others seek to evaluate constraint at the production levels. Sial and Carter (1996) evaluate the shadow price of capital of small Pakistani farmers consecutive to participation in a credit program. In a different context, Banerjee and Duflo (2008) compare the marginal productivity of capital of Indian firms taking advantage of a change in subsidized lending in India.

a bank. Karlan and Zinman show that demand elasticity is relatively flat when interest rates are below lenders' standard rates but very elastic when prices are above. However, Karlan and Zinman's experiment has some limitations. First, it considers a specific type of clientele (those who were already clients). Second, their past experience might bias downward the elasticities of demand when the rates are above the current standard interest rates. Third, their focus is limited to two credit attributes: interest rate and maturity while other factors might be important in the decision to apply for a loan such as the size.

This article contributes to the analysis of the gap between supply and demand of credit using empirical results from a study carried out in rural areas of Serbia where there is a combination of substantial credit constraints and a very low outreach (and demand for?) of microcredit services. In this context, we try to understand the determinants of inadequate matching between the type of credit offered by microfinance institutions and demand from households.

Without directly analyzing the households' credit behavior, we evaluate credit demand of rural households through the analysis of consumer preferences, using choice-based conjoint (CBC) methods, commonly used to analyze demand for products that have many attributes.

Empirical results of this article are based on data from the follow-up survey of the Living Standard Measurement Surveys (LSMS) 2002, conducted on a representative sample of around 2,000 agricultural households.

This article is organized as follows. Section 2 describes the use of financial services rural Serbia; Section 3 analyzes credit demand of agricultural households in rural Serbia using choice-based conjoint methods. Section 4 concludes by looking at the factors impeding the development of microcredit.

2 Credit Market in Rural Serbia

In the rural areas surveyed in Serbia, agricultural activities represent the main source of income. Around 40 percent of households rely directly on agriculture while the second most important income source are the social transfers. Revenues from non-agricultural businesses remain very limited.

Agricultural households in Serbia do not use a wide array of financial services. In the year before the survey (2007), almost one-third (29 percent) of agricultural households had credit transactions with only the informal sector; 15 percent of households had access to some loan in the formal

Table 20.1: Access to credit.

Access to credit	
Outstanding debt	40
Bank	7.2
Micro-credit	0.6
Cooperative	0.85
Relative	9.92
Friend	11.56
State credit programs	4.5
Municipal program	3.6
In kind (shopkeeper, suppliers, etc.)	25
Usurer	1.31
Other	0

sector; and 60 percent were not engaged in any credit transactions at all. The most frequent credit source among households is the consumer shop followed by friends and relatives. Credit from banks concern only 7 percent of the households and are slightly more frequent than credit from input suppliers (6 percent). Moreover, 5 percent of agricultural households had access to subsidized credit from a government program (that started in 2004) in the past year. It is important to note that figures on the use of informal credit sources might be slightly underestimated as they are particularly difficult to capture with household survey questionnaires.

Table 20.1 shows also, at the time of the survey, that microfinance was relatively non-existent.

2.1 *Latent demand*

Access to credit is not only measured by the proportion of households having an outstanding debt or by the amount of the loan size secured. Some rural households ask for some credit and receive less than demanded or are refused while others are excluding themselves from the credit market, even though their demand for credit is different from zero.

In rural Serbia, 38 percent of households were willing to borrow more at market conditions and 28.5 percent of them had a need for credit that they did not ask for, in the year before the survey. This self-exclusion from the credit market is explained by the fear of being turned down, the fear of not being able to repay a potential loan or because of the lack of appropriate

Table 20.2: Latent demand issues.

Proportion of households	
Willing to borrow more at the market conditions	38
Need of credit in the past year, not asked	28.5
Main reasons of no demand	
Fear of being turned down	7.1
Fear of not being able to repay	24.4
Not having appropriate collateral	8.14
Credit demand refused	7

collateral. Moreover, 7 percent of households have been refused in their credit demand in the year before the survey. See Table 20.2 above.

Although these latent demand estimates are only an approximation of credit constraints, their conjunction with limited transactions on the formal and informal sectors demonstrates that there is a significant need for credit that is currently not addressed by existing financial sources and show the potential for some intervention in the credit market.

In the following section, we evaluate credit demand with a new approach.

3 Evaluating Demand from a Choice-Based Conjoint Analysis

In this section, we investigate the role that credit product typology plays in the demand for credit. One way to assess the impact of the terms of credit on financial demand is through the analysis of consumer preferences by using specifically stated choice methods such as choice-based conjoint analysis (CBC),[2] commonly used when a product has many attributes. Credit products have indeed many attributes that are simultaneously affecting demand.

CBC methods have their foundations in consumer theory — utilities for goods can be decomposed into separable utilities for their characteristics or attributes — and random utility theory, which states that utility is a function of the characteristics or attributes.

In CBC experiments, respondents are presented with combinations of attributes presented as different products. Respondents usually have

[2]A comprehensive description of the methodology of conjoint analysis can be found in Green and Srinivasan (1978 and 1990).

difficulty in accurately determining the relative importance they place on a given product attribute. That is, individual attributes in isolation are perceived differently than in the combinations found in a product. Moreover, rather than presenting every possible combination of attributes and attribute levels, CBC experiments present a subset of the possible combinations of product, selected randomly. Respondents are asked to pick up only one product out of several product offers. The process therefore determines the comparative valuation of each attribute and which level of each attribute is preferred. The benefit of the method is to recreate as much as possible the conditions of the market by suggesting some figurative examples that are close to reality.

To our knowledge, this is the first attempt to evaluate financial demand with a choice-based conjoint approach. Applied to agricultural households in rural Serbia, it will allow for identifying the preferred terms of credit for each credit characteristic and which credit characteristic (size of the loan, interest rate, etc.) is most valued by households and has the most effect on the decision to take a loan. The CBC also allows the evaluation of the demand for the existing supply that is available in some parts of Serbia. This is of particular importance in rural Serbia where the outreach of the conventional banking sector is still limited and where there are some potential programs aiming at improving access to credit such as a large-scale subsidized credit program from the government or microfinance interventions.

3.1 *Design of choice based conjoint analysis*

The design of the choice sets of the CBC is very important in order for the results to make sense in a specific context (that they are believable by the respondent) and would be close to reality if the contingent products were actually present in the market. In rural Serbia, the choice sets of the CBC experiment are based on the most valued attributes by the households (according to a prior qualitative survey[3] on households' perception and use of financial services) and the attributes' levels that were commonly used by the government credit program, by banks and by microfinance institutions.[4]

[3]Twelve focus group discussions were conducted in four regions of Serbia. Participants were asked to mention all loan attributes that mattered to them. After aggregation across groups, the five most important attributes were selected.
[4]The attributes and values reflect somehow the existing supply in the Serbian rural credit market but as Churchill and Iacobucci (2002) suggest, the range for the various attributes

Table 20.3: Attributes and Levels.

Factors/Attributes	Level
Interest rate	4% 12% 15%
Loan duration	1 year 2 years 5 years
Loan size	400 € 1,000 € 6,000 € 16,000 €
Grace period	1 year None
Euro linkage	Linked Not linked
Repayment frequency	Monthly Semi-annually Annually

The choice-based conjoint design consists of six attributes[5] reflecting the most important attributes, set at several levels (see Table 20.3) representing approximately the existing credit contracts in Serbia. For instance, banks usually charge interest rates of around 12 percent per annum, provide large loans (16,000 euros on average), with a loan duration of generally one year or longer, a grace period and semi-annual or annual repayment. Banks' credits are usually linked to the Euro. The government-subsidized credit program is characterized by lower interest rates, ranging from 3 percent to 5 percent (for long- and short-term credit respectively). The 4 percent interest rate suggested here is an average of the two. Loan sizes vary between 1,000 (short-term) and 16,000 euros (for long-term), they have a grace period and the loans are reimbursed annually. Long-term credits are linked to the Euro while short-term credits are not. Microcredit organizations generally provide small loans (400 euros on average) with higher interest rates (15 percent), to

might be somewhat larger than the range normally found but not so large as to make the options unbelievable.

[5]According to Dufhues, Heidhues and Buchenrieder (2004), it should not exceed 20 attributes.

be repaid every month during a year, without a grace period, and generally not linked to the Euro.

The permutation of these six attributes and the associated levels (2, 3 or 4) provides 432 (2*2*3*3*3*4) possible combinations (a "full factorial"). An orthogonal design of 18 orthogonal factors (six factors * three cards per task) is constructed resulting in 64 different tasks.[6] The tasks were divided into 16 blocks of four tasks[7] (as one respondent cannot evaluate 64 tasks) and each respondent had to evaluate only one block, all blocks being rotated among respondents. Choice sets of each task consisted of four alternatives: three credit contracts — described with words and images to increase respondent understanding — and an option: "none, I would not choose any of these." In each case, respondents were asked to choose option A, option B, option C or the "none" option. An example of a choice set is provided in Figure A.1 (Appendix).

3.2 *Estimation strategy*

As agricultural households were asked to choose only one alternative from each set of profiles, a random utility model (RUM) is used to estimate how choices are related to attribute levels (and later to some socioeconomic characteristics). The choice-based conjoint analysis is estimated by a conditional logit specification (Maddala, 1983). In a conditional logit model, alternative specific variables that vary by outcome (j) and individual (i) are used to predict the outcome that is chosen. In the conditional logit model, the predicted probability of observing the outcome J is given by

$$P(Y_i = J) = \frac{e^{\beta' z_{ij}}}{\sum_{j=1}^{J} e^{\beta' z_{ij}}}$$

where J is the outcome choice from the J existing alternatives; β is a vector of parameters that we are interested in estimating and z_{ij} the characteristics levels of the loan attributes for the individual i and outcome j.

The key assumption of conditional and multinomial logit model analysis (MNL) is the independence of irrelevant alternatives (IIA). Thus, the

[6]One task was dropped as it contained the same cards in the task (where the choice is evident), resulting in 63 tasks and nearly an orthogonal design.

[7]Following Bennett (1999), the minimum number of people in a sub-sample should be around 50, in order to ensure a sufficient power or statistical significance between subjects of interest.

comparison between the choices presented to respondents is assumed to be unaffected by the possibility that other profiles could be chosen.[8]

Furthermore, the parameters are specified through a linear utility model, allowing for the calculation of the tradeoffs between independent variables.

3.3 *Results*

Simple observed frequencies of the choice-based conjoint analysis are displayed in Table A.1 (Appendix). In total, 7,974 different tasks were presented to respondents — each with three different choices corresponding to three different loans and the "none" option. One of the first interesting outcomes is that the option "none" was selected in 75.8 percent of the cases, meaning that respondents were interested in taking up a credit in only 24.2 percent of the cases. Moreover, 58 percent of agricultural households refused all loan contracts.

The effects of loan attribute levels on take-up are estimated with the conditional logit model presented in Section 3.2. The conditional logit results are displayed using odds ratios and z statistics in parenthesis. Odds ratios give the proportional change of odds to choose the loan contract for a unit increase of the variable (in comparison with the base category).

Table A.2 (Appendix) displays the results of the conditional logit model. The most striking result, as mentioned above, is the large odds ratio and significance level associated with the "none" option, showing that an important proportion of agricultural households reject all loan contracts, no matter what loan options are offered.

The direction of effects of loan attribute levels on take-up turn out generally as expected, although the relative importance of each attribute and their levels is less straightforward. Interest rate is the strongest determinant of take-up (largest odd ratio). The probability of accepting a loan is 4.4 and 1.25 times higher when the interest rate is 4 percent and 12 percent respectively than when the interest rate is 15 percent, meaning that the elasticity rate for a 3 percent decrease interest rate is 1.25 while it is 4.4 for an 11 percent decrease in interest rate.

As expected, respondent utility decreases with price. There is a sharp decrease of demand when interest rates are close to market rates (Table A.1

[8]The IIA assumption is tested by a Hausman–McFadden test, under the null hypothesis of no violation.

in the Appendix shows that only 3 percent of the loan options with the 15 percent interest rate are selected). This low acceptance at market rates may be due to the existence of subsidized loans (provided by the rural credit scheme) distorting consumers' expectations, the limited credit experience of agricultural households or by the low expected returns on investments from agricultural households.

In terms of loan duration, the preferences reflect the need to have repayment schedules adapted to the agricultural production cycle. A five-year repayment period raises the probability of choosing a loan by 1.4 compared to a one-year repayment option (and by 1.2 compared to the 2 years' option). On repayment schedules, annual repayment is clearly preferred to monthly repayment (raising the probability to take a loan by 1.42) and slightly preferred to semi-annual repayment (raising the probability by only 1.08).

The results on loan size show that there are preferences for medium-sized loans. Respondents are reluctant to select small-sized loans (400 euros), which diminishes the probability by a factor of 2.4 percent and 2 percent compared to loan sizes of 1,000 euros or 6,000 euros respectively. They are also reluctant to choose large loans (16,000 euros) where the probability of choosing a loan decreases by a factor of 2 percent and 1.8 percent compared to loan sizes of 1,000 and 6,000 euros respectively. Agricultural households are not interested in very small loans which are clearly insufficient to address their needs, but are also averse towards larger loans. A loan of 1,000 euros is preferred over the three other loan sizes available in the conjoint analysis.

Finally, the existence of a grace period is a strong determinant of accepting a loan contract (raising it by 1.7) while the linkage to the euro has a smaller effect (it lowers the probability of choosing the loan by 1.1).

Agricultural households are generally more likely to accept a loan contract if the interest rate is lower, the repayment period is larger, the loan has a grace period, and is not linked to euro and the repayment schedule is longer. The impact of loan size is less straightforward as medium-sized loans of 1,000 and 6,000 euros are preferred over both small (400 euros) and large (16,000 euros) loans. All levels of attributes have a statistically significant effect on the loan choice.

3.4 *Interaction effects with individual characteristics*

The estimations above provide the direction and magnitude of the average effects of attributes levels on demand for credit. These effects are likely to be heterogeneous across households and farm characteristics. As these characteristics have some interaction with the alternatives and affect the choice of loan contracts, a mixed model, combining the features of the conditional and the multinomial logit model, is specified and estimated. The model includes the alternatives or attribute levels (as before) and new variables of interactions between the attribute levels and specific household characteristics. We specifically look at how demand varies with household size and wealth, age of household head, investment needs, but also with the experience of agricultural households with the credit market (existence of a credit history). As such, the following individual variables are interacted with the attributes' levels: consumption level (as a proxy of wealth level), household size, age of agricultural household head, farm size (as a proxy of investment needs) and formal credit experience.

Tables A.3–A.6 (Appendix) display the results for each individual characteristic added separately to the model.

As the majority of respondents (58 percent) have refused all loan contracts, it is noteworthy to see how the individual characteristics interact with the probability that the "none" option is selected over the alternative loan contracts. Overall wealth, farm size, credit experience and household size lower the probability of rejecting all loan contracts while the age of the household head increases it. All coefficients associated with the interaction between the individual characteristics and the "none option" are significant.

An increase of 100 Dinar (around US$20 at the time of the survey) of consumption per unit level diminishes the probability of rejecting all loan contracts by around 15 percent, illustrating that poorer households are less willing to ask for a loan. Having one acre[9] of land lowers the probability by approximately 16 percent, showing that bigger farms have greater need of credit. The chance of rejecting all credit contracts is more than three times higher for households who did not have access to at least one formal loan in the last 12 months compared to those who had, reflecting existing demand and also a better understanding by the household of formal loan requirements. In terms of household characteristics, the chances of rejecting credit contracts decreases as household size increases (one member reduces the chance by 20 percent) suggesting that credit demand is linked to consumption needs (expected to rise with the size). On the other hand, the age

[9]1 hectare is equal to 100 acres.

of the household head raises the probability of rejecting a loan contract by around 3 percent per year. The latter finding is an important figure as the average age of the household head in rural Serbia is 62, and around half of the heads of household are retired. With regards to age, credit needs are first expected to increase with the productive experience of the household and then diminish. Age, however, also affects access to credit as some people are not eligible for credit after a certain age limit. This is a potential explanation for the high refusal rate.

Turning now to the interactions of each individual characteristic with the loan attributes, Table A.3 (Appendix) shows that most interactions with consumption levels are not significant, except for two which are marginally significant. A unit increase of consumption decreases the odds of choosing a loan with 400 euros rather than a loan of 1,000 euros by 7 percent (although not significant at the 10 percent level). Demand, measured by loan size, thus marginally increases with wealth.

Farm size (Table A.4, Appendix) has a clearer interaction with loan attributes. There is a positive effect on farm size and loan size demand; one acre of land increases the chance of choosing a loan of 16,000 euros versus 1,000 euros by 10 percent and decreases the chance of choosing a loan with 400 euros rather than 1,000 euros by 12 percent. Farm size also increases the odds of choosing a loan with a grace period and a longer repayment frequency, levels linked with larger loans, but has no effect on loan duration suggesting that larger farms are able to take larger loans, to repay them annually, with a grace period, but do not necessarily want to repay on a long- term basis.

Experience with the formal sector (Table A.4, Appendix) also has some significant interactions with loan attributes. Households having had access to formal credit are more willing, although this is only marginally significant, to take loans at the market rate (15 percent) and are more interested in credit of 1,000 euros with a grace period. These interactions are potentially affected by the knowledge of the rural credit program, although it is interesting to see a clear preference for loans of 1,000 euros, but not for lowest interest rates (two characteristics of the rural credit program).

Finally, household head age (Table A.6) significantly increases the chance of choosing small loan contracts. (Increasing age by one year increases the preference for a credit contract with 400 euros rather than 1,000 euros by 1.4 percent).

3.5 *What is the demand for existing credit sources and microfinance in rural Serbia?*

Without including interaction effects, discrete choice models allow estimating of the expected utility for each loan contract by adding up the effects of its component attribute levels.

Results of the conditional conjoint analysis are compared to the current situation of credit supply in rural areas of Serbia and to the main loans that are available to agricultural households.

However, attribute and levels selected for the conjoint analysis cannot represent every loan contract available in the market as there are many players providing credit in rural areas: at least six commercial banks (to some extent), the rural credit scheme (channeled through commercial banks) and microcredit institutions. Moreover, conditions and terms of credit are likely to vary with borrowers' characteristics. Thus, credit conditions of each type of provider described below are approximated with the attribute and levels selected for the conjoint analysis.

Table 20.4 describes several formal credit contracts available to agricultural households: microcredit products offered by microfinance institutions that operate in rural areas; short-term and long-term credit from the rural credit scheme, series of loans with different characteristics from financial organizations and commercial banks providing credit in rural areas.

The analysis of household utility derived from the products in the potential formal credit supply in rural Serbia (Figure 20.1) shows that loan structures of short-term and long-term credit from the rural credit scheme are preferred over the loan structure from banks, mainly because of the differential of interest rates and the existence of a grace period. The range of commercial loans also has different utility levels. For example, agricultural

Table 20.4: Credit providers.

	RCS Short-term	RCS Long-term	Non Bank1 Short-term	Non Bank2 Short-term	Bank3 Long-term	Bank4 Short term	Micro Credit1	Micro Credit2
Interest rate (%)[10]	4	4	15	15	12	15	15	15
Loan duration (year)	1	5	1	1	5	1	1	1
Loan size (Euros)	1,000	16,000	1,000	6,000	6,000	1,000	400	400
Grace period	Yes	Yes	Yes	Yes	No	No	No	No
Euro linkage	No	Yes	No	Yes	Yes	Yes	No	No
Repayment schedule	Annually	Semi-annually	Annually	Monthly	Monthly	Monthly	Monthly	Monthly

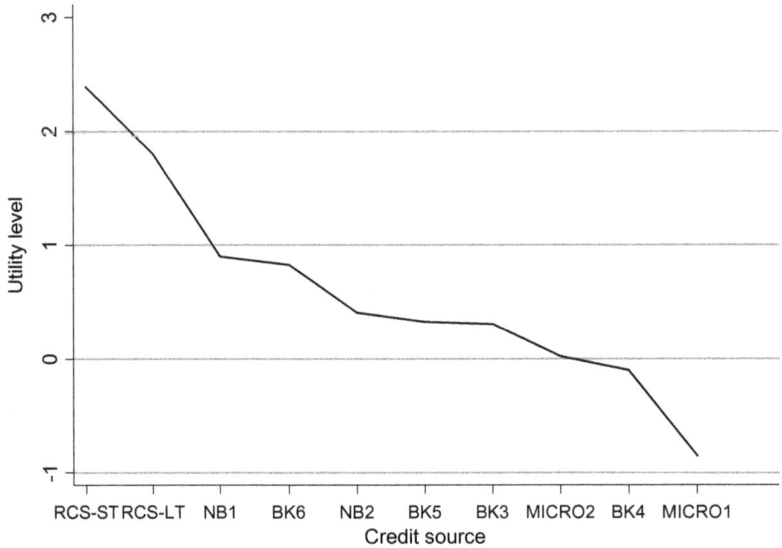

Figure 20.1: Utility derived from different credit contracts.

loans from organization Non-Bank1 have several characteristics with positive effects on the probability to take a loan such as a grace period, an annual repayment schedule, the loan size of 1,000 euros although the interest rates are the highest. There is clearly a trade-off between loan characteristics and price. Medium-term credit from Bank 5 are at a lower price (12 percent), but have a lower demand as they have no grace period and are linked to the euro.

In terms of demand for microfinance, the typical loan structure of microcredit organizations is the least preferred. Indeed, most of the attributes of microfinance products reduce the probability of agricultural households to take a loan: high interest rates, short repayment periods, no grace period and to a lesser extent, the small loan size. This low acceptance for microfinance product might reflect the inadequacy of microcredit products to agricultural needs. Monthly repayments and the inexistence of a grace period are not adapted to production cycles and does not solve inter-temporal maximization problems of agricultural households. Very small loan sizes (400 Euro) from some MFIs might also limit the possibility to undertake long-term investments, needed in the agricultural context. Furthermore, agricultural households are averse towards microfinance interest rates that are close to

[10]Interest rates vary over a greater range than the one proposed in the conjoint evaluation. For instance, interest rates from Pro-credit are clearly over 15 percent.

market levels. But this is not specific to microfinance as some conventional banks are charging the same interest rates. This important aversion toward market interest rates explains the popularity of the government rural credit program, which provides the greatest utility according to the CBC results and is also confirmed by a strong demand (exceeding by far the supply) in the areas where it is available.

4 Conclusion

Rural areas of Serbia are characterized by the importance of agricultural activities, significant credit constraints and a low use of formal financial services. The objective of this paper is to understand the potential of microfinance interventions to address the credit needs that remain unsatisfied. The potential take-up for microfinance is low as typical microfinance products may not be particularly adapted to rural activities specificities. As such, the capacity of microfinance to lower credit constraints seems limited.

Evaluating financial demand using a choice-based conjoint method in rural Serbia shows that the majority (58 percent) of agricultural households are not interested in any loan currently available in the market. A few key characteristics of the rural population affect the demand for credit: wealth, farm size, credit experience and household size raise the overall demand for credit while age of household head diminishes it. The most important credit attributes affecting credit demand are the interest rate, the loan size and the existence of a grace period.

Agricultural households are more likely to accept a loan contract, everything else being equal, if the interest rates are lower, the repayment period is larger, the loan has a grace period and is not linked to the euro, and the repayment schedule is longer. However, comparing household demand to the existing formal credit supply in rural Serbia suggests that microfinance has a very limited potential. Indeed, most attribute levels that are typical of microfinance products significantly lower the probability of taking a loan: the level of interest rates, the loan size (for some products), the inexistence of a grace period and, to a lesser extent, the repayment schedule. Moreover, the microfinance product is the least preferred of all existing financial products. The significant aversion towards interest rates at market levels, charged by both microfinance institutions or banks, might reflect a relatively slim profitability of agricultural activities, uncertainty of production levels and also lack of familiarity with credit and private banks. Agricultural activities need reimbursement schedules, delays in reimbursement (grace period) and maturities that are adapted to the production cycle. Finally, a part of agricultural households' credit needs are not addressed by microfinance loan sizes and might divert farmers away from long-term investments.

Thus, it seems that there are several factors that are potentially hampering the outreach of micro-credit. The specificities of microcredit products — small loan sizes, monthly repayment schedules, group guaranties — may not be adapted to agricultural activities.

Microcredit institutions might adapt their products to answer the specific needs of the population in these rural areas by developing repayment modalities that are more adapted to the production cycle and by increasing loan sizes.

However, if the diversification of financial products would increase household satisfaction and demand, this would not be neutral for MFIs' operations. Increasing the variety of products could generate extra costs. Product changes suggested above might affect the risk of loan defaults and increase the intensity of monitoring. However, some recent findings put these threats into perspective. For instance, Field and Pande (2008) show that monthly versus weekly repayment does not affect default in India.

Even though the inadequacy of products is one of the key determinant for low demand for microfinance services, there might still be a significant proportion of agricultural households that would benefit from a microloan (generating larger returns than interest rates) and still not take it up. Indeed 58 percent of agricultural households in Serbia refuse all contracts. There are perhaps some other factors impeding credit demand that are at play such as risk aversion or important uncertainties characterizing agricultural activities that could be mitigated with other interventions such as insurance mechanisms.

References

Amin, S, A Rai and G Topa (2003). Does microcredit reach the poor and vulnerable? Evidence from Northern Bangladesh. *Journal of Development Economics,* 70, 59–82.

Armandariz de Aghion, B and J Morduch (2005). *The Economics of Microfinance.* London: The MIT Press.

Banerjee, A and E Duflo (2008). Do Firms Want to Borrow More? Testing Credit Constraints Using a Directed Lending Program. Working Paper.

Bennett, JW (1999). Some Fundamentals of Environmental Choice Modelling. Research Report 11, University of New South Wales.

Churchill, G and D Iacobucci (2002). Market Research, Methodoligical Foundations, 8th ed. London: Harcourt Publishing.

Crépon, B, F Devoto, E Duflo and W Parienté (2008). Poverty, access to credit and the determinants of participation to a new microcredit program in rural areas of Morocco. Ex Post Impact Analyses Series 2, Agence Française de Développement, Paris.

David, C and R Meyer (1980). Measuring the farm level impact of agricultural loans. In *Borrowers and Lenders: Rural Financial Markets and Institutions in Developing Countries*, J Howell (ed.), pp. 201–234. London: Overseas Development Institute.

Dufhues, T, F Heidhues and G Buchenrieder (2004). Participatory product design by using conjoint analysis in the rural financial market of Northern Vietnam. *Asian Economic Journal*, 18(1), 81–114.

Evans, TG, AM Adams, R Mohammed and AH Norris (1999). Demystifying nonparticipation in microcredit: A population-based analysis. *World Development*, 27(2), 419–430.

Field, E and R Pande (2008). Repayment frequency and default in microfinance: Evidence from India. *Journal of European Economic Association*, 6(2–3), 501–509.

Filmer, D and L Pritchett (2001). Estimating wealth effects without expenditure data or tears: An application to educational enrollments in states of India. *Demography*, 38(1), 115–132.

Gine, X, T Harigaya, D Karlan and B Nguyen (2006). Evaluating Microfinance Program Innovation with Randomized Control Trials: An Example from Group versus Individual Lending. Asian Development Bank Economics and Research Department Technical Note Series, 16.

Godquin, M and M Sharma (2005). If only I could borrow more! Production and consumption credit constraints in rural Philippines. IFPRI mimeograph.

Green, PE and V Srinivasan (1978). Conjoint analysis in consumer research: Issues and outlook. *Journal of Consumer Research*, 5, 103–123.

Green, PE and V Srinivasan (1990). Conjoint analysis in marketing: New developments with implications for research and practice. *Journal of Marketing*, 54, 3–19.

Iqbal, F (1986). The demand and supply of funds among agricultural households in India. In *Agricultural Households: Models Extensions, Applications and Policy*, I Singh, L Squire and J Strauss (eds.). Baltimore and London: John Hopkins University Press.

Jappelli, T (1990). Who is credit constrained in the US economy? *Quarterly Journal of Economics*, 105(1), 219–234.

Karlan, D and J Zinman (2008). Credit elasticities in less developing countries: Implications for microfinance. *American Economic Review*, 98(3), 1040–68.

Maddala, GS (1983). *Limited-Dependent and Qualitative Variable in Econometrics*. Cambridge University Press.

Navajas, S, M Schreiner, L Meyer, C Gonzalez-Vega and J Rodriguezmeza (2000). Microcredit and the poorest of the poor: Theory and evidence from Bolivia. *World Development*, 28(2), 333–346.

Paulson, AC and R Townsend (2004). Financial constraints and entrepreneurship in North Thailand. *Journal of Corporate Finance*, 10, 229–262.

Rosenzweig, MR and HP Binswanger (1993). Wealth, weather risk and the composition and profitability of agricultural investments. *Economic Journal*, 103(416), 56–78.

Sial, MH and MR Carter (1996). Financial market efficiency in an Agrarian economy. Micro-econometric analysis of the Pakistani Pubjab. *The Journal of Development Studies*, 32(5), 771–798.

United Nations (2005). *The Millennium Development Goals Report 2005*. United Nations Department of Public Information.

World Bank (1990). *World Development Report 1990: Poverty*. New York: Oxford University Press.

World Bank (2007). Rural Credit Household Survey: Republic of Serbia. Unpublished report.

Zeldes, SP (1989). Consumption and liquidity constraints: An empirical investigation. *Journal of Political Economy*, 97(2), 305–346.

Appendix

Table A.1: Frequencies of attribute selection.

Attributes	Level	Presented (%)	Selected (%)
Interest rate (%)	4	0.50	0.13
	12	0.24	0.04
	15	0.26	0.03
Loan duration (years)	1	0.50	0.07
	2	0.25	0.09
	5	0.25	0.09
Loan size (Euros)	400	0.24	0.05
	1000	0.25	0.11
	6000	0.26	0.10
	16000	0.25	0.06
Grace period of 1 year	Yes	0.50	0.10
	No	0.50	0.06
Linked to Euro	Yes	0.50	0.07
	No	0.50	0.09
Repayment frequency	Monthly	0.51	0.07
	Semi-annually	0.25	0.09
	Annually	0.25	0.10

Table A.2: Determinant of loan contract choice (1).

Estimated odds ratios[11] from Conditional Logit Regression	
Interest rate: 4%	4.42 (19.06)
Interest rate: 12%	1.25 (2.28)
Loan duration: 1 year	0.73 (−5.35)
Loan duration: 2 year	0.89 (−1.7)
Loan size: 400 Eur	0.83 (−2.15)
Loan size: 1000 Eur	1.99 (9.86)
Loan size: 6000 Eur	1.74 (7.77)
Grace period	1.69 (10.5)
Euro linkage	0.89 (−2.43)
Repayment: monthly	0.70 (−5.97)
Repayment: semi-annually	0.92 (−1.28)
None	30.32 (29.73)

Note: Odds ratio and T-stat are in parentheses.

[11] As only 12 parameters can be estimated (obtained by adding the total number of levels and subtracting the number of attributes), some levels for each attribute are used as the base category (interest rate: 15%; loan duration: 5 years; loan size: 16,000 Euros; no grace period; no linkage to euro; repayment frequency: annually).

Table A.3: Determinants of loan contract choice (2).

Estimated odds ratios from Conditional Logit Regression with interaction effects on Household consumption		
Interest rate: 4%	4.54	(10.10)
Interest rate: 12%	1.39	(1.78)
Loan size: 400 Eur	0.50	(−4.87)
Loan size: 6,000 Eur	0.90	(−0.88)
Loan size: 16,000 Eur	0.53	(−4.75)
Loan duration: 1 year	0.69	(−3.38)
Loan duration: 2 year	0.83	(−1.54)
Grace period	1.60	(5.06)
Euro linkage	0.78	(−2.71)
Repayment: monthly	0.64	(−3.91)
Repayment: semi-annually	0.84	(−1.32)
None	21.12	(15.24)
Consumption*interest rate: 4%	0.9999	(−0.19)
Consumption*interest rate: 12%	0.9996	(−0.71)
Consumption*loan size: 400 Eur	0.9993	(−1.50)
Consumption*loan size: 6,000 Eur	0.9998	(−0.43)
Consumption*loan size: 16,000 Eur	0.9998	(−0.47)
Consumption*loan duration: 1 year	1.0002	(0.56)
Consumption*loan duration: 2 year	1.0003	(0.68)
Consumption*grace period	1.0002	(0.69)
Consumption*euro linkage	1.0005	(1.63)
Consumption*repayment: monthly	1.0003	(0.94)
Consumption*repayment: semi-annually	1.0004	(0.83)
Consumption*none	0.9986	(−2.10)

Note: Odds ratio and T-stat are in parentheses.

Table A.4: Determinants of loan contract choice (3).

Estimated odds ratios from Conditional Logit Regression with interaction effects on land cultivated		
Interest rate: 4%	4.44	(0.91)
Interest rate: 12%	1.12	(0.44)
Loan size: 400 Eur	0.70	(−2.06)
Loan size: 6,000 Eur	0.71	(−2.20)
Loan size: 16,000 Eur	0.31	(−5.93)
Loan duration: 1 year	0.69	(−2.56)
Loan duration: 2 year	0.77	(−1.52)
Grace period	1.27	(1.91)
Euro linkage	0.84	(−1.42)
Repayment: monthly	1.06	(0.37)
Repayment: semi-annually	1.12	(0.63)
None	28.33	(12.32)
Land*interest rate: 4%	1.0022	(0.06)
Land*interest rate: 12%	1.0188	(0.39)
Land*loan size: 400 Eur	0.8932	(−3.46)
Land*loan size: 6,000 Eur	1.0466	(1.59)
Land*loan size: 16,000 Eur	1.0926	(2.51)
Land*loan duration: 1 year	1.0068	(0.25)
Land*loan duration: 2 year	1.0238	(0.75)
Land*grace period	1.0564	(2.37)
Land*euro linkage	1.0122	(0.53)
Land*repayment: monthly	0.9160	(−3.13)
Land*repayment: semi-annually	0.9577	(−1.35)
Land*none	0.8645	(−2.95)

Note: Odds ratio and T-stat are in parentheses.

Table A.5: Determinants of loan contract choice (4).

Estimated Odds Ratios from Conditional Logit Regression with Interaction Effects on Formal Credit Experience		
Interest rate: 4%	4.72	(15.14)
Interest rate: 12%	1.41	(2.72)
Loan size: 400 Eur	0.51	(−7.41)
Loan size: 6,000 Eur	0.88	(−1.61)
Loan size: 16,000 Eur	0.54	(−6.88)
Loan duration: 1 year	0.78	(−3.4)
Loan duration: 2 year	0.93	(−0.89)
Grace period	1.60	(7.42)
Euro linkage	0.84	(−2.72)
Repayment: monthly	0.76	(−3.62)
Repayment: semi-annually	0.95	(−0.66)
None	22.74	(22.95)
Credit*interest rate: 4%	0.88	(−0.78)
Credit*interest rate: 12%	0.74	(−1.47)
Credit*loan size: 400 ur	0.57	(−3.48)
Credit*loan size: 6,000 Eur	0.98	(−0.15)
Credit*loan size: 16,000 Eur	0.79	(−1.6)
Credit*loan duration: 1 year	0.82	(−1.63)
Credit*loan duration: 2 year	0.89	(−0.79)
Credit*grace period	1.22	(1.93)
Credit*euro linkage	1.15	(1.31)
Credit*repayment: monthly	0.78	(−1.99)
Credit*repayment: semi-annually	0.91	(−0.64)
Credit*none	0.30	(−5.68)

Note: Odds ratio and T-stat are in parentheses.

Table A.6: Determinants of loan contract choice (5).

Estimated Odds Ratios from Conditional Logit Regression with Interaction Effects on Age		
Interest rate: 4%	3.71	(4.02)
Interest rate: 12%	2.01	(1.70)
Loan size: 400 Eur	0.18	(−5.25)
Loan size: 6,000 Eur	0.84	(−0.68)
Loan size: 16,000 Eur	0.30	(−3.99)
Loan duration: 1 year	0.55	(−2.30)
Loan duration: 2 year	0.59	(−1.81)
Grace period	2.64	(4.46)
Euro linkage	1.30	(1.23)
Repayment: monthly	0.68	(−1.49)
Repayment: semi-annually	1.11	(0.37)
None	2.98	(2.45)
Age*interest rate: 4%	1.0035	(0.60)
Age*interest rate: 12%	0.9917	(−1.15)
Age*loan size: 400 Eur	1.0148	(2.64)
Age*loan size: 6,000 Eur	1.0005	(0.10)
Age*loan size: 16,000 Eur	1.0089	(1.73)
Age*loan duration: 1 year	1.0048	(1.08)
Age*loan duration: 2 year	1.0074	(1.45)
Age*grace period	0.9922	(−2.10)
Age*euro linkage	0.9931	(−1.86)
Age*repayment: monthly	1.0003	(0.08)
Age*repayment: semi-annually	0.9967	(−0.68)
Age*none	1.0285	(3.62)

Note: Odds ratio and T-stat are in parentheses.

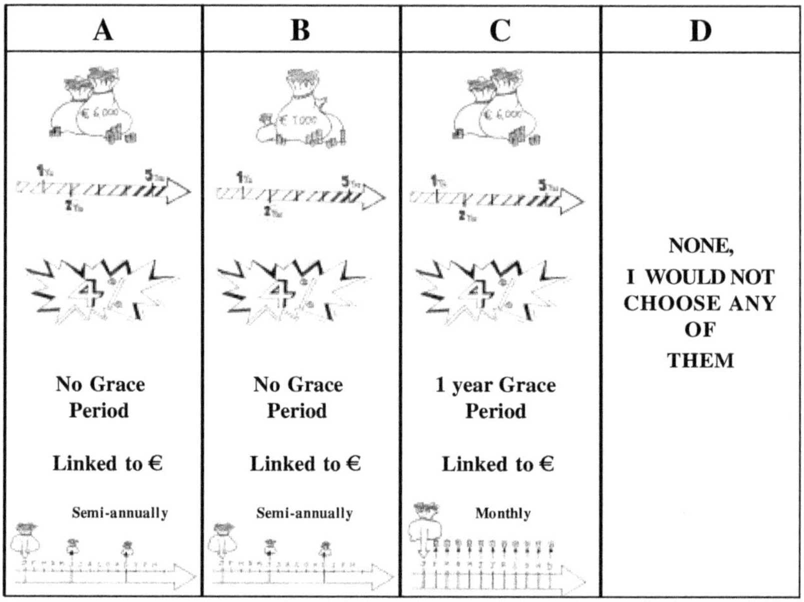

Figure A.1: Example of a choice set for the conjoint analysis of loan demand.

Rural Microfinance and Agricultural Value Chains: Strategies and Perspectives of the Fondo de Desarrollo Local in Nicaragua

Johan Bastiaensen
Institute of Development Policy and Management (IOB), University of Antwerp

Peter Marchetti*
Fondo de Desarrollo Local and AVANCSO, Guatemala

1 Introduction

In recent decades, microfinance has become a consolidated industry in maturing urban as well as small rural town markets. Outreach in deep rural areas however, continues to be weak and the development of rural microfinance related to agricultural activity remains very much a "frontier issue" (CGAP, 2006: 9). Yet, more than two-thirds of the world's poor live in rural areas and the majority of them — despite a significant diversification of the rural economy — still depend to a large extent on agricultural activity. For that reason, many economists have rightly identified growth in agriculture output and a strengthened participation of smallholders as key dimensions of a strategy to reduce (extreme) poverty (World Bank, 2008). Obviously, the lack of deep rural and in particular agricultural outreach constitutes a major problem for an industry that claims to play a crucial role in the global fight against poverty.

Not all agricultural growth, however, will automatically produce poverty reduction. In the current context, scholars and policymakers need to take

*With the collaboration of Julio Flores, Elizabeth Campos, Manuel Bermúdez, Arturo Grigsby, Francisco Pérez, Miguel Alemán, Lea Montes, Alfredo Ruíz, Marcelo Rodríguez.

due account of the dramatic changes in world agricultural markets. These markets are witnessing a rapid integration of developing country processors into ever more demanding worldwide agro-food chains which are increasingly governed and dominated by a small number of concentrated global players (Ruben *et al.*, 2006; Gonzalez–Vega *et al.*, 2006; Vermeulen *et al.*, 2008). Traditional dispersed and poorly linked on-the-spot markets are gradually replaced by consciously governed value chains. While these globalised agricultural value chains in principle offer both opportunities and threats for local smallholders and other poor stakeholders in developing countries, in practice, they all too often tend to produce more income concentration and social exclusion as well as detrimental environmental consequences (particularly in the Latin American context). All too often, smallholders are unable to connect to the new dynamic chains under favorable conditions and remain trapped within the less dynamic spot market segments. The key issues here are how these global chains actually become shaped up to the local level (Roduner, 2004); how their articulation into living local societies is mutually crafted by the intersecting actions and interests of a multitude of actors with unequal power at intertwined local, national and global levels to produce the reality of globalization (Hart, 2002); and which of the potential value chains actually come to be deployed (or not) in each particular context.

Today, awareness of the importance of agricultural value chains for inclusive development and poverty reduction is growing (Ruben *et al.*, 2006: preface). Yet only recently have analysts started to link this awareness to the debate about microfinance (e.g., Gonzalez–Vega *et al.*, 2006; Quiros, 2006; Meyer, 2007; Miller and Da Silva, 2007; World Bank, 2009). From the side of value chain analysis, the attention for the financial components has been weak (Meyer, 2007: 5) and is often limited to "embedded" financial mechanisms operating within the chain, like trader credit, contract farming or warehouse receipts (Fries and Akin, 2004). Thus, the mainstream debates about agricultural value chains and microfinance have very much been two worlds apart. The key point of our contribution is that this gap needs to be closed in order to develop more appropriate models that can improve strategies of microfinance for a more inclusive rural development. In particular, we will argue for a proactive rather than passive role of microfinance in the making and reshaping of agricultural value chains in view of enhancing efficiency, social inclusion and gender justice. This view will also bring us to argue for a "finance plus" approach, emphasizing the need to articulate microfinance with underlying social change processes and complementary services. Without such an approach, the contribution of rural microfinance risks becoming tied into the current exclusionary, male-dominated and environmentally destructive agricultural growth model.

We will contextualize our argument referring to the experience of the Fondo de Desarrollo Local (FDL) in Nicaragua. The FDL is a maturing microfinance institution specialized in financing agricultural production (62 percent of its almost US$ 70 million portfolio in 2008), with a significant share in longer-term investment credit, priority for solidarity groups of productive women, and a client drop-out rate of only 5 percent in agriculture.[1] After having created a sustainable client-enterprise interface and pioneered an entrepreneurially viable technology with multiple financial products, the FDL now is partially and gradually evolving towards a more integrated value chain approach, in which both financial and non-financial services (provided by its allied founder institution, Nitlapán, as well as others) are combined to enhance the participation and benefits of small-scale rural producers in agricultural value chains.

In what follows, we will first develop our theoretical framework. Part one begins with a short discussion of "development" and "poverty reduction". Referring to the experience of the FDL, we then elaborate on how social embeddedness and institutional entrepreneurship are key in reducing transaction costs and establishing a viable governance structure for microfinance. We then link these issues to our framework for the analysis of value chains and their transformation. In the second part, we apply our framework to the case of Nicaragua and the FDL. We start with a brief overview of recent tendencies in agricultural growth and value chain development in Nicaragua, indicating their exclusionary and environmentally destructive characteristics. We then present an analysis of how the FDL, in alliance with other actors, tries to evolve towards a more integrated strategy with the potential to strengthen alternative pathways of growth that can successfully challenge current evolutions. The emerging transformative strategies in the critical cattle sector are analyzed in more detail. We conclude with initial evaluations of how FDL's strategy signals possibilities for better uses of international subsidies in the struggle against poverty.

[1]The FDL has won the 2005 Prize for Excellence in Microfinance for Non-regulated Institutions, granted by the Inter-American Development Bank (IADB), the 2006 Central American Bank for Economic Integration Prize for Microfinance Management, the 2006 CGAP Certificate of Transparency, and was recognized again in 2008 by the Central American Microfinance Association, Redcamif, as having the best financial indicators in Central America.

2 Microfinance and Inclusive Value Chain Development: A Theoretical Framework

2.1 *An actor-oriented approach to development*

Our framework starts with Amartya Sen's argument that "*the core of development is the enjoyment of freedom — the freedom of individuals to lead valuable lives*" (Sen, 1999). We focus in particular on what Sen calls "*agency freedom*": the practical ability of people to co-shape the life and livelihoods of their preference and to replicate, contest and change the conditions which enable them to do so. We complement Sen with Long's claim that human agency critically depends upon the capacity to enroll other human beings in "projects" that sufficiently match one's own "project" (Long, 2002: 17).[2] The analysis of the matching, contestation and negotiation process about this mutual enrollment must therefore go beyond a neoclassical view of unrelated livelihood strategies of diverse actors. As indicated by De Haan and Zoomers (2005: 32), the livelihoods of people need to be understood as "*going beyond the economic or material objectives of life*"; they quote Wallmann (1984) saying that a "(l)*ivelihood is never just a matter of finding or making shelter, transacting money, getting food to put on the family table or to exchange on the market place. It is equally a matter of ownership and circulation of information, the management of skills and relationships and the affirmation of personal significance and group identity.*" A livelihood is thus just as much a matter of material well-being as it is about relationships and socially validated knowledge and meaning. It is therefore also as much an individual as it is a social-relational process that is shaped at the intersection of individual strategies and multiple collective action, giving rise to collective pathways of change that broadly enable and constrain actors' individual strategies. This is why we need to address the interface issues of the diverse life-projects that are inevitably at stake in the accommodation, manipulation and contestation of any development initiative, whether we are talking about actions and interventions in value chains, financial markets or any other domain.

2.1.1 *Systems of exchange and livelihood opportunities*

Besides property rights over resources, access to markets and non-market exchange systems enable and constrain the environment of individual livelihood strategies. As contributions to existing exchange systems, we

[2]This is why "poverty" fundamentally has to be understood as a relational process (see De Herdt and Bastiaensen, 2008, for a more elaborate discussion).

argue that integrated development of rural microfinance and agricultural value chains can make a difference. Evidently, transactions of goods or services between buyers and sellers are the core of any exchange system and market. Such transactions are enabled or constrained by available *infrastructure* (roads, communications, electricity, market places) as well as the provision of supportive public or private *services* (transport, storage, legal and information services, technical assistance, financial services). Inescapably, they are also dynamically rooted in the *broader institutional environment*, i.e., in existing social networks, prevailing formal and informal "rules of the game" and acknowledged meaning systems, and in the conflicted/concerted rules between the poor and microfinance and value chain entrepreneurs (Gibson *et al.*, 2004: 12; Rankin, 2001, 2002, 2008).[3]

Williamson (1991) distinguished between the ideal-type forms of a horizontal "market", with autonomous actors guided strictly by prices, a vertically integrated "hierarchy", governed by a central authority without any strict reference to market prices, and hybrid combinations of both. In practice, value chains are always particular hybrid mixes of "market" and "hierarchy" strategies, largely depending on the characteristics of the goods or services exchanged as well as the nature of the institutional environment and power relations in which they are rooted. Microfinance and agricultural value chains, today, seem to be moving in opposite directions in terms of the governance of transactions. Microfinance evolves towards more impersonal financial markets, substituting so-called "informal" personalized financial services rooted in interlocking market transactions tied to patron-client relationships between producers of unequal power or between producers and politicized financial services delivered by state-development banks or the NGOs that filled in the vacuum left after the demise of those banks. The emphasis in the discourse about rural (micro)finance is clearly on market creation in the midst of dysfunctional non-market financial configurations.[4]

Agricultural value chains, on the other hand, are increasingly evolving toward more conscious, hierarchical coordination among the actors of

[3]Distancing ourselves from liberal theories of social capital, we do not see social capital as a "zone beyond politics" but highlight the agency of the poor without obscuring "the structural sources of inequality produced by the present political-economic conjuncture" with due attention to the "darker side" of both the local social networks of the poor and the international ones of microfinance institutions (Rankin, 2002: 11–15).

[4]This does, however, not necessarily imply that there would no longer be a role to play by all kinds of complementary "embedded" financial transactions, ranging from services among family and friends over credit tied to trade or contract farming in value chains or to "clientelistic" transactions with "patrons" or even politicized state institutions.

the entire chain for diverse reasons. Early experiments with unaccompanied liberalization of dysfunctional state-led marketing boards failed. At the same time, the share of retail through supermarkets rose vertiginously and entailed rapid changes in world food markets which made product quality, timing of delivery, processing, food safety and environmental certification crucial, particularly in higher value segments of the market in both rich and poorer countries (Ruben *et al.*, 2006; Reardon *et al.*, 2004). Reflections and conscious attempts were made to create and improve higher value market niches (Quiros, 2006). Usually multinational corporations took the lead and gained control over these new opportunities. Primary agricultural producers are thus facing strong and increasing power of global buyers in the chain, even when today many of the transactions are not yet directly governed by a central authority. For primary producers, integration into more consciously and better coordinated hierarchical agricultural value chains thus entails both a challenge of deepening dependency and an uncertain promise of higher income.[5] As is rightly stressed by Roduner (2004: 5) "*how*" producers become connected to agricultural world markets therefore becomes more important than the mere fact of gaining access to these markets. Under certain conditions of powerlessness and high competition among primary producers, there is a risk of a race to the bottom by which increased participation in world agricultural markets could open up a pathway of "immiserizing growth".

As the observed changes in world food markets are obviously critical for the prospects of any renewed agricultural development strategy — key for world poverty reduction — we believe it is necessary to draw a more explicit connection between such a strategy and the policies to develop rural microfinance. We examine how some of the prevailing mainstream views of the nature of the microfinance revolution might be incomplete and partially misleading, and thus obscure opportunities for weaving together microfinance and agricultural value chain development strategies.

2.1.2 *Rural microfinance*

It is received wisdom in the microfinance industry that the creation of rural and agricultural (micro)financial markets is more difficult than urban (micro)financial markets. Rural and — even more so — agricultural finance

[5]Even when the primary producer might lose in terms of relative value added — as can be expected — s/he might still gain in terms of absolute value added. In fact, in the absence of other measures, farmers will not be willing to participate if this condition of increase in their absolute value added is not met.

is associated with both higher transaction costs and higher risk (Zeller, 2006). Co-variant climate risks, fragile connections to segmented and volatile markets, and the lack of access to complementary private (e.g. business training, legal assistance) and public services (education, health) do make agricultural financing a more intrinsically risky affair than urban financing.

Higher risk, however, should not be assumed to be commensurate with higher transaction costs. Also rural poverty and vulnerability themselves are held to be detrimental to the capacity and willingness to pay for credit services. Moreover, they are thought to be responsible for a low effective demand for commercial credit serving entrepreneurial purposes (Gonzalez–Vega, 2003). We argue against these inevitabilities of poverty and low effective demand for agricultural credit and posit that the stable supply of agricultural credit at reasonable interest rates, especially when adequately articulated to broader dynamics and additional services, stimulates demand. To do that, transaction costs must be lowered, efficiency lifted (ROA), and profitability (ROE) reduced to around 4 or 5 percent.

Higher transaction costs in rural areas are held to be caused by physical conditions (low population density, spatial dispersion of clients, markets and organizations, deficient roads, poor electrical and communication infrastructure) as well as detrimental institutional conditions (complex heterogeneous and pluralistic normative frameworks that make reliance on legal enforcement mechanisms problematic, and in particular makes it usually impossible to take recourse to conventional collateral in order to guarantee loans).[6] Except for the physical conditions in the rural space, we believe, however, that most of these factors can be mitigated by appropriate strategies of embedding rural financial services in local territories.

In the FDL, counterintuitive to the received wisdom and standard story about agricultural financing for small producers, *embedded* agricultural microcredit actually developed with lower transaction costs than *non-embedded* urban microcredit. What is surprising about the FDL is that it has sought developmental impact in the agricultural sector by embedding itself in local communities and specializing in agricultural financial products. That has meant simultaneously increasing efficiency while lowering profits. The calculations in Table 21.1 give us some comparative data on the FDL's transaction costs in its key agricultural and urban financial products accounting for nearly 80 percent of its portfolio. The first thing to note is that the FDL

[6]Even when the loans are appropriately secured in legal terms, in particular the sale of mortgaged land can turn out to be locally illegitimate and give rise to strong resistance and rejection of the financial institution.

Table 21.1: Transaction costs, interest rate composition, portfolio weight and average size loan — June, 2008.

Key Financial products	Effective Interest Rate/1	Financial Margin/2	Provisioning for Arrears/3	Operative Costs/4	Profit/ Subsidy	% of Portfolio	Average Loan Size	Interest Rate in Relation to Average Interest Rate of the FDL
			Urban					
Small and medium-sized urban enterprise.	27.58%	19.58%	4.20%	8.78%	6.59%	2.75%	6,684	102%
Urban commercial, Service, Industrial Investment.	25.96%	17.96%	4.17%	8.78%	5.01%	4.00%	3,004	96%
		Urban Subsidized Financial Productos/5						
Urban micro-enterprise.	32.19%	24.19%	2.84%	21.82%	−0.46%	4.00%	1,138	119%
Urban solidarity groups (commerce and services).	40.97%	32.97%	1.97%	37.77%	−6.77%	3.64%	317	152%
Wage earners (multi-purpose loans).	27.58%	19.58%	3.52%	22.35%	−6.30%	5.00%	225	102%
Housing loans.	27.58%	19.58%	4.18%	16.21%	−0.81%	4.19%	697	102%
			Agricultural					
Agricultural and Cattle <$5000.	25.36%	17.36%	1.46%	11.30%	4.61%	9.92%	3,479	94%
Agricultural and Cattle $5000–$10,000.	24.44%	16.44%	1.46%	11.30%	3.69%	22.77%	6,987	91%
Agricultural Investment Loans.	21.58%	13.58%	3.11%	9.45%	1.02%	7.43%	2,410	80%
		Agricultural Subsidized Financial Products						
Agricultural Solidarity Group Loans.	26.85%	18.85%	3.05%	20.70%	−4.89%	7.30%	278	99%
Development portfolio (green package).	16.54%	8.54%	2.98%	11.14%	−5.58%	4.00%	1,973	61%
Rural solidarity loans (investment for women producers).	21.58%	13.58%	3.05%	11.29%	−0.76%	1.74%	469	80%
Rural solidarity loans (investment for women) with technical assistance.	16.54%	8.00%	3.67%	11.29%	−6.96%	1.00%	511	61%
Development Portfolio (Cows, Specialty Coffee and Irrigation).	16.54%	8.54%	2.98%	11.14%	−5.58%	0.63%	612, 1,078, and 1,337	61%

(1) Includes commissions and all other costs charged to clients.
(2) Financial margin = interest rate − average financial cost (8% for the FDL in 2008).
(3) Provisioning for arrears, a key factor for calculating transaction costs, is highly sensitive to entreprise size for urban products, less so for agricultural.
(4) Central and decentralized overhead costs were charged to each product according to its weight in the total portfolio of the FDL.
(5) These products were subsidized only partially by medium urban enterprises with most of the subsidies coming from more efficient agricultural products.

imposes a lower ceiling on its interest rates for agricultural activities since agriculture is known to be quite less profitable than urban activities (see Bastiaensen and Marchetti, 2007: 150 for estimates of relative urban and agricultural profitabilities).[7] Urban interest rates ranged from 102 percent to 152 percent above the average interest rate of the FDL, while agricultural rates ranged from 61 percent to 99 percent of the average rate. More importantly, the operational costs and the provisioning for arrears for the agricultural loans are consistently lower than those of the urban loans. At the same time, Table 21.1 shows that transaction costs logically remain sensitive to loan size, but in FDL practice, they clearly remain relatively lower for the agricultural financial products. One key to lowering operating costs and arrears in productive agricultural microfinance is its product design of long-term financial products for investment combined with short-term loans for working capital for equally long-term clients. Nevertheless, we believe that the FDL's social embeddedness in local communities, practices, and norms (see below) held the key to its success in lowering agricultural transaction costs.

We thus find that urban microcredit is not particularly efficient, but still quite profitable in the segment of larger loans to small and medium-sized enterprises, whereas highly efficient embedded agricultural credit for smaller clients is still in need of internal subsidies. Overall, the relative profitability and efficiency map translates into a picture of cross-subsidization in which the larger urban and agricultural loans subsidize the smaller urban and agricultural loans, including the more highly subsidized rural developmental investment loans. As such, Table 21.1 illustrates the FDL strategy to balance profitability with development considerations by subsidizing financial products for priority sectors, and, in this way, to avoid mission drift. It also indicates that comparatively lower transaction costs and moderate needs for internal subsidies in the countryside have also permitted subsidizing loans to poor urban women and microenterprises.

This implies that once a development-oriented initiative like the FDL has mastered its transaction costs in agricultural activities, a sophisticated system of cross-subsidies can be developed in order to target both poorer peasant farmers and extremely poor urban microenterprises that are of little

[7]Fears of a stricter imposition of maximum interest rate legislation have somewhat reduced the opportunities to charge relatively higher urban rates in 2009, thereby reducing the space for internal urban-to-rural subsidies. Of course, this leads to the paradox that insisting on low across the board interest rate caps might actually increase rural interest rates, or, worse, reduce the space for viable rural finance.

interest to the more commercially-oriented MFIs. These results allow us to hypothesize that the real reason that agricultural financing remains a frontier issue for microfinance is not so much because of the higher transaction costs as such or the higher intrinsic risk in agriculture but rather because microfinance cannot generate as much profit in agricultural activities as in urban ones. As we will argue below, the FDL's lower rural transaction costs have more to do with socially embedding microfinance activity in local territories than any other factor. Therefore, also the "professionalization" of microfinance promoting impersonal procedures and legal techniques plays its part in explaining mission drift away from the poorest enterprises and particularly away from agricultural financing where the answer to extreme poverty lies. Here lies the bottomline for why microfinance remains urban-based. Most "successful" MFIs therefore concentrate their portfolios in the urban areas keying in on small and medium enterprises and charging higher interest rates to microenterprises than the FDL does. The FDL's counter-intuitive agricultural and rural performance runs against the received wisdom and microcredit raters are simply incredulous until they evaluate how embedding financial services actually works. Due account should be taken here (and more research could be usefully done) of how the intense "historical" consultation and conflict within local agrarian networks around the initial establishment of the FDL practice led to its social embeddedness and the local legitimation of its embedded, "capitalist commoditized" financial transactions (for details about this history, see Rocha, 2002; Bastiaensen, 2000; and Bastiaensen and D'Exelle, 2002). The theoretical sections that follow are thus not simple speculation but borne out by FDL practice.

The FDL success in lowering costs of transaction in agricultural financing were a necessary condition for its and Nitlapán's interventions to synergize agricultural financing with value chain development analyzed below. Those interventions would have been impossible without the FDL's strategic use of internal subsidies to targeted agricultural development portfolios for poorer microenterprises. In this context, we should certainly start investigating and questioning the illogical use of international public subsidies to mainly subsidize highly profitable urban and rural commercial microfinance institutions, while agricultural microfinance all too often finds itself obliged to finance the synergy between microfinance and value chains from the pockets of somewhat better-off urban and rural microfinance clients.[8] However, we

[8]To add to this irrationality, agricultural microfinance institutions interest rates to poor urban women in the FDL are normally several points below the international subsidized microfinance institutions.

should not only be thinking about the need for internal transfers to cross-subsidize operational costs of the more expensive rural financial products, but also of additional subsidies for tied-in technical assistance and commercial support (in a Finance Plus perspective [see Section 3]). Actually, the FDL's and Nitlapán's new frontier of tying microfinance to value chains in part moves forward more slowly than would otherwise be possible, due to misdirected subsidies in the global microfinance and development industry (see also Section 2.1.3 below).

We also think that the tendency to view the rural microfinance challenge as just a matter of replicating urban — or even creating new rural — contractual innovations has been quite detrimental to the required "bottom up" and site-specific crafting of appropriate client-MFI interfaces. A key issue here is "social embeddedness" with which we want to stress that financial market transactions are inevitably embedded in a broader local institutional environment made up of a variety of social networks and associated normative and cognitive frameworks as well as daily practices, none of which show pristine "bureaucratic order and completeness".[9] Microfinance organizations certainly correspond to what Cleaver (2001: 13) calls "bureaucratic institutions", i.e., "*formalized arrangements based upon explicit organizational structures, contracts and legal rights*", which she contrasts with socially embedded institutions "*based on culture, social organization and daily practice, commonly but erroneously referred to as 'informal'*". She stresses rightly that both categories are not neatly distinguishable and that bureaucratic institutions may actually be or become socially embedded as the outcome of processes of "institutional bricolage".[10] Our point is precisely that rural

[9]It should be stressed that there is nothing politically innocent about this social embeddednes, just as in the case of the "*capital* in social capital" (Rankin, 2001, 2002: 15) or the resulting relationships in institutional "assemblage" (Rankin, 2008) or "bricolage" (Cleaver, 2001).

[10]Cleaver (2001: 28) observes that "(a)*rrangements which rely on a blueprint derived from abstract and universalized 'design principles' may result in inadequate institutional solutions as they fail to recognize the depth of social and cultural embeddedness of decision-making and co-operative relations.*" She therefore strongly questions "institutional theory", i.e. the social engineering approach that proposes to transfer improved "modern" institutional designs into developing contexts characterized by "widespread institutional deficiencies" (sic). Although she refers to water management, her observations are quite important for any serious attempt to work with actor-networks in value chains and microfinance, in particular since she rightly stresses the primordial importance of actor agency in the functioning of institutions, in particular with respect to their invisible and intangible aspects. She therefore arrives at the conclusion that even the most sophisticated institutional bricolage analysis is not capable to inform the kind of social engineering that institutional theory proposes (Cleaver, 2001: 29).

microfinance can become viable beyond the usual "possibility frontier" to the extent that it manages to deeply embed its transactions in the concrete interfaces between itself and clients and between clients and other actors.

Such social embeddedness emerges in the domain of contestation, compromise, and incomplete agencies in microterritorial politics, and "works" if the microfinance institution manages to successfully engage in that arena, adopting and/or adapting principles, values and norms of the inherited territorial repertoire so as to operate through existing social networks in order to create a workable social interface that adequately supports contractual financial transactions. In other words, the prevailing institutional environment and practices can provide the social and normative templates to be mobilized during the transactions taking place at the interface between the microfinance institutions' rules and organizational set-up and its clients. As all financial contracts are inevitably functioning in such broader, location-specific environments, it is evidently not at all illogical to find that some successful "contractual innovations" have turned out to be ineffective in other areas or for certain types of clients. Although certain aspects of the local institutional environment indeed can be detrimental to the functioning of financial markets,[11] the tendency to view the prevalence of rural "informal institutions" as a mere hindrance for the emergence of "modern" markets guided by formal rules and legal systems represents a grave danger for the rural and particularly for the agricultural "microfinance promise". The present-day tendency towards the conventionalization of rural microfinance will inevitably exclude many of the poorer agricultural clients and significantly shift the financial possibility frontier backward again.[12]

[11]See Bastiaensen and D'Exelle (2002) for an analysis of how the values, cognitive frameworks and social networks of prevailing patron-client relationships in poorer rural villages were a serious hindrance to the development of an appropriate credit culture in the historical experience of the FDL.

[12]Bastiaensen and Marchetti (2007) provide an analysis of the current threats for the development of rural microfinance. We question the mainstreaming paradigm for its stubborn ideological insistence on the integration of MFIs in the financial industry without much concern for possible anti-developmental consequences of the current regulatory frameworks, almost directly imported from the international private banking industry. Its exclusive reliance on formal business documentation and the state-backed legal framework inevitably excludes a significant part of rural clients, in particular those who cannot present formal documents or property titles. It also implicitly implies the unquestioned imposition of imported contractual designs and associated norms, enforced by outside legal authority backed by state force, in our view violating one of the key principles of

We contend that the success of the contractual innovations that lie at the origin of the "Microfinance Promise" (Morduch, 1991) was not just due to the innovative properties of the contractual forms, but also due to their connection and reliance on existing social networks and prevailing cognitive forms, practices, norms and rules — such as the mobilization of principles related to women's honor as a means to strengthen female willingness to repay within the new context of financial transactions in Bangladesh.[13] The creation of viable agricultural microfinance therefore inevitably requires the mutual crafting and conflict resolution, between clients and MFIs, of an innovative social and normative realm around financial transactions based upon relatively inflexible contracts. In the making and remaking of this realm "at the interface", recourse can and needs to be taken to those available social templates (networks, rules-norms, perceptions and motivations) that are conducive for successful financial market development, in particular in terms of "contract culture" and entrepreneurial values. It requires a kind of combative "institutional entrepreneurship" (Bastiaensen, 2000), a bricolage of MFI's and local actors' initiatives, which is able to assemble different bits and pieces of the available institutional repertoire, negotiating them together through innovative contractual and organizational practices around the financial transactions.[14]

In the Nicaraguan context, the FDL tries to mobilize the principles of the poor's "anti-subsidy culture" in their mutual relations; their dream of peasant autonomy and their strong work ethics; whereas keeping far away from the principles of unequal exchange of prevailing patron-clients relationships (Bastiaensen and D'Exelle, 2002).[15] At the same time, it is also

the original microfinance innovations and the necessary "institutional bricolage" that can adequately embed financial transactions in local rural institutional spaces. Additionally, also the usual imposition of a shareholder charter for regulated MFI-banks is highly questionable and unnecessary. In fact, as argued by Mersland and Strom (2008: 600) pro-poor banking has been dominated "*by mutual and non-profit ownership, not by investor ownership*". They also indicate that no relationship can be found between ownership type and operational efficiency.

[13]Group solidarity financial technology is no panacea; actually it remains one of the more conflictive and complicated arenas of the micropolitics of microfinance.

[14]"Institutional entrepreneurship" needs to be distinguished from "institutional engineering". In the latter, outside institutional designs and rules are imposed upon local realities; in the former it is about the capacity to interact, negotiate and sufficiently align inside and outside institutional designs and rules into a workable new practice.

[15]We believe it is quite probable that both the more positive and negative institutions remain present in the rural social space. They key point is that the agreed-on negative institutions must not become associated and mobilized within the social interface that

evident that it is necessary to rely on and connect to local networks in order to generate cheap and effective information for the selection of clients as well as to safeguard local legitimacy and (possibly also) effective participation in contract enforcement. The creation and social maintenance of a workable interface between clients and financial institutions therefore has the character of a continuous discursive and practical "struggle" to generate an innovative societal realm, building upon, but at the same time changing, the balance of existing values and networks that has the potential to contribute to the strengthening of a rural market society. Especially if the MFI is capable of effectively transacting with previously excluded "unbankable" clients, there is a possibility that significant institutional externalities are generated through their association with an actor-network of contractual and entrepreneurial practices and relationships. In the same vein, producer organizations and other actors will make use of some social templates in microfinance; resist, subvert, eschew or transform others. This can both effectively strengthen and signal their capability and trustworthiness in order to improve their "market citizenship" beyond the financial transactions between MFI and poorer clients, opening up real windows of opportunity for the poorer clients to graduate out of mere survival livelihood strategies. And it is precisely here that opportunities need to be found for associating the creation of a social realm that enables financial transactions with the strengthening of actor-networks of agricultural value chains and in particular for mitigation of the tendency towards the exclusion of poorer actors in the more beneficial, but also more demanding, chains.

This implies that we give a more proactive role to agricultural finance than, for example, the approach exemplified by Gonzalez–Vega *et al.* (2006). We agree with them in their argument that "*existing or potential value chain relationships facilitate access to a broad range of financial services ... increasing credit worthiness of producers*" and thus permit exploring "*ways in which expanded financial intermediation facilitates increased smallholder participation in modern chains*" (Gonzalez–Vega, 2006: 5). They, however, do not analyze the need for transformation of the MFIs nor of the existing governance of the food chains; they rather seem to argue that the current dynamism of existing and potential value of food chains influences "*the pace*

governs the financial transactions. This principle also explains why rural clients are rather easily capable of distinguishing between "soft" and "hard" financial institutions. Lack of "credit culture" prevailing in the former need not necessarily affect the transactions of the latter.

and style of rural financial deepening" (2006: 5). In other words, they give the impression of assuming that existing microfinance and existing food chains will almost automatically lead to financial deepening and even the democratization of agricultural microfinance. Gonzalez–Vega *et al.* (2006) seem to envision the existing and potential chains strictly within a mainstreaming commodity framework where getting the prices right is the recipe for success, while hardly any attention is given to the deeper institutionalities at stake and to the "social currencies" distinct from "priceable" values that are crucial for democratizing value chains and incorporating less capitalized producers into them (Long, 2003: 115–25). We believe a more proactive and, at the same time, more humble change strategy is both possible and necessary if we want to develop microfinance institutions that contribute to inclusive rural development and poverty reduction.

2.1.3 *Value chains*

As we have indicated above, significant changes are taking place in world agricultural markets. The shift away from agricultural bulk commodities towards differentiated and (often) processed higher value, specialty products further increases the need for intense and deliberate *ex ante* and *ex post* coordination, especially if the actors want to upgrade the overall performance of the chain. This is more likely to be achieved by organizing production and exchange into hybrid value chains with a mixed market and hierarchic governance or even vertically integrated enterprises rather than through indirect, *ex post* coordination in spot market transactions only. Many systems of exchange for agricultural products therefore take the form of value chains.

How do we conceptualize a value chain? A popular definition identifies it as an institutional arrangement that "*describes the full range of activities which are required to bring a product or service from conception, through the phases of production (...), delivery to final consumers, and final disposal after use*" (Kaplinsky and Morris, 2000: 4). A useful complementary perspective to this rather technical-economic definition of the value chain is given by Goletti (2004) who conceptualizes it as the connections or linkages among different economic actors which organize together to enhance productivity and value added of their activities, bringing benefits and improving competitiveness.

The concept of "value chain" is inspired by several complementary historical sources, with each contributing key perspectives to its analytical capacity. A first relevant historical background is the French "filière" approach (IRAM, 2006). In its essence, this approach consisted of a static, descriptive representation of physical product flows at a sectoral, bulk commodity level — often related to a colonial export product. The analysis usually stopped at national borders and restricted itself to simple commodity pricing analysis. Initially it dedicated little attention to the governance and interrelations of actors in the chain (implicitly assuming centralized colonial management), although this came to be included in the approach later (IRAM, 2006). Key ideas from the "filière" approach were taken over and further elaborated in the sub-sector approach of Michigan University (Boomgard *et al.*, 2002). A second contribution is Michael Porter's Value Chain analysis (Porter, 1985). Here the primary focus is the competitiveness of individual firms and its connection with the nature and organization of its upstream suppliers and downstream marketing chain. Porter stresses both the importance of the system's cost efficiency and the creation of monopolistic market niches through product differentiation as key sources of value creation and profitability. The interconnection of firm value chains of suppliers, primary producers, processors, wholesalers and retailers is called the "value chain system". The effectiveness of vertical coordination among firms is crucial to achieve competitiveness. In this perspective, the network of horizontal interactions (clusters) among firms in a value chain system, even among apparent competitors, is also of great importance as it generates significant and often critical agglomeration rents in terms of mutual learning, shared actionable knowledge as the basis for effective collective action, vision of the future and motivation. Such cluster-dynamics are the key, especially for SMEs, to their competitiveness and survival (Parrilli, 2007).

Another approach in value chain analysis is the political economy perspective of Global Commodity Chain analysis (Gereffi and Korzeniewizc, 1994; Gereffi, 1999). Implicitly, this approach is a critical vision of what is left unmentioned but quite operative in the Porter approach. Here, the focus is rather on the commodity or value chain as a whole, i.e., as a usually cross-border international network linking localized producers through a whole range of intermediaries with global consumers. The political economy perspective also implies that the discursive emphasis shifts from firm competitiveness to power relationships and the distribution of value added that results from the unequal control over key resources and networks within the global chain.[16] This approach also stresses the importance of

[16]It should be clear, however, that both approaches are not necessarily incompatible as "firm competitiveness" is evidently linked to relative power.

governance, i.e., the necessity to count with key actors that have the capacity to provide and impose guidance in the chain in order to coordinate the relevant participants in the chain. Such governance is needed in order to guarantee and improve the systemic efficiency and competitiveness of the chain, and thus to increase the total value added generated. Gereffi (1999) points out, however, that there is usually one or a few dominant actors in chain governance, controlling one or another key resource, which not only affects the total amount of value added, but also its distribution among chain participants as the dominant actors have the capacity to appropriate rent.[17] Unequal power between actors in the chain thus affects income distribution and can induce both "opportunity hoarding" (the protection of the "competitive edge" through shielding of lucrative phases from potential competitors) and "exploitation" (disproportionately low compensation for the efforts of the weaker parties). Agricultural value chains are usually buyer-driven chains, implying that chain governance is increasingly dominated by a few (multinational) enterprises with significant control in processing and access to the more lucrative, higher value consumer markets (brands, supermarkets, export chains).

Related to both the generation of aggregate value added and its distribution is the strategic/tactical concept of "upgrading", which can be understood at the level of specific actors in the chain as well as the whole chain. Upgrading refers to innovations done to achieve higher levels of value added; they must be understood as improvements in products and/or processes, which are new to actors of the chain, and which permit the structure as a whole to carry on and maintain its competitive position in the face of constantly changing standards (Giuliani *et al.*, 2003). Four different types of upgrading can be distinguished: *process upgrading* (increasing the efficiency of internal process within individual links in the chain and between the links in the chain); *product upgrading* (introducing new products or improving old products); *functional upgrading* (increasing value added by changing the mix of activities conducted within firms or moving the locus of activities to different links in the value chain); *and chain upgrading* (moving to a new, qualitatively better value chain).

For economists, governance is mainly a matter of managing individual businesses and inter-firm relationships, which it, of course, also is. The

[17]Rent can have several origins, both endogenous (e.g. technological advantages, access to key human resources, organizational or relational superiority, marketing control) and exogenous (e.g. key resources, infrastructure, favorable policy environment, financial costs).

sociological perspective of Norman Long (2002), however, adds an important point, which is especially relevant in less commoditized (peasant) rural societies. Long stresses that a value chain is always a social process that is promoted by particular actors who have the capacity to sufficiently enroll relevant others, e.g., a number of processing/exporting firms interested in one or another agricultural commodity linking up with a network of traders who can in turn mobilize and tie together the efforts from a vast array of primary producers. Similar to the case of microfinance, the creation of this product "market" involves the management of a number of social interfaces within a complex actor-network, inevitably rooted and articulated to the broader local institutional context (networks, rules, norms, practices, perceptions and values).

The organization and functioning of particular value chains is therefore always the result of complex social and discursive struggles over the nature of livelihoods pathways, economic and non-economic values,[18] images of the "market", technological models. Given the tendency for the poor to "*end up at the losing end of the multiple bargains*" (Bastiaensen *et al.*, 2005, p. 981), their social exclusion and relative lack of discursive and organizational power is one of the reasons for their deficient access to beneficial value chains as well as for the absence of chains that are more in accordance with their capabilities and motivations. As indicated by Dorward and Kydd (2005), such social exclusion adds to the problems of transaction failure and deficient control over assets and other resources necessary for poor households to respond to existing opportunities. An increase in the participation of SMEs in agricultural value chains usually requires simultaneous change at all three levels (institutional and organizational change, transaction costs, and assets).

Finally, care must be taken not to lock our analysis of rural and even agricultural dynamics into a fragmented view of separate value chains. The functioning of particular value chains usually depends upon their insertion and articulation to a broader knowledge and support system — a web of vertical (chain) and horizontal (cluster) networks among enterprises as well as with providers of complementary input, including financial institutions — and

[18]In these on-going process, non-commoditized values and relationships can be contested and changed (e.g., gender norms prohibiting female labor force and entrepreneurship in segments of the agricultural chains); but they can also turn out to adapt and accommodate to the market logic in the value chain (e.g., when unpaid female or child labor contributes to the profitability of market activity).

upon their overall match with networks, practices and cognitive-normative frameworks of the territories that they cross-cut. Often a part of the actors in the chain, and in particular the primary producers, will also be engaged in diversified livelihood strategies which will interfere positively or negatively with their achievements in the chain. Successful value chain development will therefore also partially depend upon the synergy that can be achieved with the broader development and dynamics of the rural territories. The same quality of human interactions and compatibility of motivational and cognitive frames that is critical for the success of complex value chains will also determine the nature of the success of territorial development (Schejtman and Berdegué, 2003; Echeverria and Ribero, 2002).

Wrapping up the different conceptual contributions, we find the following complementary dimensions with which to think about the articulation of a "Finance Plus" approach with processes that enhance beneficial participation of rural SME's in agricultural value chains:

(a) *systemic efficiency and competitiveness* of the agricultural chain in question, which can take the form of improving (the participation of SMEs in) existing chains or that of articulating new agricultural chains with enhanced opportunities for SME's;
(b) *equitable and proportional distribution of value added*, which make it dynamically (more) worthwhile for SME's to participate in the chain and in particular avoids the dangers of "immiserising growth";
(c) *exclusion* of SMEs due to lack of critical assets and organizational resources, transaction failures or discriminatory social process, which translate into a need for economic and socio-cultural emancipation of the excluded groups;
(d) *struggles over value and meaning*, the outcomes of which determine whose views and interests will dominate in the choice to concentrate collective efforts in the development of particular value chains and the way they are organized and governed. As this is a matter of "voice" and relative power of different actors and their respective networks and epistemic sub-communities, it is closely related to the issue of social exclusion.

2.1.4 *A transformative value chain approach to microfinance: "Finance plus"*

All of the above brings us to argue for a transformative value chain approach. Much too often, poor agricultural producers remain exclusively tied into producing risky, rain-fed and/or undifferentiated bulk products for traditional and often local spot markets in which little value added can be generated; risk and vulnerability are high, and traditional social practices of hierarchical, unequal exchange often dominate transactions within the market. Both for the income prospects of these poor producers as well as the prospects of developing a viable rural microfinance sector, this offers only limited prospects of beneficial development. In our view, a more vibrant microfinance sector with the capacity to contribute to inclusive rural development thus inevitably goes together with the promotion of consciously governed value chains in both traditional and non-traditional agricultural sectors in which the poor and excluded sectors participate in a beneficial way. It is clear, however, that such beneficial participation is all but evident and requires substantial investment and conscious actions for change.

Here is an important potential role for rural microfinance as it requires social embeddedness and institutional entrepreneurship in order to establish a negotiated social-institutional realm, characterized by contractual relationships between equal parties, in order to solve its pressing transaction cost problem. This often quite innovative institutional realm can serve as a platform for broader institutional re-articulation of transactions and social relations in the value chains to which it is inevitably articulated. From here, microfinance can be managed as an active actor that is promoting both investments and institutional innovations to create and transform agricultural value for the benefit of excluded rural groups, such as land-poor and landless farmers and other entrepreneurs, women and youth. In such a "Finance Plus" strategy, we should not consider microfinance as a disconnected reality,[19] but rather accept that it can only deliver on its promises to the extent that it links up with strategies of other relevant actors, in particular movements and associations of client-beneficiaries, capable of articulating their preferred pathways of change and subsequently having their voices heard to mobilize the minimally required cooperation of the state, private entrepreneurs, NGOs, etc. to make these pathways possible.

A transformative value chain approach linked to a "finance plus" strategy, particularly if its wants to be successful with less capitalized productive enterprises, inevitably requires additional subsidy for the required

[19] In this sense, part of the current heated debate about the (lack of) beneficial impact of microfinance might miss an important point in ignoring this crucial point about the necessary and often location-specific co-evolution of several of these variables for the hoped-for impact to emerge.

investments and social learning. These subsidies cannot be generated solely from internal sources: i.e., profits made in the financial operations with the somewhat better-off clients. A key question is therefore the generation and, even more importantly, the quality of the utilisation of scarce external subsidies. In this respect, we believe the widespread failures of the agricultural and rural investments financed by international development cooperation contrasts sharply with the FDL's much better use of internally and externally generated subsidies. It is our conviction that current internationally financed programs are all too often plagued by clientelistic populism and elite capture, and therefore end up supporting inefficiency and exclusionary tendencies rather than reducing either of them. This could be changed if these subsidies would be better articulated with market-based institutional transformation of rural governance and sustainable financing done by microfinance institutions with the capacity to penetrate the agricultural sector and in particular to articulate to promising value chain development and transformation. We are in full agreement with the World Bank (2008) concerning the very high social and economic pay-off of rural investments in terms of growth and sustained poverty reduction, but do believe that such a more appropriate institutional articulation of rural economic and social governance is a key condition for the success of substantially increased rural investments.

3 Towards a Value Chain Approach in Agricultural Finance: The FDL in Nicaragua

3.1 *National context*

Nicaragua is the most rural and most agrarian of the Central American countries, and the only one where the agricultural sector has been growing in recent years (Grigsby and Pérez, 2007). Some 1.4 million people are directly active in agriculture as farmers; 59 percent of these farmers are poor subsistence farmers. Besides a small better-off minority, most of the non-farmer rural population is landless and, to a large extent, dependent on wage labor. Remittances from temporary or permanent migration, mainly to neighboring Costa Rica, are an important complementary source of incomes for a large, but unknown percentage of the rural inhabitants.[20] Yet, the

[20]In 2006, some 60,000 Nicaraguans would have been active in Costa Rica agriculture on a permanent or temporary — during harvest time — basis.

poorest sectors of rural society seem to benefit relatively less from migrant income, due to insurmountable barriers to migration. Income inequality is very high in Nicaragua and seems to be increasing. UNDP estimated that the Nicaraguan Gini-coefficient for income inequality was equal to 0.56, which ranks among the highest in the world. Poverty continues to be high in comparison to its Central American neighbors. In 2005, 47 percent of the Nicaraguan population was considered to be poor (below the US$ 1 poverty line), with 16 percent "extremely poor". This poverty definitively has a rural face, with 75 percent of the poor living in rural areas. Despite strong rural and agricultural growth in the last decade, progress in rural poverty reduction has been slow and disappointing.

As to the agricultural sector in Nicaragua, the integration into the more dynamic global and national food chains has been slower than in neighboring countries with more systemic competitiveness. Nevertheless, Nicaragua has been catching up quickly with Costa Rica and other Latin American countries with, for example, supermarkets already accounting for 10–20 percent in the early 2000s (Reardon *et al.*, 2005: 4) and significant upgrading in several agricultural chains. Globalization, and in particular the several free trade arrangements now prevailing in Nicaragua, offer both threats and opportunities for the rural economy. With rising food and agricultural prices some optimism has surfaced, but with the onset of the current recession, Nitlapán's attention centred even more clearly on the need for value chain improvement. In this context, the main challenge is to upgrade production-processing-marketing chains in order to become/remain competitive in increasingly demanding national and external consumer markets. In Nicaragua, significant and relatively successful efforts are underway in value chains related to (specialty and biological) coffee, milk-dairy production, cacao, root crops/vegetables for supermarkets and — more timidly — rural tourism. Because of their national outreach, Nitlapán and the FDL are participating in all of these chains.

This reemerging rural value chain dynamism, particularly its most dynamic sector in meat/dairy transactions, is, however, not translated into inclusive development and poverty reduction as this process shows clear signs of increasing exclusion of the small and medium-sized producers in the dynamic chains. The current model of rural growth thus points in the direction of increasing polarization and has clearly contributed to rising inequality in the country, explaining also why results of recent growth in terms of poverty reduction are so disappointing. Another key problem in the majority of agricultural activities is environmental degradation; it is in particular a critical threat for the sustainability in booming dairy and meat chains. Most of the rural economic expansion — in particular extensive cattle-raising — is based upon the incorporation of ever more land at the agricultural frontier and thus the destruction of the remaining tropical forests. According to the Nicaraguan Ministry of the Environment, the current extensive path of the agrarian system is incorporating 70,000 hectares a year to agriculture at enormous environmental cost.

3.1.1 *FDL and Nitlapán response*

With rising concerns about exclusionary and environmental tendencies in an otherwise dynamic rural and agricultural growth (Grigsby and Pérez, 2007, 2008), the FDL endeavored to reconcile its mission to support peasant and SME-based rural economic development with being a highly efficient microfinance institution. Once the FDL had created workable social interfaces in several deep rural areas, enabling it to solve the transaction cost problem, it started at first to develop an overwhelmingly agricultural portfolio, also including substantial long-term investment financing for rural producers (see Table 21.2). In particular, the dairy and meat portfolios have expanded exponentially.

Rapidly, the Boards of Nitlapán and FDL became aware, however, that social impact required a more deliberate effort in linking finance with agricultural value chains and in supporting smaller producers to get beneficial access to them. Up until 2003, the role of Nitlapán/FDL in value chains had been the organization of supply for wholesalers and processors, principally in the western and northwestern areas of Nicaragua with oil-seed markets (sesame seeds, groundnuts, soybeans). Much of these efforts were executed through elite negotiations with minimal participation from rural producers. These initial efforts benefited both the FDL and producers by making markets more predictable, thereby significantly reducing price risks, but they did not necessarily make these markets more equitable or efficient for the clients, even though small producers' access might have marginally improved. After 2005, the emphasis turned to addressing value chains in a more coherent manner in chains connected with coffee, vegetable-fruit, milk, cheese, and meat production. Given the exclusionary tendencies identified above, the key strategic challenge of the emergent comprehensive approach to finance for value chain development is the need to improve the access and the position of smaller producers within these chains and — if possible — to contribute to the overall upgrading of the chain in order to increase national value added.

Table 21.2: Loan portfolios of FDL and associated development programs of Nitlapán (2008).

	Clients	%	Portfolio (US$)	%	Average loan size (US$)
Overview Loan Portfolio — FDL					
Non-Agricultural Portfolio.	39,835	48	26,296,122	38	660
Agricultural Portfolio.	42,501	52	43,640,372	62	1,027
— *Long term agricultural loans.*	21,009	26	*31,202,787*	*45*	1,485
— *Investment (subsidized risk capital).*	1,271	2	*4,813,800*	*7*	3,787
— *Development Portfolio (risk capital + technical assistance/ value chains).*	7,438	9	*7,419,644*	*11*	998
Total portfolio FDL	**82,336**	**100**	**69,936,494**	**100**	**849**
Development Portfolio — FDL					
Investment loans — rural women (cows).	3,791	58	*1,896,300*	*33*	500
Green package (silvopastoral cattle intensification).	1,163	18	*2,349,700*	*41*	2,020
Solar Panels.	956	15	*895,300*	*15*	937
Genetically improved dairy cattle.	280	4	*258,200*	*4*	922
Irrigation equipment (vegetables-fruits).	173	3	*219,800*	*4*	1,271
Reconversion coffee.	164	3	*166,900*	*3*	1,018
Total development portfolio FDL	**6,527**	**100**	***5,786,200***	***100***	**887**
Development Portfolio — Nitlapán					
Meat cattle franchising.	171	19	*596,290*	*37*	3,487
Leasing dairy cows.	425	47	*518,985*	*32*	1,221
Equipment and machinery.	299	33	*489,700*	*30*	1,638
Access to land + technical assistance.	16	2	*28,489*	*17*	1,779
Total portfolio Nitlapán	**911**	**100**	***1,633,444***	***100***	**1,793**
Total development portfolio FDL/Nitlapán	*7,438*		*7,419,644*		*998*

Source: FDL, Nitlapán.

At the same time, the Board also started to emphasize that special attention should be given to the access of small producers, and in particular also rural women, to productive, agricultural and other investment credit rather than just the customary short-term credit for working capital in petty trade and service activities. A final important concern was the environmental sustainability of the agricultural activities that were financed, particularly of the dairy and cattle production which comprised about 40 percent of the agricultural portfolio and was clearly linked to the environmentally destructive expansion of the agricultural frontier. Using part of its profitability margin, implicitly transferring profits from the most profitable operations, the FDL therefore started to develop an internally subsidized "development portfolio" with a number of often longer term investment products at a somewhat lower cost directed at less capitalized agricultural SME, and rural female clients (see Table 21.2).

In 2008, about 60 percent of the clients and around 40 percent of the investments in this "development portfolio" were destined for a variety of small-scale agricultural and some industrial investments for rural women: e.g., homestead vegetable, root crop or fruit production; small livestock (poultry, pigs, sheep); cows; small mills and local food processing activities. Except for the solar panels, the other products in the "development portfolio" are linked to investment needs of small enterprises that want to upgrade their position in coffee, dairy- and meat-cattle and vegetable-root crop-fruit chains. The development portfolio is concentrated in the dairy/meat chains (over 75 percent of the portfolio), also because the majority of rural female productive activity is related to double purpose cattle and because of the environmental issues in cattle (see below).

The structure of the development portfolio gives a good reflection of the current "state of the art" of the FDL and Nitlapán in taking the first steps towards a more integrated value chain approach. In fact, the capitalization and financing of small peasant production in cattle produces rapid and significant results even without further transformations in the value chain. Successful advancement of small enterprises in coffee, fruits and vegetables depends more upon further transformations in the chain and results are more difficult to attain as FDL and Nitlapán's experiences in the marketing and processing stages are incipient. We must also add that compared to 2007, the average size of loans have increased by 20 percent. This reflects the difficulties of incorporating less capitalized producers into value chains. Typically, many of the less capitalized do not show a performance meritorious of continuing in the development portfolio, but this is also a reflection of misplaced international subsidies in agricultural development which often remains out of their reach.

Trying to address the environmental threat for the future sustainability of the current dairy-cattle development pathways, one of the key financial products (with nearly half of the investments and a quarter of the clients in the development portfolio) is the "green package" with moderately subsidized rates of interest to induce silvopastoral-based intensification of livestock production, which represents the envisaged route towards long-term sustainability and the protection of soils, water and forests from the destructive effects of extensive cattle raising. Nitlapán and FDL are also making co-investments in innovative Payments for Environmental Service schemes (earlier in a successful pilot project financed and executed with the Global Environmental Facility, the World Bank and CATIE and today in new, improved schemes supported by the IADB and CABEI).[21] These efforts are also connected to the normal portfolio of cattle loans for medium-sized and larger producers.

Directly linked to these and other investment products is the strategy to complement the FDL financial services with complementary technical and marketing assistance mostly paid for by the FDL. The motivation behind this strategy was the empirical finding that credit alone was often not enough to enable poorer clients to implement the more substantial changes that are necessary for a more beneficial access and participation in markets and chains. Over the period 2004–2008, the FDL financed on average 50 percent of the non-financial services that were provided to its clients by Nitlapán. The rest was supplemented by development agencies who, up to that time, had rarely used their funds to promote synergy between financial and non-financial services. Today, the FDL also intermediates business services for its clients through alliances with other actors in value chains: other NGOs like Technoserve and Clusa, private suppliers of farm input and machinery, and the "Enterprise Incubation" Programs of Nitlapán. The corresponding funding amounts, however, remain below the investments made by the FDL itself.

The full potential and final impact of the credit, leasing services, investment products, technical and marketing assistance, and so on, can however only be appreciated by analyzing how they operate interactively, between themselves and interfacing with clients and other actors, to promote socially

[21] See Van Hecken and Bastiaensen (2009) for a detailed analysis of the FDL–Nitlapán experiences with PES and silvopastoral intensification.

and environmentally more beneficial pathways of change in the value chains under question, in particular whether the more integrated services indeed succeed in linking up with the priority groups and in addressing the key binding constraints for a more beneficial participation and thus overall development of the value chain. As we only have limited space here, we will focus our presentation on the dairy-cattle value chains where the FDL–Nitlapán presence is most developed.

3.1.2 *Dairy-meat cattle value chain*

Without doubt, dairy and cattle activities are among the more profitable and secure agricultural activities in Nicaragua.[22] However, as indicated above, neither the participation of smaller-scale producers, nor the environmental sustainability of the current extensive growth model is guaranteed.[23] Traditionally, smaller and even medium-sized cattle producers have double-purpose systems that are not specialized in (genetically adequate) milk cows, nor engage in the more rewarding "finishing" stages of the fattening process of meat cattle. Very few of the FDL clients have the resources to become actors in the rewarding finishing stage. Key in this is their lack of access to remunerative milk or meat markets for upgrading their herds. In the meat-cattle chain, the smaller producers generally sell their young male animals to large specialized fatteners, who control vast pastures and thus manage very extensive cattle systems with substantial, but environmentally dubious cost advantages. The larger producers as well as a limited number of cattle traders also have the scale and the capacity to reach sufficient volume to program their cattle deliveries throughout the year in agreement with the industrial slaughterhouses and thus to gain direct and more beneficial access to the higher value added segment that serves supermarkets and relatively more lucrative export markets.[24] This market control as well as

[22]The current decline in meat and milk prices due to the international recession represents the first blip in the meat and dairy sector in over 15 years.

[23]In the epicenter of milk value chains in Nicaragua (Matiguas), international enterprise has hastened the development of the network of purchasing fresh milk from producers. In 15 years, smaller producers along with capable "colono" producers working the lands of large landholders have been eliminated, leaving salaried laborers in their places. The process of dispossession was accompanied with intense intervention of international agencies like PRODERBO UE, FondeAgro–ASDI as well as extremely deep penetration by both the FDL and Nitlapán (Baumeister and Fernández, s.d.).

[24]Nicaragua's insertion in the international meat export-market is quite deficient, selling a substantial amount of live animals for slaughter in neighboring countries and largely unprocessed meat to be used for hamburgers and the like in US fast-food chains.

their access to financial capital allows this segment of large producers and traders to engage in cattle sharecropping with land-owning, but capital-poor large and medium-sized farmers in order to fatten more animals. This sharecropping operates in terms of local cattle prices, such that the large producers and traders reap most of the benefits following their monopoly on the access to the slaughterhouse and the much higher prices paid there. When small and medium-sized farmers succeed in fattening animals (which they hardly ever do) or need to sell their aged, unproductive cows, they are dependent upon local informal butchers and municipal slaughterhouses, which cater to the less demanding, poorly paying local markets, or they need to sell to local intermediaries who pay only marginally better prices. Despite the poor articulation of the Nicaraguan cattle and meat markets into the international context, the cattle operations are quite profitable for all parties, albeit the rates of return logically change according to the kind of activity and articulation to the markets, clearly to the detriment of the smaller farmers. In large part, this can be explained by the very extensive nature of all cattle-raising and thus by its dependence on the availability of abundant and cheap land. In 2007, the FDL estimated that investments in dual purpose, mixed cattle generated a return in a 40–60 percent range; in the development phase of cattle-raising between 60 and 90 percent, and in the finishing-fattening stage of 120 to 150 percent. Although we lack precise data, it is also clear that the larger part of Nicaraguan value added is captured by the industrial slaughterhouses and the national and international cattle traders. Guesstimates by Nitlapán indicate that the supermarket retailers capture some 14 percent, the slaughterhouse 39 percent, national traders 12 percent, local traders 5 percent and producers around 30 percent of total national value added.

Given the importance of cattle and its overall profitability, the FDL has a substantial exposure to the different actors in the meat-cattle chain extending "normal" loans between 12 and 24 months at a 21.6 percent to 24.4 percent interest rate (2008) for dual purpose cattle and the development and fattening stages of cattle raising. However, aware that this financial response to existing solvent demand might produce both socially undesirable concentration and be environmentally damaging, the FDL in association with its partner institution, Nitlapán, has started to take initiatives to try to

Substantial value added could be captured through more adequate processing and direct commercialization, in particular starting with the neighboring markets in Mexico and Central America. (Flores and Delmelle, 2006).

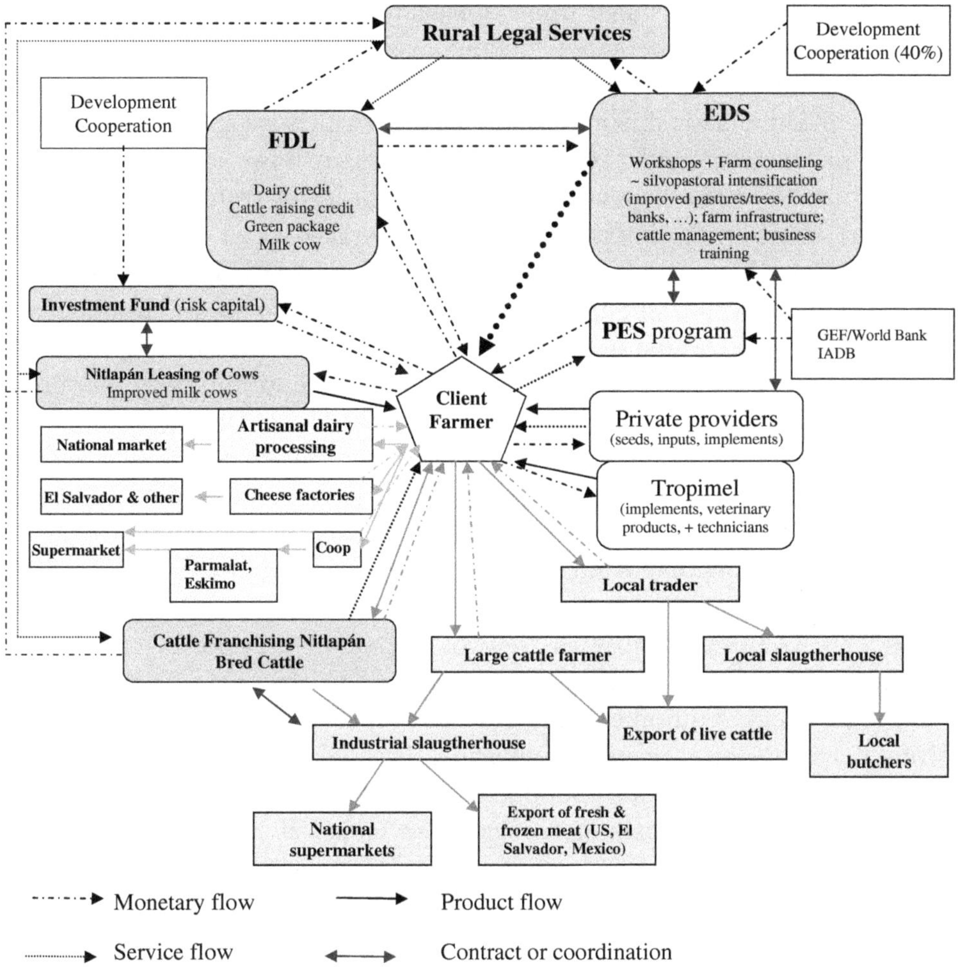

Figure 21.1: FDL alliances in the dairy and meat chains.

support both socially more inclusive and environmentally-sound intensive, silvopastoral cattle systems. Alliances with other institutions and initiatives deliberately trying to induce and support changes in this direction are a key strategy in this respect. Figure 21.1 summarizes the main alliances and relationships.

A basic alliance is that with the "Entrepreneurial Development Services" (EDS) program within Nitlapán. FDL buys technical assistance services at commercial rates from EDS for its clients — cattle farmers. This technical assistance consists of local workshops about preselected themes and (limited) on-farm tailor-made consultancy services. Up to now, technical assistance has mainly focussed upon silvopastoral intensification, in particular the establishment of higher yielding pastures and permanent fodder banks, which allow significant increases in pasture carrying capacity and reduce the feeding crisis during the dry season (which is especially relevant for dairy production) and the need for farmers to have access to second farms further down the agricultural frontier in order to transhumance their cattle. The substantial efforts in this area have also been connected to a pilot project in "Payments for Environmental Services (PES)" (carbon storage and biodiversity conservation) financed by the Global Environmental Facility (2003–2007), and a more recent IADB–PES project, paying farmers *ex post* for increased carbon storage in fodder banks and improved pastures (with or without trees). Other important topics of technical assistance are the establishment and maintenance of basic farm infrastructure (e.g. clean milking conditions and practices) as well as better management of cattle (reproduction, sanitation, genetic improvement). In the context of this operation, complementary commercial alliances have been forged with private providers of improved seeds and farm implements (mainly grinders to cut fodder). A special case is the network of small-scale local enterprises (Tropimel) for technical assistance services, tied to the sale of farm implements, solar energy equipment and veterinary products. These small innovative enterprises, often also engaging in a broader range of petty trading activities, are themselves also supported by FDL-credit and EDS business training services. EDS business services also make efforts to support producer access to markets, for example, organizing visits to milk collection centres and industrial slaughterhouses. Impact has however been very limited as access to information is clearly not the only problem affecting smaller farmers' lack of opportunities to participate in certain market segments. Up to now, however, Nitlapán's technical and training services to support collective marketing initiatives have not gone beyond the planning stage, nor has a policy been developed to link with strategic local partners (like dairy cooperatives).

More significant prospects for changing the marketing system are achieved by the "meat cattle franchising operation" of Nitlapán. In this case, Nitlapán adapted the traditional cattle share-contract, where richer and poorer cattle ranchers equally share the proceeds calculated at local market prices, into a very different "modern" and contractually transparent and formalised setting. The basic mechanism is that the franchising enterprise and a farmer-associate join together in an explicit and detailed formal contract to raise meat cattle (either development and/or final fattening) under more intensified production conditions. In mutual agreement with the farmer, Nitlapán buys the initial better quality animals, puts in technical assistance, veterinary and other necessary inputs; the farmer provides land, appropriate conditions (infrastructure, water, pastures and fodder crops) and his labour time. Both parties share the risk of the operation. As in any share-cropping contract, net proceeds are shared among the parties — after a formal receipt with all the details as well as the support documents for all the components of the calculations is delivered. The promotion of mutual transparence in the contractual operation is held to be very important as practices of mutual cheating are widespread in the Nicaraguan countryside to such an extent that they become an impediment for the improved and more complex cooperation that is often needed to reap more benefits in agricultural value chains (as is the case here).[25] Here we also find an important link to the positive externality associated with the promotion of "contract culture" in the financial transactions of the FDL. We believe this is an important factor in explaining the difference between the relative success of investments within the FDL-realm and the dismal results of the politicized, clientelistic state investment programs, which continue to be financed with official development aid (see above). Overall, less capitalized, mainly medium-sized producers who could never dream of operating in the fattening have upgraded their participation in the cattle chain.

Crucial is that Nitlapán coordinates and plans the entire operation after negotiating the entire batch of about 2000 heads of cattle with an industrial slaughterhouse. In this way, it gains significant price advantages, not only because it can offer a huge batch of cattle at once, but also because it guarantees cattle of appropriate weight, a better than average quality (young animals, no prohibited substances) and arriving according to an agreed schedule. Contrary to local traders and traditional share-cropping, Nitlapán pays the share of its farmer-associates according to these slaughterhouse prices and not — as is normally the case — at local prices. In March

[25]Despite local embeddedness and careful selection, moral hazard problems caused by cheating producers remain a serious challenge. Especially in the context of the current economic crisis, the temptation to opt out of contractual obligations and even to sell (i.e. to steal) the share-cropped animals seems to have surged in some cases. Also, the ambiguity of the present government in its weak stand against the so-called "No Payment Movement", which is asking for cancellation of debt obligations with "usurious" microfinance institutions, is not very helpful, as it translates into practical difficulties to take recourse to legal action or support of the local police to enforce contractual obligations (and even to recover stolen animals in some cases).

2009, local market prices were below C$ 26.3/lb; whereas Nitlapán in that period obtained between C$ 42.9/lb for the animals offered in the slaughterhouse, i.e., a price premium of 63 percent. Taking account of the additional costs and the 50 percent–50 percent share-arrangement with the program, this translates in an additional net income of about US$ 42 per animal for an eight months fattening operation, or 77 percent increase compared to the estimated income from a similar operation valued at local prices and with the usual less intensive practices. An important — at least potential — advantage is precisely also that the franchising operation enables smaller and medium-sized farmers to participate in the more rewarding fattening phase (especially those who are too far away from the roads to engage in more intensive milk production) and not only in the less profitable development phase (although many smaller farmers still do not have the conditions or the motivation to engage in the fattening phase).

Up to now, most efforts were directed towards the setting up of the operation and less attention has been given to articulating poorer cattle ranchers, who do not yet have the necessary conditions on their farms (mainly the capacity to feed the animals). Efforts are therefore underway together with training services and the small Nitlapán unit, Tropimel, in order to incubate more of the small farmer enterprises with the required conditions to engage in joint venture contracts.

Here, Nitlapán manages a small non-reimbursable investment fund from which to finance the more risky initial investments (farm implements, veterinary products, seeds, barbed wire) of those small farmers.[26] The franchising enterprise often also complements FDL cattle credit (e.g., in the current IADB–PES project), since the FDL is very careful not to give too much credit, and the producer therefore usually still has substantial idle capacity on his farm. As the animals held in the joint venture agreement remain the property of Nitlapán, it runs less risk than the FDL in the similar operation. As part of its environmental concerns in cattle raising, the Incubation Enterprise also engages significantly with very small-scale cattle raising in the more developed and more densely populated Pacific Region of Nicaragua where there is more market competition, making it easier to incorporate less capitalized producers. Again the investment fund for risk capital is used to finance, for example, innovative fattening of meat cattle

[26] As part of its risk management, the FDL is very hesitant to give credit to farmers who have not yet been able to prove their capacity. Once such a small farmer has demonstrated his capacity to operate his/her improved farm, the FDL usually takes over.

in stables, using chicken dung and improvised fodder mixes including sugar by-products, stubble and vegetable waste.

A final initiative is the leasing enterprise in improved milking of cows. More than the previous operation, this enterprise plays an important role in the capitalization of land-poor women and men, but it does not actively engage in the commercialization phase. For a poor farmer, having access to one or two cows not only makes a huge difference in terms of family diet, but often also enable him/her to engage in a more successful accumulation strategy. The leasing operation gives these poor farmers the opportunity to gain access to a good breed milking cow without immediately having to buy the animal. The lease contract allows the farmer to minimize the initial risk to the cost of the rent (which also includes a contribution for technical assistance). Experience shows that if the operation is successful, the capitalization process can proceed quite rapidly, mainly through the calves which become the property of the lessee. Technical assistance is crucial as the genetically improved cows — they are not pure breeds, of course, but still higher yielding cows — need regular and appropriate feeding. Again this matches the strategy to intensify Nicaraguan cattle raising, certainly in this case including the promotion of very intensive dairy cattle in the Pacific Region. Several experiences indeed show that even having access to land is not necessarily a condition for successful milking cow management, as one vegetable farmer has proved by handling five milking cows with only 0.17 hectares of land. He manages his 8–10 litre per day cows in a stable, collects the manure to fertilise his vegetable plots and feeds the animals with chicken dung and vegetable waste from his own field, other producers and nearby supermarkets.

Trying to tentatively evaluate the impact of these articulated interventions, we can say that in the meat chain, the package around bred cattle franchising has been effective both in promoting value chain competitiveness and improving the distribution of value added among the partners. The initiative has yet to upgrade the value chain for the majority of poor producers beyond ineffective national slaughterhouses by gaining direct access to differentiated, higher value meat markets beyond the traditional "hamburger connection" (Flores and Delmelle, 2006). Up to now, the program has been less effective in connecting small farmers, except in the denser Pacific region where risk capital has been used to deal with poor producers. Similarly, the program needs more international subsidy or more profits from the FDL to intensify the training component of technological transformation. It has also achieved significant results in making cattle ranching environmentally more sound, combined with PES. Nevertheless, more concentration of less capitalized producers with their intrinsic rationality of intensifying production in improved pastures and fodder banks could produce a higher environmental plus than current PES initiatives.

The dairy chain work shows a strong impact in capitalization of poorer producers, in particular in the better connected areas, but to a lesser extent also in the more remote areas. For its concentration at the production stage, its impact on chain competitiveness remains less clear. In the more densely populated areas, capitalized and upgraded dairy producers have become more competitive, taking advantage of road infrastructure and increased consumer demand. In the deep country regions, lack of roads and incapacity to compete with transnational cheese makers who hoard opportunities impose stronger constraints. Typically, the poorer producers face significant "barriers of entry" to the more dynamic chains and — if they have access — their modalities of access are clearly less beneficial. They suffer most from a lack of access to roads and have financial constraints that make it difficult to meet fresh milk quality standards. Furthermore, for lack of insurance, they often show strong risk aversion and prefer disadvantageous, but flexible inter-locked contracts, in particular with the intermediaries of the "Salvadoran" cheese-makers. As a consequence, it is the larger dairy producers who continue to disproportionally benefit from the advantages of the dynamic fresh milk chains, leading also to increasing land concentration in the connected milk-producing areas and expulsion of poorer farmers to the more marginal land in the agricultural frontier. More radical transformations seem to be necessary to put feet under the dream of small-scale industrial dairy production and upgrade this chain at the national level. These transformations include socioeconomic incidence with local populations and mayors in the deep countryside.

From a microperspective, maximum impact for smaller farmers requires the combination and synergy of different interventions and services. Strong territorial articulation of the different lines of action is crucial for this. At present, FDL and Nitlapán performance is not yet optimal at all in this respect. Both institutions and their different programs operate (and have to continue operating) with autonomy and they often respond to the quite varied organizational logic of a microfinance, a leasing, a franchising, a legal and a technical consultancy enterprise, some of them with outside subsidies and others with internally generated funding only. Recently, steps are therefore taken to start training the staff in adopting a strategic territorial view, among others, by engaging actively them in participative action-research for the joint evaluation and policy development of the ongoing interventions and products.[27] To the extent possible, it is also the intention to actively associate other local actors, like cooperatives and other producer associations, private entrepreneurs, municipalities, local representatives of line ministries and NGOs, in this process towards the creation of a territorial development view that functions as actionable knowledge for joint action among FDL, Nitlapán and other allies in specific territories. In order to be successful, a key challenge will be to find appropriate ways to jointly articulate strategic projects for the excluded sectors of small enterprises, self-employed and wage-laborers and let their voice be heard and taken due account of in the local development process. This will evidently require envisaged participatory action-research to seriously engage with struggles and negotiations at the dynamic social interfaces between the different local and outside actors involved.

4 Concluding Remarks

Albeit still very imperfect, the above case of the increasingly articulated FDL and Nitlapán interventions in the meat and dairy sectors substantiates the main proposition of this contribution, i.e., the potential and necessity of a more proactive role for microcredit in promoting and rearticulating promising agricultural value chains towards increasing efficiency, equity and environmental sustainability. Such a proactive role requires the creation of synergy among financial and additional non-financial services, such as technical assistance, legal services, input provisioning, marketing support and so on. Equally or more important is the alignment with other relevant local and supra-local actors who share similar (or at least not too dissimilar) strategic views about the development of agricultural chains and the participation of small-scale producers who can get involved in a joint social learning process. This alignment needs to be deeply rooted in a broad process of local institutional transformation of rural societies and their economic governance. Building upon the innovative institutional platform of the locally embedded "contract culture" — crafted in order to reduce transaction costs for microfinance and achieve high efficiency in rural financial transaction — offers a promising avenue for such broader institutional rearticulation. The

[27] A pilot project, financed by the Flemish Inter-University Council (VLIR) and the Belgian Development Cooperation, has recently started.

FDL's institutional entrepreneurship in the negotiation of actor networks, rules of the game, and perceptions with and around their clients provide a possible stepping stone towards enhanced management and "democratisation" of agricultural value chains. This socially innovating governance context can also afford a way out of the enduring problems of the inefficiency, inequity and gender injustice of the current use of public subsidies for rural development in the prevailing context of political clientelism and elite capture. Similarly in an industry that purports to combine sustainability with poverty reduction, poorly spent subsidies to commercially-oriented MFIs through lower interest rates, better loan terms and outright grants for their transformation into banks should be transferred to initiatives based upon clear conscious developmental and transformative orientations such as those exemplified by FDL. In this way, it should also be possible to guarantee a better use of the much needed national and international funds to co-finance such deeper institutional transformation and related investments.

We must however correctly understand the challenge and not underestimate the task ahead. Today, value chain interventions are becoming increasingly popular in the development industry (Merlin, 2005; USAID, 2009) Usually they are quite adequate in indicating the component of value chain analysis and interventions, but there are doubts about the capacity to avoid the pitfalls of Big D development. Big D development, with its connotations of social engineering and top-down intervention from the developed centre to the benighted periphery, supposedly began with Harry Truman's speech in 1949 and has evolved through innumerable reincarnations into the 21st century (Hart, 2001). What Big D development planners miss is the importance of what is really taking place in "little d" development, "*the development of capitalism as geographically uneven but spatially interconnected processes of creation and destruction, dialectically interconnected with discourses and practices of Development*" (Hart, 2009). In our view, this entails the ongoing complex struggles and negotiation processes around meaning, networks, rules and interests among the actors involved from the local to the global space. Planners of value chain transformation overlook not only the darker sides of their transformations but the enormous weight and power-laden salience of the diverse trajectories of capitalist development to bedevil best laid plans. Supposed change is not all it seems as Casolo has shown in her analysis of women's access to land in Honduras (2009).

Big D paradigms for upgrading chains and actors in those chains risk remaining simultaneously hegemonic and homogenizing, as the problem is that all of the key conceptual boundaries are preestablished before arriving in the local territory. Following the current popularity of "participative" (sic) development approaches, those boundaries are often firmly implanted through processes of popular consultation and subsequent financing for local organizations around the agenda imposed. When Long (1999: 19) indicates that "*interface analysis grapples with the multiple meanings made up of potentially conflicting social and normative interests, and diverse contested bodies of knowledge*", we take him to mean that neither of the multiple meanings, nor the different organizations nor the social strata of empowered and excluded really exists without the other value-laden practices of others. The global commodity chain does not exist without its local expression. The categorical and social boundaries that make up the framework of "actionable knowledge" at the basis of joint action in value chains should thus be mutually produced in the multiple encounters at the interface, and not redefined, refined or adjusted by simply "listening to the people". A proactive role of microfinance in value chain development fundamentally requires finding ways to facilitate and articulate to ongoing struggles as well as cooperative actions in the multiple political arenas of "little d" development.

References

Agarwal, B (1994). *A Field of One's Own: Gender and Land Rights in South Asia.* Cambridge, UK: Cambridge University Presss.

Bastiaensen, J (2000). Institutional entrepreneurship for rural development: The Nitlapán banking network in Nicaragua. In *Rural development in Central America*, R Ruben and J Bastiaensen (eds.), pp. 151–170. Houndsmill: Macmillan.

Bastiaensen, J and B D'Exelle (2002). To pay or not to pay? Local institutional differences and the viability of rural credit in Nicaragua. *Journal of Microfinance*, 4(2), 31–56.

Bastiaensen, J and P Marchetti (2007). A critical review of CGAP–IADB policies inspired by the Fondo de desarrollo local, Nicaragua. *Enterprise Development and Microfinance*, 18(2/3), 143–157.

Baumeister, E and E Fernández (s.d.). Políticas de transformación agraria y contextos locales: el caso del municipio de matiguas durante la revolución sandinista, 1979–1990. Mimeograph.

Boomgard, J, S Davies, S Haggblade and D Mead (1992). A subsector approach to small enterprise promotion and research. *World Development*, 20(2), 199–212.

Casolo, J (2009). Gender levees: Rethinking women's land rights in Northeastern Honduras. *Journal of Agrarian Change*, 9(3), 392–420.

CGAP (2006). Good Practice Guidelines for Funders of Microfinance. Microfinance Consensus Guidelines (2nd Ed). Washington DC: CGAP.

Cleaver, F (2001). Reinventing Institutions: Bricolage and the Social Embeddedness of Natural Resource Management. In *Securing Land Rights in Africa*, TA Benjaminsen and C Lund (eds.), pp. 11–30. London: Routledge.

Collins, D, J Morduch, S Rutherford and O Ruthven (2009). *Portfolios of the Poor: How the World's Poor Live on $2 a Day.* Princeton University Press.

De Haan, L and A Zoomers (2005). Exploring the frontier of livelihood research. *Development and Change*, 36(1), 27–47.

De Herdt, T and J Bastiaensen (2008). The circumstances of agency. A relational view of poverty. *International Development Planning Review.* 30(4), 339–357.

Dorward, A and J Kydd (2005). *Making Agricultural Markets Systems Work Better for the Poor: Promoting Effective, Efficient and Accessible Coordination and Exchange.* Project Report, Preparation of the DFID RNRA Team Working Paper 2: Making Markets Work for the Poor.

Echeverri, R and MP Ribero (2002). *Nueva ruralidad. Visión del territorio en América Latina y el Caribe.* San José: Instituto Interamericano de Cooperación para la Agricultura (IICA).

Flores, S and G Delmelle (2006). Detailed Market Chain Analysis for Smallholders Affected by the CAFTA Agreement in Nicaragua. Draft Report to IFPRI. Proyecto 2005X138NIT.

Gereffi, G and M Korzeniewicz (eds.) (1994). *Commodity Chains and Global Capitalism.* Westport, CT: Praeger Publishers.

Gereffi, G (1999). International trade and industrial upgrading in the apparel commodity chain. *Journal of International Economics*, 48(1), 37–70.

Gibson, A, H Scott and D Ferrand (2004). *Making Markets Work for the Poor. An Objective and an Approach for Governments and Development Agencies.* Woodmead: ComMark Trust.

Goletti, F (2004). The Participation of the Poor in Agricultural Value Chains. A draft Research Program Proposal. Ha Noi, Vietnam, Agrifood Consulting International for Making Markets Work Better for the Poor Project, Asian Development Bank.

Gonzalez-Vega, C (2003). Deepening rural financial markets: Macroeconomic, policy and political dimensions. Paper presented at *Paving the Way Forward for Rural Finance: An International Conference on Best Practices.*

Gonzalez-Vega, C, G Chalmers, R Quiros and J Rodriguez-Meza (2006). Hortifruti in Central America. A case study about the influence of supermarkets on the development and evolution of creditworthiness of small and medium agricultural producers. *MicroREPORT* No. 57, USAID, Rural and Agricultural Finance Program. Available at: http://www.microlinks.org/evø2.php?ID=12564_201&ID2=DO_TOPIC

Grigsby, A and E Pérez (2007). Structural Implication of Economic Liberalization on Agriculture and Rural Development in Nicaragua. First Phase: National Synthesis.

Grigsby, A and E Pérez (2008). Procesos de Diferenciación en la Población y la Economía Rural. Segunda fase del proyecto "Structural Implication of Economic Liberalization on Agriculture and Rural Development in Nicaragua." Managua, Nitlapán-University of Michigan.

Hart, G (2001). Development critiques in the 1990s: *Culs de sac* and promising paths. *Progress in Human Geography*, 25(4), 649–658.

Hart, G (2002). *Disabling Globalization: Places of Power in Post-Apartheid South Africa.* California Studies in Critical Human Geography. Berkeley: University of California Press.

Hart, G (2009). Developments after the meltdown. *Antipode*, Special Issue, 41, 117–141.

Hulme, D and P Mosley (1996). *Finance Against Poverty.* London: Routledge.

IRAM (2006). L'Analyse de Filières et les Enjeux Actuels des Politiques Agricoles. Note Thématique, 2.

Kaplinsky R and M Morris (2000). A Hand Book for Value Chain Research. Available at: http://www.acdivoca.org/acdivoca/

Legovini, A (2002). The Distributional Impact of Loans in Nicaragua: Are the poor worse off? World Bank Nicaragua Poverty Update, Annex 8.

Long, N (1999). The Multiple Optic of Interface Analysis. Unesco Background Paper on Interface Analysis http://www.utexas.edu/cola/insts/llilas/content/claspo/PDF/workingpapers/multipleoptic.pdf (accessed on 30 March 2009).

Long, N (2001). *Development Sociology: Actor Perspectives.* London: Routledge.

Marconi, R and P Mosley (2004). The FINRURAL impact evaluation service: A cost-effectiveness analysis. *Small Enterprise Development*, 15(3), 18–27.

Merlin, B (2005). *The Value Chain Approach in Development Cooperation*, 2nd Ed. Eschborn: GTZ.

Mersland, R and R Stroem (2008). Performance and trade-offs in microfinance organisations. Does ownership matter? *Journal of International Development*, 20, 598–612.

Meyer, RL (2007). Analyzing and financing value chains: Cutting edge development in value chain analysis. Presentation at the *3rd African Microfinance Conference: New Options for Rural and Urban Africa.* Kampala, Uganda.

Miller, C and C Da Silva (2007). Value chain financing in agriculture. *Small Enterprise Development and Microfinance.* 18(2/3), 85–108.

Morduch, J (1999). The microfinance promise. *Journal of Economic Literature*, 37(4), 1569–1614.

Parrilli, MD (2007). *SME Cluster Development: A Dynamic View of Survival Clusters in Developing Countries.* Basingstoke and New York: Palgrave-Macmillan.

Porter, ME (1985). *Competitive Advantage.* New York: Free Press.

Quiros, R (ed.) (2006). Financiamiento de las cadenas agrícolas de valor. Resumen de la conferencia *Financiamiento de las Cadenas Agrícolas de Valor.* Costa Rica.

Rankin, K (2001). Governing development: Neoliberalism, microcredit, and rational economic women. *Economy and Society*, 30(1), 18–37.

Rankin, K (2002). Social capital, microfinance, and the politics of development. *Journal of Feminist Economics*, 8(1), 1–24.

Rankin, KN (2008). Manufacturing rural finance in Asia: Institutional assemblages, market societies, entrepreneurial subjects. *Geoforum*, 39, 1965–1977.

Reardon, T, J Berdegué and CP Timmer (2005). Supermarketization of the "Emerging Markets" of the pacific Rim: Development and trade implications. *Journal of Food Distribution Research*, 36(1), 3–12.

Reardon, T, P Timmer and J Berdegué (2004). The rapid rise of supermarkets in developing countries: Induced organizational, institutional, and technological change in agrifood systems. *Electronic Journal of Agricultural and Development Economics*, 1(2), 168–183.

Roduner, D (2004). (Draft) Report on Value Chains. Analysis of existing theories, methodologies and discussions of value chain approaches in the development cooperation sector. Bern, LBL, mimeograph.

Ruben, R, M Slingerland and H Nijhoff (2006). Agro-food chains and networks for development. Issues, approaches and strategies. In *Agro-Food Chains and Networks for Development*, 1–28. Dordrecht: Springer Verlag.

Schejtman, A and J Berdegué (2003). *Desarrollo Rural Territorial.* Santiago de Chile: Centro Latinoamericano para el Desarrollo Rural (RIMISP).

Sen, A (1999). *Development as Freedom.* Oxford: Oxford University Press.

USAID (2009). Microlinks. Enterprise development and Value Chain Resources. http://www.microlinks.org/ev_en.php?ID=9651_201&ID2=DO_TOPIC, (accessed on 30 March 2009).

Van Hecken, G and J Bastiaensen (2009). The Potential and Limitations of Markets and Payments for Ecosystem Services in Protecting the Environment. IOB Discussion Paper 2009–1. Antwerpen, University of Antwerp, IOB.

Vermeulen, S, J Woodhill, FJ Proctor and R Delnoye (2008). Chain-wide learning for inclusive agrifood market development: A guide to multi-stakeholder processes for linking- small-scale producers with modern markets. International Institute for Environment and Development, London, UK, and Wageningen University and Research Centre, Wageningen, the Netherlands.

Williamson, O (1991). Comparative economic organization: The analysis of discrete structural alternatives. *Administrative Science Quarterly*, 36.

World Bank (2001). *World Development Report 2001. Attacking Poverty: Opportunity, Empowerment, and Security.* Washington DC.

World Bank (2008). *World Development Report 2008: Agriculture for Development.* Washington DC.

World Bank (2009). *Moving Out of Poverty. Success from the Bottom-Up.* Washington DC.

Zeller, M (2003). Models of rural financial institutions. Paper presented at *Paving the Way Forward for Rural Finance: An International Conference on Best Practices*, Washington DC, 2–4 June 2003.

PART V

Meeting Unmet Demand: Savings, Insurance, and Aiming at the Ultra Poor

Women and Microsavings*

Beatriz Armendáriz
Harvard University,
University College London, and CERMi

1 Introduction

The vast majority of microfinance clients are women. Women are also the poorest.[1] The 2006 Microcredit Summit Campaign estimates that as many as 69 million out of 82 million poorest clients are women.[2] The trend is on the increase: From 1999 to 2005, the number of women clients increased by an astonishing 570 per cent. These numbers might please donors and socially responsible investors in microfinance, for women are not only the poorest, but also the main brokers of health and education.[3]

Microfinance women clients, however, are still facing severe saving constraints. As argued by Armendáriz–Morduch (2010), poor households are able to access microloans and other financial services from microfinance institutions (MFIs), but saving products are scarce and/or plagued with difficulties due to "high frequency" microsavings involving soaring transaction costs.

Poor households have a strong desire to save and can do so, albeit in small amounts, hence the word microsavings.[4] Relative to their male counterparts,

*I thank Marc Labie for useful comments on an earlier draft.
[1]See United Nations (2000).
[2]See Daley–Harris (2009).
[3]See United Nations (2000).
[4]Attempts have been made to distinguish micro from non-microsavings (see, notably, Hulme–Moore–Barrientos, 2009). The main problem is that microsavings are context-specific, and often scarce. For the particular case of MFIs, the authors provide some MIX market data indicating that, with myriad qualifications, microsavings account balances held by MFIs might range from 0 to US$ 5,514.

however, poor women are interested in saving and have low discount factors. However, savings accumulation is not possible due to myriad reasons. Chief among them is the lack of secure hiding places and commitment saving products, which most MFIs cannot profitably offer as yet.

Women not only demand security, but also flexibility and desired commitment. Flexibility because women often face the need to draw from their own microsavings to meet frequent repayments (i.e., weekly or biweekly) on their loans contracted with MFIs, and/or for unforeseen contingencies (Wright, 2005). And desired commitment for women often self-select themselves into microfinance programs and/or informal savings arrangements such as ROSCAs, which force them to save either because of hyperbolic preferences or because formal or informal savings arrangements are perceived as a device to preserve their tiny savings from pressing demands for consumption from their male partners and/or relatives and friends.

Drawing from existing studies conducted in Africa and the Asia, this essay argues that informal ways of saving by women in microfinance are a response to MFIs' failure to offer adequate (e.g., secure, flexible, and commitment) microsaving products. Rotating credit and saving associations (ROSCAs) in countries like Kenya, for example, represent an informal and convenient venue for women to protect their tiny savings against claims by their husbands for immediate consumption (Anderson–Baland, 2002).

Desired commitment to save is also well-documented among low-income households using informal venues such as deposit collectors (Rutheford, 2000). The introduction of SEED, a commitment savings product by an MFI in countries like the Philippines, on the other hand, shows that women review discounting preferences favoring future over present consumption, and are conscious of self-control problems, which suggests that a vast number of women would welcome the introduction of SEED-style products (Ashraf–Karlan–Yin, 2006). A more recent study, also in Africa, suggests that informal saving venues like ROSCAs also involve women's "desired commitment" to save (Gugerty, 2007). However, if informal venues offer convenience, security, and desired commitment, one wonders what the role of microfinance in microsavings really is. Specifically, this essay address the question straightforwardly: Can microfinance facing exceedingly high transaction costs really help poor women clients to remove microsaving constraints and thereby smooth consumption over time and/or pay for household expenditures in health and education?

The essay is organized as follows. First, it shows that the persistence of ROSCAs in Kenya and elsewhere in Africa might be a response to MFIs' saving failures vis-à-vis their women clientele. Second, it illustrates that MFIs in the Philippines and elsewhere in Asia can potentially boost savings via the introduction of adequate saving products for women. But, also, that informal venues can meet demand for desired commitment, possibly more effectively. Third, it highlights the constraints faced by most MFIs when trying to collect microsavings, and the possible ways to circumvent such constraints in practice. A corollary: it seems rational for women to turn to MFIs for microcredit, but not for microsavings as informal venues offer greater security and flexibility on the one hand, and desired commitment on the other. The essay concludes by highlighting the potential for mobile banks and branchless telephone banking to propel high volumes of women's microsavings in low-income economies.

2 Why Have ROSCAs Prevailed Alongside MFIs?

Microfinance is often portrayed as a formal venue for borrowing small amounts of money, and for keeping women's microsavings conveniently secured. This is partly true. Take the example of the Grameen Bank and its replications worldwide. The main mission of the bank is to help poor women to pull themselves out of poverty via access to financial services, microsavings included. Traditionally, Grameen and its numerous replicators worldwide have offered two types of microsaving facilities, namely, a "compulsory savings" account, which can be withdrawn if and when the client leaves the organization — on condition that the client had already saved for at least five consecutive years; and "voluntary savings" account, which, at least in principle, offers microsaving clients the possibility of withdrawing from their accounts at any time during the duration of loan cycles.[5] In response to growing concerns about the lack of flexibility of compulsory savings (often criticized as a hidden form of collateral), however, an improved version of the classical Grameen microsavings model emerged as part of the so-called Grameen II model, introduced in 2003. Grameen II offers more flexible microfinance products; most popular among them is the Grameen pension scheme.[6] Yet, microsavings are not enough to meet demand for microcredit. Outside sources of funding are needed. With some exceptions, the gap between microsavings and microcredit is not filled by commercial

[5]Women's World Banking (2003).
[6]See Dowla–Barua (2006).

banks, international donors, socially responsible investors and/or charities, unless MFIs have a proven self-sustainability record.

Similar efforts by other MFIs, including those by fully-commercial microfinance banks, cannot claim to be collecting enough microsavings to fully fund the growing demand for microcredit. This might be partly due to the fact that women's microsavings are being diverted, that is, intermediated via informal institutions such as ROSCAs, which operate alongside MFIs. Indeed, recent anecdotal evidence on ROSCAs being a widespread conduit for women's microsavings mobilization nowdays abounds.[7] Moreover, ROSCAs prevail everywhere, even in countries that are thick in microsavings such as Indonesia, which hosts the world's most famous microsavings-based bank, namely, the Bank Rakyat of Indonesia (BRI).[8]

What makes ROSCAs so attractive even in countries like Indonesia? Typically, ROSCAs participants self-select themselves into a group of women. The group meets regularly for a pre-determined period of time to pull each participant contribution into a common "microsavings pot", which is allocated to one participant at each meeting. The woman who gets the pot at an early meeting is socially pressurized to continue making contributions to the (pulled) microsavings pot, up until all participants have gotten hold of the pot.[9] Pot allocation is generally random or predetermined. Rationality suggests that the last woman who gets it must at least be as well — off as if she had saved the money on her own, throughout the entire duration of the ROSCA.

There are many interpretations regarding the attractiveness of ROSCAs. In a seminal paper, Siwan Anderson and Jean–Marie Baland (2002) report on their survey on ROSCAs in Kenya, and suggest their findings to be valid in most African households. Two main convincing explanations are worth highlighting from the Anderson–Baland's field work. First, married women have conflicts with their male partners who prefer immediate consumption over savings for household expenditures in, for example, health and education. To get around this problem, women either hide participation in saving and borrowing via a "secret" ROSCA, or husbands turn a blind eye on their wives' ROSCA participation because men have time-inconsistent preferences, e.g., men allow their wives to participate in a ROSCA as a

[7]See Bouman (1995) for a comprehensive review.

[8]In Indonesia, ROSCAs are called "Arisan" or "Simpan Pinjam" (Hosps, 1995).

[9]Gugerty (2007) estimates that the average ROSCA recipient in Kenya gets a microsavings pot of about US$ 25, which is equivalent to one third of the national average of monthly household expenditures.

self-discipline device, which they wish to impose upon themselves. Second, collegial support among participants empower each member in her daily interactions with her male partner. More generally, ROSCAs reinforce solidarity among women via numerous mechanisms aimed at minimizing tensions between each participant and her male partner.

While the term "solidarity" is often used in the microfinance jargon in connection with within-group members self-help for repaying the MFI under a joint liability clause, the existing solidarity that the Anderson–Baland's article suggests for the particular case of ROSCAs in Kenya differs in that there isn't a "third party", e.g., a loan officer, forcing solidarity over repayments, which do not pertain to members' own resources. Standard theories predict that solidarity regarding repayment and compliance is stronger if side-transfers, e.g., saving and lending, are linked to members' own resources (Stiglitz, 1990). Simple put: relative to MFIs, the incidence of moral hazard in ROSCAs is lower because of the absence of outside sources of funding. And in the case analyzed by Anderson and Baland, microsavings funds and side-transfers among women also finance intra-household conflict minimization, the authors suggest. Exclusion from the group for malfeasance becomes a credible and powerful threat, particularly when ROSCA participation is secret.

Let us now turn to microfinance. Carrying out exclusion from future refinancing threats for non-repayment is questionable at best, impossible to implement at worst. In practice, microfinance in Grameen-style solidarity groups do not involve exclusion of the entire group in case of default by a member, and Grameen II has explicitly abolished joint liability and exclusion threats for non-compliance, for such threats seem to create tensions within the group, not solidarity (Yunus, 2002; Dowla–Barua, 2006; and Armendáriz — Morduch, 2010).

Unlike microfinance, social cohesion and true solidarity seem to be the rule rather than the exception in informal institutions such as ROSCAs. Side-transfers among ROSCA members carry a great deal of weight, particularly because such transfers are perceived as loans, and because these loans are made out of members' own resources thereby reducing the incidence of moral hazard. Tensions, yet another issue often invoked in the group – lending microfinance literature, are minimum or non-existent in ROSCAs. Such an informal way of propelling and mobilizing women's microsavings has therefore virtues. These cannot be replicated by MFIs using loan officers who typically impose solidarity and consequent use of microsavings, which are not necessarily welfare-enhancing.

A qualifying remark is important here. When comparing microsavings between microsavings via MFIs and ROSCAs, I am referring here to Grameen-style solidarity groups where participants are linked by a "joint liability clause" — implicit or explicit — according to which, a member who does not repay creates a negative externality on other members' resources, microsavings included. The joint responsibility methodology might have an effect on repayment rates, within-group tension (positive or negative), and on microsavings.

If tensions among group members who should otherwise help each other emerge — due to the joint responsibility clause imposed by the MFI, such tensions can only exacerbate and/or add intra-household frictions between women and their male partners. The result might be the disempowering of women, whose financial needs to meet expenditures in health and education can be potentially disrupted by frictions (Armendáriz–Roome, 2008).

Thus, the answer to the question as to why ROSCAs have prevailed is that the incidence of moral hazard is lowered when compared to that of MFIs. More social cohesion, enhanced solidarity among group members, and the scope for side-transfers (or microloans) geared towards minimizing intra-household conflict, and securing microsavings from male partners, are all virtues of informal microsavings arragements such as ROSCAs.

Microsavings via informal venues is not confined to ROSCAs. Unlike dissatisfaction with microsavings facilities expressed by women in microfinance (see Women's World Banking, 2003), in his 2000 study, Stuart Rutheford reports on clients' satisfaction on more than a dozen informal microsavings venues, including deposit collectors.

The downside of such type of informal venues, however is that, unlike microfinance, informality goes unfunded by outside-the-community resources. It follows that it seems rational and welfare enhancing for women to smooth consumption over time and make lump–sum investments via microloans from MFIs, in parallel to mobilizing their microsavings via informal venues such as ROSCAs and/or deposit collectors for expenditures in health and education. Informal institutions offer added security due to lower incidence of moral hazard, flexibility because strong solidarity involves side-transfers or microloans à la carte, and commitment, an issue to which we turn next.

3 Demand for Commitment: Can it Be Met by MFIs?

The fact that women clients desire some kind of discipline and/or wish to commit themselves to a saving product is well documented. Take the example of deposit collectors in West Africa.[10] A deposit collector will turn up daily to collect an agreed sum from a well-established clientele of households for a predetermined fee. If the woman household-head saves less than thirty times per month, she pays an additional fee in proportion to her lapses. This in turn induces discipline. Commitment savings products feature prominently in such type of informal arrangements. If women express the desire to commit themselves into a microsaving product so explicitly, as they actually do vis-à-vis the deposit collector, why do MFIs seem to have a hard time mimicking informal microsaving mechanisms?

Ashraf–Karlan–Yin (2006) take the demand for commitment issue seriously. In particular, the researchers partnered with an MFI in the Philippines in order to carry out a random experiment. The experiment involved a sample of women randomly assigned into treatment and control groups. Baseline surveys were previously carried out, that is, prior to random assignment. This in turn enabled the researchers to learn about the characteristics of the MFIs' clientele. Women in the treatment group were offered a "commitment product", which was labeled SEED (Save, Earn, Enjoy Deposits). Clients in the treatment group who opted for opening a SEED account had restricted (self-imposed) withdrawals, and such restrictions were not compensated via higher-than-market returns on deposit accounts. Out of the 710 women assigned to the treatment group, approximately 200 women took up the commitment savings product.

Two interesting questions are addressed in the Ashraf–Karlan–Yin article. First, if some women — those exhibiting hyperbolic preferences — demand SEED-style products, why there seems to be no market for such microsavings products in the first place? Second, does the introduction of a new microsavings product by the MFI have a long-term positive effect on microsavings?

To answer the first question, the researchers invoked informal mechanisms such as ROSCAs to argue that demand for microsavings commitment products such as SEED is being met, albeit informally, so the market exists, and that MFIs are slowly catching up. Save More Tomorrow or the SMarT savings product offered in the United States by formal financial institutions is similar in spirit to the SEED microsavings product introduced in the Philippines, the researchers would argue.

---

[10]See S. Rutheford's report for CGAP (2006).

In addressing the second question, Ashraf, Karlan and Yin offer a convincing answer by relying on supply-side considerations. In particular, if MFIs estimate that the demand for commitment savings products is large, such products are expected to be profitable and will therefore be introduced at a larger scale. Relying on stylized facts, they argue that the impact of introducing SEED-style products is long lasting, for other branches of the partner organization in the Philippines as well as other rural banks are already contemplating implementation.

Their results deserve some qualification, however. In particular, the 200 hyperbolic preferenced women were the more educated. Also, they were more sophisticated in that they seemed to have already realized that they had a self-control problem, which hindered their ability to save, to make lumpy investments in health and education.

The problem is that the meager 24 per cent (or the 200 women) take-up of highly educated and sophisticated clients expressing a strong desire to commit themselves into a microfinance product in the Philipinnes experiment might (a) be too small to make the commitment saving product profitable for MFIs, (b) be perceived as a relatively successful commitment product in the Philippines but might not be as successful if introduced by other MFIs operating in other parts of the world, and (c) might be reaching out to wealthier borrowers.

4 The Challenge

The problem facing MFIs seems to be that women's demand for microsavings is really a demand for "a package". The package should at least include the following three ingredients: security, flexibility and commitment. Typically, low-income women would like their tiny savings to be secured for the marginal loss of losing a dollar is huge. They would at the same time demand flexibility because the incidence of idiosyncratic and aggregate shocks in rural economies is high due to drastic changes in weather conditions, low levels of education, and poor health, among other considerations. Women also like to commit themselves to saving tiny amounts, not only because of hyperbolic preferences as suggested in the Asharf–Karlan–Yin (2006) article, and because intra-household conflict like in the Anderson–Baland (2002) article in Kenya, but also because of social pressure: Women often find it exceedingly difficult to refuse demands for their readily available microsavings — for religious events, and for helping family members and friends, for example — while microsavings are kept in their homes (Jean–Philippe Platteau, 2000).

To meet women's demand for such a highly complex package to effectively mobilize microsavings represents an enormous challenge for MFIs. Some stylized facts suggests that "commercialization" and "age" can make it happen. On commercialization, Marguerite Robinson (2006), for example, argues that only fully-regulated and well-supervised MFIs (e.g., commercial MFIs) can profitably collect deposits if at least some of the following three prerequisites are met. First, the country where the commercial MFI is located must be politically stable and have a decent regulatory framework. Second, the MFI in question must review a strong institutional performance record, an extensive knowledge of the microfinance market, a wealth of expertise in financial intermediation, and a great deal of expertise in suitable investment strategies for dealing with excess liquidity. And, third, commercial MFIs must collect small and large deposits simultaneously, because this strategy will raise average deposit size thereby make savings mobilization profitable (Some sort of cross-subsidization à la Armendáriz — Szafarz, 2010 in this volume). Robinson provides three examples of successful savings mobilization MFIs. These are displayed in Table 22.1.

A more complete picture should include the percentage of women's microsavings being mobilized, however. In the particular case of the Kenyan bank, to which we will come back to below, mobile banking and the use of new technologies seems to be the way forward for microsaving constraints faced by women to be lifted, at least partially.

In contrast with Robinson's observations, the World Bank (1999) emphasizes the age of the MFI as the main determinant of success in microsaving

Table 22.1: MFIs savings growth in Indonesia, Cambodia, and Kenya.

Institution	Savings Accounts	Savings Accounts	Savings Deposits	Savings Deposits
BRI (Indonesia)	15,979, 848	29,869,197	2,599,686,690	3,244,874,360
Year	(1996)	(2003)	(1996)	(2003)
ACLEDA Bank (Cambodia)			180,622,000	423,401,000
Year			(2006)	(2007)
Equity Bank (Kenya)	155,883	252,186	27,869,571	44,465,375
Year	(2002)	(2003)	(2002)	(2003)

Source: Goodwin-Groen (2006), ACLEDA Bank Plc Annual Report (2008), and CGAP Agricultural Microfinance Case Study 4, (2005).

mobilization. From a sample of 206 organizations, saving banks and commercial banks mobilize over 90 percent of the low-income household deposits. With the exception of the BRI, which dates back to the late 19th century, neither the Cambodian nor the Kenyan bank feature as main actors. And the main reason why this might be so, the report suggests, is that both institutions are much too young relative to those institutions which pre-date microfinance, namely, saving institutions and commercial banks.

In line with the World Bank's findings, the World Savings Bank Institute (2007) reports that nearly 70 million — approximately half the estimated figure for microfinance clients — use saving banks in India, Mexico, Tanzania, and Thailand alone. Critics might however argue that saving banks are not necessarily serving the poorest of the poor. In response to such criticisms, the World Savings Bank Institute delivers results from clients' surveys. Based on those surveys, it has been suggested that nearly 16 percent of the 70 million savers are poor. Again, data on microsavings by women is, however, scarce.

5 Concluding Remarks

This essay has argued that MIFs have so far failed to meet demand for microsavings by women. High transaction costs might explain such a failure. MFIs have not fully internalized women's concerns about security, flexibility, and desired commitment, however. Security seems to correlate with age: Informal institutions such as ROSCAs date back to at least a few centuries, and the origins of formal MFIs such as the BRI can be traced back to the 19th century. Relatively new, fully-commercial MFIs such as ACLEDA, on the other hand, might be delivering a misleading picture for such institutions might be serving a relatively wealthy clientele of microsavers on the one hand, and because the unreported proportion of women clients as well as average deposit levels appear suspicious at best, and a negative by-product of commercialization at worst. More generally, recent commercialization trends do not appear to be favoring women anyway.[11] Thus, the demand for microsaving security by women is unlikely to be met by newly-created MFIs, even if these commercially-oriented institutions are fully regulated. More is needed.

The prospects for meeting women's demand for flexible microsaving products seem brighter with the advent of technology and mobile banks.[12]

[11]See Cull *et al.* (2009).
[12]For more on IT and savings, see, Mas (2009).

In particular, MFIs such as Kenya's Equity Bank seem to be offering greater flexibility, thanks to the bank's adoption of new technologies, notably GSM networks — as part of branchless telephone banking. Under the sponsorship of the UK government's Department for International Development, Kenya's Equity Bank is using mobile banks and mobile phone technology to collect microsavings and carry out microcredit transactions instantly. It offers security too, as its four- wheel banks are endowed not only with trained staff and money, but also with security guards.

Mobile and branchless banking offer commitment too, as the trucks show up every week at a pre-specified time in remote villages where GSM technology operates via satellite dishes. Introducing SEED-style product to meet demands for stronger commitment should be easier to implement. Kenya's Equity Bank mobile banking is currently reaching up to 45 percent of rural women clients in remote villages.

Thus, to meet demand for microsavings by women requesting security, flexibility, and commitment, MFIs might need to adopt new technologies, following the lead of Kenya's Equity Bank's mobile banking and GSM technology. The adoption of new technologies for microsaving mobilization requires donors' support, however.

But even if donors' support for introducing mobile banking and branchless technology massively was to take place, the issue on intra-household conflict and social pressure from friends and relatives remains. In particular, the virtues of, say, "secret" ROSCAs in terms of women's control over their microsavings and solidarity are difficult to be replicated by MFIs.

Fostering solidarity networks among women wishing to better meet their health and educational objectives while minimizing confrontation and social pressure remains a challenge. And as this essay goes to press, I am unaware of such a challenge being taken on explicitly by MFIs, either because of lack of data and/or because it is impossible to deal with such delicate issues. It all seems to depend on traditional norms and behaviours — typically biased against women — which are exceedingly difficult to change.

One hope is that the speed of economic development will be high — with the help of better microfinance; the other one is that proactive non-governmental organizations (NGOs) in defense of women's rights will work in tandem with mission-driven MFIs. Donors should, however, be cautious about trying to take advantage of potential complementarities between NGOs and MFIs because "third party" intrusion into intra-household conflict and obligations to relatives/friends might not be welcomed by a large majority of women microsavers.

References

ACLEDA Bank (2008). *Annual Report.*

Anderson, S and JM Baland (2002). The economics of ROSCAs and intra-household resource allocation. *The Quarterly Journal of Economics*, 117(3), 963–995.

Armendáriz, B and J Morduch (2010). *The Economics of Microfinance*, 2nd Ed. Cambridge, MA: MIT Press.

Armendáriz, B and A Szafarz (2010). On Mission Drift in Microfinance Institutions. In *The Handbook of Microfinance*, B Armendáriz and M Labie (eds.). Singapore: World Scientific Publishing.

Armendáriz, B and N Roome (2008). Gender Empowerment in Microfinance. In *Microfinance: Emerging Trends and Challenges*, S Sundaresan, (ed.). New York: Edward Elgar Publishing.

Ashraf, N, D Karlan and W Yin (2006). Tying odysseus to the mast: Evidence from a commitment savings product in the Philippines. *Quarterly Journal of Economics*, 635–672.

Bouman, F (1995). Rotating and accumulating savings and credit associations: A development perspective. *World Development*, 23, 371–384.

CGAP (2005). *Equity Building Society of Kenya Reaches Rural Markets.* CGAP Case Study No 4. Washington DC.

Cull, R, A Demirgüç–Kunt and J Morduch (2009). Microfinance meets the market. *Journal of Economic Perspectives*, 23(1), 167–192.

Daley–Harris, S (2009). *State of the Microcredit Summit Campaign Report.* Microcredit Summit Campaign.

Department for International Development, Financial Deepening Development Fund (2008). Kenya — Access to Finance, http://www.financialdeepening.org/default.asp?id=717&ver=1

Dowla, A and D Barua (2006). *The Poor Always Pay Back: The Grameen II Story.* Bloomfield, CT: Kumarian Press.

Goodwin–Groen, R (2006). *Where Are They Now? The Performance of Seven Microfinance Deposit-Taking Institutions From 1996–2003.* Washington DC: CGAP.

Gugerty, MK (2007). You can't save alone: Commitment in rotating savings and credit associations in Kenya. *Economic Development and Cultural Change*, 251–282.

Hospes, O (1995). Gender Differences in ROSCAs in Indonesia. In *Money-Go-Rounds: The Importance of ROSCAs for Women*, S Ardener and S Burman (eds.). Oxford: Berg Publishers.

Hulme, D, K Moore and A Barrientos (2009). Assessing the Insurance Role of Microsavings DESA Working Paper 83.

Mas, I (2009). The economics of branchless banking. *Innovations*, 4(2), 57–75.

Platteau, JP (2000). *Institutions, Social Norms and Economic Development.* Amsterdam: Harvard Academic Publishers.

Robinson, M (2006). How can Commercial Banks Mobilize Savings from the Poor? In *Poor People Savings, Q&As With Experts.* Washington DC: CGAP, http:// www.cgap.org.

Rutheford, S (2000). *The Poor and Their Money.* New Delhi: Oxford University Press.

Rutheford, S (2006). Why Do Poor People Save? In *Poor People Savings, Q&As With Experts.* Washington DC: CGAP. http://www.cgap.org.

Stiglitz, J (1990). Peer monitoring and credit markets. *World Bank Economic Review*, 4(3), 351–366.

United Nations (2000). *Human Development Report.*

Women's World Banking (2003). What do microfinance costumers value? *What Works* 1 (1). New York: Women's World Banking. Also at http://www.swwbb.org.
World Bank (1999). *A World Bank Inventory of Microfinance Institutions, Sustainable Banking With The Poor.* Washington DC: The World Bank.
World Savings Bank Institute (2007). *Who Are The Clients Of Savings Banks?* Brussels: WSBI.
Wright, GAN (2005). *Understanding and Assessing the Demand for Microfinance.* Nairobi, Kenya: MicroSave, Market-led Solutions for Financial Services.
Yunus, M (2002). *Grameen Bank II: Designed To Open New Possibilities.* Dhaka: Grameen Bank. http://www.grameen-info.org/bank/bank2.html.

Boosting the Poor's Capacity to Save: A Note on Instalment Plans and their Variants

Stuart Rutherford

SafeSave Bangladesh and Brooks World Poverty Institute, University of Manchester

For households in wealthy countries, regular periodic instalments are by far the most popular way to save, buy insurance, and repay loans. In developing countries, microfinance providers have pioneered instalment plans for the poor, first as a repayment schedule for loans, and later as a deposit payment schedule for "commitment" savings accounts[1] and for insurance. Indeed, it is still not widely understood that the opportunity to save or repay in frequent bite-sized amounts is the main driver of microfinance's success — far more important than other better-known aspects such as group-formation, joint liability,[2] and the focus on investments in microenterprises. This note uses evidence from Bangladesh first to demonstrate the power of the instalment plan as a financial tool for the poor, and then to describe how it can be combined with other innovations to help poor households boost their capacity to save.

1 The Dominance of the Instalment Plan

Most loans made to individuals or households in developed countries are repaid in periodic instalments. This has long been the case. Loans for

[1]In a commitment savings account, the saver makes a regular periodic deposit for a set term, and is rewarded with a better rate of interest than in ordinary or "passbook" savings accounts.

[2]Joint liability: the obligation on a member of a group organised by a microfinance organisation to jointly guarantee the loan or otherwise ensure that the loan is repaid.

homes are repaid monthly over many years, following pioneering work early in the 20th century by lenders such as Bank of America. Cars, another expensive item, are commonly bought on monthly instalment credit. Education loans may be repaid in the same way. Even for less costly items like household goods, retailers may offer credit with periodic instalments. In some countries, notably Japan, it is routine for department store customers to be asked whether they want their credit or debit card to be debited once, or several times for smaller amounts against a regular schedule. Credit cards themselves offer the option of deferred payments, extending the use of the instalment device to every kind of purchase.

Finance is the trick of moving money through time. The instalment payment plan makes it possible to buy a house now out of income you have not yet earned. The loan contract is a promise by the borrower to deposit with the lender a series of regular savings out of future income until enough has been amassed to repay the loan. To keep things simple, the price of the service — the interest payable — is also chopped up into regular monthly bites and added to the instalment. It is by offering instalment payment plans that lenders have been able to turn consumer finance into such big business. Few lenders would offer, and few borrowers would accept, a home loan scheduled to be repaid in a single lump sum 20 or 25 years later. Faced with such a proposal, the borrower would likely seek a regular savings plan to make sure she puts away enough to repay the loan, and the lender would almost certainly require her to hold those savings at his bank: and that arrangement is, of course, precisely what the instalment-based home loan achieves.

Similarly, most of the savings held in individual or household savings accounts in western banks originate from instalment saving, usually deducted automatically or voluntarily, from regular periodic income. As households age, more of their money may be held in fixed deposit accounts (CDs) or other non-contributory devices, but much of the money that sits there was originally amassed through periodic saving, or from interest earned on it, or from assets generated by using instalment plans, such as when a home that was bought with a loan is sold up and the proceeds put in the bank. When savings are directed to a defined end-use, and kept with a specialised provider, they, too, depend on periodic instalments: pensions and almost all forms of insurance are the most obvious examples.

2 But the Poor Need to Intermediate, Too

The World Bank estimates that about 2.5 billion people, or one third of humanity, live on incomes of $2 a day or less.[3] Some enjoy regular wages or salaries, but, for most, the income comes from casual or self-employment, and may be not just small but also irregular and unreliable. At that level of income, the bulk of earnings is spent on absolute necessities — food and the means to cook it — and even that basic task requires careful money management, so as to ensure that there is food on the table every day, and not just on days when some income flows in. As a result, poor households spend time and energy seeking small-scale ways to build stocks of grain, or squirreling away a bit of reserve cash, or searching out neighbours willing to offer them short-term loans in cash or kind. We know this from careful observations of money-management in low-income households carried out through the "financial diary" research methodology, and reported in the 2009 book, *Portfolios of the Poor* (Collins *et al.*, 2009).

But poor people do not spend their entire income on basics. Though your wardrobe may be small and shabby and your home cramped and ill-built, being poor doesn't relieve you of the need to spend on clothes and shelter. You will aspire to some home comforts — a fan, a stove, a radio or TV, a connection to the electricity grid, perhaps even some sturdy furniture. During the life of your family, you will have to find sums that are large, relative to your income, for childbirth, child-raising, education, marriage, job-seeking, old age and funerals. You will need money to celebrate the major festivals of your culture. The poor quality of your environment and the rough and ready nature of your work may make your family more vulnerable to illness and injury than better-off people, and treatment may require large-scale expenditure. You are more likely than the better-off to suffer from natural or man-made disasters: during the financial diary research, which lasted for one year, one in five of the Bangladeshi households under scrutiny lost their homes to fire, flood or bulldozing; four in five of the South African households had to find large sums to pay for funerals, many of them resulting from AIDS-induced deaths; and two in five of the Indian households faced expenditure for health problems that severely strained their household finances.

[3]These incomes are calculated at "Purchasing Power Parity" which irons out wrinkles in market exchange rates between currencies to ensure that $1 in the USA buys the same as a PPP$1 elsewhere.

With very small incomes, poor people rarely have enough ready money to fund even a fraction of this long list of spending needs. Constantly, they need to find a way to dig into past income (through savings) or into future income (through borrowing) to pay for them. It turns out, then, that it is precisely *because* of their poverty, and not *despite* their poverty, that the poor's need for financial services is greater than that of the better-off. Greater, that is, not in terms of value — poor people obviously spend less than the rich do — but in terms of frequency and intensity.

And yet few poor people have bank savings accounts, let alone access to mortgages, consumer loans, pensions and insurance cover. Again, the financial diary research produced insights into how they seek equivalent services and devices. We noticed, first, the bad news: all too often the poor fail to put together the money they need, and an illness goes dangerously untreated, a chance to buy a bicycle is lost, and an attractive marriage offer for the eldest daughter is foregone. Next, we saw how assets were sold, often at knock-down prices, to meet a more urgent spending need. This is a form of (dis-)saving, since the asset sold represents income earned in the past, but it is an unattractive way to use savings, not just because the price realised is low, but because the asset sold — the family's cow, or their roof-sheets, maybe — will almost certainly need to be replaced, adding to the list of things for which further saving or borrowing will be required.

3 The Instalment Plans of the Poor

The good news is that many poor households manage, more or less successfully, to set up their own instalment plans. Those with iron discipline can do quite well on their own at home: "piggy banks" of one sort or another are common, and some people manage to stick to a vow to put something into the piggy-bank every day. But savings held at home are vulnerable to theft, loss, and trivial spending, so many poor people get their savings out of the home and into the hands of a "money guard": a friend, relative, or employer who can be trusted to take care of it. Such schemes work best when the saver has regular cash transactions with the guard, as when a rickshaw driver regularly saves a few cents each day with the person who hires him the rickshaw, or a domestic cleaner has her employer hold back part of her pay.

In some places, poor people are served by unlicensed but reliable deposit collectors. In the *susus* and their variants in West Africa, the collector calls on the saver regularly (often daily) and returns the accumulated savings at the end of a defined term (monthly, mostly, in West Africa; somewhat longer in South Asia), deducting a fraction which the collector keeps as his or her fee. Savers thus pay to save (or, put another way, receive a negative interest rate on their savings) but such is the value of being able to rely on accumulating a lump sum at a given time — say, enough to pay for school books and clothes at the start of the school term — that many savers regard the price as reasonable. Elsewhere, the inverse of the deposit collector is available — a moneylender who collects repayments in regular (daily, weekly or monthly) instalments. They tend to be more expensive than the deposit collector, for obvious reasons: they have to put up the capital and bear the risk of default.

The most sophisticated informal schemes are savings clubs of one sort or another, which necessarily involve a group of people. Sometimes the idea is just to add discipline and regularity to your saving by doing it at the same time as a group of friends. More elaborate clubs pool regular periodic savings and lend to their members, usually on interest which is returned to the savers at the end of a cycle. In effect, these "ASCAs" (accumulating savings and credit associations) are like miniature credit unions or thrift and loan co-operatives. An alternative format is the ROSCA (the rotating savings and credit association) in which every member makes a defined deposit at each of a series of meetings, and at each meeting one member walks away with the whole sum. Thus, 10 of us may meet weekly for 10 weeks and put $10 each on the table each time: and each of us will take away $100 once. Descriptions of these devices, which are widespread, and an analysis of their place in the poor's efforts to manage their money, can be found in the book, *The Poor and Their Money* (Rutherford and Arora, 2009).

The ROSCA neatly demonstrates the value the poor put on instalment payment plans. Note that in the ROSCA that we described in the previous paragraph, each member, over a 10-week period, paid in $100 and took out $100. There was no profit. There were no financial costs, either, but the members had to go to the bother of organising their ROSCA, and run the risk that one or more of them might disrupt the device's rhythm with delayed payments or by trying to get away without paying at all. So what was the point? The point is to enjoy the magic of the instalment plan — to turn a series of small payments into one usefully large sum that can be used to meet one of life's many larger-scale spending needs.

Our 10-member, 10-week ROSCA also demonstrates how instalment plans work as both a saving and as a loan-repayment device. After all, during the run of the ROSCA, most of the members (all except the first and last to take the "pot") start off as savers, making weekly deposits of $10, and then they take their "pot" and turn into borrowers, using their weekly $10 to "repay" the balance of their $100 not yet subscribed. In the "auction" or "bidding" variant of the ROSCA, common in southern India, East and Southeast Asia, and some parts of Africa, members bid for the right to take the early pots. Their bid-money is divided among all the members, so that those who choose to use the ROSCA primarily as a savings device, rather than as a borrowing device, do well: by taking their pot later on in the cycle, they receive a share of others' bid-money that is greater than the bid-money they themselves pay out, and the balance rewards them with an equivalent of interest on their savings.

Not every ROSCA works well (and ASCAs probably have an even poorer success rate), but as you sit and read this, they are running in every country of the world, in their millions.

4 Adding Value to the Plan: Reliability

Starting in Bangladesh in the 1970s and in South America a few years later, microfinance organizations have brought a reliable version of the instalment payment plan to growing numbers of the world's poor. Perhaps one in five low-income households now have an account at an MFO, though the worldwide distribution of the service is skewed, with South Asia doing best and Africa, above all rural Africa, doing least well. Earlier efforts to popularise the device among the poor failed to scale up. The credit union movement, for example, a developed form of the ASCA, launched and relaunched itself throughout the late 19th and the 20th century, sometimes with government backing. But it never managed to set up management systems that were at once simple enough and cheap enough to give the movement traction among the very poor. (Credit co-operatives were also vulnerable to being used as channels for subsidies by governments seeking the favour of voters.)

Despite its startling success, the place of the instalment payment plan at the heart of MFO work has still not been fully appreciated. Microfinance pioneers embraced ambitious aims, such as ending poverty, fighting discrimination against women, and promoting the growth of small (or "micro") enterprises, and it was the heady promise of these ambitions that caught the public imagination.[4] Newspapers and TV producers found that their

[4]See, for example, Yunus, M (2007). *Banker to the Poor.* New York: Public Affairs.

microfinance stories had far more resonance if they featured downtrodden women hauling themselves out of poverty by taking a small loan to start a sewing business, than if they explained how a village boatman managed a decent funeral for his father by borrowing from a microlender.

There was some public interest in microfinance's lending mechanism, but it centred less on the instalment payment plan than on "joint liability" — the system under which members of a borrowing group were required to co-guarantee each other's loans. The idea appealed to our yearning for social solidarity, playing on a contrast between our own selfish ways and the "community spirit" of poorer folk. Joint liability also attracted some economists who enjoyed arguing about how, exactly, it worked. But joint liability, at least in mature microfinance markets like that of Bangladesh, has been largely abandoned. It has the unfortunate effect of hitting your best clients hardest — penalising those who do pay in order to guard against those who don't.[5]

The instalment payment plan, by contrast, was there at the start of modern microfinance, and has survived as microfinance has evolved. In Bangladesh, the standard loan repayment plan of 50 weekly instalments was in place by the end of the 1970s, and went on to dominate microlending until, at the start of this century, loan terms of other than one year were introduced.[6] Even then, the weekly schedule remained the norm. Some major providers, such as BRAC,[7] experimented with a shift to twice-monthly or monthly instalments, but soon fell back to the weekly rhythm. In Latin America's system of Village Banking, starting in the 1980s, weekly payment plans were also used, although the loan term was 16 rather than 50 weeks.

In 2002–2005, I carried out a "financial diary" study of microfinance clients in rural Bangladesh.[8] A selection of such clients, from three different

[5]For a discussion of the waning of joint liability in Bangladesh see (Rutherford, 2009), especially chapter 7, pp. 132–134.

[6]When, in 1976, Muhammad Yunus started his experiments with lending to the poor that went on to become the Grameen Bank, he first used daily collections of repayments. That was soon abandoned as too clumsy, and Grameen quickly settled on the weekly repayment rhythm.

[7]BRAC is Bangladesh's biggest and best known non-government organization (NGO) and, by some counts, the biggest in the world. It has a microfinance operation as old as Grameen Bank, which it rivals in size.

[8]The study (Rutherford, 2006) was part of a bigger study commissioned by MicroSave, an initiative to improve the quality of financial services for the poor.

districts of the country and chosen to be broadly typical of microfinance's clientele as a whole, were visited at least once a month for three years, and a record kept of their money management behaviour. This included a close and continuing look at the loans they took from MFOs.

Altogether, 239 MFO loans were scrutinised in detail. The disbursed value of these loans totalled $39,000 and represented somewhat more than half of the total value of loans from all sources used by the "diary" households in the three-year period, the balance being accounted for by loans from family and neighbours (some with, some without interest), credit from shopkeepers and the like, loans from savings clubs of the sort described above, and a few loans from formal banks.

When we looked at how the microfinance loans were used, we found that about 30 percent of them (representing about 40 percent of total disbursed value) went into stock for small businesses, mostly in retailing but some in small-scale production or craftwork. A further 16 percent of the loans (about 14 percent of loan disbursed value) went towards buying assets, some of them for business, some for domestic use. So very roughly half of the loans and of their value went into so-called "productive" uses — business inventory or assets.

The other half of loans went into a wide mix of uses — mostly consumption of all kinds (food, health, festivals, education, shelter and clothes, and so on), with some on-lending to others, and some used to pay down other debt. For those who believe that all microfinance lending is, or should be, for microenterprise development, this is a surprising, even alarming finding, though MFO workers who meet their clients weekly at the meetings have long known that their efforts to persuade all their borrowers to use loans exclusively for business uses are only partly successful.

Moreover, the figures given so far — proportions of loans taken and of loan value — tell only one part of the story. When we looked at the borrowers, we found that a minority of them took most of the loans that went into business uses. They were households that run a thriving shop or small production unit, take as many MFO loans as they can (many have accounts at more than one MFO), invest in their businesses, prosper, and borrow again. Other client households may also be "entrepreneurial", in the sense that they run their own businesses, but because they find many other priorities for their borrowing, choose not to put their MFI loans into their businesses. Yet others, perhaps the majority, derive most of their income not from businesses they own but from casual labour in the market or day labour in the fields or self-employment as a rickshaw driver or boatman or the like. They borrow to maintain their lives rather than to start or grow businesses. For them, the MFO loan is a basic intermediation device that allows them to form usefully large sums of cash that can be spent on life's many needs.

What makes it possible for them to use the loans for consumption and other purposes, rather than for business, is the instalment payment plan. The plan chops the loan up into 50 small weekly bites that can usually be found from normal weekly cashflow, irrespective of how the loan is used or of whether its use produces an income stream. In effect, MFO borrowers receive a year's worth of weekly savings bundled into a lump sum, which they can spend on whatever happens to be their priority when they take the loan. And that's exactly what they do.

This effect holds, of course, only as long as the weekly payment can be found from regular cash-flow (aided from time to time by the informal devices that we reviewed earlier). When this relationship is broken, problems arise. We saw this most clearly around the end of the 1990s, when, believing that all loans were being invested in businesses and that the businesses were growing with each loan cycle, MFOs injudiciously increased loan values beyond what many households could repay comfortably in 50 weekly instalments. The mistake, worrying though it was at the time, had a happy outcome: MFOs, above all the flagship Grameen Bank, overhauled their products (Yunus, 2002; and Dowla and Barua, 2006). Grameen introduced a wider range of loan term lengths and allowed borrowers to "top up" loans half way through the repayment schedule (thus extending the payment plan at the same level for a further six months). Even more significant were the changes made to their savings products. A passbook savings account was introduced and proved popular: clients could now withdraw reserves from saving when circumstances made it hard for them to find their loan repayment. Better still, Grameen introduced a commitment savings plan with a 10-year term of small monthly deposits. It proved popular. Now, Grameen clients have instalment plans on both the saving and the borrowing side. The effect of all this was seen very clearly in Grameen's balance sheet: customer deposits held went up from about 50 percent of the loan portfolio just before the crisis, to about 140 percent of it now.[9]

The MFOs use of the instalment payment plan mirrored the way the savings clubs worked. But the MFOs achieved much more than that. They

[9]Updates on Grameen Bank's performance can be seen at www.grameen-info.org.

brought a new level of reliability to the plan. ASCAs were always popular in rural Bangladesh, but failed too often. ROSCAs, more popular in the urban slums, work better than the ASCAs but are not wholly reliable. The MFOs brought reliable services right into the heart of the village or slum: rain or shine, the men and women who serve as their front-line staff turn up on time each week, disburse their loans on the dates promised, and charge no more or less than the rule-book says. Most poor and many near-poor households in Bangladesh hold at least one MFO account, testifying to the degree to which they appreciate the unaccustomedly reliable service.

5 Adding Value to the Plan: Flexibility

But the instalment payment plan can be harder for poor people to manage than for people living in the rich world, because, for many of the poor, income is seldom regular and reliable. It is easy for a worker in the rich world to have an employer divert a fixed sum from her weekly or monthly pay packet into a saving or loan repayment plan. But a typical worker in the poor world lacks employment of this kind and, even where she does, the transfer mechanisms may not exist, or may be unreliable.

Thus, in the 1990s, as Bangladeshi microfinance grew strongly, observers noted that the rigidity with which the repayment plan was applied did not suit every client, and that the poorest households were the most disadvantaged. Landless folk who work as agricultural day-labourers, for example, suffer sharp seasonal variation in their income, with periods lasting several weeks during which work is hard to come by. With the standard microfinance repayment plan lasting for 50 weeks, they found themselves able to pay most weeks, but not every week of the year. Their difficulties were compounded by the fact that MFO staff were instructed not to accept "pre-payments": so that should a household sell an asset such as goat, or get their labouring wages in a lump at the end of the harvest, they were not allowed to make several weekly payments ahead of schedule. At the same time, MFO savings plans were undeveloped, so these clients also lacked the option of storing surplus cash short-term in savings accounts.

As a result, these kinds of households began to drop out of the microfinance system. Other similar households, observing this, decided not to open an account in the first place. When Muhammad Yunus of the Grameen Bank noted, during a microfinance conference in Dhaka in the mid 1990s, that providers like his were having trouble reaching the poorest 20 percent of the population, a flurry of interest in how to solve the problem broke out (Wood and Sharif).[10]

In 1996 *Safe*Save started as a pilot project in a Dhaka slum. This small MFO, of which I was the founding chairperson, was set up to test variants of the standard microfinance delivery methodology, and was interested in the problem of the rigidity of the typical MFO loan repayment plan. *Safe*Save took seriously the idea that microfinance, on both the savings and loan side, could be a useful service to poor households who wished to manage their money better: it was, perhaps, the first MFO to set itself up as a "general purpose" money management service rather than as a provider of finance for microenterprise. *Safe*Save wanted to be a better financial partner to poor households than the savings clubs, money-guards, money-lenders and self-help home-based savings devices that such households traditionally fell back on to help them manage their money.

Rather than bring clients together in groups, *Safe*Save transacted with them as individuals, and instead of holding meetings *Safe*Save sent a "collector" to their homes or workplaces. In this, it was inspired by the work of Indian deposit collectors. From the start it offered both savings and loans: adult clients (men as well as women) could choose to save, or to both save and borrow, and children under 16 could save. For the collection of savings and of loan repayments *Safe*Save was anxious to avoid the rigidity problems that made MFO membership difficult for the poorest. It therefore softened the harshness of the payment plan: clients could deposit or repay as and when they liked, in any amount they liked.

This step had obvious dangers: a plan that allowed you to pay whenever you chose was hardly a plan at all. *Safe*Save had to find something to substitute for the discipline that a rigid plan provided. It found it in a combination of regularity and *frequency*: *Safe*Save collectors called on their clients every day, six days a week. At each visit, clients were given the *opportunity* to pay, but were not *obliged* to pay, though of course the collectors became skilled at persuading clients to save or repay what they could whenever they could, and they soon learnt what time of day was best for a visit to each of their clients.

This softened form of the instalment plan worked. On average, *Safe*Save clients who borrow (some 25 percent choose never to borrow but use only

[10]The conference was organized by Proshika, a Bangladeshi NGO and microfinance provider, in Dhaka in August 1996, called *Who Needs Credit? Poverty and Finance in Bangladesh*. See Wood and Sharif, 1997.

the savings services) repay their loans faster than do clients in conventional Bangladesh MFOs, taking about nine months instead of the standard one year. There was considerable variation in the way that individual clients responded to the daily opportunity to pay. Some made a payment every day — a savings deposit, or a loan repayment, or both. Some made daily loan repayments while they held a loan, and reverted to daily saving when they were not borrowing. Others, perhaps because they were familiar with MFO conventions, paid in on a weekly basis, though they used the daily visit to catch up if they fell behind, or to pre-pay when they had extra liquidity on hand. Others paid in with a less obvious regularity, sometimes reflecting an unusually structured income stream, sometimes, we supposed, simply reflecting personality.

*Safe*Save now has about 15,000 clients served by branches in eight slum locations, and is able to make a surplus each month using a price structure under which it charges 3 percent a month[11] on loans (making it about 25 percent more expensive than conventional Bangladeshi microlending) and pays about 6 percent annually on savings. Although *Safe*Save received some donated funds at the beginning of its life, it is no longer subsidized, and is financing its expansion using client savings, bank loans at commercial rates, and, increasingly, retained earnings. Its fortunes can be tracked at www.safesave.org.

6 Adding Value to the Plan: Using Liquidity to Boost Savings

Microfinance clients form more of the lump sums of capital they need through borrowing than through saving. How do they choose between the two strategies?

Sometimes, borrowing turns out to be the easiest way to save. Standard MFO loans are not infrequently used to "buy" savings. This is not irrational. Among the long list of expensive expenditure needs that face even the poorest households, a stock of savings is as important an asset as any. For example, I have seen MFO microcredit borrowers, especially women, using their loans to buy jewellery that can serve as a hedge against uncertain future prospects such as divorce, desertion or widowhood. The question

[11]This is a "declining balance", not a "flat" rate: clients are charged, each month, 3 percent of the loan outstanding balance at the end of the previous month.

arises, why did she choose to use an expensive loan to acquire her jewellery instead of saving up for it?

*Safe*Save clients in the Dhaka slums are offered a daily chance to save, repay borrowings, or both. But repayment volumes exceed saving volumes by a big margin. Why? One obvious reason is that clients lack trust in their deposit-taking institution and prefer their provider to carry the default risk. But, in *Safe*Save's case, we can dismiss this. There, savings on deposit exceed the outstanding loan portfolio: it is in the *volume of transactions*, not in the value of the resulting balances, that loans hugely exceed savings. *Safe*Save clients do patiently build up big savings balances over the years — but, along the way, they take and repay loans at a much more furious pace. Their propensity is to form usefully large lump sums via borrowing far more *often* than through saving.

It is tempting to believe, given this behaviour, that MFOs would do well to focus uniquely on their lending — just as they did in their early years. After all, as lenders, MFOs have fewer opportunity to cheat their clients than they do if they accept deposits, so they can be more easily tolerated by regulators acting in the public interest. Clearly, it is much easier to make money from lending than from collecting savings. So if clients find ways to use borrowing to satisfy their savings needs — by using a loan to buy gold to be stored as savings, for example — why not let them do so? I have some sympathy for this point of view, having often urged MFOs who find it difficult to start savings services (for practical or regulatory reasons, or both) to concentrate instead on flexible, frequent instalment loans and not to insist that all loans go into microbusinesses.

But in the rich world, the market has evolved to offer savings as well as loans, and for good reasons: people may prefer to save rather than borrow, especially for long-term needs, and prefer to avoid the costs of borrowing; and providers need to mobilise savings to fund their loan books. Why shouldn't the same become true for the poor?

Conversations with clients at both *Safe*Save and conventional MFOs suggest that their propensity to borrow more intensively than they save is indeed induced by circumstance, not preference. "Of course I'd rather save up than borrow", runs the typical remark, "but other spending needs take priority over saving, and when I need a large sum urgently, I haven't yet built up enough savings to cover it, so once again I end up borrowing. Then I'm on the repayment treadmill again, and it's even harder to save".

What might be done to redress this, and to help poor households direct more of their spare cash-flow to saving deposits instead of the more expensive and stressful option of loan repayments? One approach is to subsidise the saving effort. In the United States, for example, there is a movement for "matched savings", in which the state encourages poor households to save by topping up some of their savings with public subsidy. In the US, poor households typically lose out on many of the subsidies available to better-off ones, because they lack the kind of assets (such as expensive housing) that governments choose to subsidise. To compensate for this, it is argued, it makes sense to subside savings (Schreiner and Sherraden, 2007).

But might there be a better and more direct way than using expensive subsidies to boost the savings of the poor? Can it be done, if not profitably, at least without massive subsidy? What can we learn from the MFO borrower who used a microloan to buy a stock of savings, and from *Safe*Save clients who would like to save rather than borrow but find that making savings deposits always comes third in line behind expenditure needs and loan repayments? At its experimental rural branch outside Dhaka, *Safe*Save is piloting a further innovation which tries to load the dice in favour of savings, and we close this note with it.

The approach taken in *Safe*Save's "Product 9" (P9) could scarcely be more straightforward. If liquidity shortfalls constrain saving, why not provide clients with the liquidity from which they can save? P9, therefore, offers clients a series of interest-free loans, with each loan rising in value, but as each loan is taken, one-third of its value is put into a long-term savings account in the client's name which cannot be withdrawn without penalty until a target sum has been reached. Thus, each time a loan is taken, its liquidity is tapped to make painless savings, but two-thirds of its value (rising in value with each cycle) is available to meet pressing expenditure needs.

Loan value increments are structured so that after the fourth loan is taken, the client's savings balance exceeds the outstanding amount of her loan (see the English translation of the product rules, appended to the note). From then on she is borrowing her own savings, and her loan repayments are in reality savings deposits. Still, to her, they *feel* like loan repayments, and the illusion is strengthened by the fact that she has most of the proceeds of her loan in hand, available for expenditure.

The loans are interest-free for three reasons. First, the idea of interest-free loans is immensely attractive, especially in Bangladesh with its majority Muslim culture: it compensates for the less attractive parts of the product when conceived of as a loan service, above all losing one-third of the loan at disbursement. Second, clients regard the "no-interest savings matched by no-interest loans" as reasonable: after all, except for the first four loans in the cycle, the client is borrowing her own savings.[12] Finally, *Safe*Save's P9 financial costs are low, since loan-loss risk is negligibly small and the cost of funds is zero, with clients funding their own loans through zero-interest deposits. *Safe*Save takes income from P9 in alternative ways: by a small loan disbursement fee of 1 percent of the loan value, and by interest earned on the excess of savings held over loans outstanding.

In other respects, P9 follows *Safe*Save norms. Collectors visit clients daily at their homes or workplaces, and the client may pay in as much or as little (including zero) at each visit. There are no meetings, no groups, no guarantors, no joint liability. Clients are given a passbook and a short set of rules in simple Bengali.

The tests faced by P9, then, are clear. First, does this product induce a more rapid growth of client savings than standard *Safe*Save products, and second, can it cover its own costs without subsidy?

The product was launched in the spring of 2007, but client recruitment was deliberately slow at first, so that the median age of the 475 accounts opened by end September 2009 was only 9.5 months. Nonetheless, at end September 2009, the average client savings balance, at $70, exceeded the average outstanding loan by $12. Between them, clients had accumulated $34,500 in savings and owed *Safe*Save $27,000 in loans. Transaction velocity had been as high as in earlier *Safe*Save products: by end September 2009, P9 clients had borrowed $140,000 and repaid $103,000, but P9's design had directed a third of those borrowings into savings. Of the $43,500 thus saved, $9,000 had been withdrawn — but nearly all of those withdrawals were by clients who had reached the target savings (of $300 each).

Box 23.1: How P9 works for a family of five.

Gautam and his wife Anjana have three children: two boys and a younger girl, Sabitri. Gautam and his sons make a living by stripping rice of its husk and selling it in the market — a common form of self-employment for landless, poor, uneducated villagers. Their monthly income varies with season and weather and luck, but is usually around the equivalent of 75 cents per person per day (or about $1.90 at Purchasing Power

[12]Unless the client chooses to keep her savings on deposit after she has achieved the target savings balance — see the rules.

rates). The couple are keen to keep their daughter Sabitri in school so in April 2007 they opened a P9 account in her name, hoping to save a good sum to secure her school costs. They repaid the first loan, of 2000 taka ($30) before the end of the month and the second (of $45) by mid May. Then they took the third loan ($60) using it, as usual, to buy stocks of unprocessed rice, and got into a rhythm of repaying 50 taka (about 75 cents) every day when the *Safe*Save collector called, but making bigger payment whenever they had the cash to do so. Sometimes, when their P9 loan was issued, Gautam would immediately save more than the mandatory one-third if he had enough rice in stock at the time — this helped push up his savings even more quickly. All this proved a successful strategy and by the end of October, they had taken *and repaid* eight loans, totalling just over $1,000, and built up savings of $340. They then started a second round of P9 borrowing and saving, starting again at the entry level loan of $30. They moved smoothly through the borrowing and lending regime for another five months, saving another $45. But in March 2008, misfortune struck when the older son fell seriously ill. To get proper treatment was expensive, so the P9 savings made in Sabitri's name was in the end used to pay hospital fees for her brother. As a result, the son is now almost cured, and the rest of the family is back at work, trying to make up for the time and money they lost while worrying about and caring for the son. As a result, they can spare less cash for their P9 account, but they still pay in every day when the collector calls, even though the amount has dropped to around 30 cents or sometimes even less. Nevertheless, their current statement shows them to have $102 saved in their P9 account, and just $32 still to pay on their most recent loan. Sabitri is still in school. They seem determined to persevere with their P9 account, and look forward to reaching their second $340 savings target.

P9 is still new, so it is not appropriate to make more than the preliminary conclusion that its design has helped clients like Gautam (see Box 23.1 above) to save more substantial sums more quickly than earlier *Safe*Save products, and to arrive very much more swiftly at the point where clients hold more savings than debt. Nevertheless, the outcome so far is promising.

There are also encouraging signs that P9, expanded to a minimum of 1,500 clients per branch, would cover most and maybe all of its costs. At that scale, the 1 percent charged on all loan disbursements would cover the costs of the front-line staff (the "collectors"), who are paid via a 0.75 percent commission on all repayments collected plus a small guaranteed monthly income. The earnings on the investment of the excess of savings over loans should cover all remaining costs. Progress can be tracked at http://sites.google.com/site/trackingp9/.

7 Conclusions

The instalment payment plan is the workhorse of successful financial intermediation by poor households. That has always held true in informal devices and services that the poor contrive for themselves, such as savings and loan clubs, deposit collectors and periodic money-lenders. The microfinance revolution has improved matters immensely: that fraction of the world's poor with access to good MFOs now almost always enjoy reliable instalments plans when they repay their loans, and increasingly when they make their savings, too.

Nevertheless, the constant liquidity crises that typify life on very small and often irregular incomes continue to push the poor to intermediate more often through borrowing than through saving, even though many poor households would prefer the lower costs, lower risk, and greater sense of security that saving brings. Work done in experimental MFOs, such as *Safe*Save in Bangladesh, demonstrate, however, that careful product design can help to correct this bias.

More broadly, we see once again that progress in product development comes from careful patient observation of what the poor themselves do, and what they say about it, as they face the complex challenges of managing money when there is so little of it.

References

Collins, D, J Morduch, S Rutherford and O Ruthven (2009). *Portfolios of the Poor: How the World's Poor Live on $2 a Day.* Princeton, New Jersey: Princeton University Press.

Dowla, A and D Barua (2006). *The Poor Always Pay Back: The Grameen II Story.* Bloomfield, CT: Kumarian.

Rutherford, S (2006). *Grameen II: The First Five Years.* MicroSave, www.microsave.net.

Rutherford, S and S Arora (2009). *The Poor and Their Money: Microfinance from a Twenty-First Century Consumer's Perspective.* Rugby, UK: Practical Action Publishing.

Rutherford, S (2009). *The Pledge: ASA, Peasant Politics, and Microfinance in the Development of Bangladesh.* New York: Oxford University Press.
Schreiner, M and M Sherraden (eds.) *Can the Poor Save? Saving & Asset Building in Individual Development Accounts* (2007). New Brunswick, New Jersey: Transaction Publishers.
Wood, GD and IA Sharif (eds.) (1997). *Who Needs Credit? Poverty and Finance in Bangladesh.* Dhaka: University Press.
Yunus, M (2002). *Grameen Bank II: Designed to Open New Possibilities.* Dhaka: Grameen Bank.
Yunus, M (2007). *Banker to the Poor.* New York: Public Affairs.

Appendix: Translation from the Bengali of the P9 Rules ($1 = 68 Bangladeshi *taka*)

Borrow and save at the same time using Shohoz Shonchoy's interest-free loans!

Shohoz Shonchoy introduces a new account for people with low and irregular or unreliable incomes who have difficulty finding somebody to lend money to them, and who find it difficult to save. It is designed to provide you with liquidity while you build up your savings. It will not suit everyone, but if building up savings is important to you, you may like it.

Borrowing

As soon as you open your account, you can take an interest-free loan of 2000 taka and repay it whenever you like. As soon as you have repaid it in full, you can take another bigger loan, and as soon as you have repaid that one, you can take yet another loan. Loans rise in value by 1000 taka each time until 5000 taka, and then by 2000 taka each time until 15,000 taka, and then by 5000 taka each time. These are the maximum amounts allowed but of course you can always take a smaller loan if you want to. *All* these loans are interest-free, & you repay them whenever you like.

If you need extra cash while you are holding a loan, you can "top up" your loan before you have completely repaid it. You may top up to the value of your current loan, or to the value of your current savings, whichever is greater. Suppose you took a loan of 7000 taka, and you have already repaid 4000 taka: now you can take 4000 taka again if you want to — or even more, if your current savings balance is greater than 7,000.

Saving

Each time you take a loan, or top up a loan, you place one third of its value into a long-term savings account in your name at **Shohoz Shonchoy**. **Shohoz Shonchoy** will hold this money for you until it reaches 20,000 taka.

When your savings reach 20,000 taka you have three options:

***Option one*:** You can stop borrowing and take back your savings.

***Option two*:** You can continue borrowing and build up your savings to an even greater value.

***Option three*:** You can stop borrowing but keep your savings in **Shohoz Shonchoy** and start earning profit on them.

Operating the account

You must visit our branch office to take or to top up loans. But **Shohoz Shonchoy** will send a collector to your home or workplace every few days to collect your loan repayments. You do not have to make a repayment every time she calls, but we strongly encourage you to repay as quickly as you can. By repaying quickly, you can get bigger loans more quickly, and your savings grow more quickly. This is an individual service: there are no groups, no meetings and you are never responsible for other people's loans.

Costs

The loans (and top-ups) are completely interest-free. When you open an account, you must pay an account opening fee of 100 taka, which covers your passbooks and photo. Each time you take a loan or top-up, you pay a disbursement fee of 1 percent of the loan or top-up.

If you succeed in building your savings to 20,000 taka, you pay nothing else. If you want to take back your savings *before* they reach 20,000, you can, but **Shohoz Shonchoy** will keep back 5 percent of their value as a fee for early termination of the contract.

Open an account with **Shohoz Shonchoy** today!

Insurance for the Poor: Definitions and Innovations

Craig Churchill*

International Labour Organization

This paper describes the diverse roots of microinsurance, including affinity groups, microfinance providers, social protection advocates, and insurers seeking their fortune at the bottom of the pyramid. It defines microinsurance and explains its key differences from traditional insurance, as well from other financial services that target the poor. It highlights the importance of taking a broad view of microinsurance so that it is not seen as just another financial service offered by MFIs. This article then illustrates some innovations that are emerging in product design and distribution that may have the potential to provide improved protection to the poor.

"When the early Victorian insurance companies were first approached with suggestions that they should offer (insurance) to the poor, the short answer generally given was, in effect, that security was a luxury for which the poor could not afford to pay.

The suggestions, however, were pressed. It was observed that for many centuries the poor had somehow contrived, by their own co-operative thrift, to provide some sort of financial security for themselves; and with some misgivings experiments were launched to see whether such security could be sold to them on commercial terms which would both give them at least as good a return as they were deriving through their spontaneous organizations, and enable the sellers to live on the proceeds of the trade. This is the origin of industrial

*Microinsurance Innovation Facility, Social Finance Programme, International Labour Organization.

> assurance, which is simply life assurance adapted to the needs of weekly wage-earners.
>
> Industrial assurance began timidly and on a small scale; but it met a felt need, and consequently developed at a pace for which its founders were unprepared. While it was most rapidly expanding it was already being extensively reconstructed, as the mistakes of the experimental stage were discovered and retrieved".
>
> Dermot Morrah, *A History of Industrial Life Assurance.*

1 Introduction

Microinsurance is a new tool in the arsenal to fight poverty and reduce vulnerability, or at least the term has only been in common use since the late 1990s. But in truth, microinsurance is not really new, as the quote above so clearly demonstrates. Some of today's large insurance companies began in 1800s as mutual protection schemes among low-income workers. In the early 1900s, many insurers built their business by selling industrial insurance at factory gates. Over the years, however, insurance became increasingly sophisticated and more relevant for complex risks, and wealthier policyholders.

As such, microinsurance can be described as a back-to-basics campaign for insurers that enable them to reach an under-served market. It can also be a mechanism that allows government social protection schemes to extend coverage to workers in the informal economy who lack benefits such as health insurance and pensions often available to workers in the formal sector. And microinsurance is a way for affinity groups to protect low-income members through the solidarity of risk-pooling. Indeed, microinsurance is a big tent, with a diversity of ideologies and approaches, but a common objective: to enhance the protection of vulnerable population segments.

This paper begins by describing the diverse roots of microinsurance. Next, it defines microinsurance and explains its key differences from traditional insurance, and from other financial services that target the poor. This article then clarifies the relationship between microinsurance and microfinance, and illustrates some innovations that are emerging in product design and distribution that may have the potential to provide improved protection to the poor, although it is too early to assess their impact.

2 The Emergence of Microinsurance

Microinsurance is primarily a phenomenon in developing countries, in part because insurance penetration is low and government social protection schemes only cover a small minority of citizens. Consequently, microinsurance is emerging from four largely parallel entry points to fill this gap.

First, to cope with risks, many low-income persons form their own mutual benefit associations, burial societies and the like. Some of these unregulated insurance schemes have grown quite large, posing a dilemma for regulators (see Box 24.1). Indeed the cooperative movement has a strong claim to being microinsurance pioneers. Even though they did not use the term "microinsurance" or focus exclusively on the low-income market, many agricultural and financial cooperatives have long offered insurance protection to the poor. Popular insurance provided through people's organizations indeed predates the current discourse on microinsurance. Furthermore, cooperatives represent a natural risk pool and an ideal delivery channel to extend insurance to persons outside the formal economy.

Box 24.1: Informal insurance in South Africa.

In South Africa, a number of schemes offer products that closely resemble life insurance. In the informal sector, there are an estimated eight million members of informal burial societies contributing US$ 1 billion per annum in "premiums" towards coverage for the risk of death. Some schemes are quite large. The Great North Burial Society, a registered Friendly Society, has more than 20,000 lives covered, but is unable to access reinsurance as it is not a licensed insurer.

Consequently, a catastrophe would pose a serious threat to the solvency of such a scheme. In addition, the growth of informal schemes can pose a threat to sustainability, e.g., when burial societies become larger, the efficacy of the member-governance system is undermined. At this point, the burial society also accumulates substantial assets, which increases the risk of fraud or theft to a degree that member governance cannot control.

If regulators intervene and force the formalization of informal insurance schemes, they could be trying to force a round peg into a square hole, since insurance regulations were not designed to accommodate this type of organization. Should they shut down informal schemes since they are essentially illegal? If informal schemes are allowed to operate, how should they determine the threshold that mandates regulatory intervention? Or is there some middle ground that could expand access to insurance with some degree of consumer protection?

Source: Adapted from Genesis Analytics, 2005.

Second, some non-governmental organizations and international agencies, including the International Labour Organization (ILO), have encouraged persons excluded from commercial and social insurance schemes, such as workers in the informal economy, to create risk-pooling mechanisms, especially to address health risks. These risk-pooling mechanisms, such as *mutuelle de santé* and community-based health insurance (CBHI) schemes, are ultimately intended to link to government support in order to facilitate a redistribution of resources from the rich to the poor, thus providing sustainable social protection.

Such a result is emerging in India where, in 2007, the government launched Rashtriya Swasthya Bima Yojana (RSBY), a health insurance scheme for households living below the poverty line. Eligible families are entitled to more than 700 in-patient procedures with a maximum annual benefit of INR 30,000 (US$ 600) for a nominal registration fee of INR 30 (US$ 0.60). In the districts where RSBY is starting, microinsurance schemes are devising ways of combining the government's benefits with their own, since of course in-patient procedures are just part of their health insurance needs.

Where links with government programmes are not available, however, many CBHIs remain small and independent, often run by volunteers, and unable to provide significant benefits (despite their streamlined cost structure) because of the limited purchasing power of their members. Many schemes experience low premium collection rates and high dropout rates, which combine to undermine their viability. However, federations of CBHIs have emerged in some countries, including Benin, Mali and Senegal, to help overcome some of these limitations (Fonteneau and Galland, 2006).

Third, microinsurance has emerged on the coattails of microfinance. After providing credit and perhaps savings to the poor, many microfinance institutions (MFIs) have dappled in insurance as well, either to protect their loan portfolios, or protect their customers, or both. Indeed, the motivations why MFIs might be interested in providing insurance include:

- **Lower credit risk:** One of the primary reasons why borrowers do not repay their loans is because they experience a shock — a death in the family or illness — that creates a financial stress. If insurance can help that family cope with shocks, it will also reduce the MFI's loan losses.

- **Improve customer loyalty:** MFIs often realize that they need to offer a variety of products to enhance retention, so that even when clients do not want a loan, they may still appreciate a savings account, a wire transfer service or insurance protection.
- **Enhance product profitability:** A diverse product menu allows cross-selling opportunities and spreads the acquisition costs for a client across multiple products, enhancing product profitability.
- **Diversify income streams:** Microinsurance provides an additional source of income either from profit if the scheme is provided in-house (and well-managed), or from fees if done in partnership with an insurer. The latter situation is particularly interesting to MFIs, which welcome opportunities to earn income without taking risks.

Of course, there are also disadvantages for MFIs to offer insurance. It is a different business from savings or credit, requiring different expertise. Even offering insurance products in partnership with an insurer can be time-consuming and demanding. Some MFIs may be willing to purchase credit life coverage to protect their loan portfolios, but are less interested in providing other benefits to their customers because of the additional work required that may distract them from their core function.

The fourth entry point are the insurers themselves. Often building on their exposure to the low-income market from partnerships with MFIs, some insurers see the vast number of low-income persons in developing countries as a new market opportunity, although others engage in microinsurance to demonstrate their corporate social responsibility.

Following the *Fortune at the Bottom of the Pyramid* logic articulated by Prahalad (2005), insurers have begun investigating whether they can redesign their delivery systems, products, and institutional culture to serve the low-income market. Based on examples from various industries — including construction, financial services, consumer goods and healthcare — Prahalad identifies common principles to be considered when innovating for the bottom of the pyramid (BOP). Even though he does not analyse insurance case studies, these principles are remarkably applicable to the provision of microinsurance.

In particular, when serving the BOP, the basis for returns on investment is volume. Even if the per unit profit is minuscule, when it is multiplied across a huge number of sales, the return can become attractive. This attribute is a perfect fit for insurance and the Law of Large Numbers, whereby actual claims experience should run much closer to the projected claims when the risk pool is larger. When projections can be estimated with a high degree of confidence, then the product pricing — in theory — does not have to include a large margin for error, making it more affordable to the poor. As the BOP concept filters through the insurance industry, many companies are beginning to look at the low-income market a bit differently, especially when the results from vanguard insurers show that it is possible to provide microinsurance profitably (see Box 24.2).

Box 24.2: Profitability of microinsurance.

Can microinsurance make a positive contribution to an insurance company's bottomline? Some initial findings can be gleaned from the microinsurance case studies published by the ILO on behalf of the CGAP Working Group on Microinsurance (now the Microinsurance Network). Based on an analysis of AIG Uganda, which provides a group personal accident product to more than 20 microfinance institutions, McCord *et al.* (2005) show very clearly that microinsurance can be a profitable line of business for commercial insurers, particularly for a basic product that is mandatory for all borrowers. According to this study,

"For AIG, the microinsurance product is profitable, operating with a combined ratio of 73 percent including a loss ratio of 32 percent. Using the results of the first five months of 2004 to project for the remainder of the year, AIG Uganda will earn just under US$ 200,000 from the microinsurance product or about 25 percent of its earnings.

Microinsurance produced almost 17 percent of the AIG Uganda net income in 2003. This makes it nearly the highest producing product line for the insurer, and likely the highest in 2004. Although financial data specific to this product is not readily available for the years before 2003, it appears that it has steadily provided increasing net income... (T)he claims ratio is very low at between 23 percent and 31 percent. The profit margin at 18 percent and 23 percent is also rather healthy for such a product."

Similarly, the credit life product offered by Madison Insurance and four MFIs in Zambia had loss ratios below 50 percent, well below in most cases (Manje, 2005).

But for other products, the results are less clear cut. According to Roth and Athreye (2005), the endowment microinsurance policies sold by Tata–AIG in India were expected to break even in three to four years if the insurer experiences continued high growth rates and high levels of persistency. At Delta Life in Bangladesh, which also offers endowment policies, the insurer presumed that its microinsurance products were profitable, even though administrative cost ratios were close to 50 percent, because the claim ratio was below 10 percent (McCord and Churchill, 2005). But the insurer was not able to provide sufficient data to verify that the products were profitable. Since these are voluntary insurance products sold on an individual basis, they are naturally much more expensive to distribute and service than the mandatory group policies linked to loans.

In fact, insurers are generally more eager to enter the low-income market than their colleagues in the banking world because of the different risk and trust relationships. If bankers are lending to the poor, the bankers are taking the risk that poor will not repay their loans. Whereas with insurance, it is the poor policyholders who are essentially taking the risk, not knowing for sure if the insurer will fulfil its obligations and act on its promises if the insured event occurs. These contrasting relationships also partly explain why the demand for microcredit is much greater than the demand for microinsurance.

These four distinct sources of microinsurance have created a big tent. Under the tent are many different types of organizations, approaches and risks that are being covered. Often the cacophony of discussion around the word "microinsurance" can create considerable confusion because it has different meanings to different people.

3 What is Microinsurance?

In 2003, the CGAP Working Group on Microinsurance (now the Microinsurance Network) defined microinsurance as "the protection of low-income people against specific perils in exchange for regular premium payments proportionate to the likelihood and cost of the risk involved". This definition is essentially the same as one might use for regular insurance except for the clearly prescribed target market: *low-income people.* However, those three words make a big difference.

The following key characteristics illustrate how insurance for the poor may differ from conventional insurance:

- **Relevant to the risks of low-income households:** Coverage should be linked to the greatest areas of vulnerability for low-income households, but often what is currently available from insurers does not really address the needs of the poor.
- **As inclusive as possible:** While insurance companies tend to exclude high-risk persons, microinsurance schemes generally strive to be inclusive. Since the sums insured are small, the costs of identifying high-risk persons, such as those with preexisting illnesses, may be higher than the benefits of excluding them in the first place. Many exclusions can be just administrative nuisances that undermine efficiency rather than important controls for insurance risks.
- **Affordable premiums:** At the end of the day, microinsurance schemes have to be affordable to the poor, otherwise they will not enrol in the scheme nor benefit from the coverage. Various strategies could make microinsurance affordable, including having small benefit packages, spreading premiums' payments over time to correspond with the household's cash flow and supplementing premiums with long-term subsidies from governments or donors.
- **Grouping for efficiencies:** Group insurance is more affordable than individual coverage. Insurance for the members of women's associations, informal savings groups, cooperatives, labour unions, small business associations and the like enable insurers to reach the market cost-effectively, while reducing insurance risks such as over-usage and moral hazard.[1]
- **Clearly defined and simple rules and restrictions:** Insurance contracts are generally full of complex conditions, conditional benefits, written in legalese that even lawyers struggle to discern. Although the rationale for the fine print may be consumer protection, if the consumers do not understand what is written, its very purpose is defeated. Moreover, its content can give the insurance company an excuse not to pay a claim. Microinsurance has to be kept as simple and straightforward as possible so that everyone has a common understanding of what is and is not covered.

[1]Moral hazard is a risk that occurs when insurance protection creates incentives for individuals to cause the insured event; or a behaviour that increases the likelihood that the event will occur, for instance, bad habits such as smoking in the case of health insurance or life insurance.

- **Easily accessible claims documentation requirements:** The process for accessing conventional insurance benefits can be so arduous that it discourages all but the most persistent claimants. While controls have to be in place to avoid paying fraudulent claims, for microinsurance to be effective, it has to be easy for low-income households to submit legitimate claims.

Key differences between microinsurance and commercial insurance are not just in the products themselves, but also in how they are made accessible to poor persons. As summarized in Figure 24.1, microinsurance products and processes are not just scaled down versions of existing practices.

How poor do people have to be for their insurance protection to be considered micro? The answer varies by country. Generally, microinsurance is

Commercial Insurance	Microinsurance
Premium collected mostly from deductions in bank account.	Premium often collected in cash or associated with another financial transaction; should be designed to accommodate customers' irregular cash flows, which may mean frequent payments.
Agents and brokers are primarily responsible for sales.	Agents may manage the entire customer relationship, perhaps including premium collection and claims settlement.
Targeted at wealthy or middle-class clients.	Targeted at low-income persons.
Market is largely familiar with insurance.	Market is largely unfamiliar with insurance.
Screening requirements may include a medical examination.	If there are any screening requirements, they would be limited to a declaration of good health.
Sold by licensed intermediaries.	Often sold by unlicensed intermediaries.
Large sums insured.	Small sums insured.
Priced based on age/specific risk.	Pre-underwritten with community or group pricing.
Limited eligibility with standard exclusions.	Broadly inclusive, with few if any exclusions.
Complex policy document.	Simple, easy to understand policy document.

Source: Adapted from McCord and Churchill (2005).

Figure 24.1: Illustrative distinctions between commercial insurance and microinsurance.

for persons ignored by mainstream commercial and social insurance schemes, particularly persons working in the informal economy. Since it is easier to offer insurance to persons in the formal economy with a predictable income than to cover informal economy workers with irregular cash flows, the latter represent the microinsurance frontier.

Some countries have moved toward specifying product features for microinsurance compared to insurance that is not micro. For example, in India, microinsurance includes policies that have a maximum benefit or sum assured of INR 30,000 (US$ 600) or 50,000 (US$ 1,000) depending on the type of cover. Whereas in Peru, microinsurance is defined either by the maximum sum assured of PEN 10,000 (US$ 3,300) or a monthly premium payment below PEN 10 (US$ 3.30).

These quantitative definitions are needed when regulators are creating special conditions for microinsurance. In India, microinsurance agents require less training than regular insurance agents; or in Brazil, tax breaks are being considered for microinsurance providers. The problem with identifying a specific value where upmarket insurance ends and micro starts is that it can bifurcate the market, leaving a gap above where the special conditions start. It also creates incentives for policies to be kept artificially low, or for people to take out multiple policies, and it does not accommodate the graduation of low-income policyholders out of poverty.

Microinsurance is significantly different from other microfinance services because it straddles the boundary between a market-based service and social protection. In microfinance, "best practices" have pushed MFIs to charge sufficient interest rates to cover their costs, and therefore to become self-sustainable (if not profitable). In microinsurance, however, sustainability can take on a different meaning. Instead of covering the costs purely from premiums, for some types of insurance, such as health, one might find public-private partnerships that are partly subsidized by the State (see Figure 24.2), which is justified because the scheme is providing a statutory benefit. However, care must be taken to ensure that the presence of subsidies does not allow the scheme to become inefficient.

By itself, insurance for low-income households can only have a limited effect. Insurance is an effective means of protecting against occasional large losses, but it is not an efficient means of coping with frequent small losses. Consequently, for comprehensive risk management, insurance needs to be combined with savings, credit and risk prevention services to provide more effective protection to the poor.

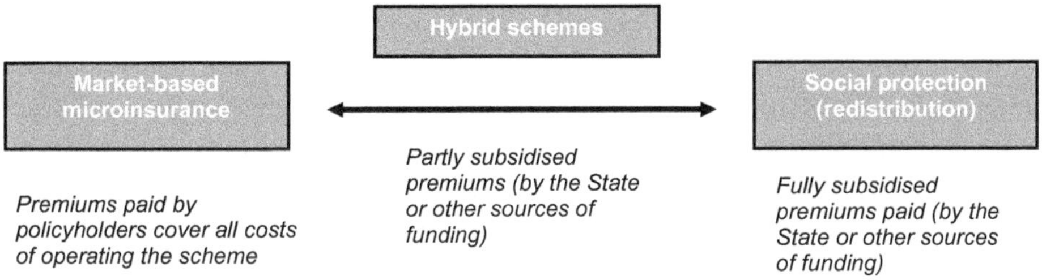

Source: IAIS (2007).

Figure 24.2: The microinsurance continuum.

4 Microinsurance and Microfinance[2]

As described above, microfinance is just one of the roots of microinsurance. A microfinance perspective sees insurance as just one of several financial services offered by MFIs, often combined with credit, and sometimes savings, to reduce the costs that would be associated with an insurance-only transaction. But this viewpoint is too narrow since it would limit the potential market for microinsurance to those persons reached by the MFI. A microinsurance perspective sees microfinance institutions as just one of many delivery channels that could be used to sell and service insurance products for the low-income market, as summarized in Figure 24.3.

Briefly looking at the issue from the microfinance perspective, if a MFI wants to offer insurance to its clients, there are four main institutional options to consider: a) partnership with an insurance company, b) creating its own insurance brokerage, c) self-insuring, or d) creating its own insurance company.

Under what circumstances is one option preferable to the others? Certainly, if no insurance company is available or willing to offer protection through the MFI, then it could go on its own. However, the possibility

A microfinance perspective on microinsurance	**A microinsurance perspective on microfinance**
One of several financial services that could be offered to the poor	One of several distribution channels to extend insurance to the poor

Figure 24.3: Microinsurance and microfinance: different viewpoints.

[2]This section is adapted from Churchill and Roth (2006).

of not being able to find an interested insurance partner is becoming increasingly less likely as more insurers seek opportunities to reach new markets. MFIs are also becoming more convincing, arming themselves with arguments and experiences to persuade insurers that this is indeed a valuable market opportunity for them. In general, if an MFI cannot entice an insurer into a partnership, it is probably not effectively communicating what it has to offer.

The creation of a MFI-owned insurance brokerage is essentially a more sophisticated version of the partner-agent model. This approach, often used by credit union networks, facilitates access to formal insurance for MFIs and members alike. As with the partner-agent model, this arrangement has the advantage of outsourcing the risk to formal insurers.

The advantage of the brokerage arrangement over the basic partner-agent model is that a organization affiliated to a MFI (or a group of MFIs) develops insurance expertise to negotiate the best deals. The brokerage is not tied to any one insurance company, so it can explore various options on behalf of its two main customers, the MFIs and their clients. In addition, the brokerage is not limited to using MFIs as the distribution channels. Once it understands the needs of the low-income market, it can explore other strategies for extending insurance to the poor, such as through cooperatives, community organizations, and even retailers. Examples of this model include MicroEnsure, created by Opportunity International, and the First Microinsurance Agency created by the Aga Khan Agency for Microfinance.

A third option is for MFIs to self-insure; in other words, to carry the risk themselves. There are compelling reasons why some microfinance institutions would want to self-insure, as well as some strong arguments against it. One argument for self-insurance is a belief that the MFIs (or their customers) will have to pay extra for the insurer's overhead. For the most basic products, like credit life, that logic might be valid. However, basic credit-life insurance largely benefits the lender since it means the MFI does not have to solicit loan repayments from the deceased's survivors.[3] If the MFI

[3]There is some debate about the usefulness of credit life insurance. Some MFIs feel that it is a complicated means of dealing with loan losses due to death, and they prefer to write off the loan and provision accordingly. This argument might be valid for predictable loan losses due to death, but would not be appropriate if a MFI experiences a natural disaster or other co-variant risks. The provisioning approach is also not relevant: for small MFIs that cannot afford to write off loans; if a MFI starts issuing larger loans, creating a concentration risk; or if the mortality rates are volatile or changing, as in an area with high incidence of HIV/AIDS.

really wants to reduce the vulnerability of its customers, more complicated products are required — products that a MFI probably cannot offer on its own.

Both TYM (Vietnam) and CARD (Philippines) had negative experiences trying to enhance customer value on their own. They provided credit life on a self-insurance basis and generated significant surpluses. Consequently, they thought it would be a good idea to offer additional benefits, by including other family members or by covering additional risks. They added these benefits, however, without assessing the impact that they might have on claims. As a result, CARD's pension plan nearly bankrupted the company (McCord and Buczkowski, 2004), and TYM's hospitalization benefit threatened to do the same even though the benefit was extremely modest (Tran and Yun, 2004)).

Another concern surrounding self-insurance is the extent to which a MFI will cope if it experiences catastrophic losses. The primary reason why MFIs should not self insure — besides not having the expertise to price and design products appropriately — is because they will have difficulty meeting claims if many clients are affected by a peril at the same time. Since they are not formal insurers, they do not have access to reinsurance, which is how insurers cope with co-variant risks.

VimoSEWA (India) learned this lesson the hard way. After several years of negative experiences with insurance partners, it began offering in-house health insurance in 1996, and then added asset insurance in 1998. Initially, VimoSEWA's transition to self-insurance had positive financial and service benefits — claims were paid faster and not rejected, and VimoSEWA began building up some reserves. However, when the January 2001 earthquake struck Gujarat, over Rs 3.4 million (US$ 75,000) were required to satisfy claims, causing a severe financial strain. Prior to the earthquake, annual payouts for asset protection were below Rs 30,000 (US$ 662). This experience helped VimoSEWA appreciate the need for reinsurance, and led the organization back to the partner-agent approach (Garand, 2005).

The main point is that a self-insuring MFI must think carefully about how it will control co-variant risks. One approach is to exclude disasters from the coverage, but this abandons clients when they need the help most. Moreover, excluding cover does not help the MFI manage its credit risk in a disaster situation. Alternatively, a self-insuring MFI could solve this problem by buying catastrophe cover with an insurance company, so the MFI covers idiosyncratic risks in-house while outsourcing co-variant risks to an insurer.

A further argument against going solo is that it may be illegal to offer insurance without a licence. Regulators generally do not bother with small schemes. Some organizations manage to disguise their schemes by calling it a member benefit instead of insurance. Insurance regulators may be willing to look the other way, or may not even realize that the scheme exists. However, once it achieves significant scale, it is bound to attract attention. In addition, regulated MFIs are probably not allowed to keep insurance liabilities on their balance sheets, so for them (or MFIs planning to transform), self-insurance may not be an option.

Some MFIs self-insure because they do not want to share the insurance profits with another organization. Similarly, if going solo means lower overhead costs, the coverage could be cheaper for the clients. Consequently, some MFIs contend that they can provide greater customer value without involving an insurer.

Another aspect of customer value is the service standard for claims payments. For MFIs that have tried working with insurers and given up, problems with claims — including delays and rejections — are probably the number one reason for the divorce. If the MFI self-insures, it can pay claims quickly and impose less onerous documentation requirements on the beneficiaries. For example, when the MFI Spandana was collaborating with the Life Insurance Corporation of India, claims often took two to three months or more to be paid. After it moved the scheme in-house, it was able to settle 73 percent of claims within seven days (Roth *et al.*, 2005).

In sum, self insurance might even be preferable to the partner-agent approach if the following set of challenging conditions are met: (1) the MFI is large enough to pool risks (at least 10,000 members) and those risks are reasonably homogeneous; (2) the product is kept simple; (3) the MFI obtains catastrophe coverage from an insurance company; (4) the MFI accesses appropriate technical assistance to help with product design, pricing, data management and performance monitoring; and (5) regulators will allow it.

The fourth option is for an MFI, or an association of MFIs, to create their own insurance company. In many countries, credit unions and cooperatives have satisfied their insurance needs through insurers owned by the association and its members. The typical approach has been for the credit unions to create a brokerage company that facilitates access to insurance for the credit unions and members alike. Over time, the brokerage builds up sufficient expertise in underwriting, settling claims and managing data, and amasses sufficient funds to form a credit union-owned insurance company. Similar experiences have emerged in microfinance, for example, CARD had set up a mutual benefit association (MBA) to manage its insurance services, and in Peru, MiBanco has created its own insurance company, Protecta, under the mainstream regulations although the insurer targets the low-income market.

Compared to the partner-agent approach, an MFI-owned insurance company allows the MFI greater influence on product design and service standards. Furthermore, it enables any profits to be redistributed to the policyholders. However, the management of the insurance company should be kept at an arm's length from the MFI so as not to jeopardize the soundness of its insurance decisions. In particular, careful consideration should be given to the investment strategy, since it is unwise to mix the credit and insurance risks by investing a significant proportion of premiums in the MFI's loan portfolio.

The transformation of an informal scheme into an insurance company is not without its challenges. In some jurisdictions, there may be significant start-up and reporting requirements that do not justify the effort. For years, SEWA has had its sights set on creating an insurance company. However, it has not been able to raise the minimum capital requirement, and the Indian insurance regulators are not interested in making an exception for microinsurance.

5 Supply and Demand Challenges

If one takes a wider view, where microfinance is just one delivery channel to distribute insurance to the poor, then it might be possible to reach many more people since there is a natural limit to the outreach of microfinance. To do so, however, there is a need to overcome a series of challenges that occur on both the supply side (insurers and delivery channels) and on the demand side (prospective poor policyholders).

5.1 *Supply challenges*

From the supply side, it is necessary to consider why mainstream approaches do not reach the poor. Although insurance companies are beginning to notice the vast under-served market of low-income households, they must overcome numerous obstacles if they are to offer quality insurance products to low-income people.

As with microfinance, one of the primary stumbling blocks is the transaction costs associated with managing large volumes of small policies. In serving the poor, insurers incur significant expenses in marketing to a clientele that may be unfamiliar with insurance, collecting premiums from persons who may not have bank accounts, and assessing and paying out small claims. As a percentage of the premiums, these costs are relatively higher for smaller policies, so there is very little to share with delivery channels and sales agents, and therefore limited incentive to sell. Plus, the system of brokers, agents and direct sales used by commercial insurers is generally appropriate for corporate customers and high-value individual customers, but does not reach the poor.

Similarly, the products generally available from insurers are not designed to meet the specific characteristics of the low-income market, particularly the irregular cash flows of households with breadwinners in the informal economy. Premium collection is a challenge since the poor may not have money when premiums are due, and they may lack a cost-effective means of paying premiums. Other key product design challenges include inappropriate insured amounts, complex exclusions and indecipherable legal policy language, all of which are inappropriate or irrelevant for the low-income market. Plus, while it is generally assumed that low-income men and women are more vulnerable to risks than the not-so-poor, insurers do not have data to accurately interpret the vulnerabilities of the poor. Without relevant data, actuaries build in significant margins into the pricing in case the claims experience is higher than expected, which can also price the product out of the low-income market.

Furthermore, insurers do not have the right mechanisms to control certain insurance risks, such as adverse selection[4] and fraud, among the low-income market. For example, the claims documentation requirements and the verification techniques that are used to ensure that someone with a US$ 100,000 life policy is not defrauding the insurer are inappropriate for a US$ 500 policy.

There is also an important cultural barrier. The people who work for insurance companies are usually unfamiliar with the needs and concerns of the poor. They assume that the poor cannot afford insurance. Plus, the culture and incentives in insurance companies reward and encourage salespersons to focus on larger policies, more profitable clients and discourage staff from the ridiculous idea of selling insurance to the poor.

[4]Also called anti-selection, the tendency of persons who present a poorer-than-average risk to apply for, or continue, insurance. If not controlled by underwriting, it results in higher-than-expected loss levels.

5.2 *Demand challenges*

On the demand side, a major challenge in extending insurance to the poor is educating the market and overcoming its bias against insurance. Many poor persons are sceptical about paying premiums for an intangible product with future benefits that may never be claimed. If the insured event does not occur, they often expect to get their money back, not appreciating the risk-pooling and solidarity aspect of insurance. Consequently, many schemes have low-retention rates as poor policyholders feel that they have wasted their limited resources.

In the low-income market, there is often an inherent distrust of insurance. For example, a study by Giné and Yang (2008) with maize farmers in Malawi revealed that they were even less likely to adopt more expensive but higher yielding varieties of groundnuts if insurance was part of the loan contract (20 percent take up rate) than if the loan did not have insurance (33 percent), even though there was no additional cost for the coverage. Those who did take the insurance were less poor and better educated. This evidence suggests a bias by the poor against insurance as a risk management tool.

But there are important social and cultural factors at play on the demand side besides income and education. In Southern Africa, for example, there is a high demand for funeral insurance. A proper burial has important cultural implications (see Box 24.3), and funerals can cost up to 15 times monthly income (Roth, 2002). Most households manage such costs through a reliance on family and friends, various burial society memberships, and sometimes several formal insurance policies, which threatens their current cashflow management because of the over-expenditure on premiums and society contributions.

Box 24.3: Why are funerals so expensive?

Five broad explanations were given for the large expenditure. The first reason, and a reason common to all respondents, was a belief that the dead (or at least some of them) become spirit ancestors. These spirit ancestors are believed to exert a powerful influence over the fate of the living. All respondents believed that it was necessary to have an expensive funeral to show proper respect for the ancestors. Some respondents stressed the importance of meeting close relatives after the funeral in which the household was reconstructed. These respondents felt that the elaborateness of the funeral helped impart importance to the meeting. Thirdly, as one respondent put it "we are poor in life, let's not be poor in death". The respondent believed that by holding an elaborate funeral, she demonstrated the dignity of her household. Fourthly, conspicuous consumption was clearly evident. Most respondents felt that mourners were aware of the costs of coffins and would gossip if the coffin was an inexpensive one. Finally, funerals seem to be a rotating social event. If one were to ask middle-aged township dwellers what they did over the weekend, it is quite probable that the response is likely to be that they attended a funeral. Funerals are opportunities to put on one's "Sunday best" and meet friends from distant places that one has not seen for a long time.

Source: Roth (2002).

In sum, the demand for many microinsurance products needs to be cultivated and encouraged, but for some products in some cultural contexts, like funeral insurance in South Africa, there is significant demand. The challenge is to stimulate similar demand for other insurance products, to design them so that the poor can afford to purchase them, and to distribute them through channels that are convenient for, and trusted by, the target market.

6 Emerging Innovations[5]

To overcome the range of supply and demand challenges, microinsurance providers have been keen to experiment, both on product design and distribution.

6.1 *Product innovations*

Microinsurance can cover a variety of different risks, including illnesses, accidental injuries, and death and property loss — any risk that is insurable

[5]Many of the innovations discussed in this section are being developed or tested by grantees of the ILO's Microinsurance Innovation Facility. For more details about these organizations, their products or the Facility, see www.ilo.org/microinsurance.

as long as the product is affordable and accessible for low-income households. One way of categorizing microinsurance is into productive and protective functions:

- **Productive:** Some microinsurance products are designed to support investments in productive activities. For example, agriculture insurance enables farmers to access loans for agricultural inputs, since without the protection banks would be more cautious about lending. Similarly, insurance for livestock or microenterprises can help the working poor to protect their income-generating assets.
- **Protective:** Although all insurance is essentially protective, this refers specifically to personal or family protection, including life and health insurance, as well as cover for personal property.

Perhaps the most significant innovation regarding productive microinsurance is the emergence of index coverage, for example for rainfall. Historically, multi-peril crop insurance has been fraught with adverse selection, moral hazard and fraud problems, not to mention the high costs associated with claims adjustment (see, for example, Roth and McCord, 2008; GlobalAgRisk, 2006). To overcome these issues, index insurance has emerged as a possible alternative since the claim is based on an objective and verifiable indicator — e.g., the lack or excess of rain in a specific period of time — which is not subject to the influence of individual farmers. Index insurance pilots have been launched in many countries, including Malawi, Ethiopia and India, although there have been key teething pains. In particular, the lack of weather data makes it difficult to design and price the product, and the weather stations need to be close to the farmers so that their losses closely correlate with the index, and the farmers accept the results.

Livestock insurance is also challenged by moral hazard and fraud problems. The claims experience of IFFCO–Tokio in India has been five deaths per hundred, whereas the actual mortality rate should be closer to three per hundred. This suggests that 40 percent of its claims may be fraudulent. Typical controls in livestock insurance include the involvement of a veterinarian to verify the health of the animal and to tag the ear for identification purposes. If the animal dies, the ear is cut and submitted to the insurer as part of the claims process. Judging from IFFCO–Tokio's experience, there are a fair number of Indian cattle with missing ears, and the vets are often complicit in the duplicity. To overcome this problem, the insurer is experimenting with Radio Frequency Identification Devices (RFIDs) that are injected into the animals instead of tagging. The technology also has other potential uses by the farmers and cooperatives, for example, to monitor vaccinations, milk production and other relevant data. If the insurer can show the cooperatives the advantages of the RFIDs, then the coops may want all of their animals to have them, regardless of whether they are insured, which could then make the insurance even more affordable.

For protective insurance, in most countries, the greatest demand is for health coverage, which is also among the most difficult to provide. Health insurance is a particularly tricky issue since ideally all persons would have access to universal coverage. However, the ideal does not exist in developing countries (nor many developed countries), and where government health schemes are available, they are often unable to reach workers in the informal economy. Microinsurance therefore can play two roles vis-à-vis social protection for health: a) helping to extend benefits to un-served segments of the population; and b) providing supplementary benefits for those who want additional coverage, or access to different health care providers, than are provided by the government.

Health insurance, micro or not, is plagued by problems of adverse selection, moral hazard, fraud and overusage, not just by the policyholders but by health care providers, pharmacies and system administrators as well. For the products to be affordable to low-income households in the absence of subsidies, benefits must be rationed (Radermacher *et al.*, 2006).

Therefore the primary innovation has been to restrict coverage to low frequency, high cost events such as hospitalization. For example, the Yeshasvini Cooperative Farmers Health Scheme in India started in 2003 and covers 1.45 million members. Yeshasvini's benefit package includes more than 1,600 surgeries and a maximum annual benefit of INR. 200,000 (US$ 4,545) for a per capita premium of INR 120 (US$ 2.70). Members can claim the benefits in one of 150 hospitals aligned with the insurance scheme (Radermacher *et al.*, 2005).

In situations where the health care costs are not high compared to the opportunity costs of being away from one's work or business if hospitalized, then microinsurance benefits may be limited to per diem payments and transportation costs. This type of "hospital cash" coverage has the advantage of not involving the health care provider, and therefore avoiding fraud or overcharging that might come from the provider.

However, by focusing attention on inpatient care, these schemes may encourage policyholders to delay treatment, therefore potentially increasing the costs of health care. So how can inpatient and outpatient coverage be viable for the poor? Certainly subsidies would be the right answer, but where they are not available, some organizations are experimenting with health savings accounts for outpatient and preventative care, combined with insurance for hospitalization. It is still early days to see if it is possible to strike an effective balance between the two, but the concept is promising.

Another challenge with health microinsurance is the lack of health care facilities, especially in rural areas. Experiments with tele-medicine and call centres for initial triage and basic treatment may make some headway, especially if the technology can also be used for insurance enrolment and premium payments, but in many developing countries, additional investments in health care facilities and personnel are really what is required.

Health products that respond appropriately to potential policyholder needs will help to generate demand among the poor. The key strategy to achieving this goal is to involve policyholders (or prospective clients) in the process of making hard choices between benefits and price. The poor cannot afford comprehensive coverage, so which benefits are they most willing to pay for, and how much are they willing to pay? Tools that can enable clients to see the trade-offs and voice their preferences — such as CHAT (Choosing Health Plans All Together) developed by the Microinsurance Academy — will go a long way towards achieving appropriate product design.

Life insurance is fairly straightforward, and by far the most prevalent form of microinsurance (Roth *et al.*, 2006). Often linked to loans, life insurance can easily be made available to low-income borrowers, although they might not know that they are covered. In fact, the low claims rates one finds among compulsory coverage is certainly a cause for concern. Besides educating the clients about the coverage, microinsurers need to find ways of de-linking life insurance from credit so that poor people do not have to be in debt to have insurance.

As mentioned above, many microinsurance products have a challenge with retention, especially among policyholders who did not claim in the previous period. Consequently, insurance that includes a savings component, building value over time, is a particularly attractive proposition because policyholders have something to show for their premium payments even if they do not have a claim. However, typical endowment or whole life policies generally do not provide good value as a high percentage of premiums are used to cover commissions and the insurer's costs, and they are particularly poor value if the policy lapses because the policyholder had difficulty keeping up with the premium payments (see Box 24.2 again). To overcome this problem, Max New York Life in India has designed a non-lapsable savings and insurance product that allows poor customers to pay premiums when they have small amounts of surplus funds. Similarly, L'Union des Assurances du Burkina Vie (UAB) plans to roll out its existing savings plus life insurance product, customized for informal sector entrepreneurs, with the use of smart card technology to overcome the high costs and fraud associated with frequent premium collections in the market place.

Another line of personal protection that generally receives the least amount of attention is personal property insurance, such as housing. In demand research, the poor do not express significant interest in property insurance unless they live in environments that are prone to fire or theft. Still, it is a line of business that requires some significant innovation, particularly if the housing covered is informal, without clear ownership, or combines business and residential spaces. Hollard Insurance in South Africa is experimenting with this type of product, using inexpensive claims assessors to help identify the property that is insured without incurring the costs of visiting the house. Similarly with claims, Hollard is using inexpensive claims assessors who take pictures with mobile phones and send them back to the head office for the actual loss adjustment process.

The poor are vulnerable to numerous risks and often do not make a philosophical distinction between coverage for personal or income-generating activities. Consequently, some organizations provide composite products which enable them to cost-effectively provide more comprehensive coverage that responds to the diverse needs of the target group. Indeed, if the microinsurer is going to go to the effort of reaching low-income people, there is justification to include additional benefits and provide as comprehensive a product as possible, as long as the product remains simple and includes coverage that the poor really want. In India, the insurance unit of the Self-Employed Women's Association, VimoSEWA, provides an integrated product of life, hospitalization, accident and asset coverage for poor workers and their families, with covers underwritten by two insurance companies, one life and one non-life.

Similarly in Kenya, the Cooperative Insurance Company (CIC) offers its Bima Ya Jamii (Insurance for the Family) to low-income, rural households through SACCOs and other cooperatives. This composite product provides inpatient health, accidental death and disability, funeral and loss of income benefits, with the health component underwritten by the government's National Hospital Insurance Fund (NHIF). Consequently, CIC is enabling NHIF to extend government benefits to workers in the informal economy and in rural areas that the government scheme would otherwise not be able to reach.

6.2 *Innovative institutional models and delivery channels*

Insurance can be delivered to low-income households through a variety of channels and institutional models. Microinsurance risk carriers include small community-based schemes, mutuals and cooperatives, as well as joint stock companies and government-owned insurers.

To reach poor households, risk carriers often partner with delivery channels that already have financial transactions with the low-income market. The most common arrangement is with microfinance institutions that provide credit and perhaps savings services, and therefore microinsurance essentially becomes *bancassurance.*

However, delivery channels can also include cooperatives, community organizations, small business associations, trade unions and even retail companies that cater to the low-income market. La Positiva in Peru is collaborating with water associations to extend coverage to rural areas; in Colombia, Mapfre distributes insurance through the utility company; while Colseguros sells small insurance policies off the shelves in Carrefour; Hollard is selling insurance through cell phone airtime salespersons; National Insurance Corporation in Uganda is delivering insurance through schools; Pioneer in the Philippines is selling insurance to school and church groups; in India, ICICI Prudential collaborates with tea plantations; Max New York Life distributes its non-lapsable product through mom-and-pop retailers, and Basix sells products for different insurers through Common Service Centres (CSC), e-governance outlets where rural citizens can access numerous government and private services. Basically any organization that engages in financial transactions and has the trust of the low-income market could potentially be an effective distribution channel for microinsurance.

From the experiences thus far, all of the institutional models that provide insurance to the poor have advantages and disadvantages. Consequently, it is important to encourage collaborations between different types of institutions, or even hybrid models to leverage the advantages and minimize the disadvantages. For example, in Mexico, Seguros Argos is an insurance company that is naturally going to encounter some resistance from the low-income households that may not trust insurers. So Argos is helping rural associations, such as cooperatives and women's groups, to form mutual insurers, a special regulatory option under Mexican insurance law. Argos provides capacity-building support to the mutuals, underwrites the products, and the mutuals and the insurer share the risks and returns.

7 Conclusions

The volume and diversity of innovation taking place in microinsurance is certainly encouraging. Some of these ideas are bound to work, resulting in better insurance coverage for more low-income households. But there is a need to push the frontier further, to minimize operating costs and stimulate greater demand.

There is no room for fat in a microinsurance budget. The industry must continue to improve products to provide better value to the poor. When cost structures and commissions devour the majority of the premium income, it is impossible to return sufficient benefits to low-income households. Greater attention must be given to reducing operating costs and enhancing efficiencies so that a higher proportion of premiums can benefit the poor. In fact, some insurance companies that have ventured into microinsurance have done so in part to learn how to become more efficient, so that the lessons from microinsurance will benefit their conventional lines of business.

Great expectations are placed on the potential of technology to enhance efficiency. Technology can improve the microinsurance business because of the information-processing nature of the sector. Besides upgrading their management information systems, microinsurers must take advantage of ways of improving efficiency, including reducing errors and fraud, through the use of smartcards, mobile phones, point of sale devises, biometrics, the Internet and wireless communications, among others (Gerelle and Berende, 2008).

Technology will not be a magic wand that solves all of the product problems. Indeed many organizations are struggling with customer retention challenges, which cannot be significantly aided by technology solutions. Instead, some organizations are experimenting with the provision of additional services so that their policyholders see that they are receiving some benefits from the insurance even if they do not have a claim. Some additional services can have the additional advantage of reducing claims and therefore may even pay for themselves. For example, Microcare in Uganda provides subsidized mosquito nets and cans for water purification to its policyholders, providing tangible evidence of their coverage while reducing claims. Similarly, VimoSEWA is testing the effect of health education on the most common preventable diseases, which could enhance retention while lowering claims costs.

The demand for microinsurance requires some coaxing. There is certainly a need to develop techniques to convey the usefulness of insurance to an illiterate or uneducated market. For example, some organizations rely on unconventional communication methods, such as street theatre and soap opera-style videos. Efforts to sell insurance to the poor will be more effective if they are preceded by a financial education campaign that helps poor persons understand how insurance works, what it can and cannot accomplish, and how it complements other financial services. Communication and education efforts have to move beyond sales to create an insurance culture. In many developed countries, it took generations before people commonly turned to insurance to address their risk-management needs.

Paying a claim — delivering on a promise — is arguably the most important opportunity to reinforce the value of insurance. Yet insurers are notorious for being quick to take the policyholder's money and slow to pay it out. Microinsurance has to prove otherwise. The best marketing opportunity for an insurer, the best way to change the opinion of a lukewarm and sceptical market, the best way to demonstrate its trustworthiness, is to pay claims. Ironically, to increase the acceptance of insurance as an effective risk-management tool among the poor, insurers should actually encourage claims! At least, insurers should take great pains to avoid rejecting claims, for example, by keeping the product simple, making sure policyholders are crystal clear about what is and is not covered, and requiring only the most basic claims documentation which is easy to access.

References

Churchill, C (ed.) (2006). *Protecting the Poor: A Microinsurance Compendium.* Geneva: ILO.

Churchill, C and J Roth (2006). Microinsurance: Opportunities and Pitfalls for Microfinance Institutions. In *Protecting the Poor: A Microinsurance Compendium*, C Churchill (ed.). Geneva: ILO.

Fonteneau, B and B Galland, (2006). The Community-based Model: Mutual Health Organizations in Africa. In *Protecting the Poor: A Microinsurance Compendium*, C Churchill (ed.). Geneva: ILO.

Genesis Analytics (2005). A regulatory review of formal and informal funeral insurance markets in South Africa. Johannesburg: FinMark Trust.

Gerelle, E and M Berende (2008). Technology for Microinsurance: Scoping Study. Geneva: ILO's Microinsurance Innovation Facility. www.ilo.org/microinsurance.

Giné, X and D Yang (2008). Insurance, credit, and technology adoption: Field experimental evidence from Malawi. *Journal of Development Economics*, 89(1), 1–11.

GlobalAgRisk (2006). Index Insurance for Weather Risk in Lower-income Countries. Washington DC: USAID.

IAIS (2007). Issues in the Regulation and Supervision of Microinsurance. International Association of Insurance Supervisors and CGAP Working Group on Microinsurance, www.iaisweb.org.

Manje, L (2005). Madison Insurance, Zambia. CGAP Working Group on Microinsurance, Good and Bad Practices Case Study 10, Geneva: ILO's Social Finance Programme.

McCord, MJ and C Churchill (2005). Delta Life, Bangladesh. CGAP Working Group on Microinsurance, Good and Bad Practices Case Study 7, Geneva: ILO Social Finance Programme.

McCord, MJ, F Botero and JS McCord (2005). AIG Uganda: A member of the American international group of companies. CGAP Working Group on Microinsurance, Good and Bad Practices Case Study 9, Geneva: ILO's Social Finance Programme.

McCord, MJ and G Buczkowski (2004). CARD MBA, The Philippines. CGAP Working Group on Microinsurance, Good and Bad Practices Case Study 4, Geneva: ILO's Social Finance Programme.

Morrah, D (1955). *A History of Industrial Life Assurance.* Routledge.

Prahalad, CK (2005). *Fortune at the Bottom of the Pyramid: Eradicating Poverty Through Profits.* Upper Saddle River, NJ: Wharton School Publishing.

Radermacher, R, I Dror and G Noble (2006). Challenges and strategies to extend health insurance to the poor. In *Protecting the Poor: A Microinsurance Compendium,* C Churchill (ed.). Geneva: ILO.

Radermacher, R, N Wig, O Putton–Rademaker, V Müller and D Dror (2005). Yeshasvini Trust. CGAP Working Group on Microinsurance Good and Bad Practices Case Study 20, Geneva: ILO's Social Finance Programme.

Roth, J and MJ McCord (2008). Agricultural Microinsurance: Global Practices and Prospects. Appleton, WI: The Microinsurance Centre.

Roth, J, MJ McCord and D Liber (2006). The Landscape of Microinsurance in the World's 100 Poorest Countries. Appleton, WI: The Microinsurance Centre.

Roth, J and V Athreye (2005). TATA–AIG Life Insurance Company Ltd. India. CGAP Working Group on Microinsurance: Good and Bad Practices Case Study 14, Geneva: ILO's Social Finance Programme.

Roth, J (2002). Informal Micro-finance Schemes: The Case of Funeral Insurance in South Africa. ILO Social Finance Working Paper 22, Geneva: ILO's Social Finance Programme.

Reaching the People Whom Microfinance Cannot Reach: Learning from BRAC's "Targeting the Ultra Poor" Programme

David Hulme

Brooks World Poverty Institute,
University of Manchester

Karen Moore

(Formerly) Chronic Poverty Research Centre
and University of Manchester;
(currently) Education for All Global Monitoring Report,
UNESCO

Kazi Faisal Bin Seraj

BRAC International Programme

> "The poorest are not like the poor but 'a little bit poorer'. They may benefit from policies to help the poor, but need other policies as well".
>
> Sen and Hulme (2006:8)

1 Introduction[1]

BRAC (formerly known as the Bangladesh Rural Advancement Committee) has been providing poor people in Bangladesh with microfinancial services since the 1970s. Its programme has expanded massively and by 2008, it had more than 8 million members in the village organizations (VOs) through which it makes loans and around 6.4 million of these were borrowers. Its

[1]Our thanks to Bangladesh's poor people and BRAC's staff for helping us learn from their experiments and experiences. Particular thanks to Fazle Abed, founder-director of BRAC; Imran Matin, Munshi Sulaiman and the entire BRAC–RED team involved in research on CFPR–TUP; and Rabeya Yasmin, CFPR–TUP programme coordinator.

outstanding loans portfolio stood at more than US$ 660 million and its sustainability outmatched most of the industrialised world's big-name banks by a long measure. While there are heated academic debates about exactly how much BRAC's microfinance has improved poor people's lives, millions of Bangladeshi women choose to regularly use BRAC loans and savings services to manage their cash flows and achieve their household goals.

But microfinance is no panacea for the poor, despite the grand pronouncements of Professor Yunus of the Grameen Bank (one of BRAC's competitors). In the 1990s, BRAC became concerned that its microcredit, and other services, were not reaching the poorest people in Bangladesh. As a result, it started experimenting with special programmes that sought to give a "hand up" for the poorest people so that they could "graduate" into using BRAC's microfinancial services. This experiment has now matured and many other microfinance providers are looking at whether they can learn from BRAC's experience.

This paper commences with an examination of the evolution of this programme — designed to reach the poorest people in Bangladesh, to improve their immediate situation and to give them the assets and other skills to move out of poverty and dramatically reduce their vulnerability — BRAC's Challenging the Frontiers of Poverty Reduction/Targeting the Ultra Poor Programme, or TUP. It then reviews what is known about the impact of TUP, and finds evidence that the programme is both reaching significant numbers of Bangladesh's poorest people and improving their economic and social condition, in many cases such that they "graduate" to being able to use mainstream BRAC microfinancial services. The concluding sections draw lessons from the TUP about the types of programme design features and the processes required to develop such ambitious initiatives.

2 The Context of the Targeting the Ultra Poor (TUP) Programme

***Bangladesh*:** Bangladesh has been doing well in recent times (Drèze, 2004) with reasonable rates of economic growth, improving social indicator levels and strengthened resilience to environmental shocks (floods, storm surges and drought). The headcount poverty index dropped from 52 percent in 1983/84 to 40 percent in 2000, although the fall in extreme poverty has been more modest[2] (Hossain, Sen and Rahman, 2000). The UN's Human Poverty

[2]Figures vary from source to source but all indicate a substantial reduction in income/consumption poverty.

Index (HPI), based on income poverty, illiteracy and health deprivation measures, fell from 61 percent in 1981/82 to 41 percent in 2007/8. Despite these improvements, life for many remains characterised by severe deprivation and vulnerability, with around 31 percent of the rural population trapped in chronic poverty and 24 percent of the entire population experiencing extreme income poverty (i.e., with consumption expenditure at less than 60 percent of the government's official poverty line). Between 25 to 30 million Bangladeshis have seen little or no benefit from democracy or the country's significant and consistent economic growth.[3]

Chronically and extremely poor people — the "ultra poor" to use BRAC's terminology — "... face a complex structure of constraints that mainstream development approaches [including the country's social protection policies][4] have found difficult to address" (Hossain and Matin, 2007:381). Ultra poor people have not been able to improve their lives through (i) accessing employment opportunities created by the growth of the formal sector (e.g., garment industry, fisheries, services); (ii) benefiting from the "green revolution" that filtered across the country in the 1980s and 1990s; or (iii) participating in the self-employment and casual employment opportunities of the dynamic informal economy that has been supported by Bangladesh's much-praised microfinance industry (Hulme and Moore, 2007). Market-related opportunities, governmental social policies, and non-governmental organisation (NGO) programmes miss the ultra poor because they lack the material, human, financial and social assets to engage, and/or they live in areas or belong to ethnic/social groups that are bypassed or excluded.

In particular, rural people living in remote areas or difficult environments (e.g., the seasonally eroded *chars* or seasonally flooded *haors*) and disadvantaged women are likely to be ultra poor. The ultra poor are not a distinct group, but a heterogeneous assemblage of different people usually experiencing multiple deprivations. Commonly, they are casual labourers (in agriculture or services), migrants or displaced people, ethnic or indigenous minorities, older people and those with severe disabilities or ill-health.

For analytical purposes, we can recognise both the economically active ultra poor, commonly surviving through their precarious, multiple livelihoods, and the economically inactive or dependent ultra poor (frail old

[3]For more detail on economic, social and poverty indicators in Bangladesh, see Sen and Hulme (2006).

[4]For an inventory, see World Bank (2005).

people, the physically or cognitively impaired, chronically sick or destitute).[5] BRAC's TUP has chosen to focus on the economically active ultra poor. The inactive ultra poor remain dependent on ultra marginal economic activities and support from family, relatives, neighbours, NGOs and community-based organisations and, sometimes, government social policies such as old age pensions.

BRAC: BRAC was established in 1972 to provide humanitarian relief to the tens of millions of Bangladeshis suffering after the war of independence and later environmental disasters. Subsequently it moved on to development work, and has evolved into the world's largest service delivery NGO. As of June 2008, BRAC was working in over 69,000 villages and over 1,000 urban slums, in every district of Bangladesh. It claims to cover 110 million people, almost entirely women, with an annual expenditure of over US$ 485 million. Nearly 1.15 million children were enrolled in a BRAC school, and more than 3.8 million have graduated. The NGO employs over 57,000 full-time staff, over 62,500 community school teachers, and tens of thousands of poultry and community health and nutrition workers and volunteers. There are now international programmes in Afghanistan, Sri Lanka and East and West Africa, as well as in the United Kingdom and United States (BRAC, 2008). In Bangladesh, BRAC's major programmatic foci are the promotion of self-employment (microfinance, and technical support) and human development (non-formal education and health services). BRAC, the NGO, is at the centre of a corporate network including BRAC University, BRAC Bank, BRAC Printers, Aarong (a network of tens of thousands of artisans and cooperative groups, retail shops and marketing specialists), the country's largest cold store company, and several other businesses.

Three key points must be noted:

- BRAC has the capacity to manage operations across Bangladesh that rivals the business sector and often outperforms the government;
- BRAC has substantial experience in programme experimentation and learning; and
- BRAC's economic programmes are heavily loan-driven and envision poor people as microentrepreneurs.

[5]When this division is empirically operationalised then, it is often found that the "economically inactive" are actually heavily involved in low- or no-pay work such as gleaning, caring for children or older people, and begging.

3 The Evolution of the TUP Programme

BRAC launched the TUP programme in January 2002 as an experimental initiative that recognised two key findings from BRAC field experience and research:

- BRAC's highly regarded microfinance programme rarely reached the poorest women, despite conventional wisdom to the contrary.[6] This was partly because of self-exclusion — the poorest women report being very worried about the consequences of not being able to make weekly loan repayments (*kisti*) and so do not join BRAC's village organisations (VOs). It is important to note that while interest rates are substantially lower than those offered by local moneylenders, they are still high enough to exclude those with the lowest and most sporadic cash flow, and those with the least confidence in their business skills. Partly it was due to social exclusion — many VO members do not want to associate with the very poor for both economic and social reasons. And partly it was because BRAC's loan-driven approach to microfinance does not match the needs or preferences of the poorest. BRAC has been aware of this issue since the mid-1980s when it began to experiment with new programmes to reach the poorest (see next section).
- For many years, the World Food Programme (WFP) operated a Vulnerable Group Feeding (VGF) scheme that provided poor women with 31.25 kg of wheat per month for two years. In 1985, BRAC began working with WFP to create a "laddered strategic linkage", the Income Generation for Vulnerable Group Development (IGVGD) programme that would allow food aid recipients to climb out of poverty by graduating to BRAC's microfinance groups and self-employment initiatives. WFP's food aid would be complemented by the savings programmes, social development, income generation training and, eventually, microcredit services provided by BRAC. The IGVGD has received favourable evaluations and continues to operate,[7] but at least 30 percent of IGVGD participants do not progress to microfinance programmes and these are usually from the

[6]This is true for most of the country's microfinance institutions (Zaman, 2005) and is likely to be the situation internationally (Hulme and Mosley, 1996). The growing concern with reaching the poorest is also neither limited to Bangladesh nor the microfinance sector (see Barrientos and Hulme, 2008; Lawson *et al.*, 2009).

[7]In its 2003/04 annual cycle, the IGVGD model took on 44,000 new beneficiaries (Hashemi, 2006: 5).

poorest and most vulnerable households (Webb *et al.*, 2001). In addition, a significant minority of "new" IGVGD participants have taken part in the programme previously but have failed to improve their livelihood security (Matin, 2002).[8]

These two experiences indicated that BRAC's programmes were having problems assisting the poorest. TUP was launched to build on existing knowledge and the organisation's commitment to the very poor. TUP was overseen by BRAC's founder-director, Fazle Abed, and systematically monitored by BRAC's Research and Evaluation Division (RED).[9]

The programme used the concept of a "laddered strategic linkage"; however, its approach was "... more systematic, intensive and comprehensive, covering economic, social and health aspects" (Hossain and Matin, 2007: 382). The idea behind the TUP approach is to enable the ultra poor to develop new and better options for sustainable livelihoods. This requires a combination of approaches — both promotional (e.g., asset grants, skills training) and protective (e.g., stipends, health services) — as well as addressing socio-political constraints at various levels. TUP employs two broad strategies: "pushing down", and "pushing out" (Matin, 2005a):

- "Pushing down": TUP seeks to "push down" the reach of development programs through specific targeting of the ultra poor, using a careful methodology combining participatory approaches with simple survey-based tools. Within geographically selected areas, certain exclusion and inclusion conditions must be met. The selected households are then brought under a special two-year investment programme involving asset transfer, intensive social awareness and enterprise training, and health services.
- "Pushing out": TUP also seeks to "push out" the domain within which existing poverty alleviation programs operate by addressing dimensions of poverty that many conventional approaches do not. This involves a shift away from conventional service delivery modes of development programming to a focus on social-political relations that disempower the poor, especially women, and constrain their livelihoods. Building links and

[8]For detailed discussions of BRAC's learning from the IGVGD, see Matin and Hulme (2003) and Matin (2005).
[9]This "Learning Partnership" is supported by the Canadian International Development Agency (CIDA) via the Aga Khan Foundation-Canada (AKF-C). Working papers can be downloaded from www.bracresearch.org.

support networks with other groups and organisations is key to "pushing out".

It is important to note that the "Targeting the Ultra Poor" programme in fact targets two groups of ultra poor people:

- the "Specially Targeted Ultra Poor" (STUP), who are supported with the complete package (called the "Special Investment Programme"), which includes asset grants; and
- the "BDP (BRAC Development Programme) Ultra Poor", changed to "Other Targeted Ultra Poor" (OTUP) in the second phase of CFPR–TUP, who do not receive asset transfers, only skills development, more intensive staff support, and health support.

The STUP are organised into microfinance groups after 18–24 months, while those OTUP who are not already BDP microfinance members join groups immediately. In this paper, we are only concerned with the STUP, who receive asset transfers as a key part of the programme.

By late 2003, after experimentation and redesign, the programme had nine main components (Table 25.1) that were carefully sequenced and linked. It carefully targets the poorest[10] (Table 25.2), provides them with a monthly stipend and health services to provide basic security, provides social development and income generation training,[11] transfers assets to participants (e.g., poultry and cages, milch cows and stables), and provides technical support, inputs and advice. BRAC's experience had shown them that the ultra poor need such extra support as they rarely have the resources — assets, money and time — or knowledge and skills required in order to give them the space to both provide for themselves and their families as well as act entrepreneurially.

The initial TUP plans envisioned that TUP members would graduate to joining BRAC VOs, but a number of problems in the field led to a redesign (Hossain and Matin, 2007:383). In particular,

- TUP members became heavily dependent on BRAC staff for assistance and advice, rather than on VOs, effectively treating BRAC as a patron;

[10]The 2002 baseline survey found that of the ultra poor, 54 percent were totally landless, 50 percent ate two meals or less a day, 70 percent were dependent on irregular, casual labour and 95 percent lived without sanitation facilities (BRAC–RED 2004).

[11]The social development component focuses on functional literacy, but BRAC fieldworkers believe its main contribution is to build the confidence of TUP participants.

Table 25.1: TUP programme components and their purpose.

Component	Purpose
Integrated targeting methodologies.	Identify and target ultra poor.
Weekly stipends.	Consumption smoothing, reduce vulnerability, and reduce opportunity costs of asset operations.
Social development (functional literacy).	Confidence building, and raise knowledge and awareness of rights.
Health support.	Reduce morbidity and vulnerability.
Income generation training and regular refreshers.	Ensure good return from asset transferred.
Income generating asset transfer (e.g., poultry, livestock, horticulture).	Significantly increase the household's asset base for income generation.
Enterprise input and support.	Ensure good returns from the asset transferred.
Technical follow-up and support of enterprise.	Ensure good returns from the asset transferred.
Establishment of village assistance committee and mobilisation of local elites for support.	Create a supportive and enabling environment.

Source: Adapted from Hossain and Matin (2007: 383).

Table 25.2: TUP programme targeting indicators for STUP.[12]

Exclusion conditions (all selected households must satisfy all conditions.)	Not borrowing from a microcredit-providing NGO. Not receiving benefits from government programmes. At least one adult woman physically able to put in labour towards the asset transferred.
Inclusion conditions (all selected households must satisfy at least three conditions.)	Total land owned less than 10 decimals. Adult women in the household selling labour. (In Phase II, changed to "Household dependent upon female domestic work or begging".) Main male income earner is disabled or unable to work. (In Phase II, changed to "No male adult active members in the household".) School-aged children selling labour. No productive assets.

Source: Matin, 2005a.

[12]The targeting parameters for OTUP are slightly wider, particularly in terms of the maximum land ownership requirement of 30 decimals.

- many VO members resented TUP beneficiaries, as they had not received "gifts" but had to repay BRAC for assets and services; and
- the assets transferred to poor women experienced relatively high levels of theft or damage, sometimes due to such jealousy.

This led to the design of Village Assistance Committees[13] (VACs) that are to enlist the energies of local elites to support TUP participants, and the poorest more generally, in their village. The VACs have seven voluntary members — a BRAC fieldworker, a TUP participant, two VO members, and three members of the village elite.[14] The contribution of these committees to TUP performance, and more broadly to local level social and political change, are complex and difficult to assess. However, Hossain and Matin (2007: 390) judge them to be a "modest success" and a challenge to those who automatically assume that the involvement of local elites in development programmes will always be negative.[15]

4 The Present Status of the TUP

The TUP aims "... to build a more sustainable livelihood for the extremely poor, by providing a solid economic, social, and humanitarian foundation, which would enable this group to overcome extreme poverty ..." (Hossain and Matin, 2007:382). In its first phase, TUP operated in 15 of Bangladesh's 64 districts, reaching 100,000 STUP participants, with a geographical focus on the north of the country and especially areas experiencing seasonal hunger (*monga*) on an annual basis. In its second phase, the coverage is even broader. Starting from January 2007, CFPR II now has 200,000 STUP participants in 23 districts, and plans to expand to 17 more districts (as of November, 2008).[16] Because not all districts, and not all villages within

[13]In Bangladesh, these are known as *Gram Shahayak Committees* (GSCs). For a detailed description and analysis of these, see Hossain and Matin (2007).

[14]These are described as "...respected individuals in the local community [chosen] through a process of guided selection" (Hossain and Matin, 2007: 384–5). Often they have strong religious beliefs and reputations for being publicly-minded.

[15]We must confess to being rather cynical about this innovation when we heard of it in 2003 — "is this an act of desperation?" we wondered. However, fieldwork in 2004 revealed its potential — in effect, empowering some local elites to pursue a social mission that, for religious and other reasons, they valued.

[16]In fact, the proposal for the second phase of CFPR–TUP proposes greater differentiation for effective targeting and learning purposes, with a total of 800,000 beneficiaries:

- STUP Model I (full package): 200,000.

them, are reached, the total number of participants is a fraction of those who would be eligible nation-wide.

Some CFPR–TUP beneficiaries have had previous experience with microfinance, but found that they were too poor and vulnerable to use it. For this reason, and because other community members had excluded them from village organisations due to their poverty, many more have never been involved in microfinance at all. It is difficult to estimate the number of CFPR–TUP beneficiaries who have previously been involved in a microfinance programme, or who are inactive members, not least because there are so many microfinance programmes in operation in most Bangladeshi villages, but also because many people would not want to disclose their microfinance status, thinking it may harm their chances of joining CFPR–TUP. Evidence focussing on OTUP suggests that between 30 percent and 40 percent of participants were either participants in (~15–20 percent) or dropouts from (~10–25 percent) microfinance (Das and Ahmed, 2009). However, as OTUP members are specifically selected from among existing "weak" members of microfinance and dropouts, as well as other disadvantaged ultra poor women, it is likely that these figures are higher than those for STUP members.

The entire CFPR–TUP programme is funded by a donor consortium[17] which has contributed about US$ 65 million over the period 2002 to 2006 and committed a further US$ 155 million over the next five years. The total budget for the second phase is US$ 223 million. By 2006, the high initial costs of the "Special Investment Programme" were reduced by over 40 percent

- STUP Model II (full package, but with a lower average asset value, a lower daily subsistence allowance, and a lower staff:client ratio): 100,000.
- OTUP Model I (as STUP Model II, but with soft loans rather than asset transfers, and a lower staff:client ratio: 100,000.
- OTUP Model II (as OTUP Model I, but with a regular loan, no subsistence allowance, and a lower staff:client ratio): 400,000.

Anecdotal evidence from BRAC staff at the time of finalising this paper suggests that these goals for numbers of beneficiaries have been met. The OTUP Models are an experiment to determine the extent to which, for some of the rural Bangladeshi ultra poor, it is sufficient to provide loans with subsidised or regular microfinance interest rates rather than assets if some level of additional training support is also available.

[17]Made up of the United Kingdom's Department for International Development (DFID), the Canadian International Development Agency (CIDA), the European Commission, Novib (Oxfam Netherlands), and the World Food Programme (WFP), and recently joined by AusAid. During the first phase, BRAC itself contributed over US$ 4 million, and plans to contribute US$ 5 million over the 2007–11 period.

to US$ 268 per recipient (BRAC, 2006c) as the programme scaled-up and found ways of reducing costs.

TUP already receives a flow of international visitors, usually funded by aid agencies, who are keen to learn from it. Interestingly, the TUP has already begun to influence other programmes in Bangladesh, with DFID's Chars Livelihood Programme redesigning itself from a broad-based capacity building initiative to an asset transfer programme.

5 The Achievements of the TUP

The large majority of data collection and assessment of TUP performance is undertaken by BRAC–RED. This includes the maintenance of a panel dataset that tracks key indicators for a sample of selected ultra poor households (SUPs) who have participated in the TUP since 2002, and non-selected ultra poor households (NSUPs) who have not participated in the TUP. At the pre-programme baseline study stage, both SUPs and NSUPs were objectively ranked in the "poorest" group in the villages. However, NSUPs were not selected for the programme because their household scores were close to the cut-off line between the "poorest" and "poor" categories – i.e., NSUPs had higher welfare scores than SUPs. In addition to the panel dataset of objective indicators, BRAC–RED also conducts regular subjective assessments of SUP and NSUP poverty and welfare indicators and change.

Rabbani, Prakash and Sulaiman's (2006) analysis of the TUP panel dataset provides evidence of TUP recipients (i.e., SUPs) improving their livelihoods more rapidly that the NSUP control group.

***Asset accumulation*:** Over the period 2002 to 2005, TUP participants had a greater rate of asset accumulation than non-participants in all asset domains — financial assets (savings and credit), physical assets (a range of livestock, household and productive assets), natural assets (access to cultivable and homestead land), social assets (social and legal awareness), and human capital (household demographic structure, education, health and sanitation). Figure 25.1 provides a diagrammatic comparison of SUP and NSUP asset pentagon dynamics. Although the human capital picture is relatively complex and overall improvements are very small for both groups, as many of these changes can take longer to emerge, nutritional improvements are already apparent. Figures 25.2 and 25.3 illustrate the dynamics for human capital in terms of food and calorie intake; SUP households also have improved the quality of their food intake to a greater extent than

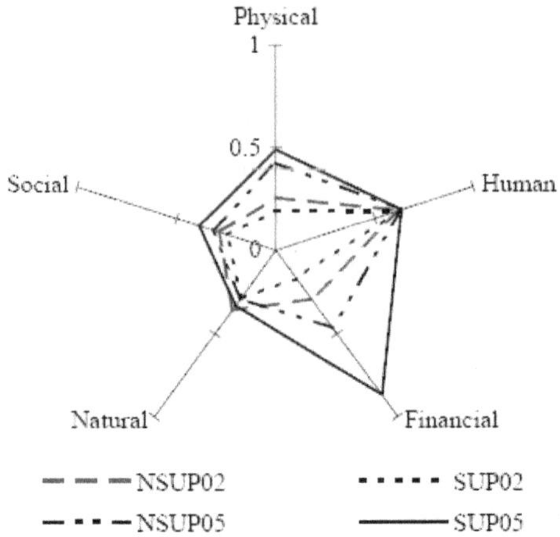

Source: Rabbani, Prakash and Sulaiman (2006: 16).

Figure 25.1: Asset pentagon dynamics — comparing SUPs and NSUPs over time.

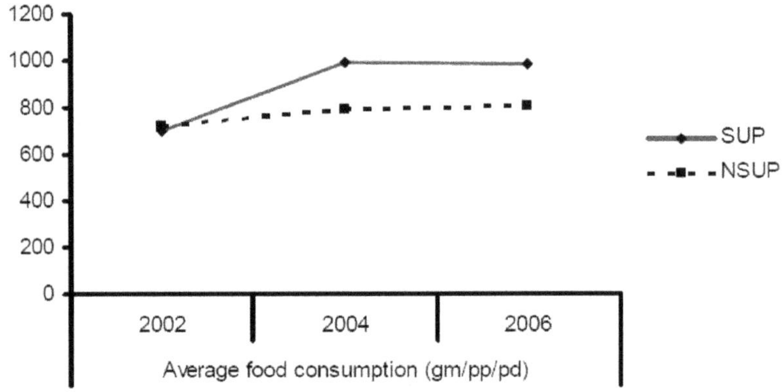

Source: Matin, 2006.

Figure 25.2: Change in food consumption — comparing SUPs and NSUPs over time.

NSUPs (see, also, Haseen, 2007). It is also notable that a greater proportion of SUP households have been able to improve their situation in terms of combinations of multiple types of assets than NSUP households, suggesting that improvements may be more sustainable over time.

***Vulnerability*:** In 2002, SUP households' self-reported higher levels of food insecurity (occasional and chronic deficit) than NSUP households. In 2005, both groups reported improvements in food security. But the food security of NSUPs had improved only a little while SUP food security had significantly ameliorated, with food deficit reports reducing from 98 percent to 70 percent

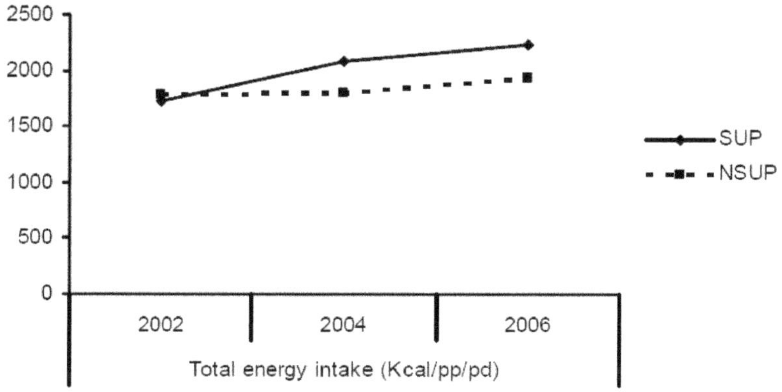

Source: Matin, 2006.

Figure 25.3: Change in energy intake — comparing SUPs and NSUPs over time.

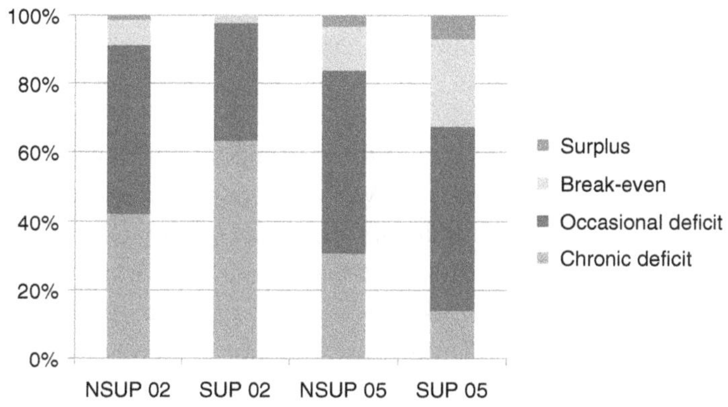

Source: Rabbani, Prakash and Sulaiman (2006: 24).

Figure 25.4: Self perception of food security — comparing SUPs and NSUPs in terms of changes in availability of food in one year.

(Figure 25.4). The TUP was associated with a reversal of SUP and NSUP status — SUPs now reported greater food security than NSUPs. Further, while both SUPs and NSUPs are equally vulnerable to various crises — with the newly asseted SUPs perhaps more vulnerable to livestock death — subjective assessments suggest that the SUPs can expect to recover from shocks sooner than the NSUPs.

Subjective poverty dynamics: Community-level assessments of changes in household poverty status reported SUPs as having experienced significant improvements in their welfare. This contrasted with NSUPs who

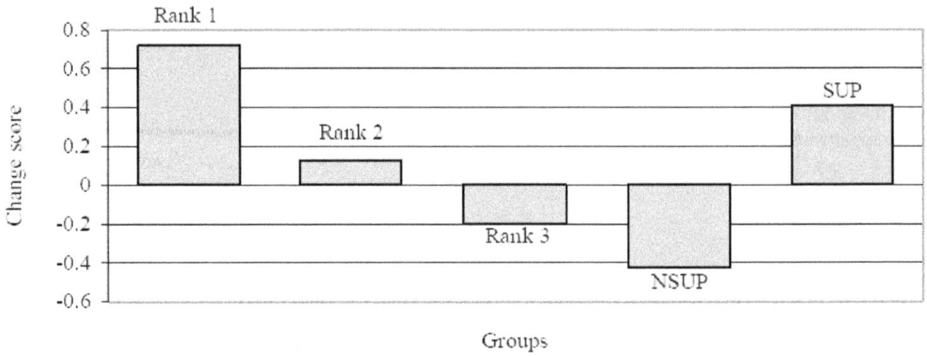

Source: Sulaiman and Matin (2006: 8).

Figure 25.5: Average change score over period 2002–2005 of households in different wealth rankings as assessed by community meetings.

were reported to have experienced a downturn in their circumstances (Figure 25.5).[18]

***Graduation to mainstream BRAC microfinance*:** By 2004, the first TUP participants had completed the two-year special investment phase and were organised into separate village organisations. They were being offered a full range of BRAC's development services, including microfinance. Based on previous experience, BRAC takes a flexible, experimental and member-driven approach to credit provision, and it generally seems to be working. About 70 percent of these women had taken and regularly repaid a first loan, and about 98 percent of them were found to have cash savings. BRAC continues to strive to assist those 30 percent who were unable or unwilling to take a small loan, or had trouble repaying. Graduation can be something of a double-edged sword. On the one hand, for those who quickly become eligible for and are able to repay a loan, both their self-confidence and status in the community may rise, helping to create a virtuous cycle. On the other, a too quick graduation may lead to default, with the opposite effect. Thus the ultra poor — with limited social resources to draw on — are necessarily very cautious about taking a loan, and it can be seen as good money management that more save than are willing to take a loan.

[18]It should be noted that while the objective assessment of assets (Figure 25.1) and subjective assessment of poverty dynamics (Figure 25.5) are consistent for SUPs, with both showing an improvement, there is inconsistency for NSUPs.

During the first phase, however, the programme realized that the above mentioned microfinance-based indicator takes a very narrow view on graduation of the ultra poor, as it overlooks other factors such as improvements in social and human assets. This realization led to a revision of the graduation criteria. A set of indicators based on programme experience and research findings were put forward for CFPR II evaluation. The objective indicators, most of which can be regularly collected by the programme, are listed in Table 25.3. It is expected that after two years, 90 percent of the participants will satisfy at least five of the indicators.

Importantly, participants' own reflections on graduation are also taken into account, alongside the more objective indicators noted above. For example, during focus group discussions to identify graduation indicators, it was often noted by TUP participants that they now are more confident in their behaviour, or they are now "smarter" than they used to be. Also, most participants mentioned that they now have a voice in local village meetings. These changes can also be considered as important indicators of

Table 25.3: Indicators of graduation.

No.	Indicator	Objective
1	The household has at least three income sources.	Livelihood diversification to foster sustainable growth.
2	The household can afford at least two square meals a day.	To foster hunger reduction and eradication.
3	All school-aged children of the household are going to school.	To foster intergenerational well-being and escape from poverty.
4	The household has access to a sanitary latrine.	To foster better health and hygiene.
5	The household drinks safe water.	To avoid water-borne diseases.
6	Home gardening • If the household has space in homestead, it has at least four fruit trees. • The household grows appropriate vegetables on the house roof. • The household grows chillies and lemon.	To ensure a sustainable nutritional supply, especially micronutrients, throughout the year.
7	Eligible couples have adopted family planning.	To ensure that increased income translates into increased per capita consumption.

Source: Adapted from BRAC CFPR-TUP programme documentation.

graduation from ultra-poverty, but collecting and analysing such indicators is less straightforward, and requires more nuanced research expertise.

***Independent verification*:** An independent review of the TUP in 2004 concluded that the programme had resulted in extremely poor women improving their livelihoods, had been relatively cost-effective, and had been more effective than comparable initiatives targeting the poorest (Posgate *et al.*, 2004 in Hossain and Matin, 2007). In addition, our personal fieldwork and interviews with TUP participants provide support for these generally positive assessments and has not yielded any data to challenge such conclusions.

6 Concerns about TUP

While TUP performance has generally been regarded as high, there are concerns about some aspects of the programme. In particular, the lack of impact on child development, the financial viability of the TUP VOs and the sustainability of the Village Assistance Committees are issues that BRAC is examining at present.

***Child development*:** There has been particular concern about the lack of progress for children in TUP households. Nutrition status among the under-fives and primary school enrolment rates have changed little or not at all. This may be because of time lags associated with changes in such indicators, or patterns of intra-household resource allocation. These findings have led to deep debates in BRAC, concerned about interruption of intergenerational poverty, about modifications to the TUP approach.

***Financial viability of TUP microfinance*:** As discussed above, in most areas TUP graduates have not been able to join standard BRAC VOs but have been organised into TUP VOs. These TUP VOs are generally smaller than standard VOs (recent fieldwork indicated memberships of only around 20 women per group against BRAC's target of 35 women per standard microfinance group). In addition, the TUP graduates prefer to take smaller loans — according to field staff in Rangpur, only about two-thirds of the average loan size of standard borrowers. With smaller groups and smaller average loan sizes, but fixed costs for servicing each group, this means that the TUP VOs may require cross-subsidizing or, alternatively, women in TUP VOs will need to be charged higher loan rates to make up for the smaller loan portfolios of their groups. Neither of these options is attractive.

***Sustainability of Village Assistance Committees (VACs)*:** The innovation of establishing VACs has worked better than many people believed was possible but these organizations only receive administrative and motivational support from BRAC for their first two years of operation. While there is no evidence that they "collapse" soon after two years, there are doubts from field staff about whether VACs will keep running indefinitely and also about whether they will maintain their present levels of activity. As a result, VACs are being monitored and there is the possibility of BRAC providing visits from social development staff and/or "refresher" events to maintain and/or raise the commitment of VAC leaders.

7 Learning from the TUP

The most obvious lesson from the TUP is that the very poor can be reached and supported through carefully designed and targeted programmes. Moreover, with appropriate support, the poorest households can develop the capacity to engage with the economy in ways that permit them to sustain their improved welfare position without further subsidies or transfers. The poorest are not a residual group to be ignored or put on permanent social assistance until the growth process "trickles down" to them: with a strategic "hand up", they can engage in the economy and share in the benefits of growth.

However, one needs to be cautious about drawing wide-ranging conclusions from the TUP, as it is a highly context-specific initiative. It is very dependent on the capacity of BRAC to experiment, innovate, learn and develop service delivery systems that can operate across the country. This demands high level analytical and management skills, alongside the ability to "win" substantial financial resources to run the programme. In particular, BRAC's technical capacity to advise on poultry, dairy and horticultural activities should not be taken for granted. The broader environment in Bangladesh has also been supportive — steady economic growth, improving physical infrastructure (e.g., the Jamuna Bridge, easing access to the north for people and goods, as well as local roads and electrification), high population density, and socio-political stability.[19]

[19]Many might challenge this latter point, but compared to many other countries with high levels of ultra-poverty — Afghanistan, Nepal, Democratic Republic of Congo, Sierra Leone, Somalia — Bangladesh's recent political problems and violence are enviable.

For analytical purposes, we can divide the potential lessons into two main types — the design features that are TUP's "context" and the "process" features that describe how the TUP evolved. In practice, successful programmes need to integrate both of these elements — an effective process has to generate content that can develop into a standardised package for delivery at scale.[20]

8 Design Features

(1) ***Laddered strategic linkages*:** At the heart of TUP is the idea that the poorest people cannot benefit from a single "magic bullet" (microcredit, bed nets, women's groups). Rather they need a carefully sequenced set of supports that provides livelihood security; confidence building and business/technical skill development; an asset transfer; and support for and institutionalisation of their improved position within the local economy and society. BRAC's experience suggests that programmes for the poorest need to be relatively complex, involving several different elements of social protection, income generation and local organisation building, which are carefully related to each other.[21]

(2) ***Asset transfer*:** One of the highly innovative features of the programme is that it involves the transfer of what is, in local economic terms, a substantial asset grant to each poor household. The relatively low level of initial assets of the poorest, allied to their ability to accumulate assets because of the frequency of adverse shocks that they experience, requires that they be given a "hand up". In effect, this means a "one-off"[22] gift of a micro-business so that they have both the material (e.g., poultry, cages, veterinary support) and non-material (technical skills and social standing) resources to engage with the economy. Organisations learning from TUP will need the ability to identify

[20]See Korten (1980) who recognised BRAC's capacity for innovation and service delivery at an early stage, and Johnston and Clark (1985) who eloquently explain the need for effective programme development to both "think through" and "act out" its components.

[21]See Krishna, Poghosyan and Das (2010) for a description of how the CFPR-TUP places explicit attention on what the authors call the five "Cs" of community-level development: confidence, cohesion, capacity, connections and cash.

[22]One of the design features of the TUP that is not yet clearly specified is how it deals with women whose TUP projects fail (e.g., their milch cow dies, their horticultural products cannot be marketed). Our own fieldwork indicates that such women are usually given a "second chance", but this seems to be at the discretion of field level staff rather than as a formal programme component.

and support such micro-businesses and the financial capacity to meet the costs involved.

(3) ***Financial costs and impact assessment*:** The unit costs of the Special Investment Programme — running at US$ 280 in 2005, 84 percent of which is asset transfer (Matin, 2005b) — are relatively high. For an aid donor or charity, that works out at 3,571 households assisted per US$ 1 million. To encourage donors and sponsors to meet such costs, organisations maintaining such programmes will need to be able to demonstrate that there are substantial benefits occurring and that, to a high degree, these are sustained after the initial investments. Similar programmes will only be feasible (i) in contexts where there is substantial donor commitment, and (ii) for organisations that have the capacity, or can contract the capacity, for high quality programme monitoring and evaluation that can be externally validated.

(4) ***Local institutional development*:** Perhaps the most challenging aspect of TUP, and the one that demands the most "acting out" in the field, is the institutionalisation at the local level. This is not about the service delivery agency but about the "new" village level organisations and the modified social norms and practices that are needed to ensure that short term programme gains continue into the future. BRAC's early design — the TUP participants will join existing BRAC village organisations (VOs) after two years, access services through these and have an enhanced social position because of VO membership — proved to be problematic. Their revised approach — developing the TUP VOs that can work directly with BRAC, and establishing local committees that enlist the support of the local elite to assist TUP participants economically and socially — shows substantial promise, but success is by no means guaranteed. It is highly original in challenging the entrenched idea that, in Bangladesh, local elites are always exploitative and must be bypassed and/or disempowered (Hossain and Matin, 2007). In effect, the TUP assumes that local elites are segmented and that while same may mirror the well-substantiated, rapacious stereotype of academic and popular literatures, others are more humane and socially-minded. Further, this second group can be developed by promoting the pre-existing social norms of cooperation and the better-off helping the less well-off (Uphoff, 1992).

This local institutional development component is perhaps the most context-specific and least transferable of the TUP design. It is highly dependent on the programme "process".

9 The TUP Process

(1) ***A process approach*:** The processes out of which the TUP has evolved is akin to the idealised notions of adoptive management and learning process approaches that have been written up in the development management and rural development literatures over many years (Bond and Hulme, 1999; Johnston and Clark, 1982; Korten, 1980; Rondinelli, 1993). BRAC diagnosed a problem with its existing programmes, systematically reviewed its own experience and that of others, and moved into a carefully monitored experiment with a new programme. This experiment was "learned from" by encouraging field staff to voice concerns and propose ideas about what might be done, through both process documentation and baseline studies by RED and the guiding hand of Fazle Abed. Uncomfortable "errors" were embraced — such as the admission that existing VOs were not keen to admit the ultra poor to their organisations — and the programme modified. From a strong knowledge base, the TUP was expanded (from 5,000 to 50,000 new households per annum) and cost-reduction measures made to permit increased staff caseloads and reduced financial costs. The programme continues to experiment with the frank admission at head office that the VACS are by no means a proven social technology.
The main difference between the TUP experience and the idealised process approaches relates to the balance between technical analysis and beneficiary participation. The TUP has been driven by the technical analyses of BRAC's directors and field managers. BRAC listens carefully to TUP participants and documents their experiences; indeed, they are encouraged to use their "voice". But this is not a participatory approach as envisioned by Robert Chambers (1997) and others. It is much more akin to the private sector model of having a "customer orientation". BRAC also listens carefully to field staff and elicits their ideas about how the TUP could be improved. However, data analysis is a task for the head office, and decision-making for a small handful of staff.

(2) ***A service delivery approach*:** The TUP is managed by a standardised business-type approach, with clear organisational structures, lines of responsibility, financial controls, and input, output and outcome monitoring. As knowledge is gained, it is routinised in the programme through documentation, training and supervision. BRAC operates a tight administrative "machine" which seeks to reward performance (especially through promotions within expanding programmes), reduce

costs and encourage poorly performing staff to move on. This is not a worker cooperative, rather it is an effective business with a strong social mission.

(3) ***Partnerships***: "Partnerships" is such an all-embracing term that it can become meaningless. However, BRAC has built on a set of strategic partnerships that allow it both to pursue its goals and acquire support where it lacks capacity. Its partnership with donors, and especially with DFID and CIDA through its AKF-C partnership, provides the finance it needs but permits the flexibility and learning for TUP that is essential. A whole set of other donors, who would want a blueprint and would engage in micro-management, are strategically avoided by BRAC — they have the money but lack other qualities. BRAC has also built links with independent researchers, and with those at both local and overseas universities, to help strengthen its learning and verify its evaluations. However, the most adventurous partnership of TUP is its engagement with local elites. Conceptually, this is an extraordinary step; hopefully as the experiment unfolds, the news will continue to be positive.

10 Conclusion

BRAC's TUP programme started because its standard microfinance programmes rarely reached the poorest people in Bangladesh. Its recent performance demonstrates that the poorest people can be reached and, with a carefully sequenced set of programme components, supported to a position in which they have a high probability of sustaining their enhanced levels of welfare and assets. Many TUP women are able to "graduate" into microfinance programmes.

Many potential lessons might be drawn from TUP including both its design features and the process from which it has evolved and continues to evolve. On the "content" sides its major innovations are (i) the transfer of a substantial set of assets to very poor households — in effect, a redistribution of assets from the taxpayers of aid donor countries to the ultra poor in Bangladesh, and (ii) the recruitment of village level elites to local committees to support TUP participants and other very poor people. The latter is a radical idea in terms of the social engineering of a more pro-poorest context in rural Bangladesh.

In terms of "process", the TUP, like most of BRAC's other programmes, has benefited from many of the elements idealised in "learning process approaches" and "learning organisations". It has built on experience, mounted carefully monitored experiments, standardised and scaled up its delivery systems, and gradually reduced the programme's unit costs. While this process has listened carefully to TUP participants and field staff, it is far from the "participatory" approach lauded by some development theorists. The experiment is closely controlled by BRAC's upper echelons.

In the future, it will be important for other agencies — NGOs, donors, governments, pro-poor elites — to learn from the TUP experience, but two notes of caution must be sounded. First, the TUP is a very complex programme and only organisations, or partnerships of organisations, with high levels of analytical and management capacity are likely to be able to mount such initiatives at scale. Secondly, the TUP cannot reach all types of ultra poor people. The economically "inactive" ultra poor (frail older people, AIDS orphans, people in chronic ill-heath) and socially excluded or adversely incorporated people (bonded labourers, refugees, indigenous people in remote areas) will need more conventional forms of social protection — old age provisions, humanitarian aid, "free" health services, and child grants.

References

Barrientos, A and D Hulme (eds.) (2008). *Social Protection for the Poor and Poorest.* London: Palgrave Macmillan.

Bond, R and D Hulme (1999). Process approaches to development: Theory and Sri Lankan practice. *World Development*, 27(8), 1339–1358.

BRAC (2009). BRAC At A Glance. Available at: http://www.brac.net/downloads.

BRAC (2006b). CFPR II Project Proposal. Unpublished.

BRAC (2006c). CFPR Progress Report. Unpublished.

BRAC–RED (2004). Towards a profile of the ultra poor in Bangladesh: Findings from CFPR/TUP baseline survey. Dhaka: BRAC-Research and Evaluation Division/Aga Khan Foundation Canada. Available at: www.bracresearch.org/highlights/cfpr_tup_baseline_survey.pdf.

Chambers, R (1997). *Whose Reality Counts? Putting the Last First.* London: ITDG.

CPRC (2004). *The Chronic Poverty Report 2004–05.* Manchester: Chronic Poverty Research Centre. Available at: www.chronicpoverty.org/resources/cprc_report_2004-2005_contents.html.

Das, NC and S Ahmed (2009). Profile of the other targeted ultra poor. In *Pathways Out of Extreme Poverty: Findings from Round I Survey of CFPR Phase II.* Dhaka: BRAC Research and Evaluation. Available at: http://www.bracresearch.org/publications/CFPRII_Baseline.pdf.

Drèze, J (2004). Bangladesh shows the way. *The Hindu*, September 17.

Haseen, F (2007). Change in food and energy consumption among the ultra poor: Is the poverty reduction programme making a difference? *Asia Pacific Journal of Clinical Nutrition*, 16(1), 58–64.

Haseen, F (2006). Change in Food and Nutrient Consumption Among the Ultra Poor: Is the CFPR/TUP Programme Making a Difference? CFPR/TUP Working Paper 11. Dhaka: BRAC Research and Evaluation Division/Aga Khan Foundation Canada. Available at: www.bracresearch.org/workingpapers/changeinfnconsumption.pdf.

Hashemi, S (2006). Graduating the Poorest into Microfinance: Linking Safety Nets and Financial Services. CGAP Focus Note 34. Available at: www.cgap.org/portal/binary/com.epicentric.contentmanagement.servlet.ContentDeliveryServlet/Documents/FocusNote_34.pdf.

Hossain, M and I Matin (2007). Engaging elite support for the poorest? BRAC's targeted ultra poor programme for rural women in Bangladesh. *Development in Practice*, 17(3), 380–392.

Hossain, M, B Sen and HZ Rahman (2000). Growth and distribution of rural income in Bangladesh: Analysis based on panel survey data. *Economic and Political Weekly*, 35(52/53), 4630–37.

Hulme, D and K Moore (2007). Why has microfinance been a policy success? Bangladesh (and beyond). In *Statecraft in the South: Public Policy Success in Developing Countries*, A Bebbington and W McCourt (eds.). London: Palgrave MacMillan.

Hulme, D and P Mosely (1996). *Finance Against Poverty*, Vol. I and II. London/New York: Routledge.

Johnston, BF and WC Clark (1982). *Redesigning Rural Development: A Strategic Perspective.* Baltimore: Johns Hopkins University Press.

Korten, D (1980). Community organisation and rural development: A learning process approach. *Public Administration Review*, 40, 480–511.

Krishna, A, M Poghosyan and N Das (2010). How Much Can Asset Transfers help the Poorest? The Five Cs of Community-Level Development and BRAC's Ultra-Poor Programme. BWPI Working Paper 130. Manchester: Brooks World Poverty Institute. Available at: http://www.bwpi.manchester.ac.uk/resources/Working-Papers/bwpi-wp-13010.pdf.

Lawson, D, D Hulme, I Matin and K Moore (eds.) (2009). *What Works for the Poorest? Knowledge, Targeting, Policies and Practices.* Colchester: Practical Action.

Matin, I (2002). Targeted Development Programmes for the Extreme Poor: Experiences from BRAC Experiments. CPRC Working Paper 20. Manchester: IDPM/Chronic Poverty Research Centre. Available at: www.chronicpoverty.org/resources/cp20.htm.

Matin, I (2005a). Addressing vulnerabilities of the poorest: A micro perspective from BRAC. Paper presented at the *Annual Bank Conference in Development Economics.* Amsterdam. Available at: www.BRACresearch.org/publications/addressing_vulnerability_of_the_poorest.pdf.

Matin, I (2005b). Delivering the "fashionable" [inclusive microfinance] with an "unfashionable" [poverty] focus: Experiences of Brac. Presentation at *ADB Microfinance Week*, Manila. Available at: http://www.adb.org/Documents/Events/2005/ADB-microfinance-week/presentation-day1-03-matin.pdf.

Matin, I (2006). Towards a bolder microfinance vision for attacking poverty: The BRAC case. Presentation at DFID, London.

Matin, I and D Hulme (2003). Programs for the poorest: Learning from the IGVGD program in Bangladesh. *World Development*, 31(3), 647–665.

Posgate, D, P Craviolatti, N Hossain, P Osinski, T Parker and P Sultana (2004). Review of the BRAC/CFPR specially targeted ultra poor (STUP) programme: Mission report. Dhaka: BRAC Donor Liaison Office Unpublished report.

Rabbani, M, VA Prakash and M Sulaiman (2006). Impact assessment of CFPR/TUP: A descriptive analysis based on 2002–2005 panel data. CFPR/TUP Working Paper 12. Dhaka: BRAC Research and Evaluation Division/Aga Khan Foundation Canada. Available at: http://www.bracresearch.org/workingpapers/impact_tup.pdf.

Rondinelli, D (1993). *Development Projects as Policy Experiments: An Adaptive Approach to Development Administration.* London: Routledge.

Sen, B and D Hulme (eds.) (2006). *Chronic Poverty in Bangladesh: Tales of Ascent, Descent, Marginality and Persistence.* Dhaka/Manchester: Bangladesh Institute of Development Studies/Chronic Poverty Research Centre. Available at: http://www.chronicpoverty.org/resources/cp43.htm.

Sulaiman, M and I Matin (2006). Understand Poverty Dynamics: Examining the Impact of CFPR/TUP from Community Perspective. CFPR/TUP Working Paper 14. Dhaka: BRAC Research and Evaluation Division/Aga Khan Foundation Canada. Available at: http://www.bracresearch.org/workingpapers/TUP%20Working%20Paper_14.pdf.

Uphoff, N (1992). *Learning from Gal Oya.* Ithaca: Cornell University Press.

Webb, P, J Coates, R Houser, Z Hassan and M Zobaid (2001). Expectations of Success and Constraints to Participation Among IGVGD Women. Report to WFP Bangladesh. Mimeograph Dhaka: School of Nutrition Science and Policy/DATA Bangladesh.

World Bank (2005). *Social safety nets in Bangladesh: An assessment.* Report 33411–BD. Washington DC: Human Development Unit, South Asia Region, World Bank. Available at: http://siteresources.worldbank.org/BANGLADESHEXTN/Resources/FINAL-printversion_PAPER_9.pdf.

Zaman, H (2005). The Economics and Governance of NGOs in Bangladesh. Consultation draft. Washington DC: Human Development Unit, South Asia Region, World Bank. Available at: http://www.lcgbangladesh.org/NGOs/reports/NGO_Report_clientversion.pdf.

PART VI

Meeting Unmet Demand: Gender and Education

The Gender of Finance and Lessons for Microfinance

Isabelle Guérin

Research Unit "Development and Societies"
(Institute of Research for Development/Paris I-La Sorbonne).
Project Leader "Microfinance and Employment:
Do Processes Matter?" (RUME), and CERMi

Introduction

Women are a prime target of microfinance both for reasons of efficiency and equality (Armendariz and Morduch, 2005; Mayoux, 2001). But do women have specific financial needs and if so, what are they? We will not seek here to offer miracle answers or standardized solutions, as gender norms and practices, including financial practices, vary greatly between and within different cultures, regions and temporal periods. "Women" as a category is indeed so diverse that there is little to be gained by looking to list women-specific services. Rather than presenting a list of "best practices" or success stories, our goal here is to highlight the gender of finance, which we argue is much more complicated than a matter of access and credit rationing (Johnson, 2004). Improved understanding of the gender of finance, we shall argue, would help the microfinance industry to design services which are better suited to the distinct demands of women (Vonderlack and Schreiner, 2002).

The first part of this article explains what we mean by "gender of finance". The second part gives examples of women-led financial circuits. Analysis, or at the very least awareness, of preexisting female financial practices helps us better understand how both women and men make use of microfinance services, or fail to. The analysis of the workings and rationale behind Roscas will highlight both the scope and limitations of female financial solidarity, offering useful lessons for group lending. In the same vein, in-kind women financial circuits will be shown to demonstrate undeniable comparative advantages that are instructive for the design of more demand-responsive microfinance services.

1 The Gender of Finance

What do we mean by "gender of finance"? The gender of finance is shaped both by supply and demand (Johnson, 2004). Firstly, financial providers adopt specific rules which are more or less gender-biased and adapted to constraints faced by men and women, based on procedure, type of collaterals and criteria used for the construction of creditworthiness. Secondly, in most societies men and women have specific financial rights and financial obligations, such that the gender of rights and obligations largely shapes the gender of financial needs.

The gender of finance most commonly translates into restrictions for women. Such restrictions may be formal and explicitly defined, for instance, when married women are not legally permitted to open a bank account without the consent of their husband. In many cases however, these restrictions are implicitly defined and take indirect routes.

As far as formal finance is concerned, for instance, although gender differences are still poorly documented, the unity of analysis systematically being that of the household (Fletschner, 2009), globally it is highly probable that women face greater difficulties in accessing formal banking (Armendariz and Morduch, 2005; Fletschner, 2009; Mayoux, 1999; World Bank, 2001; World Bank, 2007). These inequalities result from accumulated access restrictions to various institutions. These include lower rates of job market participation, confinement to traditional sectors with relatively lower profits, fewer growth opportunities and harsher competition, limited access and control of assets and especially land, restricted spatial mobility not only due to domestic obligations but also social restrictions, and finally lower education levels, which limit women's ability to deal with bureaucratic procedures. For all of these reasons, women are barely able to utilise the formal enforcement mechanisms usually required to be eligible for formal banking.

Exclusion from formal finance does not mean poor financial intermediation (Collins *et al.*, 2009): many women are financially hyperactive and already juggle a large number of mainly informal financial instruments. This might be for business purposes: in different parts of the world, women are highly engaged in small market-based activities which require regular cash flows. But this might be also, and probably more commonly, for domestic purposes (Collins *et al.*, 2009; Vonderlack and Schreiner, 2002).

Whatever the context, even if household budget management systems feature fascinating variations between and within societies, we can point to a recurring constraint: women are called to secure the balance of the family budget, with access not only to limited but sometimes poorly controlled resources. They have little control over their own income in the cases where they have one (especially in highly patriarchal societies) and even less control over their spouse' income. Whatever the allowance they receive, and these amounts are often uncertain and arbitrary, spouses and children should be fed and dressed, school fees paid on time, and social and religious ceremonies should be decently organised. Women are also expected to respond to unforeseen demands such as health problems, visitors or unexpected ceremonies. In the event of shortfall, the women are readily accused of bad money management or of being spendthrifts. Assuming this role of manager without complaint or "begging" is often taken as a question of personal honour.

Numerous monographs from the past decades conducted all over the world have revealed that the paradox of having to make ends meet without having control over income is still a strong feature of everyday life for many women (Bruce and Dwyer, 1988). Many women are forced into financial dependency whilst remaining fully responsible for the management of the household budget, and have no choice but to deploy multiple strategies of saving, borrowing, lending and creating their own financial circuits.

Whilst there is even less empirical data on informal than formal finance, it seems that the gender of finance translates into differences as much in the *nature* of financial practices as their restriction. Informal finance usually incorporates three types of collaterals, namely physical goods, personal relationships and employment (interlinked transactions) (Adams, 1994). All such collaterals usually exhibit gender differences, such that men and women own and control different goods, belong to different social networks and occupy different jobs. As a result, they have different patterns of building creditworthiness, approach different financial providers and are engaged in different financial circuits.

Thus, the nature of employment that men and women are engaged in can significantly impact upon their access and need for credit and saving services. Whilst employers are often a source of credit through interlinked contracts, not only the frequency but also regularity of income flows condition cashflow management systems and hence financial needs and reimbursement capacities. Small and regular income flows from petty business or casual wage labour, which as activities are more commonly a female preserve, do not bring about the same demand for credit, nor the same capacity for saving lump sum flows, as those for instance coming from agriculture or certain forms of migration, which are more often male-led activities. The segmentation of financial circuits along gender lines is also a deliberate choice on the part of women and/or men, allowing to maintain discretion and to facilitate the development of activities that escape spouses' control (Shipton, 1995).

The restricted access to finance of women is, above all, a matter of unequal power. There is no doubt that throughout history women's oppression has been largely based on their exclusion from the market sphere, including the financial sphere (Lemire *et al.*, 2001). But the gender of finance is also a matter of *identity*. Historical and anthropological studies teach us that in many societies, both past and present, women control the circulation of certain goods and crops (Weiner, 1976). These goods usually have a specific social and cultural value, but most also act as paleo-money in as much as they are saved, borrowed, lent and exchanged (Rivallain, 1994; Servet, 1984).

Gender differences with respect to access also reflect differences in socialisation processes (Johnson, 2004). Conversely, financial bonds shape social bonds, in as much as the choice to use a particular financial service or to favour a particular financial provider serves as a means to maintain, cement, reinforce, and preserve social bonds, or, on the contrary, to weaken or circumvent them (Servet, 2006; Shipton, 1995, 2007). These bonds include gender bonds (Guérin, 2003, 2006; Villarreal, 2004), as we shall now see.

2 Women-Led Financial Circuits

In order to cope with penury and inadequacy of income and expenses, women engage in permanent juggling between various sources of income, savings, loans or reciprocal gifts. Moreover, this juggling often takes the form of underground and secret practices in order to escape or at least limit household control. Roscas and saving in kind are two examples of the gender of financial circuits: both reveal power and resource asymmetries, but also differences in identity and socialisation processes.

2.1 *Roscas: The scopes and limits of female "solidarity" and lessons for group lending*

Roscas are a primary example of women-led financial circuits. According to the available literature, it seems that women more frequently use them, at least in some regions such as Kenya (Anderson and Baland, 2002; Johnson, 2004), South Africa (Burman and Lembete, 1996), Senegal (Dromain, 1995; Guérin, 2006), Ghana, Tanzania, Nigeria (Steel *et al.*, 1997), China (Pairault, 2003), Indonesia (Hospes, 1996) and urban India (Smets, 2006).

Why is this the case? As argued by Ardener (1964) and again by Swaan and Van Der Linden (2006), the gendered aspect of Roscas probably deserves more attention, but the question has already been raised, and various explanations have been put forward (Ardener and Burman, 1996; Anderson and Baland, 2002; Johnson, 2004).

Firstly, given the difficulty of access both to formal credit and saving for the reasons above, Roscas are sometimes the only means to obtain a lump sum, by way of credit for the first beneficiaries of the group, and forced saving for the others. It is now well recognized that the poor have a fascinating capacity to create their own constraints, especially as regards financial management (Collins *et al.*, 2009). In various contexts, it has been observed that Roscas are a way to enforce compulsory savings and act as a self-discipline mechanism (Aliber, 2001; Bortei–Doku and Aryeetey, 1996; Collins *et al.*, 2009; Guérin, 2006; Gugerty, 2007; Handa and Kirton, 1999; Kane, 2001; Rutherford, 2001; Southwold–Llewellyn, 2001). As Senegalese women say, Roscas avoid "eating money" and "obliges us to work".

Secrecy and discretion are a further factor. Various monographs put forward as primary factors the ability to save secretly and to escape or at least limit kinship control (Ardener and Burman, 1996). In rural southern India, Mayoux and Anand (1996) and Sethi (1996) consider female Roscas as a very important secret way of saving and keeping money. In Cameroon, Niger–Thomas (1996) consider the secrecy of Roscas as fundamental. In Kenya analysis carried out by Anderson and Baland, (2002) makes the same conclusion that Roscas provide "a forced savings mechanism that the woman can impose on her household and thus help to increase the household's saving rate" (Anderson and Baland, 2002). Papanek and Schwede (1988) make similar observations for Indonesia: *Arisan* (Roscas) are regarded largely as a means to separately control income use when their husband has the tendency to control and misuse it.

The preference for illiquidity and discretion, given the ceaseless demands of the entourage, often also holds true for men (Shipton, 1995). However, given the paradox discussed above, where women bear heavy responsibility for budget management control without controlling income, it can be assumed that secret savings are frequently more prevalent among women.

The degree of discretion and the means for its organisation might vary depending according to context. This is obviously easier when Roscas are made up only of women, and this is probably more often the case in contexts where women are allowed to manage their budgets independently and to access public spaces, for instance, in Kenya (Johnson, 2004); Senegal (Guérin, 2006); Cameroon (Niger–Thomas, 1996); South Africa (Verhoef, 2001). In such contexts women-led Roscas are well-known and considered as legitimate. Men are usually aware that their wife is a Roscas member and do not impede them, making saving in Roscas a socially sanctioned excuse. In some cases, men also help their wives to pay their regular contributions (Niger–Thomas, 1996). However, they do not know when she will get her turn, and women elaborate various ruses to hide this information (Niger–Thomas, 1996). Sometimes women refuse heavy male involvement, a matter of controlling not only funds but also *information* (see Nelson, 1996, in Kenya; Burman and Lembete, 1996, in South Africa).

In other contexts, perhaps owing to greater restrictions on female mobility and practices of pooling income, it seems that the Roscas themselves are held clandestinely. Transactions are conducted secretly and discreetly, with women taking advantage of the daytime absence of men. Given the extent of male control, and in some cases the control of the extended family, underground practices are the only solution (Guérin, 2008).

It would be misleading, however, to consider Roscas only in terms of female resistance to male domination. Some men actively support their wife's Rosca membership, for instance, by way of regular participation to the financial contribution. Some Roscas are family-based with membership being held on behalf of the household. This has been observed for Korean Roscas in Los Angeles (Light and Deng, 1996) whilst, in South India, we have observed similar practices.

The variety of incentive mechanisms might also explain the gendered aspect of the Rosca. In many contexts, it seems that women are more sensitive to social pressure and to feelings of shame, as Susan Johnson (2004) has examined in the context of Kenya. Here men clearly state that they have a more "individualistic" culture and that they do not like the rigidity of the Rosca rules, and that informal sanctions do not work. In contrast, women are more responsive to social and moral pressure. They have always had the habit of assisting one other with agricultural labour, the organization of ceremonies and daily survival. Not only are they accustomed to group working, but group membership is integral to their status and identity (Johnson, 2004).

This observation is probably valid in other contexts. In some places, it seems that the first Rosca were run by women and stemmed from the transformation of preexisting collective practices which included mutual assistance to meet social obligations such as marriages and funerals as examined by Ardener in Sudan (1964), the circulation and management of surplus of cereals as in South India as described by Sethi (1996), and rotating labour, such as in Senegal, as examined by Dromain (1995).

In Senegal, it is usually said that *tontines* (Roscas) are a "women's matter" (Dromain, 1995; Guérin, 2006). Women are often engaged in several *tontines* for economic reasons with the amount and frequency of payments being adapted to the diversity of their needs, but also for social reasons of prestige and reputation. Membership of a particular *tontine* is a matter of demonstrating one's membership to a particular social network.

The social, human and emotional benefits of Roscas for women have been closely documented (Ardener and Burman, 1996), showing that Roscas provide social status (Burman and Lembete, 1996; Niger–Thomas, 1996), and are a source of solidarity and mutual support (Buijis, 1998), especially in urban settings with weakened social and kinship networks, or for one-parent families (Burman and Lembete, 1996; Verhoef, 2001). They also act as a platform for learning new skills such as the ability to participate in collective discussions and to manage collective affairs (Niger–Thomas, 1996). The Rosca may be used to strengthen family networks but also to separate off from them and to create new networks, or indeed for both of these, if women combine several memberships (Ardener and Burman, 1996).

The social dimensions of Roscas are not, however, automatic, and this includes women-led Roscas. This is the case for instance in some parts of China (Pairault, 2003), India (Mayoux and Anand, 1996; Guérin, 2008) and Sri-Lanka (Southwold Llewellyn, 2004) where Roscas are sometimes limited to financial operations. No meetings are held and the organiser handles all of the transactions, whilst members do not necessarily know one other. Motivations in these cases are purely financial.

Roscas are a fascinating and remarkable financial system in terms of their dynamism, variety of forms, mechanisms and distribution, relative stability and adaptability to both moments of financial insecurity and increased industrialisation and monetarization (Ardener and Burman, 1996; Bouman 1977, 1994; de Swaan and van der Linden, 2006). The gendered aspect of Roscas is also noteworthy and illustrates women's capacity to resist and create their own spaces and circuits. However, caution should be exercised to avoid naïve or romanticised visions of Roscas.

As with any form of group action, Roscas engender their own sources of hierarchy and exclusion, including within homogeneous groups of women. Members are carefully chosen and acquire a source of social status owing to the selective nature of the process. In Kenya, Nici Nelson (1996) discusses the hierarchical workings of Roscas and the powerful position of their leaders. Thierry Pairault (2003) reports how Chinese women who enjoy full legal financial independence use Roscas in order to speculate and practice money lending. Similar observations have been made in rural South India, where women are very active in auction Roscas (Guérin, 2008).

As with any financial relationship, women-led financial circuits are two-faced, serving both as a vehicle for solidarity and hierarchy. Women-led financial circuits and financial strategies are strongly embedded in socio-economic power relations. For the poorest members, financial bonds act as a safety net, but they also reinforce their dependence upon creditors. For the better-off ones, lending is one strategy to increase their power and influence over others. Informal financial practices used by women might simultaneously highlight and reinforce existing inequalities among women (Guérin, 2006).

Such considerations should be kept in mind to avoid overestimating the potential of women's collective action in the context of financial services. Collective lending has long been and still is regarded as one of the central innovations of microfinance (Armendariz and Morduch, 2005). By allowing moral guarantees to substitute physical collaterals, whereby group members are accountable to one other for repayments, collective lending as a principle has expanded the boundaries of financial markets. Collective lending has also modified our conception of creditworthiness.

The "Grameen model" is probably the best-known collective lending approach.[1] Each borrower can obtain access to credit if he or she belongs to a group of four to seven mutually bonded members. Village banks are another approach and are based on larger groups of 20–50 people, but with a similar notion of joint liability. Beyond access to credit, village banks are often designed to promote collective capabilities and empowerment. This kind of arrangement was initiated by FINCA in Latin America and CIDR in West Africa, and is now used by organizations such as Pro Mujer and Freedom from Hunger. Self-help groups are a further method, which was

[1]This model was already practiced in various parts of the world in the early period of development credit policies (Gentil, 2004), but has been made popular within microfinance by the Grameen Bank of Bangladesh, as well as by BancoSol in Bolivia.

pioneered in Indonesia and has been replicated on a very large scale in India since the end of the 1990s. SHG resemble micro banks and are made up of 15–20 people. Partnerships with banks are a major specificity of SHG, and, here again, joint liability is the main principle.

Several global databases indicate that the customers of village banks and group lenders are largely women (Cull *et al.*, 2006; D'Espallier *et al.*, 2011), whilst the same holds true for Indian Self-help groups (Srinivasan, 2009). Various factors related to efficiency and equality can account for this. On the one hand, women are thought to be more skilled at operating in groups, participating in group meetings, and accepting social pressure (Armendariz and Morduch, 2005; Mayoux, 2001). On the other hand, at least some forms of collective lending are considered an effective means to promote collective action, "social capital" and empowerment, of which women are in greater need.

Over recent decades, the idea of group lending has become very popular, and has been promoted both by advocates of transaction costs reduction and by empowerment programs. Empirical evidence, however, provides a mixed picture as far as outcomes are concerned.

In some instances, group lending does not function at all, or only very poorly, mainly as a result of a lack of preexisting "social capital" (Bhatt and Tang, 1998; Bastelaer and Leathers, 2006; Chao–Beroff, 1997). Such outcomes can be seen in urban but also rural areas, especially those distinguished by large migrants flows (Chao–Beroff, 1997).

Group meetings can be very time-consuming (Guérin and Palier, 2005; Lazar, 2004; Molyneux, 2002), time management being precisely one of the major sites of inequalities between men and women. Women cooperating for financial purposes are not necessarily in a position to spend large amounts of time together.

The basic principles of collective lending include transparency and democratic workings, for instance, through leadership rotation and collective decision-making. These are both a question of good governance and a means to convey norms which are expected to facilitate self-management and self-organization (Doligez, 2002 ; Baumann, 2002). Indian SHGs are eligible for external loans if their notebooks are correctly managed, for instance. This, however, does not always suit the imperative for confidentiality to which women, as well as probably some men, are bound. Many women belonging to the same group are already bound by multiple, but hidden, cross debts. Such constant need to act surreptitiously in order to escape male domination as well as the ongoing entourage demands is not well suited to a collective and transparent operation. Such openness could lead to questions of an awkward nature, such as why a particular loan has been granted to a given person, given that the lender has owed another party money for several months.

The "matching problem" is another weakness of collective lending. Women's needs are too often considered as homogeneous. Over time, members' needs may evolve and diversify, but group lending may be unresponsive to these, as a minimum of uniformity in financial services is demanded (Mknelly and Kevane, 2002; Morvant–Roux, 2007; Paxton, 1996). Internal and hidden arrangements between borrowers, as observed in Kenya (Johnson, 2004), Mexico and India (Morvant–Roux and Guérin, 2009), can be a way to circumvent the rigidity of group lending, allowing for greater flexibility. But internal arrangements may also encourage manipulation by the most powerful members, as well as over-indebtedness, since the amounts lent may exceed repayment capabilities.

Negative effects for borrowers have also been reported. Excessive pressure may induce considerable social costs (Lazar, 2004; Montgomery, 1996; Rahman, 1999), whilst problems in repayment or in the selection of borrowers may lead to intra-individual conflicts and individualist behaviours (Molyneux, 2002). Group lending might be an opportunity for the better-off to acquire or monopolize the resources of the group, which includes financial services but also the strategic contacts with which they are associated (Coleman, 2006; Guérin, 2003; Mayoux, 2001; Molyneux, 2002; Rankin, 2002; Wright, 2006). As a consequence some authors suggest that group lending should be used only in egalitarian contexts (Gentil, 2004).

For all of the above reasons, group lending has been subject to increasing criticism, even to the point of being considered as primarily a way to transfer transaction costs onto female borrowers (Guérin and Palier, 2005; Mayoux, 2001; Molyneux, 2002; Rankin, 2002; Rao, 2008; Wright, 2006). Without a doubt, a naive and "romantic" vision of group lending has two major risks, namely those of a "forced" cooperation that underestimates the costs of group participation, especially in terms of time (Molyneux, 2002), and the risk of increased inequalities and hierarchisation, including gender hierarchies. But should we completely abandon the idea of collective lending or consider it only as a "second-hand" method (Harper, 2007)? We would argue that collective lending in itself is neither good nor bad, but entirely depends upon local contexts, contingent circumstances and the way in which collective lending is implemented. The following elements, if taken into account, would certainly facilitate better use being made of the collective approach:

(1) Women are too often assumed to "prefer" group membership, when in fact female solidarity is more a gender policies myth than a reality (Cornwall, 2007). Female solidarity might exist in certain places and at certain periods of time but in no case should it be taken as a universal rule. Only an analysis of local circumstances can indicate whether it makes sense or not to provide credit on a collective basis.
(2) When local female solidarity exists, for instance through Roscas, it does not necessarily follow that women *prefer* collective lending. As with any form of social network, many Roscas act both as a source of protection and oppression owing to hierarchical relationships. Women might in fact prefer individual lending, which could serve as a means to at least partially mitigate the weight of local social networks to which they belong.
(3) Joining a Rosca moreover does not give its members the spontaneous ability to efficiently manage collective loans. Running formal borrowers' groups necessitates induction into the specific rules of conduct and regulations. Empirical evidence has confirmed that training is instrumental in the good functioning of group lending, both in terms of repayment (Paxton, 1996) and in terms of group member empowerment (Voelvet, 2002). However, microfinance promoters all too often neglect group management training.
(4) Empirical evidence also shows the key role of leadership in effective group lending. This is again true both in terms of repayment performances (Paxton, 1996), and for empowerment effects. In India, for instance, it has been observed that its groups leaders are the ones who obtain the most benefits, both economically and socially (EDA, 2005). Leadership is an integral part of collective action of any nature, and we cannot expect group lending to be an exception. But at least, specific training and monitoring measures can help to attenuate the negative effects of leadership, and especially the reinforcement of preexisting hierarchies.
(5) Much attention has been given to the issue of homogeneity and relatedness between group members, whether in terms of ethnicity, caste or occupation, from which conflicting evaluations have emerged. On the one hand, higher levels of relatedness may induce better repayment performance, as mutual knowledge improves screening and monitoring

processes. On the other hand, higher levels of relatedness may reduce the pressure members put on each other to repay loans; it may also induce collusions and domino effects owing to co-variant risks. Empirical evidence offers contrasted results and there is no obvious ready-made solution: this once again depends on local socioeconomic circumstances.

(6) As regards the risks of excessive social pressure, two recommendations can be made. Firstly, microfinance promoters should be aware that such pressure exists and include it in their monitoring systems. Secondly, the principle of joint responsibility cannot discharge individual incentives, such as progressive lending or regular repayments (Morduch, 1999; Lapenu *et al.*, 2000).

(7) The lack of transparency in many borrower groups should not necessarily be taken as symptomatic of a lack of democracy or a symptom of funds abuse. It might in fact reflect the need for discretion or improved flexibility. In such cases it could be useful to design financial services that are more responsive to these factors.

2.2 *The gender of saving in kind: Lessons for the mobilisation of saving*

It is often much more beneficial for the poor to save in kind by means such as cattle, jewels, beads or clothing. Goods used as savings fulfil several functions, which are both economical and social in nature (see Guérin *et al.* in this volume). They often differ along gender lines.

Firstly, access to property is very often restricted for women such that the range of goods they can own and control is limited. Secondly goods, crops and natural resources also have a social and a gendered value. As argued by Magdalena Villarreal (2004), the calculation of value includes complex webs of meanings and actions. She argues that local processes of valuation often have more to do with social relations and identity, including gender identity, than with proper titles or legal documents.

The author cites cattle valuation and ownership, whereby in rural Mexico, poultry is characteristically a female wealth preserve, such that women manage the resource, decide when to sell it and also retain control over the money earned. As an important source of protein, eggs and poultry are important for the quality of the household food. As a frequently exchanged, borrowed and sold resource, they are considered as short-term capital and are also instrumental in strengthening social links and solidarity. In contrast, cows are a male preserve, and whilst women might be involved in cow rearing and sometimes may even be the legal owners, selling and buying are the preserve of men, the money obtained is controlled by them, and the social status derived from cattle possession is above all a male status (Villarreal, 2004).

The segmentation of ownership and valuation along gender lines varies significantly among and within cultures. In some places including Gambia, cattle are a male resource while gold and silver jewellery tend to be thrust into the women's domain (Shipton, 1995).

Similar segmentations can be found with respect to certain crops and the management of natural resources. In rural areas in Morocco until recently, the fruit of the argan tree was one of the main forms of female savings for women (Jaussaud, 2003). In Burkina Faso, shea kernels play a similar role (Saussey, 2009). In both cases, these fruits fulfil multiple functions, which are nutritive, medical, owing to the fact that argan oil and karité butter have strong therapeutic values, as well as energy value for oil lamps. Argan and karité fruits also serve a buffer function, where nuts are stocked at the time of the harvest and later sold in cases of emergency. The production and circulation of nuts also shape social relationships between women. Firstly, the various stages of the production process, namely collection, production and transformation require collective work. Secondly, they are intensely and continuously circulated between women, both for specific events and also in case of emergencies.

In rural southern India, gold is the most common form of saving, especially for women (Guérin, 2008). This is one of the few properties that women own, inherited at their marriage. In practice, many men do not hesitate to appropriate it, either to sell or for pledging. However, such male appropriation is limited for various reasons.

Some forms of jewellery are very discrete (e.g. taking the form of very small spheres [*kundumani*] which women hang on their necklaces). Much jewellery circulates among women and their reciprocal exchange is instrumental in the creation and strengthening of women's solidarity. Men often find it difficult to assess their monetary value, and women are more experienced in separating gold from gold-plated jewellery, establishing genuine from fake, and evaluating depreciation due to wear. Women play with these aspects in order to underestimate what they possess, and are sometimes more effective in dealing with pawnbrokers, visiting in groups in order to negotiate prices in a context where interest rates vary little, but the amount of cash per gram does. In contrast, men dislike going in groups and prefer discretion, since pledging gold is considered a women's domain.

Gold can be considered as a buffer, with jewellery pledged and sometimes very often sold in case of problems. When women are asked how they cope with emergencies, their first reply is often: "The things I wear on my ears and hands". Gold can also be considered as a form of long-term saving. Women try to buy gold regularly for the marriage of their children, to prepare for the ceremony and the many gifts they will have to distribute. But gold is first and foremost an ostentatious item and an outward sign of social status. Women display their jewellery at social and religious rituals, particularly marriages and puberty ceremonies. Alongside clothing (*sarees*), jewellery is a true marker of local hierarchy. Last but not least, gold is a very efficient means of speculation as the gold rate constantly grows. One can thus easily understand why women are more inclined to save in gold than in cash.

The social meanings of assets and value, the social fabric of value and the segmentation and hierarchisation of value along gender lines all help explain how and why women, as well as men use, or fail to make use of microfinance services. In particular, it is often argued that women "prefer" saving than credit services because they are more risk-adverse. Here, too, this might not be true everywhere. Moreover even if women are inclined to save, they have their own criteria, which might differ from those provided by microfinance institutions.

For instance in the case of India, it is difficult for MFIs to mobilise women to save, even within the SHG which are supposed to promote savings. Women prefer to invest their cash surpluses in their own circuits and do not like the transparency required within group lending workings. They prefer to expand and strengthen their own "underground" networks and to purchase gold (Guérin *et al.*, 2009).

In some cases, attempts made to create male SHG have failed as the men refuse to be associated with practices that are currently identified as "female". This is a matter of identity and reputation, but also discretion, as they also have their own financial circuits, part of which lies outside the village at their workplace. This is a means to preserve their anonymity amongst the village community and their own kin, including their wives.

Offering unsuitable services can also have negative side effects, as in rural Morocco, where it appears that the creation of saving cooperatives and women's credit has greatly distorted organised local women's circuits based on argane fruit circulation (Jaussaud, 2003).

If one wishes to offer financial services which are well adapted to local specificities and constraints, it is probably highly useful, if not indispensable, to firstly have minimal knowledge of local women's and men's financial circuits, both in cash and in kind: how people save, for what purpose do they save, what are the criteria that are given importance (security, anonymity, liquidity, low transaction cost, self-discipline, social identity, speculation, etc.) and then, how could microfinance complete existing practices? Most of the following suggestions apply equally for men and women, but in each case gender specificities, if any, should be taken into account.

(1) In certain cases, it might appear that women need above all credit services. In West Africa, the *Confédération des institutions financières*, a network of microfinance cooperatives with a predominantly male membership, over the last two decades has developed a number of innovations specifically designed for women. While 'saving first' is a fundamental principle of the cooperative movement, most of these innovations are credit-based. In such a context, experience reveals that many women are not interested in cash saving as the income-generating activities they are engaged in require high working capital turnover rate (Ouadréagago and Gentil, 2008).
(2) In response to time and mobility constraints, both of which affect more women then men, providing home-based or work-based services might be a good way to encourage women to save (Vonderlack and Schreiner, 2002). Informal saving collectors operate in some but not all places, and some microfinance institutions have successfully implemented home-based services. This is the case for instance of the Sewa bank in Gujarat (India). Sewa is a women-based cooperative bank, with around 175,000 mainly female members. Saving collection is one of the cooperative's strengths. Their provision of a doorstep service since the 1970s is probably an explanatory factor in their success. Mobile agents known as "handholders" call at clients' doors at intervals chosen by the client, usually daily or weekly, collecting both savings and loan repayments. The higher transaction costs for the cooperative are counter-balanced by improved repayment rates and greater saving mobilisation stemming from reduced transaction costs for the clients.
(3) Safe-deposit boxes kept at home are an alternative strategy for promoting daily savings without the costs of daily transactions. This has been implemented by various microfinance NGOs in Pakistan, Bangladesh and India (Guérin *et al.*, 2005), and probably elsewhere. The main purpose of this approach is to combine low transaction costs and liquidity, in an adaptation of an existing informal system whereby people collected savings in a clay pot. In contrast to the pot, which needs to be broken to access funds, the metal box balances liquidity and security. The locked box is kept at home, and every two weeks the NGO staff

open the boxes and give savers the choice between withdrawing their savings or transferring them to a bank account. The fact that the savings facility is private prevents a public airing of intra-family inequalities. Safe deposit boxes have been successful in some places, such as former bonded labourer camps in Pakistan (Guérin *et al.*, 2005), but not everywhere. For instance in rural Tamil Nadu, safe-deposit boxes worked well at the start of the project, but were quickly abandoned. Where there are strong social networks, more usual forms of saving, for instance gold and reciprocal lending, are better matched to local aspirations and constraints.

(4) Given the importance of saving in kind, saving incentives based on specific goods that are highly valued locally might also be a better way to meet demand. Here again the example of Sewa is instructive: the cooperative provides long-term saving plans with bonuses in gold, and such schemes seem to be very popular.

(5) Usually people save for a specific purpose, and the principle of contractual savings can act as an incentive to this (Manje and Churchill, 2002; Collins *et al.*, 2009). When men and women have distinct financial responsibilities, it might be necessary to design these services along gender lines. Some informal services can offer a model for this. For instance in India, moneylenders provide a one-year saving scheme for *Dipawali*, one of the most popular Hindu festivals. Women save a regular amount monthly and at the time of the festival receive a lump sum in the form of gold and sweets, at below market price. This practice could be adapted to other anticipated events such as births, the start of the school year, home improvements or religious ceremonies. Johnson and Kidder (1999) have examined such a service in Mexico, where savings deposits are made weekly but withdrawals can only be made three times a year, either to tie in with the school year or for a birth.

(6) Last but not least, microfinance promoters should not forget that saving mobilisation over and above all requires *trust* (Servet, 1996). This is equally true for both sexes, but the building of trust might demand distinct processes for men and women.

3 Conclusion

The targeting of women is one of the specificities of contemporary microfinance, and should be acknowledged. As targeting women has been rather uneven in the history of formal credit for the poor (Lemire *et al.*, 2001), this is already a great step. With the increasing commercialisation of microfinance, however, such focus on women is a cause for concern (Cull *et al.*, 2008; Mayoux, 2007, *this volume*). Moreover, much work remains to be done if financial inclusion worthy of the name is to be achieved. This should not only be a matter of *access*. Policy makers should also examine how people *make use* of financial facilities. We argue that improved understanding of preexisting financial practices and the gender of these practices would facilitate the design of financial services better adapted to the needs of women. Beyond the specific recommendations for collective lending and saving mobilisation given above, broader lessons can also be learnt as regards finance and gender.

(1) Improved identification of demand is the first lesson, and demands knowledge of local socioeconomic realities. The examples given in this paper provide evidence of the multiple motives and rationales underlying financial practices, and it is not certain that microfinance promoters have understood the diversity and complexity of women's motivations. As argued by Susan Johnson (2004, 2007), any attempt to understand the role of gender in shaping the demand for financial services and the effects of financial services requires a local and contextualised analysis of the variety of obstacles and constraints faced by women. Two questions arise from this:
(2) The first concerns financial practices: What are the main sources of men and women's expenditure and funding patterns? Which is problematic and in which cases is it both desirable and realistic for microfinance to intervene? How do both men and women save, where and from whom do they borrow, and according to which conditions, modalities, collaterals and incentive mechanisms? What are the strengths and weaknesses of these preexisting practices? Mapping local financial landscapes and practices and their segmentation along gender lines can help to identify unmet needs and potential complementarities with microfinance.
(3) The second deals with social issues: a basic identification of local social networks may also help to design adapted collaterals. What are local practices in terms of gatherings, discussions, meeting and collective action? Along which lines are they organised and what is the role of gender, alongside categories such as community, profession, religion or friendship? A mapping of the segmentation of networks along gender lines and the degree of hierarchy they imply can help to identify those

elements on which it is possible to build. Answering these questions can help to determine not only the type of service, but also the degree of mixing. In other words, in a given context, do we need specific program for women or not?

(4) Building on informal practices is often very useful, and ultimately many financial innovations only slightly improve preexisting practices. But some are a source of inequality, both between women, as discussed here with respect to group lending, but also between men and women. Social pressure, either from group lending or public pressure, is one of the main innovations of contemporary microfinance (Armendariz and Morduch, 2005). In a context of intense competition, increasing regulation constraints and up to the recent economic crisis, the principle of social pressure, as anticipated to overcome lack of collateral and thus to reduce inequalities, can easily drift into coercive enforcement methods. Yet it is the most marginalized people, particularly women, who are liable to be more sensitive to coercive enforcement methods. As with any development project, the ongoing challenge consists of drawing on existing local practices and networks in order to achieve the social integration and appropriation of projects, however, without perpetuating and reproducing preexisting inequalities.

(5) It is equally fundamental to accept the heterogeneity of women. Women are not a homogeneous group, although they are often considered as a group with common interests. A diversification of services based on a diversity of profiles is often necessary. The *Confédération des institutions financières* in West Africa has been successful in expanding its membership to women. Many of the first experiments had limited success for various reasons. These included inadequacy of the "saving first" principle owing to women's financial constraints, group lending and joint-liability malfunctions, excessive focus on collective projects, poorly adapted and standardized supply in view of the diversity of women's profiles, and lack of professionalism. Finally, after a decade or more of various experiments and trials, it seems that the rise of women's membership mainly results from the diversification of services in terms of the amount loaned, the loan period, and collateral set, etc. (Ouadréagago and Gentil, 2008).

(6) There is no doubt that women encounter specific restrictions in accessing finance, and for this reason, they deserve specific attention. However financial exclusion is not only a "women's problem", but a matter of concern for many other marginalised groups such as young people, members

of low castes and ethnic minorities (Johnson and Nino-Zarazua, 2010). Not only are many men as much in need of microfinance services, but male exclusion might be counter-productive or even dangerous, since it runs the risk of increasing tensions within the household, neighbourhood or the local community (Mayoux, 2001).

References

Adams, DW (1994). Using contracts to analyse finance. In *Financial Landscape Reconstructed: The Fine Art of Mapping Development*, Bouman F and O Hospes (eds.), pp. 11-2;11-7. Boulder, CO: Westview Press.

Aliber, M (2001). Rotating savings and credit associations and the pursuit of self-discipline: An Institutional Perspective. *World Development*, 26(4), 623–637.

Anderson, S and J Baland (2002). The economics of Roscas and intrahousehold resource allocation. *Quarterly Journal of Economics*, 117(3), 963–95.

Ardener, S (1964). The comparative study of rotating credit associations. *Journal of the Royal Anthropological Institute of Great Britain and Scotland* 94(2), 201–29.

Ardener, S and S Burman (eds.) (1996). *Money-Go-Rounds: The Importance of Rotating Savings and Credit Associations for Women.* Washington DC: Berg.

Armendariz, B and J Morduch (2005). *The Economics of Microfinance.* Cambridge: MIT.

Baumann, E (2001). Burkina Faso: heurs et quelques malheurs de la microfinance. In *Exclusion et liens financiers. Rapport du Centre Walras 2001*, Servet, JM and D Vallat (eds.), pp. 214–226. Paris: Economica.

Bhäre, E (2006). Changing independencies and the State. How financial mutuals have changed in south Africa. In *Mutualist Microfinance Informal Savings Funds from the Global Periphery to the Core?* Swaan, A and M Linden (eds.), pp. 31–66. Amsterdam: Aksant.

Bhat, N and S Tang (1998). The problem of transaction costs in group-based microlending: Seed loans in Southern Zambia. *World Development*, 34(10), 1788–1807.

Bortei–Doku, E and E Aryeetey (1996). Mobilizing Cash for Business: Women in Rotating Susu Clubs in Ghana. In *Money-Go-Rounds: The Importance of Rotating Savings and Credit Associations for Women*, Ardener, S and S Burman (eds.), pp. 77–94. Washington DC: Berg.

Bouman, F (1977). Indigenous savings and credit societies in the third world: A message. *Savings and Development*, 3(4), 181–218.

Bouman, F (1994). Roscas and ascras: Beyond the financial landscape. In *Financial Landscape Reconstructed: The Fine Art of Mapping Development*, Bouman, F and O Hospes (eds.), pp. 22/1–22/10. Boulder, CO: Westview Press.

Bruce, J and DH Dwyer (eds.) (1988). *A Home Divided: Women and Income in the Third World.* Stanford: Stanford University Press.

Buijs, G (1998). Saving and loan clubs: Risky ventures or good business practice? A Study of the importance of rotating saving and credit association for poor women. *Development Southern Africa*, 15(1), 55–65.

Burman, S and N Lembete (1996). Building new realities: African women and Roscas in Urban south-Africa. In *Money-Go-Rounds: The Importance of Rotating Savings and Credit Associations for Women*, Ardener, S and S Burman (eds.), pp. 23–49. Washington, DC: Berg.

Chao-Bernoff, R (1977). Developing financial services in disadvantaged regions: Self-managed villages' savings and loan associations in the Dogon regions of Mali. In *Microfinance for the Poor*, Hartmut S (ed.), pp. 87–108. Paris: OECD.
Coleman, B (2006). Microfinance in northeast Thailand: Who benefits and how much? *World Development*, 34(9), 1612–1638.
Collins, D, J Morduch, S Rutherford and O Ruthven (2009). *Portfolios of the Poor: How the World's Poor Live on $2 a Day.* Princeton: Princeton University Press.
Cornwall, A (2007). Myths to live by? Female solidarity and female autonomy reconsidered. *Development and Change*, 18(1), 149–168.
Cull R, A Demigüc–Kunt and J Morduch (2008). Microfinance meets the market. Policy Research Working Paper 4630, Washington DC: World Bank.
D'Espallier, B, I Guérin and R Mersland (2011). Women and repayment. A global analysis *World Development.*
de Swaan, A and M van der Linden (eds.) (2006). *Mutualist Microfinance Informal Savings Funds from the Global Periphery to the Core?* Amsterdam: Aksant.
Doligez, F (2002). Microfinance et dynamiques économiques: quels effets après dix ans d'innovations financières? *Revue Tiers Monde*, 43(172), 783–808.
Dromain, M (1995). Un adage à l'épreuve des faits: La place des femmes dans les tontines au Sénégal. In *Épargne et liens sociaux. Études comparées d'informalités financières*, JM Servet (ed.), pp. 121–140. Paris: AEF/AUPELF-UREF.
EDA (2005). *The Maturing of Indian Microfinance. Findings and Policy Implications from a National Study.* New-Delhi: EDA Publications.
Fernando, JL (eds.) (2006). *Microfinance Perils and Prospects.* London: Routledge.
Fletschner, D (2009). Rural women's access to credit: Market imperfections and intra-households dynamics. *World Development*, 37(3), 618–631.
Folbre, N (1986). Hearts and spades: Paradigms of household economics. *World Development*, 14(2), 245–255.
Gentil, D (2004). La caution solidaire, une histoire ancienne. In *Exclusion et liens financiers. Rapport du Centre Walras 2003.* Guérin, I and JM Servet (eds), pp. 433–440. Paris: Economica.
Guérin, I, G Venkatasubramanian and C Churchill (2005). Bonded labour, social capital and microfinance. Lessons from two cases studies. *Indian Journal of Labour Economics*, 48(3), 58–72.
Guérin, I (2003). *Femmes et économie solidaire.* Paris: la Découverte.
Guérin, I (2006). Women and Money: Multiple, complex and evolving practices. *Development and Change*, 37(3), 549–570.
Guérin, I (2008). Poor women and their women: Between Daily Survival, Private Life, Family Obligations and Social Norms. RUME Working Paper 2008–3.
Guérin, I and J Palier (eds.) (2005). *Microfinance Challenges: Empowerment or Disempowerment of the Poor?* Pondicherry: Editions of the French Institute of Pondicherry.
Guérin, I, M Roesch, G Venkatasubramanian and O Héliès (2009). Microfinance and informal finance: Substitution or leverage effects? *RUME Working Paper* 2009–01.
Gugerty, MK (2007). You can't save alone: Commitment in rotating savings and credit associations in Kenya. *Economic Development and Cultural Change*, 55, 251–282.
Handa, S and C Kirton (1999). The Economics of Rotating Savings and Credit Associations: Evidence from the Jamaican Partner. *Journal of Development Economics*, 60, 173–194.

Harper, M (2007). What's wrong with groups? In *What's Wrong with Microfinance?*, Dichter, Th and M Harper (eds.), pp. 35–49. Warwickshire: Practical Action Publishing.

Holvoet, N (2005). The impact of microfinance on decision-making agency: Evidence from South India. *Development and Change*, 35(5), 937–962.

Hospes, O (1996). Women's Differential Use of Roscas in Indonesia. In *Money-Go-Rounds: The Importance of Rotating Savings and Credit Associations for Women*, S Ardener and S Burman (eds.), pp. 127–149. Washington, DC: Berg.

Jaussaud, E (2003). La participation des femmes au développement local en zone rurale marocaine, Mémoire de DESS 'Ingénierie des organisations de l'économie sociale et solidaire', Université de la Méditerranée Aix-Marseille II, Marseille.

Johnson, S (2004). Gender norms and financial markets: Evidence from Keyna. *World Development*, 32(8), 1355–1374.

Johnson, S (2007). Gender impact assessment in microfinance and microenterprise: Why and how? *Dialogue*, 37, 83–88.

Johnson, S and M Nino-Zarazua (2010). Financial access and exclusion in Kenya and Uganda. *The Journal of Development Studies.* Forthcoming.

Johnson, S and T Kidder (1999). Globalization and gender: Dilemmas for microfinance organizations. *Small Enterprise Development*, 10(3), 4–15.

Kabeer, N (1995). *Reversed Realities. Gender Hierarchies in Development Thought.* London/New-York: Verso.

Kane, A (2001). Financial Arrangements across Borders: Women's Predominant Participation in Popular Finance, from Thilogne and Dakar to Paris. A Senegalaise Case Study. In *Women and Credit: Researching the Past, Refiguring the Future*, Lemire, B *et al.* (eds.), pp. 295–317. Washington, DC: Berg.

Kevane, M and B Wydick (2001). Microenterprise Lending to Female Entrepreneurs: Sacrificing Economic Growth for Povery Alleviation? *World Development*, 29(7), 1225–1236.

Lapenu, C, M Zeller and M Sharma (2000). *Constraints of Market Failures and Rural Poverty for Microfinance Institutions: How Innovations Can Increase Outreach and Sustainability. BMZ Report, part II, Institutional-level Analysis*, Washington DC: IFPRI.

Lazar, S (2004) Education for credit development as citizenship project in Bolivia. *Critique of Anthropology*, 24(3), 301–319.

Lemire, B, R Pearson and G Campbell (eds.) (2001). *Women and Credit: Researching the Past, Refiguring the Future.* Washington DC: Berg.

Light, I and Z Deng (1996). Gender differences in Roscas participation within Korean business households in Los Angeles. In *Money-Go-Rounds: The Importance of Rotating Savings and Credit Associations for Women*, Ardener, S and S Burman (eds.), pp. 217–240. Washington, DC: Berg.

Lont, H and O Hospes (eds.) (2004). *Livelihood and Microfinance Anthropological and Sociological Perspectives on Savings and Debt. Delft: Eburon Academic Publishers.*

Manje, L and C Churchill (2002). The demand for risk-managing financial services in low-income communities: Evidence from Zambia. *Working Paper No. 33*, Geneva: ILO Social Finance Programme.

Mayoux, L (1999). Microfinance and the Empowerment of Women. A Review of the Key Issues. ILO Social Finance Unit Working Papers 22. International Labour Organization, Geneva.

Mayoux, L (2001). Tackling the down side: Social capital, women's empowerment and micro-finance in Cameroon. *Development and Change*, 32(3), 421–50.

Mayoux, L and S Anand (1996). Gender Inequalities, Roscas and Sectoral Employment Strategies: Questions from the South Indian Silk Industry. In *Money-Go-Rounds: The Importance of Rotating Savings and Credit Associations for Women*, Ardener, S and S Burman (eds.), pp. 179–98. Washington DC: Berg.

Mencher, JP (1988). Women's Work and Poverty: Women's Contribution to Household Maintenance in South India. In *A Home Divided: Women and Income in the Third World*, J Bruce and DH Dwyer (eds.), pp. 99–119. Stanford: Stanford University Press.

MkNelly, B and M Kevane (2002). Improving design and performance of group lending: Suggestions from Burkina Faso. *World Development*, 30(11), 2017–2032.

Molyneux, M (2002). Gender and the silences of social capital. *Development and Change*, 33(2), 167–188.

Montgomery, R (1996). Disciplining or protecting the poor? Avoiding the social costs of peer pressure in micro-credit schemes. *Journal of International Development*, 8(2), 289–305.

Morduch, J (1999). The microfinance promise. *Journal of Economic Literature*, 17, 1569–1614.

Morvant-Roux, S (2007). Microfinance institution's clients borrowing strategies and lending groups financial heterogeneity under progressive lending: Evidence from a Mexican microfinance program. *Savings and Development*, 2, 193–217.

Morvant-Roux, S and I Guérin (2009). Lending groups' strategies to make microfinance offer more flexible: Evidence from rural Mexico and India. *Communication to the Boulder-Bergamo Forum on Access to Financial Services*, Bergamo: Bergamo University.

Nelson, N (1996). The Kiambu group: A successful women's rosca in Mathare Valley, Nairobi (1971 to 1990). In *Money-Go-Rounds: The Importance of Rotating Savings and Credit Associations for Women*, Ardener, S and S Burman (eds.), pp. 49–70. Washington, DC: Berg.

Niger–Thomas, M (1996). Women's Access to and the Control of Credit in Cameroon: The Mamfe Case. In Money-Go-Rounds: The Importance of Rotating Savings and Credit Associations for Women, S Ardener and S Burman (eds.), pp. 95–110. Washington DC: Berg.

Ouadréagago, A and D Gentil (eds.) (2008). *La Microfinance en Afrique de l'Ouest. Histoires et innovations*. Paris: Karthala/CIF.

Pairault, T (2003). Women, property and social practices in China. In *Microfinance: From Daily Survival to Social Change, Pondy Papers in Social Sciences 30*, I Guérin and JM Servet (eds.), pp. 75–98. Pondicherry: French Institute of Pondicherry.

Papanek, H and L Schwede (1988). Woman are Good with Money: Earning and Managing in an Indonesin City. In *A Home Divided: Women and Income in the Third World*, JM Bruce and DH Dwyer (eds.), pp. 80–98. Stanford: Stanford University Press.

Paxton, J (1996). Determinants of successful group loan repayments: An application to Burkina Faso. *Unpublished doctorat thesis*. Ohio: The Ohio State University.

Perry, D (2002). Microcredit and women moneylenders. The shifting terrain of credit in rural Senegal. *Human Organization*, 61(1), pp. 30–10.

Rahman, A (1999). Micro-credit initiatives for equitable and sustainable development: Who pays? *World Development*, 27(1), 67–82.

Rankin, KN (2002). Social capital, microfinance and the politics of development. *Feminist Economics*, 8(1), 1–24.

Rao, S (2008). Reforms with a female face: Gender, liberalization, and economic policy in Andhra Pradesh, India. *World Development*, 36(7), 1213–1232.

Rivallain, J (1994). *Échanges et pratiques monétaires en Afrique du XV au XIX siècles à travers les récits des voyageurs.* Lyon/Paris: Musée de l'Imprimerie et de la banque/Musée de l'Homme.

Rutherford, S (2001). *The Poor and Their Money.* Oxford: Oxford University Press.

Saussey, M (2009). Les organisations féminines au Burkina Faso: Limites et paradoxes des dispositifs de valorisation d'un produit local, le beurre de karité. Thèse de sociologie, EHESS, Paris.

Servet, JM (1984). *Nomismata. Etat et origines de la monnaie.* Lyon: Presses Universitaires de Lyon.

Servet, JM (1996). Risque, incertitude et financement de proximitè en Afrique: Une approche socioéconomique. *Revue Tiers-Monde*, 17(145), 41–57.

Servet, JM (ed.) (1995). *Épargne et liens sociaux. Études comparées d'informalités financières.* Paris: AEF/AUPELF-UREF.

Servet, JM (2006). *Banquiers aux pieds nus: La microfinance.* Paris: Odile Jacob.

Sethi, RM (1996). Women's Roscas in Contemporary India society. In *Money-Go-Rounds: The Importance of Rotating Savings and Credit Associations for Women.* Ardener, S and S Burman (eds.), pp. 163–179. Washington DC: Berg.

Shipton, P (1995). How Gambians save: Culture and economic strategy at en ethnic crossroad. In *Money Matters. Instability, Values and Social Payments in the Modern History of West-African Communities*, J Guyer (ed.), pp. 245–277. London/Portsmouth (NH): Currey/Heinemann.

Shipton, P (2007). *The Nature of Entrustment. Intimacy, Exchange and the Sacred in Africa.* New Haven & London: Yale University Press.

Smets, P (2006). Changing financial mutuals in urban India. Practice, function, trust and development trajectories. In *Mutualist Microfinance Informal Savings Funds from the Global Periphery to the Core?* A Swaan and M Linden (eds.), pp. 151–182. Amsterdam: Aksant.

Southwold, LS (2004). Public versus private domains: A case study of Sri Lankan Rosca. In *Livelihood and Microfinance Anthropological and Sociological Perspectives on Savings and Debt*, H Lont and O Hospes (eds.), pp. 173–194. *Delft: Eburon Academic Publishers.*

Srinivasan N (2009). *Microfinance in India. State of the Report* 2008. New-Delhi: Sage.

Steel, W, E Aryeetey, H Hettige and M Nissanke (1997). Informal financial markets under liberalisation in four African countries. *World Development*, 25(5), 817–830.

Verhoef, G (2001). Informal financial service institutions for survival: African women and Stockvels in urban South Africa. *Enterprise and Society*, 2, 259–296.

Villarreal, M (2004). Striving to make capital do "economic things" for the impoverished: On the issue of capitalization in rural microenterprises. In *Development Intervention: Actor and Activity Perspectives*, T Kontinen (ed.), pp. 67–81. Helsinki: University of Helsinki.

Vonderlack, R and M Schreiner (2002). Women, microfinance, and savings: Lessons and proposals. *Development in Practice*, 12(5), 602–612.

Weiner, A (1976). *Women of Values, Men of Renown: New Perspectives on Trobriand Exchange.* Austin, London: University of Texas Press.

World Bank (2001). *World Development Report: Engendering Development. Through Gender Equality in Rights, Resources and Voice.* New York: World Bank and Oxford University Press.

World Bank (2007). *Finance for All? Policies and Pitfalls in Expanding Access.* A World Bank Policy Research Report. Washington DC: The World Bank.
Wright, K (2006). The darker side to microfinance: Evidence from Cajamarca, Peru. In *Microfinance Perils and Prospects*, JL Fernando (ed.), pp. 154–172. London: Routledge.
Zelizer, V (1994). *The Social Meaning of Money.* New York: Basic Books.
Zelizer, V (2005). *The Purchase of Intimacy.* Princeton: Princeton University Press.

Taking Gender Seriously: Towards a Gender Justice Protocol for Financial Services

Linda Mayoux*
International Consultant with WEMAN, Oxfam Novib

Gender equality of opportunity and women's empowerment are now widely recognised as integral and inseparable parts of any sustainable strategy for economic growth and pro-poor development:

- Women are statistically the global majority. As the global majority, women cannot be treated as "a special case". Their needs and interests must be as integral a part of any development policy as those of men.
- Gender equality of opportunity and women's empowerment are essential for economic growth. Studies by World Bank and others have shown that countries that have taken positive steps to promote gender equality have substantially higher levels of growth.[1]
- Gender equality and women's empowerment are essential components of poverty reduction strategies. Gender inequality and women's disempowerment are key factors in creating poverty.[2] Gender inequality means women have higher representation amongst the poor and therefore women's needs

*This paper is a shortened version of a paper for Oxfam Novib's Women's Empowerment Mainstreaming and Networking (WEMAN) program for Gender Justice in Economic Development (Mayoux, 2009a). It draws on work since 1997 by the author and others funded by DFID, ILO, Levi Strauss Foundation, Aga Khan Foundation Canada and Pakistan, the Open University UK, UNIFEM, World Bank (Mayoux, 2008) and IFAD (Mayoux, 2009b). Further details, reports, resources and case studies can be found at www.genfinance.info. Any comments, suggestions and additions gratefully received — please contact the author at l.mayoux@ntlworld.com. This paper does not necessarily represent the views of any of the sponsors of the work on which it is based.
[1] Blackden and Bhanu, 1999; Klasen, 2002.
[2] See, e.g., DFID (2000).

are the majority norm rather than minority interest in poverty reduction strategies. Women also have prime responsibility for children and family well-being which makes them key actors in poverty reduction.

- Women themselves, when given an opportunity to talk openly through the use of well-conducted participatory methods, want to change gender inequalities in incomes, control over resources, decision-making, division of paid and unpaid labour and gender-based violence, and their effects on the well-being of women and their children. Moreover many men also support these changes because they too are constrained by existing norms of masculinity and resulting peer pressure and responsibilities.[3]
- International agreements on women's human rights have been signed by most governments and aid agencies, whereby gender equality of opportunity and women's empowerment are goals in and of themselves on the assumption that "women are also human".

Gender issues cannot therefore be seen as a marginal concern for the financial sector, particularly an inclusive sector which receives funding from development agencies based on claims to reduce poverty and contribute to pro-poor growth.

From 1997, "reaching and empowering women" has been the second theme of the MicroCredit Summit Campaign.[4] Donors and microfinance providers have produced many manuals outlining ways of increasing women's access to microfinance.[5] However until very recently, despite female targeting of small loans and savings and frequent use of the term "empowerment" in promotional material, explicit attention to gender issues within the microfinance movement has been negligible, even in recent discussions on promotion of an inclusive financial sector.

The practical ways in which gender equality and women's empowerment can be most effectively promoted differs between financial service providers

[3]For detailed discussion of findings using the Gender Action Learning System (GALS) methodology in Uganda, Pakistan, India and Peru, see Mayoux *et al.*, 2009 and Mayoux, 2010. In Uganda where 70 percent of 500 men in participatory research admitted to stealing money and crops from their wives, violence and alcoholism, hundreds of men are using GALS and stopping theft, alcoholism, adultery and violence, because they now realise that these are not the ways to happiness and prosperity — let alone a good sex life! They now discuss family affairs with their wives. Many have signed over land to give their wives some security and status. Many are working with other men to help them change.

[4]Microcredit Summit Declaration and Plan of Action RESULTS 1997.

[5]For older Manuals and Guidelines, see, for example, UNIFEM 1993, 1995; Binns, 1998; Johnson, 1997.

depending on the type of financial institution, context and capacities. Nevertheless, there are steps which financial institutions of ALL types can take: from banks, through MFIs to NGOs with savings and credit as part of an integrated development program. Moreover, although some of these strategies will require "a different way of doing business", and some shift in priorities for resource and funding allocation, they are likely to increase rather than undermine sustainability. This is not a question of "women's empowerment projects" as optional add-ons, although, if well-designed, these can also have their role. It involves mainstreaming gender and empowerment throughout program design in order not only to benefit women, but also in the process, improve the longer term financial and organisational sustainability of the services themselves and the sustainability and dynamism of the economy in general.[6]

This paper discusses a draft Gender Justice Framework Protocol[7] proposed by WEMAN Network partners in South Asia, Africa and Latin America based on their experience and research in the sector which is discussed in detail elsewhere (Mayoux, 2009b). The draft Protocol aims to be a catalyst for serious debate about ways forward, and is being used as a starting point for lobbying by the WEMAN network to establish consensus on an agreed protocol for the sector. The framework assumes a commitment to a diversified financial sector, where different players from commercial banks and MFIs to women's organisations may have different focuses and roles, but where each would make a firm commitment to gender equality of opportunity and women's empowerment and adapt and integrate these principles into their organisational structure, product and service delivery and role at macro- and policy levels.[8]

[6]More details on many of the issues described here can be found in Mayoux (2008, 2009).
[7]This gender justice draft protocol was presented at the Asia Regional MicroCredit Summit in Bali in July 2008 and signed by over 400 participants, including prominent figures in the microfinance movement including Mohammad Yunus and Lamiya Morshed of Grameen Bank and Sam Daley Harris and Michele Gomperts of the Summit Campaign, Nirmal Fernando of Asian Development Bank, and NABARD.
[8]As part of the WEMAN program, the Protocol, and also the evidence and practical innovation underpinning it, is being progressively developed through workshops in Latin America, Asia and Africa and as contribution to the MicroCredit Summit Campaign.

1 Gender Justice Framework Protocol for Financial Services[9]

Gender justice for the purpose of this Protocol means:

- removing the all-pervasive institutional gender inequalities and discrimination which constrain both women and men at every level, enabling both to realise their full human potential;
- affirmative action to empower women (currently the most disadvantaged sex) to access and benefit from these changes;
- working with men to change attitudes and behaviours which not only harm women, but also children and often men themselves.

1.1 *Framework*

- organisational mandates, vision and objectives of all financial service providers have explicit commitment to gender equality of opportunity and women's empowerment.
- organisational gender policies support this commitment, developed through a participatory process with staff and clients, integrated into all staff training and including gender equitable recruitment, employment and promotion.
- removal of all forms of gender discrimination in access to all forms of financial services as an integral part of product and service development, including technological innovation.
- financial services contribute to women's empowerment through effective design of products, non-financial services including financial literacy, and client participation.
- gender indicators are an integral part of social performance management and market research.
- consumer protection and regulatory policies integrate gender equality of opportunity and empowerment.
- gender advocacy in areas like women's property rights and combating gender-based violence essential to removing gender discrimination and empowerment are an integral part of the advocacy strategy.
- the specific needs and interests of very poor and vulnerable women are included in all the above.

[9]Mayoux (2009a).

2 Why a Gender Justice Protocol for Financial Services?

A concern with gender issues in financial services is not new. Nor can it be dismissed as a Western or donor-imposed agenda. From the early 1970s, women's movements in a number of countries, notably India, became increasingly interested in the degree to which women were able to access and benefit from poverty-focused credit programs and credit cooperatives. The problem of women's access to credit was given particular emphasis at the first International Women's Conference in Mexico in 1975, leading to the setting up of the Women's World Banking network. In the wake of the second International Women's Conference in Nairobi in 1985, there was a mushrooming of government and NGO-sponsored income-generation programs for women, many of which included savings and credit. Then in the 1990s, microfinance programs like Grameen Bank and some affiliates of Finca and Accion International began to increasingly target women, not only as part of their poverty-targeting mandate, but also because they found female repayment rates to be significantly higher than those of men.

Increasing women's access to financial services, particularly microfinance, has been seen as contributing not only to poverty reduction and financial sustainability, but also to a series of "virtuous spirals" of economic empowerment, increased well-being and social and political empowerment for women themselves, thereby fulfilling gender equality and empowerment goals. Some of the dimensions and interlinkages between the different "virtuous impact spirals" identified in the literature are shown in Figure 27.1.

Firstly, increasing women's access to microfinance services can potentially lead to women's economic empowerment (see linkages in the centre of the diagram), increasing women's role in household financial management. In some cases, this may be the first time women are able to access significant amounts of money in their own right. Access to money in turn may enable them to start their own economic activities and/or invest more in existing activities and/or acquire assets and/or raise their status in household economic activities through their visible capital contribution. Increased participation in economic activities may enable women to increase incomes and/or their control over their own and household income. This in turn may enable them to increase longer term investment and productivity of their economic activities, and increase women's engagement in the market.

Secondly, increasing women's access to financial services can potentially increase household well-being (see linkages on the left of the diagram). This is partly through economic empowerment, but may occur even where

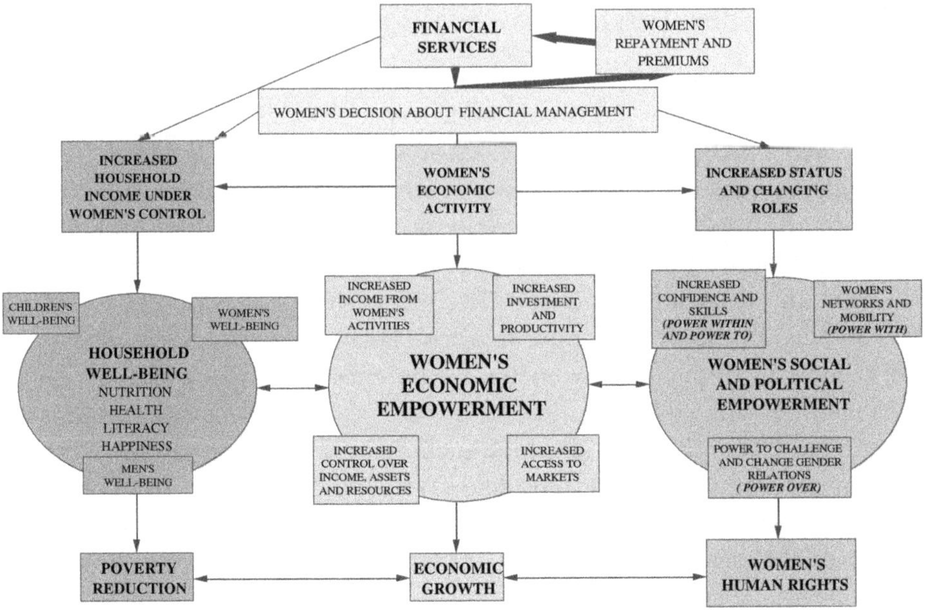

Figure 27.1: Microfinance and women's empowerment: virtuous spirals.

women use the financial services for activities of other household members, e.g., husbands or sons. Even where women are not directly engaged in income-earning activities, channelling credit or savings options to households through women may enable women to play a more active role in intra-household decision-making, decrease their own and household vulnerability and increase investment in family welfare. This may in turn benefit children through increasing expenditure in areas like nutrition and education, particularly for girls. It can also lead to improved well-being for women and enable women themselves to bring about changes in gender inequalities in the household. It is also likely to benefit men.

Thirdly, a combination of women's increased economic activity and increased decision-making in the household can potentially lead to wider social and political empowerment (see linkages on the right of the diagram). Women themselves often value the opportunity to be seen to be making a greater contribution to household well-being, giving them greater confidence and a sense of self-worth. The positive effects on women's confidence and skills, expanded knowledge and support networks through group activity and market access can lead to enhanced status for all women within the community. In some societies where women's mobility has been very circumscribed and women previously had little opportunity to meet women outside their immediate family, there have been very significant changes. Individual women who gain respect in their households may then act as role models for others, leading to a wider process of change in community perceptions and male willingness to accept change.

Most microfinance providers can cite case studies of women who have benefited substantially economically and socially from their services. Some women who were very poor before entering the program, started economic activity with a loan and built up savings, thereby improving well-being, relationships in the household and becoming more involved in local community activities:[10] Some women, and many women in some programs and contexts, show enormous resourcefulness and initiative when provided with a loan or given the chance to save without interference from family members. Impact studies which differentiate by poverty level generally find benefits to be particularly significant for the "better-off poor" who have some education and contacts to build on for successful enterprise.[11]

Finally (see linkages along the bottom of the diagram), women's economic empowerment at the individual level has *potentially* significant contributions at the macro-level through increasing women's visibility as agents of economic growth and their voice as economic actors in policy decisions. This, together with their greater ability to meet household well-being needs, in turn increases their effectiveness as agents of poverty reduction. Microfinance groups may form the basis for collective action to address gender inequalities within the community, including issues like gender-based violence and access to resources and local decision-making. These local-level changes may be further reinforced by higher level organisation, leading to wider movements for social and political change and promotion of women's human rights at the macro-level. Moreover these three dimensions of economic empowerment, well-being and social and political empowerment are potentially mutually reinforcing "virtuous spirals", both for individual women and at household, community and macro-levels.

Nevertheless, despite the potential contribution of financial services to women's empowerment and well-being, there is still a long way to go before women have equal access to financial services, even microfinance, or are able

[10]For an overview of the literature on women's benefits from microfinance, see Kabeer (2001), Cheston and Kuhn (2002), and Kabeer (1998).

[11]Gender impact assessments rarely distinguish between women by poverty level, but see, for example, the study of Women's Empowerment project in Nepal by Ashe and Parrott (2001).

to fully benefit.[12] In many regions, despite some advances, women's access to microfinance is still unequal beyond very small savings and loans. Large numbers of women, particularly in rural areas, do not have access to financial services. Moreover women's access to loans decreases compared to that of men as NGOs transform to formal institutions, become more profitable and "mature".[13] This is partly because of the move to larger loans and many women's lack of confidence to use such loans. However, there are also often changes in gender balance of staff, attitudes and ways of relating to clients which are less favourable to women.[14]

Evidence also indicates that, despite the undoubted considerable potential contribution, none of the assumed linkages between women's access to financial services and empowerment can be automatically assumed to occur. Microfinance may even disempower women.[15] The degree to which women are able to benefit from minimalist financial services which do not take gender explicitly into account depends largely on context and individual situation.

None of the above implies that financial services should cease attempting to target women — women have a right to equal access to financial services and removal of all forms of gender discrimination in financial service providers. This right is enshrined in international women's rights agreements and national equal opportunities policies. Moreover the marginalization of (and often overt hostility towards mention of) gender issues, misses the important contribution which gender equality and women's empowerment can make to both the financial services sector and development in general. Promoting gender equality within organisations and targeting women are beneficial even in commercial terms.[16] More empowered women are

[12]For more detailed discussion and references on potential negative effects, see Mayoux, 1999, 2000, 2001, 2008, 2009b.

[13]Cheston (2006); Frank *et al.* (2008).

[14]Many clients in different contexts interviewed by the author in the course of consultancy report applying for larger loans for profitable businesses, but were turned down or given smaller loans because of discrimination by male staff. In some cases, smaller loans meant they were forced to invest in substandard equipment which led to unnecessary losses.

[15]This was the firm conclusion of a recent well-respected and rigorous impact assessment in Pakistan funded by EU for 5 of the main microfinance institutions: Zaidi, Jamal, Javeed and Zaka (2007).

[16]In 2004, a study by the American organisation Catalyst found that financial performance was higher for companies with more women at the top. The experience of Wells Fargo Bank in the US also indicates the benefits of targeting women as a client group (Cheston, 2006).

potentially more profitable clients: able to profitably use larger loans, save more and needing less support — providing the institution takes their needs seriously in order to maintain client commitment. The failure to pay serious attention to gender strategies misses an important opportunity to discuss the many positive gender innovations which are taking place in relation to organisational gender policies, products, non-financial services, client participation and macro-level policies, and promote these as an integral part of good practice in the sector as a whole.

Given the potential negative impacts and contextual and institutional constraints, gender justice in financial services requires more than increasing women's access to small savings, loan, and microinsurance programs or to a few products designed specifically for women. Achieving gender equality and empowerment goals depends not on expanding financial services per se, but on the specific types of financial services that are delivered in different contexts to women from different backgrounds and by different types of institutions or programs. Addressing gender issues will therefore require a strategic gender justice approach — not only to mainstreaming gender equality of access, but also strategies to ensure that this access then translates into empowerment and improved well-being rather than merely feminisation of debt or capturing female savings or insurance premiums for program financial sustainability. The best way of integrating gender policy within existing practices and contexts can be assessed through a gender assessment or a well-designed participatory process.[17]

3 Organisational Gender Policy: The Commercial Bottomline

In all types of financial institutions the most cost-effective means of maximizing contributions to gender equality and empowerment is to develop an institutional structure and culture that is women-friendly and empowering, and that manifests these traits in all interactions with clients.[18] A focus on diversifying management and staff in order to reach the huge female market

[17]See, for example, checklists at the end of Mayoux (2009b) and Cheston (2006). A participatory methodology is being developed as part of Oxfam Novib's WEMAN program based on the Gender Acction Learning System methodology. For details, see http://www.wemanglobal.org.

[18]For more detailed discussion of frameworks and methodologies for institutional gender mainstreaming, see, for example, Groverman and Gurung (2001, 2008); ILO (2007); Macdonald *et al.* (1997).

for products and services is an accepted part of good commercial practice and management. Indeed, for an organisation to fail to have a gender policy is likely to be in contravention of national equal opportunities policies and international agreements on women's human rights.

All financial service providers can contribute to gender justice goals through having a clear vision and commitment to gender equality and women's empowerment throughout their advertising and promotion in order to attract women clients and also change attitudes towards women's economic activities in the wider community. This is possible even within financial sustainability constraints. Even at this commercial level, there is the possibility of a financial services sector which promotes a vision of women as successful and competent entrepreneurs and farmers and acts as a significant force for change in attitudes and behaviours — and, in the process, opens up a large and profitable commercial market for financial service providers. This is not an issue of cost, but of vision and inspiration in regard to gender justice on the same level as, for example, HSBC Bank's promotion of cultural diversity, and commitment in some quarters to environmental sustainability.

Many formal sector banks have gender or equal opportunities policies for staff. These internal measures are consistent with financial sustainability. In fact, mainstream banks are sometimes way ahead of nongovernmental organizations in implementing staff gender policies (examples include Barclays in Kenya — dating back to the 1980s — and Khushali Bank in Pakistan). The promotion of diversity, of which gender is one dimension, is a key element of best business practice in the West.[19] Commercial banks increasingly have gender or equal opportunity policies to encourage and retain skilled female staff. Many commercial banks have childcare facilities and proactive promotion policies for female staff. Increasing the number of female staff is essential to increasing the number of female clients in many social contexts. Both female and male staff will, however, require gender training integrated into general induction training.

Many of these strategies, such as recruitment and promotion, and sexual harassment policies, cost little. Although a gender policy may entail some costs (for parental leave, for example), the cost is likely to be compensated by higher levels of staff commitment, efficiency and retention. Unhappy

[19]An interesting study by Fortune magazine of the most profitable businesses found that these had good representation of women in high management positions (Cheston, 2006).

and harassed staff members are inefficient and change jobs frequently, and training new staff is costly. In many social settings, increasing the number of female staff is essential to increasing the number of female clients.

4 Equality of Access as Integral Part of Product and Service Development, Including Technological Innovation

The accelerating commercialisation of microfinance, together with recent advances in technology, have the potential to significantly increase access to cheaper and better financial services for women as well as men. Market competition has stimulated:

- product diversification and client-centred product development through market research;
- technology improvements in information and delivery systems, particularly mobile and e-banking.

There is also increasing discussion of ways in which financial services can better integrate into wider economic development processes e.g., value chain finance and local economic development. These are areas where even commercial banks are developing strategies. So far, the measures proposed have been gender-blind, potentially leading to further marginalisation of women.

Many formal sector banks have been at the forefront of product innovation. It is now generally accepted that participatory market research and "knowing your clients" is good business practice. SEWA's services have always been based on consultation with clients. Grameen Bank undertook a four-year reassessment and redesign based on extensive client research. This significantly increased outreach and sustainability.[20] ICICI Bank in India also conducts both participatory market research and funds in-depth research on the needs of microfinance clients through its support for Centre for Microfinance Research in Chennai. Many microfinance staff have been trained in Microsave's market research tools and/or are using some

[20]In the three years to December 2005, Grameen's deposit base tripled and its loans outstanding doubled. Profits have soared from around 60 million taka in 2001 to 442 million taka (about US$7 million) in 2004. Dropouts are returning, and even some old defaulters are repaying and re-joining.

variant of one or more of these tools to design products for women as well as men.[21]

Ensuring gender equality of access, however, requires more than introduction of a few small loan products for women's activities. It requires looking at financial services of all types — for large and medium-scale women entrepreneurs and farmers who are potential role models and providers of market linkages and employment, as well as microentrepreneurs. It requires viewing women as capable and valued economic actors, not victims who are lucky to get a little loan or need to be taught thrift in use of their scarce resources. And designing processes which enable women then to progress and graduate from small savings and loans to accessing larger loans and accruing significant assets.

Mobile and e-banking, particularly in the commercial sector, potentially promises much wider and also cheaper access to financial services, particularly in rural areas which are more costly to reach than urban centres. Mobile banking has great potential to reach women who have less mobility outside the home than men either because of domestic responsibilities and/or social restrictions on their independence and interaction with men. However, here there are important questions to be asked about:

- who owns and accesses the mobile technology?
- where are facilities like ATMs located — in male or female space?
- how are credit histories and credit ratings established? As individuals or as households?

It is crucial that mechanisms are developed to ensure discrimination-free access for women as the industry rapidly expands.

There has recently been a renewed interest in the provision of complementary services ("credit-plus", as it is often called). Apart from their savings and credit initiatives, many NGOs and an increasing number of MFIs provide a range of other, separately funded interventions for women and men. This as both an efficient means of development, and a means of enhancing client — and hence organizational — financial sustainability. Examples include literacy, health and HIV/AIDS awareness.[22] None of these recent developments is necessarily gender-sensitive, yet there are ways for them to

[21]For details of MicroSave tools, see www.microsave.org.
[22]For a discussion of the complementarities between microfinance and other development interventions, see, for example, Magrner (2007), and Watson and Dunford (2006).

take gender dimensions into account. It is crucial to include women fully into training, extension, and other interventions, regardless of whether they are conventionally viewed as being of interest only to men, especially technical training for new agricultural crops and technology and other livelihood development programs. Conversely, encouraging men to come to training normally targetted at women on e.g., family welfare, and including discussion of gender issues in training for men can lead to significant changes in men's attitudes and behaviour. This requires not only targeting and promotion to women, but also to men, examination of all training content from a gender perspective.

Most of these measures have minimal cost but would enable expansion of number of female clients and increase repayment rates. They would therefore enhance, rather than detract from, financial sustainability. This would entail some initial cost, but costs are likely to be recouped in the longer term through better outreach to good female clients, and more responsible repayment by men.

5 Financial Services Contribute to Women's Empowerment through Appropriate Design of Products, Non-Financial Services Including Financial Literacy and Gender Action Learning

One of the reasons why calls for women's empowerment strategies have been largely dismissed by the commercial sector is because they are generally seen in terms of "empowerment add-ons" for women — and hence not attainable through a financially sustainable model. However, although effective, cost-efficient and sustainable empowerment methodologies are certainly important as part of strategies in the sector as a whole, there are also many ways in which mainstreaming empowerment within financially sustainable institutions can have significant impact — if strategically planned as an integral part of design. This includes:

- mainstreaming gender and empowerment in core activities;
- participatory market research to identify products which can contribute to empowerment;
- non-financial services which contribute to empowerment, including financial literacy;
- client participation which really strengthens women's networks for collective action.

Focusing first on what can be achieved by mainstreaming then enables scarce resources and energy for empowerment methodologies per se to be targeted where they are really needed.

There are ways in which core activities of financial services providers can be adjusted to contribute to empowerment. Financial institutions lacking the scope to introduce non-financial services can promote a vision and commitment to empowerment through the questions asked during the application process. The application process for products or other services involves asking questions about the applicant's background and capacities. Without increasing the time needed to answer these questions, they could be reworded or adapted to promote a vision of empowerment and challenge assumptions about power and control in the household for both women and men. For example, the wording can treat women as individuals who can make their own decisions, eliminating references to — and automatic, often erroneous assumptions about — male heads of households. Some microfinance institutions that require husbands' signatures for their wives' loans also require wives' signatures for their husbands' loans. Others do not require a spouse's signature for any loan and accept female as well as male guarantors. The sequencing of questions, types of detail required and way the interview is conducted can help applicants think through their financial planning — focusing on helping them think through their capacity to repay loans and save, and the types of insurance etc. they need, rather than treating this just as a policing exercise for the institution.

An empowerment vision can also be integrated into basic savings and credit training and group mobilisation without increasing costs of core training. Many issues within the household and community need to be discussed to enable women and men to anticipate problems with repayment, with continuing membership, and so on. Discussions need to equip women and men to devise solutions that also address the underlying gender inequalities that cause the problems in the first place. Even if men are not members, many women want their male family members to be invited to these meetings.

As noted above, participatory market research is now an accepted part of "good business practice" in MFIs, and also increasing in the commercial sector. However, participatory market research in itself does not necessarily produce products which will benefit women — even when women are targetted and information gender disaggregated. It may only point to products which can be profitably sold to women and/or men — which cannot be assumed to be the same thing. However, without additional costs, there are ways in which sampling and questioning can be adjusted to explicitly look at gender issues of access and control, empowerment impacts and gender-specific areas of vulnerability and need.[23] This can lead to design of products which increase women's incomes and control over incomes, and role in household decision-making. Examples include:

- loans or savings products to increase women's asset ownership, including land and housing;
- mechanisms to enable women to graduate from small to larger loans without discrimination, provided they have a good credit record;
- loan products and sponsorship of enterprise competitions to encourage women's enterprise in non-traditional activities and also in services needed by women;
- introduction not only of products specifically targeted at women, but revising the loan conditions for all products to ensure that there is no gender discrimination;
- encouragement of male savings for education of girls, assets for their daughters to take with them on marriage so that men's responsibility for the future of their daughters is encouraged and enable female savings to be used for enterprise investment;
- pension and long term savings products.

Banks generally use individual rather than group-based lending and may not have scope for introducing non-financial services. This means that they cannot be expected to have the type of focused empowerment strategies which NGOs have. However, there is now increasing acceptance of the idea of "smart subsidies" in relation to increasing poverty reach and/or complementary interventions on HIV/AIDS. Women's empowerment strategies are arguably the most effective means of addressing both poverty reach and household well-being, and also HIV/AIDS.

A key area of current discussion in relation to capacity building is financial literacy so that clients know their rights and can understand the information given to them in order to best use the services given. A number of financial literacy courses and methodologies have been developed. SEWA, Microfinance Opportunities with Freedom From Hunger,

[23]Gender-sensitive adaptations of market research tools are currently being developed by the author and participating MFIs in Oxfam Novib's WEMAN program. Drafts and updates will be found on www.genfinance.info from March 2010.

Womankind Worldwide and Siembra in Mexico have developed manuals for women's financial literacy.[24]

So far, financial literacy programs have been developed mostly for women. However, financial literacy for men, if it incorporates, for example, men's discussion of financial planning with their wives and equal participation in financial decisions, could contribute significantly to changing men's attitudes and behaviour. If such training were a condition of access to loans, it is more likely that men would attend such courses rather than generic gender training. There are, however, some potential dangers in financial literacy being delivered by individual MFIs as it could become merely another way of persuading clients that their products are the best. It might be more appropriate to provide this through BDS providers, or even as part of adult education.

Evidence from WEP–Nepal and FINCA–Peru suggest that delivery of women's enterprise training and/or financial literacy can not only increase client incomes, and hence repayment capacity, but also increases client retention and satisfaction and hence has substantial financial benefits for the institution (Valley Research Group and Mayoux, 2008; Frisancho *et al.*, 2008). In WEP–Nepal, the training of savings-led credit groups enabled these groups to not only survive, but also replicate themselves during the insurgency, when nearly all other village organisations broke up. Benefits for both clients and organisations do, however, very much depend on the relevance and effectiveness of the training on offer (Mayoux, 2005).

A current innovation being developed by the Oxfam Novib WEMAN program with partners LEAP in Sudan and GreenHome and Bukonzo Joint Savings self-managed microfinance in Uganda for both women and men, is a combined market research and financial literacy methodology. This is based on experience with Gender Action Learning System[25] for working with people who cannot read and write. The underlying idea is that simple diagrammatic tools can be used both as part of any organisation's market research process and/or on an ongoing basis by microfinance groups themselves as a

[24]Examples from a joint initiative from Microfinance opportunities and Freedom from Hunger can be found at www.microfinanceopportunities.org or www.ffh.org, from Womankind Worldwide at www.womankind.org, for Siembra at http://www.genfinance.info/Chennai/Case%20Studies/SiembraManual_Chapter%203.pdf and for SEWA at http://coady.stfx.ca/resources/abcd/SEWA%20Financial%20Literacy%20Manual.pdf. An early version of "EAT THAT FAT CAT" currently being further developed can be found at http://www.lindaswebs.org.uk/Page3_Orglearning/PALS/PALSIntro.htm.
[25]For details of GALS Tools, see www.wemanglobal.org.

continual process of participatory product development. At the same time, the tools are designed to increase participants' understanding of their situation and financial literacy and hence are an empowerment process in itself. The finished diagrams can be used as business plans and loan contracts with MFIs or even banks. In Sudan, India and Uganda, groups now use some of these tools with very little external supervision for purposes like increasing poverty inclusion of their groups and developing their own livelihood plans. Individuals are also teaching others in their household and communities the individual planning tools. This methodology therefore has potential to be self-replicating and once established, the peer learning financial education, instead of being a cost to the organisation, could be an effective means of self-recruitment of reliable new clients able to credibly communicate their own financial needs.

There are a number of ways to offer capacity-building in a more effective, cost-efficient and sustainable manner:

- Mutual learning and information exchange within groups could meet many basic training needs if systems are properly set up and funded initially (see Box 27.1). This training does not substitute for professional (expensive) training, but it enables such training to be targeted at those areas where it is really needed and builds peoples' capacities to absorb, benefit from, and disseminate such training.
- Implement a cross-subsidy: charge better-off clients (including men) for some services, such as business services and business registration and/or charging clients for more advanced training after they have taken subsidised basic courses.
- By developing formal or informal links with providers of other services, microfinance programs can increase their contribution at a minimal cost and give providers of other services ready access to a sizeable, organized constituency of poor women, which would in turn contribute to the sustainability of their own services. Interorganizational collaboration between microfinance programs and specialist providers of other types of service could take several forms. A microfinance program could advertise complementary services available from other organizations, such as advice and information about legal rights offered by local women's organisations. A microfinance program could refer clients to other organizations or make special arrangements for programs, groups, or individuals to pay for particular services. Collaboration could also take the form of sharing the costs of developing training programs and innovations or conducting research.

Box 27.1: Integrating gender indicators in social performance management and management information systems.

Possible gender indicators for insertion into social performance management.
Clients (from a rating survey — if MFI does not have this information):

- Percent of women clients who know and understand the terms of the financial services provided by the MFI (including different products available, cost of credit — interest rate [declining], if savings — then interest paid, if insurance — then premium paid, and terms of payout)
- (in mixed-sex program) percent of women accessing larger loans and higher level services; percent of women in leadership positions
- Percent of women clients with enterprise loans who themselves are working in the economic activity for which the credit is used (either by themselves, or jointly with husbands in a household enterprise disaggregated)

Source: Frances Sinha Indicators related to gender for social rating (unpublished draft for MI–CRIL).

Any or all of these means could be combined to increase cost-effectiveness over time. For example, after an initial focus on identifying mutual learning possibilities, collaborating organizations could apply for donor funds to develop them. They could then introduce service charges for their better-off members or non-members at a later date. In other cases, although the financial service providers themselves may be financially sustainable, complementary services may need to be treated as ongoing commitments to be met through donor funding — especially when services are seeking to reach very poor women.

In many rural areas, particularly more remote areas with very badly developed infrastructure, separating the delivery of financial services from other types of complementary support is not necessarily the most cost-efficient strategy, because it entails parallel sets of staff, high transport costs, and other duplicative costs. The desirability or undesirability of separating functions needs to be judged on the basis of the balance between a number of factors e.g., level of expertise required for the types of financial and non-financial services needed, levels of expertise of organizations and staff, availability of services from specialist training providers, and the relative costs in any particular context of e.g., transport and staff. It is also possible to separate the costs of delivering different services without separating their operational delivery.

In all the above, it is vital to stress that gender equality of access and women's empowerment are not "complementary" or "credit-plus" like literacy or business training. They are cross-cutting strategies that must be mainstreamed through the delivery of financial services themselves and other complementary interventions. At the same time, gender mainstreaming measures must complement rather than substitute for gender-specific services, particularly women's rights training for women (and men) as well as legal and other support for women with very difficult household situations.

6 Gender Indicators Are an Integral Part of Social Performance Management

A key element in gender mainstreaming is integration of gender indicators into information systems so that institutions are aware of what is happening in regard to gender equality of access, and also empowerment. The extent and type of gender-based information will obviously differ from institution to institution, depending on the nature of their existing management information systems.

In recent years, much of the innovation in microfinance has focused on poverty targeting and poverty depth. Some of the energy for this has been in response to the U.S. law passed in 2003 requiring the development and use of cost-effective poverty measurement tools by the United States Agency for International Development's (USAID's) microenterprise grantees. This has led to the compilation and refinement of a range of different tools for poverty assessment so that MFIs applying for funding from USAID, and also more widely, can assess the degree to which they are reaching the poorest.[26] The poverty assessment tools are based on a household measure divided equally by members of the household to give a dollar a day individual measure of income poverty. This has numerous pitfalls and methodological problems including how to account for non-market incomes, inter and

[26]For more details of these tools, see http://www.povertytools.org/index.html

intra-national variation in purchasing power and in expenditure and consumption patterns and needs, and reliability of client response.[27] All of these have gender dimensions which remain to be addressed.[28] In particular, they are unlikely to be able to accurately assess individual dollar a day poverty without addressing intra-household inequalities. Failure to address inequalities within the household may further decrease the access of women in households just around the poverty line i.e., the main target group of financially sustainable MFIs. This is the case even though women themselves may be extremely vulnerable within these households and well below the dollar a day cut-off in terms of their own incomes and expenditure.

The recent advances in Social Rating and Social Performance Management[29] seek to include social indicators and social audits incorporating areas like poverty reach as an integral part of rating and performance assessment alongside financial indicators. However, SPM is not necessarily gender-sensitive and, like the poverty tools, may even militate against female targeting. Gender is treated as one possible dimension of an organisation's mission against which performance would be assessed. The degree to which social performance management will therefore promote gender issues will depend on whether or not gender is already part of the organisation's vision and mission, and whether or not it has the tools already to assess performance in relation to gender and/or has conducted gender impact assessment. Unless gender is an explicit and integral part of the definition of "social", there are dangers that gender equity in terms of both access and empowerment will become completely swamped in the other range of performance indicators.

A detailed discussion of the complexities of gender and empowerment impact assessment, particularly intra-household impact assessment, is outside the scope of this paper.[30] Some writers have proposed gender impact indicators like those in Box 27.1 which could be easily integrated into SPM

---

[27] A full discussion of these issues is outside the scope of this paper; however, some very interesting critical papers can be found on the links page of the poverty tools site http://www.povertytools.org/Links/links.htm.

[28] See Mayoux (2002) http://www.povertytools.org/Project_Documents/Gender%20Issues%20draft%20072104.pdf, Chant (2003) http://www.eclac.cl/publicaciones/xml/6/13156/lcl1955i.pdf and Gammage (2006) http://pdf.usaid.gov/pdf_docs/PNADH568.pdf.

[29] See for example, IFAD (2006: 1287).

[30] See, for example, questionnaire at end of Zaidi *et al.* (2007) and discussion in Mayoux (2004a).

and other information systems, provided the application, follow up and particularly repeat loan and exit assessments are properly conducted in the interests of client understanding, not just rapid institutional expansion. This is an area where much more discussion is needed on how gender indicators can be integrated into management information systems of different types — particularly the trade-off between manageability and depth of information to make any conclusions meaningful.[31]

7 Consumer Protection and Regulatory Policies Integrate Gender Equality of Opportunity and Empowerment

A recent area of concern because of both the proliferation of products and the increasing numbers of competitors in the microfinance market has been the issue of consumer protection: Do people, particularly the poor, know what they are signing up for, and how can they be protected from abuse? Since at least 2003, many microfinance networks, including ACCION, have been developing and implementing consumer protection guidelines covering both relations with clients and quality of products and services.[32]

These guidelines currently contain no explicit references to women, but potentially offer some protection to both women and men, for example, the specifications of treatment with respect, privacy and ethical behaviour. However, in order to make them effective in protecting women as well as men, it is desirable to make explicit reference to women and also make sure they cover specific forms of discrimination and vulnerability which women are likely to face. In addition, these guidelines, including the gender dimensions, need to be included in all staff training and induction and in client application processes and financial literacy training.[33]

It is also unclear how seriously financial service providers would take such principles on an individual institutional level. Ideally these would be

---

[31]See Sinha (2009). A manual for integrating gender in SPM is also currently being prepared by Frances Sinha and others. For further details, see http://www. genfinance.info.
[32]See in particular SEEP (2006) and an overview of the October 2006 discussion on MicroLinks available at http://www.microlinks.org/file_download.php/SC+15+Summary+Document.pdf?URL_ID=13137&filename=11618091991SC_15_Summary_Document.pdf&filetype=application%2Fpdf&filesize=933903&name=SC+15+Summary+Document.pdf&location=user-S/
[33]See proposals at http://www.genfinance.info.

part of the overarching regulatory framework at national level, and required part of any support from government and donors.

8 Gender Justice Advocacy

Many of the forms of discrimination which prevent women from both accessing and benefiting from financial services involve wider systems of inequality in access to and control over resources, gender-based violence and overwhelming responsibility for the unpaid care economy. It was recognised even in the "Bible" of financial sustainability by Otero and Rhyne in 1994[34] that advocacy and change in women's property rights was an essential pre-requisite of women making substantial progress. However, gender advocacy in these crucial areas has disappeared off the agenda of the microfinance movement.

Group-based savings and credit for women was seen as a key innovation of microfinance, combining efficiency and effective poverty targeting with empowerment (Otero and Rhyne, 1994). Many microfinance programs have engaged in collective action on land rights, violence and political participation.[35] Savings and credit groups can provide an acceptable forum for women to come together to discuss gender issues and organize for change. For example, women's groups in Zambuko Trust in Zimbabwe spontaneously invited a woman to give talks on "how to manage your husband and mother-in-law" (Cheston and Kuhn, 2002). In South Asia and Africa, microfinance groups have demonstrated their potential to promote change with respect to domestic violence, male alcohol abuse, and dowries.

In some organisations, microfinance services have provided the basis for increasing women's ownership of land and women's property rights. Property rights are fundamental to women's ability to access and benefit from financial services and are key elements in poverty reduction and rural and enterprise development. Within the financial sustainability literature, women's equal property rights are explicitly regarded as an essential part of the enabling environment for gender and microfinance (Otero and Rhyne, 1994). A number of strategies have been employed by microfinance programs

[34]Otero, M and E Rhyne (eds.) (1994).

[35]See for example initiatives by SEWA in India www.sewa.org, ANANDI in India www.anandiindia.net and LEAP in Sudan www.leap-pased.org and the Gender Action Learning System being developed as part of Oxfam Novib's WEMAN program http://www.palsnetwork.info.

to support improvements in women's property ownership and rights through microfinance initiatives. This is in addition to development of specific products like Grameen Bank's Housing loan and land-leasing products.

Group-based financial services can also provide a potentially large and organized grassroots base for political mobilization, increasing women's awareness of wider political processes and their leadership capacities to participate in politics. In India, many organizations are involved in promoting women's leadership in local council bodies. SEWA, for example, promotes women's unions and organizations. Grameen Bank and other MFIs in Bangladesh disseminated voter education material to women through their organization before the last elections.[36] In Africa, CARE–Niger has been very effective in developing women's leadership to compete in local elections. By increasing the participation of half the population, group-based financial services can significantly contribute to improving local governance and developing democratic systems.

A number of organisations with microfinance programs have developed other innovations to put their women's groups at the forefront of citizen development in rural areas. Rural Information Centres were developed by Hand in Hand, Swayam Shikshan Prayog, ANANDI (India) and LEAP in Sudan to help women obtain information from the Internet and as a resource for the groups or clusters to generate income. Illiteracy no longer needs to be a barrier to using such facilities. Software and technology can now make a lot of information accessible through voice transmission, video, and other formats. Despite support from numerous donors, however, many centers remain under-used for lack of community organization and training, or they are dominated by male youth (in some places, for downloading pornography). When managed by women's self-help groups or cluster organizations, the centers often can be managed effectively for the community.

It is important that commercial financial services providers link with and support these type of initiatives — both as a means of accessing a bigger market, and to support their existing clients in an empowerment process. This could be done through targeting of their charitable funds at such initiatives and/or supporting community-led initiatives. Gender justice advocacy also needs to be an integral part of "mainstream" advocacy and lobbying activities for the financial sector.

---

[36]Mohammad Yunus in "Empowering Women" Countdown 2005, MicroCredit Summit Campaign.

9 The Specific Needs and Interests of Very Poor and Vulnerable Women Are Included

In all the above, mainstreaming gender and women's empowerment can be largely achieved through better design of financially sustainable financial services and existing capacity building. Many women from households just above or just below the poverty line, in combination with the other resources at their disposal, can make significant steps forward if they are given a level playing field with men.

There are however specific challenges when working with the poorest women, as with the poorest men. These challenges have not only poverty but also specific gender dimensions:

- Lower levels of literacy;
- Lower levels of access to and control over resources — even "female-specific" assets like jewelry — which can complement financial services as inputs to economic activities;
- Lower levels of access to networks and human resources who can assist and support;
- Greater vulnerability to sexual exploitation and abuse at the community level, if not the household level.

This means that it is crucial that better poverty assessment tools are developed to incorporate these gender dimensions of vulnerability and poverty, and that the specific needs of the poorest women are taken into account in product development, market research, financial literacy, consumer protection etc.

10 Promoting an Enabling Environment for Gender Justice in Financial Services: Role of National Networks, Government and Donors

As indicated above, underlying this paper is the framework of a diversified, inclusive and sustainable financial sector capable of making a significant contribution to economic growth, pro-poor development and civil society strengthening. Gender justice, gender equality of opportunity and women's empowerment are essential components of any claims to inclusion, pro-poor development and civil society strengthening, and also significant contributions to economic growth. However, despite the considerable potential contribution of the commercial sector and positive interlinkages between gender justice and financial sustainability, it is unlikely that significant progress will be made through reliance on the commercial sector alone — given the current trends, pressures for rapid expansion and short-term financial sustainability and overwhelming strength of gender discrimination and vested interests.

It is therefore crucial that governments and donors take steps to honour their gender mandates in terms of support for an enabling environment for gender justice within which the commercial sector will play its part, but in the context of an appropriate policy environment and in collaboration with a strong gender justice movement of NGOs and civil society organisations.

There are a range of potential measures which government and donors can take at the intermediate and national levels to provide such an enabling environment, in particular promoting collation of information and exchange of experience on gender innovations of the types discussed above. Many of the more costly non-financial services might be better provided through a network of providers. Financial literacy, for example, as noted above, is arguably best provided by impartial organisations e.g., capacity-building NGOs or integrated into adult education programs rather than by financial service providers to avoid them being used as just one more form of marketing to clients. There is a need to collect comparative information on gender access and gender impact from different types of providers to assess the best strategies. It is also important that these good practices, and women's own strategies and perspectives move from being "marginal gender specialisms" to being an integral part of mainstream training for bankers and other staff — essential as they are to ensuring that over half of potential microfinance clients benefit from their services.

The implications for donors of all these institutional possibilities is that they are likely to need to draw on gender expertise for organizational gender assessment and training to help financial service organisations identify the most efficient and effective ways of implementing strategies like those outlined above. Ideally, there would be a set of agreed organizational gender indicators and a gender performance rating system — differentiating those of their partners and projects who are at the forefront of innovation on gender and who could thus provide examples to others, those who are open to change but do not yet have capacity and who thus require capacity building, and those who are not interested in change. Over time, the decision would need to be made as to whether to continue to fund the last, as their development contribution is likely to be far less than the other two.[37]

Many donor agencies operate not only through promoting and supporting rural financial institutions and stakeholder participation, but also promoting a conducive policy and regulatory environment. Enabling and promoting the above gender strategies requires gender justice to be mainstreamed at this macro-level, in regulatory frameworks, consumer protection, advocacy strategies of microfinance networks and mainstreaming gender in other supporting interventions.

Firstly, if all financial service providers promoted by governments and donors were required, or at least encouraged to mainstream gender justice in some of the ways discussed above, then this would go a long way not only to increasing gender equality of access, but also a conducive environment for women's empowerment. If all members of microfinance networks and banks promoted a vision of women's empowerment in promotional materials, advertising, and in interactions with their now millions of clients, this would be a significant contribution not only to empowerment of their clients, but to changing attitudes towards women's economic activities and social roles in the community and internationally.

Secondly, microfinance institutions and banks are increasingly concerned with their impact on local and national economies, both in terms of market distortion and also environmental sustainability. There has recently been increasing interest in value chain finance from donors and institutions themselves in order to better target credit to parts of the value chain which can best promote increased production, incomes and employment.[38] Most value chain analysis and development have so far been gender-blind, with the likely outcomes of further marginalizing women. It is therefore crucial that gender issues are fully mainstreamed in this new development. Ways of mainstreaming gender in value chain development are discussed in detail by the author elsewhere.[39]

Finally, many microfinance networks are involved in advocacy on issues affecting the sector. However, gender issues are rarely part of this advocacy — despite early recognition of the importance of changing property legislation to enable women to take real advantage of financially

[37]A system like this has been introduced by some international NGOs like Oxfam Novib. See Mukhopadhyay *et al.* (2006).

[38]See, for example, Shepherd (2004), Chalmers (2005), Jansen *et al.* (2007).

[39]For ways in which this can be done, see, for example, Mayoux and Mackie (2009).

sustainable financial services (Otero, 1994:2). There is a need for these networks to include lobbying and advocacy on issues like women's property rights, informal sector protection and violence which affect their clients, and hence sustainability as well as the whole development process.

References

Ashe, J and L Parrott (2001). PACT's Women's Empowerment Program in Nepal: A Savings and Literacy Led Alternative to Financial Institution Building. PACT.

Binns, H (1998). Integrating a Gender Perspective in Micro-finance in ACP Countries. Brussels, European Commission.

Blackden, M and C Bhanu (1999). Gender, Growth and Poverty Reduction, World Bank Technical Paper 428,Washington DC.

Chalmers, G (2005). A fresh look at rural & agricultural finance. Retrieved Nov 2007, from RN__1_A_Fresh_Look_at_RAF[1].pdf.

Chant, S (2003). New contributions to the analysis of poverty: Methodological and conceptual challenges to understanding poverty from a gender, perspective. Mujer y desarrollo, Santiago, Chile, CEPAL, Women and Development Unit, United Nations.http://www.eldis.org/cf/rdr/rdr.cfm?doc=DOC14786.

Cheston, S and L Kuhn (2002). Empowering women through microfinance. In *Pathways Out of Poverty: Innovations in Microfinance for the Poorest Families.* S Daley–Harris (ed.). 167–228. Bloomfield, Kumarian Press.

Cheston, S (2006). Just the Facts, Ma'am: Gender Stories from Unexpected Sources with Morals for Micro-finance. *Micro Credit Summit*, from http://www.microcreditsummit.org/papers/Workshops/28_Cheston.pdf.

DFID (2000). Poverty Elimination and Empowerment of Women: Target Strategy Paper. Retrieved Nov 2011, from http://www.dfid.gov.uk/pubs/files/tspgender.pdf.

Frank, C, E Lynch and L Schneider–Moretto (2008). Stemming the Tide of Mission Drift: Microfinance Transformations and the Double Bottom Line. New York: Women's World Banking.

Frisancho, V, D Karlan and M Valdivia (2008). Business Training for Microfinance Clients: How it Matters and for Whom?, Poverty and Economic Policy Research Network. PMMA Working Paper 2008–11. http://www.microfinancegateway.org/p/site/m//template.rc/1.9.30264.

Gammage, S (2006). *A Menu of Options for Intra-Household Poverty Assessment.* Washington: USAID.

Groverman, V and JD Gurung (2001). *Gender and Organisational Change: Training Manual.* Katmandu: ICIMOD.

Groverman, V, T Lebesech and DS Bunmi (2008). Self-assessing your organisation's gender competence: A Facilitator's Guide to support NGOs in assessing their gender competence and in planning for gender mainstreaming.

IFAD (2006). Assessing and managing social performance in microfinance.

ILO (2007). *FAMOS Check Guide and Methods.* Geneva: ILO.

Jansen, A, T Pomeroy, J Antal and T Shaw (2007). Mali Value Chain Finance Study: Using a Value Chain Framework to Identify Financing Needs: Lessons learned from Mali. From mR_81_Mali_Value_Chain_Finance_Study[1].pdf.

Johnson, S (1997). *Gender and Micro-finance: Guidelines for Best Practice.* London: Action Aid-UK.

Kabeer, N (1998). Money Can't Buy Me Love? Re-evaluating Gender, Credit and Empowerment in Rural Bangladesh. Brighton, IDS.

Kabeer, N (2001). Conflicts over credit: Re-evaluating the empowerment potential of loans to women in rural Bangladesh. *World Development*, 29(1), 63–84.

Klasen, S (2002). Insert of the Holy Grail: How to Achieve Pro-poor growth? Munich, University of Munich, Department of Economics.

Macdonald, M, E Sprenger and I Dubel (1997). *Gender, and Organisational Change: Bridging the Gap between Policy and Practice.* Amsterdam: Royal Tropical Institute.

Magner, M (2007). Microfinance: A Platform for Social Change. http://www.grameenfoundation.org/pubdownload/dl.php.

Mayoux, L (1999). Questioning virtuous spirals: Micro-finance and women's empowerment in Africa. *Journal of International Development*, 11, 957–984.

Mayoux, L (2000). *Micro-Finance and the Empowerment of Women — A Review of the Key Issues.* Geneva: ILO.

Mayoux, L (2001). Tackling the Down Side: Social Capital, Women's Empowerment and Microfinance in Cameroon. *Development and Change*, 3(32), http://www.microfinancegateway.org/files/18143_Tackling_the_Down_Side_Cameroon_.pdf.

Mayoux, L (2004a). Intra-household Impact Assessment: Issues and Participatory Tools. Available at: http://www.sed.manchester.ac.uk/research/iarc/ediais/EINOctø4.pdf.

Mayoux, L (2004b). Gender Issues in Developing Poverty Tools. Draft, Washington DC, USAID/AMAP. http://www.povertytools.org/Project_Documents/Gender%20Issues%20draft%20072104.pdf.

Mayoux, L (2005). Learning and Decent Work for All: New Directions in Training and Education for Pro-poor Development. Draft. Geneva, ILO. http://www.microfinancegateway.org/p/site/m/template.rc/1.9.24903/.

Mayoux, L (2008). Module 3: Gender and Rural Finance. *Gender and Agriculture Source Book.* Washington DC: World Bank.

Mayoux, L (2009a). *A Gender Justice Protocol for Financial Services: Framework, Issues and Ways Forward.* The Hague: Oxfam Novib.

Mayoux, L (2009b). *Reaching and Empowering Women: Gender Mainstreaming in Rural Microfinance: Guide for Practitioners.* Rome: IFAD.

Mayoux, LC (2010). Diamonds are a Girl's Best Friend: Experience with Gender Action Learning System. In *Elgar International Handobook on Gender and Poverty*, S Chant (ed.), pp. 84–94. Edward Elgar.

Mayoux, L and G Mackie (2009). *Making Stronger Links: Gender and Value Chain Action Learning, A Practical Guide.* Geneva: ILO. Available at: http://www.ilo.org/empent/Whatwedo/Publications/lang-en/docName-WCMS_111373/index.html.

Mayoux, LC, P Baluku *et al.* (2009). Balanced Trees Grow Better Beans Community-led change in gender relations in Uganda. www.wemanglobal.org

Mukhopadhyay, M, G Steehouwer and F Wong (2006). *Politics of the Possible: Gender Mainstreaming and Organisational Change: Experiences from the Field.* The Hague: Royal Tropical Institute and Oxfam Novib.

Otero, M and E Rhyne (eds.) (1994). *The New World of Microenterprise Finance: Building Healthy Financial Institutions for the Poor.* London: IT Publications.

Results (1997). *The Micro Credit Summit Declaration and Plan of Action.* Washington DC: RESULTS.

SEEP (2006). Consumer protection Principles in Practice: A Framework for Developing and Implementing a Pro-Client Approach to Micro-finance. Progress Note 14 October, 2006. http://www.seepnetwork.org/content/article/detail/4664.

Shepherd, AW (2004). Financing agricultural marketing. Retrieved Nov 2007, from http://www.fao.org/ag/ags/subjects/en/agmarket/markfinance.pdf.

Sinha, F (2009). Integrating Gender Equity into Social Performance Management in Microfinance: Workshop Report. Gurgaon, India, EDA Rural Systems.

UNIFEM (1993). *An End to Debt: Operational Guidelines for Credit Projects.* New York: UNIFEM.

UNIFEM (1995). *A Question of Access: A Training Manual on Planning Credit Projects that Take Women into Account.* New York: UNIFEM.

Valley Research Group and L Mayoux (2008). *Women Ending Poverty: The Worth Program in Nepal — Empowerment Through Literacy Banking and Business 1999–2007.* Kathmandu, Nepal: PACT. http://www.microfinancegateway.org/p/site/m//template.rc/1.9.34360.

Watson, AA and C Dunford (2006). From Microfinance to Macro Change: Integrating Health, Education and Microfinance to Empower Women and Reduce Poverty. *Microcredit Summit*, Halifax. http://www.microcreditsummit.org/papers/UNFPA_Advocacy_FINAL.pdf.

Zaidi, S Akbar, H Jamal, S Javeed and S Zaka (2007). *Social Impact Assessment of Microfinance Programmes.* Study Commissioned by and Submitted to the European Union–Pakistan Financial Services Sector Reform Programme, Islamabad.

Higher Education Through Microfinance: The Case of Grameen Bank*

Asif U. Dowla†
St. Mary's College of Maryland

1 Introduction[1]

Nurjahan was a typical teenager growing up in rural Bangladesh. She was a good student who loved going to school and spending time with her extended family. She received merit scholarships from the government for excelling in regional-level examinations at the primary and junior levels. However, her carefree days of being a 15-year old came to a halt when she was married off because her family could not afford to pay for her continuing education. But, because her father could not afford to pay the agreed-upon dowry, Nurjahan was divorced within four months of the marriage. When she returned home, Nurjahan resumed her education undeterred. She paid for part of the cost of her education by working as a tutor for the children of rich families and passed the Secondary and Higher Secondary Certificate examinations with distinctions. Nurjahan's lifelong dream was to become a physician. However, while she and her family could pay for her educational expenses at the high school level, medical school expenses were beyond their reach. In addition, Nurjahan's family also had to pay school fees for all her siblings and the family was not rich enough and did not have enough collateral to qualify for a loan from the private and nationalized commercial banks.

*I thank the scientific committee for comments on the draft version of the paper. I am grateful to Lindy McBride for editorial assistance.
†Hilda C. Landers Endowed Chair in the Liberal Arts, Department of Economics, St. Mary's College of Maryland, USA.
[1]This is an updated version of part of chapter 7 of my book co-authored with Dipal Barua (Dowla and Barua, 2006).

The family was dependent mainly on the meager incomes of Nurjahan's father, who was a teacher in the religious school, and her mother, who had a home-based tailoring shop funded by loans from Grameen Bank. Fortunately, because her mother was a member of the Grameen Bank in good standing, Nurjahan qualified for an education loan from the bank. She used the loan to pay for her tuition and room and board while in medical school. Today Nurjahan is a practicing gynecologist who repaid her loan before it was due so that the money could be used by others less fortunate than she was.

Nurjahan's story reflects the main idea of this handbook — that there is a "mismatch" between what the potential clients demand and what MFIs offer in terms of financial products. Prior to the introduction of education loans by Grameen Bank, a student, especially a female student such as Nurjahan, would have had to give up her dream of becoming a doctor. She would probably have received a general education in the local college and her family would have gone into debt trying to marry her off again. Now, thanks to the education loan of Grameen Bank, she is a self-confident, independent woman who is helping other people.

2 Grameen Bank and Education

In the last two decades, Bangladesh has made a remarkable turnaround in expanding access to primary and secondary education for the poor and for girls. This was made possible through large investment in schools, materials and teachers funded by the donors, the government, communities and the households (Hossain, 2004). More importantly, there was a dramatic change in the cultural norms about the value of female education (Hossain and Kabeer, 2004). Almost 75 percent of the sample in the World Bank Gender Norm Survey of 2006 believed that girls should have as much education as boys (World Bank, 2008). In 1991, only 20 percent of Bangladeshi females could read and write, making them among the least educated females in the world. By the end of the 20th century, the gross enrollment rate in primary education was over 100 percent, and the gender gap in education at the primary level had been eliminated (Hossain and Kabeer, 2004). Similar improvements occurred in secondary schools. Since 1994, the enrollment of girls in secondary school has increased at a rate of 13 percent per year, while boys' enrollment has increased by 2.5 percent per year (Khandker *et al.*, 2003). Bangladesh is one of the few countries in the developing world that has achieved this degree of parity across gender lines and it now has one of the largest primary education systems in the world (Hossain, 2004). This success is attributable to political commitments, change in the norms and values regarding the importance of girls' education, and, more importantly, to several incentive programs implemented by the Bangladeshi government to redress gender inequity in enrollment (Hossain, 2004).[2]

Grameen Bank started in 1978 when the poor deemed education as a luxury that they could not afford. Through its long experience in dealing with poor clients, Grameen Bank was aware of the borrowers' aspirations to educate their children. When borrowers are queried about their dreams for their children, a common response is that they hope their children will not be members of Grameen Bank. Even though such a response seems paradoxical, there is a valid rationale for it. Grameen Bank is a bank for poor people, and, like all good parents, borrowers do not want their children to be poor as adults.[3] The majority of borrowers hope that their children will become educated and join government service, become successful businessmen, or get involved in another respectable occupation (Rahman *et al.*, 2002). This rising aspiration for children's education and future is fairly widespread among all classes in Bangladesh (Hossain and Kabeer, 2004; World Bank, 2008).

From its inception, Grameen Bank has always encouraged its members to send their children to school. Grameen's original focus on female membership was due to the staff's realization that to make a fundamental change in the lives of the poor, credit must be channeled to the women. A fact borne out empirically in Bangladesh, as well as many other parts of the world, is that when women have financial resources, they use them primarily for the welfare of their families. Within the family, significant additional financial resources are used for the welfare of the children, especially for costs such as school fees and educational supplies. The borrowers codified this emphasis on the importance of children's education into the Sixteen Decisions, the social charter adopted by the members in 1984. Decision 7 states, "We shall educate our children and ensure that they can earn to pay for their education." The borrowers adopted the Sixteen Decisions in 1984. At that time, mostly the sons of rich families in rural and urban areas were going to

[2]The government initiatives include free primary education, Food-for-Education, Cash-for-Education, and the Female Secondary School Assistance Program.

[3]This notion of greater class mobility is widely accepted as a fact in rich countries. However, in poor countries, class mobility is rather limited; a poor person's children are more likely to be poor, and the most important means of improving class mobility is higher education.

school. Despite widespread aspiration for education, the poor families were unable to send their boys to school because of high direct and indirect costs, and there was little support for educating the girls (Hossain and Kabeer, 2004, and Todd, 1996). So, the bank had to use Sixteen Decision to inculcate the norm of educating the children irrespective of gender.[4]

During its earlier days, the bank promoted children's education by helping to establish schools in the centers. Borrowers contributed to pay for a teacher, buy textbooks at cost from the bank, and set up one room school in the center house where they met weekly to pay off the installments. The teachers were members' children and local youths. Instruction in reading, writing, arithmetic, and forms of physical and creative expression were provided in center houses in the mornings and evenings. In 1990, around 4000 such schools were managed by the centers (Jain, 1996). However, with the rapid expansion of government schools in the rural areas and with parents opting to send their children to those schools, the center schools eventually became unnecessary. To directly encourage the borrowers' children to get educated, Grameen Bank started a monthly scholarship program in 1999. The scholarships reward excellence in national tests in the fifth, eighth, 10th and 12th grades as well as extracurricular activities.

Anecdotal evidence suggests that the increased income that results from the use of credit is put towards children's education and that access to credit has increased the demand for children's education. Theoretical analysis suggests, however, that increased credit may have an ambiguous effect on children's schooling. This ambiguity occurs because children are both consumption and production goods: the family derives satisfaction from having children and benefits from their use in family enterprises. An increase in income due to credit, then, will lead to higher demand for education of the children, or what theoreticians call "income effect". Credit that facilitates owning and using more capital, however, could increase the productivity of children's work, thereby making it too costly to send them to school instead of using them in a family enterprise. This is known as the "substitution effect". However, the higher income that is made possible by the increased productivity of children will increase the income of the household in the long run. This change at long-term wealth induces borrowers to raise more and better-educated children.

[4]It is true that the borrowers do not put into practice some of the Sixteen Decisions, such as the pledge not to pay and receive dowry. This is because of a lack of social sanctions against violating this norm and the pre-existing norm of buying offspring's happiness by paying dowry trumps the new norm of not paying (Dowla, 2006).

In addition, many MFIs, including Grameen Bank, provide members with non-credit services or social intermediation, such as vocational training, organizational help, and social development instructions aimed at improving health, literacy, leadership skills, and social empowerment (McKernan, 2002). Chase (1997) suggests that these non-credit services could also lead to higher demand for children's education by increasing its perceived benefit.

Wydick (1999) identifies two effects of microcredit on children's education. He labels the first one the "family-labor substitution effect". Wydick suggests that credit, through the increased use of capital, could increase the productivity of family labor and, as a result, increase the cost of sending the children to school. This echoes the "substitution effect" mentioned previously. He calls the other effect the "household-enterprise-capitalization effect". In this case, an increase in credit may lead the family to substitute hired labor for child labor if the credit relaxes the constraint on working capital needs. Using data from Guatemala, Wydick found that the relationship between access to credit and schooling is not unequivocally positive.

Maldanado, González–Vega and Romero (2003) identify several more routes through which credit might affect schooling. Research shows that when households face interruptions to their income due to crises, they tend to take their children out of school as part of a coping mechanism (Jacoby and Skoufias, 1997). By providing access to regular and emergency loans and promoting the build-up of income-earning assets, Maldanado and co-authors believe that the use of credit from the MFIs makes it less likely that children will be withdrawn from school in response to adverse shocks. They call this the "risk-management effect". However, these researchers also point out that additional activities made possible through credit may also increase the demand for child labor. In this respect, their findings are similar to Wydick's "family-labor substitution effect".[5] The empirical exercise of Malanado and co-authors, however, shows that, credit from MFIs increases children's schooling, mainly through income and risk management channels.

This research team also points out that, compared with men, women show a greater desire to educate their children. MFIs' specific targeting of women for delivery of credit will help increase their power to influence household schooling decisions. The improved bargaining position and empowerment of women gain through access to credit, these researchers believe, will increase the schooling of children, an outcome they term "gender effect".

---

[5]Maldonado and his co-authors label the increase in demand for children's schooling due to non-credit services provided by MFIs as the "education effect".

In the context of Bangladesh, a different gender-associated effect is also pertinent. An increase in credit-related activities causes the female to reduce the time she spends on household chores; this slack must be picked up by the children, most often the female child, thereby reducing her schooling (Pitt and Khandker, 1998).

This brief survey of theoretical results suggests that credit can have an ambiguous effect on the education of children. To find the truth among the various theories regarding the credit-education relationship, researchers have tried to verify empirically whether credit from Grameen Bank increases the likelihood of borrowers' children enrolling in school. Although her results were based on a very limited sample, Todd (1996) found that 100 percent of the female children of Grameen borrowers had some schooling, compared with only 60 percent of girls in the control group of households that qualified for a loan from the bank but chose not to participate. In the case of boys, Todd found that the participation rate was 80 percent for borrowers compared with 62 percent for non-borrowers. Todd also measured schooling by observing the number of years of schooling annually completed by each child as a percentage of the number of years he or she should have completed, given the child's age. This measure is an attempt to capture the true effect of credit on schooling. Once again, the Grameen borrowers came out ahead with 62 percent of possible school years completed, compared with only 44 percent for the control group children. Todd suggests that girls are receiving more schooling than boys because "boys can earn cash income for their families as young as eight years old". Such a simple comparison between the borrowers and the control group and the use of a small sample make the results, however, subject to many biases.[6]

A World Bank study (Pitt and Khandker, 1998) corrected for these biases by using a better methodology and scientifically choosing a larger sample size. It found that a 1 percent increase in credit to women by Grameen Bank increased the probability of a girl's school enrollment by 1.86 percent. However, similar increases in credit to men did not affect a girl's enrollment. The response for boy's schooling, however, was much higher: a 1 percent increase in credit provided to women and men increased the probability of boy's schooling by 2.4 percent and 2.8 percent, respectively. This suggests that there is a strong preference for boy's schooling among Grameen Bank members at the time, despite attempts to increase member awareness of the

[6]For a more detailed explanation of these biases, see Pitt and Khandker (1998).

benefits of educating female children. More importantly, Pitt and Khandker (1998) report that, among the three organizations serving the poor in their data set, education of girls is only significant when the clients borrow from Grameen Bank, not from the other two. They suggest that the reason for this may be that a girl's activities form a close substitute for a woman's activities for the other two organizations. It is the female child who assumes the mother's household responsibilities when the mother becomes involved in a self-employment project. They could not verify empirically if the positive result for Grameen Bank was due to the Sixteen Decisions.

Using the same data set with a slightly different estimation technique and a different measure for educational attainment, however, Jessica Chase (1997) was able to replicate Pitt and Khandker's results for boys' school enrollment. She found that boys in Grameen families have a higher probability of school enrollment as well as greater levels of educational attainment. Unlike Pitt and Khandker (1998), she did not examine how credit to men and women affect the schooling of boys and girls. Nor did she find any evidence of an effect of Grameen membership on girls' schooling. Rather, Chase (1997) found that credit had a neutral effect on the schooling of girls: neither the demand for more education nor the demand for more household labor had an effect on Grameen girls' school attendance. She suggests that the different impacts of Grameen's credit on male and female children may involve circumstances beyond the bank's control. If given an opportunity to educate one child and keep one at home, Chase believes, the family may choose educating the boy over the girl because the family is more likely to reap the benefits of investment in a boy's education. The family may perceive that the return on the education of a male child is higher than that of a female child. One of Todd's respondents noted that "daughters need some education, but not too much. If we spend a lot of taka on the daughter's education there is no return to us, she will take it all to another household".[7] The same sentiments were captured by a survey conducted by Chase to identify the reasons for a lack of current enrollment in school: 8 percent of boys in the sample mentioned their "parents did not want" them to have an education, compared with 27 percent of girls citing this reason. In retrospect, we should point out that these studies were conducted in the early 80s and 90s before the massive investment in the education sector by the government and the changes in social norms for female education took hold.

---

[7]Todd, H (1996). *Women at the Center: Grameen Bank Borrowers after One Decade*, 200–201. Boulder, CO: Westview Press.

3 Higher Education Loan

Grameen Bank is now more than 27 years old. The first generations of borrowers are close to retirement age, and many of their children are entering university. From the very beginning, the bank has been committed to making qualitative changes in the lives of its borrowers — a commitment it continues to fulfill by encouraging borrowers to educate their children and helping them to do so. In addition to the scholarship, the bank is also helping to improve children's education by providing additional sources for paying for their schooling, especially at the undergraduate and graduate levels.

The bank's internal survey shows that significant numbers of borrowers' children are, in fact, attending school. Despite the significant progress in enrollment at the primary, secondary and higher secondary levels, however, the survey also reveals that there was a dramatic drop in enrollment in post–higher secondary education programs in the year 2000. The same trend is also observed at the national level. In 2005, the gross enrollment rate in the tertiary sector was 6 percent compared to 92 percent, 62 percent, and 41 percent in primary, secondary, and higher secondary level respectively (Al–Samarrai, 2007). The bank's survey also revealed a much greater drop in the enrollment of female students after higher secondary education, due mainly to the cultural prerogative that females should be married and raising a family by a certain age.

A similar trend is observed at the national level. The gender gap is widest at the tertiary level — approximately two male students for each female student. Such disparity is in sharp contrast to the extremely high demand for higher education revealed by a focus group discussion with adolescent girls (World Bank, 2008). Several recent changes in the economy and the society also increased the demand for higher education by the parents, especially for the girls. Increasing economic opportunities fuelled by significant economic growth and increases in public sector employment opportunities have encouraged investment in higher education. Population growth and increased pressure on the land have reduced the profitability for farming as a profession and have therefore increased the demand for educated sons. Rising divorce, dowry and desertion suggested that, instead of marriage, women need economic security through employment, made possible through higher education. The emergence of the export-oriented garment industry in the 80s increased women's employment opportunity and this has increased the demand for educating girls (Hossain, 2004).

Despite the bank's efforts and the value attached to higher education in the society as a whole, cost is an impediment to children's continued education. The high cost of education beyond the post-secondary level is cited in the 2000 internal survey as one of the top reasons for the drop in school enrollment of borrowers' children.[8] Even though primary education is free, families end up paying hidden fees or bribes to teachers for these so-called free services (Tietjen, 2003). Moreover, the schools face serious problems with absentee teachers and poor-quality instruction.[9] As a result, families that can afford the costs end up using private tutoring, which adds to the overall price of education. The private cost of education increases at a growing rate with the level of education. The cost of post-secondary education increases rapidly because of the student's need to leave home, stay in a dormitory, and pay for room and board. According to the Household Income and Expenditure Survey of 2005, poor households spend 4856 (US$ 71) Taka per student compared to the 18, 225 (US$ 282) Taka paid by rich households annually for tertiary level education. The higher cost burden on the rich is reflected in the different enrollment rates between the rich and poor: the gross enrollment rate for the poor household is 1 compared to 8 for the rich household (Al–Samarrai, 2007).

To ease the burden of the cost of university-level education, in 1997, the bank introduced an education loan for the children of borrowers. Unlike the situation in wealthier countries where the government provides such loans, Grameen Bank — a member-owned institution — decided to provide these loans to finance higher education for the children of its members. All children of borrowers who have a loan, whether a basic or rescheduled loan, with the bank and have been members of the bank for at least a year are eligible to receive such loans.[10]

The loan finances all costs of higher education from admission to a course to the successful completion of that course, including admission fees, education supplies, tuition, room and board, and so on. The loan is given to students pursuing graduate or postgraduate degrees and professional education

---

[8]The monthly scholarship amount provided by the government secondary school program is equal to what a child can earn from two to four and a half days of work.

[9]A recent World Bank study reports that, on average, 15.5 percent and 17.6 percent of teachers are absent in primary and secondary schools, respectively. Chaudhury N, J Hammer, M Kremer, K Muralidharan and H Rogers (2005). *Roll Call: Teacher Absences in Bangladesh.* Washington DC: World Bank.

[10]Adopted children and other dependents of the borrowers do not qualify to receive such loans.

in medicine, engineering, agriculture, and teaching, in both public and private institutions. The amount of the loan depends on the nature of the course and its duration. Table 28.1 shows the loan amounts for various courses. Table 28.2 provides the breakdown of annual costs for some representative courses.

This cost schedule applies only in the case of a public institution. Although private universities are much more expensive, the bank is still willing to pay for such an education if the private university agrees to exempt 25–50 percent of the expenses. Once a student provides such assurance from

Table 28.1: Loan amounts for various types of courses.

Type of Course	Duration in Years	Loan Amount
MBBS (medicine)	5	105,000 taka (US$ 1616)
BDS (dentistry)	4	84,000 taka (US$ 1293)
Engineering	4	75,000 taka (US$ 1154)
BA (honors), B.Ag., and BBA	4	77,000 taka (US$ 1185)
Postgraduate (M.Ag. and MBA)	2	38,000 taka (US$ 585)

Table 28.2: Breakdown of annual costs for some representative courses.

Year	Admission, Tuition, Supplies, and Other Costs	Room and Board	Total (Budget)
	MBBS (Medicine)		
1	15,000	16,000	31,000
2	—	16,000	16,000
3	10,000	16,000	26,000
4	—	16,000	16,000
5	—	16,000	16,000
Total	25,000	80,000	105,000
	BA (Honors), B.Ag, and BBA		
1	4,000	16,000	20,000
2	3,000	16,000	19,000
3	3,000	16,000	19,000
4	3,000	16,000	19,000
Total	13,000	64,000	77,000
	Master's, Including M.Ag. and MBA		
1	3,000	16,000	19,000
2	3,000	16,000	19,000
Total	6,000	32,000	38,000

a private university, the bank will finance the rest of the expenses. The specified cost schedule assumes that the course will run and finish on schedule. In the case of a schedule delay of six months, the zonal manager can increase the amount of the loan to pay for the added expenses of room, board, and educational supplies.

Once the loan is approved, the amount is transferred to a current account owned jointly by the borrower and the student. The student can withdraw the amount allocated for tuition and other fees at the beginning of each year, and the yearly funding for room and board is transferred on a quarterly basis. The area manager examines the progress report of the student and, upon satisfaction, approves the transfer of funds for the next year's education. No interest is charged on the loan during the course of study. A month after the student's receipt of the final approved installment amount of the loan, a 5 percent service charge is added to the outstanding amount from that day onward. A year after the successful completion of the course, the student begins repaying the loan through monthly installments that include a principal amount plus the service charge. The monthly installment amount is determined in consultation with the student.

The student must pay back the loan over the same number of years for which the loan was approved; a student must, for instance, pay off a five-year loan plus the service charge for a medical degree in five years. The student can, however, repay the loan earlier than the scheduled time by paying higher installments. Students do not have to pay a service charge if they can repay the entire loan amount before the start of installment payments. Table 28.3 reports the status (as of December 2008) of the education loan.

A 5 percent interest rate is less than the commercial rate and less than the rate charged on a typical loan from Grameen Bank.[11] This low interest rate thus amounts to a subsidy from the bank to the borrowers, because the alternative cost is a lot higher. Given that the return to education at the tertiary level is 12.8 percent, investment in higher education by using the bank's education loan will yield a net benefit (Asadullah, 2006a). The bank is willing to subsidize the higher education of the borrowers' children because it will fulfill the borrowers' lifelong dreams of seeing their children become educated so that they will not have to become members of the bank. In return, the borrowers will be loyal to the bank and feel that they are being rewarded for their ownership of the bank. In addition to loans for higher

[11] A private commercial bank is charging 18 percent for similar loans. See http://positive-bangladesh.wordpress.com/2008/01/21eximbank-launches-interest-free-loan-for-students

Table 28.3: Status of the education loan program (cumulative up to December 2008).

Course of Study	Number of Students			Total Approved Amount (Hundred Thousand Taka)	Total Disbursement up to December '08*	Number of Students who Repaid the Loan up to December '08
	Male	Female	Total			
Bachelor's (honors): general subjects	23,293	6,755	30,048	21223.21	9193.94	350
Master's: general subjects	1,191	258	1,449	452.69	259.78	86
BBA	412	52	468	330.65	77.79	4
MBA	49	3	52	14.82	10.73	4
Bachelor's: agriculture/veterinary/fisheries	326	57	383	255.53	112.04	9
Master's: agriculture/veterinary/fisheries	104	6	110	51.50	26.84	4
Bachelor's: engineering/textile/computer and marine engineering	745	56	801	509.95	153.67	7
Medicine and dentistry	290	91	381	318.77	118.22	7
Total	26410	7278	33688	23157.12 ($35 ml)	9952.97 ($15 ml)	471

*Amount disbursed is less than the approved amount because the loan amount is given out in installments.

education, the bank extends "coaching loans" for preparatory courses so that students can score high on the admission test and thus get admitted into an undergraduate program in a university. Borrowers' children who have attained a Grade Point Average (GPA) of 4.0 in both Secondary School and Higher Secondary School Certificate examinations qualify for such a loan.[12] The loan can only be used for the fees for such courses; students have to arrange their own funding for room and board. A service charge of 5 percent is applied to the loan amount from the day it is sanctioned. If a student is successful in achieving admission into an undergraduate program and wants a higher education loan, the coaching loan will be added to the higher education loan. Although the student will have to pay a service charge on the coaching loan, he or she will receive the higher education loan interest-free until the end of the program. Students who fail to enter a university and do not want a higher education loan will have to repay the bank for the prep courses through installments within a year of the loan's sanction.

By providing education loans, the bank is trying to correct an imperfection in the capital market. If the capital market was perfect, as stipulated in the literature and in textbooks, anyone wishing to pursue higher education would be able to finance it by borrowing from a financial institution. The borrowers would pay off the bank in the future by means of higher, predictable income streams made possible by an education financed through credit. Unfortunately, financial institutions are unable to provide such loans for human capital formation. One reason is that, unlike land and other non-movable assets, expected future income cannot be used as collateral against a loan. Financial institutions cannot take ownership of the human capital acquired through loans and sell it to pay off the debt in the case of default. Moreover, they do not know if the student will be able to complete the program or will be able to get a job to pay off the debt. Milton Friedman (1962) suggested that imperfection in the credit market would lead people to under-invest in education to acquire human capital. Such under-investment will be more pronounced in the case of the poor. Critics argue that microcredit cannot solve the problem of poverty by remedying the imperfection in only one market — the market for financial and physical capital that conditions

[12]The GPA is calculated by converting letter grade for a course into points (4 points for an A, 3 points for a B, and so on), adding up the points for all the courses, and dividing the sum by the number of courses. The highest possible GPA is 4.0 and a GPA of 4.0 will be the same as getting a first class degree in the United Kingdom.

the lives of the poor (Sobhan, 2005). So, by providing an education loan for the children of borrowers, Grameen bank is attempting to remedy the imperfection in another market: the market for human capital.

In advanced countries such as the United States, as well as in many developing countries and countries in transition, the government provides education loans to remedy such imperfections in the capital market. In the United States, the interest rate on a student loan is lower than the rate for other forms of commercial credit such as mortgages, credit cards, and consumer loans because of the federal government's explicit guarantee against default to the lending institution. In Bangladesh, it is Grameen Bank, a for-profit company that is providing the loan. There are, however, some interesting similarities between Grameen's program and the government programs in advanced countries. In both cases, for example, repayment is secured from the future income of the students. This is known as "deferred payment" or "income-contingent repayment".

While these similarities exist, Grameen's loan program differs from many other student loan programs in a fundamental way. Lending to students can be disaggregated into several distinct functions: (1) originating the loan, (2) providing the capital, (3) guaranteeing or bearing the risk of default, (4) subsidizing some of the cost of borrowing, (5) and servicing and collecting (Johnstone, 2001). Unlike Grameen's student loans, in the loan programs of other countries, these functions can be performed by separate entities. For example, the private banks or the universities themselves can originate the loan, and the parents bear the risk. Also, all loan programs entail subsidies, explicit or implicit, from the government. In the case of Grameen's education loan program, the bank performs all five functions. Even borrowers who are on a flexible loan (which is akin to a rescheduled loan) can qualify for an educational loan. By giving such a loan, the bank signals to its borrowers that it genuinely cares about their welfare without regard to their credit history. A recent paper reports that only 9 percent of young people from poor households are enrolled in college, compared with 24 percent for the entire population (Ahmad, 2003). These loans will redress the longstanding inequality in access to higher education for the benefit of children of the poor.

Education loans can serve as insurance. In case of income shocks, the first casualty may be the expense of higher education of the children. The family may want the children to drop out to take up employment so as to supplement the family income. In the case of a female, the consequences of income shock may be even worse. Instead of being asked to look for work, she may be married off. If the family has more than one child going to college, the female child may become the sacrificial lamb for the family. However, higher education may be a means of breaking the poverty trap. Research suggests that there is persistence in educational attainment across generations, especially among men: sons of fathers with low educational attainment tend to attain low education levels as well (Asadullah, 2006b). Education loans and the attainment of higher education will allow the borrowers' offspring to break such intergenerational poverty traps. Thus, the loans, by educating the children of the poor and improving their job prospects, will also help to reduce the problem of inequality.

4 Conclusion

In this paper, we examined how Grameen Bank, by providing loans for higher education, is signaling to its members that it genuinely cares for the welfare of their families. The introduction of education loans suggests that Grameen Bank is developing new financial products to match the changing needs of its borrowers. Despite the improvement in enrollments and the reverse gender gap in the primary and secondary levels, female enrollment in tertiary education is lagging behind male enrollment. This is a mismatch that Grameen Bank is trying to close by providing education loans.

We have mentioned several benefits of the loan to the borrowers as well as society. The education loan program has not been evaluated yet. Anecdotal evidence suggests that the parents and the children find the program useful, and increasingly larger numbers of students are using the loans to fund their education. The unexplored question is whether the program leads to increased debt burden for the child as well as for the family if they are unable to get a job to pay off the debt. So far, the default rates on the education loan are negligible.

Even though Grameen now has seven and a half million borrowers, only close to 34,000 students, 78 percent of whom are male, have taken advantage of the education loan. The loan was developed for the children of older borrowers who were about to enter university for undergraduate and graduate education. That cohort is not as big as the older children of recent members. However, the number of students using education loan is still a smaller fraction of those who would have qualified for such a loan. It is possible that the tight job market for the educated youth and the resulting risk of indebtedness is dissuading the borrower's children from pursing higher education. Or it may be that the simple cost-benefit calculation suggests that education beyond secondary or even primary level is not economic for many of the children. Asadullah (2004) reports that the return to education is lower for primary and secondary level of education and the rate of return is lower in the rural areas compared to urban areas.

The success of the program raises the question as to why the government is not providing education loans. While the government's lack of resources is the obvious answer, it is also not clear that a government-run program would be as successful as the Grameen Bank's. The benefits of a government-run program may be captured by the better-off; in addition, the government would not be able to utilize the efficiency and transparency that is inherent in a member-owned organization such as the Grameen Bank. Despite the good wishes of the bank, there are still two types of "mismatch" caused mainly by the lack of demand for the higher education loan. The first one is revealed by the low participation rate in the education loan program overall. The second one is that fewer females are taking advantage of the loan.

The bank has expanded rapidly since the early 2000s: At one point, the bank was opening two branches per day (Dowla and Barua, 2006). Such rapid expansion means that more students will be in the pipeline to take advantage of the higher education loan of the bank. One hopes that the bank will identify why more borrowers' children are not taking advantage of this product, especially the females, and if necessary, change the product design and the terms of the loan so that it can be scaled up rapidly.

References

Ahmad, A (2003). Inequality in the Access to Education and Poverty in Bangladesh. Part of the ongoing project Access to Secondary Education and Poverty Reduction in Bangladesh.

Al-Samarrai, S (2007). Education spending and equity in Bangladesh. Background paper for Poverty Assessment of Bangladesh. Mimeograph World Bank, Washington DC.

Asadullah, MN (2006a). Returns to education in Bangladesh. *Education Economics*, 14, 453–468.

——— (2006b). Intergenerational economic mobility in rural Bangladesh. Paper presented at the *Royal Economic Society (RES) Annual Conference*, University of Nottingham.

Chase, J (1997). The Effect of Microfinance Credit on Children's Education: Evidence from the Grameen Bank. Unpublished undergraduate honors thesis in economics, Harvard University.

Chaudhury, N, J Hammer, M Kremer *et al.* (2005). *Roll Call: Teacher Absence in Bangladesh.* Washington DC: World Bank.

Dowla, A (2006). In credit we trust: Building social capital by Grameen Bank in Bangladesh. *Journal of Socio-Economics*, 35(1), 102–122.

Dowla, A and D Barua (2006). *The Poor Always Pay Back: The Grameen II Story.* Bloomfield, CT: Kumarinan Press.

Friedman, M (1962). *Capitalism and Freedom.* Chicago: University of Chicago Press.

Hossain, N (2004). Access to Education for the Poor and Girls: Educational Achievements in Bangladesh. A case study prepared for Government of China/World Bank conference on *Scaling up Poverty Reduction*, Shanghai.

Hossain, N and N Kabeer (2004). Achieving universal primary education and eliminating gender disparity. *Economic and Political Weekly*, 39(36), 4093–4100.

Jacoby, HG and E Skoufias (1997). Risk, financial markets, and human capital in a developing country. *Review of Economic Studies*, 64(3), 311–335.

Jain, P (1996). Managing credit for the rural poor: Lessons from the Grameen Bank. *World Development*, 24(1), 79–89.

Johnstone, DB (2000). *Student Loans in International Perspective: Promises and Failures, Myths and Partial Truths.* International Comparative Higher Education Finance and Accessibility Project, Center for Comparative and Global Studies in Education, Graduate School of Education. Buffalo: SUNY.

Khandker, S, M Pitt and N Fuwa (2003). *Subsidy to Promote Girls' Secondary Education: The Female Stipend Program in Bangladesh.* Washington DC: World Bank.

Maldonado, JH, C González–Vega and V Romero (2003). The influence on the education decisions of rural households: Evidence from Bolivia. Paper prepared for the *Annual Meeting of the American Agricultural Economics Association*, Montreal, Canada.

McKernan, SM (2002). The impact of microcredit programs on self-employment profits: Do non-credit program aspects matter? *Review of Economics and Statistics*, 84(1), 93–115.

Pitt, M and S Khandker (1998). The impact of group-based credit programs on poor households in Bangladesh: Does the gender of the participants matter? *Journal of Political Economy*, 106(5), 958–996.

Rahman, A, R Rahman, M Hossain and S Hossain (2002). *Early Impact of Grameen: A Multi-Dimensional Analysis.* Dhaka: Grameen Trust.

Sobhan, R (2005). A Macro-Policy for Poverty Eradication through Structural Change. Discussion Paper 2005/03, World Institute for Development Economics Research.

Tietjen, K (2003). The Bangladesh Primary Education Stipend Project: A Descriptive Analysis. Partnership for Sustainable Strategies on Girls' Education.

Todd, H (1996). *Women at the Center: Grameen Bank Borrowers after One Decade.* Boulder, CO: Westview Press.

World Bank (2008). *Whispers to Voices: Gender and Social Transformation in Bangladesh.* South Asia Region. Washington DC.

Wydick, B (1999). The effect of microenterprise lending on child schooling in Guatemala. *Economic Development and Cultural Change*, 47(4), 853–869.

Index

Ingram Content Group UK Ltd.
Milton Keynes UK
UKHW032257290323
419396UK00008B/215

9 789814 295659